MW01408231

THE PERFECT CAR

THE BIOGRAPHY OF JOHN BARNARD

EVRO PUBLISHING

The Perfect Car:
The Biography of John Barnard

John Barnard

SIGNED BY JOHN BARNARD

Evro Publishing certifies that this is a genuine signed copy

THE PERFECT CAR

THE BIOGRAPHY OF
JOHN BARNARD
MOTORSPORT'S MOST CREATIVE DESIGNER

BY NICK SKEENS

EVRO
PUBLISHING

© Nick Skeens 2018

All rights reserved. No part of this publication may be reproduced or stored in a retrieval system or transmitted, in any form or by any means, electronic, mechanical, photocopying, recording or otherwise, without prior permission in writing from Evro Publishing.

Published in June 2018

ISBN 978-1-910505-27-4

Published by Evro Publishing, Westrow House, Holwell, Sherborne, Dorset DT9 5LF

Edited by Mark Hughes
Cover design by Paul Harpin
Internal design by Richard Parsons
Back cover image by Rainer Schlegelmilch

Printed and bound in Slovenia by GPS Group

Every effort has been made to trace and acknowledge holders of copyright in photographs and to obtain their permission for the use of photographs. The publisher apologises for any errors or omissions in the credits given throughout this book and would be grateful to be notified of any corrections that should be incorporated in future reprints or editions.

www.evropublishing.com

This book is dedicated to my rock and my love, Sue 'the Professor' Sullivan, without whom I would never have finished it, and to my three boys, Daniel, Mark and Rob, those lights of my life.

CONTENTS

	PROLOGUE	9
	INTRODUCTION	15

Part 1
ABOUT A BOY — 21
1. The toy-maker (1946–61) — 23
2. Chariots of fire (1954–64) — 40

Part 2
LEARNING THE ROPES — 51
3. Whatever Lola wants, Lola gets (1965–71) — 53
4. Head start (1971–72) — 68
5. To McLaren, and the M23 (1972–73) — 79
6. First World Championship (1974–75) — 94

Part 3
AMERICA — 105
7. California dreaming (1975–76) — 107
8. American revolution (1976–78) — 124
9. The Chaparral high (1978–79) — 137

Part 4
McLAREN — 163
10. Conceiving the carbon car (1979–80) — 165
11. The pillar of Hercules (1980–81) — 190
12. Changing of the Guard (1976–80) — 203
13. The Prince of Darkness (1980–81) — 214
14. Barnard and the White Tornado (1979–82) — 223
15. Racing the carbon car (1981) — 235
16. Turbo-powered takeover (1982) — 249
17. Coke is it (1983) — 270
18. The perfect car (1984) — 285
19. Mr McLaren (1984–86) — 295

Part 5
FERRARI (1) 311
20 The Maranello bypass (1986–87) 313
21 Reinventing the wheel (1987–88) 336
22 The secret car (1987–88) 350
23 The miracle of the duck (1988–89) 368
24 Man on fire (1989) 393
25 Work of art (1989) 403

Part 6
BENETTON 413
26 The Godalming Scud (1989–91) 415
27 The true colours of Benetton (1991) 437
28 Tomfoolery (1991–92) 454

Part 7
FERRARI (2) 463
29 Pure genius (1992–94) 465
30 Death and daylight robbery (1994) 484
31 The last V12 (1994–96) 495
32 The coming of the King (1995–97) 500

Part 8
B3 AND BEYOND 513
33 The last Barnard car (1996–98) 515
34 Prost goes pop (1998–2002) 521
35 Bye bye B3 (2002–08) 527
36 Was he all that? (1969–2008) 534

EPILOGUE 543
TECHNICAL MILESTONES 560
GLOSSARY 562
INDEX 578

PROLOGUE
HOW THE MOUNTAIN CAME TO MOHAMMED

This book is about a genius, a poet of engineering, a man who produced some of the most brilliant and beautiful race cars of the modern era while battling enormous odds to do so. One mission drove him throughout his professional life — his attempt to create the perfect car.

The word 'genius' is often overused and some quite rightly feel it should be reserved exclusively for the greatest of humans — Shakespeare, for example, or Mozart, Newton and Einstein among a handful of others. Genius, then, is only to be applied to humanity's greatest minds, people who brought their particular disciplines to such a high degree of brilliance that all who followed or preceded are eclipsed. Their creative contribution to the world was so breathtakingly 'other' that they changed the way humanity thinks and acts.

However good he is, John Barnard is certainly not in this league. And yet, in his chosen field of motorsport, he was himself a Colossus. He completely changed the way that top designers created race cars and made them significantly stronger, safer, lighter and faster. Famed motorsport commentator Murray Walker said it best at the British Grand Prix in 2012: 'John was and is a genius, and there aren't many of those about.'

Geniuses, whether greater or lesser, tend to have led fascinating lives, undergoing intense periods that sparkle with luminescent creativity while often labouring under enormous pressure. This book tells the story of a man who rose from humble beginnings to the very top of an elite profession on the cutting edge of technology where he created important innovations that remain in use today. Does that qualify him as a genius? Given the broad spread of meaning assigned to the word today, so broad that it allows footballers, businessmen, comedians and even politicians to revel in the title, then perhaps even the most fastidious and pernickety might agree that Barnard was, at least, some kind of genius.

The backdrop to his tale is motorsport's most demanding incarnation, Formula 1, the rocket science of the sporting world. But to read this book you need no prior knowledge. Every term, every innovation, every context is, I hope, fully explained, either in the main text or in the glossary. And, I would further claim that if you read this book, you will have under your belt a detailed introduction to the engineering of modern race cars, because there have been no major, lasting innovations in motorsport created by a single designer since John Barnard put away his Formula 1 drawing board.

The idea for this book emerged in an interview I conducted with furniture designer Terence Woodgate for *Creative Island II*, a book about British design. The subject was his award-winning Surface Table, a carbon-fibre dining table of supreme elegance. Light and long, it is unnervingly perched on four thin legs and yet able to support a Mini car in the middle without flexing more than a couple of inches.

Terence waxed lyrical about it for a while before suddenly changing the subject, as if drawn away from his own story to an astounding and all-but-forgotten tale about his collaborator, John Barnard, who handled the Surface Table's construction. Terence's detour went something like this:

'Barnard's incredible; he's the greatest living Formula 1 designer, bar none. So good, in fact, that Ferrari begged him to come to Italy and work for them. And Barnard said, "No". Then they added a series of zeros to his proposed salary but still he wouldn't come. Why? Because he wanted to go home every day and have lunch with his family.

'In a final and dramatic last offer, Ferrari said, "Okay, we'll come to you." The greatest team in motorsport swallowed its Italian pride and said, "We want this Englishman so much that we'll relocate part of Ferrari F1 to Godalming, and build it to this Englishman's specifications." They had made Barnard an offer he couldn't refuse. The mountain moved to Mohammed.'

How had I not heard of Barnard? How come most of us haven't? Surely his name should be up there with the household names of Formula 1?

After the interview, I found myself trying to think of equivalents. Would Manchester United build a multi-million pound training ground in Spain to secure the use of a Spanish coach? Might a comparable British racing team, say, McLaren, brave patriotic fury to move its Formula 1 operation to a village 30 miles from Paris to secure the services of a French designer? The answer to the latter is a definite 'No', because world motorsport's greatest design talent lives and works in southern England, a fact that itself owes much to the work of John Barnard.

Terence suggested I call Barnard to interview him but he issued a caveat: 'Take care; he is notoriously difficult to talk to; he was known in Formula 1 as the Prince of Darkness.'

So, with some trepidation, I called him. The Devil Incarnate, happily, was keen to help, delivering the technology behind the elegant Surface Table with patience and clarity.

When I called again to check my writing for accuracy, I asked why he hadn't published an autobiography. It turned out that he had been approached but had failed to be impressed by potential biographers' demands for too much of the proceeds. However, irritated as he was and is by inaccurate, dismissive summaries of his work within the motoring press, he felt that now, yes, perhaps the time was right to set the record straight.

In the summer of 2009 we met for lunch in London at the Royal Society for the Encouragement of Arts, Manufactures and Commerce (the RSA) in London, where Barnard enjoys the distinction of being an RDI, a Royal Designer for Industry — a chosen member of Britain's design elite.

He asked what I knew about motorsport. 'Not a lot,' I said. 'But I write about a wide range of design.' And then the sleight of hand. 'Do your children understand what you have done?'

'No,' he conceded. They had never taken much interest beyond enjoying their father's status by securing, from Bernie Ecclestone, cherished passes to occasional races.

'There should be a book about your life that everyone can understand,' I said, 'not only motorsport fans, but people like your children, the layman, anyone interested in creative minds and how they do what they do.'

And so the conversation blossomed. The more I talked to him, the more fascinated I became, and the more questions bubbled in my mind. How does a self-conscious, self-doubting boy grow up to become a design legend? How does he rise from what I discovered was a working-class childhood to do battle in the world's most competitive sporting arena, and win? And how did he manage to bring so many major innovations into a sport already replete with brilliant minds?

There are many elements in John Barnard's life that have fed his genius and natural creativity. His supportive parents played a crucial role, so did his teeth-clenching determination, his hatred of compromise, his obsession with detail and perfection, and, of course, that essential ingredient, Lady Luck, without whose mercurial beneficence there can be no success. I saw in my mind a book that could trace that adventure from birth to senior citizenship and even thought it could open up to the uninitiated the extraordinary world of motorsport and the astounding characters who inhabit it.

John Barnard is one of the most innovative designers in Britain, a country that boasts perhaps the strongest creative sector in the world and certainly the most impressive lineage of invention and innovation on the planet. He is responsible for bringing the Space Age to motorsport, introducing carbon-fibre composite technology, making significant advances in aerodynamics, creating innovative uses for titanium and other 'exotic' materials, making huge strides in gearbox and suspension design, and dramatically improving the quality, strength and safety of the cars.

He has done it all against the odds, against his humble beginnings, the relative paucity of his education and the dramatic effects of his own character flaws that, so many have argued, prevented him from achieving even greater heights. But the truth is that his startling innovations have been copied throughout the world of motorsport and are still in use today, and almost certainly could not have been achieved had he not been the flawed character that he is.

His principal achievements are these.

He conceived and developed the first carbon-fibre car, creating what was, at the time, one of the most complex carbon-fibre structures in existence. This car was faster, lighter, stronger and safer than its aluminium competitors.

He invented the paddleshift gearbox — the first electronically operated transmission in which the gears are operated from levers, or paddles, on the steering wheel. Ever since, race drivers have not had to take their hands off the wheel — another major contribution to safety as well as speed — and the concept has transferred to road cars. He was also the first to move the dashboard instruments onto the steering wheel.

He created the aerodynamic 'coke-bottle' body design of Formula 1 cars.

He was the first in Formula 1 to commission and direct a turbocharged engine made specifically for a Formula 1 car rather than one derived from a production engine.

There were many, many other innovations, all ground-breaking, almost all copied by rival teams, but the first three of these achievements — carbon, paddleshift and coke-bottle body shape — were major changes that are still in use today. To find anything comparable, you have to go back to before Barnard's time, to the work of John Cooper and Colin Chapman.

And beauty. Barnard's design ethos was instinctive: 'If it looks beautiful, then it's going to go quick.' So he would often draw the concept and then refine it in wind tunnels to make it slip through the air like a supersonic jet. In fact he had to redesign the wind tunnels to meet his needs; another area of Barnard pathfinding. More perhaps than any other race car designer, Barnard was all about poetry in motion.

He utterly changed the way race cars were built, raising the standards from the comparatively slap-dash, oil-soaked, spanner and hammer, 'weld, rivet and hope' methodology of the '50s, '60s and '70s to today's antiseptic, aerospatial, clean-room, CAD-driven, carbon-fibre palaces of motorsport technology. He completely reorganised Formula 1 engineering, bringing a long-needed uniformity in methods, tools and parts and ensuring that everything on any top-level race car was the best that it could possibly be. This also made the cars far safer.

Nor were his triumphs only in Formula 1. Like so many great creative British people, he conquered America too, creating a race car that helped precipitate a revolution in the running of Indycar. He also designed the first 'ground-effect' Indycar and it became a favourite with the fans. At the peak of his career, almost everything Barnard designed turned to racing gold.

What all this really means, how it was achieved, and how Barnard's remarkable mind created the ideas that revolutionised both Indycar and Formula 1 is a story that hasn't yet been told. It's time that it was.

Nick Skeens
Burnham-on-Crouch, Essex, March 2018

INTRODUCTION
THE ITALIAN CRASH 1981

British racing driver John Watson believes in the mysterious power of the 'sixth sense', that warm rumble in the guts that warns of imminent danger. But those feelings never fluttered his stomach on that rainy day in northern Italy as he stepped into his revolutionary McLaren MP4 from the 'lucky' right-hand side of the car. The date was 13 September 1981 and the race, at Monza, was the 13th of the Formula 1 season. It was a day that would indeed be unlucky for some and one on which 'Wattie' would himself dice with death.

The paddock — that elite preserve of teams, VIPs, rich enthusiasts and motorsport journalists — was already expecting trouble. Ulsterman Watson was driving a car created by the new kid on the block, John Barnard, a man who, as fate would have it, had been born on the same day 35 years earlier and who shared a taste for the superstitious. The car was revolutionary because it was made of carbon-fibre, a new material with a dreadful track record in sport. Some paddock pundits predicted that in a crash it would shatter into razor-sharp shards or turn to dust.

Not that these opinions mattered to Barnard. He had no time for ill-informed journalistic doubters or indeed those designers and engineers who had dabbled in the new technology by securing carbon-fibre panels to their Formula 1 cars with rivets, all in a misguided effort to add strength without weight via this super-strong, super-light material.

To Barnard that method made no sense at all. After working with boffins at British Aerospace, he had concluded that there was only one way to do it, and that involved the most painstaking design process and the use of financially crippling clean rooms and autoclaves — giant ovens that cooked the wonder material under pressure. His competitors' efforts had generally ended in failure, with panels ripping off at their weakest points, the rivets, and then disintegrating into their poorly cured component parts.

Motorsport journalists, ever hunting a story, had fresh in their memories the Fastnet yacht race tragedy just two years earlier. During a severe storm 14 yachts racing in the 1979 Fastnet lost their carbon-fibre rudders with tragic results — the loss of 15 lives. Some journalists duly predicted disaster for a carbon-fibre car.

Monza is the fastest Formula 1 circuit in the world because it has long straights and relatively few corners. Quick and dangerous, it is somewhat fittingly shaped like a pirate's pistol. The bottom of the handgrip is made up of the two *Lesmo* curves, *Lesmo 1* at the heel and *Lesmo 2* at the front, leading up into the long, fast *Curva del Serraglio* towards the trigger, the *Ascari* chicane, with straights along the bottom and top of the barrel, the gun's business end being the *Curva Parabolica*. Watson was well aware that the newly introduced, ever more reliable turbo-powered cars were going to be very hard to beat, his McLaren having a normally aspirated Ford Cosworth engine.

Qualification for the race had not been ideal. Watson's McLaren teammate, Andrea De Cesaris, had spun out in practice and Wattie himself had experienced recurring problems with his car's electronics. As a result he was seventh on the starting grid and would have to take significant risks if he wanted to get anywhere near his glorious triumph in the British Grand Prix at Silverstone eight weeks earlier. Since then he had recorded two disappointing sixth positions and a retirement, so the pressure was on.

That burden increased dramatically when the race began. At the end of the first lap Wattie found himself down in 11th place, but he was known for his ability to overtake and by lap 16 (of 52) he was back where he started and brimming with confidence despite the rain that had just started, sending three cars spinning off the circuit. Now he was stuck behind Didier Pironi's Ferrari and on lap 19 he decided to do something about it.

'As I approached the two Lesmo corners, I conceived a cunning plan,' Watson said. 'I'd drop back marginally and attack *Lesmo 1* in such a way that I'd leave *Lesmo 2* faster than Pironi, allowing me to pick up his slipstream and take him on the upcoming *Ascari* chicane. It would have been a sweet move.'

It could hardly have turned more sour. He found himself running wide as he screamed out of the second *Lesmo* at 150mph, accelerator pressed to the floor.

'Bad mistake. As I came out of *Lesmo 2*, the left-side wheels ran up the kerb and dropped over the outside edge onto the grass border. The car bottomed out and pivoted on the kerbing. Suddenly I was in a looping spin, skidding back across the track and I knew it wasn't going to be good. I shut my eyes, ducked my head and held on to the wheel.'

Watson's car slammed backwards into the steel barrier on the right-hand side of the track, sparks flying on impact. Engine, suspension and both rear wheels were torn off as a unit and cartwheeled across the track, spinning through a rolling fireball full of flying bodywork panels. This fiery mass missed Carlos Reutemann by inches as he sped by in his Williams at 150mph, swerving through the smoke onto the grass verge and side-swiping the metal barrier.

Simultaneously Watson, still strapped into what was now only half a car, shot away in the opposite direction to his engine, bouncing off the barrier and sliding backwards down the road towards *Curva del Serraglio*.

'As I slowed down, I lifted my head and I saw a Cosworth engine sliding across the track. I thought, "Who the hell is that? Jesus, somebody else has gone off because of my shunt!"'

The remains of his McLaren came to rest some 60 metres from the first impact. Watson unstrapped, climbed out and looked behind. Realisation flooded through him as he stepped over the car's shattered back end: 'Shit, that's *my* engine in the middle of the road!' But still he couldn't make sense of it: 'The impact didn't feel all that bad; substantial, but no big deal'. He looked into the cockpit and felt more confused: 'I couldn't work it out; something was missing... Christ, where's the gear stick?'

He spotted it as he walked along the edge of the track, his competitors still tearing by. It was still attached to the gearbox, which itself remained wedged in the barrier. During the crash, the gearbox had been driven backwards into the barrier, where, like a wrecking bar in the hands of a Tolkienian troll, it had forced the barrier's upper and lower sections apart and become trapped. As the car bounced away, the engine was wrenched from the rear of the cockpit, causing the gear linkage and gear lever to be yanked out of the cockpit through the back of the car, miraculously missing Watson's hip.

Three factors were crucial to Watson emerging unhurt from this accident. The first was that it was now mandatory in Formula 1 to have dry-break connectors on the fuel lines; this self-sealing valve system prevented petrol from continuing to spew out of a severed pipe so that the explosion was reduced to a mercifully brief flash. The second was that the gear lever had not ripped through Watson's pelvis on its way out of the back of the MP4. The third was that he was in a car built by John Barnard.

Wattie remains convinced that Barnard's extraordinary innovation saved his life: the McLaren's monocoque chassis had proved itself to be one of the strongest boxes on the planet. Had the chassis been aluminium, as was the case with other Formula 1 cars flying round the Italian circuit that day, the powerful rear impact might have driven the engine forward through the bulkhead at the back of the monocoque, puncturing the fuel tank behind Watson's seat.

'Aluminium would have ripped,' says Watson, 'I could have burned. The carbon-fibre just flexed and stayed together.'

Happily, Barnard had also designed the engine mountings as 'frangible fittings', meaning that in just such an accident the engine would be ripped away, providing further protection of both driver and chassis.

Having survived, now chief in Wattie's mind was how he was going to explain to Barnard, a designer with a reputation for preferring the nuclear option, how he had destroyed his car.

'I felt guilty for letting the team down with the Canadian Grand Prix just two weeks away. At the very least I'd created a mountain of work.'

For millions watching the race on the BBC, commentator Murray Walker described the moment in his revving engine of a voice: 'Seventh is John Watson and out of the points at the moment is Carlos Reutemann: there he is, storming along behind John Watson… WHO LOSES IT! That's John Watson and a very nasty one indeed: he's torn the whole of the back off the car. That's a very, very bad one indeed.'

It is the sort of commentary that, over the years, had been all too often the prelude to a grim announcement about severe injury or death. If you watch the YouTube video, you can detect the surprised relief in the voice of co-commentator James Hunt, the 1976 World Champion, as he spots Watson emerging from the cockpit: 'He's perfectly alright, he's got out of the car and walked away… They come out of that corner at about 150 miles an hour and he hardly slowed down at all. A very nasty shunt for John Watson; that was a great shame because it looked like a little bit of an error in concentration: he just let the car ride up the kerb a bit and then failed to control it.'

Barnard went through a similar emotional process: horror followed by relief.

'We were watching on TV monitors in the pits. I saw the flash fire, and thought, "Oh God, that looks bad." It's the worst fear for a driver, getting burned. It's particularly stressful to see that. So it was a relief to see him walking along the track.' Barnard's mood soon changed: 'Then I'm thinking, "Why did he crash? Was it my fault, did something break on the car?" I'd have been absolutely desolate. It turned out, of course, to be Wattie's mistake, though when he came back to the pits he didn't exactly admit that. "Not sure what happened," he said. "I might have touched the kerb."'

But what put a slightly smug smile on Barnard's 35-year-old face was the simple fact that, as he had known all along, those paddock pundits had got it wrong and now the whole motorsport world knew how wrong they had been. The carbon-fibre monocoque had not shattered or turned to dust; it had, instead, very possibly saved a driver's life. Suddenly the paddock was being fed with its own words and forced to think the unthinkable: 'We really are going to have to follow the new boy.'

A revolution on the cutting edge of motorsport had just begun. It would shake the windows and rattle the walls of the world's racing team headquarters, forcing every engineer onto a crash course in aerospace composites. It would drag the level of Formula 1 engineering up to a totally new plane and push team budgets through the roof. John Barnard had arrived in Formula 1 and John Watson, for one, was mightily relieved that he had.

… PART 1

ABOUT A BOY

CHAPTER 1
THE TOY MAKER
1946–61

John Barnard's early life shares much in common with a *Boy's Own Annual*, a Norman Rockwell painting or the *Ladybird Book of Things to Make*. Those of a certain age will remember the skilfully drawn images of an attentive son, still in his school uniform, looking up to his pipe-smoking father in the ideal garden shed workshop, receiving benign and patient instruction in the art of carpentry or metalwork.

Such was the young John Barnard's experience, except for one clear difference: his mother was as capable as his father in all things technical, which was and perhaps still is a relatively rare thing. And something else remarkable happened in John's youth: despite his parents' long experience in the mechanical world, John became the engineering authority in the household early on — in many ways John was the father to the man.

John Edward Barnard was born in Edgware General Hospital on 4 May 1946 to proud parents Edward (known to most as Ted) and Rose Ellen Barnard, a working-class if entrepreneurial couple who lived at 99 Llanover Road, North Wembley, London. After earlier miscarriages, Rose Ellen, aged 37, was delighted to have a son and soon gave up work to devote her life to her baby.

Perhaps there were omens. That year motorsport's governing body, the Fédération Internationale de l'Automobile (FIA), standardised the rules for Grand Prix racing, so creating the Formula 1 category, specifying the 'formula', the limits within which the cars must be designed. And while the infant John was on his way into the world, on that very day John Watson was also yelling out his new-born lungs, minding Belfast that they were to pay close attention.

John Barnard's earliest memory happens to be of a major sporting event — the 1948 London Olympics. He insists that he can remember, at just two years old and watching from his pram, an athlete jogging eastwards along East Lane over the North Wembley hump-back railway bridge, just 100 metres from 99 Llanover Road, towards the famous stadium. Bright in Barnard's mind is the fact that the runner was carrying the Olympic Torch. Such recall would suggest Barnard has a remarkable visual memory — an essential aid to any successful designer.

He certainly remembers the steam locomotives that used to thunder under the North Wembley bridge, the smell of the steam and the coal as the smoke wrapped around him, the pumping and pushing of the coupling rods, the sound of steel rim on shining steel rail, and the roar of the *Flying Scotsman*, the most famous train in the world, as it swept down the line towards Kings Cross station. John Barnard, then, was born and brought up in a tough, working-class environment set amid world-class sporting excellence and world-beating engine power.

There is much to suggest that John inherited his penchant for innovation more from his mother than his father. In John's words, 'Mum was the entrepreneurial person; she was always up for having a go; my father was the rock, the anchor.' Rose Ellen's brothers, Bert and Tom, had a small business that built houses and flats, so the entrepreneurial spirit was in the family.

Ted and his elder brother John (known as Jack) also had business flair; together they had a small engineering firm called Johnsteds, which was eventually based on Jack's farm near Sevenoaks in Kent. Ted also ran a small transport business; John recalls Ted telling him how he used to pick up tiles from barges moored at Richmond Bridge that had come from Holland.

So if the Barnards' roots were working class, the aspirations and achievements of his parents set them on a rung further up the social ladder. During the Second World War, both worked at Glacier Metal Company, later to become GGB, one of the world's biggest manufacturers of bearings. Ted's was a Reserved Occupation, his skills in making marine bearings more valuable to the war effort than a fighting role, and Rose Ellen became the boss of the grinding shop, a rare elevation at the time for a woman and made possible by the shortage of male labour during the war. As John says, 'My parents weren't typical working class. Working for yourself was fairly well entrenched in our DNA.'

Despite the status she enjoyed at Glacier's, Rose Ellen didn't think twice about giving it all up to look after their only son. She devoted herself to John, waiting until he was 14 before returning to full-time work, when she took over a greengrocery business attached to their house. This meant getting up at 4am each day to drive with Ted to Covent Garden or Brentford Market to buy fresh fruit and veg before Ted went on to a day's work at Glacier's.

John's parents were opposites in many ways. His mother was a powerful force, a leader in the workplace. His father was a more reserved man who would calmly stand his ground before giving in for the sake of peace and quiet. The contrast led to some dramatic rows, a trait that passed on to John and came to both help and hinder his career. But it was clear to John that his parents' love for each other was strong and that their love for him was even stronger.

In September 1951, 40-year-old racing legend Juan Manuel Fangio was battling away, and failing, at Monza, a setback in a season that saw him eventually secure the first of five Formula 1 World Championships. That week things were not going well for John Barnard either. He had spent his first day at the infants' school in nearby Park Lane and hadn't liked it.

'There were some 40 children in my class, all strangers with their strange smells and strange words, and a teacher droning on and on. I cried all morning, so much in fact that the teachers called my mother at lunchtime and she had to come and pick me up.'

After that he went home every lunchtime, initially ferried back and forth on a bike Rose Ellen had equipped with a back seat for him. Lunch with the family was to become a controversial habit throughout his life.

Such odd behaviour must have brought sneering from his peers: 'Where's John — is he a mummy's boy?' He didn't care; he was a loner. His isolation also fed his perfectionism.

Barnard was, and is, perpetually motivated to prove his superiority as a way of staving off his fundamental fear that he simply wasn't up to it. He fought hard against this fear.

'Throughout my childhood I was always worried about being good enough,' he said, 'and I feel that even to this day. I think it is this aspect of my character that has given me the drive to achieve, to be better, to make things as perfect as possible. I'm never satisfied with what I've done and what I've built.'

This didn't make for a harmonious interaction with the human world. If things weren't perfect in his household, he would take control, shouting at his father, berating a friend. Was it bullying? In a sense, it probably was, but it wasn't out of any delight in cruelty, any relishing of another's pain, it was out of insecurity driven by a fear of things being out of control, less than perfect. If he was hard on others, he was just as hard on himself, merciless with his own shortcomings and hating in others what he hated in himself. If the school and his peers looked down on him for going home at lunchtime, so what? They would never be better than him; Barnard would see to that. His way was the right way for him.

In 1953, the year in which Alberto Ascari in a Ferrari pipped Fangio to his second Formula 1 World Championship, seven-year-old John Barnard moved from the Park Lane infants' school to Wembley Manor Junior, a relatively new school in East Lane where boys and girls were taught together in the same class — a comparatively novel practice in British schools. Like many post-war primary schools, resources were at a premium. Lessons were often held in the dining hall, with several classes working together, before they had to pack up and rearrange the tables for lunch. That made no difference to John, who continued to go home for lunch anyway.

In many ways he was a strange and fastidious child, his strangeness coming from his extraordinary focus on detail. It was at around this age that he developed the sort of superstitions that come from an organised and tidy mind. He began to do things in a certain sequence and should the sequence be thrown out he would find it traumatic.

One such ritual occurred while putting on his shoes and socks: 'I always put on my left sock and shoe first. Always, without fail.' If he couldn't find his left sock, he couldn't put on his left shoe, his right sock or his right shoe. One summer break he was with family friends at a holiday camp. 'We were in this cabin, and I was looking for my left sock and couldn't find it anywhere. The parents asked, "What's wrong, John?" I said, "I can't find my left sock!" Well, they laughed at me.'

John was unable to join in the joke. To him, the matter was serious: 'When you put socks on for the first time they form around the shape of your foot, the big toe stretching the inside edge, so the next time you put them on you'll be able to see the difference between the two.' What he means, of course, is that anyone ultra-fastidious, who automatically laser-focused in upon the tiniest of details, would be able to see the difference; most mortals consider they have better things to do.

Things just had to be right; they had to fit right, be formed right and feel right; and if they weren't right, there was a crisis. Contempt for imperfection would go on to dominate the rest of his life, whether it was contempt for himself or contempt for others who just didn't get how important perfection was. It's not an attractive trait — as he says of his eldest daughter, also a perfectionist, 'It will drive you mad.'

Which meant he made a difficult friend, and still does. He had buddies but was never really close to them; they didn't quite meet his standards, there was always something he was tempted to criticise, and, no doubt, would discuss their failings with his parents, further emphasising his sense of otherness. He didn't trust people to be careful with his possessions and with reason — none had his focus, his attention to detail, his high-speed solution-spotting capacity, and, especially, his care for tools or toys.

John recalls being very protective about the things he made. He was known for his temper — he had no compunction about screaming at friends or even adults if they dropped a model or mishandled a tool or a piece of machinery he had made. His perfectionism had an impact on his social life and he found himself reluctant to bring friends home because he fretted about their clumsiness: 'They could be pretty rough with delicate work. I was a perfectionist from a young age, something that my parents and my friends had to put up with.'

The following year, 1954, the Barnard family moved west across the humpback bridge to 3 Peel Road, close to the busy thoroughfare of East Lane. This was the house of his maternal grandmother, Mrs Martin, Martin being Rose Ellen's maiden name.

Set beside the massive Hop Bine pub[1], 3 Peel Road had a sizeable plot that included a greengrocer's shop separated from the three-bedroom semi-detached house by a gated alley. Wide enough for a car, the alley led into a spacious garden soon complete with workshops, garages, a vegetable garden and greenhouse. One of John's uncles, known as Bert the Builder, often stored his building materials in the outhouses.

Both the greengrocer's and the house were set back from Peel Road behind a forecourt and a hedged-in front garden. John would later construct large gates for the forecourt that he closed at night to prevent drinkers from the pub next door relieving themselves on his parents' property. A self-sufficient hive of DIY activity, 3 Peel Road was the crucible for Barnard's success, the very place

---

[1] *The pub was designed by Truman Brewery architect A.E. Sewell and is now, lamentably, a Tesco Express.*

where the young engineer would one day design one of the most famous cars in American motorsport history.

So in many ways, his childhood, while secure and relatively free, was private and self-sufficient, an only child of similar-minded parents. Barnard talks of no great social gatherings at his house; he and his parents were never party animals. They minded their own business and got on with their own stuff, and often worked together on building projects of various types. They were beholden to no one and that's precisely how they liked it.

The young John experienced a more outdoors life than is common today. With friends he often went down to the railway embankment and sat there on the grass for hours watching the trains go by. On one occasion a goods train approached, slowing down for a signal. The driver leaned out of the cab and called down to the boys: 'Fancy a ride on the footplate?' John takes up the tale:

'We clambered aboard and the driver released the brakes, blew the whistle and set off. Time meant nothing to us as we raced south-east along miles of track; we had watched so many trains go by and to actually be on one, in the driver's cab, was such a thrill.

'The driver pulled into the sidings at Willesden Junction and told us, "That's it boys, the ride's over." It suddenly struck us that we were some five miles from home. We started walking and got back very late. My mother, I dimly remember, was very angry.'

But not so angry or so worried that she called the police. In those days it was a common view that children had to learn to fend for themselves, an attitude forged in a Britain steeled by two world wars and that certainly contributed to the young engineer's legendary self-reliance. Fending for himself and solving his own problems are major factors in John's mental make-up.

John's childhood was peppered with risky adventures that were typical of a '50s childhood. He recalls taking his closest friend, Clifford, to stay at Uncle Jack's farm in Kent. They would play in an old First World War flat-bed lorry, a five-tonner, that his uncle used for collecting hay. It was usually left parked on a grassy slope next to the farmhouse with chocks under the wheels to prevent it rolling away.

The boys, being boys, used to release the handbrake, go through the gears and turn the steering wheel, although they never plucked up the courage to start the engine — that was expressly forbidden. One afternoon, after his older cousins had been driving the lorry, John and Clifford hopped in the cab and began to pretend to get it started. Clifford moved the gear lever to neutral and John pulled the handbrake off:

'Suddenly we were rolling down the hill! We panicked and leapt out of the open doors. Then, madly, we ran after it, trying to grab the wheels to slow it down. No chance — we were lucky not to lose our hands. It sped off down the lane and crashed through a ten-foot holly hedge into a yard full of chickens. It came to a stop amid a squawking cloud of dust, leaves and feathers.

'We looked at each other, and both decided escape was the best option, belting off to hide in the hayloft. Happily for us, our cousins got the blame; they'd parked it and hadn't replaced the chocks.'

Tragically, Uncle Jack died in the infamous Lewisham train crash in December 1957. Caused mainly by thick fog, this disaster killed 90 and injured over 100 more. John recalls his father being absolutely devastated.

A seminal moment in John's life came when he was 10. His father took him to see his uncle's house in Willesden, north-west London, just a few miles from home. Uncle Charlie had rented the bottom floor to an old man whose name now escapes John but whom we shall call Mr Pilkington.

Mr Pilkington had lost his only son in the Second World War and his wife had died a few years later. Lonely, but self-sufficient, Mr Pilkington had spent his oceans of spare time in the garden shed, which he had converted into a workshop. There he beavered away making toys for grandchildren that would never come to play with them. Now he was dead too, and his home was about to be cleared by relatives.

John remembers stepping into the front room of the dark, musty, detached house: 'I was in an Aladdin's Cave. All around me were shelves, tables and sideboards loaded with the most amazing models I had ever seen; six-foot railway locomotives in gleaming brass and red-and-green paint, five-foot motor torpedo boats complete with torpedo tubes and working rudders.

'The models weren't built for speed, but were geared for pulling heavy loads — perhaps a child could ride them. Almost all the floor space was taken up with boxes upon boxes of miniature engineering parts, each one full of treasure — shiny bolts, oily nuts, springs, metal strips and engineering wonders I couldn't yet understand. It was a wonderful expression of a model-maker's art.'

At the time John was building balsa-wood boats and planes and gluing together Revell plastic kits of car models, Rolls-Royces and gangster-style Duesenbergs rather than race cars. But what he saw in Mr Pilkington's flat had a powerful impact, amplifying his ambitions in his model-making and sowing the seed for his engineering future. He moved around the room, taking in all the detail, the immaculate perfection, the tiny working boat winches finished in brilliant detail, railings cunningly wrought from copper and brass, bollards, steering wheels, fuel tanks, gear levers, half-built carburettors, pistons and crankshafts.

Scattered on the table in that small, brown-painted room were detailed engineering drawings, blueprints and guides to the construction of these wonderful models. Opening a cupboard door revealed some 20 internal combustion engines, each hand-crafted by Mr Pilkington, each fully working, one a four-cylinder, four-stroke petrol engine just six inches long.

John had been given his first model railway, a Trix Twin 00-gauge set, at the age of five. Every year relatives would buy him a new locomotive, his favourite being a pre-war maroon Princess 4-6-2 that he still possesses. But the larger train models in this room were in another league, far beyond anything he had ever made or owned.

In the garden, Mr Pilkington's workshop, a small wooden shed, revealed yet more marvels of miniature model-making, all set out in ordered chaos. John's eye fell on the tools: grinding wheels, drilling machines, a small lathe for turning metal and wood and curious devices that he couldn't fathom, that he had never seen before.

John returned home inspired and was further uplifted when, a few days later, his father came home with the tools from the shed and a selection of boxes of engine paraphernalia, having collected enough money to make a decent offer to Mr Pilkington's relatives. The booty all went into Ted's workshop, a small room lit by a single electric bulb, part of a white-painted outbuilding behind the greengrocer's.

The Barnards even had a small forge made out of an old steel grating, firebricks and a vacuum cleaner motor to act as a bellows. They used it render metal parts white hot so they could beat them into the shapes they needed. John began making new models with gusto, including cars, boats and planes, all inspired by Mr Pilkington.

The family took pride in being able to make everything themselves, an approach that engendered in John his belief that, given a little ingenuity and a lot of hard work, a solution could be found to every mechanical problem. This philosophy, grounded in practical skill, was his childhood gift: 'My great joy was making things; that was the keynote of my youth. With both parents in engineering, and both intensely practical, we often worked together upon projects that would both save money and give us the intense problem-solving satisfaction that successful DIY always brings.

'My parents supported me in everything I wanted to do, and seemed at times to live for me, rather than themselves. If I wanted to do something and didn't know how, one of them would always find a way to help me out.'

They were a tight-knit family unit, their arguments intelligent, if sometimes severe, and their love expressed in that typically British post-war manner, with the minimum of physical contact but with a powerful sense of familial bond. It was amid this atmosphere of disciplined, explosive, reasoned and energetic industry that John's character was formed.

Another attitude that was to inform and perhaps even restrict his future career came in his family's approach to money: 'We didn't believe in borrowing. If you wanted something, you saved up for it. If you needed it quickly, you hired it. If you couldn't afford either, you went without. You *never* asked to borrow other people's things; it was rude and put them under an obligation, making it awkward for them to refuse. We didn't believe in credit — the only loan acceptable was for a mortgage on a house. It was a practical philosophy driven by war shortage; it was tough but it was fair.

'Today, I look at the modern credit society and think — were we wrong? Could we have had a better life on credit? But then, one look at the world economies shows the wisdom of my parents' attitude. I think you lose something when you use credit; you lose self-reliance and the value of things. I'll tell you one thing: when we bought stuff, we really did appreciate it!'

Without a doubt, John Barnard wanted money but he wasn't going to borrow in order to get it. That restriction turned out to make him particularly good at getting and keeping hold of money, but the question remains for some, as we shall later see, as to whether he might have made a good deal more had he not been so averse to borrowing.

When John was 10 his parents wanted to move him from Wembley Manor Junior into a nearby small private school, Buxlow Preparatory, but they were unable to. Here the 40 or so pupils were intensively trained for the 11-Plus exam, a nationwide test that was taken by most 11-year-old schoolchildren. If you passed, you would go to a grammar school, with a better chance of going on to university. If you failed, and most did, you were all too often considered a 'thicky', destined for the much-maligned Secondary Modern school system and a career trajectory likely to lead straight to the factory floor.

The 11-Plus was a major hurdle for Britain's schoolchildren and many of those who failed it felt cast aside and demoted to an inferior league. John became one of the many young, talented people who it tripped up.

'The first time I saw an 11-Plus paper was in the exam hall itself and I found it extremely confusing. I'd never seen questions laid out in that way and I spent too long working out what they were asking. I don't think I got through enough of them.'

When the results came through, it was traumatic; perhaps John's biggest upset since that dreadful first day at school. He admits even today that he still carries the chip upon his shoulder.

'It gave me a lasting sense of inferiority. I could actually feel people thinking that I was too dim to get into grammar school.' One might imagine what hell it must have been for a perfectionist like John to consider himself branded as sub-standard. He was aghast.

Happily, there was an upside. His failure amplified his competitive streak and made him brutally determined to succeed, to prove that the system had got it wrong, to show that he wasn't mere cannon fodder for the factories. It was in the furnace of this public shame that the steely edge of his temper was forged.

John went to East Lane Secondary Modern (now Wembley High Technical College) where he was immediately given another exam, this time in a format he could understand. Looking at the results, a teacher remarked, 'You shouldn't be here, you should be up the road', referring to the grammar school. The teacher made some effort to get him moved but nothing came of it and John was assigned to the Technical Stream, where he settled down to work, a smart and tidy-minded boy.

Unlike many of his peers, John took a particular pride in his appearance. His uniform was always smart, his shoes polished to a sunny shine, his Mackintosh raincoat immaculate — the sartorial projection of a highly organised mind. In the scruffy rough-and-tumble of shabby post-war Britain, this wasn't calculated to win him many friends.

He recalls once walking the third of a mile to school, when, out of the blue, he was jumped on from behind by a boy from his year, Michael Moran. Apparently infuriated by the sight of a such a smart softie lording it on East Lane, Moran took it into his head to show off his combative prowess to his own mother and sister. It didn't go well. As the boys tumbled to the pavement, John fought back and the exchange of blows sent the young bully scuttling back to his mother, where he found no sympathy: 'Serves you right for being such a bully, you little idiot.'

'He never came near me again,' said Barnard. 'I think he learned to fear me. He must have realised that I wouldn't stop to think that I'm actually killing this bloke, that it wouldn't bother me at all.'

As a consequence, John passed through the rest of school unmolested by any other bullies. They knew he was not to be messed with.

Barnard landed on his feet at East Lane Secondary Modern. Despite their reputation, these schools were improving all the time and many of today's British business and creative leaders owe much of their personal success to the solid and wide-ranging education they provided. Maths, Sciences, English, History, Geography, Religious Education and French made up the core of John's education, together with metalwork, woodwork, workshop technology and technical drawing: 'I had some fantastic teachers: they were strict but inspirational, and were always keen to help you get on.'

One teacher, Mr Peggs, who was in charge of woodwork and metalwork, stood out for John. Each year Mr Peggs would set the classes to build something practical that they could take home. Some might elect to build chairs and tables, the more ambitious might look to create a wood-framed canoe.

But 15-year-old Barnard had an ambition of an altogether different order. He had no interest in doing what everyone else did and was developing his penchant for always going at least one better. So he asked Mr Peggs if he could build a full-size speedboat. When the teacher quizzed John about his request, it soon became clear that the boy was serious. 'Right,' said Mr Peggs. 'You are to build it at the front of the entire class, under the blackboard. We'll push some workbenches back and people will just have to cram in.'

This was the first of many 'sink or swim' situations that defined Barnard's life. Mr Peggs was a boating man himself and kept a cabin cruiser on the Thames at Windsor, where Ted Barnard also kept a boat. Mr Peggs introduced John to a local boat-building firm that sold him some plans for a wooden speedboat as well as all the necessary materials and fittings. John chose a design that was 16 feet long (4.9 metres), with a beam (width) of 5 feet 6 inches (1.7 metres).

The first job was to make the wooden ribs — the boat's skeleton. When they were shaped according to the plans, Mr Peggs, ignoring all protocols about respect for school property, allowed John to screw them upside-down into the classroom parquet floor to hold them steady. Thus John was able to fit the wooden stringers that joined the ribs together and attach a keel. He could then 'skin' the whole structure, covering the frames in marine plywood shaped into the required complex curves through the time-consuming agency of hot cloths dipped in boiling water and applied to the panels to make them supple.

Only one lesson a week was assigned to this project, so John had to work in his free time. After 'tea' (the evening meal), John and his father, who had done a full-day's work at Glacier's, would go to the school and work late into the night. During lunchtimes the young designer had help from his classmate and friend Bob Dunham.

Mr Peggs also secured for John permission to use a Yankee screwdriver, in effect a pump-action screwdriver that considerably eased the laborious task of driving home the hundreds of screws required in the boat's construction. The trouble with a Yankee, as anyone who has used this brilliant tool will know, is that if you get it wrong, you're quite likely to drive the bit through a finger.

John was working under the tutelage of a perfectionist and Mr Peggs's influence lasted a lifetime. On one occasion the pupil made a wooden bracket that he fixed under the foredeck to help brace the dashboard. He cut a piece of teak for the job but he rushed it: 'I looked at what I'd done and realised it was a bit rough and ready but figured that no one would see it, so I screwed and glued it into place.'

And then in walked Mr Peggs. He checked over John's work, looked behind the panel to see how it was fixed and spotted the dodgy wooden bracket. He looked John straight in the eye.

'What a horrible piece of work,' said Mr Peggs.

'But no one will see it!'

'It's sloppy. Every part of your work should be as good as every other part, even if it cannot be seen. I don't ever want to see that sort of shoddy work again.'

John smiles when he remembers this lesson: 'To this day I've never forgotten his passionate disgust and have never taken such a short cut since. Here I am, at 70, and I can still hear his voice and his anger. Mr Peggs was one of a number of teachers who had a really profound influence.'

The speedboat took six months to complete and, when John and his father wheeled it out on the trailer one summer evening, someone from the school called the local paper, *The News*, to take a photo of it.

The story ran on 10 August 1962: 'The launch, the biggest it was possible to build, was squeezed out of the woodwork room at the end of term and taken to John's home for painting. Total cost was about £55, given by his father.' The paper then quoted Mr Peggs: 'John is one of the best craftsmen we have had.' His reward, from his father, for this moment of local fame was a 40-horsepower Evinrude outboard engine from Ted's boat. John would later trail his speedboat to Frinton-on-Sea in Essex, some 70 miles away, where he used it for water skiing.

The speedboat project reveals a number of John's developing character traits: perfectionism, attention to detail, problem-solving and, most dramatically, his short temper. One evening, a teacher popped in to see how the Barnard father-and-son team were getting on, only to witness John shouting at his dad: 'No! No! No! No! NO! Not like that! You've got to do it like THIS!' The teacher passed no comment at the time, but John still remembers being conscious of what he must have been thinking and not particularly caring.

It's worth noting that John cannot remember giving his speedboat a name, a fact that perhaps reveals one of his core attitudes to the machines he made; he was fastidious about them but never sentimental; his passion lay not so much in the machine itself but in its construction, its economy, its looks and its performance.

John has no interest in motor racing beyond what the races tell him about the machines that he created. He's not obsessed by the beauty or glamour of a machine; he's primarily interested in its functionality. In his career he made some of the most beautiful cars in motorsport, but that was mainly a side effect of efficiency. To Barnard, as will be seen, it was all about the numbers. He says, 'I often drew my cars with flowing lines that were pleasing to the eye, but it was always about function rather than style.' In his initial concepts, John was guided by the simple maxim, 'If it looks right, it probably is right', an approach that became his design starting point.

The speedboat project wasn't Barnard's first brush with media exposure. He gained a brief burst of national recognition in July 1961 on an ITV game show called *Friday Island*, where teenage boys and girls were challenged to solve practical problems on air. The children were tasked with helping castaways Robinson Crusoe (Mike Hall) and Man Friday (Peter Ling) on their studio-built island by identifying and assembling things that had supposedly washed up on the beach.

After a selection interview in which 15-year-old John solved the problem of obtaining drinking water on a desert island, by means of boiling sea water and condensing it on a large flat rock, he was teamed up for the programme with a girl — 'horror!' At that age, despite the immense practicality of his mother, he believed girls to be 'pretty useless creatures'.

On the programme itself, broadcast live, the tasks were made all the more onerous for John because he had his arm in plaster up beyond his elbow. At school a few days earlier, he had tripped while playing softball and snapped his forearm, leaving it hanging at right angles. He recalls calling out, 'I've broken my arm!' and receiving the typical disbelieving abuse from his mates before they ran over, took one look at it and turned away, retching.

Apparently it wouldn't do to allow '60s TV viewers to see he was at a disadvantage, so the producers asked him to wear an American cowboy-style, chequered, long-sleeved shirt to conceal the cast. With a cruel sense of humour they then set him the first task — to hang wallpaper. 'It didn't go well,' says John.

But he came into his own when presented with a disassembled meat mincer to put back together against the clock. In front of an audience of millions he reassembled it in record time, his opposition only managing a partial assembly that had various bits the wrong way round. He and his team-mate won the programme, and John and she were declared Champion Castaways.

Besides revealing John's extraordinary tenacity against the odds and his determination to succeed at a high level, this story showed another remarkable aspect of his character — he was supremely unbothered by dramatic, public success. He didn't boast about it and didn't celebrate it. It happened and he moved on. Any compensation for past failure was quickly forgotten — his low opinion of himself remained undiminished.

As for school sports, he was neither particularly interested in them nor good at them. The only thing he remembers about East Lane sporting life was being part of a school 'house' team called Meyer, which was represented by the colour green. Barnard hates that colour with a superstitious anger: 'It's my all-time hateful colour.' Later he would work for a man with a similar name — Teddy Mayer at McLaren. They never got on.

The first time John saw television was at the age of seven, when his mother's aunt, Great Aunt Maud, bought a set especially for Queen Elizabeth's coronation in 1953. Ted considered it pointless to have a television until the tiny screens got bigger and didn't buy one until the late '50s, when he plumped for an English Electric model with a 21-inch screen.

The common interests of his peers held little appeal to him. Rock-n-Roll was only so much noise to the young Barnard — his family didn't own a record player. Music has never played a large part in his life, although after racking his brains he does confess a liking, aptly enough, for the music from the former capital of America's motor industry, Detroit: 'I do like old Motown.' Otherwise he finds music distracting, preferring the lilting voices of BBC Radio Four in the background to accompany any domestic pottering.

Even the glittering products of Hollywood were of comparatively little interest to him, although he does recall being captivated by one film in particular. In 1952 his father took him to see *The Crimson Pirate*, a swashbuckling romp that starred Burt Lancaster in the eponymous role. It's the only film that sticks in his mind from childhood and one scene in particular set his mind racing.

The pirate, Captain Vallo, is set adrift from his ship with two crew-mates in a rowing boat, without oars and chained to the thwarts. In a moment of Archimedean inspiration they decide to capsize the boat, which turns turtle and sinks to the bottom, upside-down. With the boat above their heads and the pirates breathing from a trapped air bubble, they walk ashore — a trick stolen by the producers of *Pirates of the Caribbean* over half a century later. This wheeze gripped John's imagination and he found himself in regular reverie, teasing the idea apart: 'How long would the air bubble last? Surely the trapped air would make it float? Could it work? It might, if the boat weighed...'

The Barnards, then, were all about practicality rather than fantasy. Even the family dog showed some technical genius. Buster, a Border Collie cross, was John's closest companion: 'He'd be with me all the time.' Born on Uncle Jack's farm, Buster was an intelligent, free-roaming dog who happily wandered the local streets and estates on his own as the mood took him, and even did his own shopping.

'At first I used to take him to the grocer's about 70 yards away, buy some Pal dog food, put the can in his mouth and he'd carry it home. Later we wrapped the right change in newspaper, put it in his mouth and off he'd pad up the road to the grocer's, where he'd put his paws on the counter and drop the cash in return for a tin of meat.' One day Buster came in with a rusty tin of Pal, covered in dirt. Rose Ellen noticed it first: 'Where did he get that? He can't have got it from the shop.' So John kept an eye on Buster, following him across the road to a patch of wasteland. There the dog began to dig, unearthing his secret stash of dog food.

A visit to the grocer's solved the conundrum. 'The cunning hound had been wandering into the shop, spotting a tin in some hapless woman's shopping bag and helping himself. He must have felt some guilt because instead of bringing it home, he would bury it across the road.'

Academically, the young Barnard did well, steadily improving with the passage of school terms until, in his final year, he passed more exams with higher marks than any of his class-mates. In the summer of 1962 the Associated Examining Board for the General Certificate of Education awarded him five Ordinary Level qualifications — English Language, Craftwork Metal, Mathematics, British Constitution and Geometrical Drawing (Engineering).

He also secured, from the Royal Society for the encouragement of Arts, Manufactures and Commerce (RSA), his Technical School Certificate, which included passes in English Language, Civics, Physics, two papers in Mathematics (both with credit), Mechanics, Geometrical and Technical Drawing, and Metalwork with Drawing (all also with credit). It wasn't the last honour he would receive from the RSA.

His success prompted his Form Master, Mr Russell, to make a natural presumption: 'I assume you'll try for university?' It took John aback: 'It sounded to me like flying to the moon. In my mind I was firmly ensconced in the mechanical world, and university was not in my vision.'

He elected instead to leave school and go to Acton Technical College in West London to do a two-year Ordinary National Diploma (OND) in Engineering. The college was tied into the Brunel College of Advanced Technology and Barnard took some of his courses there, all of which, he says from the perspective of over 50 years, he enjoyed.

But the work was tough. While the young Barnard scored highly in homework and laboratory work, his examinations in the spring and summer of 1963 were, in the main, disappointing, with his Head of Department commenting in April, 'Satisfactory progress has been made but from your examination marks it is obvious that Heat, Light & Sound and Mathematics must be given the attention they require.' His Mathematics immediately improved, his score of 75% the following July earning a 'very good', but in Heat, Light & Sound his 'disappointing exam result' scored just 46%, although not for want of trying as his homework mark in the same subject was 74%.

Barnard was a character who liked to work at his own pace and in his own way. He was not a natural at exams, which only goes to show, given how later he would excel under enormous pressure but always at his own pace, that exams cannot be an accurate test of ability for everyone.

By the end of 1964 he had secured an Ordinary National Certificate in Electrical Engineering, Applied Mathematics, Applied Heat, Principles of Electricity and Workshop Technology, with a higher level OND in both Electrical and Mechanical Engineering. His scores at Acton were merely average to good, providing no signal whatsoever about his extraordinary future. John, it would seem from this, was just an ordinary Joe.

CHAPTER 2
CHARIOTS OF FIRE
1954–64

John was nine when he built his first winner. It was a soapbox trolley, or go-cart, the fastest on East Lane.

Using a plank of wood for his chassis, he took the four wheels off the pram in which his mother had shown him the Olympic torch-bearer — nothing was thrown away at Peel Road — and put the bigger ones at the back and the smaller ones at the front. He even installed suspension: at the front he fitted a coil spring over the bolt that connected the axle to the plank; and to support the rear axle he made a metal A-frame that incorporated two long springs. The seat was simply a wider piece of wood screwed to the plank. Thin ropes from each side of the front axle allowed him to steer by pulling one rope or the other.

'We used to race down the pavement on either side of the hump-back bridge, a stone's throw from my house,' says Barnard. 'The pavement was wide enough for two box trolleys and our mates used to give us a push-off from the top of the hill. At the bottom of each side of the bridge was a crossroads. If you were lucky, you stayed on the pavement, but quite often it was impossible to take the corner without slipping off the kerb, so you regularly flew into the road.

'The trick was to do it when no cars were coming, which was a lot easier in the '50s than it is today. The suspension really helped keep up speed despite the sharp bump off the pavement and onto the road. I made several of these machines and used to lend out the older models to my mates for races.'

At around the same time John decided he needed a bicycle. The family budget wouldn't stretch to a new one, so he made his own from bits and pieces, buying an old bike for seven shillings and sixpence (equivalent to about £5 today) and rebuilding it using parts from other broken bikes.

Soapbox cars and scavenged bikes had their obvious limitations, serving mainly to feed Barnard's burgeoning interest in cars. At the age of 10, he helped to fix the clutch on his father's Morris 10 saloon: 'This is my first recollection of being involved with the inner workings of a proper car. The Morris 10 "wet" clutch was an odd affair; basically a metal disc that ran in oil and featured two rings of corks set into the steel to help the pressure plate grip. My job was to go down to the chemist, ask for some of the corks used in their medicine bottles, and then cut them down to replace the worn ones in the plate.'

His father always had some vehicle or another parked in his garage undergoing repair and John soon learned the core skills of a motor mechanic. 'From the age of 11 I understood what the distributor did, what made the pistons move, how they turned the wheels, and how the gearbox functioned.'

By 15, he was fixing cars entirely on his own. His two uncles had a small building firm and a van that often needed attention; John loved taking its engine apart to make it run more efficiently, removing the cylinder head and cleaning off the accumulated coke.

He felt no early draw to the motor racing world, despite his mastery of the East Lane death run. He recalls being taken by 'Uncle Terry' to Brands Hatch in the early '50s, perhaps aged seven, and watching Les Leston drive to victory in a rear-engined Cooper 500. He also visited Snetterton in Norfolk a few times. But otherwise he was 'not massively fired up' by motor racing, and never went to a Formula 1 race in his youth, preferring to immerse himself in making things. But, aged 13 or so, he did start reading *Autosport* magazine and so began to develop a solid background knowledge in the technology and history of the sport.

He also liked motorcycles. Sometimes he visited Wembley Stadium with school friend Mick Cottingham to watch speedway races. 'He was always great fun to be with but my parents regarded him as a dodgy influence,' comments Barnard. Apparently Mick was a good-looking chap — in those days it was about quiffs and big hair — but he had a cocky air that didn't endear him to adults. 'He used to come round and pick me up for the speedway, dressed like a Teddy Boy complete with shining, winkle-picker shoes. Of course, I was never allowed such frippery. But Mick used to bring a spare pair of winkle-pickers that I'd slip on in the shed before creeping out before my parents could spot me.'

Speedway championships, emphatically defined by the heady, creamy smell of Castrol R racing oil, provided a powerful teenage thrill. 'Mick and I would often stand by the bend where the most action and accidents were likely to be. At the very least we'd be sprayed with cinders from the track as the bikes skidded round the corners.'

This stimulating experience prompted John to dream of a bike of his own: 'We used to stand outside Tommy Price's workshop in North Wembley, staring at the speedway bikes in the window, discussing their various merits. A few years later, when we were 16, Mick got his own motorbike, making me intensely jealous, so I went home and told mother that I was old enough to have one, that I needed it to get to college. She replied, "If you get a motorbike, I'm leaving home." So that was the end of that.'

So it was the bus for young Barnard. He recalls being 'bloody cold waiting on the bridge at Willesden Junction' on his daily journeys to Acton Technical College, six miles from home. But he did get to do some driving. At 16, John was given the keys to his parents' old Trojan van and was set free to drive it around Sudbury Court, a local housing estate, to make fruit and veg deliveries for his mother. The legal driving age, then as now, was 17, but at that time police were inclined to turn a blind eye to lads who were slightly under-age if they were using a vehicle for work. One night John drove it to a dance at the community hall on the estate and on the way a policeman stepped off the pavement, put out his hand, and stopped him.

'What are you doing, lad?'

'Delivering groceries.'

'At this time of night? Dressed like that?' John was wearing his best suit. The policeman went round to the back of the van and opened it. On the floor sat a hessian bag half-full of potatoes, all that was left from John's earlier round. 'Okay, lad, carry on.'

When John turned 17 in May 1963, the month in which Graham Hill took the first of his five victories in the Monaco Grand Prix, his parents duly bought him a second-hand Austin A35 van. It would have boasted an attractive rounded bonnet and white radiator grille had these not been smashed in an accident, and the gears were also making a horrible noise. It was an inspired gift and summed up the parental approach: 'Here is your birthday present, at least some of it, now get on and sort out the rest.'

He got to work straight away, dismantling the gearbox and installing a new first-gear cog. To fix the van's damaged front he went a little way up Peel Road to a garage owned by a Mr Dick, from whom John bought oxyacetylene welding equipment at a knockdown rate. A generous and helpful soul, Mr Dick set up the equipment and taught him, there and then, how to use it, showing him how to connect the welding torch to the gas bottles, how to get the right flame and which nozzle sizes to use for the various steel thicknesses he was likely to encounter.

John dragged the heavy gear home, and, with great delight, torched the front off the Austin. He then rebuilt it, welding replacement panels into position and replacing the lights, bumper and grille, all rescued from cars in a local scrapyard. He also decided to fit windows into the rear side panels.

The next thing to do, as any young blood knew, was to make it go fast. He bought a second-hand supercharger and fitted it with metal brackets made up in the workshop. He attached a belt drive to power the supercharger from the crankshaft, installed a better exhaust system, and adopted other tuning bits and pieces. The changes meant that the car, to use a popular phrase from the time, 'went like shit off a hot shovel'.

Barnard then made his first major mistake: 'I remember my father warning me about the dangers of this increased power, but, being a cocky teenager, I thought I knew better than the old man. I couldn't afford new tyres and the brakes were old, but I figured they'd do.

'I was coming back from Acton one evening, racing along the North Circular Road in the rain, when a car braked hard ahead of me. It was at that precise moment that I learned the importance of uprating your tyres and brakes to match the power of a supercharged engine. I ran straight into the back of the car and destroyed all the work I'd done just a few weeks before. The owner of the car I hit wasn't too happy either.'

John couldn't face bringing the Austin home in that state, so he borrowed the keys to a nearby lock-up garage owned by his uncle and set to work fixing the car there. In the end he realised it would be a lot easier if he confessed to the accident and repaired it at home. 'My father wasn't angry. He just shook his head and said, "I told you so." My mother was simply relieved I wasn't hurt.'

In repairing the Austin, John improved his welding and sheet metalwork and learned how to spray-paint. A friend in South Wales had some spray gear so he drove the car there for painting, but by the time he got back to Peel Road the new paint was bubbling off, a cause of some stress. He took the lesson on board: 'That's how I learned the importance of prepping; how important it is to rub down the metalwork thoroughly and use the right primers and paints.'

John sold the Austin A35 for a figure close to the cost of the entire rebuild project and began to look at sportier cars. Around this time Rose Ellen recruited a young man to manage the greengrocer's and he arrived proudly in a black Rover 14 sports saloon.

'This was a fascinating-looking beast,' says John, 'with a long bonnet leading back from a tall front grille to running boards that you could stand on, like a Chicago gangster in a movie. It also boasted a chopped top [a low roof] which gave it a really racy feel.'

John envied the car but knew it was out of his price range. That situation changed abruptly when, one fortuitous day, the young man arrived for work with the back smashed up. John bought the Rover for a tenner. He then examined the damaged back end and quickly concluded that repair was beyond his skills — 'the boot and rear doors were totally crumpled.'

So he decided to go in an entirely new direction. He torched off the boot, rear doors and back-seat area. He then welded in a steel bulkhead behind the front seats, cutting out a section of it and installing a rear window. 'It looked, well, interesting, with its long bonnet, low windscreen, running boards and a cab like a pick-up truck. The rear consisted of nothing more than the open chassis.' On this he built a tongue-and-groove pine open-topped box with a hinged tailgate that really did turn it into a pick-up truck — ideal for making deliveries for his mother.

'The car got a lot of quizzical looks and wry comments,' remembers Barnard, but he didn't give a hoot about those. He was learning another important life skill — to ignore critics.

There then occurred a violent incident that powerfully demonstrated the tightness of the Barnard family unit. Mr Dick had sold his garage to a Mr Brown, whom Barnard describes as a 'car-dealing spiv out of the mould of Arthur Daley', referring to the unscrupulous trader played by George Cole in *Minder*, the '80s British TV series. Brown specialised in selling used cars and, having run out of room on the garage forecourt, began parking the cars up and down Peel Road, sometimes blocking the Barnards' drive. This, reports, John, drove his family 'potty'. One day, upon seeing yet another Brown car parked in front of her shop, Rose Ellen went out to 'give Mr Brown a piece of her mind'. She received a torrent of abuse and returned to the house even more angry.

Her distress lit the blue touch paper, prompting Ted and John to march out of the house together and 'put things straight'. Within a few moments of Ted telling Mr Brown what he thought of him insulting his wife, four other men appeared and started a fight. When one of them threw a punch at Ted, John and Ted 'went berserk' and John recalls 'lashing out with his fists and catching a guy on the nose, which immediately burst into blood.' He remembers little else of this, his second street fight, other than 'in short order, they all ran away', having learned the folly of tangling with Barnard males defending their womenfolk.

Mr Brown, clearly sure that he had a right to park where he liked without being beaten up, called the police, who came round the following day. 'They took one look at me, a 17-year-old, my mum and my dad and concluded, "Okay, we can see what happened here", and that was the end of the matter.' Mr Brown never again parked his cars in front of the Barnards' drive.

One lasting effect is that Barnard still dreams of building a house 'in the middle of 30 acres as far away from pesky neighbours as is practical'.

While at college in Acton, John honed his car-building skills, taking on a series of semi-wrecked Triumph TR two-seater sports cars, his favourite being a TR3A that he sprayed black and to which he fitted a steel hard-top. 'The TR3A had a gorgeous four-cylinder engine which made a throaty roar as I shot along East Lane. But I was always pushing to get another car.'

John even started looking at kit cars, which enthusiasts put together from parts supplied by manufacturers and in so doing avoided the need to pay purchase tax. He went to look at a completed one with Ted: 'The owner proudly claimed it could do 95mph. My dad sniffed and turned to me: "I wouldn't buy you anything like that — don't know who has put it together."' The phrase found purchase in John's mind; from now on he would seek workmanship of the highest quality and where he couldn't afford it or find it, he would do it himself.

Then came the car that was the young Barnard's coming of age, his ambition personified, his growing talent realised. He began looking at thoroughbreds, the cars created by master craftsmen.

Shortly after his 19th birthday, in 1965, John and his father went to view a second-hand Aston Martin DB2/4, a car probably best known for its role in Alfred Hitchcock's *The Birds*. John was struck by its style and beauty: 'There on the drive stood a gorgeous silver-grey car complete with its bowler-hat grille. There was a 3-litre engine under a long curved bonnet and it had wire wheels.'

The owner was friendly enough to speak a word of warning: 'Listen chaps, I don't want to teach you people to suck eggs, but this is quite a powerful car. You do know what you're doing?' Ted assured him they did and paid him £480 — 'a fitting price for a car with the registration PCD 480'. It was also a substantial sum, representing more than a third of the annual average wage at the time. The car was 10 years old and in good order, but its paintwork was tired and the upholstery worn.

They drove it home but decided not to do any work straight away — John wanted to enjoy it. He recalls doing summer work in a banana-packing factory for Geest, driving to work in the Aston and getting ribbed for being so flash. He enjoyed the banter and revelled in the envy, as far as Barnard would or could revel in anything. That is, until the engine blew up.

'I was tooling along one evening towards London on Western Avenue, the A40, not far from Northolt Aerodrome, at a healthy 80mph, when there was an enormous bang. The entire front of the car was engulfed in smoke, which cleared as suddenly as it appeared.

'I pulled over, the engine still running, and checked the rev counter — all seemed fine. So I hopped out, lifted the bonnet, and found myself looking right through a hole in the engine block to the road beneath. One of the con rods had disintegrated, its broken arm cutting two long slots, top to bottom, in the engine block. The piston was jammed at the top of the bore but the other five pistons were still running.'

He nursed it home wondering where he could get another Aston engine. He soon heard about a 3-litre engine block for sale in Birmingham for £25, but when he brought it back to Peel Road he discovered he had been misled; the engine was the 2.6-litre version. Despairing, he decided to go direct to Aston Martin in Newport Pagnell, where he found a 3-litre engine block. The only problem was the price — £250. 'Given that I needed to add con rods, liners, pistons and bearings, it was rapidly becoming clear I couldn't afford the rebuild.'

At the time he used to hang around at The Chequered Flag garage on the Edgware Road watching the mechanics prepare race cars. He told them the sorry tale of his Aston and was advised to 'just shove something else in her'. It was, momentarily, a dilemma. To switch engines would have been to break a purist's rules, but he was young and raring to go. He started looking for 'an engine with a bit of poke' and found a 4.7-litre Chevrolet V8 in good condition, complete with a four-speed Borg-Warner gearbox, for £250. This was a more powerful proposition altogether, but still John felt the need to buy twin Carter four-barrel carburettors to supply even more fuel. This car was going to move.

Now to fit a quart into a pint pot. First he had to install the V8 in an engine bay designed for a straight six. He quickly discovered he would have to rebuild the footwells at their inboard sides in order to accommodate the Chevy's bulk.

The engine also required a completely different exhaust system and gearshift/clutch mechanism, and he even had to relocate the battery further back.

The process was an education: 'I learned how to adjust the engine cooling and how to trim the airflow through the front grille, I mastered pedal ratios and basic motor electronics. I was learning all the time.' After two months' hard graft, John had the engine in place and running perfectly. He soon found, to his utter joy, that the acceleration, enhanced by the Carter carburettors, was on a par with an E-type Jaguar.

Then his perfectionism kicked in. The Aston DB2/4 was powerful, but it needed to look a lot smarter. So he decided to respray it in his father's garage. He built his own paint-spraying system by using a discarded electric motor to power an old air compressor that provided the pressure for the spray gun. For the colour he chose Rolls-Royce Shell Grey.

The job finished, he peeled away the masking tape to reveal immaculate work. On his first journey out, someone leaned through the window at traffic lights and asked him who had done the spray job. 'I did it myself,' he beamed as he roared away.

The only thing wrong with the Aston now was its 10-year-old upholstery. Barnard wanted it to look new, but to replace it would be highly specialised job. This was outside his skill set, and definitely beyond his budget. One evening he raised the issue at the dining table and received an answer he hadn't expected. Rose Ellen, in her no-nonsense style, said, 'Upholstery can't be that hard, son. We can work it out and do it ourselves.'

The next day Ted and John went to an upholsterer's in Wembley to talk through the practicalities and came home with two halves of cowskin, one grey, the other black: 'These were straight off the animal, treated and dyed, but otherwise half a cow.' Now they had a plan. John took the old seats out of the car and carefully cut the stitching, reducing the old upholstery to its component panels. He gave these, together with the new leather, to his mother. Using the old panels as patterns, she cut the grey leather to match the shapes of the seat bases and backs.

Meanwhile, John and Ted began working on her ancient Singer sewing machine, replacing the old treadle with a foot-operated electric motor and rebuilding the sewing foot and needle clamp to cope with needles strong enough to pierce multiple layers.

The seat backs featured vertical pleats that had to be carefully packed with wadding to achieve a comfortable-looking padded effect. They presented no problem to Rose Ellen, who took the originals apart, worked out how they were made and then created identical new ones. She used the black leather to make the piping that ran round the edges, sewing the hide tightly around lengths of cane and leaving a flange of material so the finished piping could be joined to the rest of the upholstery. She soldiered on until the entire job was done, to Aston Martin standards.

John looks back on the achievement in amazement: 'It was the toughest thing I'd ever asked mum to do, and it was absolutely perfect. At the time, it made me feel that as a family we could do anything, that whatever we wanted to make, however complex, however diverse the skill set required, we could do it ourselves, and do it as well as the professionals — there was nothing to stop us.'

If you've spotted that there's no input here from John's relatives, it's because none have survived. If you've noticed that none of his childhood friends have contributed, it's because he has lost contact with them all — a mark of his peculiarly insular character. But that character, and all that had contributed to its making, guided him towards the profession in which he would excel, although his future direction was yet to crystallise — and at this stage it wasn't even an ambition.

Perhaps there was nothing particularly special about Barnard's childhood. True, he had engineering-minded parents and an ability to build cars, but that didn't mean he was remarkable; there were probably tens of thousands like him across the country.

He did, however, possess another attribute that would make him stand out from the pack — his ever-developing, intense, perfectionist drive, created in part, as he says himself, by his early failure of the 11-Plus exam. He also had a natural inclination towards leadership, which was exemplified by his forthright, dominant and sometimes angry relationship with his father.

Perhaps these traits are best summed up in this revealing observation: 'As I got older, I remember feeling a strange pressure — that I was the leader, the head of the family, the one with real drive to succeed. My parents really didn't do anything but go to work; and if they did anything else at all, it was nearly always for me. It was a great gift, and I don't mean to sound ungrateful, because I'm immensely grateful, but sometimes it felt like a burden.'

A great gift indeed — for if it weighed him down it also lifted him up, like a plant pushing through a pavement. An extraordinary creativity had been born — now all it needed was room to blossom.

PART 2
LEARNING THE ROPES

CHAPTER 3
WHATEVER LOLA WANTS, LOLA GETS
1964–70

In May 1964, when Graham Hill scored the second of his five victories in the Monaco Grand Prix, John Barnard was completing his college course in Acton, acquiring an Ordinary National Diploma (OND) in engineering. It was a respectable result, although John admits, 'I spent all my free time building cars, and my homework suffered for it.'

That September he started part-time study at Watford College of Technology on a three-year course for an engineering Higher National Certificate (HNC). This was an important next step towards an engineering career, although the fact that this qualification didn't equate to a university degree status would bother him for ever more. The course proved to be ideal for him, teaching such fundamentals of engineering as how various materials behave under various loads and stresses, and the basic mathematical formulae that he would use time and again throughout his motorsport career.

'The course taught me to think problems through and to analyse structures in a way that proved very useful later on,' John says. 'I gained a feeling for materials and a hands-on sense of how machines work. I learned the vital skill of deriving formulae from first principles.'

By the summer of 1967 he had completed modules in Mathematics, Strength of Materials, Theory of Machines and Applied Thermodynamics. He did reasonably well, scoring grades that were average to good, Bs and Cs for the most part.

The Watford course also required John to work in Wembley at the Osram Lamp Division of GEC (General Electric Company), a massive British conglomerate. He was assigned to the Lamp, Machinery Design and

Development Department, which designed machines for making lamps and light bulbs.

Working with a senior engineer, his first major project was to design and build an industrial machine that crimped electric terminals onto the end of cables. One unit was sold to a factory in Birmingham and John was duly despatched to see if it was working properly. He drove up in his Aston Martin DB2/4 and confirmed that all was in order, but while there he was mercilessly ribbed by bored female workers who obviously enjoyed some sport with a boy so evidently wet behind the ears.

The HNC's combined practical and academic methodology provided a solid foundation, fostering in Barnard an instinctive understanding of machines and materials, what he describes as 'a feel for the beating heart of machinery... A good engineer develops this by playing with the things, taking them apart and rebuilding them by hand. It gives a feel for scale, for the strength of components, for the power a machine can generate.' Barnard, in fact, was unusual in his feel for machinery; his engineering instinct formed the core of his unique talent.

His education served him well, but it was serving a brain blessed with that most rare and valuable combination of talents: a drive to create new solutions combined with top-class practical skills. Tyler Alexander, a McLaren director who worked with Barnard, put it well: 'John was very, very good at designing and making things — he knew how they worked. It's a key thing that a lot of people don't have. He had both sides of it — he knew what he wanted and he knew how to make it work, because he knew how to make it. That, to me, was a major part of his success.'

Another talent John seemed to develop early was a knack for financial success, some of which was a result of a bright, money-conscious mind nurtured by his family's thrifty outlook, and some of which came with the territory. He was paid £1,400 a year at GEC, a princely first salary for a part-time employee, £150 more than the average UK full-time salary.

When the price of petrol suddenly shot up by 50% in 1965, from five shillings to seven shillings and sixpence per gallon, John, ever frugal, responded by swapping the thirsty Chevrolet engine in his Aston Martin for a Ford Zodiac straight six that he found in a breaker's yard. It was clear to him that fuel prices were, as a general rule, only ever going to go up.

A few months later he sold the DB2/4 to a friend for a profit that allowed him to buy, for £750, a dark blue Aston Martin DB4, the model Michael Caine drove in *The Italian Job*. Its 4-litre six-cylinder engine had a habit of draining oil out of the crankshaft when parked overnight, so when John came to start it in the morning it had no oil pressure. To fix this, he removed the engine and replaced the bearing shells, as well as cleaning out the cylinder head and polishing the ports. He also resprayed the body.

Cars were now an obsession: 'I would work on my various cars almost from the moment I got home until bedtime, burning the midnight oil on Friday and Saturday nights.' Which, it must be said, had a debilitating impact on his love life. 'I wasn't really into girlfriends at the time; cars were just too intoxicating. I didn't get out much either.'

His life wasn't entirely bereft of romance; he remembers the educational joys of having a girlfriend, Annie, two years older than him, with whom he went camping in France for a wonderful week of fun, using his father's Standard Vanguard estate. Driving into Dover to catch a ferry across the Channel, he discovered that the radiator had sprung a leak. He was torn — should he take it home and repair it, or carry on? Romance, or some similar impulse, got the better of him, so after a temporary repair the couple made it as far as Perpignan near the Spanish border before heading home. But something didn't spark in the relationship and they broke up soon after their return: 'She probably got fed up with me messing about with cars — that's usually what happened.'

Unsurprisingly, John couldn't see a future for himself in the Osram Lamp Division and, as his Watford College course drew to a close, he started looking for a way into the motor industry. By now it was becoming clear to him that it made sense to do what he was good at, and that simply had to involve cars.

He applied to Simms Motor Units, a manufacturer of car components based in East Finchley, North London. When John arrived at the factory gate in his DB4 he asked the guard where he should go: 'The man did a bit of a double-take, stared at the registration plate, looked up at me and said, "GEL 23! That used to belong to Mr Simms!"' John saw this remarkable coincidence as a good omen, but perhaps it was more an omen for his future in general than for the upcoming interview, because he didn't get the job.

Barnard changed direction, applying to the Hoover Company at Perivale, West London, their factory a famous example of Art Deco architecture. He got the job and a salary of £1,600 a year in the design and development department.

His role was to work alongside a man who studied competitors' washing machines and tumble dryers, taking the appliances apart and writing reports about them. The two worked alone on this low-level industrial espionage in a well-equipped workshop complete with lathes, mills and welding gear, most of which lay unused and gathering dust. John soon became bored, but his interest was rekindled when he came up with his first professional innovation.

The problem was straightforward. It could be tricky to work out what made a competitor's machine tick if you couldn't actually see inside it when it was running. So Barnard made use of the idle workshop and started cutting up Perspex sheets. Soon all the machines were fitted with plastic windows so he and his colleague could peer inside as the innards spun around.

'My superior was amazed at this,' Barnard reports. 'No one had really made use of the workshop before.' But his enthusiasm didn't last. 'There are only so many Perspex windows you can fit into washing machines before you understand their mechanicals completely.'

He relieved the tedium in his breaks by reading *Autosport* and, as he did so, began to develop a desire to get into motor racing. The ambition was also catalysed by regular weekend visits to mates at The Chequered Flag, where he watched them working on race cars. Sometimes he would go with them to watch local stock-car races.

The years were passing. It was now late 1968 and John, 23 years old, was becoming worried about his future. 'I just couldn't work with Hoover until I was 65. The very idea scared me. I began asking myself, what do I do, what do I like?' But his own self-doubt, the inferiority complex that provided so much fuel for his ambition, began putting up barriers. 'I actually thought that motor racing couldn't be for me, because it was a sport for rich boys who could afford to do it for fun.' However, he suppressed his doubts and began writing application letters.

He first contacted Bruce McLaren, the renowned New Zealand racing driver whose own McLaren cars were dominating Can-Am (Canadian-American) racing in North America and starting to make an impact in Formula 1. His enquiry was rewarded with an interview at their factory in Colnbrook, Berkshire, west of London and beneath the deafening roar of a Heathrow flight path. There he met Swiss-born designer Jo Marquart, who, after a few minutes' chat, politely informed the young aspirant that he would be better off gaining experience in racing classes of lower prestige, such as Formula Ford, before he had the temerity to come knocking on a Formula 1 door.

Disappointed but now even more determined, Barnard next wrote to Eric Broadley at Lola, the race car manufacturer that Broadley had founded 10 years earlier and named in tribute to Broadway dancer Gwen Verdon, who played the seductive Lola in the musical hit *Damn Yankees*, singing the then famous song 'Whatever Lola wants, Lola gets'. What Lola wanted, and was getting, was a series of victories for its cars in a range of motorsport categories. Broadley replied the same day, inviting Barnard to an interview the following week at the Lola factory in Yeovil Road, Slough, near Heathrow. John was taken aback to discover that the interview was actually going to be with Broadley himself, so, haunted by his failures at Simms and McLaren, he felt pretty intimidated on his 45-minute drive to the factory.

Broadley, a bespectacled, friendly-faced boffin of a man, dressed in shirt and tie, was a considerate character who immediately put the applicant at ease. Soon John was chatting away about a 'special' he was planning to build, based on the design of the Lotus Seven. The Lola boss was impressed by the young man's knowledge and passion. Suddenly he took John's hand, shook it and said: 'You can start in the drawing office.' Barnard was delighted.

'This was a big break for me. I knew I would have to raise my game and I knew I would be tested and I was nervous about that, but I was also energised and confident.'

The move to Lola meant a £200 pay cut, but that was of little concern to a young man who was making a dream, a relatively new one, come true. When he told his Hoover colleagues, with quiet pride, that he was off to Lola, it was only then that he discovered there were other people there who shared his growing fascination with motorsport, and one engineer even had his own race car. Barnard's natural habit of keeping himself to himself had excluded him from these racers.

The Lola factory was a cramped, single-storey unit on a trading estate, packed to the rafters with racing paraphernalia. It was a buzzing place replete with talent and enthusiasm.

Among the talented people John encountered were Jim Chapman and George Woodward, a quiet, modest pair who shared a dry, acerbic humour. Together they had formed Chapward Racing Services and Lola was their principal client. There seemed to be nothing they couldn't do: they built cars to Broadley's general specifications, suggested improvements, worked on the cars' set-up, and then took them to America where they acted as race mechanics for some of Lola's customers.

'They were artisan-mechanics,' says John, 'now a very rare breed. Today, a mechanic doesn't get involved in complex discussions with the engineers. They go to the store, pick up a part, fit it on, and if it doesn't fit, they take it back.'

John was part of the team designing the cars that Chapward built. Broadley would 'scheme' the basic design and John and the other designers would produce all the detailed drawings before Chapward got down to constructing the car.

Barnard's first job at Lola was to redesign the mountings for the oil cooler on a Can-Am car, the T220, which was being built for American driver Peter Revson. Can-Am cars were immensely powerful and John recalls with pleasure the thrill of just being around these racing monsters: 'They had enormous Chevy engines, bored out to eight litres. Chapman and Woodward used to wheel them out into the alley behind the factory and fire them up. The ground shook and the noise was deafening — just to be near them was fantastic.'

The T220 was duly shipped to America, where Revson wrote it off during its first race, at Road Atlanta. Jim Chapman recalls the moment: 'It was a brand new car but had arrived in America with virtually no testing. So we were actually trying to sort the thing out during the first race. Peter lost a tyre and he crashed into a bridge before being hit by another car — there was nothing left of it, but somehow Peter walked away.'

This was, unfortunately, the way at Lola, and elsewhere too. The Slough factory turned out cars thick and fast, but too often their products were not tested sufficiently before being thrown into the lion's den of racing. Lack of testing, together with Broadley's tendency to ignore lessons learned from previous cars, provided bones of contention for Chapman and Woodward, and created a challenging environment for the young Barnard.

'We were left very much to our own devices,' Jim Chapman said in an interview for this book, 'and so we did our own development, trying to improve the car for every race. When we brought all the changes, all we'd learned, back to Lola, Eric would ignore it. He was very much a one-man show. So we would end up with another brand-new, untested car for the following year, instead of it being an evolution, incorporating all the best parts of the previous year's car. In 1970, '71, and '72 the test programme for new Can-Am cars didn't last much longer than one day prior to shipping the cars to the USA for the first race.'

The 'new start' philosophy was not necessarily as misguided as Chapman suggests, and it rubbed off on Barnard. He would go on to imitate aspects of this approach and, as we shall see, keep everyone on their toes by starting afresh each year with a brand-new car.

Life at Lola was non-stop and John slipped into the frenetic work ethic like a hungry fox into a henhouse. Soon he caught the boss's eye as a possible talent. After just nine months, Broadley approached John at his drawing board and made the offer any young car designer dreams of hearing: 'Would you like to design a car on your own?'

To this day Barnard cannot recall what specifically he had done to prompt it. 'If you think I can,' was his meek reply. 'Go on lad, have a crack at it,' said Eric.

Broadley explained that Volkswagen was bringing out a new category, Formula Super Vee, intended to introduce up-and-coming drivers to open-wheel racing. One of the requirements was to use the Volkswagen (VW) Type 3 air-cooled 1,600cc engine, as fitted to the Beetle. Eric gave John the specifications and left him to it, his first blue-sky moment, his initial step into the unknown.

First Barnard formed in his mind a basic picture of the car, and then, referring to existing Formula Ford designs, he calculated the wheelbase (the distance between the front and rear wheels measured from their centres), the track (the width between opposite wheels) and the weight distribution across all four wheels. Then he began to draw a body shape to accommodate the driver, engine, fuel tanks and suspension. He designed the car around a spaceframe chassis, a triangulated arrangement of tubular steel that was the usual structure for production race cars at the time.

'In those days the regulations were quite loose,' recalls John, 'so there was more scope to place stuff where you wanted. You build up a feeling for the car you're creating by studying similar Formulas, not to copy them but to get the scale, the general feeling for the design. But this was a brand-new Formula, so it was that much more of a challenge.'

Two weeks into designing the optimum way of mounting the VW engine and gearbox into the chassis, Barnard's work was interrupted by Broadley. 'Volkswagen are dropping the Beetle engine and changing it to the VW-Porsche Type 4,' Eric commented in passing, as if this fundamental change was as easy as swapping batteries in a transistor radio. The first example of this new design of air-cooled engine, as used in the Porsche 914, arrived a few days later.

'I remember unpacking it, setting it up on a wooden box in the drawing office and being shocked at how it was such a completely different size and shape to the Beetle engine.' He paced around it, looking at the bulky air ducts that ran all over it to keep it cool. His task was quickly becoming a nightmare. 'It slowly dawned on me that accommodating this engine was going to be impossible. I felt sick to my stomach. I was contemplating my first major failure, and I was the new boy, in whom Eric had shown so much trust.'

At eight o'clock that evening, Eric came into the drawing office and saw John pacing around. When he asked what was up, John's reply was emotional: 'There's no way I'm going to get this engine in. I can't do it. It's going to be a horrible mess.'

Eric smiled and then said something that John would never forget: 'Don't worry about it, lad. Go home. It's the best thing to do. It's what I do when I've got a problem like this. Don't stand and stare at it, just put it to the back of your mind and I guarantee you the answer will come to you in two or three days.'

John is fond of remembering this moment: 'I now have his advice etched in my mind. When I get confronted with a "nasty", I worry the solution, tease it, but I don't panic. If I hit a wall, I just remember what old Eric said: "The answer will come to you in two or three days." And it always has.'

Eric's wise advice worked to inspire John's first significant motorsport innovation. Contemplating the fan that drove air through a bulky system of steel ducts, Barnard saw an opportunity to save space and weight. He realised that some of the ducts served to take heat from the engine to warm the production car's interior, so that function could be dismantled straight away — racing drivers were never afforded such luxuries, whatever the weather. There were also flaps in the system to allow air to bypass the engine in cold climates; they could go too. In the end Barnard decided to take off all the ducting so he could 'let the dog see the rabbit'.

With it all removed he suddenly saw a way to use the engine to make the car physically stronger, envisaging a means by which the engine itself could actually add to the car's strength. What if he bolted a vertical aluminium plate to the rear of the chassis? He could bolt the engine to that, which struck him as a much stronger mounting. And, what if he then attached the rear suspension arms not to the chassis, but to the gearbox? Why, then the engine would become a structural part of the chassis itself — a far more rigid set-up. For further strength Barnard also adopted two steel tubes to run from the top of the aluminium plate to the back of the engine's crankcase.

It should be noted that the concept wasn't entirely original. The first fully stressed engine in a racing car is attributed to Lotus's Colin Chapman, who used a comparable technique to secure a BRM H16 engine into the Lotus 43 in 1966, and, more successfully, the Ford-Cosworth V8 engine in his Lotus 49 of 1967. In both cases the chassis was a monocoque, made of aluminium panelling, rather than a tubular spaceframe as used by Lola. As far as Barnard was concerned, however, his idea was new.

'I hadn't seen the BRM mounting but the difference is that the H16 was designed specifically as a racing engine whereas the VW engine in the Super Vee was a standard production engine designed for rubber mounting in a road car. As far as I know, the Cosworth V8 was the first fully stressed racing engine; my Super Vee solution was semi-stressed because it had two tubes to help with lateral and vertical bending forces. It was the only Super Vee that didn't use a complete spaceframe assembly to support the engine, gearbox and rear suspension.'

His particular solution, with the bolts, aluminium plate and bracing, amounted to a new way of mounting, or 'picking up' the engine, and thereafter all Lola Super Vees were built that way. Indeed, versions of this method became Barnard's signature way of installing a racing engine.

The bit between his teeth, John now romped over the rest of the powerplant, creating a new air-ducting system in lightweight glass-fibre to replace the original steel. Happily immersed in the detail design of the rest of the car, he created a quarter-scale model using a light, fine-grained wood known as 'gelatong' to make up the chassis and then covering this in modelling clay to form the body shape. The model took about 10 days to complete, John taking it home each evening to refine it in the Peel Road workshop, shaving the clay block millimetre by millimetre to achieve a perfect three-dimensional rendition of his original concept.

This he took to Specialised Mouldings in Huntingdon, Cambridge, a company that began life in Bromley, Kent, in the south-eastern outskirts of London, as a neighbour to the infant Lola, leading Broadley to develop a close working relationship with the company's founder, Peter Jackson. The engineers there used John's model to create a full-size wooden 'buck' or 'plug' from which the mould for the glass-fibre bodywork would be made. Buck-making is a highly skilled process, as you may imagine; it's not easy to take the dimensions, lines and contours of a small model and convert them accurately into a wooden structure.

The process of mould-making is more straightforward but requires care and skill, and is explained here because later we will encounter similar but more complex carbon-fibre processes. The outer surface of the full-size wooden buck was painted with a gloss finish that was then polished and coated with a release agent. Then it was painted with gelcoat, a form of paint that bonds well with resin, dries smooth and hard, maintains flexibility and is used to create glass-fibre's outer surface.

When the gelcoat was dry, it was itself painted over with resin and covered with carefully aligned strips of glass-fibre matting. These were pressed into the contours of the buck with brushes before more layers of matting were added to make the mould thicker. Matting is extremely pliable when soaked in resin but it's easy to make a mess of its lay-up, resin being nasty, sticky, smelly stuff. After the resin had set hard, the mould was released from the buck, ready to be used to make any number of Super Vee body panels.

To make a panel, the mould's smooth, inner, hard, gelcoated surface was covered with a releasing agent so that the mould could be easily separated from the body panel. Then another coat of gelcoat would be applied, pigmented to the colour of a customer's choice, and this would make up the outer surface of the car's bodywork. Once dry, this would be coated with resin and laid up with glass-fibre matting to provide thickness and strength. When hard, this skin of gelcoat and glass-fibre would be released from the mould, *et voilà*, the smooth-surfaced bodywork would emerge in the chosen colour.

In the meantime, John's drawings flowed into the workshop where mechanics constructed the chassis, suspension, brackets and other parts. Every so often Broadley would drift by John's drawing board to ask how it was going and to make occasional suggestions about suspension geometry. The Super Vee took about three months to complete, from blank paper to gleaming racer.

Now it was ready for testing. John accompanied Frank Gardner, an acerbic Australian driver and engineer, to the track at Snetterton, near Norwich. 'I remember the feedback well,' says John. 'Frank was a no-nonsense Aussie. He would say either "OK", meaning good, or "bucket of shit", which wasn't so good. On this occasion he said "handles like a sockful of diarrhoea", meaning the suspension needed tightening up. What a start.'

But what a learning experience too. Barnard ran every part of the operation, designing and specifying every component, solving the engine pick-up, planning the body shape, calculating and laying out the complex suspension, making a model, working with the bodywork moulders, overseeing the build and taking the finished Super Vee out to be tested. Even Gardner finally acknowledged that it was 'all right'. And it now had a name as well. The Lola T250 was the first car designed entirely by John Barnard.

He recalls no real praise. 'I got a few nods and grunts from others at Lola, but nothing more.' Even his boss had little to say: 'All Eric said was, "Good job, lad."' This was fine with the young engineer; it was an approach he had become used to at home — his parents weren't given to high praise — and one that he would adopt with his own employees in the future. 'I didn't expect any more. To them, it was just another car, so no massive criticism, no great praise, it was just, "Let's get on to the next one." As for me, I was counting my lucky stars to have landed such a rare opportunity to design a professional race car.'

What was there left to do? Take it to market, of course. One morning Robbie Rushbrook, a Lola director, came up to John, looked over the Super Vee, and said: 'Well, lad, now you've finished it, you'd better take it up to the show.' So John put it on a trailer and towed it to Olympia in West London for the annual Racing Car Show, where he spent a relatively restful 10 days sitting on the Lola stand chatting to admirers and potential customers.

One day he was alone on the stand when the phone rang. A deep Texan voice asked if he represented Lola, to which John said 'yes'. Well, that was good, because the man wanted to buy two Can-Am cars — worth £100,000 each. John, out of his depth, looked around for help, only to spot, on a neighbouring stand, racing driver Peter Gethin chatting into a phone, surrounded by a bunch of mates who seemed most entertained. The penny dropped and Barnard felt a fool.

Lola sent some 60 Super Vees off to America in that first year, 1971, but as one of John's Lola colleagues commented, 'We never got any feedback, never heard whether it was a good car, bad car, what was a problem, what wasn't. Lola was producing so many cars, I don't think they ran many of them before they were shipped off to America.' This came from Patrick Head, of whom we shall hear more soon.

Despite the lack of feedback, it is more than likely that the work done by John Barnard contributed to Lola's dominance of Super Vee in the USA throughout the '70s. The T250 recorded its first win at Road Atlanta on 11 July 1971, driven by Tom Reddy. Tom Davey and Bob Wheelock went on to win the Sports Car Club of America (SCCA) Formula Super Vee championship 'run-off' races in 1971 and '72 respectively, driving Lolas.

John Barnard's first race car was a winner.

Barnard's attention turned once again towards girls. It was tricky, because six-day weeks were the norm at Lola. But he did break away on Saturday nights, accompanying Glyn Williams, a mate who had other friends in Hampstead, North London. So John slipped into a group where the girls were mainly New

Zealanders, one of whom was Pauline Douglas. A relationship began.

'Pauline and I thought we were in love.' So convinced were they that John proposed with a diamond ring, but the relationship was doomed. 'I was still spending most of my free time in the workshop at home, so, after about a year or so, Pauline decided to go back to New Zealand. It was a pretty logical conclusion, really.'

That's it. No more details on his first love, his first engagement, are to be extracted from Barnard's memory. This is mainly because Pauline was not, in fact, his first love — cars were. John had yet to develop his determination to put his love interest, his future family, before his motorsport career.

One day in late 1970, Robbie Rushbrook popped his head around the door and announced: 'We're moving to Huntingdon.'

John looked up from his work. 'Does that mean I've still got a job?'

'Well, you're coming with us, aren't you?' The design office packed up their drawing boards, loaded them into a van for the two-hour drive from Slough to Huntingdon and a new factory on an unfinished site, surrounded by mud. They walked in, set up their new office and immediately went back to their drawing boards.

Now aged 24, still living with his parents and not enamoured by the prospect of a daily four-hour commute, John decided it was time to buy his first house. His father helped him with the purchase, for a heady £4,800, of a three-bedroom detached chalet bungalow and garage at 15 Weir Road, Hemingford Grey, Huntingdonshire (now merged with Cambridgeshire). After John had taken possession, they spent the next few weekends doing it up, and, to help with the mortgage, he rented out a couple of the rooms. He had managed to buy at the bottom of the market and the house turned out to be a wise investment.

John's next job at Lola moved him up a notch when he was assigned to major work on a car to be driven by one of the biggest stars of the day. His task was to draw the monocoque chassis for the T260 Can-Am car that Lola was building for Jackie Stewart, based on a scheme drawn by Eric Broadley.

With a structure based on an aircraft fuselage, the monocoque chassis had first been introduced to Formula 1 in 1962 by Colin Chapman at Team Lotus, and gradually monocoques replaced the old spaceframe tubular triangles. The monocoque 'tub' achieved its stiffness by virtue of a series of bulkheads that were arranged in a row down the length of the car and had aluminium sheeting glued and riveted to them.

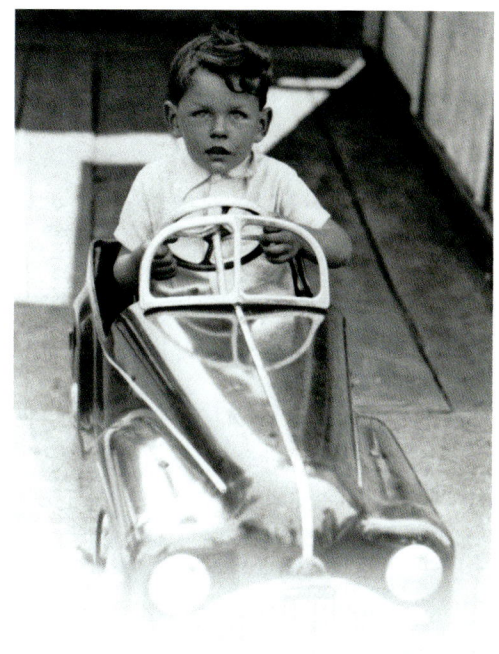

ABOVE LEFT Rose Ellen Barnard, engineer and perfect mother, and the rock upon which John Barnard's career was built. *Courtesy of John Barnard* **ABOVE RIGHT** The earliest photo of him with a car — a gift on his fourth birthday. *Courtesy of John Barnard* **BELOW** When, at 15, he visited his mother's sister Aunt Joan and her husband Uncle Gilbert in Chicago, they took him fishing in Wisconsin. *Courtesy of John Barnard*

ABOVE East Lane's Boffin Boys: Mr Peggs is seated centre, John is in the back row, sixth from left, and Bob Dunham, who assisted in John's construction of a speedboat, is also at the back, second from right. *Courtesy of John Barnard*
BELOW This item about the speedboat John built in Mr Peggs's class appeared in *The News* on 10 August 1962. *Courtesy of John Barnard*

Pictured with the new launch made at East Lane School are, left to right: Robert Dunham, John Barnard, Mr. C. F. Watkins, the woodwork master, and Mr. R. Peggs, head of the technical department

ABOVE Soon after he turned 19, John bought this 10-year-old Aston Martin DB2/4 for £480; his mother made new leather upholstery for it and he shoehorned in a Chevy V8 after its six-cylinder engine blew up. *Courtesy of John Barnard* **BELOW** John's mother, Rose Ellen, with the family cat and a Triumph TR3A, one of several TRs that he bought in a damaged state and rebuilt. *Courtesy of John Barnard*

ABOVE After selling his rebuilt Aston Martin DB2/4, John made enough profit to afford this DB4, still aged only 19; he rebuilt its engine and repainted it himself, and kept it for some years. *Courtesy of John Barnard* **BELOW** When he left his first full-time job, at Osram, to go to Hoover, his leaving card drawn by colleague and friend Brian Phillips predicted an innovative future. *Courtesy of John Barnard*

A 5 LITRE VACUUM CLEANER YOU SAY. VERY GOOD MR. BARNARD. "BUT WILL IT SELL".?

ABOVE At Lola, Barnard designed his first racing car, the Super Vee T250. He was asked by Eric Broadley to do the job on his own, from a blank sheet of paper, within months of arriving. He produced a winner. *Courtesy of John Barnard*
BELOW The car on display at the 1971 Racing Car Show at London's Olympia; at left, his father, Ted, looks on proudly. *Courtesy of John Barnard*

ABOVE Jackie Stewart in the Can-Am Lola T260 at Watkins Glen in 1971. Barnard drew the chassis detail and tested the design in the Specialised Mouldings wind tunnel, which opened his eyes to aerodynamics. *LAT Images* **BELOW** With Patrick Head, John also worked on the Lola T280 in which Jo Bonnier was killed during the 1972 Le Mans 24 Hours — a tragedy that changed his approach to racing car design. *LAT Images*

ABOVE After Lola's move to Huntingdon, John bought his first house, in the village of Hemingford Grey. *Courtesy of John Barnard* **BELOW** Working on cabbie-cum-racer Ronnie Grant's Lola-based Super Vee Taurus under the Clapham railway arches, where Ronnie still has his taxi business today. *Courtesy of John Barnard*

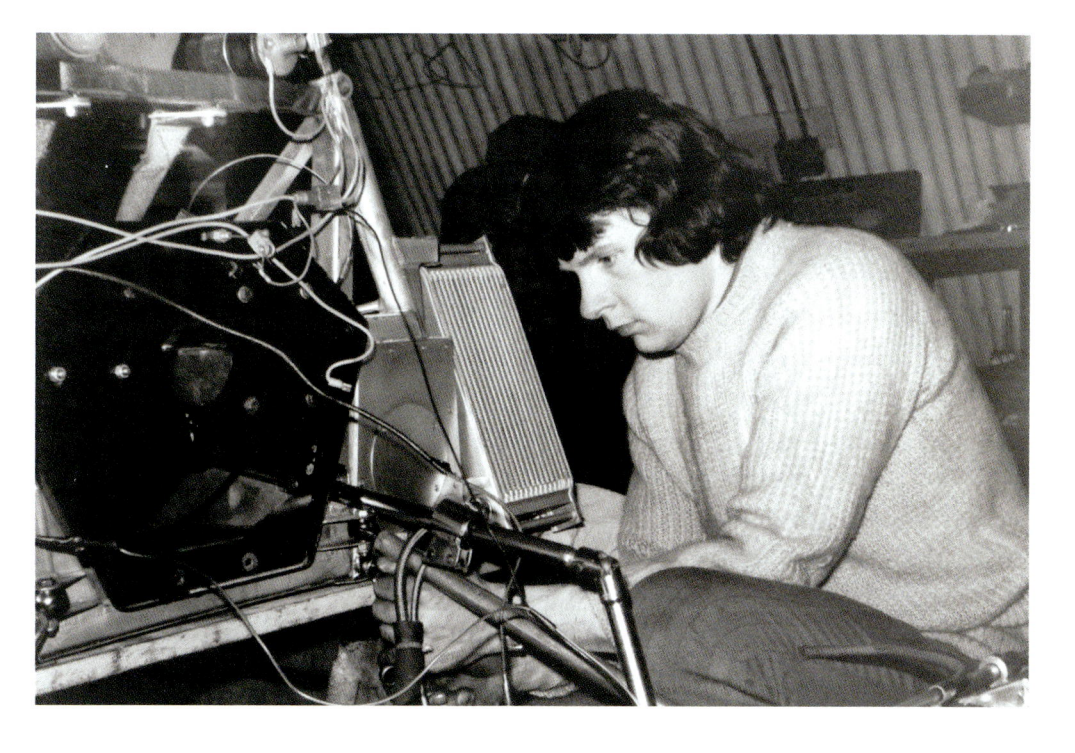

ABOVE With Patrick Head, John devoted much of his spare time in 1972 and '73 to building and developing Ronnie Grant's Super Vee, seen at Brands Hatch in '73. *K.D. Reeks* **BELOW** Ronnie (left), Patrick and John (back to camera) — at first the young designers mocked Grant for being so old for a racing driver but then they discovered how quick he was. *Courtesy of John Barnard*

As soon as Barnard had completed the T260 chassis design, Eric asked him to make a quarter-scale model. Lola's move to Huntington had put the company on the same trading estate as Specialised Mouldings, which made bodywork for Lola. They had a wind tunnel and John, intrigued, duly took the model over for testing. The tunnel had been built by Peter Wright, the pioneering British racing aerodynamicist who went on to make his name at Lotus. Wright is the man credited with the development of 'ground-effect', of which there will be more later.

Wright's wind tunnel was a simple affair consisting of a large fan at one end of a long prefabricated building. In an interview for this book Wright described it as 'a low-cost device made in composites — we couldn't afford to make it a full return circuit tunnel, so it was a straight-through tunnel. The building that housed it acted as the return circuit — conventional technology for the day; it took a bit of tuning to get it to work.' He added that Dr John Harvey from London's Imperial College provided essential expertise.

According to Wright, Eric Broadley 'wasn't sure about wind tunnels at all' but to Barnard the facility was a revelation, his T260 model becoming one of the first Lola cars to be tested in this way. John recalls that 'the car had a very rounded, chopped form to it, but the results from the wind tunnel were interesting. My work on that car opened my eyes to the difference aerodynamics could make.'

Thus was born Barnard's fascination with wind tunnels, an arena in which he would make pioneering steps. At that stage, motorsport aerodynamic technology was still in its infancy; that lack of knowledge would soon contribute to one of the most tragic episodes in Barnard's career and change the way he approached engineering design.

After Lola shipped the T260 to America, Stewart found it had 'the most God-awful front-end lift' — the front wheels wouldn't grip the road. This was something that Wright's testing in the primitive Specialised Mouldings wind tunnel had been unable to predict. In the end it was Broadley who solved the problem before the 1971 season's last two races by creating a bulky and unsightly front wing mounted on two outriggers, with a concave curve that made it look not unlike a bulldozer.

Dubbed by many as 'the cowcatcher', after the ironwork on the front of American locomotives, this device did at least work to keep the nose on the track. But the solution didn't go down very well with Stewart, who that season was suffering from stress-induced stomach ulcers, a complaint that made him tetchy. He whined to Broadley in his high-pitched, Scots brogue: 'Eric, what do you want me to do with that thing? Knock it off on the first lap?' He recalled the incident in an interview for this book: 'The cowcatcher! It was way out in front of the car, the most ridiculous thing.'

Somehow, thanks to Stewart's skills, the T260 secured two wins and two pole positions during 1971, placing the Scotsman third overall in that year's Can-Am series.

Barnard duly went on to help create two more Lola sports cars, the 3-litre T280 and the 2-litre T290, developing designs for their aluminium monocoques 'pretty much on my own'. It was work that would stand him in good stead for the future.

In 1971 Eric Broadley decided to adapt the T242, a Formula Atlantic single-seater, to create the T300 for Formula 5000, an exciting series for cars using big 5-litre engines, usually the 'small-block' Chevrolet V8, that started in North America and spread to Europe. Eric assigned John to join the team working on the T300.

'The first problem,' says John, 'was that the existing chassis just wasn't big enough. To fit it all in we had to stick the radiators on top of the sidepods, which themselves were full of fuel. It was scary.'

John's concern was that if the car side-swiped a barrier and ruptured a tank, fuel would spurt over hot radiators and burst into flames, and the radiators themselves could also shoot scalding water over the driver. This concern, and the simple fact that the basic chassis was so small and the engine so large, meant that drivers had to be brave beyond reason. As John comments: 'You needed the part of your brain that thinks about an accident to be completely closed off.'

But in the end John considers the T300 'a good call' on Broadley's part; the feared accident never happened and the car was a regular winner. Lola's test driver, Frank Gardner, became the 1971 British Formula 5000 Champion after switching mid-season from the T192 to the T300, and the car and its subsequent incarnations went on to dominate the formula for several years and on both sides of the Atlantic.

John's next project was 'The Whale', a Can-Am car conceived by Eric and built by Chapman and Woodward. Designated T310, it was designed with a longer nose to counteract the disconcerting front-lift problems experienced with the T260. On the first day of testing at Snetterton, Frank Gardner kept it well under its top speed as he found its brakes required a fair old stamp because, explains John, 'he reckoned that his legs, broken in an accident some years before, lacked the strength to stop the monster at high speed.' Back at the factory the team added a vacuum-powered brake-booster system to reduce pedal pressure.

Gardner was the subject of much derision as a result, but never to his face. He was renowned for his robust response to piss-takers, so people were wary, says John: 'Everyone knew that he spent his free time in the Australian outback hunting kangaroos with a machine gun.' So it's perhaps no surprise to learn that Barnard later declined an offer from Frank to accompany him to Australia to design cars.

The whole drawing office was now busy designing and refining Formula 5000 cars for a growing market. John had a mishap with the bodyshell of one of them when taking it to Brands Hatch for testing, strapped to the roof rack with its nose cone sticking out over his vehicle's bonnet.

'I was doing about 70mph down the A1 in driving rain when I noticed that the nose cone had simply disappeared.' Fearing he'd lost the whole shell, he pulled over to find 'the nose still attached to the rest of the bodywork, but bent up like a shark with an open mouth.' He bent it back down, secured it with string to the windscreen-wiper mountings and set off again, this time at a more conservative pace.

On his return to Lola he told the sorry tale to Robbie Rushbrook, who commented, 'Ah, don't worry, they always do that. We'll throw some more glass-fibre at it.' Lola was nothing if not a place to learn by one's own mistakes. Barnard, as it happened, was their fastest learner, but he was about to face some formidable competition.

CHAPTER 4
HEAD START 1971–74

Soon after Lola moved to Huntingdon, Patrick Head joined the drawing office. Another young hopeful trying to get ahead, he was destined to take Williams into the Formula 1 stratosphere, securing 16 Formula 1 Drivers' and Constructors' Championship titles during his career. John and Patrick hit it off pretty well, although their backgrounds were very different.

Patrick was educated at Wellington College, a famous public school in Berkshire, before plumping for a career in the Royal Navy. He then changed his mind and studied Mechanical Engineering at University College, London, graduating in 1970. When he applied for a job with Lola, in January 1971, his recruitment was even more informal than Barnard's, Broadley telling him during a brief chat to, 'Start on Monday and if you're no good you'll be gone by Friday.'

On arrival, Patrick was taken, he remembers, 'to a very small design office at the end of the factory, with glass windows on the right through which you could look out onto the shop floor.' He noticed in one corner of the office a quiet, industrious young man on his own, facing the end wall — this was Barnard, working as far away from everyone as he could get. 'I was shown to a drawing board in the middle,' says Patrick, a position that put him between Barnard and Bob Marston, who ran the design office. Designer Andy Smallman joined a little later and was placed behind Patrick.

When Patrick joined, Lola was making nearly 300 cars a year, of numerous types. 'Somehow John had managed to get himself onto small single-seaters,' Patrick says, 'and he clearly didn't get on well with Bob Marston. Whereas John is a perfectionist and would agonise over getting a solution that was acceptable,

Bob was a character who would think about a problem for five minutes, and whatever was the best idea that emerged from those five minutes was what went down on paper. If it was horrible, it didn't seem to matter.'

Patrick concedes that Marston's approach may well have been a direct result of Lola's intense production demands and that perhaps Broadley needed that attitude in the man who ran the design office. 'To give Bob his due, he then designed a perfectly sound structure around that idea. But his approach certainly didn't suit John.'

John says he got along perfectly well with Marston but agrees with Patrick about his methods. 'We nicknamed him Dural Block Bob[2] because he seemed to machine everything out of aluminium and then bolt it on the car. Probably unfair, but that's how we looked at it then.' John never recalls Marston briefing him or looking over his work — 'I just got on with my own stuff.'

The Wembley boy had created an enviable independence, and, once achieved, he was never going to give it up. 'John went out of his way to just look after his patch,' says Head. 'But I was effectively straight from university, very much under Bob Marston's eye, and given whatever project he was working on.'

Furious self-confidence balanced Barnard's weighty self-doubt and put him in control, helping him overcome the fear of failure. He was finding a new way to cope: 'In the back of my mind was the thought, "If this innovation doesn't work out, what is my back-up plan?"' It was an approach that stayed with him for the rest of his career.

Marston put Head to work on the T260 Can-Am car, which meant dealing with Jackie Stewart within his first week at work. However, as soon as Stewart saw the car's inboard front brakes, he declared: 'I'm not driving the car with this on it!'

The inboard brake system was designed, in theory, to allow more control of the wheels over bumps. As Barnard explains, 'Basically, wheels are significantly heavier when fitted with brake discs and callipers, and that means they're harder to control.' When a wheel goes over a bump, extra weight around it can cause more bounce and risk more loss of grip. Inboard brakes were an effort to limit this movement, with the brakes themselves moved from the wheels and 'inboard' onto the chassis. A rotating brake shaft ran from the axle of each

---

[2] *Dural Block, also known as Duralim or Duraluminium, was originally used to make airship frames. Containing 4% copper, the aluminium alloy has the property of hardening over time and is known for its durability. It was first developed in 1903 by German metallurgist Alfred Wilm.*

front wheel via universal joints to the chassis where each terminated in a brake disc and calliper set.

The system did bring problems. First, it was harder to cool the brakes when they were inboard rather than exposed to the airflow around the wheels. Second, inboard brakes were more difficult to service because they were less accessible. Third, and most crucially, the long brake shafts were under immense load and could snap just when they were most needed, sometimes with fatal consequences. When Jochen Rindt died in his Lotus 72 while practising for the 1970 Italian Grand Prix, a broken brake shaft was blamed.

The result of Stewart's announcement, Head remembers, was 'a great confab' in a meeting room out of which Marston emerged to say: 'Right, we're changing it all. The brakes are going back on the wheels, which will now be 15-inch diameter. Oh, and you'll have to make the necessary changes to the chassis and bodywork. And you've got just three days to do it.' John looked up from his drawing board as the team began to tackle the enormous workload, smiled, looked down and carried on with his own work. As Patrick wryly comments, 'He was completely independent and was often unaffected by these group panics.'

Patrick lodged about five miles from Lola at an old farmhouse, Upwood Farm, where he shared facilities with various people, some of whom were well-heeled racing types. He spent his free time at the farm building a Lotus Seven-style club racer. Sometimes John helped, in one instance creating large mudguards out of alloy sheet by beating them into shape over sandbags.

With fast cars and perfectionist tendencies in common, the two became friends, as Patrick asserts: 'John and I always got on well; sure, we came from different environments, but I liked him; he was always straightforward. I didn't get the impression that he had any "side"; you knew exactly where he was. Maybe he was a bit chippy in some ways, but that didn't worry me. He was an individual.'

They used to race each other along the route between Upwood Farm and the factory, through the right-angled bends of the fenland, John in his van and Patrick in his mother's Saab 96. The building site that surrounded the Lola factory became a playground where they would compete to see who could enter the loose gravel parking area with the most dramatic handbrake turn. One time Patrick was in the back of the van as John went into a stone-spraying skid that sent his new friend flying head-first into one of the windows.

John also managed to bash the front of the van when he drove into a lump of asphalt left in the middle of the road by workmen. It was night and the street was unlit when John clouted the obstacle at about 40mph, shunting the car's subframe backwards and forcing two of its struts through the floor. Furious, he reported the incident to the police before complaining directly to the building firm responsible, but he was mollified when they offered him £80 to fix the van — which had only cost £65.

He was even more pleased when it occurred to him that another sharp jolt might reverse the damage. He put weights in the back of the van, chocked the rear wheels, attached a friend's Rover 90 — a powerful, heavy old car — directly to the subframe with heavy-duty cable, revved the Rover's engine and released the clutch. The subframe was wrenched back into place with, he says, 'an almighty twang'. He patched up the floor and used the vehicle for the next few years, finally selling it for £90. All this impressed Patrick: 'Nothing was a problem for him — I liked people like that.'

And it is now that we come to a seminal moment in John's time at Lola, an event that would inform his design philosophy for the rest of his career.

Patrick and John rarely worked together on a project but there were exceptions, including the T280 and T290 open sports cars. These were conceived by Broadley with the detail drawn up by Barnard and Head, the latter concentrating on the engine work.

As Patrick recalls, 'Eric schemed the car on the Sunday and then came into the design office on the Monday and said, "Patrick, you work with John on this — you've got seven weeks to turn this into a real car."' Because some of the components were to be carry-overs from previous Lolas, it seemed feasible. The bodywork was, as ever, made by Specialised Mouldings, and they hit their deadline, but there were a few issues outstanding when testing began, as Patrick explains:

'These two cars went to Paul Ricard with one-piece bodies, not unlike a Scalextric car. The master had been made but there had been no time to make the body in sections, so when work had to be done on the car the fastenings had to be undone and the whole body lifted off.' Nevertheless, testing produced glowing reports. 'The first T290 went to Guy Edwards who immediately started winning races, more than he had in the T212 because the T290 was much easier to drive. The T280 was finished afterwards and two of those went to Jo Bonnier.'

Bonnier, a Swede, drove the 3-litre T280 in the 1972 Le Mans 24 Hours race. And then came tragedy. British driver 'Quick' Vic Elford describes it:

'Jo was back on the track going hell for leather in pursuit of the Matras. He passed me at the end of the Mulsanne straight at about eight o'clock in the morning, and I followed him, accelerating out of the corner as we began to close on a privately entered Ferrari. We were heading towards two bends on the back side of the course which are taken flat-out at about 180mph. At the entrance to the second bend I watched as Jo pulled to the right and started to pass the Ferrari. Then at the last moment he seemed to realise that he was making a mistake.'

What happened next is disputed but it seems from film footage, available on YouTube, that Bonnier clipped both the Ferrari and the barrier. Either way, his T280 took off, 'spinning into the air like a helicopter' before crashing into the woods beyond the barrier, the car carving a long track through the trees and bursting into flames. Jo, who had only recently quit Formula 1 for 'safer' racing, was killed instantly.

Barnard implies that aerodynamics could have been a factor: 'The long straight there had a gradual rise and fall. We didn't fully understand aerodynamics then. Somehow the car took off and landed in the trees. It was the first and only time I had been involved in anything that resulted in a fatal accident, and it was disturbing. I guess I was pretty removed from the actual accident — Bonnier was a customer and was running the car himself, so, although we couldn't help feeling some responsibility, that fact diminished our sense of guilt.'

It is typical of Barnard's honesty on such matters that he would seek to accept some blame for this calamity, but the truth does seem to lie, as Elford suggests, in a micro-second misjudgement by Bonnier, and, as motorsport fans know, even modern race cars can take off in a high-speed incident. Bonnier's death has never left Barnard throughout his professional career.

'It brought home the fact that we had people's lives in our hands. It was the point at which I saw the need to be much more aware that everything I drew on the drawing board had a consequence and I began thinking much harder about the role a specific part played in a car's overall integrity, concentrating a lot more about each piece I was working on, asking myself: "Is this super-critical? If it fails, could it kill someone?"

'It preyed upon us. Was the chassis strong enough? Did we do something wrong? I remember Eric being very down about it. It was like a wet blanket had been thrown over the whole company.'

From now on, John Barnard's cars would be the best made, the strongest and the safest.

Despite the Bonnier tragedy, Lola turned out to be a wonderful period for John Barnard, living up to all his hopes and expectations. He was having a great life, tooling around in his Aston Martin DB4 and working in a world he loved.

'The great thing was that you were learning all the time and broadening the scope of your involvement at every opportunity. We were being continually creative on a variety of projects, and Eric was a great inspiration. I was always thinking about creating a perfect structure, and I was being given the means to do it.'

He had fallen on his feet at Lola. Other teams, as he would discover, weren't so keen to allow such creative freedom in someone so young.

But Broadley wasn't always easy to work for. At the time he was utterly absorbed in the intricacies of suspension geometry, relentlessly searching for better ways to spring the chassis, to improve a car's balance, and to control its tendency to roll in corners, dive during braking and squat backwards under acceleration. As John reports, Eric's quest caused the Lola designers considerable pain:

'We'd be beavering away in the design office on some six different cars, trying to find neat solutions to tricky problems before passing them on to the workshop to get them built. It was usually when the car was under construction that Eric would glide in and say, "I've been thinking about these geometry points", and he'd give us a set of new ones.

'You could guarantee that these geometry points would sit in the middle of the monocoque skin, where there was no reinforcement to pick them up. It was literally back to the drawing board. We'd end up laughing about it, but it was pretty annoying when you'd just come up with a brilliant solution for the last time he'd changed his mind. But he was boss and that was his prerogative.'

John and the other designers grew to dread the sound of the soft footsteps that signalled Eric's approach. But even this most irritating of habits turned out to be excellent training for finding rapid solutions to tricky problems and served John and Patrick well in their later careers.

Eric now asked John to design an updated Super Vee. The young engineer decided to make it narrower and more streamlined, replacing the spaceframe chassis with an aluminium monocoque. He also made the sidepods, which contained the fuel tanks, taller and narrower. Only one model was made for testing and he remembers it being quick. It didn't go into production: 'It was probably thought to be too expensive for that level of racing, compared with the spaceframe T250.'

Barnard's continued work on the Super Vee brought him into contact with a minor legend of the early '70s, a man who grew close to John and had a big influence upon him. Ronnie Grant was a cabbie-cum-racing driver, and a more likely lad you're unlikely to encounter. Whether he was at the wheel of a taxi speeding through London's back streets or a coach getting punters and bookies to Epsom racecourse ahead of their rivals, Ronnie always drove fast, and enjoyed doing so. Looking for a new thrill when he reached his early 40s, he decided, despite his age, to become a racing driver.

He went halves with a friend on a Formula Vee car, and then decided to buy his own. It turned out that, despite his very late start, he was a good racing driver and soon began to win races. He got to know Derek Ongaro, a manager at Lola, who told him that a spare Super Vee chassis was available if he wanted to step up to that category. That suited Ronnie because he had a spare engine and gearbox, so a deal was struck whereby Lola gave him the chassis in return for the engine and gearbox, with the company retaining ownership of the completed car.

To John and Patrick, Ronnie's arrival at Lola was 'a bit of a laugh'. They'd been assigned to work on his car and had even heard of his success on the track, but they were completely taken aback by his age. Patrick, in an article published by *Motor Sport*[3], recalled how amused they were that this old cabbie was a racer: 'The idea that somebody could be a quick driver when he was in his 40s was a bit of a joke to us. I remember John and I almost falling about. It shows how dreadful the youth can be.'

As Head added more recently, 'Ronnie was a great guy with lots of colourful language, much use of the F-word. Really a South London geezer.' They both took to the straight-talking geezer and his infectious sense of humour. 'You never considered Ronnie's age,' said John. 'He has such vitality, and even today you don't consider Ronnie's age. And he was a quick driver.'

Ronnie's first impression of Barnard and Head was that they were 'a couple of friendly boffins. They didn't boast, they just got on with the job.' He was

---

[3] Motor Sport, *November 1997, 'How to get a Head in motor racing (and a Barnard too...)' by Adam Cooper.*

struck by their relationship and the differences between them: 'John and Patrick were chalk and cheese. John was in command — it didn't matter who else was there. But often they'd bounce ideas off each other. And they didn't really argue. John was, "We'll do it that way." And Patrick was, "Oh well." But Patrick was going places. He was very well educated, miles above my head. I knew that some day he would make it.'

During this period John and Patrick spent much of their spare time in London helping Ronnie with his Super Vee in what they dubbed 'The Black Hole of Calcutta' under the Clapham railway arches. This place was populated, as Patrick colourfully puts it, 'by cab drivers with wonderful names like Cold Hands, Rucker Renton and Jake the Bake... all with great stories to tell.'

Ronnie drove the Super Vee to a series of victories in 1971, doing so well that, at the end of the year, Eric Broadley told him he could keep the car because he had provided such good publicity. However, Ronnie knew from Barnard that this spaceframe Super Vee was old hat and that John's new prototype with an aluminium monocoque was significantly faster, but he wouldn't be able to afford one — and it didn't go into production anyway. So John offered, in his spare time and at no charge, to design a special monocoque for Ronnie that would accommodate the suspension, wheels, fuel tank, engine and other parts from his existing Super Vee. John also persuaded three Lola fabricators to build it at cut price, on the side, moonlighting at a garage in Huntingdon.

John designed this monocoque at Peel Road and even gave it a name, the Super Vee Taurus[4], after his birth sign. It was the only car he ever named. When the moonlighting Lola mechanics had finished building the Taurus, they brought it down to Clapham where John, Patrick and Ronnie put it all together. Patrick concentrated on the engine, tuning it with the help of Ronnie's dynamometer. Ted Barnard, whom Ronnie came to know as 'Ed', also helped, allowing Ronnie to observe the startling 'special relationship' between father and son.

'Ed was a bloody good engineer in his own right,' says Ronnie, 'and he thought the sun shone out of John's arse. John would set Ed to work, and, frankly, if things weren't to John's liking, he'd bollock him up and down the garage. I'd hear, "What? No, no, no, no, NO!" coming from John, and see Ed looking a bit sheepish. Patrick and I would catch each other's eye and look

---

[4] *Barnard believes that two, possibly three, Taurus chassis were built — one for a friend of Ronnie Grant's.*

away. Ed would just raise his eyebrows and do what he was told. But it sounds worse than it was — it was just John's way, and they actually got on very well. John looked after his parents. He was the apple of their eye.'

Like Ronnie, Patrick is at pains to point out that Barnard was not as severe as some might want to judge him: 'It would be a caricature to paint John as a super-difficult person who was always giving people bollockings, because he's a very intelligent person and I think there are probably quite a lot of people around, including me, who have a very high regard for him. He's a person who gives out bollockings if he thinks people are pissing him about. He doesn't have a very long fuse if he doesn't respect people — especially if he thinks they haven't put in the effort.'

This side of Barnard's character should not be overplayed, but it is a regular refrain from just about everyone interviewed for this book. What is clear is that some of his genius sprang from his anger, that his rage fuelled his determination. Racing was, and is, a tough world and the pressure meant that sometimes people simply didn't feel they had time for politeness. Test driver Frank Gardner, for example, would be brutally honest if he thought a Barnard design wasn't working, and because John expected harsh criticism he assumed that others could take it when he doled it out. This interpretation is supported by John's own view of the matter.

'I tended to be the one who directed operations,' says John. 'Dad and I used to have the odd dust-up — that was quite amusing for the rest of them, the way we used to go at it.' To John, and possibly Ted himself, it was just a 'dust-up', but to others it was eye-watering.

When Ronnie's Taurus was finished, Barnard attended the races, gaining his first hands-on trackside experience as a racing engineer. By now Ronnie was competing in both Formula Vee and Super Vee. It was a great life: he raced all over Europe and earned enough prize money to more than cover his costs, one of very few private drivers to do that. And in between he was a still a cabbie.

One frantic Saturday, Ronnie fitted in races at two different tracks, thanks to a friend with an eight-seater aircraft. The action began at Silverstone, where Ronnie qualified on pole for the Formula Vee race and then sprinted to the plane. His friend flew him to Snetterton, 100 miles to the east, and landed on the Norwich Straight, where Barnard was waiting for him in his Aston Martin DB4. Ronnie climbed into the car feeling 'green and sick', sped down to the pit lane, hopped into his Super Vee just in time for practice, and took pole again. Then he flew back to Silverstone and finished second in the Formula Vee race before returning to Snetterton to take another second place in the Super Vee. 'A plug blew out at Silverstone,' Ronnie recalls, 'and there was some drama or other at Snetterton. Otherwise I would have won both.'

If Ronnie had been amazed by Barnard's passion during the Taurus's construction, he was also impressed by his innovation at the circuits: 'John would always try something different. He even put ground-effect skirts on the Super Vee, long before F1 was trying them. He made up some mouldings in thick plastic and bolted them on, and they made a big difference. He also put a wide nose on the car to give more downforce on the front wheels — no one else had it in Super Vee.' John, however, is laconic about those 'ground-effect' skirts, which hinted at a later aerodynamic innovation that we will explore in due course: 'They were just plastic bits and other people were doing it.'

Barnard's perfectionism also impressed Ronnie: 'He was never satisfied. If I came into the pits and said, "Look, my arse is hanging out a bit around the corner", he'd gaffer-tape a strip of aluminium along the trailing edge of the wing — what we called a Gurney flap[5] — and it would give me more rear grip, and then he'd be forever fiddling with it, adjusting it, making it better. I admired his get-up-and-go, the way he would work on something until it was right — such a very, very brainy, clever engineer.'

The relationship between Ronnie and John formed the basis of the way in which John went on to work with top Formula 1 drivers — the ones he liked, that is. As Ronnie adds, 'I might come back and say, "That change was useless." And John would just look up and say, "Oh, why?", and he'd sort it out. But after most of the changes he made, I just flew. Personally, I found him easy to work with.

'You meet lots of people in racing, and I wouldn't give you tuppence for most of them, but John and Patrick are two of the nicest people. And they still haven't changed since their days at the Lola drawing office. They are both one-offs.'

The respect was mutual. Neither Patrick nor John ever charged Ronnie for the work they did on his Super Vee, despite the long hours it consumed. In summary, John says: 'He had so much energy, so much enthusiasm and surprising skill. It was always a pleasure to work for Ronnie.'

Over the years that followed, Ronnie and John spent a lot of time together. Ronnie became godfather to John's middle daughter, Gillian, and each

---

[5] *Named after American driver Dan Gurney, who conceived this type of aerodynamic aid.*

November the two families went to see the ancient cars on the London-to-Brighton Veteran Car Run come coughing and spluttering up Brixton Hill, the first major ascent on their ambitious 60-mile journey.

John's time at Lola was coming to a natural conclusion. After three and a half years, he had raised his sights still higher towards the very pinnacle of motor racing. But, as he explains, 'the trouble was, Lola wasn't interested in Formula 1, and they'd even stopped making the Indycars for which they had become so famous. I began to think about leaving. I shared my concerns with Patrick, who was also getting itchy feet.'

In the late spring of 1972, while his season of helping Ronnie Grant was in full swing, John handed in his notice. Robbie Rushbrook was sanguine when John told him he wanted to leave: 'If you've got to go, you've got to go.' So he went, but with an offer in the pipeline.

Patrick Head departed too, busying himself with building a boat in the Surrey Docks in South London. He then decided to set up a Super Vee engine production company with Geoff Richardson, a fellow engineer whose business in Kimbolton, Cambridgeshire, is still running despite an early and potentially terminal setback: 'Geoff Richardson's place caught fire and most of my engines and parts became molten aluminium — by such small things the courses of lives are changed; otherwise I might have been an engine guy.'

Looking back on his Lola days, John, like Patrick, has nothing but praise for Eric Broadley: 'Eric brought a lot of talent into the business, and I've always felt he never got the praise and respect that he deserves. But he was always building cars for other people, so the credit went elsewhere. Bob Marston, Patrick Head, Tony Southgate… We were all nobodies, coming up, scratching away. Everything was "Now! Now! Now!" at Lola, and there's no better way to learn.'

Thanks to Eric Broadley, both John Barnard and Patrick Head were all grown up and ready for Formula 1.

CHAPTER 5
TO MCLAREN, AND THE M23
1972–75

While still at Lola, John Barnard heard that McLaren was looking for someone to work alongside chief designer Gordon Coppuck, and in due course he was contacted and offered the job. He began work in June 1972 at McLaren's premises in Colnbrook at the end of David Road, set amid the reservoirs familiar to everyone who has flown in and out of Heathrow, and was given his own office. This was a privilege not accorded to the other two in Coppuck's team, Ray Stokoe and David Quill, who were both older. Barnard moved back in with his parents in Peel Road and rented out his house in Huntingdonshire.

McLaren had become one of the biggest names in motorsport, and had overcome the terrible setback of two years earlier when the founder, Bruce McLaren, was killed while testing a Can-Am car at Goodwood. Now the team was run by Teddy Mayer, an American who had trained as a lawyer but entered motor racing as manager to his younger brother, Timmy, who later joined Bruce McLaren's fledgling team in 1962 with Teddy alongside him. When, early in 1964, Timmy was killed at Longford circuit in Tasmania, the tragedy prompted Teddy, somewhat counter-intuitively, to put his full effort into helping Bruce manage the team and secure sponsorship. After Bruce was also killed, while testing a Can-Am car at Goodwood in 1970, Teddy was in two minds about carrying on but duly took command. His inspired leadership guided the team to some of its most famous Formula 1 successes, including two World Championships. Teddy Mayer is relevant to this story because of the crucial role he later played in propelling Barnard to the top.

The car that brought Mayer and McLaren such glory was the M23, conceived by Coppuck and introduced for the 1973 season. This was the racer on which Barnard cut his teeth in Formula 1, making a series of significant but largely unacknowledged contributions.

Gordon Coppuck revealed in an interview for this book why he signed Barnard: 'Mostly it was the fact that he had experience at Lola; I knew he could be trusted to work on the cars at a very competent level. At that stage in his career, he was, shall I say, not too aggressive. McLaren was sometimes a difficult place for designers — others hadn't liked the environment.'

The McLaren team had a special atmosphere created in part by the preponderance of staff from New Zealand, many of whom had been brought in by Bruce McLaren, who liked to recruit compatriots. They were and are justly proud of their famous 'Kiwi Attitude', a can-do, anti-hierarchical, easy-going approach that facilitates creative problem-solving without supervision.

The back-and-forth banter among the highly skilled team of Kiwi and British mechanics was an important part of the McLaren magic. Their creative and questioning approach was to some degree encouraged by the chief mechanic, Alastair Caldwell, who had moved from Yorkshire to New Zealand as a child and considered himself a Kiwi. But as the years went by at McLaren, Barnard would find the New Zealanders' tendency to question everything that came out of the drawing office less than helpful and increasingly irritating.

John was immediately tasked with doing the detailed design for the M23's monocoque: 'Gordon had drawn a basic shape, just an outline drawing really, at one-tenth scale. That was all I ever saw.' It was a demanding undertaking: 'Drawing such things isn't easy — you have to take account of bend lines and folding allowances, and, as the new boy, I got lumbered with all the stuff others didn't want to do.'

Coppuck's outline for the M23 was derived from his highly successful M16 Indycar, which had been introduced in 1971. Like the M16, it had an aerodynamic dart shape at the front that broke away from the time-honoured tradition of mounting the water radiator in the nose. Instead there were two radiators, one on each side of the driver, as pioneered in 1970 by Colin Chapman and Maurice Philippe on the Lotus 72 and subsequently quickly adopted elsewhere, including at Lola for the T300 Formula 5000 car on which Barnard had worked.

The M23's side-mounted radiator installation, however, differed very significantly from the Lotus approach. Whereas the 72 had its so-called hip-radiators mounted in separate sidepods attached to a monocoque of cockpit width, Coppuck's monocoque extended the entire width of the car, forming the sidepod areas as well. In making the sidepods part of the chassis itself, torsional stiffness was improved.

But John, working with fellow designer David Quill, saw a problem. The whole set-up made him nervous. He felt that the sidepods should be separate units just bolted to the chassis so that, should they be damaged in any side impact, they could be replaced relatively easily. But the parameters of Coppuck's design were fixed and Barnard had to live with it.

His answer was to toughen up the sidepod sections of the monocoque, something that would also serve to further increase torsional stiffness, but the trick was to do it without adding weight or interrupting airflow into the radiators. 'I remember thinking it was a crappy job that no one else wanted to attack', says John, 'and initially I was flummoxed as to how I could do it.'

He discussed the problem in detail with the works manager, Englishman Don Beresford, in a two-way creative flow that resulted in John drawing two glass-fibre ducts to fit inside the aluminium sidepods, and having Specialised Mouldings make them. With each sidepod now having this inner sleeve, the next step was to fill the gap between the glass-fibre and the surrounding aluminium with a hard-setting foam, adding stiffness and strength. Beresford went looking for an answer and came up with a two-part foam-injection system used to insulate refrigerators. It was a novel solution, but to execute it took considerable precision. 'You had to get it right,' explains John. 'If you sprayed in too much foam it could distort the sidepod's shape.'

John has fond memories of Beresford. Affectionately known as 'Mother', he was a wiry, excitable chap, with an endearing tendency to 'vibrate with nervous energy like an enthusiastic puppy' before getting lost for long hours in his chosen mission. As works manager, he acted as a buffer between the drawing office and the mechanics, and had a way of getting on with both — almost everyone enjoyed working with him. 'He had no thoughts about his own health and safety,' says John. 'I've seen Don covered from head to foot in filler dust from making bucks for glass-fibre moulds — not a dust mask in sight. He just didn't think they were necessary.'

The sidepod design turned out to be a complete success. Barnard was establishing a reputation for making parts that were carefully considered and extremely strong.

His next job was the airbox, the intake cowling above the engine that forced cool air into the induction system. He designed it with a square aperture above the driver's head to act as the air ram, and below this he added two nostril-like slots that served to cool the electronics and the top of the engine. He created rounded profiles on all edges to the intakes and introduced graceful, curved scallops on either side of the airbox to allow air to flow more smoothly rearwards and over the wing. It was a beautiful job.

Coppuck then asked Barnard to fit parallel-link rear suspension to stop unwanted excess movement in the wheels. Installing it required moving the starter motor from its normal position low down behind the gearbox to a new location in front of it. This move meant that the oil system and other engine ancillaries had to be rearranged. It was a typical example of how one small change can domino into a far more complex project. Barnard's suspicion at the time was that all this work 'probably made no difference, and was most likely a massive waste of time.'

Barnard also suspects that Coppuck may have been given the idea by Teddy Mayer: 'It was one of the things that used to annoy me about Teddy; he was always looking at everybody else and saying, "Oh, maybe we should do that." As soon as you're in that copy mode, you're destined for second place.'

There were plusses and minuses to the design philosophy at McLaren: 'Coppuck might say, "I want you to go and do this", but that would never be followed with any guidance as to how I might actually set about doing it. It was, "Go and make it happen."' This approach proved to be ideal for John, giving free rein to his creativity, leaving him liberated to solve problems in his own way without any interference. 'Yes,' he says, 'both liberating and annoying.' It was annoying because, having gone and made it happen, Barnard often felt his work went unnoticed.

At that stage in his career he wasn't particularly bothered by having to do something that he suspected was a waste of time; every technical challenge was honing his skills and he was beginning to see more and more how a poorly thought out initial concept could create big problems down the line.

Barnard recalls that the most difficult component to draw on the M23 was the complex top engine mounting, a piece of folded and welded sheet metal glued and riveted into the monocoque. To this mounting was bolted the engine's top mounting plate, which connected the front of the engine's cam covers to the rear of the chassis. The problem was that Coppuck's chassis outline featured a complex angle at the fixing point, giving rise to some time-consuming headaches for John.

'The bloody thing had compound angles all over it; it was a nightmare. It was really difficult to come up with something strong enough without a complex and over-weighty fabrication in steel. I thought to myself, why didn't he just straighten it all up? It would have been ten times simpler, much lighter and with no impact on the aerodynamics.'

He doesn't recall complaining about this to Coppuck, who in turn doesn't recall the problem at all. Nevertheless, the exercise provided Barnard with another valuable lesson: 'I learned how important it was to think into the detail at the concept stage; if you don't, you can inadvertently create issues down the road.'

John spent a lot of his early years in car design storing away other people's solutions so he could improve on them. His sharply critical mind was quick to spot design oversights, both in his own work and that of others. As he became more relaxed about his own position in a company, he became less chary about telling people what he thought.

This perfectionist quality made him very hard on himself, and, as a consequence, very hard on others. His facility for finicky criticism — something that he still finds hard to switch off — made him a challenge to work with, but also directly led to his achievements. As he readily admits, it was a trait that led to conflict with the New Zealand mechanics: 'I remember on various occasions having quite big arguments with some of these mechanics.'

Big rows with mechanics would become par for Barnard's course in the early '80s. For now, given his relative lack of authority, they were few and far between. One might argue that the clashes were his own fault; for example, he was always trying to save weight, something that used to infuriate the mechanics because they never believed a few ounces here or there would make a difference.

On one occasion, while redesigning the oil system to accommodate the parallel-link rear suspension, he specified that a new cover plate should be secured with a lightweight, tubular, aluminium bolt with a large hexagonal head, which he knew could shear off. To prevent this, he specified a special load-spreading washer for the fitting that would allow the mechanic to fully tighten the bolt without weakening it. For Barnard, this was the best solution; he had an instinct for the strength of materials backed up by practical and mathematical knowledge.

So imagine his surprise when, during the subsequent engine test, the bolt head failed in some style, shooting a jet of oil across the floor as it spurted up through the hollow bolt shaft and past the broken head. For a moment it crossed Barnard's mind that he'd committed a cock-up of his own. Then, for the first time in his professional career, he had an open row with a colleague. 'He was a Kiwi,' comments John, 'and therefore knew everything.'

It was a reaction created by the mechanic's decision to blame John for messing up the design, claiming that the 'aluminium bolt was too weedy for the job'. But John had already observed that the mechanic hadn't used the load-spreading washer. 'Why didn't you use the damned thing? It was designed specifically to stop you doing what you have just done!'

John was overruled by a peace-loving Coppuck and the aluminium bolt was replaced with steel, but the row turned out to be a pivotal moment. Barnard had been right and the mechanic had been wrong, and yet Coppuck had overruled him — the injustice of it incensed the young designer and broke his trust in mechanics. From now on he was going to watch them like a hawk. It was of some solace that his other weight-saving efforts ensured that the M23 was right on the weight limit in its first incarnation, although it became slightly heavier in later years.

Coppuck now set Barnard another design challenge for the M23: he showed the young designer the previous McLaren, the M19, which had a rear wing mounted on a frame. It featured a central post with tubular rods supporting the centre and either end of the wing. The rods, John suspected, created interference in the airflow and reduced the wing's efficiency. Gordon asked him if he could design a better wing mounting. This question gave rise to Barnard's first significant innovation.

His solution was to mount the wing on a single, central aluminium post, which itself was faired into a streamlined, teardrop profile. This 'aerofoil post' was almost as deep as the wing itself, supporting it for most of the distance from its leading edge to its trailing edge. The wing was fully adjustable, pivoting at the rear to allow the leading edge to be adjusted up or down, thus changing the downforce to suit different tracks. The post also provided a home for the oil catch tank.

This single-post wing, free of any extra supporting struts, was the first of its type in Formula 1 and a significant step forward in the evolution of racing aerodynamics. John was, and remains, intensely proud of the achievement. As Patrick Head recalls, John made 'a significantly good job of what was accepted generally within Formula 1 as a very nice piece of design.'

John felt at the time, and still does, that he had big input into the M23. He readily acknowledges that the initial drawing was Coppuck's and that others contributed, especially David Quill, but that the airbox, engine mounting, sidepod construction, rear suspension and rear wing were a direct result of his innovative work. He also insists that he received little or no guidance from Coppuck, apart from directions such as 'improve this' or 'make parallel suspension work'.

Coppuck, of course, as the technical director, must take the credit, because, had the car failed, he would have taken the blame. As it happened, it triumphed, and Barnard lays claim to a portion of that triumph.

The South African Grand Prix at Kyalami on 3 March 1973, the third round of the World Championship, provided a fantastic début for the McLaren M23. As only one car was ready, team leader Denny Hulme used it while regular teammate Peter Revson, heir to the Revlon cosmetics fortune, had an old M19C. Denny took pole position and might have won the race had he not suffered a puncture early on. After a pit stop, he brought the new car home in fifth place, much to the delight of Yardley Team McLaren.

Barnard, a 'back room boy', didn't go to South Africa, but he did attend the Belgian Grand Prix at Zolder on 20 May. Considering how long he had now been involved in motor racing, it is remarkable that this was his first visit to a Formula 1 race, and indicative of his supreme lack of interest in the spectacle and the glamour. His job at the track was humble enough, watching the M23s — two of them now — as they circulated, looking for problems, taking times at different points around the circuit and studying how the cars performed through corners compared with the opposition. But he does recall the magic of having an 'access all areas' pass. The race began promisingly with Hulme second on the grid, but he dropped to seventh at the chequered flag after skidding off on oil from a car in front.

The M23's first victory came at the Swedish Grand Prix on 17 June. Hulme drove a superb race, passing three important rivals in the closing stages: Brazilian Emerson Fittipaldi's Lotus and Jackie Stewart's Tyrrell both dropped out with mechanical problems, elevating Hulme to second place, and then on the penultimate lap he passed the local star, Ronnie Peterson in his Lotus, to take the chequered flag. It was a particularly galling result for the hosts — the main reason the country had decided to stage its first World Championship Grand Prix was because Ronnie, 'Super Swede', had become so successful with his famously exuberant driving style.[6]

In between races, John was busy in his office, making the necessary adjustments to improve the M23's performance. That is, he was when South African rookie driver Jody Scheckter wasn't occupying his desk: 'I used to find Jody sitting in my chair ordering furniture and carpets for a new house he'd bought. He'd move aside and I'd be working away while he was yapping on the phone.' Straight away Barnard regarded Scheckter, correctly, as a hard case, a man with a mission who 'wasn't going to wait long for anything'. The driver who would become World Champion with Ferrari in 1979 already had a reputation for being wild on the track.

Barnard's first British Grand Prix, at Silverstone on 14 July, produced high drama. This home race looked very promising for McLaren, with Hulme and Revson on the front row of the grid, second and third fastest respectively alongside Peterson on pole, and newcomer Scheckter was sixth in a third M23. In what BBC commentator Raymond Baxter described as 'a blinding start', Stewart's Tyrrell screamed through from the second row and passed the two faster McLarens before the first corner, Copse, and then overtook Peterson for the lead through the Maggots/Becketts sequence. On the Hangar Straight, Carlos Reutemann, who had started eighth in his Brabham, got by all three McLarens to take third place. It was a grim beginning for the team.

But the first lap wasn't over yet. As the field headed towards Woodcote, the awesomely fast corner leading into the start/finish straight, Scheckter was right with his McLaren team-mates, determined to show everyone what he could do. He passed Revson as they approached Woodcote and hounded Hulme into the corner, right on the limit. Coming out of the corner at 150mph, Scheckter ran wide, put a rear wheel on the grass, lost control and went into a spin, smashing nose first into the pit wall and bouncing into the path of everyone else. Revson swerved to miss him, but couldn't avoid a clip that damaged his steering. Then Jody was hit by another car at full speed: after that, chaos. The ensuing pile-up put at least eight other competitors out of the race, including the entire three-car Surtees team.

Astoundingly, Scheckter was unhurt, but Andrea De Adamich, driving for Brabham, broke his leg so badly that his Formula 1 career was finished. Luckily, there was no fire and no one was killed, but even so it was one of Formula 1's worst pile-ups. The entire paddock was livid, not just McLaren.

---

[6] *The Swedes gave up staging their Grand Prix after 1978, following Peterson's death at Monza that year.*

'It was just a mess,' remembers Barnard, 'cars and bits flying everywhere, dirt and dust up in the air. It was as if half the field had got tangled up and gone in all directions.' It also led to misgivings about the South African's wild nature: 'There were rumblings in the team about him being an expensive liability.'

Come the restart, Revson and Hulme held their ground, fighting off challenges from Austrian Niki Lauda in a BRM and rookie British driver James Hunt, driving a March for Lord Hesketh. Stewart retired after only six laps when he spun out with a gearbox problem in front of the grandstands at Stowe corner. This left the two Lotuses in the lead, stalked by the two remaining McLarens, until, in quick succession, Fittipaldi went out with a driveshaft failure on lap 36 and Revson passed Peterson for the lead on lap 39. Revson led the remaining 28 laps to the chequered flag, much to the joy of the Silverstone crowd, who loved to see a British team win, even if the car is driven by an American. Peterson was second, Hulme third and Hunt fourth, to a mighty cheer from the stands.

But was Barnard delighted with McLaren's win?

'Not really,' is his surprising reaction. He was feeling increasingly estranged from the team and much of the joy of victory was tarnished by his sense of alienation. He was increasingly irritated by the 'Kiwi Attitude', and he also sensed an 'upstairs, downstairs' approach towards the drawing office from senior management. If, for example, he worked on a Sunday to finish a complex job, it was what was expected and there were no thanks.

'It was nice that we'd won,' he continues. 'It was good for the team to win and I felt satisfaction. But I wasn't getting any recognition for my role. It seems that even now I don't get any recognition for it.' Recognition is the bread and butter for any creative individual; without it their motivation is undermined.

After the celebrations at Silverstone had ebbed away, the Grand Prix Drivers' Association (GPDA), lobbied by the many drivers who had been involved in the Woodcote crash, insisted that Scheckter be banned from racing. Teddy Mayer mollified them by agreeing to 'rest' his reckless rookie for four races.

Contemplating the mountain of work created by the accident, Barnard was sure that Scheckter's spell of absence would be no bad thing at all. In fact, it turned out to be a boon. For the next round of the World Championship, the German Grand Prix at the Nürburgring on 5 August, chief mechanic Leo Wybrott proposed that Belgian driver Jacky Ickx, who was at a loose end, should step in. Ickx was renowned as a specialist at the 14.2-mile Nürburgring, by far the most demanding circuit on the calendar.

'Ickx was spectacular,' says Coppuck, 'quicker than Peter and Denny. Talk about upset... they were absolutely furious. It was decided for the race that we would knock 500 revs off Jacky's engine and put him on the hardest tyres so he wouldn't embarrass our boys any more. He still came in third. You can't imagine that as a modern scenario!'[7] Much to the relief of Revson and Hulme, who were ninth and 12th respectively, Ickx never drove for McLaren again.

Revson won in Canada, his final Grand Prix victory[8], and the last but one round of the season. Despite all the setbacks and teething troubles, the M23 secured for Yardley Team McLaren third place in the Constructors' Championship, with Revson and Hulme fifth and sixth in the Drivers' standings. With its three wins, the M23 was widely considered to be the most promising car in the paddock.

This was good for Coppuck and Barnard, but not good enough for Teddy Mayer. He had new money and new plans. McLaren was about to begin its long association with Marlboro cigarettes as main sponsor and with that came 1972 World Champion Emerson Fittipaldi from Lotus. It was Revson rather than the loyal Hulme, a long-standing McLaren fixture, who was cast aside.

Early in 1973 Rose Ellen Barnard was diagnosed with cancer. It is a sign of those times that to this day John is unsure what type it was. 'Something to do with the lower back,' is the only light he can throw on it. 'In those days no one ever mentioned the big C.'

He wasn't even aware that his mother was ill when, soon after she received the prognosis, she suggested going with him on a trip to America, her first, to visit her sister Joan in Chicago. John managed to take a few weeks off and they stayed with his cousin Sheila, hiring a 'big Yankee car'.

'We drove bloody miles, because everywhere over there you drive bloody miles. We drove to South Dakota and saw Mount Rushmore, had a look round and went back to Chicago. But, looking back, I recall that sometimes she was uncomfortable sitting in the car for so long, but she didn't complain — she just didn't look at ease.'

After the trip, Rose Ellen went downhill quickly and was moved to a hospice in Dulwich in South London, a long haul for Ted, who, now retired, drove the 40-mile round trip every day through busy traffic. John vividly remembers

---

[7] Wagstaff, Ian, *McLaren M23 Owners Workshop Manual*, Haynes, Yeovil, 2013, p15.
[8] *Peter Revson transferred to the Shadow team and was killed while testing at Kyalami in South Africa on 22 March 1974.*

the stress of this period: 'They just kept upping the dosages of painkillers, and obviously that's what killed her in the end.'

Aged just 64, Rose Ellen died on 4 March 1974. For John, the grief was raw: 'It was such a big hole in my life.' In his engineer's way, he likens his family background to a three-legged table, with Rose Ellen, Ted and himself as the legs. 'You put something on three legs and it's firm and stable. But take one of the legs away and suddenly you're asking, "How is this table going to stand up?" It was a bit like that when my mum died.' He kept this giddy feeling of weakness to himself.

Ronnie Grant remembers John well during this period and recognised a trait emerging in him that would serve him well for the rigours of life at the top of the racing game: 'He would never tell you about the problems he faced. John's not secretive, but a lot bounced off him — it was like it didn't have any impact, like he just didn't seem to notice.'

This, as Ronnie intimates, was a demonstration of his surface armour. But anyone who knows John well realises the things that appear to bounce off often find purchase deep inside. It was a mark of his background and his post-war childhood that he showed so little of it on the surface. If John could flare up, he could bury it just as quickly.

Coppuck recalls no interruption to John's powers of concentration and innovation during that intense racing season when his mother was in decline. Despite moments of friction, he found Barnard 'straightforward' to work with: 'When you're doing new ideas all the time, sometimes you're going to have disagreements, but I never felt, "God, I wish he'd go away, he's an awful bugger." I never felt that at all.'

Perhaps it's no coincidence that shortly after Rose Ellen's death, Barnard met the woman with whom he was to fall in love. And perhaps, too, it was a factor in his attraction to her that her name was Rosie, or, more formally, Rosemary.

Born in Belfast on 2 February 1951, Rosemary was the daughter of a highly respected consultant surgeon, John Walker Sinclair Irwin (he used the name Sinclair) and the grand-daughter of Sir Samuel T. Irwin, knighted for his services to medicine. Her mother, Elizabeth ('Betty') Sherrard Fulton, was clever too, having graduated with a BSc in Biology. Rosemary grew up in a large town house at 14 Lennoxvale, south Belfast, in a calm and ordered atmosphere that, like John's childhood home environment, was not big on emotional display.

When John first met her in the summer of 1974, Rosie was living in a flat in Turnham Green, West London, with three other girls who had recently returned from holiday jobs in Germany and France, where they had gone to improve their language skills. Intelligent and pretty, Rosie was a linguist too, a graduate in French and German from St Andrew's University in Scotland. After also completing a bilingual secretarial/business course, she had spent the past 18 months working for Western Publishing, helping the owner to sell children's books across Europe.

One evening, one of the girls suggested they all go to a party in Wimbledon thrown by someone John describes as a 'weird Kiwi' whom her friends had met in Paris. It so happened that Barnard turned up at the same party at midnight, having come from another elsewhere.

'There were no fireworks,' Rosie confirms. 'We danced once — he was a good dancer — chatted a little, and exchanged phone numbers. I suppose I was attracted by his looks — he was a handsome chap.'

John recalls that she 'was a decent-looking girl, but I was a little doubtful of her sense of humour because she didn't get half of my jokes.' (No surprise there — most don't.) He remarks on the big difference in their backgrounds. 'Her dad was a bigwig, her grandad was a bigwig, who had staff, a maid and a chauffeur. She came from a completely different stratum of society.'

There were other contrasts, admits Barnard: 'Rosie is very calm. She rarely loses her temper, and when she does, you probably wouldn't notice it. She always sees the best side of everything and everyone, doesn't really think about the bad side. I am the absolute opposite, assuming the worst from the word go.'

Shortly after they first met, Rosie moved to Bryanston Street, behind Marble Arch, and John and she started going out — which, in general, involved a lot of staying in. But Rosie does recall 'many an evening in various wine bars in London; I have fond memories of the Cork and Bottle near Leicester Square.'

In his limited spare time John was still helping Ronnie Grant under the railway arches of Clapham and would often spend the weekends at race tracks or at Colnbrook. Rosie says, 'I suppose I was used to my father working weekends and unusual hours so this didn't seem strange to me.'

John and Rosie were children of post-war Britain, brought up in a rule-bound society that promoted a far more powerful work ethic than is often seen today. For John it wasn't so much romance between them as 'being in tune'. In a rare moment of philosophy, he describes what makes a relationship work:

'When you meet somebody that you just get on with and are able to be happily alongside, not necessarily saying anything, then you know she is probably a good soul mate and somebody that you will be happy to spend the rest of your life with. It's no good talking about falling in love and that sort of thing because, to me, that just ties things up in a pink ribbon which is too simplified and silly. People's marriages don't last because of that, they last because they can work together; they can agree and disagree and come back together again.' Those are wise words: his long marriage survived the inferno of Formula 1 — and few do that.

The couple formed what John describes as, ever the engineer, 'a reasonably rounded unit'. He is also aware that, in some ways, Rosie was a timely substitute for his mother: 'Rosie is much more academic but not as practical as my mum. But she was just as smart and intelligent and just what I needed and still need.' And equally tolerant too, it seems. 'To this day I tell Rosemary when she annoys me and how much she annoys me. But she knows by now that I don't really mean much of it.'

In late 1973 John made his first major foray into aerodynamic development, using wind tunnels to investigate the airflow around the M23 only to discover a particularly nasty problem.

At the suggestion of another McLaren team member, John approached the British Hovercraft Corporation (BHC) on the Isle of Wight. This company had a wind tunnel that had been used for testing Concorde and, before that, Sir Christopher Cockerell's ground-breaking hovercraft concept.

Aided by John, Don Beresford went into overdrive to create a full-size plywood replica of the M23 for testing. As John says: 'By today's standards, it was very crude, with lots of crucial details missing, such as wheels and suspension. But it was full size, and that, I think, was a first in Formula 1.' First or not, it was certainly new to McLaren.

They fitted the model upside-down to the roof of the Isle of Wight wind tunnel, connecting the rear wing post to the tunnel's measuring balance; it had to be upside-down because the tunnel was designed for aeroplanes, whose occupants much prefer to be lifted up into the air than forced down onto the ground. Turning on the airflow, they watched the balance register the downforce (or, in this inverted case, 'upforce') acting on the model by recording the car's movement up towards the roof as the wind speed climbed.

They soon noticed that the single-post wing had a fundamental flaw: as the airflow increased the wing would suddenly lose downforce, before, just as suddenly, the downforce would return. Although John had never heard drivers complaining of sudden losses of grip on the track, the model's behaviour was alarming. Could Scheckter's spectacular Silverstone accident have been caused by this 'twitch'?

This was a classic case of fluctuating stall, a periodic disturbance in the airflow that causes the wing to stop working. By sticking tell-tales — tufts of cotton — to the top of the wing's post, John noticed that, as wind speed increased, a V-shaped disturbance occurred around the post, upsetting airflow along a third of the wing's trailing edge.

He returned to the factory in Colnbrook to discuss the issue with Coppuck and the outcome was that Barnard went back to the drawing board. He was at a loss; how do you design out a fluctuating stall? Barnard felt the internal pressure rising until he remembered Eric Broadley's maxim. He duly put the problem aside.

Sure enough, back on the Isle of Wight a couple of days later, the answer emerged after he chatted to the tunnel operators about the problem. When he showed them the post, one of the crew commented, 'Your design is like the rear fin on a VC10 airliner. That had a wing sitting on top of the tail fin, similar to the way your wing sits on its post. They also had a fluctuating stall.'

'How did they solve it?' asked John.

'They just repositioned the wing away from the disturbance.'

The penny dropped. Barnard realised all he needed to do was reduce the depth of the post — its length from front to rear — so that it fitted well inside the wing's boundaries. In this revised form, the wing's leading and trailing edges extended further out in front of and behind the post, like a wide plank balanced on top of an upright tube, leaving both edges clear of any disturbances that may occur around the point where the post connected to the underside of the wing.

He rebuilt the model with a narrower post, put it in the wind tunnel and ran some tests. The fluctuating stall was gone.

Now the problem was to make the new wing adjustable to suit different tracks. He designed the post and the wing as one non-movable part, and mounted the base of the post between two vertical plates rising from the gearbox. These plates each featured a matching row of holes. Long bolts were passed through the holes on one plate, through the post and into the opposite plate, thus securing the whole unit at its base. By the simple device of choosing to put the bolts through one set of holes rather than another, the wing's 'angle of attack' could be changed according to the needs of each circuit.

John is still proud of the solution: 'At the time the single-post adjustable mounting was new. No one had done it. When you've done it, it's bloody obvious. But until you try it, I can assure you it's not.'

The experiences on the Isle of Wight proved to Barnard and Coppuck that there was much to be gained by doing more wind tunnel work. MIRA, the Motor Industry Research Association, had a large wind tunnel in Nuneaton, east of Birmingham, which was used primarily to run checks on ventilation and airflow in road cars, rather than lift and drag in racing cars. Soon Gordon, John and the team had the full-size M23 model at MIRA to study airflow through the airbox and the sidepods, testing different shapes and sizes for the ducting and even the wing mirrors.

Without the aid of advanced computer design systems, it was very much 'suck it and see'. John would come up with a design that looked and 'felt' right, and would then test it in the MIRA tunnel.

Using the facility's rudimentary measuring balances set in the floor, Barnard would watch the weight reading change as the tunnel fans started to blow, recording how much lift or downforce was being created by the car's varying design changes. 'It was a lot of work; we'd be hard at it in Colnbrook, then drive two hours to Nuneaton to run the tunnel all night because a) it wouldn't be so busy and b) the electricity rate at night was much cheaper. We'd return in the morning to work, absolutely shattered. It was a gruelling time.'

Soon he was thinking about the airflow over the entire car; what he could do with it, how he might control it to make the car grip better and go faster. He also began to think about how to improve wind tunnels themselves, an area in which he would come to make important advances.

It was all worth the effort. He was gaining useful results, and the M23 was the better for it — almost ready, in fact, for its first great triumph.

CHAPTER 6
FIRST WORLD CHAMPIONSHIP 1974–75

If the 1973 season was promising, then 1974 delivered the goods. Over the winter John Barnard and the team at McLaren worked hard on the M23 to make modifications for the new season, including the addition of three inches to its length and two inches to its rear track[9], with associated changes to the body design. During this period, however, John's sense of alienation from the team was increasing, a pattern that would repeat throughout his career.

Growing in his mind was a rising concern that he was still receiving no real credit for his work, not even within McLaren, a feeling that began to amplify his desire to get away from Colnbrook and find work where he could secure more control of, and credit for, his creativity.

Forty years on, Barnard is a little more forgiving. Having spent 20 years in charge of ever-larger design offices, he is the first to concede that a lot of work done by people responsible to him may also have gone relatively unrecognised: 'You can't give due public credit to all, to the guy who created a really zippy wing, to the other who solved a major problem with the rear suspension. The guy who is fundamentally responsible for guiding and steering the project is the one who must take the main credit, because he will take the main blame when it goes wrong. If you're good, and you put your time in, then eventually you'll get the full credit you deserve.'

But things have changed. It's very rare these days in motorsport for a single designer, a second fiddle as Barnard was, to have contributed so much to a car that went on to develop such a legendary reputation.

---

[9] Nye, Doug, 'Saving the Best 'til Last, AtlasF1.autosport.com.

And he adds an important point: 'I am accused of being a perfectionist, of worrying about the detail, but I have also seen the consequences of not worrying about the detail. I prefer to get the detail right. So I would always define, in detail, what I wanted, so much so, in fact, that people complained it was micro-management.

'Some would have other ideas and would resist doing it my way. But I needed it done my way. If it went wrong, it was my fault, but if their design went wrong, it would still be my fault because I hadn't steered them away from it… It was completely different when I was working for Coppuck at McLaren: no one was telling me how to do it, they just told me to get it done quickly.'

With the benefit of this hindsight, Barnard does concede he might have been hoping for too much: 'Perhaps I was expecting more recognition than I should have done, but I felt at the time that no one had acknowledged my contribution at all. It's bad management not to acknowledge credit at least within the company, and that didn't really happen at McLaren.'

Either way, the seeds for Barnard's future revenge at McLaren were sown. It would be a bittersweet harvest.

Despite his feelings, Barnard was now where he wanted to be, right at the cutting edge of Formula 1 with a team that was winning Grands Prix. He also reveals that by 1974 he considered himself number two in the design office: 'I was never given the position as such, it was just that the sort of work I was doing implied that role. And Coppuck had total faith in me, very rarely giving me any input as to how I should do a particular job. I suppose I just felt like second-in-command.'

John says that when he was given a design job, he would complete it and send it 'straight to the workshop without being checked by Gordon'. He now knew he was more than capable of being a racing team's chief designer.

Teddy Mayer had too many problems of his own to notice his young engineer's frustrations, dealing with the implications of the new Marlboro sponsorship for his existing sponsors, cosmetics giant Yardley. He solved the conundrum by putting Fittipaldi and Hulme in M23s decked out in Marlboro's red and white, which neatly matched the colour scheme for Texaco, another major sponsor. This two-car team would be called Marlboro Team Texaco. In parallel, Yardley Team McLaren would continue as a separate operation with a third M23 driven by Mike Hailwood, the nine-times World Champion motorcycle racer who had transferred to racing on four wheels.

The 1974 season turned into a major battle between Emerson Fittipaldi for McLaren and Niki Lauda and Clay Regazzoni for Ferrari, with the surprising wild card of Jody Scheckter in a Tyrrell making life tough for his former employers. The championship chase was pretty close up to the German Grand Prix at the Nürburgring on 4 August. At this stage, after 10 rounds, Lauda was leading the Drivers' title by a single point from Fittipaldi, while McLaren had a three-point advantage over Ferrari in the Constructors' standings. The M23 had won three rounds — two to Emerson, one to Denny.

The two Marlboro M23s made contact at the start of the German race, forcing Hulme to retire straight away and Fittipaldi to give up soon after with resultant suspension damage, so it remained with Hailwood to preserve McLaren's honour. After 12 of the Nürburgring's infamous 14.2-mile laps, with just two laps to go, he had made it up to fifth place, having qualified 12th.

A favourite spot for spectators was *Pflanzgarten*, where the cars went briefly airborne after cresting a sharp brow. Somehow Hailwood made a misjudgement at this point because he landed his M23 slightly awry and lost control. The car crashed heavily into the right-hand barrier and both of his legs and his right foot were smashed, ending his Formula 1 career on the spot — although he later made an emotional and successful return to the Isle of Man TT.

Not ones to hang fire, Teddy Mayer and McLaren partner Tyler Alexander turned to an old friend, British driver David Hobbs, to take Hailwood's place in Austria. It was an odd choice in some ways as Hobbs had never raced at the Österreichring, but he managed a creditable seventh while Hulme was second.

Now, after two consecutive non-finishes, Fittipaldi had dropped to fourth in the Drivers' standings, with Regazzoni leading from Scheckter and Lauda. As for Constructors' points, the zero yield from the Nürburgring had cost McLaren dearly, allowing Ferrari to move ahead. Fittipaldi and McLaren had to stop their backward slide and they only had three races in which to do it.

And so to Monza in Italy, where both Ferraris dropped out due to engine trouble, to the deep dismay of Formula 1's most partisan fans. Here Fittipaldi came in second, Hulme sixth and Hobbs ninth. Now McLaren's Brazilian ace was third in the standings, three points behind Regazzoni and two behind Scheckter, and McLaren were back at the top of the Constructors' table, four points clear of Ferrari.

For the penultimate battle, at Mosport Park in Canada, Teddy Mayer dumped Hobbs and replaced him with German driver Jochen Mass. This made things worse — Mass came in 16th. But Fittipaldi won, with Hulme sixth. Of the Brazilian's title rivals, Regazzoni was the only one to finish, in second place, while both Scheckter and Lauda crashed out.

Fittipaldi and Regazzoni went into the last race at Watkins Glen, in New York state, tied for the World Championship on 52 points apiece, with Scheckter still in with a remote chance, seven points behind. The tantalising prospect of McLaren winning both titles — Constructors' and Drivers' — hung in the balance, and even Barnard was showing a keen interest. The tension at Ferrari was so palpable that Regazzoni wiped out his car in pre-race testing, requiring the Scuderia to fly in a new one from Italy. Qualifying didn't go well for any of the title contenders, with Scheckter sixth, Fittipaldi eighth and Regazzoni ninth.

As the race got underway, Lauda endeavoured to hold up Fittipaldi in a cynical effort to help his Ferrari team-mate's championship chances by letting the leading cars get away. But Regazzoni was already in trouble; his untested replacement car was handling badly and he began slipping down the order. For Fittipaldi, Lauda was irrelevant as he was out of contention for the title, but Emerson had to finish ahead of Regazzoni, and, if Scheckter were to win, he had to be at least fourth.

On lap 10 there was an appalling fatality when Austrian Helmuth Koinigg, driving for Surtees, crashed head-on into an insecurely installed barrier. The lower section of the two-part guardrail buckled upon impact, allowing the car to slide beneath the upper section. Poor Koinigg was decapitated, his head still in his helmet as it bounced across the track. Today the race would have been suspended, but such was the way of things at that time that the World Championship decider carried on.

To the delight of all at McLaren, and their fans, on lap 45 Scheckter went out with a broken fuel pipe while lying fourth. Fittipaldi, who had been circulating in the South African's wake and well ahead of Regazzoni, inherited the position. A jubilant Fittipaldi duly finished in that fourth place, with Regazzoni 11th, and so secured McLaren's first Formula 1 World Championship title. McLaren also won the coveted Constructors' title for the first time.

Of course, the McLaren crew celebrated. And, of course, Barnard was happy with what the M23 had achieved. But he has no recollection of celebrating the double win with any gusto. He felt divorced from the team, unappreciated, an outsider.

By now Barnard was concentrating on making improvements to the long-running M16 Indycar, which had twice won the Indianapolis 500, in 1972 with Mark Donohue driving for Roger Penske's crack team and in 1974 with Johnny Rutherford at the wheel of a works entry. The M16 was fitted with a four-cylinder, turbocharged, 2.6-litre Offenhauser engine, the 'Offy' being the staple powerplant of Indycar racing much as the Ford-Cosworth DFV V8 had become in Formula 1.

Barnard turned his attention to the Indycar, by now in M16C/D guise, in June 1974, working alongside Hughie Absalom, McLaren's chief mechanic on the Indycar side. John got to know Hughie well and was impressed with his skills as both a fabricator and a mechanic, but their relationship at McLaren was short-lived. In 1974 Hughie left for Parnelli, also known as Vel's Parnelli Jones, an American-owned racing operation based in California — a team that would soon play a vital role in John's development as a top-class designer.

John's task was to redraw the entire monocoque of the M16C/D with the aim of reducing weight while increasing stiffness, leaving unchanged only the exterior panels, for which expensive bucks had already been prepared. He undertook a general upgrade of a design that was in its fourth season, with the specific brief to improve driver safety and comfort.

Barnard doesn't recall specific details of the changes he made to create the M16E, although it included lengthening the wheelbase and revising the suspension. The car duly finished second in the 1975 Indy 500 driven by American Johnny Rutherford and might have won had the race not been foreshortened by torrential rain. Rutherford was a true star in the works McLaren Indycar effort in this period, winning the Indy 500 again in 1976 with the M16E.

Meanwhile, tensions between John and the team continued to grow. He recalls coming up with a new engine cowling and some innovative radiator sidepods for the M16, but felt they were never given proper testing: 'It was another thing that pissed me off; McLaren had this unadventurous, super-careful approach.'

The last project to which John Barnard devoted his creative energies at McLaren was the M25 Formula 5000 car. The plan was to put it into production at Trojan Cars, based on the Purley Way in Surrey, as with previous McLaren Formula 5000 designs going back to the M10A of 1969.

To create the M25, John modified the Formula 1 M23 chassis to accommodate a Chevrolet V8 engine, and to achieve that he needed to do something radical. His first problem was similar to the one he had faced with the Lola Super Vee — how to join what was effectively a road car engine to a racing chassis.

The answer was, again, to make it a structural part of the chassis; to make the Chevy 'semi-stressed'.

His aim was to use the water pump, situated at the front of the engine, as a means of attaching the engine to the chassis, but after some load calculations he realised that the pump would have to be much stronger. So he redesigned it to incorporate mounting attachments and had it cast in magnesium, which provided the requisite strength as well as being much lighter. He reinforced the new casting with internal strengthening beams that connected to the engine's two banks of cylinders, creating fixing points on each side to provide solid mountings for bolting the front of the engine to the chassis.

On a mission to ensure more lateral stiffness for the car, he then designed two steel tubes to run from the rear corners of the chassis to the bottom rear of the engine. The engine was now so strongly supported it would help absorb the massive torsional and vertical bending loads encountered during a race. To Barnard's knowledge, this was the first time anyone had ever 'semi-stressed' a Chevrolet engine.

The first M25 was tested by Denny Hulme and it was immediately clear that the car was, as John puts it, 'bloody quick'. But for reasons that John never divined, the project was taken no further and the car was put into temporary storage at Colnbrook, on top of the roof of the lavatories. John recalls: 'I rather liked that car and I was peeved that it didn't get taken up.'

Coppuck agrees, adding in an interview for this book that 'we were really proud of it'. But he also explained that, with its Formula 1 chassis, the M25's purchase price for customers was very high compared with rival cars produced by larger production companies such as Lola: 'We all felt that if we could convince someone to pay up, and if they had the right driver, it would be a Formula 5000 winner.'

The M25 marked a new theme in Barnard's life. When he made a car and was left entirely to his own devices, he made it to the highest standards, using the best materials available. He was on his way to gaining a reputation for creating top-class race cars that cost a small fortune to build but did have the golden advantage of being extremely quick.

With Rosie to listen to his complaints on a daily basis, Barnard found himself increasingly exasperated by McLaren boss Teddy Mayer, who, as mentioned, had a habit of interfering in the designers' work. 'I found him a particularly annoying character,' says Barnard, 'a frustrated designer who was always trying to press upon us his ideas about how he thought something should be done just because he'd seen it done that way on another car, or read about it in some magazine.'

Mayer didn't understand that Barnard had made a mantra of never copying others: 'I might take an idea and improve it,' John says, 'but I did my level best never to copy someone else's solution.' This was a core philosophy for the young designer. 'I like to think it all through myself. If you don't come up with your own answers, you just won't understand it.' So when Mayer said something like, 'Have you seen what they've done on Graham Hill's Shadow? I think we should do the same', Barnard just grimaced and carried on, not wanting to waste precious time on explaining why he didn't want to follow the pack.

McLaren director Tyler Alexander remembered well the tensions between Mayer and Barnard and what it cost everyone at the time. In an interview for this book before his death in January 2016, Tyler revealed that at one stage, motivated by his frustrations with Coppuck, Barnard asked to be put in charge of the design office at McLaren.

'Teddy wasn't prepared to put John in charge and you could say that that was a big mistake on Teddy's part. John was awkward and difficult to get along with, and he was young, but he was also pretty damned clever even then; I'm saying this with the benefit of hindsight. I remember having some arguments with him and I guess I didn't really appreciate how clever he was. He was changing bits and pieces and wanted to do a lot of stuff and we were kinda against that.'

Alexander's point was that had Mayer possessed the vision to promote Barnard, the team might have escaped the clutches of future McLaren owner Ron Dennis a few years later, a humiliating takeover that still upsets many McLaren fans to this day.

Tyler went on to make a crucial point about the dangers of business people getting too set in their ways, especially if their industry is led by innovation: 'It's a trait that happens in a lot of businesses, where you've been doing something for a long time and it all seems to be OK. Then someone else comes along and says we should really do it this way or we can use these components to make it lighter and just as strong, or whatever. You kinda say, "Woh, we know our way works!" That's not unusual and still goes on today, but you learn over the years that there are better ways to deal with it.'

Barnard, however, has no recollection of asking to take over from Coppuck, although he accepts that he may have expressed some of his frustrations to

Alexander: 'My fundamental flaw is that I don't cover up my feelings about people; if I don't like somebody, they know it, and I can't help that they know it. I just never really got on with Teddy. There was no discussion about me taking over from Gordon, which, in any case, would have been a very difficult thing to do — what would have happened to Gordon?'

Mayer, who died in 2009, was a popular figure in the Formula 1 paddock, where most have fond memories of him, and he worked closely with Bernie Ecclestone on developing Formula 1's commercial potential.

Alexander again: 'Sure, Teddy was an awkward guy, but be careful how you say that because Teddy was also a guy who, no matter what you talked about, within reason, he knew better than you. And what really pissed people off about this was that most times he was right. This could be true about the race cars, and this was one of the reasons why Barnard and he didn't get on.

'Teddy used to poke his nose in and some people didn't like it. But he was interested in the cars and he had a very, very astute memory about things, and that's part of being good at going motor racing, because you remember the things that worked and the things that didn't and why.'

While Barnard might dispute the phrase 'most times he was right', he does fully accept that Mayer had a good brain: 'Teddy was highly educated and managed to teach himself to be a respectable and respected engineer as well as a highly successful racing team leader'. As we shall see, Teddy played a crucial role in Barnard's future.

Barnard was beginning, once again, to get itchy feet. Although he may not have felt he was getting full credit for his work, people in the industry were watching with interest.

In April 1975 he took a call from an old Lola associate, Jim Chapman, who was now working as team manager and racing director at Vel's Parnelli Jones, the American racing team to which Hughie Absalom had moved. Vel's Parnelli Jones, also known as VPJ, or simply Parnelli, was a forward-thinking, highly innovative and successful team that had recently decided to employ European designers and engineers to help continue their success in Indycar and break into Formula 1. Londoner Maurice Philippe, formerly at Lotus, had been employed as chief designer but, quiet and thoughtful, he had had trouble fitting in with the larger-than-life Californian racers and was now in a dispute over his proposed new contract. Jim's conversation with Barnard was to the point.

'Hi John. Maurice is leaving. Do you want to take over as chief designer?'

'Yes!'

'Okay. You'll have to move to California.'

At 29, the biggest opportunity of his life so far had suddenly landed in his lap. John's memory is of a quick conversation and a snap decision, but Chapman reports that there were 'some negotiations' during the call before he accepted the offer. It was a mark of John's growing self-confidence that he felt he could start naming his terms — and hereafter Barnard would command increasingly impressive salaries. Jim says, 'I was pleased, relieved and excited to get him, all at the same time.'

Barnard broke the news to Rosie: 'I'm off to California — as chief designer for Vel's Parnelli Jones!'

'Oh, I'll come with you,' she said, immediately, but then paused. 'But I can't come if we're not married.'

At least, that is John's version. He insists that Rosemary was the one who asked for his hand, and that this moment amounted to her proposal. Rosemary remembers it more as a mutual decision, and that it had in fact been reached before the Californian job offer. Both agree that, swinging sixties and sexy seventies apart, such were the ethics of the day that even the ever-tolerant Ted Barnard would have raised objections. As Rosemary says, 'My mother would have been horrified if I had gone off to California with a man without being married.'

The next six weeks were 'somewhat intense'. John's first move was to hand in his notice to Gordon Coppuck, who was taken aback, as he revealed decades later: 'I was quite disappointed when he left and went to Parnelli's... it was a bit of a hiccup. But I felt fortunate that John Baldwin was leaving Parnelli's at the same time. It was virtually in exchange, with Baldwin coming in to take Barnard's place as my right-hand man.' It is unfortunate that Coppuck should describe Barnard as his 'right-hand man' and yet recall so little detail of what he did for the M23. Memories fade...

But all that was behind Barnard as he put his Huntingdonshire house on the market, sold it for a good profit and then bought, in short order, a three-bedroomed detached house on a sizeable plot of land for £23,800. This was in Lightwater, Surrey, at 151 Ambleside Road, some 30 miles south-west of London and within easy striking distance of McLaren and Tyrrell.

He then travelled to Belfast to marry Rosie, with Patrick Head as his Best Man. On Saturday 21 June 1975, they tied the knot at Fisherwick Presbyterian Church in Chlorine Gardens with the same minister who had married her parents. The church was the same one too, conveniently a mere five minutes up the road from her father's house, where the reception was held. Ted was there, of course, as was his nephew, Drew, and John's Aunt Joan flew in from Chicago with her children, John's cousins Jane and John. On Rosie's side of the church there were, in John's words, 'hundreds of her Irish mob'.

At the reception Patrick stood on the staircase to make his speech, sporting safety pins for cufflinks as he wished good health to the happy couple. 'I recall it being a lovely weekend,' says Patrick, 'and thinking that Rosie's family were very civilised people who lived a very civilised life. Did I think, "Goodness me, does she know what she's in for?"'

In the early evening the newlyweds climbed into Rosie's mother's little Renault, covered as it was in white shaving foam, and, with the assembled crowd waving and throwing confetti, set off up the road trailing tin cans. They drove around the corner, stopped the car, got out and climbed into John's more anonymous Ford Escort, already loaded with their gear and free of wedding paraphernalia, before travelling another 30 miles to spend their wedding night at a hotel in the port of Larne. The following morning they caught the early ferry to Stranraer, Scotland, and drove 500 miles south to their new home in Lightwater. They then spent the next four days of their honeymoon painting and decorating, buying furniture and sorting out the garden, all in an effort to get the house ready to rent out to a McLaren colleague before they set off for California.

Friday 27 June saw them book into the 'less-than-splendid' Holiday Inn on Hawthorne Boulevard, Torrance, California, 15 miles south-west of Los Angeles and on the Pacific coast. John was at work at Parnelli early on Monday morning. By Wednesday he was working until 4am. Rosie, now somewhat at a loose end, spent her days reading and getting sunburned by the pool despite a disappointingly cloudy sky.

As for McLaren, they were going to miss their troublesome young designer. In 1975 the team, still running the M23, finished third in the Constructors' Championship and Fittipaldi managed second in the Drivers'. Glory was achieved again in 1976, still with the faithful M23, now in its fourth season, when James Hunt famously beat Ferrari's Niki Lauda to victory in the World Championship by just one point, but McLaren didn't win that year's Constructors' title and wouldn't win another crown until Barnard returned to the team at the end of the decade.

For the next four years, Barnard was committed to creating revolutions in American motorsport. McLaren, and England, would have to wait.

PART 3
AMERICA

CHAPTER 7
CALIFORNIA DREAMING
1975–76

Walking into Vel's Parnelli Jones Racing, as John Barnard did in late June 1975 just a week after his wedding, has occasionally been likened to entering a boys' toyshop. Perhaps the experience may have put John in mind of Mr Pilkington's front room, only this time on a truly American scale. The warehouse behind the front office in Torrance was an automotive treasure trove, housing dragsters, massive off-road specials, a turbocharged speedboat and even an old gas-turbine Lotus 56 Indycar.

Vel's Parnelli Jones Racing, or simply VPJ, was founded in 1969 by one of the most famous partnerships in American motorsport. Arkansas-born Rufus Parnell 'Parnelli' Jones was a bullish, crew-cut, chisel-featured man who had a big reputation as a driver, with victory in the 1963 Indy 500, despite oil streaming from his car, among his achievements. Velko 'Vel' Miletich, the only son of Yugoslav immigrants, served in the Second World War as an aerial photographer before securing the Ford dealership in his home town of Torrance. He learned early that racing and car sales went together — 'win on Sunday, sell on Monday' as the motorsport adage has it. Miletich employed top drivers, including Parnelli Jones himself, and for 10 years dominated West Coast stock car racing. Together, this dynamic duo amounted to an almost unstoppable force and in due course their team had its Midas fingers in many pies, including Indycar, Formula 1 and Formula 5000, plus off-road, dragsters and dirt cars.

Dubbed the 'Super Team' by the American press, Parnelli was the USA's first modern domestic racing team to employ full-time designers, hence its interest in Barnard. It is also reported to have been the era's largest race team, with over

60 people employed in Indianapolis, Torrance and East Carleton in Norfolk, England. At its peak in 1975, VPJ used over 30 support vehicles to transport cars and personnel to and from events, with its Formula 1 operation being flown around the world in jumbo jets.

It was one giant leap for new chief designer John Barnard, who entered a world bristling with 'Yankee Can Do' philosophy and a stronger sense of team spirit than he'd encountered anywhere before.

To be taking over from Maurice Philippe was a considerable honour. With a background in aerospace, Philippe was notable for developing Colin Chapman's innovative concepts for the Lotus 49 and 72, but he was never quite able to get his Parnelli cars to fly. As leading American motorsport writer Gordon Kirby said in an interview for this book: 'Philippe created some interesting, funky cars for Parnelli, but they didn't work out that well.'

Patrick Head is more blunt: 'Maurice Philippe was a bit of a funny mixture; certainly he can be credited with some aesthetically beautiful cars; he was the main designer on the Lotus 72, albeit with Colin Chapman keeping a close eye on it. The Parnelli Formula 1 car took a lot of its lead from the Lotus 72. But then Philippe designed some truly awful cars at a later stage, so John moved in there to replace him.'

One of Philippe's last cars was the VPJ-4, a rare instance of a Formula 1 car designed in the United States.[10] The VPJ-4 was cursed with such teething trouble that it kept Barnard from his marriage bed.

After making its début in the Canadian Grand Prix at the end of the 1974 season, a single VPJ-4 entry embarked on a full 1975 campaign in the hands of Mario Andretti, the Italian-born American who had already established a formidable reputation, thanks to many successes such as winning the Indy 500 in 1969, achieving a maiden Grand Prix victory with Ferrari in 1971, and being part of Ferrari's all-conquering World Sports Car Championship team of 1972. During the first half of 1975 the VPJ-4 showed flickers of promise, taking fourth place in the Swedish Grand Prix just a few weeks before John arrived, but there were major issues with its suspension and brakes.

Barnard's first mission was to sort out the problems. Philippe had designed the VPJ-4 with inboard front brakes but John preferred to have them outboard, for the three reasons discussed earlier (Chapter 4) in connection with Jackie Stewart's Can-Am Lola T260, plus a fourth: racing tyres, which were becoming

---

[10] *The first was Woolworth's heir Lance Reventlow's front-engined Scarab of 1960.*

ever more sophisticated, were generally made for outboard brakes, and there was a good chance they wouldn't perform as well without the weight of the disc and calliper. As John says, 'It's all a balance of compromises.'

To accommodate the brakes on the wheels, Barnard had to design new uprights, the complex fabrications that provided mountings for wheel hubs, axles and brakes. This, in turn, necessitated a total redesign of the front suspension. Barnard had just five days to complete this mountain of work before the car had to depart for the next Grand Prix, in France on 6 July. There Andretti qualified only 15th but drove strongly to fifth place — a fair start.

While her new husband worked into the early hours, Rosie busied herself first with sorting out their rented apartment on Redondo Beach overlooking the pier that stretched out into the sunny Pacific, and then she too started work at Parnelli, drawing up sales contracts for the car dealership business. Their smart new home was just a six-minute drive from Parnelli, enabling them both to get away from the office and go home for lunch.

John, meanwhile, was still trying to solve problems on the VPJ-4. He spent a lot of time working with John Edwards, a former motorcycle speedway rider who had been a draughtsman for Philippe. Barnard created new air ducts for the radiators and a new rear wing, and redesigned the front nose and aerofoil fins. He later replaced torsion bars on the rear suspension with coil springs. But without a total rebuild, the VPJ-4 was never going to be a championship-winning car.

Such was the Parnelli team spirit that Barnard even had help from Andretti himself. On one occasion, when John was working on the coil-spring bump rubbers, Mario asked if he could help. So John said, 'These bump rubbers are too hard. Take them to that lathe and machine out some of the rubber to make them softer.' Andretti did as he was told — a surreal moment for Barnard. Drivers were typically above getting their hands dirty and machining rubber requires both experience and skill, but, as John says, 'racing was a lot more like that then, even in Europe. It was about small, close-knit teams full of committed, dedicated people.' At Parnelli, to use an American phrase, it was 'all that and then some'.

It should be recognised that Philippe's VPJ-4 wasn't some dreadful cock-up of a car; it just had problems, but they were not insurmountable, despite Philippe's admission to Jim Chapman that he had designed the car 'in anger'. To compensate, Philippe's original plan had been to travel with it to races so he could develop and improve it during the season. But this eminently sensible proposal hadn't gone down well with Parnelli Jones, who insisted that Philippe instead stayed in California to develop the VPJ-6, an Indycar spawned from the Formula 1 design.

Chapman finds himself in sympathy with Philippe: 'To be honest, that was a very silly decision, because it left the Formula 1 team on the road without an engineer.' He adds that the team's owners underestimated the necessary commitment: 'I think VPJ lacked the forethought and experience to see how much more competitive Formula 1 was compared to Indycar racing. You needed to have engineers over there on the ground. Trying to ship your car from California to races around the world — well, it doesn't work. Or it can, but what a thrash! I remember it because I got thrown into the middle of it, and so was John.'

Inevitably then, and despite Barnard's best efforts, Andretti's season in the VPJ-4 wasn't exactly covered in glory. He was 12th in the British Grand Prix, 10th in the German and crashed out of the next two races in Austria and Italy. The final destination for the season was Watkins Glen and the United States Grand Prix, for which the team had high hopes. The VPJ-4 travelled ahead, the team personnel remaining behind to continue work on the myriad other Parnelli projects.

Short of time, Barnard and Chapman accepted Mario's offer to fly them across to New York in his light aircraft. The plan was to fly into John F. Kennedy international airport and then onwards to Allentown and spend the night at Mario's home in Nazareth, Pennsylvania. As they prepared to land at JFK, in darkness, John noticed they were amongst a line of jumbo jets on final approach and one came so close, just a few hundred metres away, that he feared its turbulence might send them into a spin. 'It was pretty scary. We landed on a different runway, but I made a mental note to avoid flying in a light aircraft whenever possible.'

There were compensations when they eventually arrived in Nazareth as Mario loaned them his Cadillac so they could drive themselves to a restaurant. Chapman recalls: 'It was pouring with rain and John, who was going to drive, struggled to find the light switches or wiper controls. We needn't have worried because the lights came on automatically — sensors detected the dark — and the wipers started up because they just knew. Even the headlamps would dip automatically when a car approached from the opposite direction. We were surprised and impressed.'

Interest in Parnelli was high for this 'home' race. It was even higher when Mario qualified fifth. But a spectacular end-of-season result wasn't to be; on lap nine Andretti went out with suspension failure, to a groan of disappointment from the crowd and the pit lane. He ended the season in a disheartening 14th place in the World Championship standings with just five points.

With the team's management concerned about the costs involved in Formula 1, a situation exacerbated by sponsorship difficulties and the desire to concentrate more on Indycar, the 1976 season went nowhere. Andretti did only two Grands Prix for VPJ: in South Africa he qualified 13th and finished sixth, and at Long Beach in California he started 15th and reached ninth place, managing to secure the fastest lap up to that point, before the cooling system sprung a leak and the engine overheated.

Much to Barnard's disappointment, Parnelli then withdrew from Formula 1 with immediate effect. His regret, however, was tinged with relief as he was impossibly busy across a range of Parnelli projects. Andretti went straight to Lotus, where his remarkable combination of driving skills and technical know-how helped Colin Chapman's team to its first Formula 1 victory for two years, at the end-of-season Hunt/Lauda showdown in Japan. Within two more years, in 1978, Mario became World Champion in the ground-effect Lotus 79.

The Parnelli atmosphere of 'anyone does anything' pushed everyone to their limits and Barnard suddenly found himself working in an arena in which he had no experience whatsoever. He was asked to prepare a vehicle for the Baja 1000.

The Baja (pronounced *Bah-Hah*) is an off-road rally in Mexico, raced over the dunes and dirt tracks on the Baja California Peninsula, the 1,000-mile strip of land that hangs down from California like an elephant's trunk drooping into the Pacific Ocean. The event attracted wacky minds and even wackier cars, including buggies, trucks, home-made race cars, motorbikes and VW Beetles, and custom-made racers like VPJ's radical Chevy Baja Blazer, a strong and powerful tube-frame 'jeep'.

Parnelli himself won the Baja race in 1970 and 1973, setting a record time for the gruelling journey that remains unbroken. Andretti was impressed, once describing Jones as the 'greatest driver of his era. He had aggressiveness and a finesse that no one else possessed. And he won with everything he put his hands on, including off-road.'[11]

---

[11] '*The People of IMS: Parnelli Jones*', indianapolismotorspeedway.com.

This was completely new territory for the bemused Barnard. The Baja Blazer had a robust chassis made up of two-inch diameter steel tubing, glass-fibre bodywork, four shock absorbers on each wheel, and suspension movement of over a foot (as opposed to the inch or two of a Formula 1 car). All this was designed to be strong enough to survive high-speed encounters with rocks, boulders, ruts and gullies.

John's guide in this new arena was Dick Russell, the main mechanic for the Baja cars who had been with Parnelli 'since the year dot'. John was asked to redesign the suspension, drawing all the components including the rear axle and differential: 'Talk about jumping in at the deep end!' He took to it, nevertheless, like a lizard to the desert.

Parnelli had entered the car for the spectacular Mint 400, an annual off-road race for motorbikes and dune buggies, sponsored by Mint Hotel and Casino and run through the sands and scrub surrounding Las Vegas. Also known as the Great American Desert Race, it formed the central feature in the film of Hunter S. Thompson's novel *Fear and Loathing in Las Vegas*, a fact indicative perhaps of the type of nutters the race attracted.

To test Barnard's work, Parnelli Jones suggested driving the Blazer in the desert surrounding Las Vegas. He insisted Barnard come along himself to get a better understanding of the stresses to which these remarkable vehicles were routinely subjected. 'You'll get to know just what these things are designed for,' he beamed.

'The Blazer,' reports John, 'was one helluva machine.' It had no windows or windscreen, and above the cabin, across the width of the car, ran a giant inverted wing designed to help prevent the vehicle from becoming airborne. Its downforce could be increased or decreased by adjusting a flap on the trailing edge by turning a handle inside the cabin.

This wing concealed and protected a row of powerful spotlights for night driving. When they rose up and turned on, the wing became ineffective, which meant that fast corners and jumps over rocks would be that much more precarious, but at least the driver could see where he was going.

John duly arrived in Las Vegas for a weekend's desert-driving education. Dick Russell was standing by the Blazer with Parnelli, having just installed a passenger seat especially for John. Barnard climbed in and secured the five-point harness across his body. Dick warned him to pull it tight, and John, tugging the straps, assured him that it was. Parnelli then climbed into the driver's seat, switched on the engine, grinned and floored the accelerator.

What followed was one of the most alarming driving experiences of Barnard's life: 'We set off at 130mph across the desert, bouncing, rocking, thudding and rolling. I was watching these enormous ruts approaching us, thinking, "There's no way he's getting us over those." Then, BANG, and over we'd go. The pounding was dreadful, like being slammed up and down on a concrete slab.'

Parnelli, bull-necked, teeth gritted, seethed with happy aggression. At one with the car, he was in a battle with the desert and he wasn't going to lose. Barnard was irrelevant — just a tortured witness to this macho display of calculated bravado: 'We were now flying over gullies some three feet deep. After about four minutes my seat belts were flapping like I'd never pulled them tight. BANG! BANG! It was a nightmare.'

He tried in vain to find a handhold as he was thrown around, praying that Parnelli would stop. Small chance of that, as Parnelli skidded against cacti and bounced over rocks, churning up a dust plume that could be seen for miles: 'We came to a stop after 20 minutes. I staggered out of the car feeling like I had just fallen out of a concrete mixer. It was an incredible ride, but it confirmed to me my suspicion that these guys were absolutely nuts.'

If John was having fun at VPJ, initially he was wary of Parnelli: 'You had the impression that he could explode at any moment and that, if he did, it was going to hurt.' But John got used to his ways and grew fond of him. He also liked Vel Miletich, a large-framed six-foot-five hulk of a man, the business force behind the company. A big-hearted, gentle giant, he would treat John like a brother, slapping his enormous paw on John's shoulder and making his body ring from the impact as he beamed, 'My buddy!'

The characters were larger than life and so was the location. What really caught John's eye in the boys' toyshop was the Lotus 56, the four-wheel-drive, turbine-propelled Indycar designed by Colin Chapman and Maurice Philippe. Dick Russell spotted John's interest and one day suggested rolling it out and starting it up. 'You had to heat the turbine to get it going,' says John. 'It was like lighting a big blowlamp — flames shot out the back of the thing.' Dick climbed into the cockpit as the car whistled and roared into life, drove it into the car park and managed to get all four wheels spinning and smoking. 'I thought it was brilliant. It was typical of life at VPJ — there were bits of kit lying around everywhere in the warehouse, and we'd just go in and play with them.'

American racing teams had a reputation for being a gung-ho lot dominated not by a designer, as was the European model, but by a chief mechanic. Unlike their European counterparts, there was comparatively little design effort in the individual teams. Instead, much of their activity was a form of advanced customisation of bought-in chassis. Under the direction of the chief mechanic, the crew would set up the car according to specific requirements for the driver and the tracks on which they were to do battle, making a host of changes. As journalist Gordon Kirby says, 'In the '50s and '60s the cars, both F1 and Indy, were made by seat-of-the-pants engineers.'

In contrast to his combat with McLaren's Kiwis, John had no problems with the creative mechanics at Parnelli. Perhaps this was because there was a subtle difference in attitude, a little more respect, perhaps, for talented authority.

A legend among chief mechanics, George Bignotti worked at Parnelli just before John's time, between 1970 and 1973. Bignotti holds the record for the most wins in Indycar history, more than 80, including 10 in one season, in 1964, with A.J. Foyt driving.

'Bignotti was famous for recording all the little tweaks to the cars in his notebook,' says John. 'The story went that when George set up a car he'd send everybody out of the workshop. He would have one bloke he trusted, someone who would do exactly what George told him. How to set up the car, what springs to put on, what ride, how much tilt, how much stagger and all these kind of things. He was an iconic Indycar character. But that was the way it was. The chief mechanic.'

This was beginning to change by the time Barnard arrived; he was part of a vanguard of European design influence as exemplified by Maurice Philippe. The Parnelli team helped change the mould, bringing in a higher proportion of European designers and mechanics than any other American racing operation, but avoiding the hierarchies and territorialism that were becoming more common across the pond.

Soon after his arrival, John became heavily engaged in a new project, one for which Parnelli Jones was sure he could secure sponsorship and which would attract the attention of his American audience. John was to redesign Philippe's VPJ-6 Indycar, complete with a turbocharged version of the Ford-Cosworth V8 engine used by most Formula 1 teams.

Before Barnard's arrival, the project had consumed a great deal of effort at Parnelli, all to little avail — turbocharging a Cosworth was considered by its creators, Mike Costin and Keith Duckworth, to be impossible because it would produce, Duckworth judged, a lot more power than the engine was designed for. That mattered not to Parnelli. For him, as the US Army Corps of Engineers had famously boasted, the difficult he did at once, the impossible just took a little longer.

There were other problems too. In early evaluation during practice at Indianapolis in 1975, the VPJ-6's suspension had proved too soft for the rigours of the super-quick speedway and its monocoque lacked the necessary stiffness. So the project had been sidelined, with Parnelli instead running an Offenhauser-powered Eagle for the rest of the 1975 season — a poor second best from Jones's point of view. Jim Chapman remembers his anger: 'Parnelli was really mad at the quality of the new Offy engines we received. The castings were so porous that engine oil leaked through the blocks. This meant we had to spend more time and money to make them into reasonably reliable race engines, which, in the end, we were not prepared to do.'

With the arrival of Barnard and his evident mastery of chassis design and his abilities with engines, the VPJ-6 project was reawakened. So, by the end of 1975, John was working on a redesign of the car together with developing the turbocharged version of the Cosworth engine. He was on the path to making his first major contribution to Indycar racing.

For Miletich and Parnelli, the project was a no-brainer: Maurice Philippe's VPJ-6 was small and light, and the Cosworth engine likewise; if the Cosworth could be made to work in turbocharged form, the resulting car would surely be more than a match for heavier competitors running the veteran Offenhausers.

To better understand Barnard's mission, it will help to take a look at the arena for which the Parnelli VPJ-6 was being destined and the special problems that Indycar racing threw up for an engineer. Organised by the United States Automobile Club (USAC), the Indycar series was run mostly on oval speedways, including the most famous one of all, the Indianapolis Motor Speedway. This idea of an oval track, anathema in Europe, has many advantages for the spectator, not least of which is that most of the crowd can see most of the action most of the time.

Europeans have tended to consider this form of racing repetitive and dull, just a bunch of cars whizzing round and round and round, the oval lacking the variety of a Formula 1 circuit. But this view misses the subtleties of Indycar. Each oval differs from another and there are myriad subtleties of shape, but what they all have in common is that the cars circulate anti-clockwise and therefore the turns always go to the left. There is just as much variety in the turns, in terms of track width, radius, angle of banking, surface inconsistency — and more. Each turn requires supreme concentration from the driver amid a tight pack of cars travelling at over 200mph with changing fuel loads.

Another major attraction of Indycar racing is the spectacle of sustained high speed. John recalls: 'At Indianapolis I stood right by the concrete retaining wall where spectators aren't allowed. As the cars fly by at 220mph, just three feet away, you realise how bloody fast it is, and how the smallest mistake is going to result in a serious accident. Al Unser told me that if you lose it, the only thing you can do is stand on the brake pedal and lock up all four wheels, because there's no way you're ever going to catch it. Television can't relay that speed; you just have to be there.'

Barnard did everything he could to build his Indycars well enough to withstand high-speed impact, but his job was to make them go as fast as possible. Balance was the key; he had to set up the cars carefully to accommodate the differing demands of the various turns. It was a conundrum; a car that had 'too much push' (understeer) might be hard to handle through Turn One, and yet might also be 'too loose' (oversteer) for the longer Turn Three, turning too sharply and threatening a tail-end breakaway.

The aim is to get the car balanced in a way that makes a particular driver feel comfortable, taking into account his general preference for a little understeer or oversteer, or just a neutral attitude. The key is the set-up of suspension and aerodynamics: the permutations have to be micro-adjusted and tailored for a particular driver according to the circuit, track temperature and weather conditions. It is a complex balance of compromises.

Driver feedback is crucial to getting the set-up right, but not all drivers are good at communicating a car's characteristics. Over time, Barnard became particularly adept at questioning drivers and interpreting what they said, a skill he first developed with Ronnie Grant and honed with Mario Andretti and Al Unser. Of course, driver feedback is essential in any realm of motorsport, but the Indycar ovals presented new problems to Barnard as a chief designer and he found himself much more involved in the racing than he had been with Lola or McLaren.

Perhaps the biggest difference with Indycar, Barnard found, was the relative contempt its audience had for the science of the sport: 'They don't really care whether the teams are using the latest technology and they don't give a hoot if the cars are a bit big and clunky. They prefer it if everyone is on the same level rather than someone getting a jump because they'd developed some new technology that only experts can properly understand. Above all, they want great racing.'

Parnelli was about to upset this applecart, and Barnard's focused, perfectionist energy was going to provide the push.

The mission was to create the VPJ-6B, a smaller, lighter Indycar fitted with a turbocharged Cosworth DFV engine, fuelled, like all Indycars, by methanol (alcohol) rather than petrol and with its capacity reduced as required by the regulations. In short, the objective was to make a success of Maurice Philippe's earlier attempt to convert the Formula 1 VPJ-4 into the VPJ-6. The key men, all working closely together, were John Barnard as chief designer, John Edwards as his assistant, Jim Chapman as team manager, Hughie Absalom as chief mechanic and Larry Slutter and Chickie Hirashima as engine experts.

Barnard was perplexed by the proposal and told team manager Jim Chapman that it would have been far better to start from scratch, as Chapman relates: 'John was disappointed at not having a clean-sheet-of-paper design to do. That was mainly for financial reasons, which made it more appealing for the owners to pursue the makeover of the Maurice Philippe Indycar. I was told that the budget was really being stretched. I wasn't thinking far enough ahead and in hindsight should have fought harder — we could have advanced considerably by letting John Barnard do a new design at that time. But John took over the project and did a fantastic job, especially given what he had to work with.'

Stuck with the economic realities, John redesigned Philippe's chassis to allow it to take stiffer suspension fore and aft, as demanded by the oval circuits. To that end, he double-skinned the front to make it stronger and rebuilt the forward bulkhead to accommodate new front suspension: 'As part of my efforts to make it a proper Indycar, I took the torsion bars off the rear and put them on the front, because the front bars and suspension were nowhere near stiff enough.' For the rear suspension, he replaced the torsion bars with coiled spring/damper units: 'It took some big changes to make it work on an oval track; it hadn't been done this way before.'

It was at this time that John began working with Steve Nichols, a talented American designer at Chicago-based Gabriel, a pioneer in the field of shock absorbers. At the time most Indycars used Monroe shock absorbers, which, according to Nichols, were 'standard, ugly, horrible little devices'. Under John's brief, Steve created a clever design, neat and compact, which ultimately 'helped improve the performance of those cars'.

Barnard considered the Monroes to be engineered 'quite sloppily', which allowed leakage of hydraulic oil past internal valves and seals. However, this in itself wasn't necessarily a disadvantage, as it translated into better grip than the Gabriels initially provided. Parnelli's driver, Al Unser, complained about the new-fangled shock absorbers when he first tried the VPJ-6B, prompting John to fly to Chicago and run them on Gabriel's testing machines in an effort to improve performance. Nichols suggested internal changes in the oil-leakage paths to get them to behave on track more like the Monroes. 'Once we got them responding properly,' says Barnard, 'we could tune them much better than the Monroes because they were more precise.' Soon other teams were using the new Gabriels.

Barnard also came up with an ingenious solution for improving the stiffness of the anti-roll bar, the part of the suspension that compensates for the car's tendency to 'roll' as it goes round a corner. The new system allowed the tension in the anti-roll bar to be adjusted for different circuits and circumstances.

He then took a calculated risk. A change in the rules for new Indycars in 1976 required them to have stronger, safer fuel cells incorporating bags made from a Kevlar weave. Developed for 'Huey' helicopters in the Vietnam War, this type of fuel cell was virtually bullet-proof but had the disadvantage of being, says Barnard, 'enormously stiff and unwieldy'. Unlike the existing fuel cells, it was almost impossible to fit the Kevlar type through the access apertures in the monocoque. So Barnard got round the new rule by keeping most of the old outer monocoque design, meaning that, from the outside at least, the car looked enough like Philippe's VPJ-6 to qualify technically as an existing car rather than a new one, thus enabling him to retain the original fuel cells.

Barnard replaced the old British-made Hewland racing gearbox with one made by Pete Weismann, who owned a small Indycar support operation in Costa Mesa, a 40-minute drive down the Californian coast from Torrance. Jim Chapman says of Weismann, whom he introduced to Barnard, 'Pete was another of those guys who was a real innovator, but, much like John, once he'd done something new and got it all working, he lost interest in it and went on to the next new thing.'

John found Weismann 'very clever and easy to talk to' and admired the American's approach to gearbox design: he used precision-machined, top-grade materials in his constant effort to make gear changes swifter, more reliable and less likely to cause damage at high revs. The Weismann gearbox also happened to fit the space in the car, was significantly stronger than the Hewland and had more scope for mountings and fixings. Pete was to provide vital input into Barnard's understanding of transmission design, an area that John would go on to revolutionise.

The big idea behind the VPJ-6B project was the turbocharging of its Cosworth engine. When the first Cosworth engine arrived, a few months before Barnard started work at Parnelli, Jim Chapman recalls that Larry Slutter and Chickie Hirashima in the engine shop were deeply impressed: 'Larry and Chickie carefully took it apart and measured everything for a base reference. I remember standing in the engine shop looking at all the parts neatly laid out, when Larry said, "These engines are built like Swiss watches compared to our Offy!" What a statement from Larry, who had so much experience building Offys, Ford V8 Indy engines and many types of stock-block racing engines for so many years.'

As with all Indycar engines, the Cosworth was to be run on methanol, which gives more power and mileage, and has the added advantage that, when ignited, it is extinguishable with water. To save time in the car's build, John decided to specify the same fuel filler pipe as used on Parnelli's Eagle. So he went to the workshop, slide calliper in hand, to measure the Eagle's pipe diameter, which, of course, required opening the fuel cap.

'I spotted Hughie Absalom glancing at me out of the corner of his eye but I paid him no heed,' says John. 'Big mistake. I pushed open the valve and a huge jet of methanol squirted into my groin, immediately freezing my privates and washing the blue dye of my trousers all over my legs beneath. I cried out — the mechanics were most amused.' So, of course, was Hughie, a fun-loving party animal with whom John spent some of the scarce free time he had at Parnelli.

Cosworth's Keith Duckworth thought the turbocharging project was completely nuts. It was easy to see why. To meet the regulations, the engine's capacity had to be reduced from 3.0 litres to 2.65 litres. As John says, 'When you take 400cc out of an engine, put a different fuel through it and then turbocharge the whole affair, you very soon find its weak spots.'

A major weak spot was porosity in the cylinder heads. The higher cylinder pressures created by turbocharging forced gases through microscopic flaws in the cylinder-head into the water-cooling passages, causing leaks. 'If you found porosity during a test, you had to throw the cylinder head away.' Parnelli tried to get advice direct from Duckworth but received nothing but derision.

Happily, not every cylinder head showed signs of porosity, and in any case, rather brilliantly, Slutter and Hirashima came up with a way of sealing the combustion chambers. They noticed that the copper O-rings that formed the seals between the top of the cast-iron cylinder liners and the aluminium cylinder head were prone to leaking owing to the extra pressure caused by turbocharging, which raised power from around 500bhp to 800bhp. They decided to make new rings out of Beryllium copper, an extremely strong alloy that would be better able to maintain its integrity under the higher cylinder pressures involved.

Another issue was the effect of turbocharging upon the pistons. During development a piston sometimes burned out because any deviation from the optimum fuel/air mixture could suddenly create a hotspot — and a split second later part of the piston would disintegrate. Barnard recalls Miletich's bitter complaints: 'Those bloody guys at Cosworth. When I phone them up all they do is chuckle at me, tell me that turbocharging their engine is a waste of time and cannot be done, and then bill me $100,000 for new pistons.'

Cosworth's attitude both baffled and irritated John: 'We honestly thought Cosworth would be interested in helping with the engine's development — we couldn't have been more wrong.' The direct result was that thereafter Barnard never enjoyed a good relationship with Cosworth, clashing with the company's representatives in almost every subsequent encounter. Today he still finds himself seething at the memory of the superior, know-it-all attitude of some of Cosworth's engineers.

Motivated into midnight fury by Cosworth's negativity, John and the team worked all hours designing their own pistons, con rods, oil system and valve sealing rings, all specially created to handle the increased horsepower. Eventually they had an engine that would, or should, last a race of 500 miles — but costs were becoming a major challenge.

Jim Chapman talks wistfully of the intense enthusiasm at Parnelli for the Cosworth turbo project: 'The lights in the race shop rarely went out. Huge amounts of work. Larry and Chickie in particular were doing endless nights and days. It was a massive effort when you think there were only 47 people to design our own cars, build and develop our own engines, build all the tooling and produce all our own bodywork. The engine development was sort of tedious, requiring lots of patience and in this regard John Barnard was a God-send to Larry.' John, with his sleeves rolled up, busily made drawings for the new engine parts and ancillaries.

There came a point in development when they decided they had to dump the existing fuel injection system, a brave move that ran the risk of being a time-consuming dead end. Indycars were using a fairly crude Hilborn injector that squirted a steady stream of fuel into the inlet manifold under pressure, but this presented problems for the turbos, which take time to spin up to speed (the so-called turbo lag) and pump more air into the engine. Ideally the VPJ-6B would have a fuel injection system that could correctly match the increasing amount of air with the right quantity of fuel. Slutter suggested using a far more sophisticated Lucas four-shuttle pump, which also promised significant savings in fuel consumption, enough to reduce the number of pit stops in a race.

Barnard became deeply involved in refining the installation of the Lucas system. He hunted through the stuffed cupboards at Parnelli, 'like a kid in a sweet shop', to find the necessary tools to measure injection and exhaust flow. Eventually he succeeded in creating a system that could produce the perfect fuel/air mixture at all times, taking account of throttle position, engine revs and turbo pressure. His work included the design of a canny diaphragm arrangement that would react precisely to changes in turbo pressure and override the throttle at key moments.

Initial tests looked promising, but there was a drawback. The Lucas system had been designed for petrol engines and when used with methanol, which lacks the extra lubricants added to petrol, the injector pumps were prone to seizing. That meant the team increased the risk of breaking the cardinal commandment of racing — 'To finish first, you first have to finish.' To Barnard's disappointment, but total understanding, the Lucas project was kicked into the long grass.

Barnard was learning on the fly, teaching himself, solving problems as they came in through the drawing office door, with Larry and Chickie acting as first-class guides.

'The engine project was a team effort,' says John. 'Everybody was adding their tuppence-worth; it was a good time and I learned a lot. It wasn't reams of calculations, it was basically doing it and trying it, and I was drawing stuff as and when required.'

Bit by bit, sketch by sketch and bolt by bolt, the team at Parneli solved all the problems, working in an atmosphere inspired by Barnard's renowned precision and design foresight.

He made an indelible impression, as Jim Chapman recalls: 'John was extremely focused — an intense young man when engaged in his duties. He had the passion, drive and talent to succeed in a very competitive environment —

people like that are rarely easy-going. If they are, then they are rarely successful. They just don't have time in their world for small talk, and they don't handle fools too easily.'

Happily there were no fools at VPJ. Barnard was among equally driven, equally focused people and therefore utterly in his element. He was as happy as it was possible for him to be: he was busy, creative, brilliant, respected, laughing, enjoying the ride, newly married and, a bonus, living in the California sun.

Soon tests began to confirm that the engine was stable, reliable and very powerful; the turbocharged Cosworth was a runner. But there was little time to celebrate the achievement, for Barnard was now in a headlong rush to finalise the VPJ-6B's bodywork. He took the completed car to a wind tunnel in Atlanta, owned by aerospace giant Lockheed Martin, in which wind speed could reach almost 200mph. 'It was the biggest I'd ever seen; a London bus would have been dwarfed in it.'

The tunnel featured a highly developed system of nozzles that blew air along its floor with the aim of reducing the so-called boundary layer, where the airflow met the floor and slowed down. Barnard realised that everything he did in the tunnel was going to be a compromise, one aspect of which was the fact that he couldn't simulate the rotation of the car's wheels over the track. So, heeding advice from Lockheed engineers, he added a half-inch-wide strip of aluminium to the top of each tyre in order to make the air 'trip', simulating the effect of a rotating wheel. Slowly the feedback became more and more useful.

Barnard had also learned to fix polyurethane strips, like skirts, under the car to change the airflow and so create low pressure under the car, the beginning of his ground-effect experimentation that he would take to a new level with his next employer. Increasingly he was realising that the airflow beneath the car was just as important as the airflow over it; that if you could create a low-pressure area beneath the car, then atmospheric pressure from above would help keep the car pressed to the track, improving cornering speed.

John changed Maurice Philippe's design for the rear wing, mounting it on a single post just as he had for the McLaren M23, and he now saw a way to introduce a means of rapid adjustment, so that the wing could be altered during pit stops to suit changing conditions. His method for the M23, with long bolts sliding through rows of holes in twin plates either side of the gearbox, was superseded by curved slots into which lugs on the wing post located, secured by a screw system so that the wing post could be hand-wound into the right position and quickly locked in place. John believes that this winding handle method was a first in Indycar.

The revised rear wing, together with the aerodynamic adjustments that came out of the Lockheed Martin wind tunnel, began making a noticeable difference for the Parnelli drivers who were testing the car. Now they could feel the improvements, the increase in downforce and the reduction of lift and drag.

Jim Chapman describes John's work as 'a tremendous improvement' on the Philippe design, transforming it into 'a competition-winning car'.

'The car was certainly very different,' says John. 'We had the Eagles sitting in the workshop with Offenhauser engines in them, and comparing them with the Cosworth Indycar was like putting a truck next to a Formula Ford. It was a real step.'

The VPJ-6B, now dubbed the Parnelli Cosworth, was ready for action.

CHAPTER 8
AMERICAN REVOLUTION
1976–78

The 1976 United States Automobile Club (USAC) Indycar season got off to a good start for Parnelli, with 37-year-old Al Unser putting the turbocharged Parnelli Cosworth on pole and bringing it home fourth in the opening race, the Jimmy Bryan 150 at Phoenix International Raceway, Arizona on 14 March. His older brother, Bobby Unser, won in Fletcher Racing's Offy-powered Eagle.

Come May, Al managed seventh place in the Indy 500, a race cut in half by a torrential downpour. At 225 miles, it was the shortest Indy 500 in history, won by Johnny Rutherford in a McLaren M16E, the chassis that Barnard had so painstakingly redrawn.

Al Unser finished fourth at the Milwaukee 150 in June before facing the rigours of the Pocono 500 in Pennsylvania. About two-thirds of the way through, he had a slow puncture at the rear that threw the wheel out of balance, making it shake so violently that it threatened to damage the suspension. As Unser came into the pits, Barnard had to make a rapid assessment: 'I ran to look at where the rear radius rod on the suspension joined the chassis. It looked secure, but I had to decide fast. Was it safe to carry on? Yes, I said, although my heart was in my mouth.'

With total faith in his designer, Unser drove flat out to victory, having led 109 of the 200 laps. The VPJ-6B had triumphed at last.

After the race, Barnard conducted a detailed examination of the car. To his utter horror he discovered that half of the rivets connecting key parts of the suspension to the chassis had been shaken loose by the puncture and the fast cornering that had followed it. 'I'd taken a massive risk with Al's life. If he'd crashed and been seriously injured, or worse, I would have never forgiven myself.' This was Barnard's second salutary lesson in the massive risks of top-level racing.

In Wisconsin on 22 August, Unser and the Parnelli Cosworth were entered in another race at Milwaukee, this time the Tony Bettenhausen 200. Al qualified fifth, behind Johnny Rutherford's McLaren M16E on pole, Gordon Johncock's Wildcat, Tom Sneva's Penske-entered McLaren M16C/D and Bobby Unser's Eagle. Rutherford led for all but one of the first 57 laps, then Al went ahead.

In the meantime Barnard found himself with the task of chalking instructions on the pit board for his driver to read as he flew past. This was more onerous than it sounds, especially at Milwaukee, where the cars took only 30 seconds to complete the one-mile lap.

'I stood on the exit of the final turn where the cars could either carry on or dive into the pits, so it was a pretty hairy spot. I was protected, if that's the right word, by a wall just 18 inches high, and the cars were whistling past just a few feet away. I was writing nearly all the time, looking over to Hughie [Absalom], who was feeding me the data. As soon as I'd finished writing, I'd bounce up, flash the board as Al shot past and pop down again to write more instructions. It was frantic — I was up and down like a jack-in-the-box. I remember it occurring to me that this was a) bloody dangerous and b) potentially a terminal waste of a useful designer.'

There then ensued a battle of the brothers, with Bobby passing Al for a brief spell in the lead until, finally, Al reclaimed the lead for good on the 74th lap, remaining there for the next 127 laps to take the chequered flag. Barnard was elated, not just because of the victory but also because he had survived one of the most alarming experiences of his life.

Later that month Hawaiian driver Danny Ongais joined Parnelli for a preliminary race and some testing prior to a full season in 1977, bringing with him much-needed sponsorship from Interscope, a film production company. Known as the 'Flyin' Hawaiian' or 'Danny On-The-Gas' for his foot-to-the-floor driving style, the curly-headed 34-year-old had developed near folk-hero status on the drag racing scene. To Barnard, there were shades of Jody Scheckter in his fearless 'win or bust' approach.

Ongais's one-off race, his first in Indycar, came at the California 500 at Ontario Motor Speedway on 5 September. He qualified his Parnelli Cosworth 11th but during the race lost control in a gust of wind, slamming into the wall and rolling the car. Happily, and to the amazement of the spectators, Danny escaped with only cuts and bruises.

Shortly afterwards, Ongais and Unser ran their Parnelli Cosworths at a tyre test at Phoenix, where Danny proved to be quicker down the straights despite his inexperience. This upset the senior driver, leading Al to believe that Danny had a more powerful engine — which wasn't the case.

'Al could never get it in his head that Danny didn't have a better engine,' says John. 'But Danny was utterly fearless. Unlike experienced drivers who generally favour a touch of understeer, many drivers new to the big ovals ask for their cars to be set up with a neutral balance, even slight oversteer, which tends to give them more top speed when they exit a corner, providing greater pace on the following straight.'

Experienced drivers dislike oversteer on the oval tracks because it increases the possibility of losing control of the back of the car, with the resultant spin almost inevitably followed by an extremely nasty accident. So they opt for the safety margin and increased control of having the car set up with a little understeer even though that will inevitably compromise speed out of the corners.

The last race of the season, the Bobby Ball 150 at Phoenix on 7 November, ended on a high. Al only qualified 10th, but in the race he made his way up through the pack to pass first Mario Andretti's Penske-run McLaren and then Gordon Johncock's Wildcat to take the lead on lap 89, and there he stayed for the remaining 62 laps.

This was a climactic vindication for the long hours of work spent developing the VPJ-6B and set the paddock abuzz with wonder at the team's achievement. That year's three victories for the innovative Cosworth-powered car put Al Unser in fourth place in the points, behind champion Johncock, runner-up Rutherford and third-placed Wally Dallenbach, who hadn't won any races but had been a consistent points scorer.

It wasn't the glorious achievement that had given VPJ their three consecutive USAC titles in 1970, '71 and '72 — the first for Al Unser, then two for Joe Leonard — but it was a huge step in the right direction. The Parnelli Cosworth was proving its worth.

Despite being so busy, John did manage to get away on some weekends. By now he was part of an English crowd, including Hughie Absalom, Jim Chapman (a neighbour at Redondo Beach), Jim's future wife Debbie, and a mechanic who John knew from Lola called John Saunders Rowe. They used to gather for Thanksgiving and Christmas and attend parties organised by another close friend, an extraordinary American character called Bill Yeager.

Balding, bespectacled, single and about 15 years older than Barnard, Yeager was Parnelli's fixer. He would organise the parties, invite the girls (with whom he was very popular), get the best hotel rooms and make sure the right people were at the races watching the Parnelli team perform. The life and soul of any gathering, he had his fingers in a thousand pies.

Barnard recalls getting a speeding ticket and telling Yeager about it. Bill laughed, told him he knew the local Chief of Police, and said a bottle of whisky would resolve the matter. Yeager went on to have a heart transplant and became one of the longest-lived American survivors of the operation, which, to John, 'was one hell of a surprise given his party, party, party lifestyle.'

One sunny Sunday, Yeager invited John, Rosie, Jim and Hughie aboard his sister's speedboat for a voyage from Redondo Beach to Marina Del Ray, eight miles up the coast. Their destination had just come into sight when Jim noticed the boat was filling with water — and they had no lifejackets. It transpired that the seal around the prop shaft was leaking badly. Crowded into the stern to prevent the bow from nose-diving under the swell, everyone bailed for their lives as Bill opened up the throttle in an effort to reach harbour in time.

'When we arrived,' says Jim Chapman, 'we all leaped out and the boat sank immediately. Thank you, Captain Yeager! Although we were all about to drown in the Pacific Ocean, everyone saw the funny side of it and laughed like hell, including Yeager. Everyone, that is, except me, who never learned to swim.'

John couldn't swim either and was equally unamused.

Jim Chapman felt very strongly that he had chosen the right man in John and 'interfered with his work as little as possible'. He even enjoyed John's 'really good sense of humour' — the only contributor to this book to have praised Barnard for his wit. That must be an indication of just how contented he was at Vel's Parnelli Jones.

Jim himself instigated his own little revolution that spread throughout motorsport. He had become irritated with the fact that teams were often too mean to offer food to the mechanics at the circuits. Jim thought this dumb and suggested to Parnelli that it was bad for both productivity and team spirit.

'The crew were paid "per diem", by the day, and the attitude was, "Why the hell should we provide food when they've got per diem?" I'd say, "Take the per diem away, but then if you're going to do that, let's feed them properly", which prompted the response, "Oh no, we couldn't do that!"'

Jim insisted and eventually Parnelli gave in. The move immediately brought criticism from rival teams, who feared that Parnelli was spoiling the mechanics and setting an unnecessary precedent.

'There was a ploy in all this,' adds Jim. 'You sit them down and feed them good food and they're at the track when you need them. They don't drive off somewhere to find something to eat and then gobble it down or give into the temptation to have a couple of beers before coming back to work. The best thing was to bring your crew in early, feed them breakfast at the track, good food, and have lunch there for them and dinner too.'

It was now late 1976 and Barnard was working on the revised VPJ-6C for the next season. With its carried-over monocoque still incorporating the old-style fuel cells, he concentrated more and more on aerodynamic improvements, which had the happy side effect of making the car look prettier.

The VPJ-6C was a lovely creation. Gordon Kirby recently described it in glowing terms: 'It was a beautiful, svelte little car — everything you would like to see in a racer. It moved the sport forward. Barnard had that ability to understand the real dynamic of a race car — how it works and how to make it work practically. He worked very closely with the drivers.'

Barnard refashioned the nose and front wing and remade the bodywork for the cockpit so that it faired into a smooth, aerodynamic engine cover leading into a sleek rear deck. 'Although I never tested in a wind tunnel,' he says, 'you just had to look at it to know it was going to be a better aerodynamic package.'

When he started work on the Parnelli VPJ-6C, Barnard had just lost his assistant, John Edwards, but a replacement was waiting in the wings, already employed by the team. Gordon Kimball had been taken on by Jim Chapman as a 'helper' despite lacking experience and had quickly demonstrated commitment and ambition.

'Helpers are a vital part of any race team,' says Chapman. 'A really good helper who does his job well, even if he's just washing the wheels and cleaning them after a race, is invaluable. He'll give a wheel a visual inspection and might, for example, tell you that you've got a chipped rim here, or spot a crack starting in a spoke.'

Kimball was a quiet, easy-going young man from a wealthy family; his parents owned a massive avocado ranch in Ventura, southern California. Recently graduated from Stanford University with an MSc in Machine Design, his ambition was to be a race car engineer. Jim introduced him to Barnard, who

ABOVE Barnard's new workplace in Colnbrook; he never felt part of the team at McLaren, finding himself clashing with the 'Kiwi spirit'. *Sutton Images* **BELOW** The McLaren M23, upon which Barnard did so much work and for which he received so little credit. Visible are his breakthrough single-post wing, innovative sidepods and shapely airbox. The car is seen at the 1973 Italian Grand Prix, driven by Peter Revson. *Sutton Images*

ABOVE Emerson Fittipaldi in his Marlboro-sponsored M23 at the Spanish Grand Prix, *en route* to becoming the 1974 Formula 1 World Champion — McLaren's first such success. *Sutton Images*
BELOW John hard at work at his McLaren drawing board in Colnbrook. *Courtesy of John Barnard*

ABOVE Johnny Rutherford winning the 1974 Indy 500 in a McLaren M16D; Barnard had redesigned the monocoque, reducing weight, increasing stiffness and improving driver safety and comfort. *Bob Tronolone* **BELOW** Wedding day, Belfast, 21 June 1975: Rosie's parents, Sinclair and Betty Irwin, are on the left, with John's Aunt Joan, from Chicago, and his father, Ted, on the right; Patrick Head was Best Man. *Courtesy of John Barnard*

LEFT A few days after their wedding, John and Rosie take a break from gardening at their new home in Lightwater, Surrey; Rosie, who received driving lessons from John in his Mini, is holding the remains of their wedding cake. *Courtesy of John Barnard*

BELOW One week after the wedding, John started work in California at Vel's Parnelli Jones, his first task to implement emergency suspension and brake changes for the Formula 1 Parnelli VPJ-4. Just 15 days on from the wedding, Mario Andretti duly drove the revised car to fifth place in the French Grand Prix. *Sutton Images*

ABOVE Al Unser racing the Parnelli VPJ-6B to seventh place in the 1976 Indy 500. *Bob Tronolone* **BELOW** Barnard looking alarmed at the 'bloody dangerous' pit junction in the 1976 Milwaukee 200 — 'potentially a terminal waste of a useful designer'. *National Racing Photo Services*

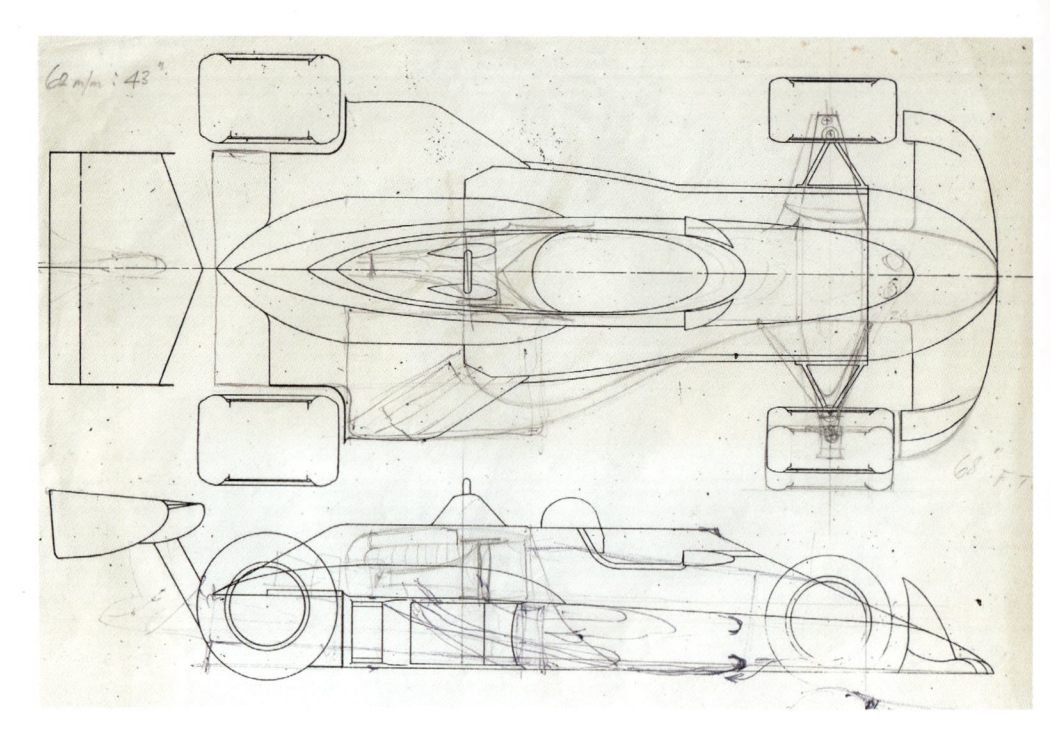

ABOVE Barnard's drawings for the Parnelli VPJ-6C Indycar; American journalist Gordon Kirby described it as 'a beautiful, svelte little car — everything you would like to see in a racer'. *Courtesy of John Barnard* **BELOW** The young designer sitting in his VPJ-6C, newly painted and without decals, during its first test at Arizona's Phoenix International Raceway. *Courtesy of John Barnard*

ABOVE During practice for the 1977 Indy 500 the first VPJ-6C proved to be immediately quick in the hands of Al Unser — until a big shunt. *Courtesy of John Barnard* **BELOW** Unser steps unhurt from the wreckage of the VPJ-6C after running over an errant turbine wheel from Janet Guthrie's car. *Getty Images/Bettmann*

ABOVE The Parnelli crew with the VPJ-6B that Al Unser raced in the 1977 Indy 500 after the VPJ-6C's crash; team boss Vel Miletich is at rear right, behind Unser, and next to him (wearing caps) are John Barnard and Jim Chapman, the Englishman who lured John to the team. *Indianapolis Motor Speedway* **BELOW** Barnard having a good think during his Parnelli period. *Courtesy of John Barnard*

warmed to him immediately. He became John's detailed design man, his 'pencil'.

The first problem to solve was the location of the turbocharger for the Cosworth. Made of cast iron, this heavy component sat up high behind the engine. 'That's a bad place,' says John. 'Weight high up in a race car will raise the centre of gravity, increasing the car's tendency to roll in corners, compromising the car's balance and performance.' It also presented a 'great lump' in front of the rear wing, which, aerodynamically, was less than ideal. 'I found myself looking at it and thinking, "That's got to be moved."'

But where to move it? 'The only conceivable place was down near the gearbox, but there just wasn't enough room. "Right," I told myself, "we need a new gearbox."'

Barnard had a new direction in mind, as pioneered in Formula 1 by Ferrari in 1975 with the 312T (T for Transverse) in which Niki Lauda won that year's World Championship. John drove down to Costa Mesa to see Pete Weismann and they discussed the practicalities of designing a transverse gearbox. The idea was simple in theory. Normally the gears are arranged inside the gearbox in longitudinal rows along the line of the engine's crankshaft, creating a gearbox that is much longer than it is wide. If they could turn the gearbox through 90 degrees, then they could liberate enough space behind it to allow the turbocharger to be sited lower down.

Fired up by the potential space-saving, Barnard redesigned the gearbox casing to accommodate a pair of bevelled gears that would allow the gear train to run at 90 degrees to the crankshaft. He also saw that by designing his own gearbox tailor-made for a specific car, he could build the casing in such a way as to avoid having to make special brackets and fixings for suspension mountings. Clearly the lesson learned from the M23 engine mounting had sunk in — think of the detail at concept stage to avoid unnecessary aggravation down the road.

But almost as soon as he started, Barnard recognised he might be creating trouble ahead for the mechanics, who often need to get into gearboxes to change the ratios. His fear was that if he installed a standard access hatch in the gearbox casing, getting at the gears inside the transverse version would require removing some of the suspension. 'I knew that wasn't an option,' recalls John. 'I would never have heard the end of it from the mechanics.'

Having discussed the possibilities with Pete, he decided to mount the gear shafts on two rails, allowing the mechanics to slide them out of the casing by the relatively simple process of removing the rear wing and one suspension link. The upside was that the system worked well. The downside was that, to accommodate the rails and give them room to slide out, he had to make the bottom of the gearbox significantly wider, which put it in the path of the exhaust pipes. He was now forced to run the exhaust around the wider gearbox base, using longer pipes with sharper bends in them. He tested the new set-up but quickly saw there was a new problem. The revised exhaust layout resulted in slightly reduced engine performance and slower turbo response.

It wouldn't do. Barnard was forced to move the turbo up behind the engine, allowing him to use shorter pipes on the exhaust but placing the heavy unit higher up than he had originally intended. It was a compromise, something that he was never happy with, but overall it was a gain: 'I didn't win as much as I wanted with the transverse 'box, but what I did gain was a 'box to which it was easier to bolt the suspension, a very simple mounting.'

Once they got past teething problems with oil circulation and overheating, the transverse gearbox was a big step forward. Jim Chapman was impressed by Barnard's efforts: 'We did a lot of testing of the new gearbox. We ran it on a giant lathe backwards, at very high speed, checking for oil distribution, power losses, that sort of thing. John did a great job, especially since it was the first gearbox he had designed.'

While Barnard was developing his version, Indycar designer Roman Slobodinsky was trying to create a transverse gearbox to go with his radical idea to lie the Offenhauser on its side in order to reduce its centre of gravity. 'Weismann did the gears for both our boxes,' says John, 'but Roman encountered serious difficulties with getting the Offy to run efficiently on its side.'

The transverse gearbox received fulsome praise from George Moore, a motorsport columnist writing in the *Indianapolis Star* on Sunday, 22 June 1977: 'John Barnard... has done more than just innovate. This gentleman has cut a brand new path in the field of transmission design and has created a gearbox for a rear-engine car which has design criteria not seen since the days of Harry Miller's front-wheel drive transmission.' Miller is widely considered to be the greatest creative engineer in American racing history. The comparison was so complimentary that Barnard kept three copies of the article in his files. Not bad, then, for his first gearbox design.

Indycar races weren't all about the big ovals; some were run on street circuits with considerable braking requirements. Street circuits, and short ovals like Milwaukee, created problems with brake cooling.

Barnard noticed that cooling air going into the front brakes on the VPJ-

6B was being deflected by the suspension uprights, so, in another bit of fresh thinking, he redesigned the uprights to include slotted vanes that guided air onto the brakes. But even this step forward wasn't good enough; the front brakes were still being shielded from the airflow by the five-inch-long axles.

Puzzling over this for a while, Barnard came up with a new way of attaching the front wheels. He replaced the existing front axle with a one-inch stub that slotted into a 'back-to-back angular contact wheel bearing' made by Swedish bearing manufacturer SKF. He had seen this arrangement on a Citroën SM road car: 'I looked at the bearing, did some calculations and realised it could easily carry the load and speed of an Indycar.'

It was such an impressive piece of engineering that people couldn't actually see how the wheel was held on. It certainly confused A.J. Foyt, the Indycar legend who was as famous for his temper as his driving skill, and thought it fine and dandy to stroll down the Indianapolis pit lane to peer at a competitor's car; as a talented engineer himself he must have found the temptation irresistible. John thought it beyond the pale.

'You never did that; you never walked down the pit lane, went up to somebody else's car and started to inspect it. But with Foyt, you just couldn't bring yourself to say, "A.J., mate, piss off." He squatted down and peered into the front upright, looking puzzled. I knew all he could see were some tiny little vanes and nothing else. He then stood up, looked at me, shook his head like I was an idiot and walked on by. I just had to have a sly grin to myself.'

When the VPJ-6C first ran in practice for the Indy 500 in May 1977, initial impressions were entirely favourable, with Al Unser on the pace straight away. As Jim Chapman recalls, 'Al was very impressed with the new car, it gave the feeling of great stability, particularly in Turn Three, which is very fast.'

On subsequent practice runs Unser was faster still, but unfortunately for him a car in front driven by Janet Guthrie, the first woman to race at Indy, lost its turbine wheel at the entrance to Turn Three and he was unlucky enough to run over it, with alarming results. The VPJ-6C spun backwards into the wall and was torn apart. Protected by Barnard's beautifully made chassis, Unser walked away from the wreckage with minor injuries, but the car was a write-off. The new transverse gearbox, the only one Barnard had built so far, was destroyed.

'It was one of my early experiences of a bad accident in which what I had done could have resulted in the guy being seriously hurt,' says John. 'As it happened he wasn't and I was mightily relieved. But it did serve to make me think even harder about the importance of building the chassis as strong as possible. It also taught me to ensure that everything else — wheels, engine, gearbox, suspension and outer bodywork — would come apart in a crash, taking the energy out of the impact.'

The loss of the new car put Parnelli behind for the rest of 1977. Al Unser and Danny Ongais, who was now doing a full season with Interscope backing, both had to run VPJ-6Bs and there were only two victories. The first went to Ongais in the Norton 200 at Michigan International Speedway on 17 July, the second to Unser in the gruelling California 500 at Ontario Motor Speedway on 5 September. But despite securing just one win, Al finished second overall to Tom Sneva in the points standings by adding three second places, two thirds and a fourth to his tally.

Jim Chapman: 'I really believed we could have been ahead of the field for the rest of the season with that car. But once the gloom and despondency subsided I realised that the new VPJ-6C John had created had really great potential to be a winner, and it was.'

Fully settled in to Parnelli and envisaging a long spell at the company, and with an eye on rising property prices and their attendant profit, John and Rosie bought a detached bungalow at the foot of Palos Verdes hill, 10 minutes south of Torrance by car, enabling them both to continue their habit of having lunch at home.

It was, Rosie says, 'a typical American house on a typical American street with the typical lawn in the front. It was owned by English people before we moved in — they'd had cats and it was flea-infested, so we had it fumigated.' Also not particularly typical was the psychedelic wallpaper on most of the interior walls, hardly to the Barnards' conservative taste — but they never got round to changing it.

What they did do was attack one of the bathrooms, humping out an old cast-iron bath to replace it with something more modern and taking off the tiles only to discover that the wall beneath was uneven. Ever the perfectionist and much to the bemusement of Rosie, John borrowed an electric surface grinder to spend five dust-laden days grinding the wall perfectly flat.

'All my domestic DIY projects take two or three times longer than anticipated,' admits Barnard. 'I end up peeling back one more layer and finding more to do.' The problem remains; his grown-up children now regard his offers to help them decorate their homes with trepidation. Although they know the work will be immaculate, they find themselves asking if they really want Dad in their homes for two weeks, taking the skirting boards and door frames back to bare wood when all they really needed was a lick of paint.

Sponsorship for 1978 had become a major difficulty and early in the season people were beginning to leave Vel's Parnelli Jones, sensing that Miletich and Parnelli were shifting their business focus away from the race track. Al Unser had decided to join Jim Hall at Chaparral, taking Hughie Absalom with him. The demise of VPJ had begun.

Cosworth's Keith Duckworth played his own part in the decline of Parnelli. The success of the team's Cosworth turbocharged engine pulled the blinkers from his eyes, and, as Barnard puts it, immediately after the 1976 Pocono win, 'He shut up and saw the light.' Duckworth poached the Parnelli team's Larry Slutter and Chickie Hirashima, appointing them to guide the development and production of the turbocharged Cosworth DFX, and set up a Cosworth factory in Torrance to build it. The DFX went on to win every Indy 500 race and every Indycar championship between 1978 and 1987. The programme became Cosworth's most lucrative ever and was an achievement that, without the Parnelli team, the company would never have embarked upon, given Duckworth's original mindset.

To this day, Barnard is annoyed about the way Duckworth exploited the situation and it galls him that, after Duckworth had poured such scorn on the idea, he should then change his mind without acknowledging it: 'I wasn't impressed with Keith for doing that. Vel and Parnelli were the ones putting their hands in their pockets and I don't think they ever got the proper credit. Cosworth steamrollered in and ran away with the profit.'

Parnelli agrees and said in a recent interview: 'We were in a *Catch 22* because you had to satisfy your sponsors and we needed to order parts from Duckworth. We could have sued him and not let him do what he did to us, but we decided not to do that. We decided to try and work with him.'[12]

An alternative perhaps, might have been to patent some of the changes they made, but such is the time pressure of the racing world that significant innovations are rarely patented, as Barnard knows to his cost; it probably never even crossed their minds, and, it must be conceded, patenting changes

---

[12] Kirby, Gordon, 'The Way It Is/Indy car racing's Cosworth revolution', www.gordonkirby.com. Accessed April 2017.

on someone else's engine might have presented some legal problems. Given the circumstances, there was nothing the Parnelli team could do to stop the poaching, something that was par for the course; had not they poached Barnard from McLaren?

Mindful of the team effort at VPJ, Barnard is keen to point out that he didn't lead the development of the Parnelli Cosworth, but that's not how his contribution is viewed elsewhere; he was the chief designer overseeing a massive team effort, so he should be accorded due credit. Gordon Kirby sums it up best: 'John is responsible for some major contributions to Parnelli, in particular bringing the Cosworth revolution to Indycar. It was a Parnelli programme but he had a vital influence upon it.'

The revolution Kirby refers to would prompt a major clash between the teams and the USAC organising committee. USAC were committed to encouraging Offenhauser engines, but the power and potential of the Cosworth turbo had been made clear to the entire Indycar paddock by Parnelli. Patriotic arguments followed, with some declaring, 'American engines for American sport', others replying, 'The Cosworth may be designed by the British, but it is a Ford.'

And then there was the money problem. A Cosworth turbocharged engine, much like a Swiss watch (to steal Larry Slutter's vivid description), was an expensive bit of kit, around three times the cost of the time-honoured Offenhauser. Now the teams were demanding more money from USAC, blaming the organisation for capricious regulation, adding for good measure complaints about badly negotiated television rights and low attendances.

Then tragedy struck USAC: in April 1978 eight key members were flying in a Piper Navajo Chieftain when it crashed in a thunderstorm just 25 miles southeast of Indianapolis, killing all on board.

Bereft, the organisation was in disarray, unable to fight back effectively when the Indycar teams clubbed together after team owner Dan Gurney issued his famous 'white paper' accusing USAC of incompetence. He distributed it to all the Indycar team owners, quickly gaining support from Roger Penske and Pat Patrick. The result was the formation of Championship Auto Racing Teams (CART), a rival series for Indycars that was overseen by the Sports Car Club of America (SCCA).

As the battles continued, teams started redesigning their cars to incorporate a Cosworth turbo. Vel Miletich and Parnelli Jones, horrified by the rows, concluded they were never going to make money from the mess that was now

Indycar. *Autosport* reported in its 27 August 1978 edition that Interscope had ceased its sponsorship.

Vel's Parnelli Jones was slipping away from the racing scene, ironically at a time when the VPJ-6C was really coming good. In 1978 Danny Ongais won five races with the car and took eight pole positions. He won every race he finished bar the last, at Phoenix, where he came fourth after starting on pole. It was his best ever year in Indycar racing, but Tom Sneva won the championship again for Penske, without winning a single race. For the 1979 season A.J. Foyt, who had viewed Barnard's work on the VPJ-6C with such disdain, also bought one, driving it to five victories and that year's championship title.

By mid-1978 Barnard was at a loose end. The workload at Parnelli had dropped significantly during the first half of the year and he had seen some good people leave, but he wasn't despondent. He was also looking across the pond to Lotus, who were making a major breakthrough with ground-effect technology. Barnard found their innovation inspirational. Slowly, in the back of his mind, a plan for a ground-effect revolution in America began to take form.

In late March, Patrick Head, now chief designer at the embryonic Williams Formula 1 team, paid a visit, accompanied by Frank Williams. They were in California for the Long Beach Grand Prix and Patrick had asked Barnard for some garage space to prepare the team's singleton FW06, his first Formula 1 design. Patrick was deeply impressed by the DFV engine conversion and John's role in it: 'I found him beavering away in the design office designing a fuel system for the new DFV. Quite clearly he'd been heavily involved in some of the drawing and I know he had worked on the adaptation of the engine to fit it into the car.'

Perhaps it was seeing his Best Man on the brink of Formula 1 success that contributed to Barnard's growing desire to join the Parnelli exodus. Part of him didn't want to go as he had learned so much with this extraordinary American racing team and had enjoyed his time there: 'I spent three years at Parnelli and by the end of it even the mechanics had learned to respect me, to give me some credit. That itself was an achievement because mechanics are notoriously tough, especially on new engineers and designers — they love to make them squirm.'

The last word on Barnard's time at Parnelli should go to Jim Chapman, the man who had plucked him from McLaren: 'I feel honoured that I was in the fortunate position to offer John his first opportunity as the chief design engineer.

He certainly did not waste the opportunity afforded him and reached the top echelon of Formula 1 design. I am thrilled by all of John's accomplishments during his motor racing design career.

'I can't think of anybody who could have come in, adapted to that environment, pulled his sleeves up and been that successful. I think Maurice Philippe had certainly missed the important points of what Indycar needed, and John put all that right. It was the start of turning the Parnelli racing team round again to put it on an upward track to be successful. The car certainly performed, won quite a few races in a very competitive field, a car that was really three or four years old in chassis design anyway.'

Barnard now had a wealth of high-level experience under his belt, with a much deeper understanding of aerodynamics and chassis, suspension and engine design. He was also developing a name for himself in the media, with *Autosport* declaring, 'Barnard is acknowledged to be one of the brightest brains at work in USAC.'[13]

He was now ready, more than ready, to build a race-winning car entirely of his own design.

He also wanted to go home.

---

[13] Autosport, *18 May 1978, p41.*

CHAPTER 9
THE CHAPARRAL HIGH
1978–79

Some time in the summer of 1978, John received a call from A.J. Foyt. The legend of the Indy 500 had gulped down some humble pie, realised that Barnard's front wheels did stay on a car even with one-inch axles, and was soon ordering a Parnelli-Cosworth for himself. Now he was courting the budding design genius to build him an Indycar.

Barnard liked Foyt: 'I secretly admired him as a big, tough, no-nonsense "see if I can get away with it" type of racer. He was a bit of a legend at the time.'

So Barnard flew down to Foyt's home city of Houston, where he visited his workshop — 'a very clean and tidy operation, not very big' — before going off to have lunch with him. It was a new experience: such was Foyt's superstar status that almost everyone they passed on the way to the restaurant said, 'Hi, A.J.!' John describes Foyt as being 'as wide as he was tall', unusual for top racing drivers who, like jockeys, are generally short, slim and light. John was conscious of feeling like a complete unknown.

Foyt saw Barnard as a means to securing a sharper edge. He told John: 'I will do absolutely anything to win.' This didn't ring the right bells with Barnard, and less than halfway into the meal he was having doubts. While Foyt furnished him with hair-raising tales illustrating his uncompromising thirst for victory, Barnard quietly decided that he wouldn't be happy working with the Houston hero.

Barnard never took up his offer, continuing to work at Parnelli for the time being, but he was always on the look-out for the ideal job, one that would give him freedom to realise a growing dream — to build the perfect race car.

Rosie Barnard considers his time at Parnelli as 'probably his happiest professional period', partly because he didn't clash with people there. 'Yes, he was happy,' she says, 'but then there was young love helping him too. It was a good time. We didn't have any responsibilities — no children.'

But when, in September 1978, Rosemary announced that she was pregnant, a balance tipped in John's mind. Now aged 32, he was looking for a route back to England.

A week or so later John took a call from Hughie Absalom, now at Chaparral Cars with Al Unser. Absalom told him that Jim Hall, Texas oil magnate and co-owner of Chaparral, had taken an interest in him. 'Would you like to build a car for Chaparral?'

Hall had already established a considerable reputation for innovation and was credited with a series of important developments in aerodynamics. In 1966 he wowed motorsport with his Can-Am Chaparral 2E, the first race car to be fitted with a high-mounted driver-adjustable rear wing. It was followed in 1967 by the 2F, which had an even bigger wing towering above its closed coupé body and took part in the World Sports Car Championship, contested mainly in Europe.

Mounted on two substantial struts, Chaparral's wing applied downforce direct to the rear wheels, improving its grip through corners. These cars also had an automatic gearbox, without a clutch pedal, but instead there was a 'wing pedal'. The driver would push this down on the straights to flatten the wing angle, spilling the downforce and so reducing the drag, similar to the way the Drag Reduction System (DRS) operates in Formula 1 today. To reinstate grip in corners, the driver simply took his foot off the pedal. It wasn't long before sporting bodies banned any aerodynamic device that could be adjusted while the car was moving.

Then, in 1970, Jim Hall did it again, producing the famous Chaparral 2J 'Sucker Car' or 'Vacuum Cleaner', a boxy beast of a machine that featured two 17-inch fans driven by a dedicated snowmobile engine. The fans were mounted horizontally in the rear so that they would literally suck the car onto the track, the effect enhanced by a system of articulated plastic skirts around the base of the car that helped 'seal' it to the ground, while the underside of the car was so shaped that it encouraged the reduction of air pressure. The 2J has been widely applauded for being the first ground-effect car, of which more shortly, but teething troubles meant it took time to achieve its potential. Almost as soon as it did, it too was banned.

Thus Jim Hall had already built a reputation for aerodynamic innovation, but that was all from an earlier period. It was his chats with ex-Parnelli staff such as Hughie Absalom, Al Unser and Dennis Swan that made it clear to him that Barnard was the man to restore that reputation.

So Barnard agreed to fly the 1,000 miles east to Midland, Texas, for a chat. For the first time, his confidence was such that he felt he could lay down some stringent conditions. He told Hall: 'I have some ideas for a new car, something a bit different, but I'll have to do it in England.'

This line in the sand was a significant moment and underlines one of the more endearing aspects of Barnard's character; whatever the demands of professional racing, his family was going to come first. It was still his intention to have a top-flight career while doing his best to get home for lunch.

'Why do you have to do this in England?' queried Hall. Barnard concentrated on the technical reasons. 'Because I know I can get it all built there. British motorsport technology is the best in the world and has all the specialist skills I'm going to need. I know all the people and the places.'

He went on to explain how he planned to update 'ground-effect' innovations created by Peter Wright for the Lotus 78. No one in the US, not even Jim Hall, had tried ground-effect quite like this before.

Hall was in a mood to listen and soon they were talking practicalities. Barnard would need to set up a British arm of Chaparral by creating a manufacturing company. Although this was completely outside the designer's experience, he didn't imagine it would be difficult. How much would it cost? Barnard came up with estimates and Hall agreed to send him sufficient money every month.

The deal looked like going Barnard's way, so he added an all-important rider that was, in part, motivated by his still burning disappointment with Gordon Coppuck at McLaren. He looked Hall straight in the eye and said, 'You understand, Jim, that I will be designing this car. That means I must get full credit for being the designer.' Hall looked a little taken aback but agreed. The deal was concluded in typical American style with a hearty handshake, agreeing that John's salary should be £15,000 a year (equivalent to about £80,000 now) plus a company car. This was probably a satisfactory rate for a chief designer then but incredibly modest compared with today's levels of remuneration at the top of motorsport.

Back in Torrance, Barnard went to see Vel Miletich to give in his notice. Vel was understanding and they parted on good terms.

There's one notable postscript to his relationship with VPJ. Just a few years later, Barnard came to Miletich's aid, loaning him £2,000 and delivering it, under cloak-and-dagger circumstances, to a Yugoslav cousin in a run-down part of London. Barnard, driving a brand-new Mercedes, was outside his comfort zone and feeling much like he was trapped in the seedy, suburban environs of a Le Carré novel as he handed the money over to a man who wouldn't step outside the door. The cousin had escaped from communism and was bound for America; John was helping him on his way, to the eternal gratitude of Vel Miletich.

And so, in late September 1978, John returned to England, leaving Rosie behind to sell their Californian home. In many ways he was sad to leave America, where the entrepreneurial spirit had taught him so much: 'The way they look at things is inspirational. Set up a company? No problem. So what if you haven't done it before! Whatever you want to do, just go out and do it!' He brought the attitude with him and he would need it immediately.

John had reached a landmark in his career. At last he had a brief to create the perfect race car from scratch, and he had the experience, skill, talent and commitment to do it. There would be no need for compromise, no frustrations arising from trying to correct another designer's mistakes. John Barnard was now bristling with energy, impatient to start and ready to make a step-change entirely on his own. There was no big operation to back him. He'd have the money, but he'd have to find the facilities — this car would be entirely his own work.

Upon his return, he immediately began setting up Chaparral Cars UK Ltd, working out of his father's front room at 3 Peel Road, their Lightwater house still being let to a McLaren employee. Rosie returned six weeks later to live with him and Ted while their Lightwater tenant moved out and a builder started extending their future family home.

For his company car, John ordered himself a Renault 30TS, the French company's top-of-the-range executive hatchback saloon, but not 'over the top'. He plumped for a hatchback to facilitate the transportation of racing parts.

So it was in the house of his childhood that Barnard conceived, drew and developed the Chaparral 2K or Yellow Submarine, so called because it stuck so firmly to the track that it appeared more like the upper works of a submarine than a race car, and because the sponsor, Pennzoil, had yellow branding.

John set up his drawing board and went to work: 'It was another blank page. I had nothing to constrain me; just the USAC regulations, which were pretty relaxed compared with F1.'

He had first come across ground-effect in the early '70s at Lola: 'I remember Peter Wright showing me an old, small, crude, one-tenth scale model he'd made of an open-wheel car, complete with sidepods, the floors of which were in the shape of an inverted wing profile — the first ground-effect design I had ever seen. He had taken this model from BRM to Lotus and worked with Colin Chapman on it. The auto-aerodynamics world was lit up by that particular innovation and Lotus led the way for quite a while.'

Wright, working at the behest of his BRM boss, Tony Rudd, with Imperial College's Dr John Harvey, had based his pioneering ground-effect work for this secret 'wing car' upon a seminal paper written by Professor John Stollery, who developed the thinking in support of Donald Campbell's ultimately tragic record-breaking projects in his *Bluebird* car and boat.

The main power of ground-effect comes from a combination of aerodynamic downforce created by air flowing over an inverted wing and a phenomenon known as the 'Venturi effect', which, put simply, is the tendency of a fluid, such as air, to move faster and, therefore, at a lower pressure when it passes from a wide pipe into a narrower pipe and then out into a wider pipe again. This is because when the air exits the constriction, it expands again, this expansion effectively sucking the air through the narrower section into the trumpet flare of the pipe's rear mouth because it is at lower pressure.

Barnard, like Wright, wasn't going to use pipes, but he would achieve the same effect by creating two giant inverted wings under the car's sidepods, each sculpted into a inverted U-shaped 'Venturi tunnel'.

Inverted wing shapes in motorsport were nothing new, experiments with aerofoils going back to at least 1928.[14] But this was a wing of a different order in scale from anything seen in Formula 1 or Indycar racing: the Chaparral 2K's under-wing profile ran almost the whole length of the car.

In each tunnel, the aerofoil shape began alongside the driver's thighs, dipped down by the bottom of his seat and then followed a long graceful curve that rose upwards beyond the rear wheels towards the integral rear wing. Just behind the driver's seat each tunnel became significantly narrower, reaching its narrowest point just in front of the rear wheel before flaring open again, ensuring that the Venturi effect would help suck the air through more quickly, further reducing pressure.

The tunnels achieved their Venturi effect with much greater efficiency by

---

[14] *'The First Launch' (Fritz von Opel's RAK 2 — 23 May 1928)* opelpost.com.

virtue of 'skirts'. Fixed along the bottom of each sidepod, these skirts, as with those used at the back of the Chaparral 2J 'Sucker Car', actually touched the track, effectively sealing off the underside of the car.

Talking about the pioneering work at Lotus, Peter Wright said in an interview for this book: 'Ground-effect was defined pretty thoroughly by John Stollery. What I did was find out how to apply it to a race car really effectively on the Lotus 78.'

Wright was working with Ralph Bellamy at London's Imperial College wind tunnel where they used a rolling road. Comprising a wide conveyor-belt loop set in the floor beneath the stationary model, this travelled at various speeds to simulate the movement of the car: 'We stumbled on the need to seal the gap between the side pods and the rolling road — I think it was me who figured it out… When we put skirts on the car, suddenly the whole thing worked.'

In the first version of the 2K, the skirts were more like boards, flexible plastic sheets that almost dropped down to ground level, and initially failed to create a fully effective seal with the track. But as Barnard points out, 'No one else was doing this in Indy, so they were as good as they needed to be.' Nevertheless, he built the sidepods to leave room for a more effective system.

Barnard's final incarnation of skirt design for the 2K was far more sophisticated, comprising sliding skirts of quarter-inch thickness made of aluminium-skinned honeycomb panels. These moved up and down inside the double wall of the sidepod between nylon rollers, sliding up when the car rolled in a corner or went over a bump, and dropping down again under their own weight. The nylon rollers prevented the skirts from getting jammed when the low pressure under the car sucked them inwards. Their bottom edges were made of a low-friction ceramic that slid along the track, a 'Lotus idea', as John explains: 'To stop the wear we attached to the bottom of the skirts an aluminium tube with the bottom cut away. Inserted into the tube were ceramic rods, like sticks of chalk. They would scrape along the track, which didn't please the track owners.'

John's designs received criticism, with people telling him that ground-effect couldn't work in Indycar racing, one contention being that it would create too much drag. As was his way, Barnard didn't argue; he just ignored everyone. The more confident he became in his own skills, the more irrelevant he considered other people's nay-saying. He certainly understood that ground-effect was great for corners but created drag on the straights, but he also knew how to arrive at the best possible balance between the two.

By now John was drawing pages of designs on the board he'd set up in the front room at Peel Road, the place where his mother, 13 years earlier, had done such a magnificent job for his Aston Martin with half a cow.

Ted, happy to have companionship again in the house after the death of Rose Ellen, was roped in to help with labelling up drawing sheets and writing out long lists of the parts John would need. Ted settled back into his old role, which mainly consisted of doing what his son asked him to do. 'That's the way I'd grown up,' says John. 'I'd say, "I really want to do this", or, "Can you do this for me?" — and that was enough. It was done.'

Rosie was busy keeping the books. 'I got on okay with Ted,' she says, but was concerned that she could 'never match up to his wife, of course, because she was very practical, so I didn't even try to.' She also noticed his tendency to fuss: 'I suppose because John's mother had had several miscarriages, he would get anxious if I went off for a walk in the snow during my pregnancy.'

The London weather was a considerable contrast to the sunny delights of California. The house had no central heating and on winter mornings they often awoke to frost on the inside of the windows.

As the winter moved on, however, he began to worry about running out of time. The aim was to get the first 2K finished and shipped to America before May 1979, the month of the Indy 500 and all of its build-up. Not only was he designing a ground-breaking car from scratch, but he also had to locate, set up and manage a team of experts to build it.

As the drawings began to take shape, Barnard went in search of an expert team. He asked Bob Sparshott, the owner of BS Fabrications in Luton, to realise his designs for the chassis, uprights and suspension, with chief fabricator Peter Burns making specialist parts. Barnard came to know Pasquali Rousseau, an apprentice at BS Fabrications who would later work for him at Ferrari. He also contacted Gordon Kimball in California and persuaded him to come and work in Luton as his 'pencil'.

As John completed the drawings for the major parts and overall schemes, he drove the 30 miles from Wembley to Luton some three times a week in his Renault. There, he would talk through his drawings with Kimball, who would then produce the detailed drawings in his office above the workshop. 'It was quite a change for Gordon,' says John. 'He was a Californian, used to the sunshine — here he was working away at a drawing board in rainy Luton. But he didn't seem to mind; for him it was all about racing.'

For the bodywork, John contacted Specialised Mouldings, the Huntingdon company with which he'd worked at Lola, and briefed a young contract draughtsman, Dave Pollard, to draw up the bodywork in detailed quarter scale. 'He was superb; he worked in ink the whole time and was very accurate.' John then blew up the drawings to full size so that Specialised Mouldings could create the bodywork buck.

Barnard now decided to take a new approach to the rear-wing design, eschewing the single post that he'd invented at McLaren, instead mounting the wing between two large endplates, each of which rose from horizontal plates fixed to the gearbox at the rear end of the ground-effect tunnels. He chose this route because he wanted nothing to impede airflow coming over the rear wing; a centrally mounted post would be an obstacle, however aerodynamically perfect it might be. The large wing endplates also helped to minimise vortexes that occur at the ends of the wings, a swirling mixture of high and low pressure — which is why you see aircraft fitted with upturned winglets. Similar endplates are common in Formula 1 today.

To ensure clear airflow rising from the ground-effect tunnels, he did his best to keep the rear suspension out of the way, mounting the rear suspension damper unit directly to the bottom of the large wing endplates rather than to the gearbox.

He made the wing endplates out of honeycomb sandwich, an aircraft method, which basically comprised strong aluminium hexagonal 'honeycomb' glued between two sheets of 22-gauge aluminium. In themselves, these weren't strong enough to support the rear suspension, so in key places he cut away the honeycomb and filled the gaps with machined aluminium blocks, or inserts — an established aerospace method of creating load-bearing strength. This technique would later inform his ground-breaking work in carbon-fibre.

All of this left the central rear section of the car as clear of obstruction as possible. His whole ethos was to completely encase the car in aerodynamically effective bodywork, something he had first attempted with the VPJ-6C: 'The rear suspension was quite a step — mounting the spring damper units to the wing endplates had not been done before. I was pushing the boat out.'

To push that boat out a little further, he turned again to Steve Nichols at Gabriel, commissioning him to design a compact shock absorber that would allow the damper to move with 'the maximum amount of stroke in the minimum space'. As Steve explained in an interview for this book, 'The new system allowed the damper's piston to travel right to the bottom and right to the top of the unit.' This was all in an effort to reduce the size of the whole unit

— Barnard's design for the Chaparral meant that he needed the same piston travel in a more compact package than anything that had gone before.

Standard dampers, just like the shock absorbers on a road car, have metal eyes at the top and bottom of the unit so they can be fixed in place. Barnard came up with an ingenious design to get rid of the eyes, replacing them with a gimbal arrangement to support the body of the damper.

In the same space-saving quest, Barnard designed his own built-in air jacks, used in pit stops for wheel changes, because the off-the-shelf versions wouldn't fit his aerodynamic profiles.

Barnard met Jim Hall only twice during the Chaparral 2K's build. In October 1978 there occurred the novelty of two Indycar races in England, at Brands Hatch and Silverstone, and Hall's team came over with its Lola T500 driven by Al Unser. Hall asked Barnard to find him a 'really good hotel', so Rosie booked him into The Ritz, on London's Piccadilly. John went there to meet him, taking along his layouts and schematics and spreading them out on the double bed in the Texan's room.

As Hall looked at the drawings, Barnard said: 'I'm not sure what to do with the gear-shift run. Should it go outside the fuel cell or through it? What do you think?' Hall, apparently, thought nothing. 'Just do what you think best,' was his laconic reply. John duly ran the linkage outside the chassis and inside the bodywork, but it was a compromise that would irritate him until he solved it almost a decade later at Ferrari. Barnard was surprised that Hall wasn't keen to have more input, claiming the man didn't study his drawings at all, merely giving them a glance. So John rolled them up and went home.

In many ways, however, Hall was the perfect boss, paying the bills on time and resisting any temptation to interfere. Later John invited Hall to visit Specialised Mouldings in Huntingdon to see the body bucks: 'I was able to show him what the car was going to look like. He just said, "Great. Carry on." That was his entire input!'

Barnard now turned to the engine, a Cosworth DFX turbo, and immediately redesigned the air inlets so they would fit under his aerodynamic engine fairing. He also took the opportunity to attack the problem he'd had on the VPJ-6C of how to get the turbocharger down low and out of the airflow.

Under time pressure, Barnard decided to draw the exhaust-pipe layout in detail himself — something he hadn't done before and has never done since. At the time and without Computer Aided Design (CAD) software to help, exhaust design was usually handled by expert fabricators experienced in cutting and welding pipes *in situ* on the first mock-up of the car, and John would have to spend hours supervising the work.

It will be recalled that with the VPJ-6C the exhaust pipes as first conceived turned out to be too long because they had to run around the wide base of the car's transverse gearbox. This had forced Barnard to compromise by relocating the turbo higher than he wanted, an outcome that had really bothered him. With no time to build a new transverse gearbox for the 2K, he plumped for a longitudinal one, built by Pete Weismann, and decided this time that the best way to get the turbo lower down was to redesign the bellhousing, the section that sits between the engine and gearbox, and contains the flywheel and clutch. This was a radical thought.

Barnard cut away the top of the bellhousing and, in place of the removed chunk, fixed a stainless-steel plate that bridged the front and rear faces of the bellhousing, effectively replacing the lost strength. He fitted the turbocharger on top of this plate, so now it was lower and less of an obstruction to airflow. The exhaust pipes entered the turbo under the plate in the space created by lowering the middle of the bellhousing.

Barnard thus became the first in motorsport to create a new bellhousing that incorporated the turbo, a design that became the method of choice for mounting turbos throughout the Indycar world for many years to come. 'I didn't get the turbo as low as I managed on the Parnelli-Cosworth, but it was a better compromise overall.'

One of the remarkable things about the 2K was that this ground-breaking ground-effect design was created without the benefit of a wind tunnel; there wasn't the time, the people or the money. The Chaparral was a product of gut instinct and experience, the most 'natural' top-flight racer that Barnard would ever build.

'This was such an instinctive car,' he says. 'It was all about what looked right, what felt right. I guess it was probably the most complete package I had created, with the minimum of compromises to get it all to fit the aerodynamic concept. There was compromise of course, a whole list of things that you're trying to get as near as you can to perfection.'

The only feedback he received on ground-effect aerodynamics during the project was from Patrick Head, who was busy designing the Williams FW07 using the Imperial College wind tunnel, as Wright and Stollery had before him. Patrick's FW07 went on to win five Formula 1 World Championship races in 1979, including the British Grand Prix with Clay Regazzoni at the wheel.

Patrick recalls the phone conversation: 'John phoned and said he'd got a job making an Indycar for Jim Hall, that he was going to do it in England but hadn't the time to do wind-tunnel work. I gave him some advice, saying, "On your underside tunnels, John, keep them as long as possible before you start the expansion and keep as much as possible as you can out of the airstream at the back — think of it as the trumpet exit. And make the car so that it keeps its edges as close to the ground as possible, get the back of the bodywork to seal up to the wheel, bring the sidepod as far forward as you can so you can run as small a front wing as possible." It was that sort of conversation, no more than that, pretty limited, no drawings, just a brief chat with general guidelines. He never sought any more information from me on it.'

And so, in early April 1979, with the Indy season well underway, Barnard arranged for the chassis, suspension and bodywork to be shipped to Midland, Texas, where the car was put together by Hughie Absalom and other former VPJ staff. Chaparral's engine man, Franz Weis, built and adapted the turbocharged Cosworth DFX, and after its installation the completed 2K was taken to Ontario Motor Speedway in California to be put through its paces by Al Unser. John flew out to attend this shakedown.

After a few laps Unser came into the pits, grinning from ear to ear. 'This thing flies!' he told Barnard, meaning, in one sense, the very opposite; that the ground-effect underwings glued the car to the track through corners. 'Fantastic,' declared Unser. 'This thing just feels right. It's an out-of-the-box success'. The car had been taken off its truck, put on the track and driven to competitive speeds with the minimum of adjustments.

Jim Hall, who had flown to the Speedway aboard his Learjet, also looked impressed. The 2K was packed up and taken back to Texas while Hall, Unser, Absalom and Barnard went back to their nearby motel, opened some champagne and toasted the Chaparral 2K. 'Everyone was happy,' says John.

But the job wasn't over; John had to leave the party early for a two-hour drive to Costa Mesa, south of Los Angeles, to pick up some spare gearbox casings from Pete Weismann. When he arrived, Pete was still busy finishing the machining of the casings, which were needed for the season's racing, so John had to hang around before he could drive to the airstrip near Ontario Motor

Speedway where Hall was waiting for him so they could fly back together to Midland. By now time was getting on, and Hall was getting impatient; he didn't like flying in the dark.

Unable to warn Hall of the delay, John weaved through the traffic at a law-breaking 80mph, ignoring the horns of protests from other drivers and smiling to himself — it had been a good day.

So when he arrived at the airstrip shortly after sunset he was surprised to find that Hall was livid: 'What the hell have you been doing? You've kept me waiting!' John didn't say anything in reply, but in his head he was angry. 'I had just bust a gut and every speed limit, and all I got were complaints and black looks.' Like so many similar moments in John's life, this one stuck in his mind. He thought, 'This guy just doesn't intend to be grateful for anything.'

He didn't need compliments from Hall; he was getting them from everyone else. Bob Sparshott was full of praise and Barnard quotes him as saying, 'It's the first car we've ever built where everything fits!' Indeed, the build was full of a serendipity brought about by Barnard's exacting attention to detail and the key principle he had learned at McLaren, to design the chassis with enough forethought and accuracy to ensure that the final build is quick and efficient.

'Everything we drew just fitted,' he says. 'Nothing had to be rebuilt or redesigned.' The only change they had to make between the test and the first qualifier for the Indy 500 was to fit stiffer front suspension springs.

The car underwent more evaluation at Chaparral's own track in the desert outside Midland known as the Rattlesnake Raceway, an aptly named place that was replete with dangers. 'There was no safety there,' says Barnard, 'no ambulance or medical facilities. But that didn't stop Franz Weis from hopping in the car and screaming round the track.' He asked Franz if the lack of rescue equipment worried him and he said: 'Not really. What really worries me is that there might be a rattler on the track; then there's a good chance my front wheel will flick it up into the cockpit.'

Sometimes rattlers would crawl up through grilles in the floor of the engine room. To deal with them, the engineers had a snake pole with a wire noose at one end. When a rattler came into the garage, they would drop the noose over its head and tighten it. They called it 'Fishin' for Rattlers' — hardly the sort of sport to be found in a Surrey workshop. Barnard found himself avoiding the engine room.

Testing at the Rattlesnake revealed a flaw in the wheels. Hall had insisted they use wheels he'd secured free of charge via a sponsorship deal with General

Motors. Barnard didn't really want to use them because they were made up of two halves riveted together and he didn't trust them. The test showed they were leaking air through the rims. Barnard phoned Hall with the problem. Such was the team owner's pulling power that he was able to call the boss of General Motors and persuade him to open up their R&D workshops in Detroit on a Sunday and fix the wheels inside 24 hours.

More entrepreneur than inventor, Hall had secured American motor oil manufacturer Pennzoil as the car's primary sponsor. With the Indy 500 just weeks away, the 2K was now ready for a new paint job. Pennzoil's colours were bright yellow — the Yellow Submarine was about to be born.

Hall flew in a top spray painter from California who brought with him a customised paint containing tiny metal flakes. He'd just completed the job when, in a dusty gust of wind, the door to the paint shop blew open, coating the wet paint in fine sand. There was no paint left to do it again, so Hall sent his private plane back to California to pick up a new batch while the car was rubbed down.

It was a setback that put Hall in a bad mood. When John flew in from London carrying more parts, he was summoned to Hall's office, where his brother Dick was also waiting. In Hall's hand was an invoice itemising the cost of the car.

'This car has cost me £220,000 and I've just had to fly some guy in from California to paint the thing for a second time!'

'It's a one-off car, Jim,' replied Barnard, calmly. 'They always cost more.' Dick chipped in: 'What the hell have you spent all the money on?'

The comment was tantamount to an accusation of embezzlement; John had to bite his lip. 'It's all listed there,' he replied.

He recalls feeling that Dick Hall had been winding up his brother up about the cost, which included John's expert design, setting up a company, hiring two draughtsmen, all the fabrication, materials and parts, and transport — as far as Barnard was concerned it was a bargain.

But Hall couldn't see it. He knew that if he'd bought a similar car off the shelf from Lola it would have been half the price. But this, of course, was not an off-the-shelf car. And in Barnard he had employed a perfectionist. John showed no emotion, instead just storing away Hall's reaction.

They were now ready for May 1979, the month of testing and qualifying for the car's début at the Indianapolis 500 on the last Sunday of the month. John left the team to it, flying back to England to build a second car as back-up.

Meanwhile the USAC/CART war was getting up steam. USAC (United States Automobile Club) was running the Indy 500 as part of the 1979 USAC Championship Car Series, but by now the new rival series run by CART (Championship Auto Racing Teams) was splitting the field, with many of the CART-aligned outfits, including Chaparral, only racing in that year's Indy 500 as a one-off because of its historical significance and popularity. Two months earlier these CART teams had boycotted the first USAC-organised race of the season, the Datsun Twin 200 at Ontario Motor Speedway.

That race was won by A.J. Foyt who, having earlier sided with the CART teams, now turned against them. Such was his will to win that he proposed that USAC should refuse to let the CART entrants enter the Indy 500. This idiotic idea would mean that Al Unser, driving the Chaparral 2K, would be excluded, together with his brother Bobby, Johnny Rutherford, Danny Ongais, Gordon Johncock and Wally Dallenbach — most of the top names in the sport. But USAC thought Foyt's ruse a marvellous one, duly rejecting entries from the six CART teams — Chaparral, McLaren, Fletcher, Gurney, Patrick and Penske — and declaring them 'harmful to racing'. Next stop, the US District Court for the Southern District of Indiana where, on 5 May, the six teams won an injunction against USAC on the grounds of restraint of trade. USAC was forced to allow them to compete, but only on the promise that the rebel teams wouldn't disrupt proceedings.

In the main and as was his wont, Barnard was happy to ignore all these shenanigans as he struggled to complete the back-up car in England. But he couldn't ignore it all. Pole Day on Saturday 12 May, at which the front rows of the grid were decided, was cut short when Danny Ongais crashed at Turn Four, where he remained trapped in his car for over 20 minutes. Grid qualification was postponed to the following day.

The next day Al Unser in the Chaparral 2K took provisional pole position with a four-lap average of 192.503mph only to be later knocked off the top spot by Rick Mears and Tom Sneva, both in Penske-Cosworths, putting Al on the outside of the three-car front row. Eight of the nine cars on the front three rows were powered by Cosworths.

A.J. Foyt was in a Barnard-designed Parnelli-Cosworth, on row two, as was Danny Ongais, back in 27th spot because of his crash. How thin the grid would have looked if USAC had had their way and disqualified all the CART racers, most of which used Cosworth engines.

While it was positive that Unser was on the front row, he was in the less-favoured outside spot. This meant he would have a longer journey around the first turn, which could lose him places to a driver or two on the inside positions of the row behind. Bob Sparshott phoned Barnard to comment, 'You could have had Al on pole if you'd been there to make some set-up changes.' John couldn't be everywhere at once; he was still working flat-out on the back-up car.

'Pressure, pressure, pressure', was the feeling John remembers from that time, and more was to come. In the early hours of Thursday 17 May, Rosie woke up with the unmistakable pain of contractions. She turned over to John: 'I think we'd better get to the hospital.'

'It's the middle of the night,' came the exasperated reply.

'Well look, I'm very sorry, but we *are* going to have to go!'

And so they did, with John driving the two miles to Northwick Park Hospital in Harrow and sitting with her until he had to leave for Kent — he had a 7am pick-up for a bellhousing casting for the back-up 2K.

So it was that their first child, Jennifer Ellen, was born while John was on the road collecting his bellhousing casting. He regrets to this day that he missed the moment.

Rosie, ever practical, was philosophical: 'I don't get precious about things like that; I knew the car was important as well. He abandoned me again four days later to go to Indianapolis! But that's just life, isn't it? It didn't really bother me; I'd seen all the work that went into the car. Obviously I'd rather he stayed but… *c'est la vie*.'

John landed at Indianapolis and collected a rental car. As he drove towards the famous Indianapolis Motor Speedway he saw in the distance a massive billboard showing a large photograph of the bright yellow 2K with Jim Hall and Al Unser standing beside it — Hall must have moved fast to get the publicity shot done in time. For Barnard it was a moment of intense pride: 'It was quite galvanising, a completely new experience to see someone I knew getting such publicity, and with my car taking up an entire billboard.'

But his feeling of pride evaporated rapidly as he got close enough to read the text: 'Jim Hall — Master of Ground Effect'. To Barnard that meant one thing: Hall was claiming credit for the design. With mounting fury, John drove into the circuit, parked the car and marched over to the Chaparral motorhome to confront Hall. Both Hall and Al Unser were inside. 'I've just seen the billboard down the road,' fumed John. 'It's just like you designed it all! Our deal was that I would be recognised as the designer.'

'Oh gee, sorry, John,' Hall responded. 'It was Pennzoil's idea. I couldn't stop them.'

Unser stood in the corner shaking his head. John turned to him: 'It's not right. That wasn't the deal!'

Al looked deeply embarrassed. 'There's nothing I can do,' he said, 'but we know what really happened.'

What really happened, at least from Barnard's point of view, was that Hall had shaken hands with him at their first meeting with the full intent of claiming all the credit. This might seem an extreme reaction on Barnard's part; after all, Hall could justly lay claim to important innovations, including the rear wing and the 'Sucker Car'. Or could he? To this day controversy rages over the origins of the 'Sucker Car': was it really Hall's idea, or was it Hap Sharp's, or did the original concept come from General Motors? Barnard reveals that when he first arrived in Midland, Troy Rogers, one of Hall's long-standing mechanics, issued a warning: 'You'll never last here because Hall always takes the credit.'

Rosie Barnard was shocked: 'I knew very well that John and Gordon Kimball had drawn every single piece of that car, and I found it incredible that somebody could lie like that and claim something that wasn't his in such a brazen way.'

Al Unser later told Barnard that he was both 'sorry and shocked' by Hall's decision to claim authorship of the 2K. Barnard keeps a photograph of the car on display at home on which Al wrote, 'At least we know who the real designer is!'

The build-up to the 2K's début continued apace, with more track action, including Bump Day on Sunday 20 May (where non-qualifiers get a final chance to 'bump' the slowest qualifiers from the grid) and Carburetion Day on Thursday 24 May (the final pre-race practice session that in older days had been the last chance to tune carburettors). Conflict between CART teams and USAC continued over various 'capricious' new regulations, with Al Unser having to use all his influence to get Danny Ongais into the race following his qualifying crash. The upshot of it all was that USAC did a lot of caving in and for the race, on Sunday 27 May, there were 35 cars on the grid — the highest number since 1933.

The Indy 500 was begun in traditional style. Tony Hulman, who had bought the dilapidated Indianapolis track in 1945 and made the race so popular, always began with the famous line 'Gentlemen, start your engines' and after his death in 1977 his wife, Mary, stepped into the role. In 1979 she announced the same, but by now with an important revision: 'Lady and Gentlemen, start your engines,' in honour of Janet Guthrie, the first woman to take part in the Indy 500 and now doing so for the third time.

The cars were started in the pit lane by mechanics using portable external starter motors. For this purpose, John had designed an aluminium tube that ran from the rear of the 2K under the rear deck and into the gearbox, through which the Chaparral pit mechanics inserted the starter motor shaft so it could turn the engine over and fire it up.

At the rolling start the field sped into Turn One and Al Unser felt the extraordinary power of Barnard's ground-effect design as he eased the Chaparral 2K through the curve. Despite being on the outside, he cruised past Sneva and Mears and into the distance.

Jackie Stewart, commentating for ABC TV, remarked as the 2K moved seven seconds ahead, 'a tremendous margin. And there you see Jim Hall, a tremendously clever man, and that car that he has been able to construct… that chassis is so good I just can't imagine how superior it is to the rest of them.' Clearly, Hall's message that the car was his design was getting through.

But it was a case of the Commentator's Curse if ever there was one, because Al was losing power and on lap 96 pulled into the pits. John takes up the tale: 'The aluminium tube that guided the external starter motor tube was burned to a cinder. It just fell out of the back. I was standing there holding this tube and there was ABC commentator Chris Economaki right on top of me: "What's the problem?" I just showed the tube to the camera.' The Weismann gearbox was overheating.

Unser roared out of the pits but it was to no avail. On lap 104 of 200, smoke began pouring from the back of the Chaparral, followed a few laps later by flames. John soon discovered that the gearbox oil pump lacked the power to push sufficient lubricant through the oil cooler and around the spinning gears to keep the gearbox temperature down, a problem exacerbated by the insulating effect of the aerodynamic bodywork covering the engine bay. The older Unser brother, Bobby, took over the lead in a Penske.

Jackie Stewart waxed lyrical about this terrible blow for the Chaparral owner: 'Jim Hall, a man that I admire… sitting in the pits there, must be really upset, one of the truly brilliant men.'

There were, perhaps, compensations for Barnard. While Mears won the race for Penske, Foyt finished second in his Parnelli VPJ-6C and Ongais, despite starting near the back of the grid, drove his VPJ-6C brilliantly, gaining 23 places to finish fourth.

Much of the rest of the season was a struggle, exacerbated by John's diminished enthusiasm after the row with Hall. He didn't attend any more races that year and the set-up of his car suffered for it. He spent his time sorting out the inevitable teething troubles such as specifying a more powerful gearbox oil pump and adding the new sliding skirts. The skirts turned out to be so effective that the extra suction under the car began to distort the sidepod underwings, which had to be stiffened up.

On 10 June Al Unser finished second to his older brother at Trenton Speedway and on 15 July he was third at Michigan International Speedway. But the race that Barnard really remembers was the one on 2 September at Ontario Motor Speedway in which Unser led for many laps before dropping to fifth at the finish — and he recorded a qualifying speed of 202.202mph. And here we shall take a diversion into the world of numbers, fate, superstition and serendipity.

The number 202.202 had a profound impact on Barnard and the reason why is revelatory: 'I saw that number. Not just 202, but 202 *point* 202. I thought, "I just can't believe this!"'

Why such a powerful reaction? 'Hard to say,' he says. 'There are certain numbers I like: 202, is one, 2 and 4 are others. Why 202? I've always thought 2 is a nice round number, dividing so neatly into 1 and 1. And 2-oh-2 has zero, the roundest of numbers, in the middle of two 2s.'

This kind of thinking has an impact on the way Barnard both designs and manages design. 'Some numbers just seem to crop up. In the drawing office I'd often be chipping in with things like, "Can we make that 14 not 13, or 2 for this or 4 for that?" If I can design using nice round numbers without any cost to performance, I will; I'm always going to prefer 176 to 176.395.'

John claims not to be 'desperately superstitious', adding that he just pretends to be 'to make people laugh'. Evidently his desire for mirth goes so far as to affect the design of his cars and the way he has run his various design offices: 'When I did the VPJ-6C, the rear deck was 13 inches above the tub zero line at the bottom, and that always worried me, so I said to myself, "On the Chaparral, I'm not going to make that rear deck 13 inches, I'll make it 14."'

He also liked 14 because it was the number A.J. Foyt used on his cars: 'Little things like that register in my head.' So much so that he would make decisions, as he did for much of the 2K, based on a gut instinct provoked by numbers he did or didn't like, all part of 'feeling good' about the car. In that sense John's cars are not only expressions of his deep understanding of mechanics and his instinct for aerodynamics; they're expressions of a personality trait.

This isn't just superstition or a form of Obsessive Compulsive Disorder — it's important from a practical point of view. 'Apart from anything else, when you're making, checking and measuring stuff, working with round numbers is much less likely to produce mistakes because you can register them in your head more readily than complex fractions.'

With his favourite numbers always having been 2 and 4 (the latter his birthday), so the balance and symmetry of 202.202 struck him as beautiful, partly because 2+2 = 4 and partly because graphically the number sits so neatly astride the decimal point. It also felt auspicious: 202.202 is a figure with a feeling of serendipity about it and seemed to him a harbinger of the car's future success.

On the subject of serendipity, 202, as it happens, has other qualities and here we divert into the world of advanced mathematics (made simple) on an excursion that may shed some light on Barnard's curious mind.

This 202 is a Smith Number, named after an otherwise anonymous American, Harold Smith. Mr Smith happened to be brother-in-law to mathematician Albert Wilansky, who, on a less than busy day, noticed that if he added together all the digits of his relative's telephone number, 493 7775, he got 42, which, famously if irrelevantly, happens to be the 'meaning of life' in Douglas Adams's *Hitch Hiker's Guide to the Galaxy*.

Wilansky also noticed that 4,937,775 is a Composite Number, that is to say, it could be divided evenly by itself, by 1 and other numbers. Why was it called a Composite Number? Because, in a sense, it wasn't a new, original, individual number. It was instead a composite, made up of other round numbers that had been multiplied to create it. For example, 9 is a Composite Number because it can be divided evenly by 9, 1 and 3. The number 7, on the other hand can only be divided evenly by 1 and 7, which makes it a Prime Number, a number that is entirely of itself and not made up of multiples of other numbers.[15]

Now, no doubt, beside himself with boffinic excitement, Wilansky then spotted that if he added the digits of the Prime Factors that produce Mr Smith's

---

[15] *Shyam Sunder Gupta, 'Number Recreations — Smith Numbers',* www.shyamsundergupta.

telephone number (i.e., the Prime Numbers that can divide into it exactly), he also came up with 42. In case you doubt him, the Prime Factors of 4,937,775 are 3, 5, 5 and 65,837. So: 3+5+5+6+5+8+3+7 = 42.[16]

So it is with 202; the only Prime Numbers that can divide into it exactly are 2 and 101 — these are its Prime Factors. Multiply them together, 2 x 101, and you get 202; add up the digits of 202, 2+0+2, and you get 4, Barnard's other favourite number; add up the digits of the Prime Factors, 2+1+0+1, and again you get 4.

'Lovely, isn't it!' comments John.

The ninth Smith Number is 202. There is an infinite quantity of Smith Numbers and finding them continues to test mathematicians and their long-suffering students. Apparently, and perhaps unsurprisingly, Smith Numbers have uses in cryptography.

But — and here's the further serendipity — the most famous Smith Number is 666, the number of the Beast, the Prince of Darkness. In addition 666 shares with 202 the fact that it is a Palindromic Smith Number (i.e., it reads the same backwards as it does forwards). Barnard, as we will discover, soon became known throughout the paddock as the Prince of Darkness.

Just a lot of coincidence? Perhaps so, but complex coincidences do have a certain awe-inspiring allure and those who have read Carl Sagan's novel *Contact* might also enjoy the concept of the 'Hand of the Great Designer', some intergalactic Super-Engineer, writing his signature deep within the infinite bowels of the definition of a perfect circle, that eternal and Transcendental number, Pi, which begins 3.14159... *ad infinitum*.

It's a lovely conceit that the fates of us all might be written deep in the numbers associated with our lives. Barnard admits, 'Sometimes I wish I had been a pure mathematician who eats, sleeps and breathes numbers. They do attract me. Sometimes I find myself just adding up numbers, just to see how they come out.'

He's further amused by the fact that 202 is also classed as a Joke or a Hoax Number. But let's leave this diversion into Barnard's brain right there and return to the tale of his car.

With all the gremlins ironed out, the stage was set, once again, for the season's climax, the Miller High Life 150 at the one-mile Phoenix International Raceway

---

[16] *'Smith Number'*, Wikipedia.

in Avondale, Arizona, where Al Unser had scored such a memorable victory in the Parnelli-Cosworth three years earlier. Now, on Saturday 20 October 1979, could he repeat that success?

Al started in second place on the grid behind Bobby but was in front before the end of the lap, leading the race up to lap 52, when Bobby took over. It was then Rick Mears's turn to lead until lap 63, when Al eased past in the Chaparral. There he remained to take victory in the last race of the season.

The Chaparral 2K was now the complete racer: fast, wonderful to drive, beautiful to look at and strong enough to handle the demands of Indycar racing. It was ready to become a regular winner. But not for Al Unser — who moved on to drive for Longhorn. By now, too, Barnard was also grazing in pastures new.

In late 1979, after Barnard's departure from Chaparral, Jim Hall received the Louis Schwitzer Award for 'the most innovative car' at the Indy 500. Hall picked up the award without inviting John, a fact that John learned from Hughie Absalom. But now, happily, the Schwitzer Award listings for that year state 'Jim Hall & John Barnard'.[17] While the credit remains somewhat misleading, it is better than nothing. As John says, 'Hall did precisely nothing but pay for my work!'

One Chaparral 2K is now on permanent exhibition at the Petroleum Museum in Midland. But, at the time of writing, neither John's name, nor the fact that the car was designed and built in England, is mentioned anywhere on the exhibit; Jim Hall once more takes all the credit. However, at the Indianapolis Motor Speedway Hall of Fame Museum, where another Chaparral 2K is displayed, the caption beneath their exhibit gives full credit to 'British Designer, John Barnard'.

The 2K, of course, cared nothing for the man who really designed it. In 1980 Johnny Rutherford, replacing Unser at Chaparral, placed it on pole position in qualifying for the Indianapolis 500 and won the race. He went on to win the 1980 CART PPG Indy Car World Series, as the breakaway championship was now called, with four more race victories and three second places in a very reliable season that saw the Chaparral retire only twice in 12 outings.

So why did Al Unser step away from the car that always looked likely to dominate the 1980 season? Indy insiders report that an important reason was

---

[17] *'Louis Schwitzer Award'*, Wikipedia.

Al's irritation with Jim Hall's attitude to Barnard. If this is so — and, to date, Al Unser hasn't gone on the record to fully explain his reasons — then it's a rare and admirable example among racing drivers of concern for others taking precedence over the irresistible desire to win, the very instinct that makes them so good.

Further confirmation of Unser's sacrifice, and Hall's uncompromising desire for the credit, comes from journalist Robin L. Miller in an email to John Barnard, written on 12 April 2012, the day of the Road Racing Drivers' Club annual award dinner, held that year in Long Beach. Miller was a writer for the *Indianapolis Star* at the time of Rutherford's first victory in the Chaparral 2K:

'I wrote that JR [Johnny Rutherford] drove the John Barnard-designed Chaparral constructed in England by BS Fabrications. I was walking through Gasoline Alley and Hall charged out and threw the paper at me, screaming, "Where do you get your information?" I said, "Come on Jim", and he yelled that the car was designed and built by Chaparral Racing. We didn't speak for the next five years but Al Unser thanked me for putting it in print and said he quit the best ride in Indy car because he was so mortified that Hall had refused to acknowledge your contribution. I'm only going tonight to see Dan Gurney and Parnelli and when they start raving about Jim Hall I'll be heading for the exit.'

A similar thing happened to American journalist Gordon Kirby. He talks of Jim Hall's 'huge pride' and how 'still to this day' Hall says the Yellow Submarine was his concept, that all Barnard did was 'put his concept into practice'. Kirby adds: 'Once I wrote in *Autosport* about the 2K, saying it had been designed by Barnard and built by BS Fabrications. That really annoyed Hall and he asked me to leave his garage!' Kirby thinks Hall and Barnard had some similar personality traits: both were 'highly motivated, driven men, clashing over ownership'. The difference, it seems, lies in John's no-nonsense honesty.

Johnny Rutherford is reported to have said: 'When McLaren pulled out of Indycar racing, I got the job with Jim Hall and the Chaparral... Jim was a thinker. Things occurred to him during his driving career that made him an innovator. What he came up with was a better way to do it — and he beat everybody doing it.'[18]

The Jim Hall legend persists, as do the question marks. Was he really an innovator or was he just good at getting the right people to work for him at

---

[18] *The People of IMS —Johnny Rutherford'*, www.indianapolismotorspeedway.com.

the right time? Such a skill is highly valuable, but Hall's mistake seems to have been that, by stealing credit from those who really deserved it, he undermined his whole reputation. More and more people now question the element in his panoply of talents that is most important to him, the genius of invention. Rutherford added, in unknowing testimony to Barnard, 'Driving the Yellow Submarine was my crowning glory because the car was so good and the fans loved it so much. It was really a dream come true.'

More recently Rutherford has changed his tune, turning up in September 2012 to a celebration of the 2K at the Indianapolis Motor Speedway Hall of Fame Museum: 'It was quite a jump what this car would let you do — it was amazing… that was the best season I've ever had in championship racing. The Chaparral was a great race car and the beginning of what we still see today. Barnard came across something that worked really well and I was just fortunate to reap the benefits and drive it.'[19]

The article from which this quotation is taken states that the 2013 Indycars couldn't do better than rebuilding Barnard's car: 'Alighting from the bright yellow racer, JR was beaming. "This is what the next Indy car should be," he exclaimed. "With all the modern safety features, of course." Many observers include the 2K among the most beautiful race cars of all time… At least two design studies have been commissioned to help shape the look of the new Indy car. But Johnny Rutherford had it right when he said that maybe they should just copy the looks of the iconic Chaparral 2K.'

As Gordon Kirby testifies: 'The 2K had a huge impact. Ground-effect technology was just coming into Indy, a year or two behind F1. Penske had done a little work in this area, but the 2K was the real definition of ground-effect. It was elegant and beautiful, carrying the science and the art to a new level. Such a cohesive design. When they rolled out the 2K at the Speedway in '79, it got everybody's attention — it clearly was the state of the art, everything a race car should be. It was a design classic. Again, everybody had to go down that route and copy it.'

Patrick Head agrees, describing it as, 'a most phenomenal piece of work, which he did with Gordon Kimball assisting, pretty much working in the front room of his dad's house, and with Sparshott on the fabrication. It was beautifully constructed and a very significant achievement in John's career; stunning from the word Go!'

---

[19] Oreovicz, John, 'John Oreovicz Blog: New car development on track for 2012', www.espn.com.

In the meantime, back in England, the Chaparral 2K's performance was being closely watched by one Ron Dennis, a young entrepreneur and racing team owner who was later to become, alongside John Barnard himself, the driving force behind McLaren's resurgence and domination of the sport. He looked at both Barnard and his car, and concluded that the English engineer was exactly what he needed. In an interview for this book, he summed up the Chaparral 2K:

'The 1979 Chaparral 2K was... quick out of the box, leading its very first race. The idea behind it was essentially simple: optimise downforce created by the underside of the bodywork, minimise drag created by the topside of the bodywork, and the result would be the best of both worlds: a race car that gripped strongly in high-speed banked oval turns yet flew down the super-fast straights incredibly quickly. It was a winning combination. Furthermore, resplendent in Pennzoil yellow, it looked good too. And it was that combination that attracted my interest. I took notice of John's success and recognised in him a kindred spirit — someone who, as I did, valued the perfect conjunction of function and form.'

Barnard describes the failure of his relationship with Hall as 'a crying shame'. He adds, 'The plan had been to build the Chaparral brand in the UK, creating a manufacturing company and a whole design office; that was the thinking behind the project from the very outset. Now I was unemployed, my ideas stolen.'

One can understand his sense of burning injustice. Aged just 33, Barnard had designed a revolutionary, highly successful car on his own, against the clock and in the front room of his childhood home, while setting up and running a motorsport company to do it. He also managed to create enormous aerodynamic improvements not through painstaking wind-tunnel research, but from his intuitive, mechanical, intellectual and aesthetic feel for a race car. Now, like a schoolboy dream come true, the car was wowing American audiences — and today it's still considered to be one of the best race cars in history. You just couldn't make it up.

It's hard to think of a comparable achievement in the history of professional motorsport. As Gordon Kirby pointed out, Barnard was viewed in America as responsible for 'back-to-back major revolutions with both the Parnelli-Cosworth and the Chaparral 2K'.

It's also hard to divine how all this came to be; perhaps the answer lies in the simple fact that no one with Barnard's background, life path, temperament, work ethic and genius had come into Indycar before from quite such a trajectory.

It was time to change that trajectory. Barnard was now ready to wow the world of Formula 1 and give the miserable, shivering Brits busy emerging from their famous winter of discontent something to cheer about.

PART 4
McLAREN

CHAPTER 10
CONCEIVING THE CARBON CAR
1979–80

You might have expected the big boys of British motor racing to be hammering on John Barnard's door after such spectacular success across the pond, but post-Chaparral he was 'hunting around for work'.

He, Rosie and baby Jennifer were now living in their newly refurbished and extended home in Lightwater, Surrey. Rosie was enjoying the mixed blessings of being a full-time mum, taking the parental pressure off John by doing night-time duties with the baby. John says, 'I probably changed nappies once or twice just to prove I could do it.' Rosie reports, 'He came out with some good excuses for not doing them, such as, "Oh, my hands are too rough!" But I didn't really expect him to change nappies as he was working all the hours in those days.'

Ted was there too, helping out with painting. Rosie had learned 'not to do top coats' because John made it clear her work was unsatisfactory, but Ted soldiered on. 'The kitchen door needed painting so Ted did it,' she says, 'but when John came home he told Ted it wasn't good enough because he could see brush strokes. So Ted did it again. I don't know how many times it was done but in the end, when it was as smooth as glass, it was accepted.'

John created more work for Ted by scratching the fresh paintwork while carrying Jennifer in her bouncy chair out of the kitchen. Says Rosie, 'I remember thinking how glad I was that he'd done it, rather than me.'

John now set up his own company, Barnard Design Consultancy (BDC) Ltd, the idea being to ensure that should he move from team to team he could do it in the most efficient way possible as regards salary, tax and pension. BDC still exists to this day.

Early in September 1979, John was contacted by Robin Herd, an accomplished designer himself who had co-founded March Engineering, the race car constructor and Formula 1 team, and was now in sole charge. Herd hired Barnard as a consultant to advise his design team, with his main focus upon March's latest Indycar project, 'The Orbiter', but also with an eye on developing a brand-new Formula 1 car the following year. 'Basically, they wanted me to show them how to design a Chaparral,' says John. 'But when I got there they were already well underway. So I gave them some pointers, such as how I had strengthened the fuel tanks and uprated the suspension.'

Barnard says his advice wasn't well received: 'It was all, "Why does this need to be so strong? Why does the front rocker have to take a 5G bump load?"' John decided that they didn't fully appreciate the forces involved in ground-effect, and increasingly felt they didn't want to listen to him banging on in his perfectionist style. 'It was a classic case of "Not Invented Here". I didn't feel welcome.' He suspects that Herd hired him to reassure sponsors that the designer of the Chaparral 2K was involved.

'The Orbiter' was a good name for a car destined to go round and round the American ovals, but, to John, that was all that was positive about it. 'It was a pretty poor effort: I didn't think it was a particularly pretty thing and I didn't think that the work they'd done on the monocoque was of a particularly high standard. But you know, it was the same old thing, "There's no time, you've got to get it made." Looking back, I shouldn't have got involved.'

He filled his time instead by drawing engine inlet manifolds for Penske. He's philosophical about his brief encounter with March: 'It was a lesson not to jump at any available deal just because I wasn't busy. It takes time to gain credibility and it can all be blown away in an instant. It was at this point that I realised I had to be in total charge of building any future car.'

The opportunity to do just that looked like arriving a week or two after the approach from Robin Herd. Héctor Rebaque Sr, a Mexican entrepreneur and architect, had set up a racing operation in order to ensure that his son, Héctor Jr, could drive in Formula 1. To run it, he appointed Peter Reinhardt, formerly team manager for German Formula 1 team ATS (Auto Technisches Spezialzubehör). At first Reinhardt acquired cars from Team Lotus, first a 78 (for 1978), then a 79 (for 1979), before being tasked to produce a bespoke Rebaque car, the HR100, which was designed and constructed by Penske Racing at its British base in Poole, Dorset.

One day early in September 1979, Reinhardt was at BS Fabrications in Luton, awaiting some parts for the HR100, when he happened into a room he shouldn't have entered. There he was confronted by, as he stated in an interview for this book, 'the most beautiful car parts I'd ever seen! They really were works of art. They were most wonderful uprights and suspension parts.'

While he was turning them over in his hands, in walked Bob Sparshott, looking alarmed. 'Peter,' he said, 'you aren't supposed to see those! They're for a ground-effect Indycar. Barnard and Kimball did them — for God's sake don't let them know you saw them!'

Reinhardt explained he had no desire to build an Indycar. Never a man to miss a trick, he also asked for Barnard's telephone number.

Before long John was driving to Donington circuit in Leicestershire, where Rebaque was testing the HR100. Says Reinhardt, 'John, being John, took a piece of paper about the size of a matchbox and sketched some ideas. We implemented them straight away and immediately the skirts started to work. I asked him to join us, offering him a partnership in the venture, subject to the old man's approval.'

John accepted the offer to join as chief designer, starting work immediately from a spare room at home, drawing up revised suspension geometry. About once a week he would drive the 100 miles to Rebaque's base in Leamington Spa, a few miles from Warwick.

Reinhardt had big plans. Bernie Ecclestone was in the process of successfully persuading the FIA that all Formula 1 teams should develop and build their own cars rather than buy from the likes of Lotus, Lola, Penske and McLaren. So Reinhardt put it to Héctor Sr that they should upgrade the whole Team Rebaque operation, saying that he had employed Barnard with this in mind. The proposed deal would include making himself and Barnard partners in a new enterprise with a manufacturing facility in Farnborough, but there was a flaw in Reinhardt's plan — Héctor Jr simply wasn't a good enough racing driver and, what's more, didn't want his father to get involved in an enterprise on this scale.

As Barnard says, 'Two months into the job, the whole thing stopped and the shutters came down.' Perhaps it didn't help that Barnard needed £500,000 up front to buy equipment for the new factory. Meanwhile, Rébaque Sr was busy coming up with a less expensive way of getting his son into a race car, persuading Bernie Ecclestone to take on his boy at Brabham in return for appropriate remuneration.

But it's an ill wind that blows nobody any good: Reinhardt would go on to work beside Barnard for most of the next decade; and during this short episode John also met Alan Jenkins, a product designer who would be at his side for some of his landmark work.

It was at this point that two pivotal characters came into Barnard's life — Ron Dennis and John Hogan.

Ron Dennis, born on 1 June 1947, is a year younger than Barnard. Recognisable for the curling tick of a smile that flicks up from the right side of his mouth, he started his career as a racing mechanic, first with Cooper and then Brabham. In 1971, after Jack Brabham retired from race driving, Dennis and Brabham colleague Neil Trundle started their own team, Rondel Racing, which became quite successful in Formula 2. By 1976 Dennis had regrouped and formed a new operation with even bigger ambitions, Project Four, in partnership with Creighton Brown, an English soldier, farmer and motorsport entrepreneur.

Based in Dennis's home town of Woking, Surrey, Project Four ran cars in Formula 2 and Formula 3 with moderate success and, in 1979, became involved in the new BMW M1 Procar Championship, a series that invited Formula 1 drivers to compete against each other in identical BMW M1 coupés during Grand Prix weekends. Ron triumphantly secured a lucrative contract to build some of the Procars, putting the project under the control of Trundle, and also signed Niki Lauda to drive for Project Four. Lauda duly became Procar Champion in 1979 with wins in three of the eight rounds of the series.

John Hogan, an old friend of Ron's, produced the Marlboro sponsorship for most of Project Four's racing operations. Born in Sydney on 5 May 1943, Hogan had worked for Ron at Rondel, where he secured sponsorship deals for the team until Philip Morris Inc., owner of Marlboro cigarettes, poached him. By 1979 Hogan was a rising star in the glittering Marlboro marketing firmament and revelled in the title of Vice-Director, Marketing Promotions, Philip Morris (Europe). As such, he was destined to help transform motorsport by pushing Formula 1 into the sponsorship big league. Together with Dennis, he devised the so-called Book of Sponsorship in which race car bodywork was divided up into different sections, each with a price tag, so that multiple sponsors could add their logos.

Hogan enjoys a powerful reputation in Formula 1. His no-nonsense Aussie style, his dry sense of humour, the twinkle in his eye, his masterful use of the English language and his obvious toughness all go towards making him a formidable negotiator. He knows where all the bodies are buried in the paddocks of world motorsport, and there hasn't been a serious book written about Formula 1 that wasn't made richer by his penetrating observations.

In November 1979, Ron Dennis invited Patrick Head to dinner in an apparent effort to lure him from Williams, saying to him, according to Patrick, 'Look, Patrick, I'm doing Formula 2 at the moment but my ambitions are Formula 1. I'm not clear exactly about the path I'm going to take but I'm very close to Marlboro so it may be with them. I'd like you to join me.'

Already happily ensconced at the front of the Formula 1 grid, it didn't take Head much more than a nano-second to reject the idea: 'I don't think Ron and I even got as far as talking about money.' Instead he told Ron about a 'really good guy' he should get in touch with. Patrick felt that the ambitious Project Four boss at that point hadn't heard of John Barnard, but Ron, inevitably perhaps, remembers it differently. Anyway, he phoned Barnard.

'I've been talking to Patrick,' Ron said. 'I understand you're looking to do something?'

'Yes, but you're a Formula 2 team, and I want to get into Formula 1,' was John's characteristically curt reply.

'Well, come down to Woking and take a look at what we're doing.'

'I'm not sure there's any point, Ron. I don't want to do Formula 2.'

'Yeah, yeah, no problem, just come down and we'll chat. It's just a talk.'

This conversation, as reported by John, is an indicator of Ron's powers of persuasion — perhaps his greatest talent — because, in short order, John drove over to the Project Four factory on Poole Road, Woking, 20 minutes from his Lightwater home. He was curious, but 'not expecting much'. The place was small, 'very neat and tidy but not like a hospital', as John puts it, referring to Dennis's later obsession with immaculate surroundings. Formula 2 and Formula 3 cars were being built on the ground floor at the back of which, about five feet up, projected a half-mezzanine over a storage area and upon which Ron had his office. On the first floor, above the mezzanine, they were building Procars.

Barnard was taken aback by Dennis's opening line: 'Actually, I want to do a Formula 1 car.' To John this sounded as if it had come off the top of Ron's head, but Dennis had been dreaming of it for years, as Hogan explains:

'Ron is Ron and he was always ambitious; from square one he had wanted to do Formula 1. Ron is still imbued with this paranoid secrecy that he picked up from Ron Tauranac at Brabham — "Don't tell anybody anything about anything!" I think it's probably as simple as that. He didn't want to tell Barnard, who, after all, was an established designer, "I want you to do me a Formula 1 car" before he had him in front of him.'

Barnard was doubtful and probed Ron about his understanding of Formula 1: 'Have you got money to do such a project? F1 is immensely expensive.'

'Just leave that to me,' insisted Ron. 'I've got enough money to start.'

Ron agrees that, at the time, John's concerns were justified: 'The reality was that I didn't have the money at that stage to make a Formula 1 car, but I wanted to start to build the resource to do one. So, it was a little bit of my strategy of under-promising and over-delivering. Getting into Formula 1 as a privateer, which is effectively what we were, was considered to be a very tricky strategy.'

'I'll want £20,000 a year plus a company car,' was Barnard's no-nonsense statement about terms. That equates to around £90,000 today — way below what any Formula 1 chief designer earns now but at the very top end then.

Ron nodded his acceptance of the figure, but Barnard was still cautious. With the new requirement for race teams to construct their own cars, it was becoming much more expensive for small new operations to gain a foothold. John added, 'So what happens if you don't have enough to keep going?'

'I'll make you a deal,' said Ron. 'If we get down the road and it doesn't go anywhere, I'll give you another year's salary.' Two years' salary guaranteed: Ron could hardly say fairer than that, although it did cross John's mind that perhaps he could have asked for more. Either way, he was beginning to feel more confident about Ron Dennis.

'If I do this, Ron, I want to do something special. It will take a year at least; it certainly can't be ready for next season.' Once more this seemed to fall in line with Ron Dennis's plans.

This, of course, occurred a long time ago, and no two accounts entirely agree. Ron Dennis recalls a meeting, perhaps to seal the deal, at John's home in Lightwater, where Ron found himself approaching the house in a state of high anxiety:

'Having set up a meeting at his home, I was so focused on not getting it wrong. It was a feeling so extreme that, if you ran a video of the first 15 minutes of this meeting, I think I could identify it frame by frame. I was walking up his path. I knocked on the door and John appeared in carpet slippers! He was clearly agitated.

'He said, "Come in", adding, "You won't believe what I have just done!"

'He was putting up what appeared to be lacquered kitchen units, and while making a hole for a fixing, he had drilled through the side of a unit. I think the hole had come through the end of the unit that was on view. I said, "I hope it wasn't me ringing the door", and he said it wasn't. So I said, "Well, John, don't worry, you can get these little plastic bungs that you put in."

'"I am not going to do that!" he replied. "I am going to leave that hole exactly there so that every time I come into the kitchen it's going to remind me that I made a mistake."

'It probably didn't prove to be the case! I don't think Rosie would have put up with it. But it became etched into my brain. It was so scary. If I had read more at that point in time, I would have said he wore a cilice.'

A cilice, as any religious devotee or, indeed, any fan of Dan Brown's *Da Vinci Code* will know, is a rough undergarment, a hair shirt, designed to keep the wearer in continual discomfort, so reminding them of their own imperfections and the constant need to improve themselves. Ron added, 'I thought this guy seemed to want to inflict psychological pain on himself. It is and was a trait of John. He is extremely tough on himself and as a consequence he doesn't suffer fools and was very tough on everybody, including me!'

John recalls that Ron later gave him a gold-coloured hook to stick over the hole, but he decided not to use it. He concedes that he really did keep the hole on show to 'teach myself a lesson'.

So Ron recognised in John a soulmate, a perfectionist endowed with an ambitious ego backed up with a powerful will to succeed.

'Engineers often have ginormous egos,' says Ron. 'Most people see that as a negative. I think ambition and ego are very close bedfellows. And if you aren't ambitious, you've got no chance. How do you drive your ambition? You drive it with your ego. It's just that sometimes the ego sticks out uncomfortably above the membrane of life and doesn't always sit very well with people. But actually the key ingredient, what drives you, is, "I'll show them."'

The main elements of an historic creative partnership were in place. It had happened before. Steam engine inventor James Watt found Matthew Boulton, a visionary entrepreneur whose breezy self-confidence and talent for the deal made them both rich beyond their dreams. Apple's Steve Jobs found British designer Jonathan Ive and the iconic iMac, iPod, iPhone and iPad were born. John Barnard now had Ron Dennis, and the sum of the whole was greater than its parts. Now the world of motorsport was about to learn what a powerful force they were.

The following week Barnard began work at Project Four as chief designer, happy to have both a mission and a free hand with which to execute it.

A 'poky' drawing office was knocked together in a corner of the upper floor of the Woking factory, raised four feet on stilts with steps running up the side to the office door. With its interior windows looking out over the Procar workshop, the office reminded the mechanics of a rabbit hutch and was duly accorded the name. Barnard moved in, set up his drawing board and began work on the first detailed concepts for what would become one of motorsport's most revolutionary cars.

From this point on and throughout the rest of his career only one thing would keep Barnard utterly committed, and that was step-change. He would show limited interest in refining his innovations year after year — that was for others to do and the very idea bored him. Barnard wanted to come into Formula 1 all guns blazing just as he had done with Indycar, his ambition to repeat his American success in his homeland.

Uppermost in his mind was to improve upon the Chaparral 2K's ground-effect by making a super-narrow chassis, a design that would allow the sidepods to be wider, creating more surface area for the inverted wings beneath them and giving the car yet more grip. But there were reasons why this hadn't been done before: a narrower chassis would have reduced torsional stiffness.

Barnard needed a material stronger than steel and as light as aluminium. An idea was developing and turning incandescent; soon it would floodlight the paddock and spread through motorsport like wildfire.

John explains: 'The bottom of the Cosworth engine was my defining point; I wanted a very narrow chassis, as narrow as the engine if possible, something that would let me maximise my ground-effect tunnels. The geometry meant compromising structural stiffness, which wasn't on. I realised I needed to use another material. Steel sheet crossed my mind but the weight penalty was too severe. I started looking at carbon-fibre, which had been around; I say "been around" — I mean that it was a word that had been used.'

Formula 1's carbon-fibre revolution was set to begin. Carbon-fibre had been tried before, but never as a complete chassis and never by the mind and hand of a perfectionist engineer like John Barnard.

At the time carbon-fibre was a miracle material that had been promising the earth for nearly 20 years but, much like Graphene (a British invention) today, had yet to live up to its billing.

American genius Thomas Edison gets the credit for the earliest work on carbon-fibre when he experimented with carbon filaments while developing the electric light bulb in 1879, but in truth he was beaten to it by British scientist Sir Joseph Swan, who, 19 years earlier, patented an incandescent electric lamp using a carbon filament. By 1875, Swan had improved the vacuum in the light bulb, which allowed a new filament made from carbon thread to glow white hot. Edison gained all the glory in the end, and for good reason; his light bulb lasted much longer than Swan's or indeed those of other rivals, a fact that made it commercially viable.

Perhaps it is fitting, therefore, that the man who instigated motorsport's carbon-fibre revolution started his professional life in a light-bulb factory.

Carbon-fibre's most remarkable properties were not unearthed until 1958, when American Roger Bacon, a research scientist at the Union Carbide Corporation in Ohio, noted that the 'whiskers' he had made out of purified carbon thread had a potential tensile strength higher than steel. But it was the British who made the breakthrough at the Royal Aircraft Establishment (RAE) in Farnborough, Hampshire, the Eureka moment arriving in 1963 when Bill Watt, Bill Johnson and Leslie Phillips invented a new method for extracting purified carbon from polyacrylonitrile fibre (also known as PAN or Acrylon) in sufficient volume to make the new material a commercial proposition. It was a classic case of the bridging of disciplines; Phillips was from the Plastics Technology Section, Watt and Johnson from the High Temperature Materials Laboratory.

Phillips, the plastics expert, suggested they use Orlon, a proprietary form of the PAN fibre that he believed would be more amenable to the carbonisation process used to create the pure carbon threads. It dawned on the team that they could ensure maximum strength for the material if they pyrolised the Orlon fibres — heated them in an inert atmosphere to boil off the impurities — while the Orlon was under tension.

Hunting around the Farnborough labs for the necessary kit, the team eschewed aerospace equipment, deciding instead to make a frame out of the children's construction toy Meccano, over which they stretched batches of Orlon strands before beginning the pyrolisation. By stretching the fibres while they were being heated and purified, the carbon molecules more readily formed themselves into the long chains that give carbon-fibre its extraordinary strength. The process also allowed the team to create carbon-fibre in much larger quantities.

Their work was awarded British Patent number 1,110,791 and was published on 24 April 1968; Roger Moreton also worked on this project but is not cited in the patent.[20] The new wonder product was then licensed out by the National Research Development Corporation, via the British Ministry of Defence, to British companies Courtaulds, Morgan Crucible and Rolls-Royce.

Working with Farnborough, Courtaulds then modified the procedure, filing 53 patent applications for processes producing a type of carbon-fibre that they called Grafil. They then granted American aerospace giant Hercules Inc. a licence to both sell and manufacture Grafil, the deal allowing for a two-way exchange of developmental information across the Atlantic. Hercules would go on to have a major role in the development of Barnard's carbon-fibre car.

Why is carbon-fibre so strong? The pure carbon molecule is considered the strongest material in the universe. Diamond, for example, is basically a lump of carbon mineral compressed and purified under immense temperature and pressure deep in the earth's mantle, before being brought closer to the surface by volcanic action. Diamond can also be formed in the ground beneath a meteor strike. Its name comes from the Greek αδάμας — *adámas* — meaning 'unbreakable' or 'cannot be tamed'; the root for the word 'adamant'. The heat and pressure create a hexagonal 'beehive' crystalline molecular structure within the carbon that gives it immense strength.

Artificial carbon fibres are produced through a process called carbonisation, which to some extent mimics the natural process within the earth. Quantities of Rayon or Acrylon are melted and the resulting residue is then forced through a spinneret to create tiny filaments of graphite carbon, five thousandths of an inch thick — thinner than the average human hair.

These filaments are then heated again to drive off all non-carbon impurities, creating a pure black carbon thread in which the atoms have been reorganised by the process to form parallel, bonded molecular chains made up of hexagonal crystals that are aligned along the filament. This molecular arrangement gives carbon-fibre a longitudinal strength far greater than steel while remaining much lighter.

The resulting carbon threads are then spun together to form thicker strands that are woven into a fabric called carbon-fibre cloth (CF cloth); this is a challenging undertaking because the fibres are brittle and can snap. This

---

[20] *Cold War, Hot Science: Applied Research in Britain's Defence Laboratories*, by Peter Morgan, CRC Press, 2005, pp65–120.

cloth can then be impregnated with an epoxy resin to create 'pre-preg' — pre-impregnated CF cloth — which typically comes off a roll a metre wide. The pre-preg is laid over a mould to make almost any conceivable shape and heated to between 130°C and 177°C under pressure in an autoclave, a specially designed oven, the heat and pressure ensuring that the resin flows evenly throughout the material.

The alternative to CF cloth pre-preg is Unidirectional Tape pre-preg, or UD Tape, created by laying, in parallel, thousands of the hair-like strands of carbon into epoxy resin, which creates a highly sticky tape supplied in rolls about 30 centimetres wide. As Barnard says, 'The weaving process for making CF cloth inevitably bends the fibres, potentially weakening it. UD cloth is theoretically a more perfect way of using the material.'

This super-material wasn't without its weaknesses. Carbon's shortcoming is its low shear strength; while it has fantastic compressive and tensile strength along the length of its fibres, it's weak in shear. If you could grip a fibre between two clamps and move one backward and one forward, it would come apart.

To counter this potential weakness, Barnard would have to undertake complex calculations to designate the number and positioning of carbon 'cross-plies', strips of UD pre-preg running at angles to each other, which, after curing in an autoclave, would ensure the correct amounts of both lateral and longitudinal strength.

He could, of course, have used the pre-preg woven cloth, but he preferred to use the unidirectional pre-preg so he could be absolutely sure of the load path (i.e., the direction in which the forces were applying stretch — tension — or compression along the fibres). If he needed the material to be more resistant in a particular direction than another, he would add the requisite extra plies of UD pre-preg to make it so. This meant that a particular part of the car was only exactly as strong as it needed to be, which minimised weight.

By the time Barnard was considering carbon-fibre for his chassis, the material had already found its way into motorsport. In an interview for this book, South African designer Gordon Murray claimed that he introduced carbon to Formula 1 in 1974, when he first started to develop carbon brakes:

'My partner-in-crime then was David North. He had come from the aerospace industry — we used to read all the aerospace magazines for inspiration. I read that carbon brakes had saved Concorde some 1,100lb, about 500kg, in weight. So I went to Dunlop, who were making these brakes, and spoke to them about the possibility of putting them on a race car. They were quite keen to do it, just out of interest. So I designed a set of brakes for which they supplied the carbon. We messed around for two years and raced them successfully for the first time in 1976. That was the first use of carbon in Formula 1 in any shape or form.'

Perhaps Murray meant only to refer to the first use of carbon in brakes, because, in 1975, British racing legend Graham Hill, working with designer Andy Smallman, produced the Embassy Hill GH1 ('Graham Hill 1'). The team employed carbon-fibre in the struts that supported the car's rear wing, with the aim of getting the best of all possible worlds: less weight, less mass, a thinner aerodynamic profile and sufficient strength.[21] How poorly the material was understood became crystal clear during a tragic and controversial race.

It was 27 April 1975 and arguments over the safety of the Montjuïc circuit in Barcelona had already prompted drivers to boycott practice for the Spanish Grand Prix. They had discovered that circuit personnel hadn't got round to securing all the crash barriers to their posts, leaving the sharp edges of the corrugated steel beams sticking out into the path of the cars. In this last year of General Franco's domination of Spain, the teams were threatened with legal action if they declined to race while Franco's *Guardia* stood in the wings ready to confiscate their cars. The teams caved in, sending their mechanics out around the circuit to work on the barriers. Defending champion Emerson Fittipaldi, still angry and rattled by a sixth sense, continued to refuse to race. It was a wise decision.

The race began with a three-car pile-up on the first corner followed by a series of shunts and gear failures, in part prompted by the bumpy, sub-standard track, laid out on public roads through a park. Disaster struck on the 26th lap when Rolf Stommelen, the leader, drove his GH1 through a left-hander at a point where fans were lining the track behind the barriers. After going over a bump his rear wing's carbon-fibre mounting failed, the wing flipping back like an opening lid. With the wing momentarily creating lift rather than downforce, the rear of the car was hoisted upwards before the aileron ripped off to go spinning high into the air.

Stommelen lost control and crashed into the barrier, which, and with awful irony, held firmly because it had just been repaired at that exact point by his own team's mechanics. The GH1 bounced off into the path of another car, collided, flipped into the air and flew over the crash barrier on the other side

---

[21] *Flux, Ian, 'Hill & back',* Motor Sport, *December 2004, p52.*

of the track, where it killed five spectators and injured ten more. Stommelen survived with a broken leg, wrist and two cracked ribs. Four laps later the race was halted — and Formula 1 never returned to Montjuïc.

Three years passed before any Formula 1 designers again tried carbon-fibre for structural elements. In 1978 Brabham's Gordon Murray used carbon panels to stiffen an aluminium Formula 1 chassis, inspired by jet fighters that were using, he says, 'woven carbon-fibre in pre-preg form — autoclave carbon — in structural components'.

Aware that Brabham team principal Bernie Ecclestone was unlikely to shell out the hundreds of thousands of pounds required for an autoclave, Murray decided to build his own. He sourced a new ship's boiler and fashioned a cooling system from a second-hand car radiator and fan plus a 600-gallon domestic water tank. He installed the autoclave and then built an oven of galvanised steel to provide the necessary heat. 'It cost just £6,000!' he boasts, although Ecclestone biographer Susan Watkins[22] quotes him as spending £12,000 on the project. Either way, Murray's claims prompted her to conclude that 'Brabham began using carbon-fibre composite materials in Formula 1 in 1978, three years before big-budget McLaren started using this material.'

Perhaps unknown to either Murray or Watkins, Barnard was working intensively with carbon in 1979. He chose to use a high-specification proprietary autoclave because he wanted the outcome to be as perfect as possible; perfection was the essence of the design revolution he was bringing to the sport.

Murray wasn't alone in his early carbon-fibre endeavours: by this stage, and for several years before, a number of teams were using the material on an *ad hoc* basis; McLaren, for example, were building their cars' underbodies in carbon-fibre and Lotus were drawing up plans to build an entire chassis out of the material.

The problem was that no one in Formula 1 except Barnard really understood how to use it properly. Some didn't use autoclaves at all, preferring to use the far simpler, and much weaker, 'wet lay-up'. This was much like the method for making glass-fibre bodywork, which had been in use since the '50s, involving little more than laying down dry carbon-fibre cloth, brushing in copious amounts of resin and letting it set. All too often carbon-fibre panels were glued and riveted in place, the rivets compromising the carbon's structural integrity.

---

[22] *Watkins, Susan,* Bernie: The Biography of Bernie Ecclestone, *Haynes, 2011, p131.*

In his former role as a product designer, Alan Jenkins, whom Barnard first met at Rebaque, had worked at RAE Farnborough, his company having been tasked by the Ministry of Defence to find uses for carbon-fibre. Now at Project Four with Barnard, he was aware of the problems.

'Glued stuff failed,' says Jenkins. 'The range of resin systems that were around weren't really strong enough. F1 teams were doing bonded joints but they were still bolting and riveting them just in case. The same was true with aircraft. There was one glue that everyone used, called Four-Ten (410); it was yellow and was instantly recognisable. It contained asbestos, it was carcinogenic and it got banned eventually, but not until it was too late for some people.'

When asked what he considers to be his own greatest contribution to motorsport, Murray admitted that it couldn't be carbon-fibre because he didn't use it correctly: 'I'd like to say the introduction of carbon, but as John made the biggest step, that's probably more important.' He went on to explain that his 1978 car was 'single skin, monolithic carbon... all I did was make a mould and start replacing single skins of aluminium with the carbon. It was the first structural use of carbon in a chassis but it wasn't the big step, with the honeycomb skinned on both sides, which John made the following year.'

Barnard didn't agree with Murray's approach: 'That's completely the wrong way to use carbon. That's a classic case of trying to superimpose carbon in place of metal. You can't design with carbon the same as you do with metal. From an impact point of view, carbon panels replacing metal do not make for a good structure. Aluminium is elastic, carbon isn't, so, in an impact, the carbon resists, shatters and leaves little behind to absorb the energy. It's a dangerous way of building a car. It's not just a lightweight replacement for aluminium.'

Barnard's vision for the material was of a different order entirely as he began to conceive a chassis made solely of carbon-fibre. This was the only solution that could satisfy his quest to make the chassis narrower without losing strength and resistance to twisting.

The concept was fraught with difficulty. One of the first big headaches was to work out how to attach heavy components (like the engine) or components under enormous load (like the suspension) to the carbon without compromising its structure; i.e., by avoiding drilling holes to accommodate bolts or rivets. With an aluminium monocoque it was straightforward to design mounting points, but how could this be done if the shell was made out of carbon-fibre? Barnard was going to need some guidance.

Around this time, Neil Trundle, in hospital for an operation, found himself in bed next to a fellow who worked for British Aerospace (BAe). One thing led to another until, a few days later, Barnard was on his way to BAe's headquarters in Weybridge, Surrey, where they had a new facility to make carbon-fibre cowlings for aircraft engines, those for the Rolls-Royce RB211 engine being the biggest sections of carbon-fibre flying at the time.

BAe was making these cowlings out of a sandwich of carbon-fibre pre-preg cloth laid over each side of an aluminium honeycomb core, a structure known as Carbon Fibre Composite (CFC) that Murray indicates above and that Barnard was considering for his race car. John watched a man drill into a block of carbon-fibre with a diamond-tipped bit, the only tool hard enough for the job, and realised that he was making an insert, the same principle that the designer had used for the aluminium inserts that helped secure suspension parts to the Chaparral 2K's large wing endplates.

Staring Barnard in the face was the solution to his engine-mounting problem. The carbon block that he saw being drilled was going to be placed inside the aluminium honeycomb sandwich before the whole assembly was covered in carbon pre-preg on both sides and put in an autoclave. 'It was all so basic,' says Barnard. 'I could have done it in my shed at home!'

His mind racing with the implications, he sped back to Project Four. If he made the chassis out of a CFC sandwich, with carbon-fibre sheets wrapped around an aluminium honeycomb, he could cut away pieces of the honeycomb and fill them with custom-made blocks of carbon (so-called 'stock blocks') made up of multiple layers of pre-preg. He could then drill through these strong points and bolt any fixing he liked — pick-ups for the engine and suspension, mountings for radiators, sidepods or bodywork — without compromising chassis integrity.

He walked into Ron Dennis's office in ebullient mood. 'You know, we can actually make the entire chassis out of carbon-fibre,' said Barnard as he paced around the office explaining the numerous advantages. Ron, having already experienced carbon-fibre in use on the BMW Procar rear wings, was quick to see the possibilities. Fired up by his designer's vision, he agreed that the new material was the way ahead. He told Barnard, 'You do what you want technically and I'll find a way of funding it. That's my deal with you.'

Barnard admired this side of Dennis's character: 'He would take momentous decisions, such as this one, completely on the fly.' As John adds, with classic understatement, 'It was a great start.'

BAe Weybridge proved to be the ideal first contact; the company was at the forefront of carbon technology and was busy developing techniques that remain in use today. Their expertise arose out of another success; under the banner of BAe's predecessor, the British Aircraft Corporation (BAC), the facility had designed and built a substantial portion of the supersonic airliner Concorde, but with the aircraft completed and flying commercially by 1976, that particular revenue stream had all but dried up. At somewhat of a loss, they decided to adopt and explore the new British invention of carbon-fibre because it held such promise for the aerospace industry. The carbon panels they swiftly created for the rudder of the Vickers VC10 airliner were possibly the first major load-bearing, structural components ever built in the new material.

BAe Weybridge had two teams working on carbon projects, all part of the 170-strong and aptly named Stress Office. One team concentrated on developing the material while the other, the Structural Applications Development Programme in Carbon Fibres, looked at structural applications. In charge was aeronautical engineer Arthur Webb, a tall, lean, sharp-minded carbon-fibre expert who was put in touch with John Barnard soon after his visit. As BAe appeared keen to provide technical advice and support to any serious attempt to employ carbon-fibre in new designs, Webb was assigned to offer advice to Barnard and Project Four in the short term. Ten years John's senior, Webb took to the young designer immediately: 'Barnard is the sort of bloke I like: dynamic, to the point, knew what he wanted to do and didn't muck about.'

Despite initial enthusiasm, however, BAe held back from getting too deeply involved in the carbon-fibre car, claiming they could afford neither the time nor the staff. Webb worked hard to persuade BAe to change its mind, and Ron too spent long hours trying to sell them the advantages of supporting Project Four, refusing to take their 'No' for an answer. Alan Jenkins recalls Dennis returning from a last-ditch meeting to persuade BAe to help: 'They say it's too big a risk,' complained Ron. 'I'm the one taking all the risk!'

Irritated by BAe's reaction, Webb decided to dedicate most of his spare time to helping John, free of charge.

Webb's first task was to expound the theoretical side to Barnard, showing him how to make stress calculations for the monocoque chassis. He admired the designer's ambition: 'Barnard didn't just want to improve the stiffness of a racing chassis by a few per cent, he wanted to make a whole step-change.'

The first problem they encountered was how to deal with carbon-fibre's biggest weakness. Says Webb: 'When we got down to the details of discussing it, it was essentially the torsional stiffness that he wanted to increase, which is dependent upon the shear stiffness for the material, which, of course, is the weakness of carbon-fibre. So calculating the carbon lay-up for a race car is not a simple or straightforward matter.'

Webb recalls an alarming incident with an experimental carbon-fibre rowing boat that illustrates the shear problem exactly. It involved the British Olympic team who, he recalls, were in Canada: 'Their boat consisted of a carbon cockpit — the channel-section cut-out where all the crew sit — plus a bow and a stern that were, effectively, two carbon cones. As they got going, they pulled hard on the oars, which made the bow dig into the water. Since the bow was buoyant, it resisted the downward plunge while loading massive stresses upon its connection to the channel section of the hull. Well, it sheared — the channel section just carried on going down, much to the distress of the rowing team who were strapped into it.'

Barnard's monocoque was similar to that rowing shell, featuring a channel section in the middle (where the driver sat) and two carbon cones, one at the front (where his legs went), the other at the back (housing the fuel tank). It might seem odd that Barnard and Webb were hoping to increase the torsional strength of a race car by using a material notorious for its poor torsional strength, but the trick was all in the calculations for the carbon ply lay-up.

It was absolutely critical to identify where on the chassis the biggest torsional stresses were likely to occur. As Barnard was to later tell the journal *Detroit Engineer*[23]: 'If you have a piece of aluminium one foot square, you can feed a load into that piece from any side and, basically, you get the same physical properties from it, the same tensile strength, shear strength and so on. But with carbon... you can only apply the load along the axis of the strand. Then, if you have a compound load — that is, one coming from several directions — you must lay up the material to account for that difference in load path. This always requires extra calculations in the basic design stage.'

Because Barnard was seeking to limit the tendency of a narrow chassis to twist, unidirectional (UD) pre-preg was his material of choice. He could have used multi-directional cloth in which the carbon fibres are arranged at right angles to each other, but, as explained earlier, he preferred UD because it was easier to calculate how stresses and loads would affect it.

For example, as a car flies round a bend, parts of its structure are subject

---

[23] 'Carbon fibre brings space-age technology to auto racing', Detroit Engineer, May 1982, pp7–10.

to powerful stretching forces. By laying sufficient UD cloth in the direction of the stretch, Barnard could ensure that the car remained stiff and stable. He would have to learn how to calculate exactly how many layers or plies of cloth he would need to achieve his target strength and weight, but the gains were enormous; you could allow for loads applied in different directions so much more precisely than with aluminium.

If Barnard and Webb got their sums right, they could increase the stiffness of the chassis by around 66% while reducing the weight by up to 30%; massive margins in the split-second world of Formula 1. The more accurate and comprehensive their calculations, the stronger the chassis — and the wider the inverted wings under the sidepods could be. The car would be quicker because it would be lighter, and, with the added grip of greater ground-effect, it would be faster through corners. This was the Holy Grail.

There were at least three drawbacks. The first was cost: carbon-fibre is around 10 times more expensive than aluminium. The second was complexity: carbon-fibre construction required an entirely new approach to car design, demanding far more time to draw and build. The third, apparently, was safety.

In addressing the second drawback, Barnard had to learn how to draw carbon-fibre lay-up, to which end Webb showed him some of the blueprints for the RB211 engine project. 'I'd never seen anything like it before,' says John. The new car would require multiple sheets of drawings for each section of the chassis, with each drawing annotated with complex tables describing the number of carbon plies, or layers, and the direction in which they should be laid in accordance with stress and load calculations.

Arthur Webb became John's tutor and between them they used pencil, paper and calculators (Arthur preferred a slide rule) to calculate likely loads, stresses and strains. 'It was very different from working with aluminium,' said John, 'more like tailoring than building a car.'

Barnard soon found that the designs for the carbon monocoque took six times the number of drawings required for a conventional chassis. 'You weren't just buying a sheet of aluminium off the shelf, you were actually creating the sheets yourself out of carbon-fibre. Everything had to be drawn and then drawn again, over and over.'

As for the apparent safety drawback, carbon-fibre was thought to be so brittle that it was liable to shatter in an accident. Some racing pundits warned that it might even explode in a crash, blasting driver and spectators with deadly shards of super-hard carbon, or that it might even 'dissolve into a cloud of black dust', an opinion Gordon Murray was offering the sports press at the time.

To be fair to Murray, he based this comment upon the direct and alarming experience of seeing his 1979 Brabham, the BT49, made with single-skin monolithic carbon, crash out in Monaco, as he explained in an interview for this book: 'The BT49 had a fairly low-speed accident at the hairpin just past the Tip-Top bar [Mirabeau] — it was raining and Piquet slid into the barrier. And the way the carbon failed really frightened me — it was a catastrophic structural failure; it doesn't fold like aluminium, it turns to dust, but turning to dust is not so bad — in a huge failure that's what you want it to do. But before it could start absorbing any energy, it just sheared and snapped in half, which frightened me.'

And he wasn't alone. Patrick Head also had his doubts: 'When carbon-fibre fails it tends to shatter. At the time I thought, "I'm not desperately convinced this is the right material to make a chassis from."'

The other theory was that carbon-fibre was too strong, that it wouldn't crumple on impact but instead would transfer all the shock to the driver, leaving him dead in the cockpit from internal trauma.

The truth was that few knew anything about carbon-fibre's crash-resistance properties. As John pointed out in the *Detroit Engineer* article, Learjets using carbon-fibre were having trouble getting flight safety certification precisely because there was so little data.

But Arthur Webb had done work on the material's impact properties that led John to decide to make the chassis out of Carbon Fibre Composite, in which plies of carbon would be laid over both sides of a sheet of aluminium honeycomb, the aluminium being the 'cheese' in a composite sandwich. Their rule-of-thumb was, in John's words, 'to maintain fibre continuity wherever possible, particularly in the fore and aft plies which provided the main bending strength of the monocoque and also picked up on the engine attachment points and the main front suspension points.'

In this, Gordon Murray tips his hat to Barnard: 'Effectively a carbon tube — that was the right way to use carbon — two thin skins and a honeycomb. That was the big pioneering breakthrough, so John overtook us. When you get it in that form you get the best performance out of carbon because it's the lightest and the stiffest; it's stabilised. Composite skins absorbed energy a lot better.'

Barnard and Webb believed that the integrity of these uninterrupted fore-and-aft plies would make a major contribution to the safety of the driver in the event of an accident. They also knew that, made properly, carbon would behave far better in a crash than most people realised. Arthur Webb:

'If an aluminium structure collides with something, it starts to collapse and buckle, with the load from the impact passing through the whole structure until and even after the buckling has stopped. But carbon-fibre shatters, it smashes almost as if it is passing through whatever it has hit, entirely dissipating the energy as it goes.

'In other words, the impact load cannot pass into the structure, because once its failure point is reached, the structure is continually shattering as the "crash front", or crush zone, moves along the structure in accordance with the amount of energy of the crash. Snap, snap, snap, all in a micro-second, with large amounts of energy dissipating with each snap.'

In other words, the nose shatters snap by snap until all the energy from the impact speed is dissipated before the nose has gone, creating an even deceleration and preventing a major shockwave from passing through the much tougher cockpit. A YouTube video of a carbon nose cone failing conveys the full impression.[24]

Applied properly, carbon-fibre has a very high failure threshold, so it takes a lot to start the shattering process. Even better, you can calculate the failure points and make specific parts of a carbon structure as weak or as strong as needed without adding significant weight, simply by adding or reducing the number of plies.

Things will bounce off a carbon chassis before it starts to break, or, vice versa, it will bounce off things. What it won't do, unless the loads are astronomically large, is cave in and trap or crush the driver, which is one of the worst qualities of aluminium. This property of being incredibly strong until it snaps makes carbon-fibre highly suited to transport technology.

This is perfectly illustrated by Barnard's and Webb's development of a carbon-fibre nose cone, work they did some years later. In the early '80s the FIA insisted that a nose cone should act as a shock absorber in a head-on crash, stipulating that it must survive a 30mph impact without damage to the car itself. To meet the new ruling, John, Arthur and new recruit Matthew Jeffreys built a test rig, as John describes:

'We made up some wooden shuttering and poured concrete into it to make an enormous concrete base. In the wet cement we set two vertical tubes to act as guide rails down which the nose cone would run. The nose cone itself was

---

[24] *'Grand Prix Insights – Monocoque (including spectacular crash test),* youtube.com, *19 June 2012; crash test at 1m 40s.*

attached to the bottom of another, smaller, concrete block that represented the weight of the rest of the car. We would then hoist up the nose cone and block some 20 feet to the top of an A-frame gantry above the concrete base. Then we'd drop it.'

This would allow gravity sufficient time to accelerate the falling model to 30mph before it encountered the steel plate at the bottom that protected the concrete base, the fall rate being measured with accelerometers. 'A simple Newtonian sum,' says Webb, blithely.

The first cone to be tested was made of aluminium and about 60 centimetres long. John found the results disconcerting: 'We dropped it 20 feet; it came out like a pancake. Even the concrete block that represented the car was split by the impact. It was terrifying to see how little energy it had absorbed. Our nose cone was probably more robust than those of our competitors, but still, that was worrying — we all shook our heads.'

In consultation with Webb, Barnard then redesigned a nose box in aluminium with a double-skinned floor and aluminium channel sections riveted in place between the skins. The idea was that, on impact, the floor and channel sections would concertina in small increments between the rivets, dissipating the energy at each point. This got them through the FIA tests, but at the cost of extra weight.

Some years later (at Ferrari) Barnard would develop a lightweight carbon alternative. To make it, Barnard and Webb used UD carbon-fibre cloth for the outer skin with some laid at right angles to give the nose cone more stability. The inside of the cone was lined with a corrugated sleeve of carbon-fibre, effectively forming carbon tubes running the cone's length.

On impact in a test, the carbon shattered to dust all the way up to the concrete, leaving an inch or two of carbon-fibre proud — all the energy had been absorbed by the moving crush front. Webb comments, 'With a bit of fine tuning, it was a complete success.' Carbon nose cones were another major contribution to Formula 1 safety — and they're still used now.

As Barnard cracked on with his car's design, aided by Arthur Webb, who was devoting days of his spare time to the project, it became clear that they needed more people. Alan Jenkins duly moved into the Rabbit Hutch, setting up a board to become John's 'pencil'.

'It was daunting,' says John, 'no question about it. But we persevered, producing all these drawings for the lay-ups and the rest of it. I'd give Alan a scheme and he would do the detailed drawings.'

Alan's first task was to redesign the Chaparral pedals to fit the emerging design of the new Formula 1 car. This was his first foray into engineering design but he rose to the challenge. He spent a fair amount of time with his mouth wide open, especially when he watched fabricators working directly to Barnard's drawings: 'In those days you'd stand and watch these guys work and you'd be in awe of them. You could produce complex fabricated pieces, like the suspension uprights that blew everybody away with their wire-eroded centres.'

'Wire erosion' is a highly accurate technique of making complex parts by shaving away material using rapidly recurring electrical current discharges. 'Back then our uprights were made up of some 19 different fabricated bits welded together in a sequence which, if you got it slightly wrong, was never going to work,' says Jenkins. 'They were a complete art form — the fabricated bits were one of John's specialities.'

With Barnard just over three months into his new job, 1979 closed in high spirits. He recalls the Project Four Christmas party: 'We were at a restaurant in Woking and it got a bit out of hand, all very un-Ron. Water was flying around and I was presented with a giant stuffed rabbit ostensibly as a gift for my daughter Jennifer [then seven months old] but actually a reference to me in the Rabbit Hutch.' Ron Dennis knew that drunken parties were good for team spirit; each year they would grow larger, more lavish and more entertaining.

But for Project Four the Christmas break was brief. Very quickly everyone was back working at full stretch, inspired by John's revolutionary new approach. Ron Dennis was busy running his various racing teams plus the Procar operation while trying to raise the cash for the carbon car.

Ron rarely visited the Rabbit Hutch although John remembers a classic moment of Dennis's own super-perfectionism: 'I'd made some little cardboard trays to put my notes in, paperwork I'd brought into the office from home. I stuck these on the desk and then one morning I came in and they'd all been replaced by neat stacking plastic trays. Beside them was a note from Ron saying, "Better than cardboard boxes." So presumably Ron was coming in when I wasn't there and having a look at the drawing board to see what was happening.'

Ron was also trying to pull his designer into his Formula 2 and Formula 3 operations. Ron's star driver was Brazilian Chico Serra, who had just won the 1979 British Formula 3 Championship. Early in 1980 Chico was testing the new Formula 2 car at Goodwood and John decided to pop down to see how it was going — an initiative that in Ron's opinion was long overdue. Barnard arrived to find himself the subject of Dennis's critical wit: 'I guess Ron had phoned ahead because Chico had laid a square of carpet in the pit lane. "This is for you, Mr Barnard," he said, "to keep Your Majesty's feet warm." Ron really did want to get me involved but I just couldn't afford the distraction.'

Barnard did eventually lower himself to do a little development work on the Project Four Formula 3 car, something that turned out to have a ripple effect. He tackled a new regulation that required cars leaving the pits to drive over a bump, an effort by the authorities to level the playing field by preventing ground-effect skirts from touching the track surface. Barnard got round this by making up some lightweight ancillary springs mounted above the normal springs: at slow speeds these would provide the necessary ride height to clear the bump but as soon as the car was out on track its downforce would be sufficient to cancel out their effect. Gordon Murray would later take the idea further, as we shall see.

A less successful intervention was an attempt to improve qualification results by putting dry ice in the air intake in an effort to keep the engine as cool as possible: 'We rigged something up but we couldn't carry enough dry ice and it only worked for about 100 yards.'

But John's main focus, of course, was the detailed design for the carbon monocoque chassis. Even with expert help, he was still groping his way in the dark. Arthur Webb: 'Once we decided to work together and agreed what we were going to make, the next big question was, how do we make it? Nobody had any idea. At Weybridge we had already been playing with making fuselages for small aircraft, but we made them in sections that were riveted together; you lose a lot of torsional stiffness that way because you can't make the joints as stiff as the carbon-fibre alongside.'

Webb emphasised to John that the key to a successful carbon structure was to have as few joints as possible. They had two choices: they could make the chassis on a female mould tool, which would mean laying the carbon-fibre on the inside of an aluminium mould; or they could use a mandrel, or male tool, and do the lay-up on the outside. They opted for the latter, and started to plan in detail how the monocoque would be made.

The first layers of pre-preg would be wrapped around the smooth outer surface of the mandrel. Then sheets of aluminium honeycomb, 10mm thick, would be laid on top of the sticky pre-preg. Sections of the honeycomb were cut away to allow room for carbon stock-block inserts, thus creating the mounting points for all heavy gear.

This, of course, meant that the exact positions of all the inserts had to be known to the millimetre and cut into the honeycomb sheets before lay-up — a considerable achievement in itself. Then the honeycomb and inserts would be covered by more layers of pre-preg and the chassis would be complete, with no joins in the main carcass.

Initially John considered creating a tubular, curved monocoque but that proved impossible. Today, designers use Computer Aided Design (CAD) software that can drive milling machines to create curvaceous 3D shapes, but at the time the sort of machinery that could achieve this was only to be found in advanced industrial aerospace facilities — it would be some years before Barnard had access to five-axis milling machines.

Instead he chose to simplify the issue, electing to give the chassis flat facets rather than curves, creating a hexagonal 'tube' rather than a rounded cylinder. The aerodynamic surfaces would come when he covered the chassis in separate and removable carbon bodywork.

So the chassis design consisted of an enclosed hexagonal tube, tapered at both ends, with a large aperture in the top for the cockpit and supported at each end and within by bulkheads. The front and rear bulkheads were integral parts of the chassis, made up on the mandrel, while the internal bulkheads were inserted after the main chassis had been cooked in the autoclave. They comprised a forward bulkhead to support the front suspension and wheels, a second to carry the steering column and dashboard, and a third to separate driver from fuel tank. Barnard also designed carbon-fibre beams to support the side panels, providing more stiffness in the cockpit, the details of which we will come to later.

The entire chassis, then, comprised the shell, three internal bulkheads and the reinforcing structure — essentially five parts. By contrast, an aluminium chassis was typically built from over 50 sections.

To get the bulkheads and reinforcing structure into the car, obviously the internal mandrel would have to be removed from the cured chassis. The question was how?

The solution was both simple and brilliant. John proposed making the mandrel in five pieces, each machined to match seamlessly with its neighbour and then bolted together. After the chassis had been fired in the autoclave, the section of mould accessible through the cockpit aperture would be removed, with mechanics reaching inside it to undo the nuts and bolts that attached it to its neighbouring sections. With the cockpit mandrel section out, the mechanics could then unbolt the remaining four sections one by one, withdrawing them through the cockpit aperture.

The calculations for making the five-part mandrel had to take into account that, once covered in the composite sandwich, it would be heated to 177°C — the temperature that would give the structure its best properties. This heating process would make the mandrel expand inside its CFC shell, growth for which John and Arthur had to make accurate allowance. It was a level of meticulous forethought never attempted before in chassis design.

This expansion, so carefully calculated, had advantages: high-quality carbon lay-up requires that the UD fibre be kept under tension, which Barnard achieved during lay-up by wrapping it around the mandrel and then pulling the pre-preg cloth taut as it was laid. Once in the autoclave, the mandrels would expand under the heat, stretching the carbon pre-preg still further, so adding more tension and therefore more strength to the final product. There was another plus: after curing, the aluminium mandrel shrank more than the carbon, which made it easier to remove from the chassis.

Alan Jenkins was in awe of John's design accuracy: 'The lovely thing about John was that he was incredibly purist about certain things. I remember having to machine the individual mandrel sections separately and then bolt them together. They all fitted perfectly. The people in this machine shop would look at me and say, "You're absolutely nuts; there's no way that's going to fit together." The way it was designed relied on the contraction of the mould tool as it cooled down so we could dismantle it, so if there were any flaws you weren't going to be able to get it out. If the resin got in the joints it would be there forever, so it had to be immaculate.'

An immaculate conception, if ever there was one, and full credit must go to Barnard and Webb for their creative design and meticulous planning. But concept is one thing and building another. Project Four was in no way tooled up to take on the task; in fact few businesses in the world had the necessary expertise. Who on earth could build the first carbon car?

CHAPTER 11
THE PILLAR OF HERCULES
1980–81

By early 1980, John Barnard had finished his overall scheme for the carbon-fibre chassis and the design of the car's glass-fibre bodywork. He tasked Alan Jenkins to find someone to make a wind-tunnel model. Among Alan's former product-design contacts was a small London design company called Random Design, who were commissioned to make a model to one-third scale. Ron Dennis, meanwhile, was still trying to secure sufficient sponsorship for what was becoming an increasingly expensive exercise.

When he wasn't wearing out pencils and speaking to old contacts, Jenkins was motoring around the country looking for companies capable of making the aluminium castings that would form the chassis mandrel — something that hadn't been made before. Jenkins found such a company near Godalming in Surrey.

He was also tasked with finding a reliable manufacturer to supply the aluminium honeycomb. Some former contacts in product design proved valuable, each showing remarkable flair in adapting to the needs of Formula 1 and the new requirements for a carbon-fibre chassis. Meanwhile, a company called Avak, which was run by Bob Coles and already did work for Project Four, made up patterns for the mandrel according to John's designs.

The carbon chassis, with its various apertures, bulkheads and inserts, was far more complex than the large engine cowling John had seen at Weybridge. This complexity became a serious issue.

For some time now, John and Ron had been on the hunt for a British company with the necessary facilities and expertise to produce the finished chassis. They desperately needed a business that could supply enough carbon-fibre, offer top-notch technical advice, help with the lay-up and cure the chassis in a state-of-the-art autoclave. They visited a series of aerospace companies but the response was the same at each one.

'We never really got past the foyers,' says John. This was an unusual experience for Ron, who was becoming more used to opening his mouth and watching people fall to his feet while reaching for their wallets.

Things looked more hopeful at Bristol Rotorway, a manufacturer of carbon-fibre helicopter blades, where the response was polite and inquisitive. John and Ron waxed lyrical about the potential for a revolution in transport technology: 'Get in on this early and you could make a fortune. Because one day all cars are going to be built from composites.' But as soon as John unrolled his drawings the mood began to change. He and Ron were told: 'This is much more complicated than anything anyone's doing in the industry. It's way too difficult; you're trying to go too far too fast.'

Ron recalls this frustrating search for a British company to help: 'Well, it was impossible! We went everywhere and I think people will be quite surprised to learn that, when we finally made the first composite monocoque, it was the biggest load-bearing carbon-fibre structure in the world. Virtually every other composite structure that was being subjected to such large forces were for filament-wound rocket motors where the tensile strength of the fibres had to cope with the huge pressures that solid propellant rockets produced. And of course this knowledge that we had gained after a few years just wasn't there back then. People in motorsport weren't even thinking about how you could go about this.'

Finding the expertise wasn't their only problem — an equally formidable hurdle was money. One day in March 1980, a delegation of Marlboro executives bowled up at the Woking factory, including John Hogan, his direct boss Dave Zelkowitz and sponsorship consultant Paddy McNally, a former motorsport journalist who was later to hit the headlines for his relationship with Sarah Ferguson, the future Duchess of York.

Ron pulled out all the stops and Hogan remembers being impressed: 'When we arrived, we went upstairs and saw Niki Lauda there, sitting in one of the Procars. Then Ron turned to a guy standing next to him and said, "This is John Barnard; he is building a carbon-fibre Formula 1 car." So we thought, "Why carbon-fibre?" Nobody had heard much about carbon-fibre at that point.'

Ron presented the Marlboro delegates with a two-feet strip of cured carbon-fibre to illustrate the motorsport nirvana to which the new material would transport them all. Zelkowitz turned the lightweight strip over in his hands and whispered to Hogan, 'The damned thing is plastic!' He then gripped the strip on either side and snapped it into two lengths with a loud crack.

'The man's face just dropped,' says John. 'I could almost hear him saying in his head, "Is this the shit the new chassis is going to be made of?"' John picked up one of the remaining half strips and demonstrated how hard it was to flex over its length as he launched into an explanation of unidirectional fibres, tensile strength and reinforcing cross-plies. The Marlboro delegation retired to consider their verdict, leaving Ron and John to get back on the road again to find someone to build the chassis.

The breakthrough came out of the blue in May 1980 when John took a call from California. It was Steve Nichols, who had helped him with shock absorbers for the Parnellis and the Chaparral, and now was keen to get into Formula 1. When asked about his current work, John admitted, cagily, that he was working on 'a ground-effect car with a narrow monocoque using new materials'.

To Nichols this could only mean one thing — carbon-fibre. He divined it immediately because as a student he had worked for Hercules Inc.: 'We had used carbon-fibre in rocket motors — if you want something skinny and stiff, carbon-fibre was the only real choice.'

So Steve told John that, if it was carbon-fibre he was talking about, he had some useful contacts within Hercules. John asked him to make some preliminary enquiries and Nichols duly contacted a friend who knew Bob Randolph, Hercules's head of Research and Development. The response was encouraging.

Since being awarded a licence to make carbon-fibre by Courtaulds, Hercules had become a major player in composite manufacture, up against Union Carbide on its own turf while in competition with Japanese company Toray Industries and Swiss Ciba-Geigy. As Nichols says, 'They were interested in expanding the use of carbon-fibre beyond the aerospace industry, and I thought they might like to go for a highly visible platform, something that would get them a lot of publicity.'

Ron Dennis called Bob Randolph: 'A very soft guy, such a pleasant personality and in the end, I can't remember how, but I talked them into seeing us.'

Bob Randolph remembers the call in more detail and recalls being cautious:

ABOVE The gorgeous Chaparral 2K, designed in the front room of Barnard's childhood Wembley home, seen here testing at Ontario Motor Speedway, California, April 1979. *Courtesy of John Barnard*
BELOW The Chaparral's ground-effect tunnels and endplate design are visible in this shot taken at the test session. *Courtesy of John Barnard*

ABOVE Barnard, Jim Hall and Al Unser confer at the Indy 500 in May 1979. *LAT Images* **BELOW** The Yellow Submarine returned to the Ontario Motor Speedway in September 1979 for the California 500 and Unser recorded a qualifying speed of 202.202mph — a figure that fascinated Barnard and went on to influence his design parameters; in the race Unser finished fifth after leading for many laps. *Bob Tronolone*

ABOVE After Barnard's's departure from Chaparral, Johnny Rutherford won the 1980 Indy 500 in the 2K. He said later: 'What this car would let you do — it was amazing... that was the best season I've ever had in championship racing...' *Bob Tronolone* **BELOW** The Rebaque HR100, seen at Monza in September 1979, shortly before Barnard's brief involvement with car and team. *Sutton Images*

LEFT First steps at Project Four towards the carbon-fibre car, with Dick Bennetts (left), later a well-known team owner, and Pete 'Butty' Turland hand-finishing aluminium moulds for the monocoque's inner panels prior to their being shipped to Hercules in the US for manufacture. *Courtesy of John Barnard*

LEFT The first carbon-fibre monocoque undergoing torsion testing at Project Four. *Courtesy of John Barnard*

LEFT These carbon inserts were made at Project Four and sent to Hercules to be built into the monocoque's honeycomb sandwich panels. *Courtesy of John Barnard*

ABOVE John Barnard, Teddy Mayer and Ron Dennis with the MP4 wind-tunnel model at the time of the merger of Project Four and Team McLaren to form McLaren International; John never clicked with Teddy, a situation that eventually led to Mayer's departure. *Courtesy of John Barnard* **BELOW** At the Canadian Grand Prix of September 1980, immediately after the merger, Mayer (left) and Barnard tend Alain Prost's M30. *Sutton Images*

ABOVE The space age comes to Formula 1 in the form of the McLaren MP4, showing off its carbon-fibre monocoque at the press launch at Silverstone on 6 March 1981. *LAT Images* **BELOW** In the MP4's first race, the 1981 Argentine Grand Prix, John Watson rose to sixth place before dropping out with transmission trouble. *Sutton Images*

ABOVE John Barnard is amused, John Watson and Ron Dennis less so, at the 1981 Monaco Grand Prix, where Andrea De Cesaris crashed the new MP4 with which he had just been entrusted. *LAT Images* **BELOW** Not an oily rag in sight at McLaren International's new state-of-the-art facility in Boundary Road, Woking, with an MP4 being assembled in the foreground. *Courtesy of Matthew Jeffreys*

ABOVE John Watson drives the carbon car to its first victory, in the 1981 British Grand Prix at Silverstone; anxious Ron Dennis screamed at his driver to slow down during the final laps. *LAT Images* **BELOW** Wattie compared the flooding euphoria of taking the chequered flag in his home race to 'getting laid for the first time'. *LAT Images*

'I replied that we were capable of doing it, but that people always wanted us to make things gratis, at no cost to them. At that time our company was unwilling to do that. Ron said, "We're quite prepared to pay." So I said, "Well, in that case, maybe we could do something. We're always interested in something new; why don't you come and see us?"

John and Ron booked themselves on the next available flight. As Ron ruefully recalls: 'To land a sponsor [today] I might spend £100,000 on a presentation. Back then we would agonise over the cost of plane tickets.' They struggled through Heathrow with their precious model of the new car, nearly five feet long, but at check-in they lost their argument to keep it with them as hand luggage and it was stowed in the hold. As John says, 'I was worried about damage as it was our only wind-tunnel model.'

On arrival at Salt Lake City, the model happily intact, they were picked up by a Hercules chauffeur to be driven out into the Utah desert, eventually arriving at a gate 'in the middle of nowhere'. This was the Hercules facility. As Ron says, 'I am sure both our mouths dropped open because beyond the gate there was nothing but desert with a road disappearing into the distance. It was remote and it was secret.'

They drove into the complex, where, as Ron explains, 'there were buildings dotted around this vast acreage, this several square miles of desert, which were all the same, different sizes but the same colour.' The driver told them that the buildings were all spaced so far apart because of the high risk that at any moment one of them 'might go off'. John adds that the buildings were partially subterranean so that, if one did 'go off', the explosion would go upwards, together with the people and everything else: 'It was pretty scary. The stuff was so volatile.'

The welcome they received at Hercules couldn't have been more of a contrast to their British experience. With Bob Randolph they had a conversation full of vision and enthusiasm, the five-foot model centre stage.

Aside from the fee, Ron soon found the lever that would persuade the American giant to get involved: 'I quickly realised that these scientists were all frustrated by one thing — they didn't have any way to talk about their technology because everything they were working on was secret. So I convinced them that the carbon car project would give them the ability to demonstrate the competence of Hercules Aerospace and show just how great these individuals were. We gave these rocket scientists the opportunity to come out of Salt Lake City and be proud about something that they'd done and be able to talk about it… It was like they had been let out of school, because they would be attending Grands Prix.'

Steve Nichols reports that. while Ron and John were in the meeting, he received a call from Hercules, possibly from Bob Randolph himself:

'He excused himself and called me to ask what I thought, should Hercules do this or not and what about Ron and what about John? I barely knew Ron but I knew John quite well, and I wanted the project to happen. So I said, "Yes, John is one of the premier Formula 1 designers in the world, fantastic designer, incredibly clever guy", and all that sort of stuff. He then asked, "What about Ron?" I told him that he had instigated this project on his own, that he was seriously dedicated, one of the best race car team managers in the business. I said, "They are both great guys and you should do it." And so they went ahead with it, which was great, because I got a job!'

After listening to Ron's pitch, Randolph declared, 'One helluva project. It looks like a real challenge. We'd love to have a go.'

That was music to Barnard's ears, the can-do chorus that he enjoyed so much. It was such a telling contrast to the attitude back in Britain.

Ron duly signed a deal for the creation of the first chassis, and, according to Randolph, agreed to pay around $60,000 per chassis. This added considerable financial pressure, but Ron, as was his wont, kept it to himself. Until recently, Barnard had no idea that Ron had taken on such a financial burden; he believed, like most in the paddock, that the reward for Hercules was mainly to have its name emblazoned on the car.

Just a week or two after the Hercules visit, John returned there with Arthur Webb over the Whitsun weekend for preliminary work. At one point the American team said, 'You've got your math wrong', rolling out documents to show how the two Brits had cocked up. Barnard raised his eyebrows before pointing out that the error was, in fact, by the Americans, who hastily rolled up their papers and put them away. The incident certainly broke the ice.

Both Webb and Barnard enjoyed working with the American experts. Bob Randolph recalls Barnard's dry humour: 'He was in the office one day and I offered him tea. When I handed him a cup of hot water with a teabag floating in it, he eyed it suspiciously and said, "Is this tea so bad you have to hide it in a bag?"' Britain might have produced the most innovative race cars in the world, but it took the country decades to trust the teabag; after all, it was an American invention and what could the Yanks possibly know about tea?

The mission now was to finish the five-part mandrel and the designs for the interior bulkheads. This was familiar territory for Hercules, who, as makers of inter-continental ballistic missiles, were practised in building cylindrical carbon-fibre casings around a multi-section mandrel that could be removed piece by piece through an aperture; rocket bodies were not dissimilar in essence to a race car chassis.

Departing from his purist mantra for the sake of speed, Barnard decided to build the forward bulkhead out of aluminium. This formed an arch over the driver's legs and had the front suspension mounted from it. He had planned to replace this bulkhead in future incarnations with carbon-fibre, but that never happened while he was at McLaren. As he eloquently explains, 'Once you start racing, you're always running beside the train you're trying to board.' His compensation was that the aluminium bulkhead 'functioned perfectly well, and carbon-fibre would have, in this case, only afforded a small weight saving'.

No doubt this compromise bugged him, but there were always other priorities. To attach the bulkhead to the chassis he made up small carbon inserts to go inside the CFC sandwich. When it came to fitting the aluminium bulkhead into the finished chassis, the mechanics would glue the bulkhead in place and then drill through the inserts and screw in the fixings.

Arthur Webb was still concerned that the shock of an impact might 'unzip the glue from the carbon-fibre'. So he suggested lines of insert-supported 'anti-peel' bolts throughout the chassis at six-inch (150mm) intervals, fastened and tightened up to stop the carbon from delaminating in a crash.

The steering and seat-back bulkheads were both made of CFC sandwich and glued and bolted into position. The seat-back bulkhead provided strong anchorage for the driver's seat, protected the driver should the engine be shunted towards the cockpit in an accident, and shielded the fuel cell.

With both torsional stiffness and driver safety in mind, Barnard further reinforced the cockpit, the weakest part of a race car and the area most likely to twist under load. For the sides of the cockpit he designed two inner panels of elongated Z section each containing a curved, carbon beam, 10mm thick and about 50mm wide, which was laid up as an integral part of the panel at the top of the Z section. These inner panels emerged from the seat-back bulkhead at the driver's shoulders and ran down either side of him, continuing through the steering bulkhead, and joined the front suspension 'horseshoe' bulkhead alongside his legs, thus cocooning him in a super-strong framework.

Building this reinforcement in carbon wasn't going to be easy; even making the mould was a challenge. One of the Project Four mechanics, Pete 'Buttie' Turland, was tasked with the unenviable mission of hand-finishing the mould, spending weeks filing, sanding and polishing to create the perfect surface upon which to lay carbon pre-preg.

Webb specified some 30 layers of pre-preg for the two curved beams, to be laid up using a method known as 'debulking'. With this process a few plies were laid over each beam's mould before being wrapped in plastic and attached to a vacuum pump to suck out all air prior to being put in the autoclave, where heat rendered the sticky resin more fluid and penetrative, so reducing its bulk — hence 'debulking'. The ply-wrapped mould was then removed from the oven and the whole process repeated until sufficient plies had been laid. As Jenkins comments, 'The results of the strength tests on this beam were mind-boggling.'

No chassis in the history of motor racing had ever seen such a high level of design. But for all this complexity, John found the whole process 'straightforward'.

'It was a learning curve, for sure,' Barnard says, 'but it wasn't, as most people assumed, some form of rocket science. There was a kind of mythology around carbon-fibre at the time; that it was too high tech for anyone but aerospace boffins, but that was just nonsense; any decent engineer could handle the material.'

Actually, it was 'some form of rocket science' because the construction methods were so alien to Formula 1. As Arthur Webb points out, 'John had an unusual capacity for learning new methods and skills remarkably quickly.'

At Hercules Bob Randolph was also impressed: 'We were in the composites industry and understood its intricacies fairly well. John was completely new, yet he was incredibly quick to pick up on the technology, which made it easy to work with him. We didn't have to waste time trying to convince him of the value of things we were trying to do. Whenever we made a technical proposal he was very quick to understand, and that was impressive to us.'

Now the main chassis mandrel plus the moulds for the interior bulkheads and the Z-section side panels were ready to be shipped to Hercules for lay-up. Barnard sent the aluminium honeycomb sheets that would form the middle of the composite sandwich to Ciba-Geigy (Bonded Structures Division) who cut them to the specified size, carving the rebates to accommodate the multitude of insert blocks before freighting them to Utah.

Soon the Hercules team was busy laying up the carbon-fibre pre-preg cloth and aluminium honeycomb, with Barnard and Webb flying out to oversee the process.

Lay-up was a particularly frustrating and time-consuming task, described vividly by Webb: 'You've got this horrid, floppy, sticky cloth in great big pieces, and you're trying to carefully position the pieces and smooth them down around a nasty shape. If you don't take a lot of care with it, you've got trouble.'

Perhaps remembering his childhood appearance on national TV, Barnard compared it to 'handling the most irksome wallpaper in the world'.

To incorporate the aluminium honeycomb, Hercules technicians used the accepted method of first laying a sheet of adhesive — basically glue set into a mesh — on the sticky carbon pre-preg laid over the mould. They would then position the aluminium honeycomb on the pre-preg and place another sheet of adhesive over it before laying the outer layers of carbon on top. When the completed structure was put in the autoclave, the adhesive would melt and 'fillet', forming areas of glue in the corners of the honeycomb cells and so bonding the carbon to the honeycomb.

During the design stages, Barnard had considered using Nomex instead of aluminium for the honeycomb. As a lightweight, fire-resistant synthetic material, Nomex appeared to be ideal for the purpose, but he rejected it for two reasons: first, he didn't think it would be strong enough; second, and perhaps more critically, Nomex was more difficult to bond to carbon-fibre cloth.

'Nomex simply didn't fillet as well,' says John, 'and it was vital that the honeycomb core bonded as strongly as possible. A lot of people used Nomex without thinking it through. Happily I had Arthur Webb and Hercules.'

Hercules helped provide a neat solution to the sticky problem of laying up the carbon-fibre onto the mould. Following a conversation with the team, John drilled a hole in the centres of the mandrel's front and rear bulkheads and passed through them a three-inch steel tube, not unlike a spit through a dead pig. This enabled mechanics to lift the entire mould onto a jig and then rotate it as they laid on the carbon-fibre pre-preg, winding it on in a continuous spiral and so making seamless lay-up much easier. After curing, the hole in the rear bulkhead was filled in, the one in the front left open to provide access for linkage to the driver's pedals.

'I was in it for the fun of it,' explains Webb, 'working in my spare time purely out of interest, rather like a hobby. Ron made some generous gestures during my time at McLaren, including giving me a car from his fleet of souped-up Mini Metros.' Given his crucial input, one can't help feeling that Webb should have been paid and paid well — but his financial reward was to come later.

He was, in fact, delighted. The chassis was all but done. All that remained was for it to be vacuum-packed before being wheeled into the Hercules autoclave to be cooked at Gas Mark Three.

Paying Webb what he was worth certainly couldn't be afforded in mid-1980, because, just as the chassis was nearing completion, Project Four simply didn't have the money. Says John: 'I remember that suddenly, in early summer, the whole carbon car enterprise was in jeopardy. It nearly died. There was so much to do and no sign of the serious money we would need to bring it off. Even the eternally optimistic Ron was saying it was getting dodgy and wasn't sure how much longer he could keep it going.'

Ron recalls this period of peril: 'Oh yes, serious financial trouble. I did not want to put myself in debt, so we only spent what we had. I was building BMW Procars and had a Formula 2 and 3 team, so it was quite a challenge to stay ahead of the spend, which of course fitted quite well with the fact that John was quite slow in the design process.' Barnard always bridles at that accusation.

One morning in June, Ron popped into the Rabbit Hutch. 'We've got a big meeting in London this afternoon. We need to take the wind-tunnel model with us, but we need it painted in Marlboro livery.' Barnard duly issued the orders and the mechanics did a rush job in the paint shop.

Barnard and Dennis contrived to leave late for the meeting, the freshly painted model wedged across the back seat of John's VW Golf GTi company car. Ron climbed into the driver's seat. 'He drove like a loon,' says John, 'passing traffic jams by speeding down the middle of the road, even racing along pavements to make up for lost time. It was like something out of *The Italian Job*.' As for Ron, who doesn't recall the drive, he says, 'Being on time for meetings was more important than my driving licence.'

They arrived in Knightsbridge, parked and rushed, as far as their five-foot model allowed them to rush, into the Capital Hotel, where they were shown into a meeting room. There Hogan and Zelkowitz were waiting with a group of other Marlboro delegates. Recalling this period, Hogan reveals how worried he was about taking such a big risk, putting his reputation and Marlboro's money behind unproven technology. 'It was me or my job, or both,' he says, smiling at the memory.

Ron and John repeated their pitch, emphasising the progress that had been made with carbon-fibre and its future potential. Ron laid out the figures needed to produce a winning carbon car. Barnard is complimentary about Dennis's skills during this period: 'He really was, and still is, exceptional at getting people to pay top dollar.' Marlboro were impressed but, to Ron's shattering disappointment, still wouldn't commit to funding the project. Undeterred, Project Four carried on, with Dennis skilfully keeping the creditors at bay.

A month later, in July, a large lorry turned up at the Woking factory. On the back was a large crate labelled HERCULES. Amid chattering excitement the crate was fork-lifted into the building and John and Alan Jenkins began prising it open. When the packing was stripped away the mood crashed. The exterior of the chassis was covered in creases and wrinkles, a result of the resin becoming more fluid than expected in the heat of the autoclave.

Arthur Webb describes John's reaction: 'Barnard went mad! Because I'd emphasised so heavily that the integrity of the fibres was paramount, that they must be kept straight, that he must avoid kinks, he thought the crinkles meant that the whole project was a failure.'

It took Webb some time to convince Barnard that there was no structural issue, that it was the resin that had creased, not the fibres. As Webb explains, 'It's not unusual for a first moulding to have all sorts of defects, so the first one-off is always a mess. In fact we had a rule of thumb at BAe, that the first two belong to the moulders because they are a learning exercise.'

But Project Four could afford no such luxuries, and 'waste not, want not' had always been a motto for the Barnard family. It was clear that this first chassis, while wrinkled, was very tough. It was taken, together with its ancillary pieces, upstairs to the workshop next to the Rabbit Hutch and mounted into a specially made jig.

The long work began of adding the bulkheads, inner panels, seat back and horseshoe beam. Drilling through the carbon to put in the anti-peel bolts had required John to design special cutting tools, made up by the mechanics and then sent off to be coated in adhesive diamond dust.

But the rough exterior caused problems more profound than cosmetics. A traditional aluminium monocoque had a dependable, smooth surface to work from and fix to. The surface wrinkles of the carbon-fibre, however, protruded as much as 2mm and couldn't be ground smooth because to do so risked breaking the fibres, interrupting their integrity.

To achieve a smooth surface at mounting points, say for a bracket to secure a radiator, John created carbon stock-block patches of about 20mm in diameter (around ¾in). These patches were glued on at the appropriate point and, when the glue set, machined down to the required depth using diamond grinders. A patch would then be drilled to take a securing bolt. John reports that the 'diamond tools wore out something awful as they worked on the cured carbon'. The workload was immense.

Despite his intense perfectionism, Barnard didn't get it right first time: 'Our first monocoque was conservative. I hadn't been able to make the weight-saving that I wanted.' The chassis was the same weight as its aluminium counterpart, but significantly narrower and more than twice as stiff; stiffer, in fact, than required. The first monocoque was duly earmarked for Italian driver Andrea De Cesaris which, as it turned out, was all to the good — some journalists dubbed him 'De Crasheris'. In later versions Barnard halved the number of layers of unidirectional CF skinning each side of the aluminium honeycomb, from eight to four, settling on a monocoque that was 70% stiffer and 25% lighter than aluminium.

Looking back, Barnard wonders at his youthful zeal: 'Today, I would have talked myself out of such an endeavour. Back then the complexity didn't faze me one iota. I never thought that it wasn't going to be possible.' He was fired up with finding the perfect solution to a problem that had foxed everyone trying to build ground-effect cars — how can you retain stiffness in a much narrower chassis without adding weight? 'I was never going to give up on that mission.'

Arthur Webb was truly impressed. 'It was incredibly brave of John to take on the carbon project. If the tub didn't work, then nothing would have worked. It was an enormous risk.'

The monocoque Barnard created was among the most advanced carbon-fibre structures in the world at the time. As Bob Randolph says, 'Advanced in its simplicity, Barnard's chassis was one of the strongest boxes ever made.'

Barnard's genius had inspired him not only to adopt cutting-edge aerospace technology, master it and introduce it to motorsport, but to actually help push forward the work of rocket scientists. His carbon-fibre car opened up new possibilities, creating fresh avenues for the material's use across many different industries, something that no other motorsport designer could claim to have achieved.

Randolph: 'When you do such a project you add a range of things to your technical bag of tricks. We learned a lot from this, about the use of honeycomb structure, about methods to ensure all parts were cured equally. The carbon-fibre monocoque drew global attention to what composite structures could do in general and what Hercules's capabilities were in particular. It was very good for us. I feel that we were very privileged to have been involved in that enterprise.'

Barnard's achievement is remarkable, and Randolph didn't hold back from further praise in a trade magazine article on the subject[25]. For the 15 chassis Hercules made for Barnard between 1981 and 1986, 'only minor adjustments were needed, because essentially they got it right from the beginning with the design and construction'.

This striving to get it right is one of the qualities that has won Barnard so much respect within the world of motorsport. He loved the challenge, revelled in creating work that was first class, first time.

As the wheel of fortune descends, so will it rise, and by late summer things at Project Four were suddenly looking up. John Hogan had been on the phone, telling Ron Dennis of new funding for the car, generating renewed excitement at the factory. Now it was time to let the world know what had been achieved, to announce the arrival of a new technology and a powerful new partnership in Formula 1.

On Tuesday 9 September 1980, five days before the Italian Grand Prix, Ron held a press conference in London to announce the breakthrough. The carbon car, in model form, caused a sensation, with national newspapers using headlines such as 'Motor racing enters the space age'.

David Smith, in London's *Evening Standard*, hailed the creation of 'a car containing hardly any metal and built instead of a material developed for guided missiles, [which] could change the shape of family motoring in the future', creating 'light, energy-saving family cars, possibly before the end of the decade'.

For a team new to Formula 1, there has never been and perhaps never will be such an impressive technological début.

In the lead-up to the public announcement of the carbon car, another big change took place: Marlboro's John Hogan brokered a merger of Team McLaren and Project Four. This was Hogan's brilliant, if controversial, solution to a major problem — the seemingly unstoppable decline of Team McLaren. By putting

---

[25] McConnell, Vicki P., 'In the fast track: composites in race cars', *Advanced Composites, March/April 1991.*

Ron Dennis and John Barnard in the driving seat, with their revolutionary new car, McLaren's fortunes could be turned around.

The carbon car also now had a name — the MP4. The 'P4' represented Project Four, but there remains to this day some dispute about the 'M'. Barnard and Hogan share the memory that the 'M' stood for McLaren, reflecting the merger, but Dennis claims that it represented Marlboro. Indeed, since McLaren's input into the car was negligible, Ron's claim has logic, whatever the reality at the time.

The reality at the time for McLaren's Teddy Mayer, Tyler Alexander and Gordon Coppuck was all too apparent. The new kids on the block had muscled into their gang and were set to take it over, with technology that, had they played their cards better, might have been theirs to command. It was all change at McLaren's Colnbrook factory: Barnard's former employers were on a train bound for the sidings.

CHAPTER 12
CHANGING OF THE GUARD
1976–80

Team McLaren was in serious trouble: they knew it, their sponsors Marlboro knew it and the public knew it. The team's last big success had been in 1976 when James Hunt won the World Championship in later versions of the McLaren M23 for which John Barnard had done so much behind-the-scenes work. The following year Hunt only managed fifth place in the points standings with Gordon Coppuck's new M26 — and it had been downhill ever since.

John Watson was a witness to the team's decline. He arrived at McLaren for the 1979 season from Brabham as a direct result of the death of Ronnie Peterson, who had been offered a seat at the team but had lost his life after a crash at the start of the 1978 Italian Grand Prix at Monza. Things move fast in Formula 1. Even as the Swede lay dying in hospital, Watson was approached by John Hogan with an offer to drive for McLaren.

As Watson said in an interview for this book, 'I knew the team was making the M28, a ground-effect car, and it sounded exciting. But it turned out to be a real disaster of a car, one of the worst in McLaren's history.' Watson describes the M28 and its successors as 'shitboxes'.

This huge setback arose from McLaren's efforts to mimic the spectacular success of Lotus's ground-effect technology, the concept that had inspired Barnard when he designed the Chaparral 2K. McLaren made the M28 as narrow and as light as possible, but things started going wrong during its first full test, at Watkins Glen in America. Says Watson, 'I went out, did a few laps and was called in. The car was taken straight to the Tech Centre to be checked out. An hour later I was told: "We're going home — there's a fundamental problem and they can't fix it."'

The problem was the front bulkhead, which the mechanics could actually distort by hand even though it should have been one of the strongest parts of the car. Watson: 'The design and the materials used were wholly inadequate. They were using an aluminium honeycomb that wasn't strong enough for this ground-effect car's narrow monocoque.'

In its efforts to strengthen the M28, Coppuck added some 60lbs in weight, so compromising the car's performance. Weight and structural integrity weren't the only issues; lack of aerodynamic expertise was also a weakness for McLaren. To improve their understanding was going to require considerably more investment, as Coppuck makes clear:

'We couldn't use our existing wind-tunnel techniques to find out what the downforce was. We needed to make a model. It wasn't any good making a model that was cheap; we needed one that was probably going to cost as much as a whole Grand Prix car. To do that you needed to have far more money coming in.'

And that was Coppuck's primary problem, created in part by Teddy Mayer's relative lack of financial acumen in this period of spiralling cost. Mayer simply didn't have Ron Dennis's 'front' and felt it incumbent upon him to prove that McLaren could get results on existing Marlboro budgets. Even though successful ground-effect design now required expensive new wind-tunnel technology, he simply couldn't bring himself to ask Marlboro for the necessary cash, or, if he ever did, present the request in a sufficiently convincing package. In Coppuck's words, 'He wasn't going to kill the goose that laid the golden egg' — although that is more or less what happened anyway.

John Hogan goes along with the view that Mayer's fear of asking Marlboro for more money contributed to McLaren's downfall: 'We'd just renewed the sponsorship contract, so Teddy had asked for the right amount of money and couldn't very well ask for more. What Teddy didn't want to do, because he was a lawyer at the end of the day, was come back and request more — doing that wouldn't have fazed Ron Dennis at all!'

McLaren also urgently needed a designer who really understood ground-effect. Hogan remembers the problem went back to the M26 when Gary Anderson, later notable for incisive technological analysis of Formula 1 for the BBC, was trying to comprehend ground-effect at the team:

'McLaren didn't have a handle on skirts,' says Hogan. 'Nobody at McLaren understood them. Gary Anderson, who was by then a kind of head engineer, chief mechanic and more, was fiddling around trying to get skirts on the M26 just by dropping things down, and saying, "That's a skirt, isn't it?" But in fairness, and I think even Gary would concede this, nobody at McLaren had a clue how the skirts worked on the Lotus 79. Not the vaguest idea.'

If the 1979 season was bad for John Watson, 1980 was worse. With the M28 a write-off, Mayer brought in designer Robin Herd as a consultant to help Gordon Coppuck on the new car, the M29. Herd introduced curves into the underbody tunnels, replacing the less aerodynamic right angles of the M28. He also proposed making the underbody out of carbon-fibre panels. The changes, says Watson, made little difference: 'It was the failure of the M28 and its successor the M29 that was ultimately responsible for bringing about the Dennis/Barnard takeover.'

But McLaren had two more shots in the locker. In a rearguard action designed to prevent Marlboro pulling out, the team produced the M30, which Watson describes as 'their last gasp at proving to Marlboro that they were technically up to speed. It was going to be the panacea, securing a future for McLaren and proving they didn't need an external group of people.'

They also had another ace up their sleeves. Hogan had found a brilliant new young driver, Frenchman Alain Prost, whom he had watched perform outstandingly at Monaco in 1979 on his way to winning the European Formula 3 Championship. Hogan told Mayer to give Prost a test drive.

So it was that, at the end of 1979, Teddy brought in 25-year-old Prost for his first season in Formula 1. Watson got on well with 'Little Napper' (a reference to Napoleon) but his criticism of McLaren's principals is scathing: 'Prost was an outstanding talent and the team focused on him as the pathfinder for the team's fortunes, rather than looking to themselves and saying, "We're not actually up to speed." They would walk around the paddock trying to eyeball rival cars and then tell the designers what they had to change. But it doesn't work like that.'

Prost's début, at the 1980 Argentine Grand Prix, was impressive for a rookie. Driving the M29B, he finished sixth while Watson retired with gearbox failure. The Frenchman managed fifth in Brazil, but that was as good as it got despite the introduction of the M29C a few races later.

Still confident that the M30 was a breakthrough, McLaren launched the car at the Dutch Grand Prix on 31 August 1980. Although Prost finished sixth, Watson, still driving an M29C, comfortably out-qualified him and ran better in the race until engine trouble intervened.

Becoming frustrated, Prost began to blame the car and its design, while the team, faced with extinction, was blaming him. Watson: 'The team was now on Prost's case, but he wasn't the problem; he was a very fine driver. The problem was with the aerodynamics of the M30; the team just didn't understand ground-effect well enough.' All that remained, it seemed, was to discover when and how Marlboro was going to pull out. Prost, meanwhile, decided that he would drive for Renault in 1981.

The departure of Prost was the final straw for Hogan, who now knew that McLaren lacked the energy, vision and design skill to recover: 'Prost came in and stayed with us for a season and left, and that hit Teddy pretty hard, because he was a young punk who said to Teddy, "The car isn't up to it." We were going in circles. That was when I was putting a lot of pressure on Teddy to do something about it.'

John Hogan was emotionally attached to McLaren and didn't relish the prospect of becoming the man responsible for destroying this historic team with a massive fan base on both sides of the Atlantic, one that had brought Marlboro so much glory. He racked his brains for a way to rescue it, but each result from the 1980 Formula 1 season just made the situation worse. Hogan was under pressure from Marlboro to pull their money out: 'It was a bit of a struggle to hold the hounds at the gate.'

In late July, a few weeks after Dennis's high-speed drive to London with Barnard, Hogan found himself chatting about the problem to Bill Murray, President of Philip Morris, another no-nonsense Aussie with an eye for quick solutions. During the conversation and by way of contrast to McLaren's paucity of ideas, Hogan was singing the praises of the exemplary Project Four operation. Murray listened patiently and then said, in his laconic Aussie brogue, 'Well, Hogie, why don't you merge them?'

The thought struck Hogan like a gong. McLaren was a big name. Project Four were unknown in Formula 1 and unproven but full of creative energy and about to introduce a radical new car. A merger could put McLaren right back at the top, bridging the technology gap at a stroke. Marlboro had everything to gain. The scheme was as beautiful as it was simple, the best of all possible worlds.

For Hogan, the future now depended upon Formula 1's new dynamic duo: 'Ron was a very inspirational person. You just had faith in him that he would get the job done and he never failed at doing any job he said he was going to do. McLaren was broke, just chasing their tail; we knew because we had looked at the books; Ron and John were the guys who would get them out of the hole.'

Hogan called Dennis to discuss the plan. It was music to Ron's ears; at last his long game with Marlboro was paying off. He wasn't dismayed in the slightest when Hogan proposed that McLaren should be the lead name in the new venture. It would be called McLaren International, with the name Project Four preserved in the title of John's carbon car, the MP4. Ron was wise enough to spot immediately the potential of arriving in Formula 1 under the McLaren banner, gaining at a stroke the kudos of a name that was as famous in America as it was in the rest of the racing world.

The deal was simple. Project Four and Team McLaren would form a 50/50 partnership. And as for control? Let nature take its course — the young bloods moving in on the old bulls. Competitive to the core as all young people in the motorsport business were, Ron and John already knew who was going to win any battle for supremacy.

Sensing trouble, Teddy Mayer invited Hogan to dinner at his house together with Tyler Alexander. That evening Hogan broke the news about this solution to McLaren's woes. Teddy wasn't impressed. Hogan: 'He didn't want to know. He thought they could survive. And I said, "Look, you're not going to survive, you've got to merge because you need Ron Dennis's expertise and John Barnard's expertise."'

But Mayer stood his ground. Mayer was 'the man'. The paddock had even nick-named him 'The Wiener', after the 'Oscar Mayer Wiener', an American hot dog sausage, in what Tyler claimed was a reference to his boss's reputed large penis. The Wiener just couldn't face the idea of a couple of Formula 1 rookies calling the shots at the team he had worked so hard to save, in such stressful circumstances, following the death of Bruce McLaren. He feared to his very bones that such a merger amounted to professional suicide.

Hogan understood Mayer's anxiety but saw no other way out and was forced to make the position crystal clear: 'I said to Teddy, "If the merger doesn't happen, we're going to pull the plug." And Tyler, ever being Tyler, said, "Now listen to him, Wiener, 'cos if you don't do it, he's going to pull the goddamned plug, you hear?"'

Teddy's back was against the wall. What could he do? Resign, and lose everything he had built? Seek another major sponsor? Who? The bank balance said there was no time, and why would anyone want to support a failing team that was reeling from the embarrassment of losing Alain Prost, the paddock's most promising star? Carry on with multiple, smaller sponsors? That could never provide sufficient money to build a ground-effect car.

Mayer needed new design expertise and there was John Barnard being dangled in front of him. He needed new energy and talent on the business front and there was Ron Dennis waiting in the wings like a famished predator. It was a shotgun wedding, with Hogan playing the affronted father with a rifle in his arms. It was heading for a showdown.

According to Ron, the showdown took the form of the Battle of the Lists: 'The first part of the discussion was along the lines of, "My company is worth this and your company is worth that." The preparation that was done for that conversation was in the form of lists. The current Formula 1 team had engines, cars, premises and suchlike. There was this enormous list from Teddy that ran to ten pages, and mine ran to just two pages. Really, my primary asset was the new carbon car. So Teddy had this smile growing across his face which said, "How are you going to match my list?"'

Ever skilled at presenting a weak position as one of strength, Ron replied, 'Well clearly it doesn't make any sense for one company to buy the other. You have a lot of things the new team doesn't need and I have a lot of things too, so why don't we just contribute those things that are needed?' Ron turned to John and asked him what he thought the new team really needed. He replied, 'All we want are the engines' — a crushing response from Mayer's point of view.

But Ron knew that to keep the team going they needed more: 'The carbon car wasn't complete so we had to have the insurance policy of having to run the old McLaren cars for the early races. We didn't need to own them, so I suggested they kept the ownership and we'd just use them and give them back so they could sell them.'

Mayer was out of his league. In his trademark 'money-no-object' style, Ron made another suggestion: 'I also realised that the worst thing we could possibly do was to put this team into anyone's existing facility, so I said that we had to have a new facility.' Project Four's Woking factory was too small and McLaren's in Colnbrook was, according to Ron, 'a dark, shabby hole under the flight path'.

Outgunned and outmanoeuvred, Mayer finally gave his assent. On 9 September 1980, the new team issued the following press release at a press conference, embargoed to the following day:

CHANGING OF THE GUARD

> *One of the best kept secrets in Formula One motor racing was revealed today with the announcement that two of motor racing's biggest teams are joining forces for an attack on the 1981 World Championship.*
>
> *The new team, McLaren International, combines Team McLaren and Project Four Racing and has the backing of Marlboro, one of the sport's pre-eminent sponsors.*
>
> *Headed by joint managing directors Teddy Mayer and Ron Dennis, McLaren International will benefit from the experience and resources of both companies' past racing programmes. It is planned to continue development of the existing Marlboro McLaren M30, which made its racing debut at the Dutch Grand Prix last weekend, along with a revolutionary new design due to be tested in late November.*
>
> *McLaren International will be based in a new 20,000 sq. ft. factory west of London. The new design and fabrication facility will be headed by John Barnard, the team's chief designer. Barnard designed the Chaparral car, which won this year's Indianapolis 500.*

As indicated in the previous chapter, the British press leaped on the story. In an article headlined 'Ferrari going Oo-la-la!', *The Sun* opened with a wayward tale claiming that Alain Prost had decided to reject Ferrari to stay with McLaren. It must have been a hectic day on *The Sun*'s sports desk because the sub-editor added, 'McLaren plan a major comeback in 1980 [*sic*] with a new factory, new car and a new design expert in Ron Dennis.' The handing of design credit to Ron was the sort of howler that would have made Barnard hop about his kitchen in a rage.

Other newspapers seemed to consider Project Four's involvement to be merely a sub-contractual arrangement to build a car for McLaren. But most got it right, leading their motorsport pages with 'McLaren make changes' (*Daily Telegraph*), 'McLaren merger' (*The Guardian*) and the prescient 'McLaren on road back to front row' (*The Times*).

Reading between the lines, the press release revealed where the real power now lay. The new facility, into which Marlboro was going to pour the lion's share of the sponsorship, would be under the design control of John Barnard. The hopeless M30 project would continue at McLaren's existing base in Colnbrook while Barnard would build his space-age race car in a new state-of-the-art factory in Dennis's home town of Woking, on Boundary Road, just a mile from the Project Four factory on Poole Road.

As for Mayer sharing the managing director role with Dennis, it was obvious to Hogan, even if not yet entirely clear to Mayer, what this really meant: 'We knew that there was going to be tension. We kind of knew that Teddy was going to be the first one to pop out, because it was already pretty obvious he didn't get on with Ron, though in a very gentlemanly way. Very bluntly, the world had passed him by.'

Just two years earlier John had drawn up the Chaparral in the front room of his childhood home. Then he had designed a race car in a spare bedroom at his own house. Latterly he had been in the Rabbit Hutch working for a team with no Formula 1 experience. Now his workplace was in brand-new premises where he was the technical chief of one of the most famous and respected racing brands.

John Barnard had arrived and, you might have thought, was feeling fantastic. He wasn't. Instead, he was scared. A key motivating factor in his perfectionism was his fear of failure; for him the devil was always in the detail. Now, here he was, centre stage with a massive spotlight shining on him, a place where he has never felt comfortable.

John discussed the new position with Rosie, revealing an important contrast between the two of them. 'I'm a glass-half-empty bloke, she's glass-half-full. So she could see all the positives.' But in the back of his mind lurked the fear of what would happen if it all went wrong: 'I told myself, "You're at the top now, you're the chief technical guy in this Formula 1 team. If it all turns to crap, it's you that people are going to say couldn't do the job. Ron had done his bit — he had got the funds. If it didn't come off, it would be logical to blame the man who made the car — that's what happened to Coppuck.'

It was all mixed emotions for Barnard: 'There was an element of, "Great — it's another step up the ladder", coupled with a kind of, "Um, how difficult is this going to be?" My natural reaction is not jubilation with these things, I don't do jumping up and down with joy. OK, I was excited, I hoped it would all be fantastic, but there was a fair amount of trepidation at the same time.'

On 14 October 1980 the deal was signed. McLaren Racing Ltd, in the physical form of Teddy Mayer and Tyler Alexander, would buy 50 shares in McLaren International at £1 each, giving them 50%; the other 50 shares for the Project Four side were distributed as 29% to Ron Dennis, 12% to Creighton Brown (Ron's partner) and 9% to John Barnard. All were to be directors of the new company.

Barnard was to be technical director, a new title for a new role, in charge of innovation and development, and hiring all design office staff. Dennis would be in charge of marketing, sponsorship and hiring personnel to manage the new company. Along with Marlboro he would also be in charge of the racing team. Mayer and Alexander were destined to take secondary roles.

Barnard's new financial status had its downside for him: 'It's all very well when someone tells you that you've got 9% of a company, but I'm rather pragmatic with things like this, something I got from my Dad. At the end of the day I was thinking, "OK, I'm technical director and shareholder, but it amounts to zero in the monthly bank balance."'

For the old Team McLaren, the future was writ large across the shabby Colnbrook walls. And Gordon Coppuck? Teddy couldn't bring himself to tell his old friend that his 15-year tenure at McLaren was over. When he finally summoned the courage, it was far too late. The humiliation was total, as Alan Jenkins recalls: 'As John and Ron were coming in through the front door at Colnbrook, Gordon was hastily throwing his stuff in the boot of his Cortina out the back. He was literally being shovelled out as we were coming in the front door — a bit of horrible realism — he barely had time to clear his desk. Teddy wasn't great at handling that sort of stuff. Ron wouldn't have done it that way. People were terribly fond of Gordon. He was a lovely bloke. And you even wonder if they ever could have worked together, John and Gordon.'

The answer to that is a deafening 'No'. It was John who had insisted on Coppuck's departure: 'You can't have two chief designers.' The fact that there were two managing directors didn't bother Ron, but then he had every intention of ignoring Teddy should they disagree.

'It was *fait accompli*,' recalls Coppuck, who bears no grudges, 'but I must say I was disappointed. On the other hand I wasn't having Formula 1 fun; I was ready to step back to Indycar. I just couldn't imagine us, as McLaren Racing, accessing the necessary money. I think the truth was that the money was there to be had, but nonetheless if you don't know that, then you are in the hard place. Leaving McLaren was a release from a very difficult situation.

'I've always got satisfaction after Ron took over, because McLaren has grown into an industry that's way beyond what I'd imagined. But I'm proud of my little bit, which was to help get it past the death of Bruce McLaren.'

When a stiff new broom sweeps through a stale old business there's bound to be a dust-up. Barnard's arrival brought much gnashing of teeth at Team McLaren;

the old guard was going to have to change their ways, and that wasn't going to be easy because they were all strong characters with major triumphs and long history under their belts.

For starters, they were facing a move from the historic Colnbrook site near Heathrow to the new McLaren International HQ under construction in Woking, giving some of them longer journeys to and from work. Worse, they had lost the gentle, easy-going, tolerant Gordon Coppuck. Worse still, he was going to be replaced by a perfectionist with a very single-minded vision, a man with whom many of the mechanics had clashed before.

John Watson remembers their frustration. He also recalls how the mechanics were a law unto themselves: 'Before Barnard they were often less than impressed by the accuracy or practicality of the designs coming out of the drawing office. They wouldn't think twice about changing some key component, defending their position by saying: "You only draw the thing — we have to build it!"'

Such was the culture at Team McLaren. If a designer made a mistake, which often happened, the mechanics would tut and huff and then redesign it their own way, sometimes without bothering to tell the designer what they had done — McLaren's mainly Kiwi mechanics were among the most highly skilled in the world.

But there was no way Barnard was going to tolerate correction of his 'mistakes', firstly because he rarely made them, and secondly because he was introducing technology that was entirely beyond their experience. The field was dressed for battle and there was only going to be one victor.

In stark contrast to the disgruntled Kiwis, John Watson was highly impressed by Barnard from the first time he met him. This auspicious moment came on Friday 25 September 1980, a fortnight after the merger, during practice for the Canadian Grand Prix in Montréal. Barnard was there to help with the M29C, which Watson was still driving, Prost having been given the newer M30. Wattie describes what followed as a Eureka moment:

'I remember Barnard asking me why I was running the car so low. "I don't know," I replied, "I'm not the engineer!" He then told me that if the car was too low, the ground-effect tunnels would stall out. So he raised the car a bit and the change in performance was unbelievable. He then suggested lifting it a little more; it was even better! We used to run rake on the car, with the front lower than the rear; he took that out too. The car just got better and better.

'It made me understand that my grasp of aerodynamics was as much use as Teddy Mayer's. Barnard's changes, which were contrary to what anyone else would have thought at McLaren, suddenly transformed the car, giving better balance, more grip, everything. For me it was the end of a very difficult period.'

Watson finished fourth in Canada, his best result in eight races. Further dramatic changes quickly followed at Team McLaren with inevitable clashes between the old guard and the new regime.

One of the first things that Ron Dennis attempted to fix was the imminent loss of Alain Prost. Ron suggested to Barnard that they have breakfast with Prost. John takes up the story: 'Over breakfast, Ron told Alain, "You've got to stay, it's all going to be different now." But Alain resisted, saying the deal with Renault was in the bag and he wanted to get away from McLaren. At a loss, Ron declared, "If you don't stay, you will regret it, you will piss blood!" I was taken aback — a stunning statement.' As for Ron, he denies using that phrase.

Prost blames his departure upon a serious crash during practice for the Watkins Glen race at the end of the 1980 season. The rear suspension on his M30 had failed on a left-hand bend and he'd struck his head on a fence post; for the first time in his career he'd seriously feared for his life. Immediately after the accident, Prost declared to Team McLaren assistant manager Tony Jardine that he would never drive for McLaren again. He later admitted, 'With Ron and John coming I was tempted to stay. But this crash… was too much. I lost all confidence. Maybe without this crash I am not sure I would have gone to Renault.'[26]

To get away from McLaren, Prost had to break his Marlboro sponsorship contract, which put John Hogan in a difficult position. Could he sue the Frenchman? In his words, 'Are you, Philip Morris, going to take Alain Prost to court in France? The answer was, "No way in the world."'

To lose such a rising star was an early blow for Barnard and Dennis. Worse was to come. Prost's replacement was also a rookie, but one who simply wasn't in the same league.

---

[26] *Folley, Malcolm,* Senna vs Prost, *Arrow Books, 2010, pp58–59.*

CHAPTER 13
THE PRINCE OF DARKNESS
1980–81

John Barnard, now also known as JB, set about laying down the law at McLaren and in doing so earned the dubious sobriquet 'The Prince of Darkness'. Coined by Tyler Alexander, the nickname flew around the paddock with a wry relish. Tyler came across the phrase in *The Verdict*, a movie in which Paul Newman was advised by his legal partner that if he did battle with lawyer James Mason, he would find himself up against 'the prince of fucking darkness'. Tyler elucidated:

'When John came, he changed the way a lot of things were being dealt with at the factory; he knew how to do things and once they were done he knew how to make them work. His ego said that he had to change the way the guys at McLaren did those things. He wouldn't allow the mechanics to do their own thing. He would be looking over Steve Nichols's and Alan Jenkins's shoulders all the time to make sure they were drawing stuff that he wanted.'

It's worth pointing out that Alexander thought it unusual that John would be checking on Nichols and Jenkins. It verifies Barnard's view that many Formula 1 teams at the time lacked rigour in their drawing offices. Barnard's lifetime habit of meticulous scrutiny of his 'pencils' also speaks to claims from several of his employees for design credit that they feel they share with Barnard; John was almost always the overseer, the guiding hand. Gordon Coppuck and Jim Hall never bothered to look at his work in detail, whereas Barnard himself scrutinised everything once he was in charge.

Alexander admits he was 'disappointed, upset and pissed off' about the Project Four invasion, but, as John Hogan had witnessed at the fateful dinner party at Teddy Mayer's house, he also understood the realities:

'I guess you could say that McLaren was a bit scruffy at the time that John and Ron came. I knew the place needed entrepreneurial people like Ron Dennis and it also needed an engineer who had a better grasp of ground-effect. McLaren had fame, reputation and a bunch of good people. It just needed some proper direction… The company was still in business, so the merger was a good thing. To me it was kind of, "Let's stop messing around and get on with it and see what happens." But the mechanics knew me and would come to me.'

Alexander was piggy in the middle, lending a sympathetic ear to the gripes of his old mates flinching under the new regime, while managing himself to make friends with their new boss. 'I don't recall ever having a row with Barnard,' he says. And John agrees. 'I got on with Tyler, he was an amusing guy, and a decent chap to go for a beer with. He was outgoing, McLaren's Mr Soundbite, always on the telly. But he always supported Teddy.'

John quickly made it clear that the mechanics weren't allowed to design anything, not even the simplest support bracket for the bodywork. It was a deeply unpopular pronouncement: Barnard effectively stripped them of their creative input, and, understandably, this upset them. Arguments between Barnard and McLaren staff ensued.

'We've been doing F1 for years, before you were out of short trousers,' a mechanic might say. 'Who are you to tell us what to do?'

'And you've been going downhill for years,' would be Barnard's stinging reply, followed by, 'and when was the last time you won a race?'

Barnard made his conditions very clear: 'I only want on the car what I have designed to go on the car. It is my responsibility, so everything MUST come through the design office. Is that clear?'

This battle with the mechanics proved to be a major turning point. Diane Holl, a future McLaren employee and later a NASCAR engineer, observed: 'When John came, everything started being drawn — everything. Properly detailed drawings and assemblies with all the nuts and bolts, torque specs — that hadn't happened before. It was a big change.'

To some it was too big a change and they resigned on the spot. Others kept their heads down but many of those also soon left. As Ron commented when interviewed for this book, 'You had to change their thinking and that was a challenge, because they had got set in their ways. There were plenty of people who got spat out, a bunch of people who just had to go in the end. And there were some who stayed behind who tried to trip us up, and that was a waste of time. There was no crack in our armour on that point.'

Alan Jenkins cites one such example as John Baldwin, who had taken over as Coppuck's right-hand man in 1975 after Barnard's departure for Parnelli: 'Baldwin drew some of the fabricated bulkheads for the chassis, but you could see that his way of doing it just wasn't going to fit. Barnard was happy to lead by example, but he didn't seem to want to go to Baldwin and say, "Look John, do it like this, eh?" The way Baldwin chose to do it would drive Barnard mad. You could see him walking away from Baldwin's drawing board, raising his eyes to heaven. You knew it wasn't going to last.'

Jenkins makes an interesting observation here. At this stage in his career, Barnard didn't teach; he didn't see that as his job. He expected people to raise their standards by themselves, copying his example, as Jenkins had done.

Another potential point of conflict arose with Steve Nichols, the man from Hercules. His laid-back style worked its way under Barnard's skin, prompting John to describe him as 'the Californian Dreamer'. Barnard adds, 'He was smart, but lazy. I don't recall him doing much drawing. He did have a good brain and he made a good race engineer. An amateur racer himself, he understood open-wheel race cars. He was a natural at working with the drivers and setting up the cars. So that's where I eventually moved him.'

As for Nichols, he recalls putting 'a helluva lot of effort into things' under Barnard, working into the early hours double checking stress calculations: 'Eventually, because he got more and more busy, he dropped off doing any calculations like that and I used to think, "It's only me that's deciding whether the wheels fall off!"'

In response to Barnard's observation that he was lazy, Nichols recalls that he regularly worked 60 hours a week at the factory, added to which were the long race weekends: 'Each day at the races would start at around 6.30am and finish around midnight or one in the morning when the car covers went on.' He recalls in 1983 spending some 150 nights in hotel rooms — five months — and working regularly overnight when the cars were being tested at tracks around Europe: 'Ron and John and all the high rollers would rarely see the hard graft that went on at tests. Didn't seem that lazy to me!'

The question of Steve's bumbling or brilliance will come up again when we address the most successful McLaren car in history — and it wasn't one built by John Barnard. But there were, happily for Nichols, plenty who thought him highly productive. Designer Matthew Jeffreys, who had joined McLaren in 1979 aged 17, explains that 'Steve came across as a very laid-back person.

People would see him with his feet up on the desk, rubbing the tip of his nose with the back of his hand and naturally conclude he was just dreaming, doing nothing, but usually he was coming up with something pretty clever, or at the very least giving a problem careful and considered thought.'

Nichols was aware of a growing sense of competitive conflict, but he was learning from it all the time: 'Occasionally I might make a mess of things and I would be sitting there trying to patch it and fix it, when his shadow loomed over and he'd be saying, "When you find a cock-up, please pass it to me to fix the cock-up!" Or he'd say, "Go right back to basics. Start over again, don't try to put a sticking plaster on it!" There were a few interesting things like that to be learned from John the perfectionist.

'In fact, I didn't screw up much, which I suspect might have irritated Barnard. I think he liked his people to screw up, because he so rarely screwed up. Looking back, it was great there, a fantastic experience because there were just a few of us at the time trying to do the whole car so you got such breadth of experience.'

Unlike some others who have been interviewed for this book, Nichols doesn't complain about Barnard's brooding presence: 'He wanted it the way he wanted it. And mostly what he wanted was very, very good and very, very detailed, exacting and precise. Nothing was too good. He'd squeeze your brain and you would dump all that you could onto the paper. He was squeezing your brain all the time to get out every last little bit.'

This mental compression was rarely rewarded. Perhaps because of the environment in which he grew up, with the absence of any praise that might go to a lad's head, Barnard rarely complimented his staff. Nichols came to the conclusion early on that Barnard was 'never going to say, "Oh, good job!", that there never would be a pat on the back, never any praise, never even the slightest bit of encouragement.' He quickly recognised this state of affairs as the 'ground rules, the playing field — and they were fine by me.'

Nichols adds, 'I found my motivation by assuming that if he hadn't chucked me out of the door, then that was as good as it was going to get! Working with Barnard was like a flat bar chart with only negative spikes — you had to watch out for the negative spikes. Otherwise, if you were bumbling along on zero, then that was good.'

John is a little peeved by the suggestion that he gave no-one any praise, and doesn't really believe it. The accusation prompts him to recall a moment when they were building the drop-test rig for the carbon nose cone and he asked

Matthew Jeffreys to design a release mechanism at the top. 'He designed an air-operated release hook. I thought it was bloody clever and a bloody good job. And I recall saying to him, "I like that, that's good." Admittedly, "I like that, that's good" is as far as I would go. I wouldn't jump around for joy because someone doing an engineering degree designed a release hook!'

Barnard adds, poignantly, 'I don't remember getting praise myself. Certainly at home, with Mum, Dad and me, if any of us did anything good, it seemed stupid patting one another on the head. We were part of a team.'

In the meantime, everyone buckled under the withering presence of the Prince of Darkness, all cognisant of what Matthew Jeffreys had been told were the Two Rules, obeyed by everyone at McLaren: 'Rule One: JB is always right. Rule Two: When JB is wrong, refer to Rule One.'

John considers the Two Rules and the Prince of Darkness nickname as 'sound-bitey ways of dealing with authority'. He doesn't particularly like the phrases but neither do they particularly offend him — they just came with the job.

'People say I blew up, but I don't see it like that,' he contemplates. 'People complain that I didn't give them enough freedom but I don't think that's true. I was happy for people to present ideas, but what they had to do was be able to defend my critique of them. If I ask questions they don't have an answer for, then, why should I take their idea over mine? Because if it's wrong, I'm the one who gets the Dunce's Hat.' Top of Barnard's mind is a moment when he did trust a designer to do something and it went dreadfully wrong, but that's a tale for later.

Jeffreys recalls how Barnard seemed to have an unfailing eye for spotting errors: 'JB instinctively knew when things were wrong or imperfect, especially things you really didn't want him to know. He could be walking past you, and you'd have this complex drawing on your board and somehow, out of the corner of his eye, he'd spot the one thing you didn't want him to see, the one item that wasn't quite right or not as he would have expected it. He would zero in on it with an uncanny focus, like it was painted Day-Glo for him. He had a natural gift for spotting the untoward.'

For all his fearsome reputation, Barnard rarely clashed with Steve Nichols, didn't row with Tyler Alexander and never had a conflict with Alan Jenkins. That is until one time in 1984, and that occasion, as we shall also see, was terminal.

One old Team McLaren man who entirely avoided the wrath of Barnard was the irrepressible Don 'Mother' Beresford, a remarkable and much-loved motorsport character. Beresford was an inspiring addition to John's technical team: 'He'd be up all night working on body bucks. He was very good and worked extremely hard.' Beresford was in favour of the merger, welcoming the new creativity and challenges and sometimes even siding with Barnard against Mayer when the going got rough. A no-nonsense man of action, he had no time for 'whinging'.

Barnard's perspective on the merger is to the point: 'It had to be done and there was no time for pussy-footing around. There was so much bickering. To innovate, to push on, to win, you all have to be singing from the same songbook.' This was no laughing party, as Elvis Costello had so vividly put it in his hit song of the previous year. Winning was what McLaren was all about.

It should be noted here, for fear of creating the wrong impression, that Barnard didn't spend his time marching around shouting at designers and mechanics. There were arguments, but he wasn't a bully, he gained no pleasure from making people squirm and, when he blew, it was just as likely to be with the two managing directors.

His occasional explosions might be seen as the whistle screaming on the boiling kettle of his perfectionist creativity and self-doubt. Matthew Jeffreys: 'He was quick to get angry but just as quick to forget it. Literally, within five minutes, he would be back to normal, speaking to you in considered, hushed tones in the drawing office, this just after looking like a beetroot and screaming like a lunatic. It's pretty difficult to get your head around that and not to take it personally.'

More often than not Barnard was a picture of calm and industry, keeping himself to himself and dealing with irritations more often with humour than anger, although often bottling it up inside. But it did have an effect on him. Jeffreys recalls the outward signs of inner angst, especially towards the end of Barnard's time at McLaren:

'You know those bits of skin at the back of your fingernails that sometimes tear back and get really painful? John was forever nipping them with his teeth and getting bleeding around them. You could tell he was suffering. The pressure to perform and come up with solutions to things must have been immense. Sure, he received personal and financial benefits, but perhaps those didn't really compensate enough.'

Equally perfectionist, although more capable of compromise, Ron Dennis had his own frustrations that caused him to boil inside, some major, others minor. A petty one was the mechanics' habit of spilling tea, which he blamed partly on the tea lady who always filled the mugs to the brim. To avoid conflict and solve the problem, he came up with the bright idea of acquiring bigger mugs and instructing the tea lady to fill them only two-thirds full. It didn't work: either she wouldn't remember or the mechanics would ask for a top-up and all Ron's protestations — 'Hold on a second, I said don't fill them up, because they spill' — fell on deaf ears. As is often the way, this top-down solution led to another irritant, as Barnard recalls: 'Not only did they still spill tea, but they wasted a third of it because no one could drink it all.' The tribulations of micro-management.

A more significant problem that wound up both Dennis and Barnard was the mechanics' casual attitude to secrecy. Barnard was keen to keep his developments under wraps, something that didn't sit well with the mechanics, who, at the time, more so than now, were a chummy bunch merrily swapping jobs, jokes and even ideas across the teams. Barnard found it hard to persuade them to close the garage doors in the pit lane: 'They enjoyed watching the girls walk past.'

He found the secrecy ethos extremely difficult to instil. 'The mechanics didn't appreciate what we were doing at first. They'd say, "Oh, the others will find out sooner or later." I'd respond, "Well then, let's make it later!"'

John Watson saw their frustration first hand: 'When Barnard designed a car it was all precision — a mind-boggling amount of work. Prior to that uplift in technology, cars were built by artisans on metal jigs, but not necessarily with the level of accuracy that the drawing may have called for. It took John to create this culture where everything was designed so that when the car was in build, there was nothing to do but follow the instructions. The McLaren mechanics were honestly surprised that the finished car worked the way it was drawn.'

Their objections receded a little when they came to work on the MP4; it was totally new to them and very impressive. As Watson adds, 'They didn't understand carbon-fibre; they'd have put a drill through it.' They needed to learn from John's example how to treat it properly, and it was a hard lesson. Slowly some of them began to come round to the new technology and see its advantages. As Tyler Alexander pointed out, his tone indicating the reservations at the time, 'With carbon-fibre Barnard was doing something that was completely new, but if you stopped and thought about it, you figured, well, this is a pretty risky thing, but it could be quite interesting.'

Mayer and Alexander were put under pressure from their old machine-shop buddies. 'Why are you changing things so fast?' they'd ask. 'We're not changing anything; they are,' would be the reply, meaning, of course, that Barnard and Dennis were the culprits. On occasion someone would approach Dennis, get him to agree in principle and then quote him in arguments with Barnard: 'They'd just say, "Ron told me it was OK to do it this way", in an effort to get me steaming into his office.'

Ron remembers how effective the strategy was: 'Sometimes someone would go into John, whose office was below mine, and say something that would pop him onto the rev limiter. There was a carpeted wooden staircase that ran up to my office, so I got an audible warning that John was coming through the door on the rev limiter by the way he cleared two steps at a time on his way up, giving me just enough time to get prepped. It was usually as a consequence of someone winding him up. After a few times we realised that "divide and rule" was clearly the objective.'

But Ron and John were a close team and efforts to sew discord ultimately found no fertile ground; the two bosses learned to check in with each other to find out the truth of things. 'It was all so petty, such a waste of time,' says John, 'but I guess it was the nature of a forced marriage.' As Ron remembers: 'If someone came along and criticised either of us, we'd launch at them. And then we'd go away and argue on our own! We had some good arguments. But I think that was mostly our finding our way.'

The relationship between the two highly competitive Formula 1 newbies was fiery but worked well: 'We were good foils,' says Ron, 'especially in that era of Formula 1 when you had to be very fleet of foot. When we were working together, we were climbing the same mountain… we were helping each other up the mountain.'

A further aspect of Barnard's superhuman workload was his involvement in the creation of the new McLaren International factory in Woking. This was his first experience at having a hand in designing a bespoke motorsport manufacturing facility — something for which he would literally 'write the book' in later years.

'Boundary Road was not planned in detail,' he says. 'It was more a case of guestimates of what we needed, where the partitions would go. Nothing like the later, bigger, high-tech facilities I'd create at Ferrari and Benetton.' He adds that it was 'mainly done by the gang of Mr Fix-Its that Ron Dennis always seemed to be able to bring in.'

Being the Prince of Darkness wasn't easy. The continual pressure and the conflict began to change Barnard. In the past he had often gone out for drinks with his team colleagues, mechanics and principals, especially at Parnelli, which was probably the happiest, most uncomplicated time of his professional life. Now, concerned about compromising his authority and hardened by his conflicts with McLaren's 'Kiwi brigade', he became less inclined to socialise.

His focus was on ensuring that the MP4 was as perfect as possible despite the various obstacles that arose, with Teddy Mayer a primary source of new tensions in the design office. Mayer had the habit of breezing into the design office announcing, 'I've come to have a look', before trying to persuade the designers that something he'd just seen elsewhere in the paddock was a good idea. This exasperated Barnard. He coped with it by raising his eyes to heaven and saying to his staff, 'Old Ted's been reading Aerodynamics in the Encyclopaedia Britannica again.' He concedes that sometimes Mayer was capable of coming up with a good idea, but his presence in the design office was adding to the pressure, rather than relieving it.

Tyler Alexander revealed that Teddy enjoyed irritating Barnard: 'He actually knew some of the phrases or words that John was using, and that would have pissed off John, and Teddy knew that. He was an awkward guy: no matter what you talked about, Teddy knew better than you. And what really annoyed people was that most times he was right. This was one of the reasons why John and he didn't get on. Teddy used to poke his nose in and some people didn't like it. But he was interested in the cars and he had a very astute memory, and that's part of being good at going motor racing, because you remember the things that worked and the things that didn't and why.'

Elsewhere in Barnard's world, other butterflies were furiously flapping their wings. The prospective carbon car was whipping up a storm of protest within the FIA and ground-effect aerodynamics were coming into question because of the safety implications of ever-increasing cornering speeds. Politics weren't yet Barnard's concern, but they were soon going to be, and would go on to play an ever-increasing part in his life despite his best efforts to step around them like so much mess on a pavement.

Aerodynamics, however, were his concern. He was now finalising the bodywork and suspension for the MP4, and to do this would require yet another significant advance.

CHAPTER 14
BARNARD AND THE WHITE TORNADO
1979–82

It would be reasonable to think that inventing the carbon-fibre car was innovation enough for John Barnard's first year in partnership with Ron Dennis. You would, of course, be wrong. He also found time to make advances in wind-tunnel technology.

Soon after starting at Project Four, early in 1980, John went to Southampton University's R.J. Mitchell Wind Tunnel, a state-of-the-art research facility, complete with rolling road, named after the designer of the Spitfire. There he saw a model of an open-wheeled March race car being tested. Its wheels were made of wood and didn't turn, each instead having a flattened base that hovered just above the rolling road. While this provided approximate information about airflow over the wheels, Barnard was unimpressed.

'I thought it was a bit of a compromise,' John says. 'Surely we can do it better than this! Why can't we run rotating wheels? I put this question to the engineer there who looked at me in surprise as if no one had mentioned it before.'

They probably hadn't: running rotating wheels on a wind-tunnel model was quite a complication. This was partly because creating accurate model tyres that would sit on the rolling-road belt like real tyres was extremely difficult, but also because, to Barnard's knowledge, no one had managed to simulate suspension movement with any useful accuracy. There was also the issue that replica wheels pushing down on the moving belt would eventually start to wear grooves in the bed beneath the belt.

But Formula 1 wheels cause considerable turbulence. Predicting that turbulence and designing accordingly was bound to give an edge. Barnard began to contemplate how to create rotating miniature wheels with tyres that would distort under pressure just like real ones, and how to design a way to mimic a race car's suspension movement as accurately as possible.

Barnard tasked Alan Jenkins to find someone to make a suitable model wheel and tyre. Rather ingeniously, Nigel Hobden at Random Design came up with a foam tyre that could be glued to an aluminium wheel.

Barnard then started thinking about a way to connect the wheels to the car. His concern was that if they rotated on axles attached to the car, as in the real thing, they would fail to accurately represent racing loads: 'At the time it was thought that rotating wheels on the sprung part of the model car wouldn't give accurate readings and it was essential that the tyre should stay flat on the belt so that any airflow around the wheel wouldn't change with model attitude change.' In other words, if the model was moved, the wheels would probably tilt at the wrong angle in respect to the rolling road.

To get round this problem, John conjured up a 'stalk' system to support the model's wheels. Each wheel was carried at the inboard end of a horizontal stalk, an aerodynamically profiled rod of several feet in length, with the outboard end sturdily mounted to the wind-tunnel floor. The wheels, running on bearings that slid over spindles on the stalks, would lightly touch the rolling road and rotate accordingly, staying level in relation to the moving surface.

The next problem was to connect these wheels to the model without transferring load from the stalks and wheels. John's solution was ingenious. For each suspension upright, he designed two protruding blades between which the stalk spindle would rest, locating the wheel in the right position relative to the upright; if the model moved up or down, the wheel always stayed flat on the rolling road.

This was just the beginning. Barnard also wanted to simulate changes in ride height to see their effect on aerodynamic performance. To do this, he suspended the model from the ceiling by a rod attached to the driver's helmet, so that, by adjusting the rod, he could raise or lower the car without affecting the contact of the tyres with the rolling road — and do so with the tunnel running.

Meanwhile, competitors were also making strenuous efforts to improve the accuracy of their wind-tunnel evaluation. The record is sketchy here — such firsts are difficult to prove — but both Patrick Head and Peter Wright talk of similar developments in this area at Williams and Lotus. But Wright comments: 'Pirelli now provides the teams with model tyres with exactly the right characteristics so they squish down the right amount. If John was the first person to make foam tyres, then he started that particular road. We used to move the body of the car through a full range of ride heights but we stopped the tunnel each time to adjust it. Our suspension simulation was unlikely to have been anything like as good as John's — it looks like he took it to a level beyond.'

Using Barnard's new wind-tunnel methods wasn't plain sailing. It was tricky to get the set-up right and the foam tyres proved problematic, requiring regular reshaping to keep them perfectly round. As Jenkins reports, 'It was a bit of a game.'

This work made John hanker after a wind tunnel of his own. Time at Southampton was restricted and he felt the tunnel operators lacked sufficient commitment to the immediate needs of motorsport: 'It was too much of a university set-up; they were more concerned with principles than the detail.' He knew that to get control of the detail McLaren must somehow acquire their own tunnel — yet another immensely expensive undertaking.

Ron Dennis reveals another factor in the growing frustration with Southampton. Both Ron and John were 'paranoid' about secrecy, so when they discovered new fixing points in the tunnel, which suggested that someone else was using a stalk method for rotating wheels, things became somewhat heated: 'We immediately realised that someone at Southampton had told one of our competition what we were doing, and they were copying us. We could have killed at that moment, we were so incensed. And whereas I was normally there to moderate John, I was actually there amplifying John! We had a sneaky suspicion who had leaked it — one of the technicians — and it was a big breakthrough at the time.'

A solution presented itself one day in the spring of 1981, when Ron came striding into Barnard's office with a newspaper in his hand: 'Have you seen this? The National Maritime Institute at Teddington is boasting about its wind tunnels.' Barnard picked up the phone and arranged an appointment. Within weeks they had a deal to hire one of the Teddington tunnels exclusively for McLaren, apart from six weeks per year during which the operators would be testing torpedoes. McLaren could even build their own rolling road.

The rolling road was designed in the drawing office under Barnard's supervision and he assigned Beresford to work with Jenkins on it, while Project Four's Neil Trundle put it together: 'These people really came into their own. They created what was without doubt the best wind-tunnel facility in Formula 1.'

The Teddington wind tunnel was a loop, with a large fan on one side and a working section on the other. The working section, where the model could be suspended from a ceiling balance, had been made especially large to accommodate work on secret torpedo projects, so it provided plenty of room for working on a race car. The new rolling road — a wide, flat, rubber-impregnated canvas belt running on rollers — would move at speeds to match the wind blowing through the tunnel, which meant the boundary layer on the 'road' surface was dramatically reduced, as John explains:

'So you now have the floor of the tunnel running at the same speed as the air in the tunnel. The model is stationary, suspended above the road on a balance, but everything else is moving. This is as close as you can get to replicating a car moving through stationary air, and the best way of getting a more accurate representation of airflow under the car.'

To keep the rolling road flat, they concocted a system of vacuum pumps under the belt to suck it down onto the rollers. Jenkins says there was serendipity in the system: 'Almost accidentally it helped reduce the boundary layer. It was a great bit of kit.'

But when the whole affair was moving at racing speeds, the rubber-coated road, sucked onto the rollers, became hotter and hotter. Eventually it began to billow black smoke that quickly filled the tunnel, bringing everything to a stop. It took a while to judge the amount of suction required at different wind speeds.

Working with the ceiling balance used for measuring the car's downforce was also tricky. Jenkins: 'It had a conventional balance, which was a wonderful bit of kit, but the bloke who'd designed it was about 93 and the only one who knew how it worked! It took a massive effort just to get the tunnel to work and keep working all day.'

McLaren's use of the Teddington wind tunnel was replete with innovation. Learning from the Southampton experience, and taking advantage of a larger, more complex balance, Barnard made the model car even more adjustable, allowing the team to alter roll and pitch as well as ride height.

First he drilled a hole transversely through the model's sidepods to take a metal rod of about 8mm diameter. Each end of this rod went into a ball joint connected to a vertical stalk that was attached to the ceiling balance. Now, with the car suspended between these two stalks, Barnard could simulate roll in a corner by lifting one or the other while also having the ability to use both to change the ride height.

To simulate changes in the car's pitch, Barnard created 'the sting', a long, thin, tapering rod projecting horizontally from the centre rear of the model. At the end of the sting a connecting wire ran up to the ceiling balance.

As John makes clear, 'With these three mounting points, we could lift the model up and down, changing the pitch and the roll angle. We could twist it like it was diving into a corner.' It was an unprecedented level of control.

The system even allowed simulation of aerodynamic bounce, or porpoising, an intermittent effect that plagued ground-effect cars. It took Barnard a while to understand its causes: 'The wind tunnel revealed that at certain points on a given circuit the car created so much suction that the skirts would be sucked inwards and off the ground. With the seal broken, air rushed in and the car would suddenly pop up on its suspension. A few seconds later the ground-effect would reassert itself, sucking the car down again, before, once more, it would bounce upwards.'

One drawback of the wind-tunnel adjustment system, because the model wasn't rigidly fixed, was that the distance between the base of the model and the rolling road couldn't be precisely determined. As John says, 'You might set the model ride height for 20mm and not see that the car had been sucked down to 15mm.' So he made a thin aluminium wheel to run on the surface of the rolling road and attached it to a lever arm that was able to turn a rotary control on a potentiometer, an electronic device much like a volume knob. If the ride height changed, the angle of the lever arm would change correspondingly, the 'volume' level would be turned and an electronic read-out would reveal how far the car had risen or fallen.

Barnard appointed Jenkins as chief wind-tunnel tester: 'This is when Alan really came into his own. He wasn't trained in aerodynamics, but he was meticulous. If he got a result that didn't seem to make sense, he would work until it did. We'd repeat and repeat to check the numbers. And if they weren't coming out the same Alan would be back there, going at it, fiddling with it, to make sure that the model produced the same numbers.

'And I tell you, when we built stuff and put it on the car, it nearly always made it quicker.'

Meanwhile, Barnard was revelling in the highly charged atmosphere of Formula 1: 'I was impressed by the sheer competitiveness of it all. Champcar [Indycar] racing is OK, but in F1 you're working hard to get onto the grid, let alone win.'[27] This intense competition led to a surprise for Barnard early in

---

[27] *Henry, Alan*, Motoring News, *'McLaren's New Designer'*, 23 April 1981, p3.

1981 when he discovered that the extraordinary Lotus 88 also had a carbon monocoque. This car turned out to be Colin Chapman's Formula 1 swansong, and here, if we may, we take a short but relevant diversion into Chapman's extraordinary world.

Colin Chapman is widely considered to have been the greatest genius in motorsport, with revolutions in suspension, monocoque design, engine development, wing technology and ground-effect all credited to him in varying degrees. Beyond all that, this instinctive, inspired engineer was also a pioneering motorsport entrepreneur, probably responsible more than anyone else for making Britain the world centre of motorsport design excellence. Chapman was, up to a point, Ron Dennis and John Barnard rolled into one.

Balanced against these extraordinary achievements is the tragic fact that at least six racing drivers died in Lotuses, including three of the sport's most famous names, Jim Clark, Jochen Rindt and Ronnie Peterson. Chapman's cars, some thought, went too far in the quest for lightness and therefore weren't always strong enough.

By the time of his sudden death in 1982 amid the ignominy of the DeLorean scandal, Chapman had built thousands of successful race and road cars, and between 1962 and 1978 Lotus had won seven Constructors' titles and six Drivers' titles in Formula 1, plus the Indy 500. He was, literally, a legend in his own lifetime.

Having led the way with ground-effect, now Chapman was up against new blood and his Lotus 88 was an extraordinary attempt at further innovation. Ground-effect had become so powerful that drivers were becoming exhausted by the muscular battle against the forces involved, some complaining of blacking out. Another negative for drivers was the super-stiff suspension, which made the ride distractingly uncomfortable and, despite ground-effect, created problems with grip.

'Before ground-effect,' says Barnard, 'we ran springs with rates of around 500 pounds per inch. Now we were talking about spring rates of 3,500. The result was rock-solid suspensions, which wasn't good, because, up to a point, the more flexible the suspension the better the grip while cornering; you need all four wheels free to move independently of each other as a car goes over kerbs and bumps, so that they all stay on the ground and stop the car sliding sideways.'

Chapman's remarkable solution was to create a 'double chassis' for the Lotus 88. The inner chassis, which housed the driver, consisted of a monocoque partly made of carbon-fibre to which the engine, main suspension, uprights and wheels were fitted. Built around this was the outer chassis, which was in effect one big ground-effect system comprising bodywork, sidepods, skirts, underwing floor, front wing and rear wing, all suspended independently via stiff rubber mounts attached to the four wheel uprights.

'It was a superb, if complex, solution,' Barnard explains. 'He had the wings effectively fixed directly to the wheels, just like the old days. On top of this he had the ground-effect tunnels similarly attached. All the downforce was diverted to the wheels via the uprights.'

The outer chassis would handle all the aerodynamics and downforce while the inner chassis would handle acceleration and braking loads. By splitting the forces between the two chassis, the car would run flatter, meaning that airflow under it would be more stable and less inclined to be disturbed by roll or bumps, while the driver, sitting in the inner chassis, would be better protected and have a much smoother ride. That, at least, was the theory, and Barnard was most impressed.

The fact that the Lotus 88's inner chassis was partly made of carbon-fibre has led some experts to claim that Chapman beat Barnard to this particular innovation. But in 2011 journalist David Tremayne revealed in the 'e-zine' *Grand Prix+* that Lotus didn't decide to make the monocoque out of carbon until late September 1980, quoting Lotus team manager Peter Collins:[28] 'The decision to make a carbon-fibre chassis for 1981 was taken just before the races in Montréal and Watkins Glen in 1980.' As the Canadian race took place on 28 September, it seems reasonable to surmise that Chapman was inspired to build a carbon-fibre chassis by Ron Dennis's 'space age' press conference that announced Barnard's carbon car to the world on 9 September, almost a year after John had made his initial decision.

More importantly, and perhaps as a result of the late decision to go for carbon, the Lotus 88's use of the material was very compromised. The inner chassis was built, in Barnard's words, 'like a Kellogg's cornflakes packet'. According to Patrick Head, 'they bonded up the carbon-fibre honeycomb in the flat under a massive press and then routed out bits and folded it up like origami.'

Lotus designer Peter Wright specified panels of carbon-fibre cloth and Kevlar

---

[28] Tremayne, David, 'Carbon Dating', Grand Prix+, numbers 78 (Malaysia 2011) and 79 (China 2011).

laid over Nomex (fireproof plastic) honeycomb to create a composite sandwich, in contrast to Barnard's use of unidirectional carbon-fibre over aluminium honeycomb. Lotus's panels were then cured in an autoclave before being fixed to an aluminium framework, by folding the panels over bulkheads and gluing them into position; Barnard, of course, fired his entire chassis in an autoclave. Lotus's method also broke what Barnard considers the primary rule of building a monocoque out of carbon-fibre — 'there should be as few joins as possible' — and didn't come near the integrity of his purist approach.

In truth Lotus's carbon monocoque was a half-way house, little more than an incremental development of the way other teams were already using carbon-fibre.

But Colin Chapman would not and could not give his designers the time or the money to perfect their use of the new material with access to aerospace expertise. In the words of Peter Collins as quoted in Tremayne's article, 'Whenever I suggested to the Old Man that the schedule would now slip, he just wouldn't tolerate it.'

Known as the 'White Tornado' for his habit of whipping through the Lotus works and blowing away anyone he thought was slacking, Chapman, aged 53, putting on weight and sporting a shock of white hair, was under severe pressure. Group Lotus was in serious financial trouble with sales of its road cars — the Esprit, Elite and Eclat — having collapsed to a third of their level of only two years earlier. Chapman desperately needed his race team to attract more sponsorship and publicity by creating another Lotus revolution on the track and to do it in short order. For the team working on the Lotus 88, which also included Peter Wright and Martin Ogilvie, there was no time to 'do it properly', as Barnard puts it.

Wright concedes the point: 'We had a completely different approach, and being Lotus, we did it all ourselves, and in about two and a half months! And Barnard's was the right solution — that's the direction in which carbon-fibre went.'

When the Lotus 88 was first tested at the Paul Ricard circuit in the south of France in late February 1981, just a week before the McLaren MP4's inaugural run, it seemed to be doomed from the outset. In Peter Collins's words, 'I don't think that it would ever have been successful in the form in which it appeared. It had... serious understeer, which made it really hard to turn in because of the massive downforce that it generated.'

In fact the Lotus 88 was never allowed to race in a Formula 1 Grand Prix.

In a stinging press release Chapman blamed 'unbearable pressure' from a lobby of rivals whom he accused of leaning on Formula 1's governing body, claiming they were 'frightened that once again we are setting a trend they may all have to follow'. His dismay was made all the sharper by the fact that the Lotus 88 was twice accepted by race scrutineers and allowed to practise before being banned each time by the FIA just before the start.

Brabham designer Gordon Murray explained at the time why he reckoned the FIA was right[29]: 'It [the Lotus 88] infringes the rule that says that any specific part of the car having an aerodynamic influence must remain immobile relative to the entirely sprung part of the car. The only way the Lotus could be changed to conform would be for the bodywork to be rigidly attached to the main monocoque. It's a bloody good idea, though, but it's not legal. We'd all like to separate the loads in that fashion, but we can't. It contravenes the regulations so blatantly that it's not really even a good try.'

Barnard's carbon car had far more significant implications for Formula 1 than anything offered by Chapman's Lotus 88 and it too would come under the political spotlight.

As the MP4 neared completion, political turmoil engulfed Formula 1, essentially in a battle over its governance. On one side, headed by Jean-Marie Balestre, was FISA (Fédération Internationale du Sport Automobile), an autonomous sub-committee of the FIA (Fédération Internationale de l'Automobile). On the other was FOCA (Formula One Constructors' Association), run by Brabham owner Bernie Ecclestone with former barrister and racing driver Max Mosley as his right-hand man.

As FOCA had steadily taken increasing control of commercial and operational aspects of Formula 1, formerly the preserve of the FIA, Balestre set out to regain the initiative. The battleground on which he chose to reassert FISA's authority was ground-effect. As we have seen, the use of ground-effect to improve cornering performance had given the Cosworth-powered teams, which were mostly British and loyal to FOCA, an advantage that the FISA-aligned manufacturer teams — the 'grandee' teams of Ferrari, Alfa Romeo and Renault, but Ferrari especially — were countering by investing in high-powered turbo engines. The bombshell, for the FOCA *garagiste* teams, came in February 1980 when Balestre announced a ban on the use of sliding skirts

---

[29] *Tremayne, David, 'Carbon Dating',* Grand Prix+, *number 79 (China 2011).*

for the 1981 season. The so-called FISA/FOCA war escalated, with FOCA threatening to run a breakaway series, until a deal was reached on 19 January 1981 at the FIA's headquarters on Paris's Place de la Concorde. Under this Concorde Agreement, FISA's responsibility for governance was confirmed — and with it the ban on sliding skirts — while FOCA acquired important commercial rights, crucially for television, an outcome that would come to enrich all Formula 1 teams and make Ecclestone a multi-billionaire.

Balestre, considered by many to be a puffed-up Machiavel, had won the support of Ferrari and Renault in part by creating rules that would favour them. So it was perhaps not surprising that anxiety was growing in high places over the carbon-fibre car, and that Balestre was attentive to Ferrari's concerns about a development completely beyond their technology at the time. John Hogan recalls that at the last race of 1980, at Watkins Glen, months before the carbon car first ran, Ecclestone approached Teddy Mayer and told him that Balestre was determined to ban it, and was planning to justify this by declaring the new material dangerous.

It never happened. Hogan believes that Chapman, as another adopter of carbon-fibre in his twin-chassis Lotus 88, may have had a hand in this because he was 'the designer nobody would argue with'. It's possible that the carbon chassis was saved from attack by Balestre because Chapman's double chassis was considered more of a threat, and perhaps Balestre realised he couldn't ban everything the British innovators came up with. Meanwhile, one person who heard nothing of this, because it was kept from him, was Barnard himself, who only learned of the move to ban his baby during the writing of this book.

At Brabham, Gordon Murray quickly found an ingenious way to circumvent the new regulations. Skirts themselves hadn't been banned, just the use of sliding mechanisms, and additionally there was a stipulation that ride height should be at least six centimetres, enforced by measurement of a car while it was at rest. So Murray equipped the BT49C with a hydro-pneumatic suspension system that lowered the car when out on the circuit, allowing the skirts — rigid ones — to make contact with the track surface. This was, in effect, a more complex version of Barnard's initiative for the Project Four Formula 3 car, which, as described earlier, used soft springs to get it over a height-measuring bump in the pit lane before full ground-effect out on track compressed the springs and put the skirts in contact with the tarmac.

Bizarrely, FISA ruled Murray's development 'legal'. Balestre's decision blew away his own arguments about the dangers of ground-effect, demonstrating what everyone in the paddock already knew, that the entire skirts issue was really little more than a political football. Balestre's volte-face was so ridiculous that it prompted journalist Nigel Roebuck to comment in the *Autocourse* annual: 'People scratched their heads in amazement. It was as if the Vatican had okayed the Pill — so long as you didn't use it to keep from getting pregnant.'[30]

Barnard recalls discussing Murray's move with Ron and concluded that it was 'a flagrant breach of regulations precisely because it was a system designed to break the regulation, and therefore how could you allow it? But it was allowed.' John himself took a different route, choosing not to develop a 'fancy system of hydraulics', which carried a weight penalty, but instead to use a variation of his Formula 3 idea.

As the 1981 season got underway, Colin Chapman, of course, was furious at being stopped from racing his twin-chassis Lotus 88, and Barnard's sympathies are firmly with him. 'I thought the double chassis was a brilliant idea. True, it pushed the rules to their limit but personally I think Ferrari, ever terrified by major innovation, moved to get rid of it. It was a great shame it was banned; it kept the aerodynamic platform stable and at a consistent height from the ground — it was the forerunner to active suspension.'

Since first becoming involved in motor racing, John had been in awe of Chapman, the only figure in the sport to have his deepest respect, except perhaps for Enzo Ferrari. As John was new to Formula 1, he only met Chapman for the first time on 12 April 1981, the day of the MP4's racing début at the Argentine Grand Prix, while waiting in the departure lounge of Ministro Pistarini International Airport outside Buenos Aires.

'I was sitting on my own when I spotted Colin Chapman pacing across the lounge. I watched him turn, spot me and come marching over. He bent down, shook my hand and said, "That's a bloody good chassis you've done there, I like that." I thought, "Oh shit, it's Colin Chapman talking to me!" I said, "Oh, thank you, Colin."'

Chapman wasn't in the habit of congratulating other designers for coming up with a design better than his own. In a symbolic sense, this moment was the passing of the torch of motorsport innovation from one British genius to another. To use David Tremayne's words, Barnard had created a revolution

---

[30] *Roebuck, Nigel, 'A year of mistakes', Autocourse 1981–82, Hazleton Publishing, 1981, p22.*

that was 'as important, as ground-breaking, as Stirling Moss's victory in Argentina in 1958 in the mid-engined Cooper; an event that changed the course of racing.'[31]

Few would now disagree that John Barnard's carbon-fibre monocoque was the greatest innovation in motorsport since the engine was moved behind the driver. There has been nothing on the same scale since, nothing, at least, that has stood the test of time.

Barnard still holds Chapman's torch. There is no one to take it from him, nor is there ever likely to be. Today a Formula 1 design office is 400-strong and backed up by computers of ever-increasing power. No single individual can make the sort of comprehensive, step-change contributions made by Chapman and Barnard. The era of the lone revolutionary in technology is over. We may never see their like again.

---

[31] Tremayne, David, 'Carbon Dating', Grand Prix+, *numbers 78 (Malaysia 2011) and 79 (China 2011).*

CHAPTER 15
RACING THE CARBON CAR
1981

It is a truth universally acknowledged that a car needs four first-class elements to make it a winner, that each element is as important as another, and that if any element is below par sustained winning is impossible. To win the Constructors' Championship, a team's cars must have the best chassis/aerodynamic package, the best engine, the best drivers and the best tyres.

At the beginning of the 1981 season, of these four McLaren had only one — the best chassis/aerodynamic package. The Cosworth engine lacked the power of its turbocharged rivals and the Michelin tyres were causing all sorts of grief. As for drivers, John Watson was very good but his new team-mate, rookie Andrea De Cesaris, was not.

In contrast to Wattie, De Cesaris never won either Barnard's respect or affection. Both Ron and John thought he simply wasn't up to the task, but he had come to the team as part of the deal with Marlboro. He had only competed in two Formula 1 races before his arrival at McLaren and hadn't finished either of them. For now they were stuck with him, as Ron explains:

'With Prost gone, we were faced with a hole in the team and that was, unfortunately, when the opportunity for De Cesaris to be imposed upon us presented itself. Aleardo Buzzi [Marlboro European President] was saying that De Cesaris's father was a distributor of [Philip Morris] product and that Andrea was more than capable of doing the job. So obviously we had to run for some time with Andrea.'

Barnard adds: 'De Cesaris seemed nervous. I thought the stress was just too much for him to handle.' John also complains that he was poor at providing feedback to his engineers — a big flaw.

By early 1981 Barnard had reinforced his design office with three existing Team McLaren people — Mike Lock, Colin Smith and John Baldwin. The team was busy fitting the MP4 with glass-fibre bodywork, newly designed front and rear suspension, and a Cosworth engine complete with a gearbox casting that Ron Dennis had secured from Tyrrell.

Work was also continuing in the wind tunnel. Alan Jenkins recalls John's typical day, which involved going home for lunch, coming back, going home for dinner and returning again: 'I remember coming back in the evening to run through the wind-tunnel tests with him. He had babies coming along, so he had a priority to spend some time with his family, and why not.'

Rosie gave birth to their second daughter, Gillian Ann, on Friday 6 February 1981 at around 8am at Farnham Park Hospital in Guildford. John made sure that this time he was there: 'I remember the nurse coming into the waiting room and declaring, "You'll want to be there at the birth", before pushing me into the room. I think I was a bit reluctant. I remember Gillian was born with no hair, and stayed bald for 18 months. I've always joked it was because the sight of her father at the moment of her birth was such a shock.' The shock, perhaps, was mutual.

The MP4 was now complete and first ran on 5 March at a test session at Silverstone. Now Ron Dennis's mission was to reward his old friend John Hogan for the massive risk he had taken in persuading his bosses to finance the fledging team and the brand-new technology. Barnard had built the most advanced and expensive race car in the world so, as Hogan had put it, 'It had better bloody well win.'

John Barnard flew back to his old California stomping ground for the first race of the season, the United States Grand Prix (West) at Long Beach on 15 March. The sights for the new car had been set high, Ron Dennis having told John Hogan, 'You've made the best investment of your life — Barnard's car will win at least one Grand Prix this year.' It was a bold claim from a man totally new to running a Formula 1 team and one that Barnard himself would never have made. Such was the bravado of Ron Dennis.

Long Beach showed how easy it is to talk the talk. Pre-race practice and qualifying sessions revealed that John Watson's MP4 had problems with fuel pressure and its exhaust system, the hot pipes of which burned the bodywork. In the end Watson qualified in a back-up M29 on the last row of the grid, one position behind his team-mate's M29. 'De Crasheris' promptly had his first crash of the season, on the first lap. Watson only made it to lap 16, retiring with engine trouble. Barnard was embarrassed: 'It looked bad, really amateur, made worse by being on Hercules's home ground.'[32]

The singleton MP4 wasn't taken to Brazil, two weeks later, after wet weather in England prevented Barnard from completing further tests with it, so its next appearance — and race début — came in Argentina on 12 April. Watson qualified 11th and got up to sixth place in the race until, on lap 35, he felt a sudden vibration at the back of the car. To a groan of disappointment in the McLaren garage, he retired soon after with transmission problems.

A second MP4 was ready for the San Marino Grand Prix at Imola on 3 May and both cars were available to Watson as Barnard wasn't yet ready to entrust one to De Cesaris. Perhaps because he was fired up in front of his home crowd, the Italian driver, to everyone's surprise, finished sixth in his M29 while the team leader in his chosen MP4 could only manage 10th after hitting the back of a Renault on the fifth lap.

The next race, at Belgium's Zolder circuit on 17 May, brought slight improvement with Watson seventh in one of the MP4s, while De Cesaris, still in an M29, went out with gearbox trouble on lap 11.

At the Monaco Grand Prix, where John and Ron bit the bullet and gave De Cesaris an MP4, things were no better — neither driver finished. As at Long Beach, De Cesaris departed the field after some wild driving on the first lap, first hitting Prost's Renault and then taking out Mario Andretti's Alfa Romeo, much to the eye-rolling irritation of Barnard. Watson lasted until lap 53, when he retired from fifth place with engine trouble.

Fortune, it seemed, was reluctant to favour the brave new car, but at least it was getting a thorough testing of its impact resistance. Ron Dennis's nervous tick of a smile was wearing out his lip muscles. But if the wheel of fortune turns downwards, then so must it rise again upon the other side, and things took a turn for the better at Jarama in Spain. Before the race Barnard made some changes, creating new skirts and adding scoops to duct air around the brakes. The outcome was that Watson qualified third, while De Cesaris also looked destined for a good grid position until he spun off and damaged the car. Come the start, Watson's MP4 was part of a race-long train at the front, one of four cars queued tightly behind Gilles Villeneuve's Ferrari, unable to

---

[32] 'Profile: John Barnard, the Man who Rejuvenated McLaren', by Doug Nye, Road & Track, March 1982.

get by because the Italian car's turbocharged power advantage outstripped the superiority of its rivals through corners. That situation stayed unchanged right to the chequered flag, with Watson third, only half a second behind winner Villeneuve. As for De Cesaris, he spun out on lap 10.

Would it get any better? The next stop was France at the Dijon-Prenois circuit. Here Watson qualified second, sandwiched by Renaults, and De Cesaris fifth. As *Autocourse* reported, 'Watson said the MP4 felt superb through the fast corners — and that's where it counted most. The slow corners still weren't right but Watson's impressively steady line and a constant engine note through the Courbe de Pouas [a long right-hander] and onto the straight left no doubt about the quality of the car. Even Andrea de Cesaris seemed able to do remarkable deeds with his MP4...'[33]

In the race Watson joined battle in sunshine and rain with his former teammate, Alain Prost, and came in two seconds behind the Frenchman's Renault. They congratulated each other on the podium, recalling the horrors of the previous year when they were driving for a dying Team McLaren.

For Prost it was an unforgettable moment, his first Grand Prix victory, achieved, like the climax to a romantic novel, on home soil with his countrymen going berserk in the stands. As he said later, 'before, you thought you could do it; now you know you can'[34]. De Cesaris finished 11th after having to pit with a loose wheel nut.

Next came Silverstone. Could Watson, like Prost, win on home soil? That would certainly be one in the eye for the yesteryear doubters within McLaren International. Could Ron Dennis fulfil his promise to John Hogan of winning at least one Grand Prix that year? Even better, could he do it at the Marlboro British Grand Prix?

As Watson recalls, 'Third in Spain, second in France... people were saying, "John, you've got to win the British Grand Prix!"'

If it was to be, Wattie could never have told from the omens, the first of which was having his VW Golf GTi broken into a few days before the race. The portents became even more disturbing when, arriving at Silverstone on race day by light aircraft, he was confronted by a jobsworth who refused him entry to the circuit on the grounds that he wasn't wearing his pass. As the most famous British driver in the Grand Prix, Watson was somewhat miffed: 'I knew

---

[33] Autocourse 1981–82, *Hazleton Publishing, p148.*
[34] *Donaldson, Gerald, 'Alain Prost',* Formula One Space — weebly.com.

he knew who I was; I guess he was having his moment in the sun.' As other VIPs passed by, Wattie had to rummage through his luggage to find proof of who he was.

Things hadn't gone exactly according to plan the previous day. Although he had been confident of pole position, Watson found himself fifth on the grid after his qualifying laps had to be interrupted by frenetic adjustments in the McLaren pits in an effort to find the elusive perfect balance that the team had managed to achieve for him in testing the week before. De Cesaris was just one hundredth of second slower — Silverstone was a circuit the Italian both knew and liked.

On Sunday 18 July the stands at Silverstone were packed, the paddock achatter about the fate of Nigel Mansell in his Lotus 88, the controversial car having been dusted off after a six-race lay-off only to be banned again. But the crowd's disappointment at one British driver going out was tempered by a growing expectation of what Wattie might achieve, despite his qualifying position and the raw power of the turbocharged opposition, particularly the two Renaults on the front row.

Watson wasn't too concerned about his grid slot; the turbos performed well in single-lap qualifying runs but their reliability and pace over a race distance were still in question. As Watson points out, 'The heavier turbocharged cars struggled a bit on their tyres in the race itself, the Cosworth-engined cars being more nimble, so as long as I could get by I would have a chance to consolidate. When you've got a good car it makes passing a lot more straightforward. Part of the skill of overtaking is putting your target under pressure and not allowing them to think that you will hold back — you come, you execute and you move on; you don't piss around.'

All good in theory, but Watson's positive thinking was undermined by a poor start. By the end of lap one he had dropped to seventh place, passed by Villeneuve's Ferrari and Alan Jones's Williams. With 67 laps to go, however, he still wasn't particularly concerned; he could feel, by lap three, that he was going to start reeling in the leaders — but as his confidence grew it all went wrong.

The incident happened in full view of the main stands at the Woodcote chicane leading into the start/finish straight. Villeneuve was just ahead of Jones, with the two McLaren drivers chasing. With vivid emotion, Wattie explained: 'That hyperactive child called Gilles Villeneuve, who was driving the Ferrari in a wholly irresponsible manner — highly entertaining for the public but much like a hooligan — lost control on the chicane: smoke everywhere.' Villeneuve skidded broadside across the track, leaving Jones nowhere to go but straight into the side of the Ferrari. Watson, a wily old fox, 'was looking beyond Alan's gearbox further through the corner, so I just had time to get on the brakes and avoid contact with anyone'. He skidded onto the grass verge and stalled while Jones and Villeneuve were still spinning in the tyre smoke.

De Cesaris showed less foresight; with his rookie eyes locked on the gearbox of Watson's MP4, he threw his car to the left to avoid the disgrace of taking out his team-mate, flew over the grass and smashed his MP4 hard into the barrier. It was a substantial shunt, but to the amazement of the doomsayers the carbon chassis stayed in one piece and De Cesaris emerged unscathed.

Meanwhile, stalled but still moving, Watson had the presence of mind to flick on the fuel pump, select second gear, release the clutch and so 'bump start' the car using its momentum.

By now three other cars had flown by — Andretti's Alfa Romeo and the Ligiers of Patrick Tambay and Jacques Laffite — and Watson lay 10th. All fired up, however, and driving beautifully, he was back in fifth place within nine laps, having overtaken all three of those usurpers and also watched Nelson Piquet's Brabham crash out at Maggots after a tyre failure.

Then came Wattie's sweetest move of the race. At the end of lap 12 he showed the crowd how the chicane should be handled by using it to overtake Carlos Reutemann's Williams for fourth place. By the end of the next lap he was third, Didier Pironi's Ferrari turbo engine having given up the ghost in a spectral puff of blue smoke. Just the two turbocharged Renaults of Prost and René Arnoux were ahead. The home crowd were getting very excited.

They were thrilled when, at the end of lap 17, Prost peeled off into the pits, retiring from the lead with a valve failure in the engine. Wattie was now second, 25 seconds behind Arnoux. Only 51 laps to go...

In truth, while the early laps had been intensely exciting, with nine cars forced out of the running by crashes or technical failure, the race now became something of a procession. But the crowd's collective ears pricked up on lap 51 when the remaining Renault suddenly began to sound off-song — something was ailing on the French car. Now Watson was catching it at the rate of two or three seconds per lap. Amid the spectators there were, as *Autocourse* put it, 'unparalleled scenes of delight'. With 13 laps to go, the gap was down to ten seconds.

Even Barnard was getting excited, and, desperate to do something but not having anything to do, he picked this moment to go for a walk towards Copse

Corner, telling Alan Jenkins and Steve Nichols to come with him. Alan thought, 'I want to stay with everyone else in the pits. We might win the bloody race!' As for Steve, it was 'a sort of relief valve — nice that he didn't just wander off on his own and that he grabbed Alan and me like he wanted his protégés with him, because he didn't normally do that sort of thing. There wasn't usually that sort of connection… so that was quite impressive.'

By lap 59 of the 68, Wattie was only 2.5 seconds behind and the crowd realised that he might actually overtake Arnoux within a few laps. The magic moment came on lap 61 as the McLaren flew down towards Copse right on Arnoux's tail. Barnard, Jenkins and Nichols watched them blast by, just a few feet apart. The next bend was the Maggots left-hander followed by the sharper right of Becketts; Arnoux braked, but Watson, having set himself up for the pass at Maggots, was able to brake later, and nipped through to take the lead; Silverstone erupted.

Alan turned to John and asked, 'Wouldn't it be a good idea to be back in the garage?' They started striding quickly back towards the pits. Jenkins adds, 'The huge thing was the crowd. We were in our McLaren uniforms and were recognised and cheered. It was brilliant, the first time I'd ever been involved in anything like that.'

Seven laps to go and Watson was trying to ignore the standing ovation he was getting each time he passed the stands: 'I could sense the crowd's expectation and anticipation. I couldn't hear it so much, but I could see in my peripheral vision that people were standing up and applauding. I tried not to let it affect me, because the most difficult thing a driver has to do at that point is not lose his rhythm and not assume it was his victory. I remember a race in 1977 that I led until halfway round the final lap. I thought I had won, but then I ran out of fuel. So I didn't want to internally acknowledge this was my race.'

This was a man on the cusp of winning only his second Grand Prix, and his first in front of his home crowd. He mustn't cock it up, but he was in a rhythm, flying round the track to his own internal beat, and he didn't dare upset it. As he came creaming past the pit lane on one of the concluding laps, Ron Dennis leaned right out over the track, terrified that the coming apotheosis would disappear with a cloud of tyre smoke or in spent fuel. He waved frantically at Wattie, screaming, 'Slow down, slow down!'

Watson remembers it with a smile: 'There was no one near me to challenge. Arnoux was slowing [soon to retire with another valve failure] and the next nearest car [Reutemann's] was some 40 seconds behind. So I gradually reduced the engine revs, which at the time we were running at 11,000 or 12,000 rpm, gradually dropping some 2,000 revs, and yet only losing a few tenths of a second per lap. Still Ron was screaming.'

As Watson zipped through the Woodcote chicane for the last time, he saw the avenue of delirious fans ahead of him and, to his right, a man furiously waving a chequered flag.

It was, he admits, one of the most glorious moments of his life. He raised his hand 'gingerly' as he crossed the line, the crowd in raptures: 'The feeling of your first British Grand Prix win is like getting laid for the first time — you dream of this moment all through your adolescence and all of a sudden it's there in front of you.'

The significance of this win cannot be underestimated. McLaren International had arrived, Ron Dennis was beaming, and John Hogan had verified to his Marlboro bosses that his risky investment was going to pay off. The Marlboro British Grand Prix had been a Marlboro triumph.

John Watson was absolutely ecstatic, his family, watching from the paddock, delighted, and Alan Jenkins was 'leaping about like a cat on a hot tin roof'. Even John Barnard allowed himself a smile or two — for him, like Watson, this was a first victory on home soil. It marked the prelude to McLaren's decade of dominance.

John explains why he took Nichols and Jenkins on that casual stroll away from the pit lane. 'I had already been in racing for ten years and had experienced big victories in the States. For Alan Jenkins, it had been a meteoric flight — from part-time work at Rebaque to F1 victory at Silverstone in just 18 months. I had learned to calm things down.'

For Barnard, it was important for his engineers and designers to come to at least some of the races and see how the car performed. But the other important factor, he claims, was to teach his team self-control: 'My approach to racing is to imagine it as a sine wave. The more I can reduce the amplitude, both plus and minus, the better; amplitude in terms of emotional response as well as in the general approach to what we're doing. I always found that the worst time was at the end of the race — the let-down. It was no better if you had won. Either way you reach the end of this incredibly highly active, highly emotional, highly stressed weekend. Suddenly, it's all gone. You get this huge trough after each race. It's common in sport, the low after the adrenalin rush. So whenever we had a big success in a race, I was always trying to nip the top off the wave so it didn't get out of control. "Just keep your feet on the ground boys. There's another race coming up, and we're going to have to be faster."'

Although Ron Dennis was happy, his day was marred by De Cesaris's accident: 'When he damaged a car, I could feel it — as far as I was concerned, every single car was an extension of my being. I can remember that when John Watson crossed the line that the elation was completely balanced by the fact that De Cesaris had crashed at Woodcote. So while everyone was crowded round John's car, all I did was to go and look at the damage to De Cesaris's car.'

Looking back from a perspective of 34 years, Ron says, 'I didn't understand why people were surprised we won, because it was obvious that we were going to win at some point. I was under no illusions — we won because of the unreliability of the Renaults, which took some of the shine off the victory.'

The carbon car had been a monumental design effort for such a small team. Rival team managements must have hoped with all their hearts it would fail, because if it succeeded they would have to change their entire approach to Formula 1 and that would take a lot of money. The sport was on the cusp of moving irreversibly beyond *garagiste* technology because no garage could make a decent carbon-fibre monocoque. Now that the MP4 had won, in its wake a wind of change was beginning to blow through the Formula 1 paddock. It would become a gale.

Ten days after the victory, as if in perfect demonstration of Formula 1's adrenalin sine wave, Ron Dennis introduced the press to the McLaren International HQ at Boundary Road. It was, he said, 'a warren of spotless, carefully planned workshops housing around £1.5 million worth of sophisticated machine plant. The offices had wall-to-wall carpeting, air conditioning and push-button telephone consoles.' Teddy Mayer, perhaps slightly put out, commented, 'All this and 65 people to keep two drivers in toys for the weekend.'

Dennis was taking his first step in building a new kind of racing team, based on Ferrari but bigger and better: 'We are trying to evolve something at McLaren International where there is no figurehead. We want the team to portray character and style. The closest example I can give is Ferrari. Any driver would want to drive for them yet they know that if they fall out they become immediate history. It's that sort of mystique, the intangible thing that we want at McLaren.'[35]

As the paddock knows well, this grand vision didn't quite play out according

---

[35] *Folley, Malcolm*, Senna vs Prost, *London, Arrow Books, 2010, pp69–70.*

to plan. Ron became very much the figurehead despite apparent contrary intentions and his growing obsession with order and clarity worked against his ambition to create a mystique led by 'character and style'. Nevertheless, McLaren International was destined to become one of the most impressive enterprises in the history of motorsport.

This first flush of success was followed, as these things are, by the frustrations of failure. The McLaren MP4's teething troubles plagued the rest of the season. The carbon-fibre car had trouble with 'bounce', the mysterious porpoise-like lurching that, as described earlier, could make the car almost undriveable. It took most of the season to sort it out, with John and Alan studying the effect in the Teddington wind tunnel. Barnard believed at the time that the problem was partly caused by super-stiff suspension creating problems with the shock absorbers.

But he also thought that the main culprit was Michelin, who had designed rear tyres that worked well on the heavier, more powerful turbo cars like the Renault and Ferrari. Says John, 'We were one of the few Cosworth-engined teams contracted to Michelin, and with the engine's lower power compared to the turbos, we just couldn't get the temperature into the tyre that we needed to make it perform as it should.'

Watson's other problem was getting the balance right. He preferred his car set up to have a little understeer, 'a car that feels glued to the track at the back', to give good traction through corners and, for him, the confidence to drive it harder, allowing him to open the throttle sooner. However, making the car feel secure at the back risked losing grip at the front. So Barnard spent long hours trying to get the perfect balance between the two. He was forever changing the stiffness of springs and anti-roll bars, altering settings on the front and rear wings, and refining the geometric angles on the suspension support to accommodate differences between the tracks and daily changes to the conditions on those tracks. When Barnard got it just right, Watson was very fast indeed, but getting it right in the limited period of practice before a Grand Prix was always a massive challenge.

It is perhaps typical of Barnard that he preferred the second place in France to the victory in Britain. He told *Autocourse* that the Dijon result was more pleasing because 'we set the car up just right and, with minimal practice changes, it was very quick. Silverstone was a sweetener, not expected but appreciated, though I was disappointed because, in test, Wattie had been able to do anything he liked with the car, and for the race we couldn't get it quite so well balanced.[36] Barnard is all about perfectionism, and, to his mind, the car had been better in France.

At the Dutch Grand Prix, De Cesaris damaged the strongest box on the planet by crashing into a tyre barrier during qualifying. Barnard was furious, refusing the Italian access to the spare car for fear he would wreck that too, so the rookie driver took no further part in the weekend. The race didn't go well for Watson, who had to retire from fourth place on lap 50 when a short between an electrical lead and a water pipe brought his car to a frustrating stop.

Then came the moment, on 13 September at the Italian Grand Prix, of which carbon-fibre sceptics had warned, as described in the opening chapter to this book. Watson lost control in Monza's second *Lesmo* turn and smashed the MP4 into the barrier, tearing the rear off the car. It was a bad shunt, the sort of accident that had claimed the lives of racing drivers in the past. So when the driver was seen climbing out of the monocoque, bewildered but unhurt, there were gasps of astonishment. The car hadn't dissolved in a spray of shards or a cloud of dust, and Wattie hadn't been shaken to death by an unyielding carbon-fibre monocoque.

Thirty years later Wattie spoke about the accident: 'I just got out and thought, "Ron's going to have something to say about this and John is going to be furious!" I had no injuries at all apart from a bit of stiffness in the shoulder and the tub was completely undamaged apart from the engine mounts being ripped out. Three days later we were back testing at Donington.'[37]

Tyler Alexander believes that Watson's survival was merely a side effect of John's genius: 'John did the carbon-fibre thing to make the car stiffer and lighter, but in my view his real contribution wasn't about stiffness, but safety, which, to the best of my knowledge, he never spoke about. Safety was a side effect; it was one of these classic things about innovation; you go down a particular road to achieve something and one of the best results that comes from it is something you weren't even thinking about.'

While this is often true of innovation, in this particular case, it isn't quite what happened. As we have seen, John always had safety in mind, perhaps more than any other motorsport designer at the time, and he consciously built cars to be strong so that they would protect the driver as completely as possible.

---

[36] Nye, Doug, 'The Nuts and Bolts of '81', *Autocourse 1981–82*, p78.
[37] Chris-R, 'McLaren celebrates 30 years of Carbon Fibre', *www.pistonheads.com*.

To him it was obvious that a carbon chassis would offer better protection.

Safety was also on the minds of the Civil Aviation Authority, whose officers had watched the Italian Grand Prix crash on television. They called Barnard the following day, telling him they were compiling regulations for aircraft of the future and asking if they could see the crashed monocoque. They arrived soon after to take photographs and notes before returning to draw up their new regulations. Which other motorsport designer can claim such an impact on aerospace design?

Hercules, too, would go on to use video of the crash as an example of the strength of carbon-fibre composite, as Watson recalled:[38] 'I believe the chassis was taken back to Hercules. They used it to display the strength and properties of the material, particularly to the US military... It was part of their sales pitch: Hercules would show the video and people would go, "Gee, how's that guy — is he alright?" And then they'd pull back the curtain and everyone would see the bare chassis.'

Bob Randolph at Hercules R&D adds that he used the chassis 'freely' to demonstrate commercial applications, stating that Wattie's 'well-known crash experience no doubt helped convince potential users of the strength, impact capability and durability of composites.' The Monza chassis was never raced again, as Barnard explains: 'When you have a major shunt like that, you're never 100% sure about what may have happened inside, so you just don't take the chance.'

Barnard and Webb monitored the torsional stiffness of the remaining chassis, making measurements after every accident and finding no significant change, meaning that despite repeated impacts, largely at the hands of De Cesaris, damage didn't spread throughout the structure. In a technical report written in 1984, they said that they had found no measurable degradation of chassis stiffness over three seasons. By contrast, aluminium alloy chassis saw degradation of at least 40% over a single season.

To Watson the carbon-fibre chassis was 'chalk and cheese' compared with the earlier McLaren aluminium monocoques. He found the MP4 far easier and more comfortable to drive. 'Apart from the Cosworth engine and Hewland gearbox, the MP4 had not one iota in common with the M29.' He also points out that the carbon-fibre chassis allowed repeatability: 'With aluminium, one car, of the same design, wasn't like another; you could build two cars to the

---

[38] Motor Sport, *March 1999, p35.*

same drawings and still have significant differences. But with the carbon tub you could ensure that both drivers had the same car. You got a much higher level of consistency and repeatability.' This meant that any changes made by Barnard or the race engineers would be certain to get somewhere close to the predicted response.

Watson also points to the more professional approach that Barnard took to setting up the car: 'When you went testing in the Teddy Mayer days, quite frequently you'd end up chasing the circuit, because it changes, sometimes quite dramatically, with the weather conditions. But John came with an agenda. You'd do a run and set a fundamental base time and then you'd start applying the changes you wanted to test. John would say, "First we will do the suspension, then aerodynamics" — whatever it happened to be. You weren't just looking for the ultimate lap time as you might under Teddy.'

After Watson's big accident at Monza, only two races remained of the World Championship season. At the penultimate round, in Montréal, Canada, he qualified ninth but finished a rain-drenched race in second place after an intense mid-race battle with crowd favourite Villeneuve, claiming the race's fastest lap.

The final race was in the unforgiving desert heat of Las Vegas, run on a curious temporary track created in the parking lot of the Caesars Palace Hotel. Shaped like a cartoon three-fingered hand, the circuit followed a series of long loops over a concrete surface that offered little grip. Few were impressed, Barnard among them:

'When you stood in the pits and looked across the concrete barriers that bordered the zig-zag track, all you could see was drivers' helmets whooshing back and forth. It was most peculiar. We ran soft tyres in an effort to get some grip, but on race day, as the temperature came up, we found that the hardest tyres worked best. Somehow the heat and the strangely shaped circuit made them work on the glassy concrete surface. All very odd to me.'

The tyres didn't work well enough. After qualifying fifth, Watson finished seventh, and De Cesaris was 12th. The race was won by Alan Jones in a Williams, with Brabham driver Nelson Piquet's fifth place being sufficient to make him World Champion by one point over Carlos Reutemann.

So the new McLaren was not covered in glory by the end of 1981, although Watson's Silverstone victory and his pair of second places were real highlights. Watson was sixth in the Drivers' standings, the best result for a McLaren driver in four years, and the team managed sixth in the Constructors' Championship,

THE PERFECT CAR

despite De Cesaris failing to complete nine of the season's 15 Grands Prix, and taking his car on no fewer than 23 'off-track excursions'.

One inevitable conclusion was that McLaren needed a better number two than De Cesaris, a man who went on to achieve an embarrassing record that still stands, as the winless driver with the most Grand Prix starts to his name — 208. An excellent solution, however, presented itself when double World Champion Niki Lauda decided to come out of retirement. Having already worked closely with John Hogan and Ron Dennis in the BMW Procar series, he was the ideal choice. But how would he get on with John Watson? More importantly, how would he click with Barnard?

John Barnard, meanwhile, was becoming troubled by another team's asset — Renault's ever-improving turbo engine. It was now clear that the way forward in Formula 1 was to have not only a carbon-fibre chassis but also a turbocharged engine.

CHAPTER 16
TURBO-POWERED TAKEOVER
1981–82

At Monza in 1981, the race at which John Watson survived his spectacular accident, John Hogan was walking through the paddock when Niki Lauda caught his eye. As described in Hogan's mimic, Lauda said, 'I vont to make a comeback' — after two years out of Formula 1. Hogan was sceptical but said he would think about it.

Ever a man for quick decisions, Hogan took the idea straight to James Hunt, who was at Monza commentating for the BBC. The former World Champion advised that return was possible, especially in Lauda's case — who could forget his heroic comeback after being so severely burned at the Nürburgring in 1976? But, as Hunt well knew from his own experience, 'Does he really still want it?'

Hogan thought he did: 'I knew Niki pretty well, and kind of knew that if he was saying something like that, he must have thought it through. He wasn't superficial about it'. Hogan also knew that Lauda Air had become a financial burden: 'He had a Lockheed One-Eleven strung around his neck at the time and was trying to get out of it.' Lauda, therefore, had two motivations — the desire to win and the need to make money. Not a man to waste time, Hogan left Hunt and went straight to the McLaren motorhome to speak to Ron Dennis and John Barnard. He reports that they had their doubts but decided to give Lauda a secret test at Donington the following week, as soon as the MP4 was rebuilt.

Watson was also asked to come along: 'I rocked up, jumped in the car and did the quickest lap I'd ever done at Donington.' Niki climbed in, set off and did four laps, but was unable to get anywhere near Wattie's time. As Barnard reports, he pulled into the pit lane looking grim, climbed out and said, 'OK, thank you very much, gentlemen. I know what I have to do. Leave it to me.'

Lauda was shocked by the changes that had occurred in two years. John explains: 'The car had moved on so much, the physical forces had changed so massively. The suspension was stiffer and the car ran round the corners with far higher G-forces.'

Ron Dennis left Donington by car with Lauda and his personal trainer Willy Dungl: 'Niki was driving, it was raining and we were coming down the M1. Willi Dungl was asleep and we were idly chatting and then there was a 30-second lull in the conversation. Then Niki said, "I want to do it." He caught me completely off guard — I had no idea that he was going to make a decision at that moment.'

Lauda had realised that he simply wasn't fit enough to drive a modern Formula 1 car, his neck muscles in particular lacking the strength to fight the G-forces on every bend. When asked in 1984 by Austrian journalist Herbert Völker whether he considered it an uplifting experience to get back behind the wheel, he responded, 'Hell, no, it was humiliating. After one lap I could hardly hold the steering wheel....'[39]

Dungl put him on to a special dietary, exercise and mental fitness programme for the winter. It is testament to Niki's will that he achieved the required improvement within a few months. As he told Alan Henry at the time: 'Getting fit is simple and straightforward. All you have to do is run for 10 minutes today, 30 minutes tomorrow, an hour the next day... run, run, train, train, and then you're fit. There's nothing easier in the world. Once you've taken the difficult decision, the mental one, there's no problem.'[40]

It is also testament to Lauda's powers of persuasion that he convinced Hogan that he should be paid a record salary to drive for McLaren: 'Niki had the first million-dollar retainer, which was really as a result of he and I deciding how to optimise the negotiations with Philip Morris.'

When Watson asked for an explanation, Hogan replied, 'you're not Niki Lauda', referring to the racing legend's global television and advertising pulling power. But the Belfast driver was assured that Lauda would receive no special treatment beyond his gargantuan pay packet; both Ron and John considered it unproductive to favour one driver over another.

With two top drivers in a revolutionary car, onlookers were thinking that

---

[39] Lauda, Niki, Second Time Around – The New Formula 1: The Turbo Era, *William Kimber & Co Ltd, London, 1984, p15.*
[40] Henry, Alan, 'Niki Lauda: a Remarkable Return', Autocourse 1982–83, p76.

the only way for the new McLaren was up. But it all looked very different from within the walls of Boundary Road. The carbon car had a significant disadvantage that was only going to get bigger and bigger, and that was its lack of a turbo engine.

Renault had introduced turbo technology to Formula 1 in 1977, entering their own team, Equipe Renault Elf, complete with a V6 based on a road-car engine. The racer was quickly dubbed 'the yellow teapot' on the grounds that it was about as much use. Renault won their first race in 1979 and followed with three victories in 1980 and again in 1981.

The writing was on the wall, especially with Ferrari following suit with a turbo car in 1981 and winning two races with it. Whereas the power output of 3.0-litre naturally aspirated Cosworth-powered cars like the McLaren MP4 was around 500bhp, the 1.5-litre turbo could generate up to 650bhp, a massive advantage once the technology got past the teething stage.

At a McLaren board meeting at the end of the 1981 season, Barnard presented his case for a turbo engine. As he told reporters at the time: 'I'm not happy to be fighting for seventh place on the grid, but there's nothing else we can hope for as we are giving away 150 horsepower to the turbo teams.'[41] It was agreed that the team had to have a turbo engine to remain competitive. The problem was, which one?

Teddy Mayer, much to Barnard's irritation, proposed the Renault engine, but John made his position clear: 'I have built a narrow chassis to maximise ground-effect. We need a narrow engine to go with it.' Somehow Mayer had got hold of some blueprint drawings of the Renault and presented them to the board. Barnard was unimpressed: 'It was based on a road-car V6 engine block, with all the ancillaries cluttered down the side of the engine. A compromise.' Even after all these years he says the word 'compromise' with a spitting venom that shows firstly his hatred of the concept and secondly his buried fury with Mayer. In opposing John on the turbo issue, however, Teddy proved to be hammering a nail into his own coffin.

In John's mind the mission was clear: 'I was still searching for the ultimate ground-effect package.' That couldn't be achieved with Renault. He needed an engine that was compact and tidy, one that wouldn't compromise the under-tunnels and rear wing.

---

[41] Folley, Malcolm, *Senna vs Prost*; London, Arrow Books, 2009, pp77–78.

Barnard and Dennis visited BMW in Munich. The company's King of Engines, Paul Rosche, showed them an impressive four-cylinder road-car turbo engine that was being adapted for racing. It featured an enormous turbocharger and belted out so much power that the exhaust pipes turned white hot, prompting John to think, 'My God, how do you handle that at the back of the car?'

John was also concerned that the BMW engine had to be carried in a tubular frame because it hadn't been designed to be a stressed member. He asked Rosche if he could change the frame's design. Rosche shook his head. John shook his head too: this engine wasn't going to work because he would be forced to build the car around it, rather than the other way round.

Once again Barnard needed Dennis's support. He laid out the parameters for the engine and made it clear: 'We can't compromise on this, Ron. It must be as compact as possible. A V6 would be ideal.' Once again Dennis fell in behind his brilliant designer. He contacted two English engine specialists, Weslake in Rye, East Sussex, and Ricardo in Shoreham-by-Sea, West Sussex, but had no joy with either.

So, in December 1981, Ron phoned Porsche's R&D centre at Weissach in Germany. Within a few days he and Barnard were on a plane to Stuttgart.

The meeting went well, with Barnard explaining in detail his requirements. The result was an introduction to the director of Porsche's motorsport department, Hans Mezger. Porsche had long experience in building cars for the world's most famous endurance race, the Le Mans 24 Hours, and Mezger told Barnard it would take two years to produce the new engine.

Then came the thorny question of money, and, again, Ron came into his own. The cost was going to be enormous, so Ron cannily broke the project up into phases. He could just about afford to pay for Stage One — design. This was critical to Barnard; if McLaren paid for this stage, then they could own the design and that meant Barnard would have control over it. This phase would be followed by the creation of a prototype, testing on a dynamometer and then production. Porsche compromised by reducing the timescale to 18 months, with design expected to take around half that period.

Thus Barnard became the first motorsport designer to direct the creation of an engine tailored for a specific racing chassis. Even Ferrari, where the engine was king, hadn't done this. For them, Mauro Forghieri's engines came first; the chassis was a subsidiary concern. Nor can the legendary Colin Chapman quite claim Barnard's laurels: the Ford-funded Cosworth DFV, introduced in 1967, was an all-purpose racing engine intended for use in a range of cars, although Chapman worked very closely with Keith Duckworth, 'huddled over a drawing board to plan both motor and machine in parallel'.[42]

Mezger offered Barnard various options to fit his criteria. One suggestion was to arrange the six cylinders in a flattened 'V' configuration of 120°, along the lines of a Ferrari engine. John felt this would make the engine too wide. He wanted the narrowest configuration possible and in the end they agreed on 80°, which would be neat, compact and ideal for creating fixing points to the rear of the chassis.

John stipulated that any pumps and ancillary equipment had to be on the front of the engine, behind the driver, rather than at the sides, making it narrower still: 'I now had the prospect of an engine that was clean and more or less the width of the oil sump — an enormous improvement in underbody geometry.'

As a Formula 1 car at the time wasn't required to carry a starter motor and attendant heavy battery, an external starter was used, as with Indycars. Barnard had a bright idea for a new type of lightweight on-board starter motor and specified that the sump casting be designed to incorporate it. He dismantled a lightweight Desoutter drill powered by air rather than electricity and fitted its compact, powerful, high-speed motor into the casting. The engine could now be started with a bottle of compressed air and a wand that plugged into an airline fitting at the back of the car.

John had to keep 'tapping the rudder' to control the Porsche design operation: 'They wanted to anchor the sump with a couple of bolt positions outside the envelope that I'd described. It would have required bumps on the underbody. I told them, "No, you must redesign it."'

Inevitably there were conflicts. As John points out, Porsche staff 'were sports car people by nature. Their understanding came from the fact that they ran races lasting 24 hours and they tried to apply that thinking to our Formula 1 engine. I was adamant that was the wrong way to think about it.'

Udo Zucker, head of Bosch's motorsport division, developed a highly innovative and relatively simple electronic fuel-injection system for the V6, but his relationship with Barnard didn't begin well. When Zucker presented Barnard with two die-cast aluminium boxes to house all the electronics, John's reaction was to the point: 'This is Formula 1, for Christ's sake. Where the hell am I going to put all that?' The result was a fiery head-to-head, which,

---

[42] *Cruickshank, Gordon, 'Tasmanian double — the Lotus 49',* Motor Sport, *June 2004, p104.*

initially, Zucker won — the first turbo-powered MP4 ran with the two boxes. If Barnard had a reputation for being difficult to work with, then so did Zucker. Wolfgang Hustedt, who ran the Bosch operation in America, described his German colleague euphemistically as 'not the easiest guy to deal with, but a genius for sure'.[43]

Eventually Barnard was able to persuade Zucker that installing everything in one box would be more efficient by saving space and eliminating some wiring and bulky connectors. It took Zucker some time to understand the weight and space parameters of a Formula 1 car, but when he did, says John, 'He was brilliant — the job he did with the electronics was fantastic.' The McLaren Porsche turbo project brought rewards for Zucker: he would soon be hailed as the 'father of electronic racing injection' as a direct result of his work on the electronic fuel systems for the MP4.

As the design stage neared its conclusion, Ron — and John — began to sweat about where the rest of the money was going to come from. They found themselves in Stuttgart once or twice a month to oversee the project and often stayed at the house of Gerd Kramer, a well-connected man who headed motorsport marketing for Mercedes. One evening over dinner he, Ron and John discussed how the rest of the Porsche engine project might be funded and Kramer suggested an approach to Mansour Ojjeh, a rich 29-year-old of French and Saudi Arabian descent who was providing sponsorship to the Williams team via Techniques d'Avant Garde (TAG), a company founded by his father, Akram Ojjeh, that had proved adept at matching money to cutting-edge technology projects. As Kramer said in an interview for this book, 'I knew Mansour Ojjeh wanted to leave Williams as a sponsor and have a different involvement in Formula 1.'

Ripe for the plucking, Ojjeh soon received an approach from Ron Dennis and Niki Lauda with the Porsche turbo proposal. When they met, in Paris, Ron was able to persuade Ojjeh to invest $5 million in the project, not as sponsor but as partner. Between them they would go on to establish TAG Turbo Engines, an enterprise that would prove to be immensely lucrative for both Dennis and Ojjeh. As for Barnard, it made his dream of having a custom-made engine for his carbon chassis a reality.

The Porsche project was a long-term one. More immediate was the fast-

---

[43] Kirby, Gordon, 'The Way it Is / Bosch's Wolfgang Hustedt has retired', www.gordonkirby.com.

approaching new season. For 1982, ground-clearance checks were abandoned, eliminating the need for fancy suspension solutions to lower the cars, and rigid skirts continued to be permitted. John's redesign of the MP4 led to the MP4/1B, based largely on the original chassis but with new, longer sidepods and underbody to accommodate longer skirts alongside an underwing that stretched, as on the Chaparral, all the way to the back of the car.

In experimenting with his high-density polyurethane skirts, looking for the optimum length and stiffness for them, Barnard finally found the solution to porpoising. The 'trick', as he describes it, was to angle the skirts inwards and to make them of the right density of material to ensure they didn't get sucked in too far, thereby allowing too much uncontrolled air to get under the car and generate porpoising. If the angle of bend could be got just right, there would be a cushion of air beneath the skirts that would reduce the amount they rubbed on the track without compromising the suction, at the same time causing less wear to the skirts. As Barnard says, 'It was a fine balance between the angle and the stiffness of the skirts.'

Getting it right, however, was very hard. Like other designers, Barnard had the MP4's skirts made by an outside company. As the method of their manufacture, by pouring liquid plastic into a mould and leaving it to set, produced inconsistent results — some skirts would be stiffer than others for no apparent reason — Barnard created a 'skirt tester' that was taken to each race. This involved clamping a skirt in a long channel of aluminium with a hinged lower section that would push on the skirt to test its flexibility, measuring the force it took to bend it a certain distance. Suddenly it was easy to choose a skirt of the correct flexibility for a given circuit.

As Barnard says, 'It was critical: if you got it just right, you could arrive at an optimal situation between air leakage under the skirt and the rate of wear that was as good as it could get for the track you were on. You could make the skirts last the entire weekend and you wouldn't get that awful porpoising.'

The paddock was watching Barnard's multi-faceted advances with both curiosity and alarm. Ferrari, realising that British technical expertise was essential to improving their chassis design, appointed Dr Harvey Postlethwaite as chief designer in 1981 and he set about creating a carbon-fibre monocoque to carry their turbo engine. Two years older than Barnard, Postlethwaite even installed an in-house autoclave with lay-up facilities at Ferrari, something that Barnard himself wouldn't emulate for some years. But things didn't go well for Postlethwaite at Ferrari.

As Doug Nye put it, 'If Ferrari ever get a halfway decent chassis, we'll never see which way they went.'[44] But he added, somewhat critically, 'Just as Ferrari had caught up with British state-of-the-art chassis building in 1963 by hiring John Surtees and Mike Parkes, so they did it again — with 100 per cent less effect on their driving strength — in 1981 by hiring Harvey Postlethwaite PhD.' What Nye meant by that, in a year in which Ferrari did well, winning the Constructors' title, will become clear.

Meanwhile, Alfa Romeo, Andrea De Cesaris's new home, rolled out three carbon-fibre cars for the 1982 Brazilian Grand Prix, the second race of the season, their monocoques made by a small factory in England.[45]

Slowly but surely John Watson and Niki Lauda moved McLaren up the grid with the 1982 car. The team's first victory of the season came at Long Beach, California, on 4 April. It belonged to Niki Lauda, who qualified second behind, of all people, De Cesaris. Lauda should have been on pole position, but in his arrogance he underestimated De Cesaris's burning ambition to make McLaren regret sacking him. After setting his best time, Lauda parked his MP4/1B in the garage before the end of the final session and walked away, confident that pole was his, but De Cesaris then clipped 0.12 second off Lauda's time. When the Italian drove into the pits and saw the joy on the faces of the Alfa Romeo crew, all the frustrations of the previous year burst through: 'I started to cry — I don't know why.'[46]

De Cesaris would feel the tears rising again the following day when, on lap 33, having just been passed for the lead by Lauda, his mind wandered and he found himself spinning off the track and into the wall. Now a full minute in the lead, Lauda calmly coasted to victory, allowing cars he'd previously lapped to repass him, now super-wary of the crumbling Long Beach track that he had so skilfully negotiated so far. Lauda was not a man to push his luck.

When asked why he'd eased up, he said in his typical no-nonsense, clipped style: 'I just slowed down. So long as you win, what difference does the gap to the next car make?' Such logic was music to the ears of Ron Dennis, who had nearly had kittens watching Watson speeding to triumph at Silverstone the previous year. Wattie himself managed a creditable sixth place.

---

[44] *'Seven of the Best'*, Autocourse 1982–83, *p42*.
[45] *Grand Premio do Brasil'*, Autocourse 1982–83, *p94*.
[46] *'Toyota Grand Prix of the United States (Long Beach)'* Autocourse 1982–83, *p101*.

ABOVE Tyler Alexander (right) explaining to John Barnard, Niki Lauda and Ron Dennis what went so wrong that Andrea De Cesaris beat Lauda to pole position for the 1982 Long Beach Grand Prix. *LAT Images* **BELOW** Lauda, duly chastened by humiliation, cruised to victory on the Sunday for the first of four McLaren wins that year; De Cesaris, as was his wont, crashed out. *LAT Images*

ABOVE Long Beach in 1983 was one of Formula 1's legendary races. Niki Lauda qualified only 22nd and John Watson (pictured) 23rd, but Ron Dennis's and John Barnard's faces, 'as long as a Lurgan spade', turned to joy as the drivers weaved their way to the front on the bumpy track. *LAT Images* **BELOW** Wattie, the more determined of the two, passed Lauda on lap 33 to take a historic win. *Courtesy of John Barnard*

ABOVE Barnard oversaw the bespoke design of the TAG-Porsche turbo engine for the 1984 MP4/2, but Niki Lauda, desperate for more power, insisted it be put into the 1983 car. Barnard said it was a mistake, and he was right. But it wasn't all bad: the decision helped iron out the bugs during a poor season in time for a triumphant performance the following year. *Sutton Images*

ABOVE Brazil, 1984: Alain Prost, in typical pose, biting his nails as he contemplates the race ahead — the new MP4/2's first test had been only three days before. *Sutton Images* **BELOW** Prost had nothing to worry about at the Jacarepaguá circuit in Rio — he scored his first win of the season and broke the lap record. *Sutton Images*

ABOVE At Monaco in 1984 Alain Prost won in the pouring rain despite Ayrton Senna passing him on the line — a famous Formula 1 controversy. *LAT Images*
BELOW But at Estoril in Portugal, the last round of the 1984 season, it was Niki Lauda who took the World Championship, beating 'The Professor' by just half a point despite coming second to him in the race. *Sutton Images*

ABOVE Barnard confers with Niki Lauda during 1984, the year in which the Austrian became World Champion for the third time in what was, by the end of the season, the perfect car. *Courtesy of John Barnard* **BELOW** Barnard's carbon-fibre McLarens were designed and built in the antiseptic aerospace environment of the team's Boundary Road facility in Woking. *Courtesy of Matthew Jeffreys*

ABOVE The McLaren design office (from left): Matthew Jeffreys, Alan Jenkins, Tim Wright, John Barnard, Steve Nichols, Bob Bell, Colin Smith and Mike Lock. *Courtesy of John Barnard* **BELOW** Prince Michael of Kent flanked by a somewhat startled Ron Dennis and John Barnard, looking every bit the Prince of Darkness. *Courtesy of John Barnard*

ABOVE Proud Ted Barnard with his now famous son at the McLaren motorhome during the first World Championship year. *Courtesy of John Barnard*

LEFT 'Mr McLaren', as Ron Dennis has dubbed him, with daughter Jennifer painting together on a Mr Men plastic tablecloth at home in Lightwater, Surrey, circa 1982. *Courtesy of John Barnard*

A peculiar feature of Lauda's winning car was its 'water-cooled brakes'. This little bit of smart thinking, not Barnard's, had been introduced at the previous race, in Brazil, by Brabham and Williams as a way to circumvent a weight limit that now favoured the 'grandee' teams. The *garagiste* teams — most of all McLaren with Barnard's carbon-fibre car — were increasingly able to build lighter cars and yet the weight limit had actually been increased for the 1981 season, from 575kg to 585kg, although there was then a small drop again for 1982, to 580kg. As the rules allowed cooling liquid to be replenished after a race before a car was weighed by the scrutineers, the crafty idea first used by Gordon Murray at Brabham and Patrick Head at Williams was to fit their cars with large tanks of water that would be emptied as quickly as possible during the race, supposedly for cooling the brakes.

With their 'water-cooled brakes', Nelson Piquet and Keke Rosberg finished first and second in Brazil, respectively for Brabham and Williams, only to be disqualified for contravening weight regulations. Ironically, Watson was a beneficiary, moving up from fourth place to second in the official results. Not put off by that penalty and keen to push against what they saw as an unfair weight restriction, more FOCA teams, including McLaren, adopted the trick for Long Beach.

In the case of the MP4/1B, Barnard used a plastic tank containing 30kg of water coupled to a windscreen washer pump that squirted it at the brakes. Says Barnard, 'Most landed on the track and evaporated. Within a couple of laps we'd be 30kg underweight and able to compete with the turbo cars. It made a farce of the weight regulations.' It also set the tone for the FOCA-aligned section of the Formula 1 paddock's attitude to FISA's arbitrary rulings: 'Find a way round them, and if you can't, then come up with a way to break them that won't be spotted.'

Unlike in Brazil, Lauda's Long Beach victory, and Rosberg's second place, were allowed to stand despite the provocative repeat use of 'water-cooled brakes'. By the time of the next race, at Imola in San Marino, FISA had officially outlawed the ploy and the leading FOCA teams responded by boycotting the race, leaving only 14 cars to take part.

FOCA then launched an attack by attempting to get turbo engines banned on the grounds that the turbos themselves were 'secondary power units'.[47] Their lobbying of both the FISA Court of Appeal and the International Chamber of

---

[47] Henry, Alan, 'A Championship Eclipsed by Tragedy and Bitterness', Autocourse 1982–83, p23.

Commerce in Lausanne failed — turbos were here to stay for the next six years. By the fateful Belgian Grand Prix at Zolder on 9 May, Barnard was having to add ballast to the McLarens to meet the weight limit.

Other major irritants were arising for Barnard, not least from his co-director, Teddy Mayer. Barnard was race-engineering for Lauda while Mayer had Watson. The seeds for conflict had been sown the previous year, when John had decided to race-engineer for De Cesaris because the Italian driver needed all the help he could get. They were at the 1981 French Grand Prix when Mayer said to Barnard: 'Watson's going quicker; I've found the big secret and I'm not telling you!' Watson finished second to De Cesaris's 11th.

'I wasn't going to stand for this,' says John. 'We hadn't set up the team to be separate entities. I reacted as if it was a joke and later learned that they had made a minor adjustment to the suspension, something that to my mind would have made little or no difference. But the fact that Teddy had come up to me crowing like that lodged in my mind.'

The same scenario occurred at the 1982 Belgian Grand Prix. Look out Mayer. John Watson takes up the story:

'The Sunday morning was abnormally warm. I went out and did a practice run; Teddy was running my car at the time and John was on Niki's car. After a couple of laps my left front tyre started to give up. Teddy said, "There's a set of tyres we had in Las Vegas the year before. Let's put them on your car." I said, "No way. They're concrete!" But he banged on, so we did it, but on the left side only, and I went out, with a very negative perspective, wanting to come back in and say, "I told you that you were wrong."'

Mayer's logic was that the long, high-speed right-handers at Zolder demanded harder tyres on the left side of the car. Despite his doubts, Wattie found that after three or four laps the car 'was starting to feel nice'. His conclusion was that Teddy's inspired idea would work if the weather stayed warm. Teddy was delighted. 'The Wiener was very happy to have made the right judgement,' reports Watson. 'That's where Teddy was clever. But the trouble was Teddy did like to stuff it up John.'

Mayer and Watson were standing in the pit lane looking rather smug when Lauda wandered over, asking what they had done to get more speed. Teddy said nothing, so Watson, more appreciative of team spirit than Teddy, told Niki the secret:

'I said, "You should run those tyres on the left side of your car, because if you don't, your left front is going to go and I'm going to piss past you." He replied he'd stick with what he had. I said, "You're nuts! Why won't you do it?" He said, "Because I haven't tried it!"

'He knew I didn't lie, that I was trustworthy, but he couldn't break out of the strict limits of the cell that he worked within. It was interesting for me to learn that because it gave me an advantage. He just couldn't go against a lifetime philosophy.'

Watson started from 10th position on the grid and drove a superb race, 'pissing past Lauda', as predicted, taking the lead from Keke Rosberg's Williams on the penultimate lap, and winning by seven seconds. Lauda, who had started six places further up the grid, finished third.

If Barnard was irritated by Mayer's lack of team spirit, he was incandescent when the scrutineers declared Lauda's car to be 1.8kg underweight while Watson's was 1kg to the good — even though both cars carried the same ballast. Barnard recalls, 'We tried to prove that the scales must be wrong, but it was a waste of time.' Lauda was disqualified, while Watson enjoyed a very popular victory. Tyler Alexander's take on the incident is highly informative:

'I suspect that John remembers it as it happened, because it would have burned a hole in him. But Teddy would have got pissed off with not being allowed to do what Wattie needed and would have finally thought, "Sod you, Barnard, I've done something to the car that works and no way in hell am I telling you about it, because you wouldn't let me do it." The shame of the whole thing was that the two of them wouldn't talk to each other. Sometimes Barnard would set the car up the way some other driver drove it... But Wattie needed something that felt a bit different.

'Teddy should have been able to talk to JB and say, "Look, Wattie's complaining like hell. He isn't driving very well. I think he ought to be quicker. He has a problem with the car and I've tried these couple of things, and Wattie's more comfortable." Barnard should have accepted that. But Teddy was getting fed up with being directed around, and he didn't like that. Going motor racing can make you a bit perfectionist, a bit all or nothing, so I understand Barnard getting a bit close-minded about Teddy.'

Lauda gave Barnard a different explanation for his failing to beat Watson, telling him that he didn't know the car well enough: 'I'm not going flat round the corners yet. I know the car will do it but I just can't convince my right foot. I keep lifting it from the throttle.' The ground-effect forces were still beyond his intuition, despite his win at Long Beach.

The Zolder episode boiled in Barnard's brain and very nearly led to the break-up of the new McLaren partnership. Before the end of the year the resulting brew would spell disaster for both Mayer and Alexander, as we shall see.

Wattie's victory at Zolder was totally overshadowed by a dreadful tragedy that weekend. Gilles Villeneuve was driving Harvey Postlethwaite's semi-carbon Ferrari during Saturday qualifying and was desperate to beat the time of Didier Pironi, his team-mate and by now also a bitter rival, following Pironi's duplicity two weeks earlier at Imola when he had cheated Villeneuve out of victory on the last lap, defying team orders. Villeneuve was on a hot lap towards the end of the session and approaching the left-hand *Terlamenbocht* corner, where he encountered Jochen Mass, going far more slowly in his March. As Mass moved to get out of his way, Villeneuve moved the same way, clipping the March's right rear wheel at around 140mph.

Villeneuve's Ferrari took off, nose-dived, cartwheeled across the grass and back onto the track in front of Mass, disintegrating on the way. Something in the carbon monocoque catastrophically failed because Gilles was catapulted out of the car still strapped into his seat. He tumbled over and over at high speed until he too crossed the track in front of Mass, before bouncing into the catch-fencing.

Watson and fellow Brit Derek Warwick stopped their cars and ran to Villeneuve, carefully dragging him out of the catch-fencing. Wattie looked into his lifeless eyes and, deeply shaken, returned to the pits where he told people that Gilles was dead. Villeneuve had broken his neck, severing the spinal cord, but somehow was continuing to breathe. He was taken to hospital. The life-support machine was turned off some six hours later, to the deep distress of his family, wife Joanne and young children Jacques, just ten, and Melanie, only eight.

Barnard's memory is more technical. Imprinted on his mind is the sight of the carbon-fibre seat-back bulkhead coming clean out of the chassis together with the seat. 'I'm afraid it was a lack of understanding of the materials. That couldn't have happened in the MP4.'

Alan Jenkins is illuminating on this issue. He was shocked to discover how backward Ferrari's carbon facilities where when he attended a job interview at Maranello three years later: 'It was depressing going to the Ferrari factory. McLaren had clean rooms and all the stuff that other people didn't have. That was John's perfectionist nature — we weren't going to do carbon unless it was all correct. So, to go to Ferrari and see the bonding equipment next to a milling machine, with cutting oil flying off it, was a little disappointing.'

A little disappointing? Dangerous and ignorant might be a fairer, if harsher, description, only going to show that despite Barnard's path-finding innovation, even highly qualified people like Postlethwaite didn't fully understand that carbon-fibre's strength relied upon good, clean bonds. It should have been impossible for the seat to have come out of Villeneuve's car.

Nevertheless, the FISA enquiry commission held into the accident on 21 May 1982 determined that 'the survival cell in Ferrari number 27 fulfilled its role considering the high speed and energy involved.'[48] The cause was cited as 'driver error on the part of Gilles Villeneuve. No blame is attached to Jochen Mass.'

McLaren claimed two more wins to take their 1982 tally to four and found themselves in serious contention for the Drivers' and Constructors' titles for the first time in five years.

The next victory was Watson's at Detroit, just two weeks after a poor showing at Monaco in which both he and Lauda went out with engine trouble. As both drivers had been unable to get good grip on Monaco's bumpy surface, hopes were far from elevated at Detroit, another street track that was even more bumpy with its tramlines and manhole covers. True to expectations, Lauda and Watson qualified only 10th and 17th respectively.

The race was halted on lap six after a pile-up. Upon the restart, over an hour later, Watson proceeded to have one of the drives of his life, passing one car after another, until, on lap 32, he overtook Lauda, Eddie Cheever and Pironi on a single lap. That left Rosberg's Williams as his only remaining target. Catching the Finn at three seconds a lap, Wattie took the lead on lap 37 and stayed there while Lauda, trying to emulate his team-mate's progress, crashed out. Invited to join in the chorus of criticism of the sub-standard track after the race, Wattie merely said, 'It's difficult to overtake', before adding, somewhat bizarrely, 'although I managed to get by okay'.[49] Watson also established a remarkable record, for no Formula 1 driver had ever won from a lower grid position than his 17th.

In the mid-July heat of the British Grand Prix at Brands Hatch, Lauda qualified fifth with Watson only 11th. But Wattie was considered the best overtaker in

---

[48] 'Grote Prijs van België', Autocourse 1982–83, p120.
[49] 'United States Grand Prix (Detroit),' Autocourse 1982–83, p139.

the pack and the great British public looked forward to another brilliant drive from him. And as an unlikely military victory in the Falkland Islands had been achieved just a month earlier, there was something triumphant in the British air. But on lap three, to the collective sinking of spectators' stomachs, Wattie ran onto the grass trying to avoid an incident between two cars ahead of him. The MP4/1B stalled and wouldn't restart — race over.

Happily, Lauda drove with supreme skill. He took the lead on lap nine after Nelson Piquet's Brabham dropped out with a broken fuel injection pump and cruised to victory, slowing down in the final laps as he had done in California three months before, Pironi almost half a minute behind him. Lauda was now third in the Drivers' Championship, Wattie second.

If Watson was disappointed, Barnard, Dennis and Hogan were supremely content, and the crowd was delirious; Lauda was a popular driver and McLaren was considered a British team for all its Kiwi roots. Dennis and Barnard had secured a second consecutive win for Marlboro at the Marlboro British Grand Prix and the team had extended its lead in the Constructors' Championship.

As in 1981, the season came to a climax in the car park of the Caesars Palace Hotel in Las Vegas. The World Championship title was still in the balance, just, as Rosberg's lead over Watson was nine points, meaning that Watson, with two wins to Rosberg's one, would become World Champion if he were to score nine points by winning the race, with the Finn failing to score. Ferrari's Pironi was only five points adrift of Rosberg, but his hopes had vanished four races earlier when, leading the championship, he had a horrific accident in the rain during practice for the German Grand Prix at Hockenheim and shattered his legs. It was also possible, if the right things happened, that McLaren could overhaul Ferrari in the Constructors' standings.

The media were cock-a-hoop even if the American public cared barely a hoot for the brouhaha. Who were all these foreigners anyway?

Before the race, Watson avoided the spotlight by nipping over to Utah to visit Bob Randolph at Hercules and check out the carbon-fibre operation. In truth he hated the Caesars Palace track with a passion, complaining to Barnard that racing between the high concrete blocks made him feel sick: 'It's a nightmare, like an ever-converging tunnel.' For Barnard, the only positive thing about the circuit was that he could walk out of his hotel and straight into the pits.

Watson didn't help his cause by qualifying only ninth, but ahead of Lauda in 13th spot. But this advantage over Lauda confirmed an interesting fact about Dennis's and Barnard's approach to their team. Unlike other British racing operations, they really were reluctant to favour one driver over another, despite differences in their pay packets.

According to Watson, on the night before the race, Ron gave Lauda some so-called team orders: 'Ron said to Niki, "John's better placed in the championship; so if he's running quicker than you, can you let him go?" I think that was the first time in Niki's life that he'd ever been asked such a thing, and, more importantly, the first time in his life that he realised it wasn't his team. The team was bigger than either driver — as at Ferrari.' In fact Watson believes that McLaren under Dennis and Barnard was the first British team to operate like the 'Ferrari model'.

Inspired by this support, Watson drove a brilliant race, taking seventh place from Rosberg on the 16th lap. On the next lap he passed Mario Andretti, the American legend having his last Formula 1 outing, for Ferrari. After one more lap he took fifth place from Eddie Cheever, the race's other American participant, driving a Ligier. If Wattie carried on like this, the championship perhaps could be his. With just nine laps to go he moved into second place, but the leader, Michele Alboreto in a Tyrrell, was 30 seconds to the good and Wattie was running out of time — and Rosberg, having found a comfortable berth in fifth position, was in sight of two points and with them the World Championship title regardless of Wattie's result.

So it was that Watson came home second, which put him third overall in the Drivers' standings behind Rosberg and Pironi, and helped to secure McLaren's second place in the Constructors' Championship behind Ferrari.

Everything was moving in the right direction for Barnard. Thanks to his growing financial comfort, he and Rosie had just moved house, to a much larger place called Rawdon on Heath House Road in Worplesdon, just a 12-minute drive from McLaren's factory. The TAG-Porsche turbo engine was progressing well and, indeed, had been announced to the world that September, despite John warning the McLaren board that it wouldn't be ready for the 1983 season.

Satisfied with the clear success of his carbon chassis, John began looking around the rest of the car in his eternal effort to improve performance and save weight. He decided that he could save some 15kg if he used carbon brake discs. This was one of those relatively rare moments in John's life when he looked at another designer's work and said, 'I want that.' In this case that designer was Brabham's Gordon Murray, who had been experimenting with carbon brakes for over five years, with mixed success.

There were many problems with the concept. The first was that carbon discs were made not of carbon-fibre but of 'carbon-carbon'. Barnard explains: 'You take a matrix of pure carbon rods, put it in a furnace and, over several stages, cook it slowly in an atmosphere of methane or acetylene which causes the molecules to grow on the original matrix. It can take months to grow a solid block of carbon-carbon from which you can make your discs.'

Five months was the norm. As Murray said at the time, 'When things change so fast in racing, carbon brakes are a problem. You've got to plan so far ahead to allow for production that by the time you've got your answer, the question has probably changed.'[50]

There were other difficulties. Carbon discs operate at around 750°C. This intense heat warms up the hydraulic oil in the brake callipers to the point where it boils, rendering the brakes useless. Murray says that with his carbon discs, 'Anything that got anywhere near the discs burst into flames — small mammals, butterflies and locusts... We'd come into the pits with the brake ducts on fire and the wheel bearing grease melted.'

Like Murray, Barnard turned to aerospace for help, contacting American company BFGoodrich (now part of UTC Aerospace Systems), which was using carbon-carbon to brake the rotors on Chinook helicopters, and also SEP of France and HITCO of California. He took a sample from each of them and machined the supplied discs to fit the standard mounting for a cast-iron disc brake.

In late 1982 Barnard tasked Lauda to test the three sets of carbon brakes at Donington along with the standard discs. Making direct comparisons at the first corner, Redgate, Niki had to start braking at 100 metres with cast-iron brakes, but with the best of the carbon options, those from SEP, that distance was reduced to just 60 metres. John was impressed: 'Wow! I thought. This is another world!' The SEP discs became the carbon discs of choice for McLaren but it would take the whole of the 1983 season to get them to work well. We will return to Barnard's solutions in the next chapter.

There was another hurdle. With carbon brakes, which presented considerably less unsprung mass, tyres took longer to come up to working temperature, but Michelin addressed this by working with McLaren to develop suitable versions of its tyres.

John had a fight on his hands trying to push through the carbon brakes project at McLaren. Teddy Mayer thought it a waste of time and resources,

---

[50] Nye, Doug, 'Seven of the best?' *Autocourse 1982–83, p43 and p46.*

pointing out, with telling accuracy, that they were no good in the rain. What Teddy didn't know was that he was about to lose his fight with Barnard.

After Watson's victory at Zolder in May 1982, and still irate about Mayer's apparent 'small-minded' lack of team spirit, Barnard warned Ron Dennis: 'Look, I'm not going to carry on working in this environment. I can't be dealing with Teddy. I don't want to discuss technical issues with Teddy just to get his approval. I shouldn't even have to try and persuade him!'

John recalls Ron's response, 'If you're going to leave, then I'm coming with you. We could do something on our own.' With Marlboro having backed Ron and John on the strength of the carbon-fibre car, the pair felt almost invulnerable. Had they gone through with this possibility, the history of Formula 1 might have been very different.

Instead, Ron came up with a less bloody and probably more sensible scheme. He suggested to John that they buy out Teddy's and Tyler's shares, 50% of a company that was now worth a good deal more than £1 a share. Before preparing an offer, Ron first talked to John Hogan to secure his backing. Hogan made it clear that it couldn't be done with Marlboro money; somehow Dennis and Barnard would have to raise the necessary funds themselves.

All these years later, Ron says that he was in no rush to get rid of Mayer. He knew the pressures the man was under and felt some sympathy. He also recalls that the first move came from Teddy: 'Life wasn't great for him at home so he used to do his paperwork all through the weekend — a clean-desk policy. There was this naked white envelope with "Ron" written on it. The message was brief and to the point: "This isn't working." I actually thought it was working quite well. I thought we were making a competitive car again.'

If Mayer had had Ron's entrepreneurial nous, he would have appreciated the strength of his position and realised that actually he should have been looking to increase his control. As it was, he felt weak and undermined. Ron sums up the situation:

'We weren't far enough down the road, thank God, that McLaren's value was high. If we'd been more successful, it would have been more painful. We had cracked most things and the revenue had gone up. John had complete control of the drawing office and effectively it was an opportune moment for them to take back control. What they didn't really expect was that we'd find a way to buy them out. I think that really caught Teddy out.'

On 13 October 1982 Dennis and Barnard offered Mayer and Alexander $1.4

million (£811,500) to buy out their shares. This meant that the two Americans would gross $1,003,500 (£582,000) between them once outstanding debts owed by the business and its owners had been paid.

Understandably, Teddy wasn't impressed. After capital gains tax, he reckoned that in reality the offer was worth $513,500 (£297,500). This would have put just £253,000 in his pocket and £44,500 in Tyler's. Or, as Teddy succinctly put it in his counter-offer, he himself would get just £14,000 a year for the 18 years he'd worked at Team McLaren, and Tyler just £2,500 per year.

He clearly thought the offer an insult and stated: 'We do not wish to retire from Formula 1, nor are we willing to give up McLaren cheaply after 18 years of involvement.'

Prepared with the thoroughness to be expected from a former lawyer, Mayer's counter-proposal included his summary of McLaren International's value. He estimated McLaren's fixed assets to be £386,000 and total assets to be £1,086,000, amounting to a net asset value of £793,000 after liabilities. He added to this £500,000 for 'goodwill and the McLaren name as a going concern', and put on top a two-year profit potential of £1,150,000 based on Marlboro's contributions of £2,555,000 in 1982 and £2,950,000 in 1983. He also reckoned McLaren International's projected incomes for 1983 from all sponsorship, including Michelin and prize money, to be £5,290,000, generating a profit of £424,000, and for 1984 he forecast an income of £5,750,000 with a profit of £726,000.

He then presented four options to Dennis and Barnard.

Option One contained a proposition about rewards for the directors. The salaries for 1983 would be: Barnard, £50,000; Dennis, £40,000; Alexander, £35,000; Mayer, £30,000; Creighton Brown, £5,000. Barnard would get 15% of all prize money (in 1982 this would have been more than £90,000) and Dennis would get 5% of all sponsorship revenue, potentially bringing him up to Barnard's income. Each would be awarded a 30% shareholding — majority control — while Mayer would get 25% and Alexander and Brown 7.5% each.

This was the option that Mayer was rooting for, his 'preferred alternative', which offered both Dennis and Barnard, in Teddy's words, 'the opportunity to make very considerable sums of money, which was your stated objective.'

Teddy's tone in these communications is detectably superior but, between the lines, there's evidence of strong emotion. Formula 1 was not about the money for Teddy, it was about the passion, the fans, the heady roar of the engines, the glamour, the status, the sheer excitement and the pursuit of victory. He had lost a brother to motor racing but still he was in it for love.

What he didn't seem to appreciate was that both Dennis and Barnard were also in it for love. It was simply that, from humbler backgrounds, and not being sons of a Pennsylvanian stockbroker nor nephews of a State Governor, they both had a keen sense of the value of money and what it's like not to have it. However, Barnard insists, 'For me, it wasn't about the money either. It was simply because I just couldn't work with the guy and I was going to leave if he didn't go.'

Mayer added ruefully, 'Obviously no one is particularly pleased by the substantial reduction in our own financial position which this offer entails, but it is made in the genuine belief that the Company will be stronger if everyone involved believes he is being properly compensated for his contribution.' Clearly he valued Barnard's contribution higher than anyone else's, and, equally clearly, most of his anger was reserved for Dennis.

There were also the three other options.

Option Three proposed that Dennis and Barnard buy all Team McLaren shares for $2.5 million, with half up front and the rest by 30 May 1983. This was Mayer's 'minimum price for an immediate sale'. He wrote, 'We do not think the price is unduly high. Moreover it is manifestly preferable and a great deal easier, for both you and your financial backer, to obtain a going concern rather than to start from scratch.' A fair point and well made.

Option Two was a compromise between One and Three. It proposed the same salaries as Option One, but smaller prize money and sponsorship percentages to Barnard and Dennis. It also offered a revised allocation of shares: Dennis 39%, Mayer 33%, Barnard 20%, and 4% each to Alexander and Brown. It also stipulated that by 30 October 1984 Barnard and Dennis would have purchased Mayer's and Alexander's shares for $1 million, with $500,000 to be paid up front a year before.

Option Four was the sting in the tail, and Mayer introduced it with some emotion: 'If you examine Option Four, you will understand why your original offer is not particularly attractive to either of us. Quite honestly we both prefer this alternative to your original offer, if only because neither of us is willing to give away something for which we have worked most of our lives.'

It proposed nothing less than the liquidation of McLaren International and examined its grim realities in forensic detail. Mayer estimated that the assets, less liabilities were worth about £500,000, that capital gains tax on that would be about £150,000 and that the balance remaining would be £340,000. Were this to be divided between the shareholders, taking into account debts that were owed by Dennis and Brown to Mayer and Tyler, Mayer would get £224,000, Alexander £61,000, Dennis £45,000, Barnard £31,000 and Brown £17,000.

Mayer was looking at liquidation because he and Alexander would refuse to sell if Dennis and Barnard didn't agree to any of the other three options. If they refused to sell, there would be nothing that Barnard and Dennis could do about it — the directors would be forced to wind up the company. Mayer also pulled another Sword of Damocles out of its sheath. He pointed it at the Marlboro sponsorship contract, which stated that should he or Dennis cease to be involved in day-to-day management, or that if Barnard ceased to be the principal designer, Marlboro reserved the right to withdraw funding just 30 days later.

Mayer then had a direct pop at his main rival, Ron Dennis: 'Discussion with John Hogan has established that he would only be seriously concerned if Barnard ceased to be the principal designer'; in such a case 'liquidation would be inevitable'.

This was Mayer's way of telling Dennis to get stuffed, that he wasn't as valuable as he thought he was, that Barnard was more important, that he, Mayer, could do Dennis's job and so could any number of other people. John was the heart and soul of McLaren International. Without him, it simply couldn't survive.

Hogan recently confirmed this analysis: 'You've got to get down to the real legal situation. It's no use throwing your hands in the air. Ron Dennis walks out the door, but you've still got John Barnard. Other way round, you get concerned because you have got to have someone to construct and build a car, someone who understood the immense complexities of the revolutions that were happening in Formula 1. You can survive Dennis's departure, you can get someone else in to manage, you could put Alastair Caldwell in charge, or Tyler Alexander. You could have done all those things. It would not have been so good, but that bit was survivable.'

Mayer's final gambit was based on his assessment that Barnard was in it for the money. This was, effectively, an offer to Barnard: 'You stay, we'll get rid of Dennis, and you'll make a fortune.' Mayer was also relying on the long history of McLaren: did these new boys really want to be responsible for the liquidation of a team so beloved by so many fans in Britain, New Zealand and around the world?

The ploy cut no ice with Barnard, who was used to divide-and-rule tactics at McLaren. Mayer had failed to appreciate how impossible it would be for Barnard to stay on working with a man who irritated him so much.

Dennis and Barnard went for Option Three, adding almost a million dollars to their original offer. Their offer of $2,344,600 meant, after tax at 30%, a net figure of $1,641,220. The record suggests that, on the following day, 22 October 1982, Mayer and Alexander accepted a rounded-up figure of $2,345,000 for Team McLaren, but asked for salaries to the end of the year plus £25,000 each in compensation for 'loss of office'. There must have been more haggling to follow because a letter on 9 July 1984 from Barnard's solicitor, Michael Jepson, to Mr G. Fisher of Baker McKenzie records the final sale figure as $2,200,000.

Only one questioned remained. Where on earth were Barnard and Dennis going to get $1.1 million each?

The answer was Barclays Bank in Woking, back in those golden days when banks were more willing to lend money. John and Ron found themselves sitting in front of the young assistant manager, his boss away on holiday. They presented their credentials together with some financial undertakings from Marlboro outlining the future security of the investment. They also presented the deeds to their homes. The assistant bank manager beamed.

This was new and deeply uncomfortable territory for Barnard. He consulted Rosie: 'I told her that this was a pretty safe bet, but it was nevertheless a significant risk. If the car failed to live up to expectations — and at the time I was putting it through a complete redesign — we could lose everything.' The decision, at odds with an upbringing that had taught him to eschew borrowing, never sat well with him.

At an Extraordinary General Meeting of Team McLaren at 199 Piccadilly, London, on 16 December 1982, ownership passed to Dennis, Barnard and Brown, and Mayer and Alexander resigned as directors 'with immediate effect'.

Now the début duo had everything they had dreamed of — complete control over their own destiny. As Ron succinctly put it 35 years later, 'Well, what you can say is that we backed our arses into McLaren quite successfully', to which John would reply, 'Yes, but it was necessary, wasn't it? They weren't thinking the right way, were they?' The old guard had been thoroughly routed. Now McLaren belonged to Dennis and Barnard and nothing, surely, could stop them from having an all-conquering season in 1983?

CHAPTER 17
COKE IS IT
1983

If 1982 closed with a shattering blow for Teddy Mayer and Tyler Alexander, it also delivered one to John Barnard. On 3 November FISA declared a ban on underwing tunnels and their attendant skirts with immediate effect, from the start of 1983. Overnight, ground-effect was dead and, with it, John's design for the MP4/2 turbo-powered car, due to run within a few months.

This was a result of a series of pressures, the most powerful from the 'grandee' lobby that had never mastered ground-effect. Their position, led by Enzo Ferrari and supported by FISA President Jean-Marie Balestre, was supported by those who felt that corners were now being taken too fast and the risk to drivers was becoming too high.

Rumours of a ban emerged about ten days before the announcement and Barnard was hoping against hope it wouldn't happen. After the ruling Ron Dennis came into John's office, keenly aware that he was well advanced in the design for the turbo-powered car, the engine for which had been specifically designed for ground-effect.

As Barnard reports, Ron said, 'They've changed the rules, John. We're going to have to run a flat bottom on the car. You'll have to redesign both the 1983 car and the turbo car.' John just stared at him, before slumping down into his seat, reeling from what he describes as a sledgehammer blow. 'We've just lost 50% of the advantages gained from the Porsche engine,' he replied with uncharacteristic softness.

He was at a loss. Such a mountain of work, such a fabulous package of aerodynamics and turbo engine, just scrapped. Today, he's unequivocal as to where the blame lies: 'Fucking Ferrari.' That alliterative epithet sums up both his view of Formula 1 politics and his fury at the time with the sign of the Prancing Horse. 'They knew they were in trouble. Their answer, classic Ferrari, was to get the rules changed.' Watson's reaction was similar: 'Bloody Balestre!'

But from the ashes of this blistering edict would eventually arise a solution that would help propel McLaren into the most successful period in its entire history, a brilliant innovation from Barnard that, once more, the entire paddock would copy and one that would emerge from the Teddington wind tunnel.

Fired up by the new regulations that took away his carefully optimised ground-effect 'wing tunnels', Barnard started trying to address the loss of downforce the rule-makers had imposed. He saw that it was now important to investigate the problem created by the wide rear wheels, which presented a barrier to air passing along the side of the car, causing a build-up of high pressure in front of each wheel, adding drag.

He ordered wind-tunnel models of various shapes and sizes; some had long sidepods, others short, and some featured a delta-shaped planform: 'I was looking for something that would jump out at me and guide me as to the best direction to bring back some downforce.'

Alan Jenkins took these ideas to model-makers Random Design but also decided to make a model himself: 'We were running out of time and I drew up a scheme with the back of the car swept in, just a way of wrapping up the radiators with a minimum plan view, which was, supposedly, the rule.

'It ended up being quite simplistic because I made it myself out of plastic sheets at a friend's model shop over a sleepless weekend. I took it to the wind tunnel on the Monday on the back seat of my car — which I remember very well because my model hit me on the back of the head as I braked for the turn-off to Teddington. That helped stop me nodding off.'

Alan's initiative wasn't warmly received. Although Barnard describes the model as 'interesting', he didn't want his designers to create models outside McLaren's normal channels because he feared security would be compromised. He also thought Jenkins's model had a fundamental flaw: 'Its biggest fault was that it lacked sidepods, which made it pretty useless really. But the fact that it was long and narrow did spark an idea.'

John took Alan's narrow chassis shape and added sidepods that were almost identical to those on the previous year's car, including the position of the radiator inlets and outlets: 'I had a feeling that, with Alan's narrower arrangement at the rear, I could take the radiators from the 1982 car and graft them on. I then drew lines from the outside of the radiators to flow inside the rear wheels to the narrow back end.'

The result was the coke-bottle shape in which the rear section of the car, when viewed from above, resembles the upper half of a bottle of Coca-Cola.

Barnard's intuitive feeling was that this new method of airflow would help the rear wheels present less of an aerodynamic barrier and that the shape would also serve to improve airflow over the rear wing. This he further enhanced by making changes beneath the car, allowing the flat bottom to rise upwards to form a diffuser, a curved carbon plate integral with the bottom of the car.

Barnard calculated that the coke-bottle sweep would speed up the air as it squeezed inwards past the rear wheels, thereby reducing its pressure. This would create a 'low' just where the air was rising from the diffuser, which would serve to suck air more quickly from beneath the car and improve the flow to the rear wing.

The design was put to the test in the Teddington wind tunnel. Able to see the effects of the airflow over and inboard of the rear wheels rotating on the rolling road, Barnard made the necessary design adjustments to find the optimum shape. This revolutionary new design was highly effective, serving to increase downforce at the rear of the car, compensating for the loss of ground-effect.

'It returned some of the performance lost by the banning of the Venturi tunnels,' says John. 'A speeding car punches a hole in the air and leaves a low-pressure hole behind it, a partial vacuum that drags on the car, slowing it down. The airflow from the coke bottle filled that hole behind the car far better, reducing that drag.'

Soon cars around the paddock were experimenting with the concept. Barnard recalls that Patrick Head at Williams briefed his aerodynamic man, Frank Dernie, who tried to replicate it based upon the appearance of the MP4/1C. Unable to copy the design accurately enough, it took him three attempts, according to Barnard, before he could get it to show any improvement.

Alan Jenkins has claimed some authorship of the coke-bottle design and is credited with its invention in several places, not least by former BBC Formula 1 technical expert Gary Anderson, who has stated:[51] 'Coming a close second to the front wing is the area inside the rear tyres known as the 'Coke bottle'. Since Alan Jenkins came up with the initial concept for McLaren in the mid-1980s, this is the area that has made single-seater race cars much more open-wheeled.'

---

[51] Anderson, Gary, 'Deconstructing Formula 1: Inside the Coke bottle', autosport.com.

In an interview for this book, Jenkins said, 'The coke-bottle shape was originally my idea. The way it was incorporated into the car John directed for sure, but the original stab at it was mine.'

While Barnard does accept that the idea sprang from Jenkins's slim-line model, he's insistent that both the concept and execution were his. He says he never saw any drawing by Alan and that the model Jenkins made had no dramatic inward sweep because there were no sidepods from which to sweep in.

'Alan played a part, no question,' says John. 'But did he invent the coke bottle? No, he didn't.'

In an effort to improve aerodynamics and to stiffen the link between the wheel and the road/spring damper, John also made a significant change to the 1983 car's suspension, and to explain it necessitates a description of two different suspension systems, push-rod and pull-rod.

In brief, the pull-rod system features suspension rods running from the top of the wheel upright to the bottom of the chassis. When a wheel goes over a bump, the rod is 'pulled' as the chassis drops relative to the rising upright and wheel. A push-rod system is the opposite, with the suspension rods running from the bottom of the wheel upright to a point towards the top of the chassis. When a wheel goes over a bump, the rod 'pushes'. In both cases the rod terminates at the chassis end in a rocker arm working on a damper and road spring.

John didn't like pull-rods because the rocker-arm mechanism was located at the bottom of the chassis, which, as he explains, 'while good for weight, wasn't good for space'. He also didn't like the fact that the pull-rod angles were shallow, whereas the push-rod angles, rising to the top of the chassis, were steeper. This steeper angle gave more stiffness to the system, which allowed the spring/damper units to exert more control over the road wheels, thus creating better ride and handling characteristics. Push-rods also had the advantage of being easier to adjust.

So John changed to push-rod suspension, in the process getting rid of the large triangular plate that had traditionally provided a mounting for the rocker arm but protruded from the upper chassis into the airflow, replacing it with a much smaller plate. But would the new method work?

He tested it in February 1983, a month before the opening race in Rio, installing the system on a 1982 MP4/1B, with encouraging results. He tested it again just before the race, this time on the 1983 MP4/1C with the full coke-bottle body. Niki Lauda found that it was a second a lap quicker and yet handled as well as the previous year's ground-effect car with skirts.

'Niki couldn't understand it,' says John, 'because it didn't feel any faster. It drove the same, balanced the same, felt the same, but was faster. This told me that the wind tunnel was giving us the right answers.'

The Brazilian Grand Prix at Rio on 13 March 1983 seemed a good omen for the season. Lauda qualified ninth and finished third, while Watson's drive was even more impressive, from 16th on the grid to third by lap 29 after a series of brilliant overtaking manoeuvres — but then his engine failed on lap 34.

But the Rio race was as nothing compared with the drama that unfolded in California two weeks later. Long Beach didn't begin well as practice and qualifying were disastrous for both drivers. They couldn't get any heat into their tough, durable Michelin tyres despite hours of fiddling, making changes to suspension and wing settings. Both qualified near the back of the grid, fully four seconds adrift of Patrick Tambay's pole time for Ferrari, Watson 22nd, Lauda 23rd. The mood at McLaren was miserable and expectations of improvement on race day were at an all-time low.

John Barnard, Ron Dennis and John Hogan were feeling the pressure. As Watson commented recently: 'Their faces were as long as a Lurgan spade, to use a Northern Ireland expression. Suddenly Lauda was an overpaid wanker and I should have retired.'

After a disappointing Sunday morning practice, Barnard ordered the cars to be returned to the factory settings and sat back in the sun in the pit lane, hoping the higher afternoon temperatures might help the tyres.

And so unfolded a legendary and surprising race. Lauda and Watson made a remarkable climb through the field, driving with supreme skill as the warmer temperatures did indeed allow the two MP4/1Cs to show their speed as the Michelins came into their own. By lap 28 of 75 the McLaren duo were third and fourth, Lauda from Watson, behind Jacques Laffite's Williams in the lead and second-placed Riccardo Patrese's Brabham. On lap 33 Watson spotted an opportunity and, much to Barnard's delight, shot past Lauda.

Wattie remembers the moment with relish: 'Niki just didn't expect me to make a bold move on him down the main straight. I got a bit of a twitch on and approached him like that, which he didn't like. But the thing that amazed me was that once I'd passed him, he didn't come back at me — there was no fight back.' It later transpired that Lauda had cramp in his right leg for those few laps.

Then Patrese, trying to grab the lead from Laffite on lap 42, made an error at the end of Shoreline Drive and had to take to the escape road, elevating the McLarens to second and third places. Three laps later Watson passed Laffite with Lauda following suit, and that's the way it stayed, although Watson's heart did 'miss a beat' on the final lap when he felt a vibration similar to the one that had heralded his engine failure in the previous race.

On the rostrum, the organisers, evidently ignorant of Ireland's explosive politics, made a misguided effort to celebrate Watson's roots in Northern Ireland by playing 'A Soldier's Song' — the national anthem of the Republic of Ireland — rather than the British national anthem.[52] Wattie was too elated to be bothered. His performance also broke his own record, set at Detroit the previous year, for the most places climbed to win a Grand Prix — and it still stands.

The rest of the season turned out to be disastrous, with Watson and Lauda finding themselves increasingly locked in combat with each other.

'Niki wasn't a difficult team-mate,' says Wattie, 'but he had all the ammunition to manipulate a position for himself in a team. If you can do all that before you even sit in the car, and then you can deliver in the car as well, then you've got the game, set and match.'

The trouble was that for the rest of 1983, Lauda, for one reason or another, didn't deliver on the track. This led to more and more tension.

'What Niki has brought, in every area of his life, is significant qualities of character, intelligence, skill as a driver and communication,' adds Watson, 'but he's also intensely selfish. On top of which if you crash and burn yourself half to death, survive and continue, you are a global icon, and it didn't help my position that Philip Morris had sponsored him throughout his career; it just looked like the McLaren team was made for him and him alone.'

Despite team spirit running through Dennis and Barnard 'like Brighton Rock', there were times when difficult situations were badly handled. For the French Grand Prix on 17 April, Cosworth, in their effort to compete with the turbos, produced an upgraded engine of DFY format, 18kg lighter than the DFV and significantly more powerful. According to Watson, Ron announced that the first DFY would go 'in Niki's car, naturally'.

The choice of words incensed Watson: 'I had a major shout at Ron and

---

[52] *Toyota Grand Prix of the United States (Long Beach)* Autocourse 1983–84, p103.

John. It was the "naturally" that got me. At that point I was ahead of Niki on championship points. I went apeshit at them both, a really good rant for about half an hour; the air was blue, so much so that Niki had to leave the motorhome. I got my engine the following day. That was the one issue where I felt the team made a misjudgement.'

The new Cosworth didn't help much as Lauda and Watson only qualified 12th and 14th respectively. Neither driver finished the race, Watson going out on lap four with a throttle linkage failure and Lauda on lap 30 with a faulty wheel bearing.

Qualifying performance was even worse at Imola for the San Marino Grand Prix, with Lauda 18th and Watson a desperate 24th, grip from the hard Michelins remaining elusive. At least Watson scored a couple of points with fifth place, but Lauda crashed on lap 12 after locking his brakes.

After long arguments with Michelin, the French company finally produced a tyre especially for McLaren with a different construction from that used by the turbo teams, with the aim of getting more temperature into the rubber. At a preliminary test at Clermont-Ferrand, Barnard found them 'immediately better'. Michelin undertook to get some sets ready for the next Grand Prix, in Monaco.

In Thursday's first qualifying session in Monaco, with no sign of the new tyres, Lauda and Watson were a dismal 22nd and 23rd. But the tyres did arrive for Saturday and during that morning's practice the McLaren duo's times improved dramatically. Then it rained. McLaren's drivers were unable to improve their times in afternoon qualifying and so failed to make the cut — only 20 cars were allowed to race.

As Lauda put it, 'Thursday — shit: Friday — nice weather, no practice; Saturday — rain. Thank you gentlemen. Good afternoon.'[53]

According to Watson, Ron Dennis was even more direct: 'Ron, bless him, turned round and said, "I'd rather you two had crashed than failed to qualify." Well, thank you, Ron. A very difficult moment.'

The pressure stoked up further a week later. After a 13-year absence, the Belgian Grand Prix returned to the remodelled Spa-Francorchamps circuit, but still the McLarens qualified far down the field, Lauda 15th, Watson 20th. And again both failed to finish, Watson crashing on lap nine and Lauda stopping on lap 34 with engine trouble.

---

[53] 'Grand Prix de Monaco', Autocourse 1983–84, p130.

At the United States Grand Prix in Detroit on 5 June, Watson delivered another brilliant performance, setting the fastest lap of the race on his way to third place, having started 21st. But Lauda could find no grip and retired on lap 50, blaming a faulty shock absorber. A week later Watson collected another point with sixth place in the Canadian Grand Prix while the Austrian spun out on lap 12.

As for pressure, for Barnard, at the mid-season point, it had become more extreme than at any moment in his career so far. It all came to a head after the British Grand Prix at Silverstone on 16 July.

With his record pay packet, Lauda was under increasing pressure to perform. As Hogan says, 'He was paid to be a second faster than Wattie and just wasn't cutting it.' Somewhat embarrassed by his lack of performance and certain that it wasn't all his own fault, Lauda decided to take control of the situation, by going straight to the top, over the heads of Dennis, Barnard and Hogan.

Aleardo Buzzi, a Swiss Italian, was now Hogan's boss, having recently taken over from Dave Zelkowitz as Philip Morris's president of the EEC region. As Hogan reports, 'Aleardo was walking down the starting grid at Silverstone and arrived at 15th position, Niki Lauda's car. He put his head down and Niki said into his ear, "You know, if vee don't have a turbo zis year, zen by ze end of zis year zis car vill not even qualify."' Barnard was in Lauda's firing line.

Ironically, Lauda scored his first point in seven races by finishing sixth at Silverstone, while Watson was ninth. As a mark of how far the turbo revolution had advanced, Lauda's McLaren was the highest-placed Cosworth-powered finisher, turbo runners occupying the top five places for the first time.

The following week Ron was summoned to Philip Morris HQ in Lausanne. When he walked into Hogan's office, Buzzi was waiting for him with a demand: 'Ron, results have been poor. We need the turbo car now.' Aware of the impact such a move would have on Barnard, Ron refused outright. In Hogan's words, 'Ron effectively blew a raspberry at Aleardo's request, so Aleardo replied, "OK, I tell you what, Ron, if the turbo car doesn't appear, I'm not paying you. You either run it or you give us our money back."'

Ron immediately phoned Barnard, who, understandably, was apoplectic. 'That's not possible, Ron, that wasn't the deal. I can't just stuff the Porsche turbo in the existing car! It can't work! I'm building a car tailored for the damned thing for 1984. That was the agreement!'

'Sorry John, but if you don't, Marlboro say they will pull the plug.'

Barnard's hand was forced. He paced around his office, fumed a little longer before bowing to the inevitable, picking up the phone to Porsche and ordering the delivery of two engines, currently in the testing phase.

Hogan accounts for Buzzi's intransigence by blaming Ron's tendency to be over-optimistic, leading Marlboro to believe the turbo car would be ready earlier rather than later: 'The problem was Ron, being Ron, couldn't help but say to the Philip Morris management, "Don't worry, it'll win straight away!", and, "The turbo will be in the car early in the season." So everybody was sitting there, waiting; we had paid for all this to happen and of course time was marching on. You could see Ron shifting from one foot to another, and you began to think the thing was never going to see the light of day, because, of course, Barnard didn't want it to run until everything was right.'

The race was now on to get the turbo into the existing car as soon as possible. The most likely date was in time for the Dutch Grand Prix at the end of August, just six weeks away. Barnard was now busy redesigning what was by then the Cosworth-engined MP4/1D to create the TAG-powered MP4/1E.

The first thing to go was the elegant coke-bottle shape, which had to be modified into a more slab-sided shape, somewhat reminiscent of the ground-effect car, to incorporate the turbo engine's larger radiators and intercoolers. The redesign was thoroughly tested in the wind tunnel. Says Barnard, 'The happy surprise was that the new configuration of the coke-bottle shape showed no significant drop in performance.'

The designer also fretted about having to use the existing Hewland gearbox with the turbo engine, but realised it wouldn't be possible to change it in time. He'd just have to hope that the Hewland package could handle the increased power, which, he figured, might be offset by its smoother delivery.

As if to symbolise Barnard's predicament, one of his cars blew up, an event that has entered the annals of McLaren folklore. This occurred when Ron Dennis and the pit team were experimenting with high-speed refuelling from a pressurised tank. Following Gordon Murray's successful initiative at Brabham the previous year of mid-race pit stops for refuelling and new tyres for his BMW turbo design, the other turbo runners gradually adopted this strategy in 1983 — and it became a factor in the increasingly poor results of Cosworth users.

Having to use pressurised refuelling was another reason why Barnard hadn't wanted the turbo mid-season. He had never been keen on the procedure — 'like priming a bomb in the pits' — and insisted on two conditions in any experimentation, namely that it be done with him present and with water rather than fuel.

So when, one day, he was out of the office, the atmosphere at Boundary Road relaxed and the mice came out to play, with Ron deciding to see how quickly the tank could be filled with fuel. He assembled the team and gleefully 'turned it up', increasing the pressure that pushed the fuel through the filler pipe. The trouble was that, in his enthusiasm, Ron hadn't given chief mechanic Dave Ryan time to secure the breather hose that let air out of the tank as fuel entered.

BANG! McLaren's eighth carbon-fibre tub exploded. With some pride, Ron admits his responsibility: 'The fuel tank was not sufficiently vented to take the flow of fuel they were putting in, and it was fine up to the point that the tank was full. And the moment the tank was full, there was a residual pressure in the refuelling rig and it just blew the back out of the monocoque — the rubber bag containing the fuel and everything. It was a mighty bang. Happily the accident gave birth to the fact that the refuelling rigs were redesigned in such a way that such an accident couldn't happen.'

Young engineering student Matthew Jeffreys recalls the smell of fear: 'Now everyone was wetting themselves about what JB would do when he got back. I have this memory of the sound of his Porsche's engine as he arrived in the car park and JB strolling through reception to his office, closely followed by Ron Dennis and Steve Nichols, like a couple of ducklings behind their mother. The door to the drawing office was open, but that was closed pretty smartly by Ron with him uttering the words, "John, don't OD but..." Despite the door closing, I heard John say, "You've blown the bloody car up, haven't you?" He knew instinctively what they had done!'

As John recalls it, 'When I returned, everyone was avoiding my eye; I just didn't know why. Ron was so worried about my reaction that he ran away for a while, fearing another explosion.'

Ron adds a little to the picture: 'It was during a lunchtime and this was one of the rare, rare moments, because the whole company was waiting for John to come back from lunch in order to see the spectacular secondary explosion of John dumping on me... so I was steeling myself for this moment. And John came in and he was totally cool... he just realised there was no necessity to make it worse.'

When John found out what had happened he might have been cool, but inside he was furious. 'The worst part was that it was a brand-new tub; it had never even been to the races and they'd split it in half.' The fact he didn't himself 'explode' is worth noting: when big things went wrong, John tended to be much calmer, instead using his periodic detonations over smaller issues as his own in-built pressure-release valve.

By mid-August the revised car, the MP4/1E, was ready for testing and flown out to Weissach, Porsche's test track near Stuttgart. Still seething with Lauda, whom he blames entirely for being forced to rush the turbo project, Barnard gave the test-driving honours to Watson. But the car didn't run well, suffering terrible throttle lag. Also present was a Porsche 956 sports racer fitted with a TAG turbo engine and one of the Porsche engineers told Watson to try that: 'I jumped in, drove it and found the throttle response much better. I don't know why that was.'

Barnard, however, did know why. When he arrived with Ron an hour later and discovered that Porsche had put his engine in another car, he hit the roof. 'I knew that the extra weight of the sports car would disguise the turbo lag. Ron thought the same, but perhaps didn't make it as clear as I did. It gave Porsche a false impression, making them think the problem was not with their turbo.'

The next test was at Silverstone, with Lauda. He went out for a few laps and on his return Barnard asked how the car felt. 'Like taking off in my Learjet,' Niki said. 'It just keeps on pushing until it gets to the top, unlike the Cosworth, which feels like it runs out of breath.' Porsche seemed happy with their engine's performance but Barnard thought there was still a lot of work to be done, as turbo lag remained excessive and the engine was burning too much oil.

Porsche's solution was to propose fitting a bigger oil tank, a suggestion that didn't go down well with Barnard. 'There's no room and that's extra weight,' he said. 'It's pretty straight-forward. Your engine is burning too much oil!' It was, he says, a classic case of an argument between engine people and chassis people. 'It will happen anywhere you go and I've encountered it numerous times. Engine says, "You haven't got enough cooling." Chassis says, "Your engine is running too hot."

'It was burning oil, not leaking it. I knew that one way to generate more power in an engine was to have piston rings that were less than super-tight. But this would use more oil.' In the end, he reports, Porsche came up with new piston rings and made some changes to the valves. Oil consumption dropped with no appreciable loss of power.

To minimise the turbo lag required a host of adjustments. The basic rule said that the larger the turbo, the more power at high speed, and the greater the lag. Conversely, a smaller turbo would give less power and less lag. By adjusting the electronics and varying the turbo sizes, Porsche, with Barnard's input, began to solve the problem. Soon they would produce different turbos to suit individual circuits: a high-speed track like Monza, with long straights and few corners, would use a larger turbo, while a winding track like Monaco would merit a smaller version.

Porsche also introduced a sequential fuel-injection system that supplied fuel to each cylinder just before each firing stroke. 'This was more efficient,' reports Watson, 'but it was a pig to start. I used to spend more time in the pits trying to start the thing than on the track.'

Lauda was given the turbo-powered car for the Dutch Grand Prix, with Watson left to face certain ignominy in the old Cosworth version. All the same, as *Autocourse* recorded, 'His casual treatment at the hands of the Marlboro McLaren management fired "Wattie" into an aggressive mood.'[54] His aggression didn't help him much in qualifying as he started 15th to Lauda's even less impressive 19th.

The TAG-Porsche turbo performed adequately in the race, helping Lauda move up to 12th before, on lap 26, he was forced to retire. Brake fluid was boiling in the callipers because the carbon brakes ran hotter as a consequence of the turbo car's higher top speed, 15mph more than the Cosworth.

But Watson, the bit between his teeth, ploughed on in the less powerful Cosworth, his carbon brakes working well. He passed car after car until he crossed the line in a brilliant third place after one of the best drives of his life. Barnard decided to return to cast-iron discs while he tried to solve the conundrum of carbon ones.

For the Italian Grand Prix at Monza on 11 September both drivers had turbo cars, but they still languished mid-grid at this 'power' circuit, Lauda 13th, Watson 15th. In the race both engines failed, Watson exiting on lap 14 and Lauda coming to a halt with electrical problems 10 laps later.

Both turbo cars ran at Brands Hatch a fortnight later in the European Grand Prix, where Watson, driving in his 150th Grand Prix, did well to qualify 10th to Lauda's 13th. Approaching half distance in the race, a damaged rear wing caused Wattie to dive into the pits, where Barnard ripped off the broken part

---

[54] '*Grote Prijs van Nederland*', Autocourse 1983–84, *p192.*

and sent the Ulsterman back out while the crew readied a new wing. Halfway round the lap, approaching Hawthorn Bend at about 180mph, the damaged wing came apart, hurling the car into the catch-fencing. Badly shaken, Wattie got out of his car and spent the rest of the race sitting quietly at the marshals' post there. Meanwhile, Lauda's engine failed again.

McLaren's dreadful 1983 season concluded on 15 October at Kyalami in South Africa, where Lauda and Watson were mid-grid yet again, 12th and 15th respectively. Just prior to the start, Wattie found his engine misfiring and headed into the pits to swap to the back-up turbo car that McLaren now had available. With moments to spare, he took up his 15th position on the grid, forgetting that, having pitted during the formation lap, he was obliged to start from the pit lane. He was running 11th when, on lap 18, he was given the bad news — disqualification.

Lauda fared much better, climbing impressively to second place. With just six laps to go, and when he was catching race leader Patrese in a Brabham, the car rolled to a halt with an electrical failure. The blame lay with Bosch, who, Barnard says, used a relay switch from a VW camper van: 'It simply wasn't able to cope with the vibrations and a wire broke inside. It was a huge disappointment.'

For Barnard there was a small sense of victory amid the general air of defeat: as he had known, the rush job of adapting the existing MP4/1D to take the TAG-Porsche turbo engine was never going to reap the benefits that Lauda and Marlboro had wished for. As John often told Rosie in his frustrated conversations at home, 'Why can't people hold their nerve and trust me?' The one plus from this debacle, however, was that the new turbo engine had now been fully tested under race conditions.

There was a reason to be cheerful at the end of the 1983 season: at last Barnard had managed to solve some of the problems caused by the carbon brakes, playing the key part in yet another breakthrough.

Carbon brakes get hot, red hot. Carbon turns kinetic energy into heat energy much faster than cast iron, so the overheating problem was immense; carbon discs can change in colour from black to red and, alarmingly, even to white under extreme loads. And, as Lauda had discovered in Holland, this heat ultimately boils the hydraulic brake fluid in the callipers. To tackle this, Barnard had introduced simple but effective air ducting to bring cooling air around the brakes on the Cosworth car, but this wasn't sufficient for the turbo.

John discussed the problem with the French company, SEP, now part of Safran Landing Systems, a world leader in carbon brakes for aircraft, and between them they came up with a solution. SEP would make the carbon discs thicker and drill into their rims multiple radial holes to help dissipate heat while also reducing weight. 'We didn't really know if these discs would work,' admits John, 'but when we tried them, it was night and day. No one had been running carbon discs with consistent reliability until this point.' The carbon disc problem had been solved, and the paddock, once more, would eventually copy Barnard's solution.

He also addressed another difficulty with carbon brakes. As with cast-iron discs, each carbon disc was bolted to an aluminium mounting disc, known as the 'bell' or 'top hat', which itself was fixed to the wheel hub. What bothered John about this arrangement was that the aluminium bell expanded more than the brake disc, and seriously so with carbon. In addition, the disc fixings wore a groove in the aluminium bell, making the expansion issue even more problematical.

Barnard's challenge, then, was to redesign the fixing method that joined the aluminium bell to the carbon disc, by devising a mounting system that would allow some sliding between the bell and the disc. His solution was to cut radial slots into the bell and fit specially made steel blocks into these slots, then bolt the disc to these blocks, complete with bushes to provide a degree of 'free float'. When the aluminium expanded, the steel blocks could slide along the slots while still keeping the disc secure. This mounting system was soon used by all teams.

Over a decade later, after Michael Schumacher won the 1994 Hungarian Grand Prix for Benetton, Barnard received a trophy from Carbon Industrie (a larger French company that absorbed SEP) to commemorate the 150th victory for a car using carbon discs. He still treasures this recognition.

Nelson Piquet became the 1983 World Champion in a Brabham powered by a BMW turbo. Watson finished sixth in the standings, Lauda eighth. McLaren was only fifth in the Constructors' Championship. No one was happy at Boundary Road. Something was going to have to give. The sacrificial lamb turned out to be John Watson.

Wattie's manager, Nick Brittan, had been negotiating for more money, quite rightfully, as his man had trounced the Austrian superstar. Discussions had reached the point where Marlboro's John Hogan agreed that Wattie should receive more, but not necessarily the million-pound retainer that Brittan was pressing for. Then, two days after the South African Grand Prix, Hogan was distracted by some hot news. Alain Prost, who had been sounding off in recent months about his Renault team's failings, had been fired after one indiscretion too many.

After phoning Prost for confirmation of his sudden departure from Renault, Hogan called Ron Dennis to tell him what was afoot and Ron duly spoke to Barnard, asking, 'Do you fancy having Prost as a driver?' John says, 'I took about three milliseconds to say "Yes"!'

The following Monday Lauda called Watson at home. 'He told me to be careful,' says Wattie, 'because they were talking to Prost about driving for the team.' Clearly Lauda also felt under threat. But by then the deal was all but done, and Watson was out. He is philosophical about it: 'I had enjoyed ten years of Formula 1, raced 151 Grands Prix, and survived. I accepted having to leave. It wasn't what I wanted, I would have liked to have continued, but it was manna from heaven for McLaren. They were getting Prost for nothing. Renault had to pay him off, so Renault effectively paid for him to drive for McLaren.'

Looking back over the years, Barnard still feels that the decision to run the TAG-Porsche turbo early was a mistake. 'I suspect they thought that we would automatically get back up to the front. My ideal scenario, and maybe I was being a bit too perfectionist, was to carry on racing the Cosworth car while running a full test programme with the turbo car on a regular basis so we could be ready for a flying start in 1984.'

Now Barnard had a rare luxury. He had several months to perfect the new MP4/2. After such a disastrous 1983, surely, finally, the only way was up?

CHAPTER 18
THE PERFECT CAR
1984

Early 1984 saw Barnard cracking on with finalising the MP4/2, his turbo car as originally conceived rather than in compromised MP4/1-based form as raced in the latter part of 1983.

Having successfully developed carbon brakes the previous season, Barnard now made another improvement to them. Owing to the extra heat from the carbon discs, the brake callipers were becoming distorted in race conditions and causing the brake pads to wear unevenly, so they had to be strengthened. New callipers were machined from high-specification, high-temperature blocks of aluminium alloy, with ribs and fins introduced to aid heat dissipation, and extra strength was added by changing the way in which the calliper was mounted and bolted to the upright.

This system looked beautiful and worked brilliantly. As John explains, 'We were able to retain a low-weight calliper that was much stronger and much more capable of handling the immense loads put on the brakes by turbo power. We were the first to win races and a championship running only on carbon brakes. The innovations were copied up and down the paddock.'

Barnard's callipers were destined to carry his magic number of 202, as related in the chapter about Chaparral: 'When I did the first calliper it would have been measured in inches but when, some years later, Brembo wanted to make a similar calliper, they asked me what centres I wanted for the fixings that attached it to the upright. They'd schemed a calliper with the centres 200mm apart. I said, "Make it 202." I think that distance stayed a long time within Formula 1.'

Turning to aerodynamics, Barnard, like most of his competitors, introduced winglets to each end of the rear wing, finding that this relatively simple addition gave the car a significant gain in downforce that wasn't sensitive to changes in attitude and ride height. This was something that Alan Jenkins was able to test thoroughly in the Teddington wind tunnel.

Straightening the sides of the chassis around the fuel tank area allowed the car to carry more fuel low down in the fuel cell, lowering the centre of gravity and helping to make the car more stable. This change also accommodated the intercoolers, the small radiators that cool the pressurised air flowing from the turbo into the engine.

Barnard also redesigned the gearbox to cope with the extra power, making most of the parts to his own specification. There were, he reports, 'a lot of detail improvements that would eventually make the gearbox much more reliable'. He also revised the rear suspension and uprights, making them stiffer and stronger so they could handle the extra power and downforce.

Steve Nichols was particularly impressed by the new uprights, each of which was made, he states, 'as a spool that housed the wheel bearing with spokes radiating out to another spool around the outside of that, and then a thin wall of sheet metal made in a fantastic shape to pick up the brake callipers and suspension points — it was a really fantastic work of art. To this day, I think these are the best uprights that have ever been made, even though people have since gone on to use die-cast titanium and machining out of metal matrix — all sorts of weird and wonderful ways.' A further ingenious detail of the 'double-spool' upright was the inclusion of a metal web between the two spools to allow better airflow over the brake discs.

Much later in Nichols's career, when young engineers working under him would come up with new solutions for uprights, he would sit back, feet on desk, back of hand to nose, thinking: 'We have had uprights like John's for 20 or 30 years; does that mean it is time to change? Or is it such an optimum design that it remains impossible to improve?'

Changing the suspension uprights and brakes prompted another advance that was soon adopted by the rest of the paddock. To allow for suspension movement, the drive shafts, which connect the gearbox output shaft to the wheel hub in each rear upright, had been fitted at each end with a constant velocity (CV) joint, as used on road cars. As John explains, 'Road-car CV joints are made to cope with much larger changes of angle than occur on a race car, but in doing that they compromise the ability to transmit high torque. Normally the angle was, say, 16 degrees, so I changed it to eight degrees. Race cars don't need the higher angles because there's nothing like the same range of movement required — for example, no potholes!'

On a regular CV joint, the central spline was surrounded by a thick outer ring containing holes for bolting the joint to a flange, such flanges being used on the gearbox output shaft and the wheel hub. Instead of bolting all these pieces together ('I always like to get rid of bolts'), Barnard designed a hub and gearbox output shaft with the outer ring of the CV joint integral within them. In doing this, he also changed the geometry to increase the torque capacity, and there was a further advantage: as the outboard CV joints were now contained deep inside the wheel hubs, the drive shafts were longer, thereby reducing their angle change when the suspension moved up and down.

The new integral joint also required the adoption of completely different rear wheel bearings, which were large-diameter, thin-section, angular-contact ball bearings fitted to the outside of the CV joint/hub package. Many people were still using taper roller bearings, which are much less efficient in terms of friction and power loss, apart from being difficult to set up.

'Now we had complete units with no bolts,' he says. 'My life seemed to be spent improving critical parts that no one would ever see!'

By now the Hercules deal had ceased and the carbon monocoques were being laid up in a clean room at Boundary Road and then transported to GEC-Marconi Space in Portsmouth for curing, an outsourcing arrangement that was facilitated by Arthur Webb's move from BAe to Marconi. McLaren were quickly outgrowing the Boundary Road facility and both Ron and John were beginning to talk about the need for more space.

The MP4/2 was first tested at the Paul Ricard circuit just a few days before the season-opening Brazilian Grand Prix — a late first shakedown by anyone's standards. Ever the perfectionist, Barnard always tried to ensure that everything was as right as possible before putting his cars through their paces.

Alain Prost jumped in the car and set off, and, as Barnard recalls, after a couple of laps came in, commenting that there was too much understeer. The front wings were adjusted to apply more downforce. Prost set off again, did some fast laps and came in with a grin on his face.

'What's it like, Alain?' John asked.

'It's fantastic. I know it's a winner,' replied Prost, before phoning Ron Dennis to tell him the good news.

Despite having asked for less understeer, Prost actually preferred more than most, as John explains: 'Nine out of ten drivers sitting in his car would say it had way too much understeer. But he had a way of easing the front end into a corner that allowed him to open the throttle earlier. That was exactly what you wanted with a turbo — it was a style that took the turbo lag out of the equation, because he was putting the throttle on before everybody else. He nearly always out-qualified Niki, who would often say, "I don't understand how he gets that half second on me. I need to look at what he does. It's really pissing me off."'

Prost's memory of this test is even more complimentary: 'I got in the new [car], and by the second lap felt ready to go for a time — really, it was as good as that. We hadn't done anything on set-up at all, but it felt fantastic, better than anything I'd ever driven. We set a new lap record that first day. When I looked closely at the car, I saw that it went together like no race car I had ever seen. The detail work was beautiful and I began to see there was something special about this man Barnard.'[55]

Like the Chaparral 2K, the McLaren MP4/2 was 'out-of-the-box' quick.

Prost qualified fourth and Lauda sixth for the Brazilian Grand Prix on 25 March 1984. Outright qualifying pace was never McLaren's strongest suit during the early days of the turbo era, as Barnard explains: 'People took all sorts of risks to get on the front of the grid. Some would remove the waste gate, which regulates the turbo pressure, and bolt a plate over the aperture, boosting the pressure sky high. You could bring the engine up to 1,000bhp. But we just didn't want to risk wrecking engines. Others could take that risk more easily — BMW, for example, made twice as many engines per season.'

Instead, McLaren's logic was that they had the best drivers in the world and the race itself was what mattered. As if to prove the point, the following day Prost won, and broke the lap record. Lauda also led, from lap 12 to 38, when he went out with an electrical failure. As *Autocourse* commented, 'The Grand Prix left a few quizzical expressions on faces in the paddock. How had McLaren got it so obviously right after so little testing? As Ron Dennis ambled in his distinctive, bouncy fashion towards the car park, that silly grin was still there, wider than ever.'[56]

Ron had plenty to smile about, and his 'silly grin' broadened further two

---

[55] 'Roebuck, Nigel, 'Fifth Column: Was it just too good to last?' Autosport, *13 June 1991*.
[56] 'Henry, Alan, 'Grande Prêmio do Brasil', Autocourse 1984–85, p105.

weeks later in South Africa. Prost qualified fifth and Lauda eighth, performance being marred by the TAG-Porsche engines having trouble running cleanly in the rarefied air; the Kyalami circuit is nearly a mile above sea level. It was a very different story in the race: they finished first and second, Lauda six seconds in front of Prost, with no one else even on the same lap.

Prost's performance was particularly alarming for the competition. His car had failed to start in time for the final parade lap and he had had to jump in the spare, which had been set up for Lauda. Recalling the horror of Watson's disqualification on the same track for the same reason at the end of the previous season, Ron ordered Prost to start from the pit lane, despite a marshal waving him onto the track. Prost proceeded to cut through the field from the back, reaching second place soon after half distance.

There was wide relief across the paddock after the Belgian Grand Prix when the McLaren cars showed major weakness. Niki and Alain couldn't get their cars to perform well at any point and neither finished, both going out with engine-related problems.

At Imola for the San Marino Grand Prix, Prost qualified his MP4/2 second, the first time in two years that a McLaren had been on the front row. He outsprinted the man on pole, Nelson Piquet in a Brabham, to the first corner and thereafter pulled away at a second per lap. The Frenchman was never headed, despite a harmless 360-degree spin on lap 23 and a tyre stop seven laps later. After four rounds of the World Championship, Prost now led the standings by 11 points.

Lauda went out in a puff of smoke with piston failure on lap 16. After investigation, it transpired that Prost's spin had been caused by a piston momentarily jamming in its cylinder before freeing off again. Barnard, of course, was on Porsche's case like a cat on the nape of a running rat. They built two brand-new engines with pistons of new specification just in time for the French Grand Prix at Dijon-Prenois two weeks later.

After another indifferent qualifying performance in France that saw Prost start fifth and Lauda ninth, the McLarens again went well in race trim. Prost was on the verge of taking the lead from Patrick Tambay's pole-position Renault on lap 28 when he had to pit to fix a loose front wheel, but Lauda was poised to take up the challenge and took the lead 13 laps later. A slow tyre change lost Niki the lead, but within seven laps he was back in front and stayed there to the end. Prost was able to resume after his pit stop and climbed back to seventh, setting a lap record on the way.

By now the World Championship was becoming a McLaren benefit, with four wins from five races, and two apiece for the drivers. In the standings Prost led Lauda by 24 points to 18, with Renault's Derek Warwick their nearest challenger on 13.

The Monaco Grand Prix of 1984 was one of those races that has passed into Formula 1 legend. The conditions on the narrow street circuit were appalling, with torrential rain that brought some spectacular crashes but, thankfully, no serious injuries. This was the race in which Ayrton Senna made his inspired progress through the field from 13th place to second, a feat that was all the more remarkable because he was driving a Toleman, which, in any other driver's hands, was never going to be a winner.

In a welcome change at McLaren, Prost put his MP4/2 on pole position, the first pole for a Barnard-designed McLaren and, indeed, the first for the team in seven years. Alain led until lap 11, when he had to avoid Corrado Fabi's stalled Brabham in the middle of the track and unavoidably nudged an attending marshal while doing so. Thankfully the marshal was more shaken than injured, but the incident broke Prost's concentration and allowed British up-and-comer Nigel Mansell, driving his Renault-powered Lotus superbly, to slip past and lead a Formula 1 race for the first time. Such was Mansell's enthusiasm, however, that he over-reached himself in the driving rain and crashed six laps later, handing the lead back to Prost. Meanwhile, Lauda had ascended from seventh on the grid and took over second place before spinning off on the 23rd lap.

The conditions were becoming ever more dangerous, the rain pelting down, with streams of water running across the track. Clerk of the Course Jacky Ickx prepared himself to make the decision to stop the race. Prost, now driving with both skill and caution, was being caught rapidly by Senna, who was in some kind of detached Zen-like dreamland of racing rhythm. He wasn't alone; German driver Stefan Bellof in a Tyrrell, the only non-turbo in the race, was catching both of them.

At the end of lap 32, less than halfway through the 78-lap race, Ickx ordered the red flag to be shown, just as Senna came roaring up the start/finish straight right on Prost's tail, passing his future McLaren team-mate and rival on the line. But rules are rules, and procedure dictated that the positions at the end of lap 31 would count. Prost was the controversial victor, Senna second, Bellof third.

Conspiracy theories abounded: it was all a French plot to promote Prost and humble Senna; it was a cunning ploy by Balestre, the French President of FISA.

This was all nonsense because Ickx was right. As he said at the time, better to stop the race a lap too soon than a lap too late.[57]

Because the race was cut to less than 75% of its full distance, only half points were awarded. This, it turned out, would have repercussions for the outcome of the World Championship.

After five McLaren wins from six races, the Formula 1 circus headed to North America for three races. McLaren had to forgo victory in Canada when the BMW turbo in Piquet's pole-position Brabham held together for once, but Lauda was a close second behind the Brazilian and Prost was a distant third with a down-on-power engine. There was a bit of a glitch in Detroit when Prost finished only fifth after Lauda went out with electronics problems, and an even bigger one in Dallas when both drivers hit the wall; they weren't the only ones as at least ten others did the same on the sub-standard, sun-baked, crumbly, concrete-bordered track.

It was around this time that Prime Minister Margaret Thatcher decided to visit Boundary Road to see for herself this high-profile example of world-beating British engineering and entrepreneurial success. Barnard recalls taking her to see the gearbox assembly area, where he enthusiastically began to explain why he had decided to run a Gleason differential. 'About ten seconds in, I noticed her eyes glaze over. It dawned on me that I should just follow her about, standing at her elbow as she shook hands with everyone in the workshop, because that was all she was interested in.'

Matthew Jeffreys's memory of this event is entertaining: 'Ron insisted everything was to be tidied up, nothing on any desks. That was typical Ron, not thinking she might actually want to see that everyone was busy and working. The night before, I went into John's office and asked him what we were supposed to do during the visit. He said, "It's all Ron's doing. I don't want anything to do with it, it's just getting in the way, it's disturbing everybody." So I expected he'd keep right out of the way.

'But when she arrived, the first place she was taken was the drawing office. And suddenly the door sprung open and there was JB ushering her in saying, "Mrs Thatcher, this is the drawing office", and he completely took over from Ron as her guide from the outset. I had to chuckle — it was completely the opposite of everything he had said the night before.'

---

[57] Henry, Alan, 'Grand Prix de Monaco', Autocourse 1984–85, p141.

Such, no doubt, is the impact of the real presence of High Office. The next visit was from royalty itself, Prince Michael of Kent, cousin to Queen Elizabeth, first cousin to the Duke of Edinburgh and grandson of Tsar Alexander II of Russia. Once more, Ron was beside himself with anxious joy, arriving at Boundary Road in his Jaguar with several pairs of skis that were to be his princely gift, secured through some deal with a winter sports company.

Barnard recalls that the royal arrival was handled with military precision, 'with Ron reporting the approach of His Highness and his police escort at regular intervals: "OK everyone, he's 20 minutes away... he's ten minutes away... Only five minutes!"' Perhaps it's typical of Barnard's attitude to the glamorous side of Formula 1 that he remembers precisely nothing else about the visit other than Ron's puppy-dog delight.

Cigarette manufacturer John Player was the sponsor of the British Grand Prix at Brands Hatch on 22 July, but, much to Marlboro's delight, victory went to McLaren. The race was a two-part affair decided on aggregate after an accident on lap 11 brought out the red flag. After the restart Prost led until lap 37, when a faulty gearbox bearing eliminated his car. Lauda, running second to Prost, received the baton and duly took the chequered flag.

After nine races, the McLaren pair now had three wins apiece. Prost was just ahead in the points standings with 35.5 (the half point a consequence of the 4.5 awarded for his Monaco win) to Lauda's 33. Their nearest challenger was Elio De Angelis on 29, thanks to his reliable Renault-powered Lotus giving him points-scoring finishes in all but one of the races so far.

Now the tight competition between Lauda and Prost was becoming an issue. At this point it should be mentioned that Prost's race engineer was Alan Jenkins and Lauda's Steve Nichols. Barnard remembers warning signs: 'Mid-season onwards, as the title race became more tense, I sensed a gradual separation between the two individual car teams. I'd catch Alan in discussion with Prost in the corner of the garage and it became clear that there were little tweaks going on with his car, that one driver didn't want the other driver to know about. Nothing major, but it was something I sensed going on. I let it ride at the time. Alan knew the McLaren rules — no one driver is given any more than the other. Equal equipment and an equal chance.'

And so the season continued, with McLaren cleaning up and the drivers alternating in victory. Prost won in Germany, at Hockenheim, with Lauda second. Niki won on his home soil in Austria, Prost having initially led the attack until spinning out on oil laid by De Angelis's broken Lotus. Holland saw another one-two, again Prost from Lauda. In Italy, at Monza, it was Lauda's turn again, with Prost suffering engine failure on the fifth lap. Back in Germany for the European Grand Prix at the Nürburgring, the pattern continued with Prost victorious and Lauda fourth.

With his superior finishing record during that run, Lauda had moved into the lead of the World Championship. With one race to go, the Portuguese Grand Prix at Estoril on 21 October, Niki had 66 points and Alain 62.5. The rest were nowhere, De Angelis still the next best but now far adrift with only 32 points. The showdown would be between the two McLaren men, with Prost facing the bigger task of having to earn four points more than his team-mate.

Whatever the outcome, it would be a resounding victory for the team, so the mood was upbeat in the McLaren pits, even if there was trouble with Lauda's engine. The Austrian qualified a lowly 11th while Prost sat on the front row alongside Piquet, who took his ninth pole position of the season in the fast but fragile BMW-powered Brabham.

A fast-starting Keke Rosberg took the initial lead in his Williams-Honda but on lap 8 Prost surged past and took command. Lauda made progress too, relentlessly moving up the field until he reached third place by lap 33.

Barnard was amazed: 'I've never seen Niki drive so hard in a race. He was driving around people, inside people. He had obviously decided when he got in the car that he was going to throw everything at it. As a consequence, he just flew.'

Flying or not, it looked like Lauda was going to be hard pressed to take the second place he needed to protect his points lead. By this time Mansell was in that position, a good half minute ahead. But the gods were smiling on Lauda: Mansell spun off on lap 52 with brake failure. Now Niki was second and there was no need for him to take any more risks: he could ease off a little, even allow himself a cautious smile. It stayed that way to the end, with Senna ominously taking third place in his less-than-perfect Toleman.

Lauda had beaten Prost to the World Championship title by the smallest of margins — half a point. On the podium Alain stepped down from the top step and invited Niki to take his place. It was a fairy-tale comeback to Formula 1's pinnacle after the horrific Nürburgring fire of eight years earlier. The McLaren drivers embraced and there were both joy and tears. Between them they had won 12 of the season's 16 races — a new record.

Steve Nichols, Lauda's race engineer, recalls the moment with deep pleasure: 'Winning that first championship with Lauda was just fantastic. It was euphoria. There's no other feeling quite like it. The only thing better than winning a Grand Prix is winning the World Championship.'

But if there was one person at McLaren who couldn't bring himself to revel in the team's victory, it was Alan Jenkins. His inconsolable misery irritated Barnard for its vivid demonstration of Jenkins's failure to embrace the McLaren team ethos. His downcast mood even moved Spanish mechanic Joan Villadelprat to the edge of violence.

'I reacted quite badly to losing to Lauda,' Jenkins admits. 'If there had been a pond to throw me in, Joan Villadelprat would have thrown me in it, for sulking after we'd won the championship. I was just sitting there in the corner, gritting my teeth when I got a big bucket of water thrown over me by Joan and I was told to cheer up and start celebrating.' Brought to his senses, Jenkins realised that Villadelprat was right and they went out to make merry.

For Barnard, less inclined to live it up, it was triumph incarnate. The Constructors' Championship was his at last, achieved by a construction that was entirely down to him. McLaren had secured a staggering 143.5 points, with Ferrari a distant second on 57.5. That truly massive margin would make Enzo himself sit up and take note of John Barnard's name. But Barnard allowed himself little time to get big-headed; the old fears and doubts began welling up. As he stated at the time, 'There is a big feeling of, "How do I follow that?"'

McLaren had made it look easy, but it wasn't easy. Throughout the season they had problems with the TAG-Porsche engine, although happily most had occurred during testing and practice. They would lose water, the electrics went wrong, the pistons were dodgy, the gearbox imperfect.

As Jenkins reports: 'It was all on a wing and a prayer — there were so many times the engine blew up in a warm-up and you'd bolt one in and still win the race. Often Mansour Ojjeh had to fly to Stuttgart on a Saturday night to get another engine. It was like that the whole time; we started to think it normal. There were so many ways we could have lost that championship — and yet we dominated.'

In the end, under Barnard's guiding hand, all the problems were resolved and the astounding victory was deservedly secured. John had achieved his dream. His car, now practically perfect, had finished the season with a 1–2 at the chequered flag and over the season it had slaughtered the competition. He should have felt like the conquering hero.

So why did he feel so empty?

CHAPTER 19
MR McLAREN
1984–86

As far as the rest of the world knew, John Barnard was on top of the world. In fact, in a rare moment of humility, even Ron Dennis would declare that 'there is no disputing the fact that John was one of the best race car designers of his time. And he was Mr McLaren.' Ron made this startling concession in an interview for this book, but if everyone else was viewing Barnard's achievements as stellar, the man himself could not agree.

There is something dangerous about total victory. It can confuse the mind, make you take your eye off the ball, throw you into a spin. With his goal achieved, his dream come true, Mr McLaren was at a loss: 'It was hard to think of new things for the following year. I was getting a bit worn out, to be honest.'

A negative mindset had begun to set in and it was taking over Barnard's head. His laser focus wavered and his attention turned elsewhere, finding more and more reasons to be unhappy with being the world's supreme race car designer. His first target was Alan Jenkins, who had, in Barnard's view, allowed his race-engineering role to go to his head.

'At the end of the 1984 season I told Alan that I wanted to bring him off race engineering and back to the wind tunnel. He didn't want to do that. He had got used to the limelight, and, having had such a successful season, that light was bright. The upshot was that Alan left. I didn't want him to leave, but I wasn't going to change my policy. I don't actually know how Prost reacted to that. I didn't really care. I felt it was better for the team.'

Jenkins will not reveal what he calls 'the true reason' for his departure but he does talk of growing pressures within McLaren, despite the victories. For example, he states that Barnard's clashes with Ron Dennis had been getting worse. 'I recall huge rows upstairs, between John and Ron, hearing the floorboards creaking above my head.'

Ron offers an explanation for this. He said that he had to be diplomatic about what he told John, because some things 'would have aggravated the hell out of him'. The trouble came when John found out that he wasn't being given the full picture, something that was happening more frequently as McLaren expanded its interests.

'The consequence of not sharing every single thing with John,' says Ron, 'was that occasionally he would find out something that I hadn't shared with him. He let moments like that undermine trust between us, irrespective of the fact that there had been a good reason not to tell him — perhaps because it would have just annoyed him or it was something that he couldn't influence.

'That was not a good thing. But in fact it was the better of the two evils, because whilst it undermined trust to a certain degree it absolutely kept him stable. Because when he lost it, it wasn't a pretty sight. Everybody around him suffered, it wasn't just me or the person he was angry with. It was like walking on egg shells when John lost his cool.'

Jenkins detected what he felt was a possible decline in Barnard's commitment to McLaren, saying he was having trouble getting John to tell him about the plans for the following year's car. Alan reports Ron approaching him on this subject and learning that Ron didn't know either. As for John, he says, 'The truth was that I didn't know what I was doing for the following year.'

Jenkins says his dilemma came to a head in a meeting with Barnard in Ron's office to try to establish what was happening on the 1985 car: 'I was, if you like, the spokesman for everyone else, trying to find out what was happening next. Barnard didn't take it very well, which pissed me off. He wasn't clear about what he wanted me to do. I was wound up. He'd say, "I'm not ready to tell you yet." I can't remember if he shoved me out or I walked out, but it ended up with me leaving and not coming back. I remember what he said but I wouldn't want it to be in a book. It's history and we've got over it. It was a heat-of-the-moment thing. The stuff on my desk ended up at the door. I didn't put it there.'

Barnard comments that he didn't put Alan's stuff by the door either, and concludes it was someone acting on Ron's orders. Either way, that relationship had come to its end.

John readily admits that another, more crucial relationship was deteriorating: 'I was finding Ron increasingly frustrating. We started having rows. Things started to niggle. Really piddling stuff.' One source of tension was the contrast in lifestyles: 'If I pointed out that I had worked all weekend at Boundary Road while he was off gallivanting with the jet set, he'd say, and he was right, "That's how I meet the right people, John. It's how I get the next sponsor." But from where I sat, I was grinding away, coping with factory problems, moans and groans, and Ron was living the high life. It started to get to me. Little things were beginning to annoy.'

They were equal partners at the top of the Formula 1 game. Why should it be so much harder for Barnard?

'I'd been pushing hard since Chaparral. We'd achieved all we'd set out to achieve. We had the World Championship, Constructors' and Drivers'. I thought, "There's got to be something more to it than this!"' For John, a man with a young family, 'this' seemed to be working nights and weekends while his relatively foot-loose and fancy-free business partner jetted round the world.

Desperately trying to drum up enthusiasm within himself for making improvements to the car, John knew he needed to make a decision but wasn't sure what it should be. For the first time in his life he felt unsure of his purpose, his direction unclear. He needed advice but had no one professional and objective to whom he could turn. He was probably suffering from depression, but even if this possibility had crossed his mind he would have dismissed it as either rubbish or weakness.

So he went back to basics, all the way back to Peel Road and the rock of familial self-reliance. He was still in massive debt and hated that. What would happen if he failed to produce a winner the following year? What would his McLaren shares be worth then? What would he have achieved for his family? He was in a fight with the brightest automotive minds on the planet. He couldn't keep on winning. He wasn't that good; no one was. The 1985 season could be like 1983 had been. He could fail. He probably would fail. Everyone failed. Even his hero, Colin Chapman, had failed.

John Barnard had fought his way to the mountain summit only to discover that the view from the top was terrifying.

Struck by crippling career vertigo, he backed away from the edge. He had to reduce the risk; if he fell his family would fall with him, and that would be unforgivable. The first thing was belt and braces. He need to secure their future. He wanted to make sure that, should anything happen to him, and he wasn't exactly sure what was happening to him, that his wife and children would be safe.

He saw his McLaren shares as 'two in the bush'. He wanted to convert them to a 'bird in the hand'. He went to Ron. 'I think I want to sell my shares.'

To Ron it was a total shock. 'What? Why?'

'I don't like the debt. I hate it. I'm no good at hanging myself on a limb financially. You don't have a family, Ron, you don't understand. It's easier for you. I want to turn my shares into hard dosh.'

Ron's memory of this moment is similar: 'John came to see me and said, "Ron, I have two ambitions in life. They are simple ambitions: I want my children to go to private school and I want to buy a really nice house. For that reason I would like you to sell my shares." He didn't sit comfortably with the commercial pressure. Was it going to be a success? Was it going to be a failure? He was distracted by the commercial side of things and it stressed him a bit. In many ways I thought that as long as he was happy with the salary and the other benefits, it didn't really concern me. I don't think at that moment in time he had any intention of leaving the company.'

Perhaps Ron could be accused of a lack of foresight. John's proposal to sell his shares would entirely change the balance of power between them and that was unlikely to be a good thing. John says that Ron proposed opening negotiations with Mansour Ojjeh, to see if he wanted to buy Barnard's shares. John owned 43% of McLaren. So did Ron. Creighton Brown had 14%.

Ron asked Creighton to try to change John's mind: 'Creighton came to see me, and asked, "Are you sure? In five years' time you will be worth at least five million!"' John's reaction was to dig his heels in: 'I thought he was just trying to stop me doing it because I was upsetting the applecart.' It was in John's nature to implacably oppose a different opinion. There was, he admits, 'an element of self-destruct. But I was telling myself: "Ron's lifestyle is better — I want to improve mine." That's how I justified it.'

John still feels awkward talking about this time, although he is, as ever, brutally honest about it. He feels that he didn't really 'have a very good reason'. One can sense an undertone of regret, even shame. But there were good reasons and certainly no reason for shame: fear of failure, fatigue, jealousy, competitiveness, confusion, anxiety, a sense of displacement, of feeling that he was under-appreciated, increasing irritation with colleagues, all these emotions that had given him so much drive, that had fed his remarkable creativity, now came together to undermine his confidence.

What he really needed was a break, a long holiday, three months or more, so he could come back fresh. But that seemed impossible; a new season was upon them. Diane Holl, a future employee of Barnard's, says he once told her, 'If I had asked Ron for six months off and Ron had agreed, then I would probably have still been at McLaren.' The request was never made.

Meanwhile, Dennis did his best to reassure Barnard, telling him, 'As far as I'm concerned, nothing will change between us. We will carry on operating as we have always done.'

Ron then concocted a deal that would secure his own financial future. Ron, John and Creighton all had shares in the TAG-Porsche engine. John and Creighton would sell their TAG-Porsche shares, and John would also sell his McLaren shares. Ojjeh would buy them all, bringing around $40 million into McLaren in return for a 60% shareholding. The investment would speed up McLaren's transformation.

As John says, 'My decision to sell turned out to be very fortuitous for Ron, enabling him to turn McLaren into what it is today. I have to hand it to him. Ron has an amazing ability to spot an opportunity and act on it and make it work.'

It was also financially fortuitous for Barnard. He refuses to reveal how much the deal was worth to him personally, but it was sufficient for him to pay off all loans, including his mortgage, and put some money aside. He had been set free.

After signing a new two-year contract on 25 October 1984, Barnard continued at McLaren as technical director with an annual salary of £100,000. His new contract included ownership of the winning car should McLaren secure a second championship; even then a championship-winning car was worth in the region of £250,000 and was likely to be an ever-appreciating asset.

Feeling a little more secure, John settled back into preparations for the 1985 season. He replaced Alan Jenkins as Prost's race engineer with Tim Wright, who had been at McLaren in the 1970s and had been working with Gordon Coppuck at Spirit Racing. According to Barnard, Wright expressed some trepidation about taking over such a high-profile role, so, in a rare moment of playing the teacher, Barnard guided him through it. Aerodynamics and wind-tunnel work he handed to Bob Bell, who had recently joined McLaren straight from graduation with a doctorate in aeronautical engineering from Queen's University, Belfast.

With new rules having outlawed the winglet extensions on the rear wing that had partly compensated for the loss of the ground-effect tunnels, Barnard returned to Teddington, briefing Bell to make changes to the diffuser and the front wing in an effort to get some downforce back. They had limited success.

Now John was sinking his teeth into a new problem, and feeling much happier. On the 1984 car, Barnard had used a very stiff rear anti-roll bar, the disadvantage of which, he explains, 'is that it effectively couples the rear wheels together, which isn't good for traction unless, as was the case in '84, you have a lot of downforce.' In an effort to regain grip for the 1985 car, the MP4/2B, he replaced the rear suspension with a push-rod system that enabled him to use a much smaller, thinner, lighter roll bar. He also revised the wheel hub package and created new front uprights. All these improvements helped compensate for the lack of rear winglets, but, as John concedes, 'the '85 car was never really as comfortable as the '84, never as sure-footed.'

John also chose not to run a heavy programme of pre-race testing, instead electing to test at the races, listening to the feedback from the drivers under race conditions to make his adjustments: 'Testing cannot give you all the answers. When the drivers race, whatever they say, they drive differently to when they're testing. They don't drive with the same style. So to get real feedback you have to race it.'

This approach must have caused eyes to pop at McLaren, but no one argued and he explained nothing to anyone. 'I did it the way I felt best, without bothering to explain.' Even more than before, he was doing everything his way.

He didn't even explain it to Prost, with whom he was developing a close technical relationship, discussing the changes to the car, and feeling deeply impressed by the driver's ability to give feedback: 'Alain had an exceptional ability to analyse his car's reactions. He could separate the feeling he got from the suspension from the feeling he detected in the tyres.' This analytical sensitivity was in part why Prost earned the nickname 'The Professor'.

Still looking for ways to reinstate some downforce, Barnard pioneered the development of the first 'barge boards' or turning vanes, the inspiration for which he attributes to Alan Jenkins, who was running the wind tunnel when the idea started to form six months earlier. These half-metre-high, vertical, curved fins, effectively upright wing sections, rose on each side of the chassis behind the front wheels from a plate attached to the underfloor. The aim was to tidy up turbulence coming off the front wheels by diverting the air around the sidepods, with the further benefit of also stabilising airflow through the sidepods to the radiators. As air turbulence from the front wheels could also upset airflow moving from the front wing and under the car, the barge boards promised to improve downforce. But it turned out that these extra pieces of bodywork sitting in the airflow added too much drag.

Barnard: 'At the time I thought barge boards weren't terribly interesting because they weren't improving my lift-to-drag ratio. Looking back on it, there were certain circuits where I probably should have run them. Somewhere like Hungary, where you can really pile on downforce and not worry too much about straight-line speed, because it's all curves and no long straights. It was an idea that sort of got away. I should have carried on with them.'

Had John persisted, this would have become a significant innovation; the concept of barge boards, or turning vanes, was further developed about eight years later and remains an important part of modern Formula 1 aerodynamic packaging. It was a missed opportunity: 'We didn't create and develop an efficient aerofoil shape for them — I just didn't push it. So although we were looking in principle at the effect, we never got it working efficiently.'

Barge boards were tried in at least one race in 1985, the German Grand Prix, the first to be run on the revised Nürburgring, nine years after Lauda's fiery accident. *Autocourse* stated, 'Both cars raced with vertical front aerofoils.'[58]

This was a race weekend that would generate another Barnard breakthrough, this time a spur-of-the-moment innovation that happens in a flash.

Prost and Lauda were experiencing serious braking problems during practice, with the Frenchman describing the brake pedal 'going down to the floor after five or six laps'.[59] This was a sure sign of overheating brake fluid, a return of the bugbear that had afflicted the development of carbon brakes two years earlier. The problem was caused by the reduction in downforce. In the 1984 car Niki and Alain had been able to brake hard and briefly, because the car's superior grip gave higher cornering speed, but now they were braking for longer, allowing time for more heat to pass from the brake pad into the calliper. John put the problem into his mind and let it percolate.

The answer came on the Friday evening before the German race. He turned to Dave Ryan, the McLaren chief mechanic, and said, 'I'm going to try something. The only heat path left into the calliper must be through the ends of the carbon brake pads. I want you guys to shave two millimetres off the ends of each pad. In the space between the pad and the calliper I want you to put a small titanium plate.' Barnard's logic was that titanium was a relatively poor conductor of heat. It was an instant success. John smiles when he recalls

---

[58] 'Grosser Preis von Deutschland — Technical File, McLaren', Autocourse 1985–86, p147.
[59] Henry, Alan, 'Grosser Preis von Deutchschland', Autocourse 1985–86, p143.

this moment: 'It was one of those quick fixes that had a lasting value. It was significant because every calliper after that had titanium slips between pad and calliper body'.

As the 1985 season approached, Barnard, ever-pessimistic, was sure that McLaren would struggle, and would be lucky to make the top three in the championship chase. A further element in his concern was that Michelin had withdrawn from Formula 1 and now McLaren were running Goodyear tyres, which proved less durable.

So it was with a deep sense of surprise and relief that, as the season progressed, it became clear McLaren was going to succeed again.

Prost convincingly won the first race, in Brazil on 7 April, setting fastest lap and lapping the entire field apart from the Ferrari of Michele Alboreto, who finished three seconds behind. In Portugal, an atrociously wet race in which a peerless Ayrton Senna achieved his first Grand Prix victory, Prost crashed out after losing control on standing water on the straight. Alain won in San Marino before being disqualified when his MP4/2B was found to be 2kg underweight.

The bit between his teeth, Prost won in Monaco. After the postponement of the Belgian Grand Prix to the end of the season, because the organisers at Spa-Francorchamps had cocked up track resurfacing, Canada came next and Prost finished third. He went out with electrical trouble in Detroit, but at his home Grand Prix in France, at Paul Ricard, he was third again.

With Marlboro once again sponsoring the British Grand Prix, John Hogan was delighted to see Prost lap the entire field and take the chequered flag in Silverstone's summer sunshine. Second in Germany, first in Austria, second in Holland, first in Italy and third in Belgium — the points piled up for Prost.

He sealed it in the European Grand Prix at Brands Hatch. While Nigel Mansell in a Williams-Honda thrilled his home crowd by winning for the first time, Alain's fourth place confirmed him as the new World Champion, France's first and only one, with 73 points to runner-up Alboreto's 53. And as the season concluded, McLaren also managed to win the Constructors' Championship for the second year in a row, with 90 points to Ferrari's 82, despite Lauda's very limited contribution. The Austrian had a terrible season, with just one victory to Prost's five, and he languished down in 10th place in the standings with only 14 points.

'It was clear early on that Niki had started to lose his edge, his will to win,' says Barnard, who recognised the symptoms all too well. 'He climbed into the '85 car and immediately saw it didn't have the grip of the previous year's. He was going to have to work a lot harder and it was clear to me that he had started to doubt.'

By the fifth race, in Canada, Barnard was convinced that Lauda was on his way out of McLaren, and probably out of Formula 1: 'He pulled in about halfway through the race. He got out of the car saying there was a problem with the clutch. We stripped the car down and couldn't find a problem. That's not to say there wasn't one, but we couldn't find it. I thought, "His heart isn't in it any more." Maybe I recognised his mood from mine. I don't know.'

Lauda announced his retirement, making the statement with his trademark dignity, before the tenth Grand Prix of the year, at his home race at the Österreichring. Having stunned the paddock with the announcement, he seemed to become fired up with new motivation to make his exit from the sport one to remember. He qualified third, by far his best starting position of the season. In the race he was second after three laps and passed Prost on the 27th to take the lead as the Frenchman stopped for fresh tyres. It was all set for an exciting conclusion, with Prost gradually catching his team-mate, until Niki's turbo failed on lap 40.

Lauda sparkled again at the next race, at Zandvoort in Holland. He elected to pit early, on lap 20, and then took the lead when Prost pitted 13 laps later. The last three laps were a desperate battle between the two, their cars inches apart as Prost weaved and dived in the high-speed struggle to get past his rejuvenated team-mate. Prost failed, Lauda won, and with it he equalled Jim Clark's achievement of 25 Grand Prix wins, which all went to prove that when Niki really wanted to win, he did. He had proved, once more, that he was a winner — no need to do it ever again.

Barnard ended 1985 in better mood. He had won two sets of World Championships back to back, for drivers and constructors, and had taken ownership of Prost's winning MP4/2B. He loaned the car for a spell to the Donington Collection of Single-Seater Racing Cars in the Midlands and later sold it to Austrian Formula 1 driver Gerhard Berger.

More than this, much more than this, Rosemary had given birth to a son. Two weeks before the end of the season, on Monday 21 October, at midday, Michael Edward Barnard was born at Mount Alvernia, a private hospital in Guildford. John was working at McLaren when the news came through that Rosie had gone into labour. He finished off some bits and pieces, hopped in his Porsche 928 and roared over to the hospital to find that it was all over, a crushing disappointment for which he had only himself to blame.

But, bliss above blisses, he had a son: 'Michael was small, and I think the consultant wanted to go to lunch, so he delivered my boy by Caesarean,' he quips. Rosie's story is slightly different: 'Michael hadn't turned in my womb and seemed insistent on coming out feet first, ready to play football.'

Rosemary, Jennifer, Gillian and Michael; John's family was complete, and it would ever be the prime focus of his life, what he did it all for.

He bought an even more splendid home called Combe Rise on Munstead Heath Road near Godalming in Surrey. Set in nine and a half acres of lawns and woodland, Combe Rise was a gorgeous six-bedroom house with a large barn and a walled garden. John embarked on a building programme and by the time it was complete the property included an indoor swimming pool, garaging for six cars and a separate flat (for Ted). The family moved in during May 1987 and stayed there until 2008.

The 1985 season had been marked by increased tension between John and Ron. This was partly caused by the change in status, with John now an employee rather an equal partner — a change that inevitably altered the psychological dynamics of the relationship.

'Ron and I were like a marriage,' John admits. 'It was a love-hate relationship. When I didn't agree, I'd go stomping up to scream and shout at him. He told me later: "I used to hate it when I heard your footsteps coming up the stairs."

'But now I wasn't a shareholder. I was still a director but it wasn't the same. There had been a tiny, subtle change in power that is hard to put in words. Almost imperceptible, but there was something there. I couldn't confront Ron in the same way I could before. I could no longer say to Ron, "Why have you just spent the last three days doing this?" or "Where the hell have you been this past week?"

Towards the end of 1985 John visited Ron's house in Pyrford to discuss plans for 1986. John could tell that Ron had something on his mind. Indeed, it was a sensitive subject. Ron said, 'I want to run this past you because it could cause problems. Mansour is offering us an executive jet at an incredibly low price. I think it would be useful for the company. But obviously I am likely to use it a lot more than you will, which you might see as a problem. I don't want it to be a problem between us.'

For a Formula 1 team principal to fly around in a company jet was still a rarity — and the ultimate calling card. John understood its potential utility. 'While we didn't want to be appearing overly flash, and we certainly didn't want sponsors thinking, "What the hell are they doing with our money?", it was obviously going to be an advantage to Ron. And it had advantages for me too — we could leave later for the races and even use it to ferry last-minute upgrades. It was good of Ron to sit down and consult me. He didn't have to do that. But he knew we needed to carry on operating the way we had before. So I said, "I think it's got to be useful. So yes."'

John now put in a request of his own. He had recently had several conversations with John Hogan who had intimated that he thought Barnard should be earning more: 'I had won a second championship. I had delivered both technically and in results. I was no longer a shareholder, so I wasn't gaining from the company's increase in value, a value that was growing because of my work. I discussed this with Hogan and he thought McLaren had got me cheaply. I wasn't really sure what other chief designers earned but I knew what the drivers got and I knew that my work was responsible for 75% of their success. I figured I was worth five times my existing salary.'

John explained all this to Ron and then asked for £500,000 a year. It would also be five times Ron's salary, but then he had valuable shares to compensate. Ron looked down and then back up at John. 'OK, I'll think about it.' That was good enough for John. He knew he was aiming high, and figured Ron would come back with something substantially lower, but that was business.

John now set about preparing the car for the 1986 season. He made a series of subtle changes to suspension and aerodynamics and sought to improve the efficiency of the two turbos.

His aim with the turbos, one on either side of the engine, was to create a ram effect by funnelling air flowing down either side of the chassis into each of them. He got a rough ride for his curious proposal to make them 'handed', with one turbo spinning clockwise, the other anti-clockwise. As he explains, 'I changed the air inlet so that I could bring the air in at the front along the side of the chassis and ram it straight into the compressor inlets of the turbos. By having opposite-spinning turbos I could do that on both sides identically. I didn't have to have asymmetric exhaust systems or asymmetric inlet systems; they could be a perfect mirror image of each other. I just felt that was the right thing to do.'

He also went to work on the gearbox, which was still having trouble coping with the increased turbo power. Each year Porsche would develop their pistons and valves to allow the car to run at higher revs, a factor that would make gear shifting more difficult with each season. Barnard had to find a solution.

Racing cars don't use synchromesh, which allows smooth gear changes, because, as John says, 'Synchromesh is too heavy and you don't mind clunky gear changes as long as they're fast.' But the higher engine revs set the clutch plate spinning much faster and, being made of a heavy metal, the plate had considerable inertia. The more revs, the more inertia and the harder it became to change gear, since it takes time for the revs to drop to match the next gear's speed.

So John created what he believes was the first carbon clutch plate, which was much lighter and therefore carried less inertia. The carbon plates were supplied by SEP and machined at McLaren. Although tests showed considerable promise, the project never reached fruition, and for that John blames himself: 'I didn't push it, partly because it needed more development and we were in the middle of racing already. I don't know — maybe I was slacking. Normally I would have forged ahead and made it happen.'

Keke Rosberg, the 1982 World Champion for Williams, was Lauda's replacement for 1986. His relationship with John started badly. Ahead of the first race, the Brazilian Grand Prix, McLaren flew out the revised car, now called the MP4/2C, to Rio a few days early for testing. In his first session for his new team, Rosberg set off at speed from the pits, made it round the 'out lap' before roaring past the pits only to lose control on the first bend. He was unhurt but the car was very badly damaged. John was furious: 'It was a brand-new chassis. This was a shakedown test. He had completely destroyed the car. I was so angry I was speechless.'

As Prost told journalist Alan Henry at the time: 'I must say I was rather taken aback by Keke's brash confidence at that Rio test. He wasn't like other drivers arriving at McLaren, who were usually meek in outlook and grateful for the opportunity. For instance, he just brushed aside John's suggestion, made at that Rio test, that he might take things easy for the first couple of laps. Instead, he put his foot hard on the throttle straight away — and duly flew off the road mid-way through his second lap… I don't think Keke and John ever quite saw eye-to-eye again.'[60]

---

[60] Henry, Alan, 'Keke Rosberg: The star who failed to shine at McLaren', www.mclaren.com.

Rosberg was back in the pit lane as the car was being dragged in. Says Barnard, 'I looked at him, looked at the car and I was busting to have a go at him but I just couldn't talk. The mechanics were shaking their heads. I think he got the message that I wasn't happy. I never did find out how he lost it on a warm-up lap. Cold tyres, a mistake, something like that.'

John also didn't take to Rosberg's driving style, which he felt was more suited to the ground-effect era in which the Finnish driver had come of age: 'Keke was the last of the late brakers. He would come hard into a corner, stand on the brakes and want to turn the car like a go-kart. It was almost the opposite end of the scale to Prost. Having developed the car over a number of seasons for Alain and Niki, who were out of the same mould when it came to braking, I knew I would be struggling to make it work for Keke.'

Barnard later spent a day with Rosberg at Brands Hatch, trying to achieve an ideal set-up for him, changing springs, altering the suspension and aerodynamics, to try to cater for the way he wanted it. 'We did get it to perform more how he wanted to drive it, but the truth was that he wasn't as good as Prost, despite looking so quick at Williams. It was surprising how differently he drove the car; he couldn't adjust his style and thought he would lose time if he tried.'

Steve Nichols, Rosberg's race engineer, takes a different view about his driver's failure to impress Barnard: 'John got pissed off with the drivers. He developed an attitude: "I am going to design the ultimate car and you will drive it in the way that suits the car." I took a more pragmatic view that we might have to adapt a car to suit an unusual driver.'

The race engineer took it into his own hands during practice for the German Grand Prix at Hockenheim: 'Keke was complaining that the car understeered horribly. By now John had kind of washed his hands of Keke, saying we could do what we wanted with him. Hockenheim is a high-speed circuit which needed minimum downforce. We reckoned we could take downforce off the front but I was afraid I was never going to get enough downforce off the rear to balance it properly. So I asked Bob Bell what we could do, and he came up with a little Gurney flap that we stuck on the bottom of the rear wing. Then I put on our softest front roll bar and took out the bump rubber to make the whole thing really soft on the front.

'John just looked at it and shook his head as if to say, "What are you idiots doing?" I remember the car went trundling down the pit lane with the Gurney flap on the bottom of the wing and Patrick Head just stared at it. Anyway,

Keke got out there and stuck it on pole! He came back in and I asked, "No understeer?" He replied, "No! Now I have understeer, before it was like the car didn't have a front end at all." We found out that the front roll bar had actually broken. I left the broken bits on the front of the car to show people how a radical set-up could work for Keke.'

For 1986, only turbos were permitted to contest the World Championship, and the season brought the most powerful Formula 1 cars in its history. Some generated over 1,350bhp in qualifying, when teams installed 'grenades', engines with unrestricted turbo boost that might blow up after two or three timed laps.

The first shock for Barnard was the realisation that Honda's new V6 engine, as used by Williams, showed signs of being more powerful and more fuel-efficient than his TAG-Porsche. Fuel efficiency was now even more essential because the FIA, which had banned race refuelling in 1984 and introduced a fuel capacity limit of 220 litres, had now further reduced the fuel allowance to 195 litres per race in an effort to keep some control over escalating power outputs. If Barnard had had his doubts about doing well in 1985, they were doubled in 1986.

He put enormous pressure upon Porsche to match the Honda engine, but the basic design was three years old and there were limits to what they could do. To demonstrate the point, this turned out to be the last season for Renault, who had pioneered the Formula 1 turbo but could no longer compete.

The 1986 season became a three-horse race between Alain Prost in his McLaren MP4/2C and the two Williams-Honda FW11s of Nigel Mansell and Nelson Piquet. The contest came down to wire: going into the last race, at Adelaide in Australia, Mansell headed the standings on 70 points, with Prost on 64 and Piquet on 63. Mansell only needed third place to become World Champion, whereas Prost needed to win with Mansell fourth or lower. It would be a thrilling finale.

Rosberg led comfortably for much of the race and looked on course for his first McLaren win until, at the three-quarter mark, a dramatic tyre failure took him out, the tread stripping away suddenly and unaccountably from one of his rear Goodyears and flailing the surrounding bodywork. That left the championship combatants in the top three places, Piquet first, Prost second and Mansell third, the Englishman perfectly poised to achieve his dream.

On the very next lap Mansell suffered the same fate as Rosberg when his left-rear tyre exploded in spectacular style at 180mph. Now his team-mate,

Piquet, only had to hold on to the lead to win the title, but Williams, fearing that the Brazilian might suffer a tyre failure too, brought him into the pits for a change. Prost shot past into the lead to become World Champion for the second time, and to give McLaren that honour for the third consecutive year. But unlike the two previous seasons, McLaren was unable to secure the Constructors' Championship, which went to Williams-Honda because Rosberg's performance over the season hadn't been good enough, with only one podium finish, second place at Monaco. Prost had scored four victories and seven further podium finishes.

It was, of course, satisfying for Barnard to know that his McLaren cars had achieved yet more honours that year and taken their tally of Grand Prix victories to 28 in the six seasons from 1981 to 1986. Satisfying, but irrelevant. His relationship with Ron Dennis had finally blown a gasket and he was already on gardening leave.

PART 5
FERRARI (1)

CHAPTER 20
THE MARANELLO BYPASS
1986–87

John Barnard was becoming ever more disgruntled about Ron Dennis as he 'swanned around' in the company jet doing deals 'for McLaren and himself'. The engineer admits an almost petulant jealousy of Ron's 'high life' and it became increasingly personal for him.

'I think I under-estimated the difficulty and importance of Ron's role,' he says, 'but I had trouble with the whole approach, treating strangers like your best friend when what you really wanted from them was their money. I couldn't understand how you could do that; either you liked them or you didn't, and it usually takes me about five seconds to find that out.'

Barnard came to feel a certain contempt for his boss, for that is what Ron now was. The partnership was long gone. Added to this was the self-imposed pressure on John to produce something new, something better: 'I really don't think Ron or anyone realised how hard it was to come up with new ideas. How do we make the fastest car even faster? It's bloody difficult. Ron's job was difficult too, but in a different way.' So, like most people under pressure, John found himself super-critical of others' faults.

But the big thing bugging John was the fact that Ron still hadn't come back on the request for a pay rise. Not a peep. Every bit as proud as his boss, John wasn't about to debase himself by chasing. In John's mind, Ron was just 'dicking him around'.

Ron, however, had quite possibly forgotten it. From the distance of 30 years he claims to have no memory of Barnard 'asking for a large number and me not addressing it'. But he does recognise that it's quite possible he did prevaricate about it.

'It's my character I suppose,' Ron states. 'If I can't immediately see a solution to a problem other than a bad one, then I would rather not take the decision. I'm probably not responsive enough — that would be consistent with my character. To this day people get frustrated if they don't get the answers fast enough. Telling people "No" isn't difficult but it isn't normally what they want to hear. So if you are trying to find compromise or trying to find a way to say "Yes", the first thing you must do is work out how you are going to finance it.'

'I can't remember it, but at that period of time, that amount would have been comparable to a retainer for a pretty top driver. It was John's mindset that he was as important as a driver and, do you know, he was right! But I also felt I was pretty important too. So possibly it was ego coming to play, which was inevitable with younger men.'

One can see Ron's conundrum. If he paid John £500,000, surely he should pay himself the same? And if he did so, where was the money going to come from? For his part, John wasn't really expecting Ron to agree to half a million, figuring on a compromise of about £300,000. Ron, it seems, got stuck on the higher figure and put it away to deal with later. And didn't.

So, feeling undervalued and ever more frustrated, John started thinking seriously about getting out.

'I was finding it very difficult to sustain my motivation,' he told journalist Alan Henry just a year later. 'We were at the top of the tree and had been there for a few years. The old flywheel had developed its own momentum… and my motivation was slipping away. And if you haven't got motivation in this game, then you just can't do it.'[61]

Arthur Webb witnessed the change in John and the deterioration of his relationship with Ron in particular: 'I found it all very sad. I thought they made a fine team.' The rows got worse and Barnard's staff began to fear him more, as Matthew Jeffreys confirms: 'Towards the end of JB's time there, it wasn't a particularly happy atmosphere, partly because he ruled as a dictator.' He adds an observation arising from John's habit of going home for lunch: 'Quite frankly, it was a relief when he went! But when at 2pm his Porsche pulled in again outside the design office — I can hear its distinctive engine growl even now — my stomach would tighten. It affected me, and most of us, for the rest of our lives.'

---

[61] 'Henry, Alan, 'Interview: John Barnard', Motoring News, 29 April 1987, p18.

Barnard's negative feelings towards McLaren were amplified in early 1986 by an approach from BMW, possibly engineered by Niki Lauda. The German car company, which had been supplying engines to Brabham and Arrows, now wanted to create its own Formula 1 team. Potentially this sounded like a very good way out of McLaren: starting or rebuilding Formula 1 teams was a deeply appealing concept to John and was already becoming his speciality; he could be in total charge and he might even have a share of the profits; and, under less time pressure, he could have the time he needed to make new advances, the aspect of motorsport that most motivated him.

BMW Sporting Director Hans-Peter Flohr contacted him to set up a meeting at the Canadian Grand Prix in Montréal in June. Turning his mind to the team he would need to make such a venture work, John contacted his old friend from Rebaque, Peter Reinhardt, who was working in Canada, in Vancouver, and flew to Montréal for the meeting.

Ron Dennis's partner, Creighton Brown, was also becoming disgruntled and expressed interest in the new BMW venture. In Montréal he was busy organising a big function for McLaren co-sponsors Shell that Ayrton Senna, the brightest new talent in the paddock, was due to attend. But when Senna said he didn't want to go, Creighton, aware that a major new Formula 1 team would need a top driver, instead delivered the Brazilian ace to dinner with Barnard and Reinhardt before rushing off to host his Shell event. According to Reinhardt, Senna listened to their discussions about BMW's intentions and concluded, 'I'm more than happy to join you guys if it is likely to come to something.'

Barnard relished the idea of building a new Formula 1 team around himself and Senna. But one thing didn't lead to another and, perhaps predictably, the deal fell apart for reasons allegedly long forgotten.

Soon after, in July 1986, Barnard began getting mysterious phone calls from 'a man claiming to be the managing director of American Express UK', telling him that a team in mainland Europe wanted to hire him. Now a little more sceptical about new ventures, John politely turned him down but remained intrigued. Who might it be?

The mystery man was persistent, calling back several times over a period of two or three weeks. The conversation moved to money, with an initial offer that John rejected out of hand. Over a series of calls the offer increased substantially to the point where, says John, 'I simply had to listen.' How much was it? Barnard won't tell, but it was probably a figure similar to the amount he had put to Ron Dennis.[62]

Still the secret agent refused to reveal the identity of his principals, adding, by way of further intrigue, that Barnard should attend a meeting in London where all would be revealed. So John duly went to the mystery man's luxurious Knightsbridge apartment and was waiting there when in walked Marco Piccinini, Ferrari's sporting director, responsible for the Formula 1 operation and one of Enzo Ferrari's right-hand men. If it had been cloak-and-dagger before, the approach now took on the flavour of a Mafia movie.

'Mr Barnard, so nice to meet you. I have heard so much about you.'

'Marco, good to see you. I figured it might be Ferrari.'

'You must come to meet Mr Ferrari, he would like to see you.'

'Thanks Marco, but that's a bit difficult. I'm still under contract to McLaren. However, I'm listening.'

'Don't worry. We can organise a private plane to fly you there and back. It will be a secret meeting; no one will know. But what more can we say without you meeting Enzo Ferrari?'

'Look, as much as I respect Enzo Ferrari, I don't want to move to Maranello. I've nothing against Maranello, but my family comes first — I'm sure you understand that. I have a wife and a family and a lovely home here. I don't want to uproot my children from their schools and I always go home for lunch. And here is the perfect place to work — southern England has the best motorsport technology on the planet.'

If there are two things that Italians understand, they are Family and Lunch, but John's statement was surely an impasse. Piccinini looked John in the eye as he produced his trump card.

'What if we built you your own design facility in England?'

The offer took John aback, and, as is his wont, he examined the horse's mouth. Recalling Gilles Villeneuve's fatal accident, he had no faith in Ferrari's composite techniques.

'That's interesting, Marco, but I'm going to need more than a design office to build a winning Formula 1 car. I would need a factory to build the chassis. I'd need to do most of it here, including the suspension.'

'All this can be talked about with Mr Ferrari. Come over and talk.'

---

[62] Yates, Brock, *Enzo Ferrari, The Man and the Machine, Doubleday/Transworld Publishers Ltd, London, 1991, p394.*

John found the notion of Ferrari moving such a critical — and expensive — part of its operation to his doorstep both stunning and gratifying.

'The very idea beggared belief — I could see I was being paid an immense compliment. Clearly Enzo Ferrari must have already agreed to the concept, because otherwise Piccinini wouldn't be proposing it. But still I was cautious.'

Why were Ferrari — even the name sounds like a revving engine — trying so hard to poach John Barnard? The answer is to be found in a famous quote from Enzo Ferrari: 'For me, the most important victory is the victory yet to come.'[63]

Ferrari desperately needed to end a prolonged lean spell. During the previous two seasons, 1984–85, the team had won only three Grands Prix to McLaren's 18. And now, during 1986, it was looking like they wouldn't win any — and indeed by season's end they hadn't. Even when they had last topped the standings in the Constructors' Championship in 1983, they had won just four times, the same as Renault and Brabham.

In particular the Scuderia didn't understand modern aerodynamics and chassis design. As Barnard says, 'Harvey Postlethwaite hadn't produced the results they wanted. We'd built a carbon monocoque that was safe — theirs was dangerous.' To get back on top, Ferrari knew that they had to get the best people, and the best people were in England.

What did McLaren have that others didn't? Others had top drivers and top management. Only McLaren had the new kid on the block in the form of the best motorsport designer in the world.

At Heathrow a few days later, early on a Sunday morning, John ascended the steps of a brand-new Dassault Falcon 900, armed only with his passport in the inside pocket of his jacket. He was impressed: 'Not your run-of-the-mill Learjet — this was serious luxury.' The state-of-the-art trijet can carry 19 passengers but this version had a mere half dozen luxurious leather armchairs.

John found himself reflecting upon the life Ron had been enjoying as he settled into his seat. He felt a rising sense of his own importance as he flicked through some magazines. He was as excited as he ever gets.

Two hours later the plane landed in Bologna where it taxied past the main terminal and stopped near a private entrance. As John descended the steps, the pilot took his passport, disappeared and then came back with it stamped, just

---

[63] Crowder, Paul, '1: Life on the Limit', Diamond Docs, Exclusive Media Group, Flat-Out Films, Spitfire Pictures, 2014; quote at 31m 20s.

as a chauffeur-driven Alfa Romeo arrived on the tarmac. Piccinini climbed out, shook John's hand, and together they set off.

Within the hour, John was gliding through the streets of Maranello towards the hallowed entrance to Ferrari, blocked by a wall of Ferrari-red steel, a sliding gate. To his alarm a man with a camera was waiting at the gate, taking photographs of the Alfa as it drew up.

'I said to Marco, "I thought this was meant to be secret!"'

'Hey, don't worry, he is a nobody,' was the less-than-believable reply.

'I should have twigged then how this was going to play out,' is John's rueful comment with 30 years of hindsight.

John was ushered into an office where, ever inscrutable, 88-year-old Enzo Ferrari sat behind his leather-topped desk surrounded by the photos and trophies of past Ferrari triumphs. John was now in the presence of the grandest figure in motorsport, a super being who, not unlike Jehovah Himself, had many names, including *Il Commendatore* (the Knight Commander, which he did not like, it having fascist overtones), *Il Drake* (a swashbuckling corsair, specifically Sir Francis Drake), *l'Ingegnere* (the Engineer, his preferred title) and, in these latter years, *Il Grande Vecchio* (the Old Man).

John was now struggling not to be awestruck: 'This is Enzo Ferrari, the next best thing to God — here I am about to be wooed by God! It was all a bit surreal. He sat wearing his dark glasses behind a big desk, saying little. The room was stylish but not over the top, dark wood furniture, nothing ostentatious but you knew where you were. And he wanted me!'

Piccinini translated as they chatted in indolent style about family and the state of Formula 1, before turning to important things, such as the sort of set-up Barnard might establish in England, where it might be, what he would design, the facilities that would be needed. Mr Ferrari complimented him on his work at McLaren, conceding that Ferrari needed to pay much more attention to chassis design — the whole point of Barnard's presence.

Piccinini then gave Barnard a tour of the factory. John found himself both surprised and disappointed by what he saw. 'I thought, God, we're miles ahead at McLaren' as he looked into the first wind tunnel to be built at Ferrari, a 'pretty basic affair' compared with the Teddington set-up. The workshops were little better, as Alan Jenkins had observed just a year before when he saw oil flying off a milling machine next to carbon-bonding equipment.

Ten years earlier Ferrari had been at the cutting edge of motorsport, as Niki Lauda testified in 1974: 'When you see all the facilities at the team's disposal it's a little difficult, at first glance, to understand why they don't win every race without any difficulty.'[64] Back then Lauda explained the mystery by reference to the great curse of Ferrari, the one factor that prevented the Scuderia from achieving its extraordinary potential — Machiavellian politics. In 1986 this fault was amplified by a failure to understand the requirements of carbon-fibre technology, despite Dr Harvey Postlethwaite's efforts.

The tour was followed by lunch in a private room at the fabled Cavallino restaurant across the road from the factory. Besides Mr Ferrari and Piccinini, the party included Piero Lardi Ferrari (Enzo's illegitimate son recently returned to the Ferrari fold) and other significant names from the extended Ferrari 'family' such as Sergio Pininfarina (the designer of Ferrari's road cars) and Sergio Scaglietti (the builder of bodies for Ferrari road cars). Various simple but delicious pasta courses were served with Lambrusco, the light, fizzy, red wine of the surrounding Emilia-Romagna region. Conversation was in both Italian and English, with John occasionally becoming the focus of attention as they talked through recent racing seasons; all of the Italian, of course, went straight over his head.

After lunch, they returned to Mr Ferrari's office, with Piero now joining them. They were discussing the details of the deal when Marco 'plonked down a letter' in front of John.

'We want you to sign this,' said Marco. 'It's not a commitment, just something to show that you are interested.'

The alarm bells began pealing in Barnard's cautious brain and, spotting his reluctance, Mr Ferrari leaned over to Piccinini and whispered in his ear. Piccinini turned to John.

'He says it's a goodwill letter, a document of intent only. Sign it please, and make the Old Man happy.'

John signed, trusting *Il Commendatore*, although aware, perhaps, that he was also termed *Il Drake* for good reason; Sir Francis Drake was respected in Italy for having been powerful, brilliant, piratical and, of course, utterly ruthless. It reminded John of *The Godfather*. 'I honestly didn't want to upset Enzo. I could have walked away but they knew the ropes and,' he quips, 'I was on them.'

An hour later he was flying back to Heathrow thinking, 'Bloody hell, I've

---

[64] *Henry, Alan,* Ferrari: The Grand Prix Cars, *Hazelton Publishing, Richmond, Surrey, 1989, p229.*

committed myself, but do I really want to do this?' Then he thought about the 'grand treatment', the astonishing monetary offer, 'meeting God', the commitment to build multi-million-pound facilities near his home — and the prospect of becoming technical director of the Ferrari Formula 1 team with all the control that implied over the engine department. As the Falcon 900 swooped down towards one of Heathrow's runways, his mind turned to McLaren, Ron Dennis, rows, frustrations and the fact that he still had received no answer to his request for a pay rise.

John did what he always did when it came to making big decisions. He drove home and talked to Rosie. 'I put the case to her, how I'd reached the end of my tether with Ron, what an enormous thing it would be to work for Ferrari, how I could still come home for lunch. And how it was Ferrari making the offer, how everyone in Formula 1 wants to have done their time there, because Ferrari is racing.' For Rosie, it was obvious. So John contacted his lawyer, Michael Jepson, and soon a 25-page contract was being worked up, the details flying back and forth over the fax machine.

'Home for lunch' could have been the subtitle of this book, because, like so much of what Barnard did, it was a preference that ran counter to the prevailing culture. The work ethos of post-war Britain was job first, pleasure second, family third. Perhaps this attitude was best summed up by Donald Campbell, who piloted his *Bluebird* cars and boats to world records in the 1950s and 1960s: 'If you are going to succeed you've got to put what you're doing first, way before your own comfort, way before your own pleasure and way before your own family considerations. You have got to.'[65]

Unlike most people around him in his working life, John had always been a stay-at-home guy, right from childhood in the secure nest of his parents' devotion. His notion of putting family first was a particularly rare thing in the higher reaches of achievement, especially in the high-flying world of Formula 1 with its promise of a life of glamour and temptation populated by people with large egos and sex drives to match.

So it was extraordinary to go home for lunch and, in doing so, John was giving Rosie and, later, his children, quality time and attention, meeting emotional needs, however undemonstratively, that were more usually ignored.

---

[65] *Gething, Ashley (Director & Producer)*, Donald Campbell, Speed King, *Tern Television for BBC Scotland, 2013.*

ABOVE The 1985 McLaren MP4/2B took Alan Prost to the first of his four World Championship titles; here he is in Monaco, driving to his second win of the season. *LAT Images* **BELOW** Organised chaos in the pit lane with John Barnard (left) staring at the dashboard, Ron Dennis replenishing coolant, Niki Lauda out of the car and Bosch man Udo Zucker holding testing equipment. *Courtesy of John Barnard*

ABOVE Barnard laying down the law at a 1985 race with Alain Prost and race engineers Steve Nichols (dark pullover) and Tim Wright duly attentive. *Felix Muls* **BELOW** Porsche engineers crowd round the MP4/2B's TAG-Porsche V6 turbo engine, chief designer Hans Mezger to the fore (white overalls). *Felix Muls*

ABOVE Alain Prost sealed the 1986 World Championship at the Australian Grand Prix in Adelaide, but by this time Barnard was on gardening leave, having been poached by Ferrari. *LAT Images*

RIGHT Proud dad: Gillian checking out the buttoning on her father's shirt, while her older sister Jennifer looks on with a critical eye, circa 1985. *Courtesy of John Barnard*

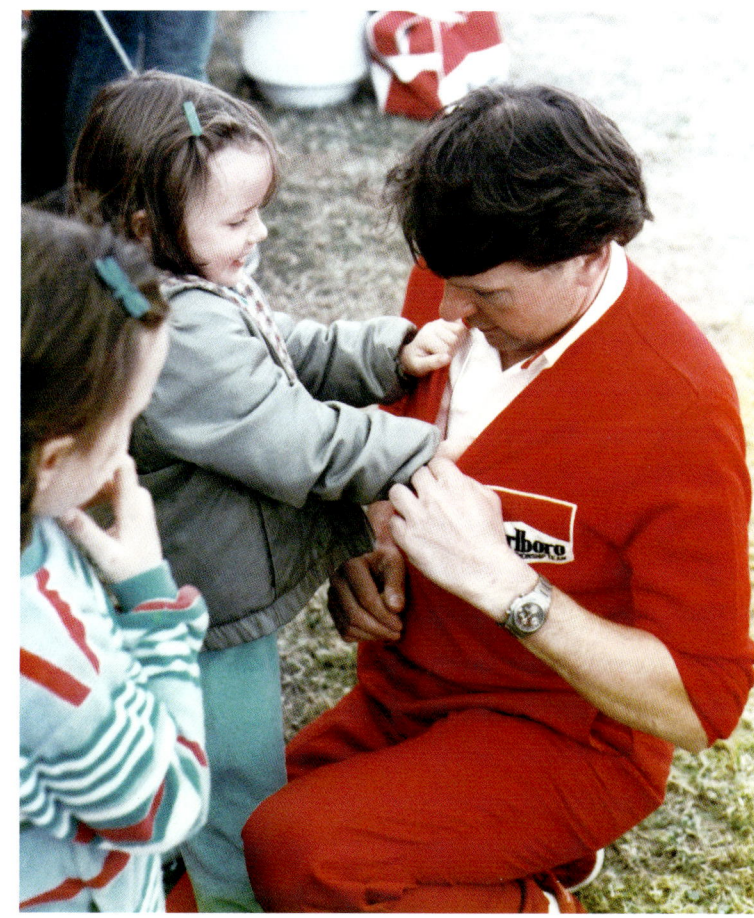

ABOVE *Il Commendatore*, the legendary Enzo Ferrari, behind his trade-mark dark glasses in his Maranello office at around the time John Barnard had his first audience with him. *Getty Images/Grand Prix Photo* **BELOW** Ferrari's approach to Barnard came via sporting director Marco Piccinini, seen with his new technical director at the annual Monaco Sporting Club dinner. *Courtesy of John Barnard*

ABOVE John Barnard posing for the press outside the Guildford Technical Office (GTO), the Formula 1 design and build facility proposed by Ferrari when they asked him to become technical director. *Courtesy of John Barnard* **BELOW** Fetching headgear — the GTO clean room. Barnard is flanked by Pete Brown (left) and Dave Owen. *Courtesy of John Barnard*

ABOVE Barnard's personal design office on the top floor of GTO's premises in River House on the smart new Broadford Park industrial estate in Shalford, near Godalming. *Courtesy of John Barnard* **BELOW** A drawing for Barnard's Ferrari 641: this revolutionary car, complete with paddle-shift gearbox, has been on display at New York's Museum of Modern Art for nearly 25 years. *Courtesy of John Barnard*

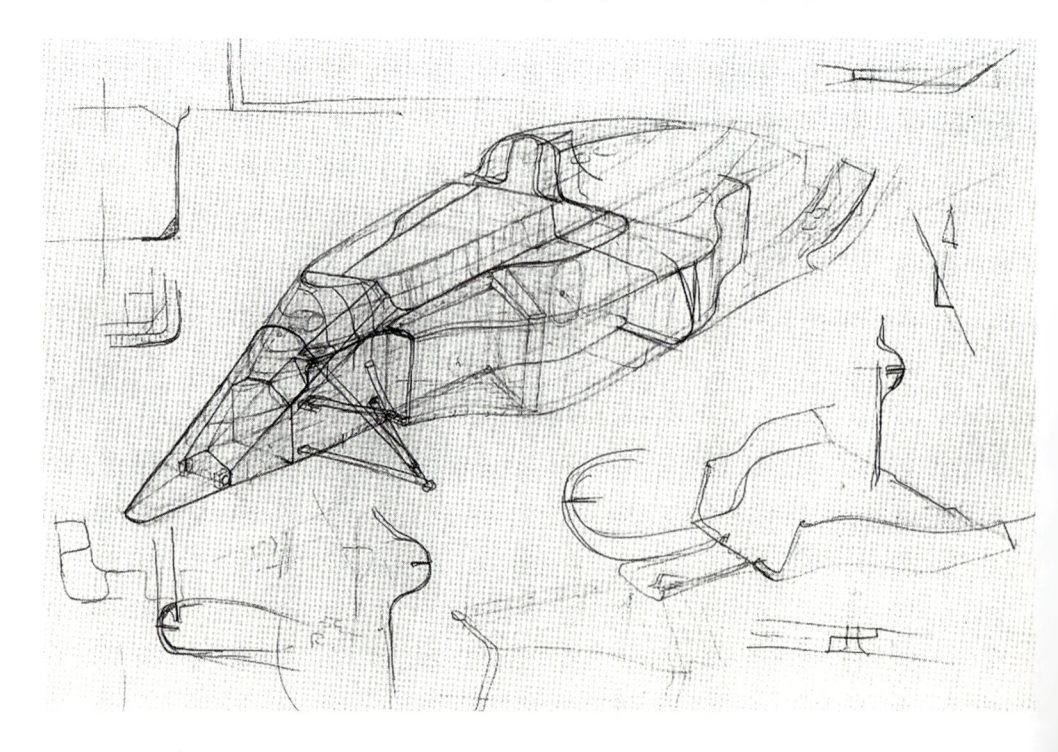

ABOVE Beast of burden: Dad carries Michael, Gillian and Jennifer on his back at Rawdon, which was the family's home in Worplesdon, Surrey, between 1982 and 1987. *Courtesy of John Barnard* **BELOW** In May 1987 the Barnards moved to Combe Rise, set in nine and a half acres of lawns and woodland that soon became a playground when the October 1987 hurricane felled many trees. *Courtesy of John Barnard*

ABOVE Michael and Gillian at the wheel of Dad's small tractor in Combe Rise's grounds, with Jennifer overseeing; John and Rosie pace behind, supremely unconcerned. *Courtesy of John Barnard* **BELOW** Family trip: outside Combe Rise, getting ready to pootle off in John's 1933 Lagonda M45 Tourer with Rosie and in-laws aboard — there's no room for Michael. *Courtesy of John Barnard*

Rosie has never been emotionally needy but that daily gesture from her husband is probably an important factor in the survival of their marriage. That and her extraordinary patience.

Barnard carried on working at McLaren as if nothing had happened. But something had happened and somehow word had started to spread. As John says, 'It didn't help that I was walking through the paddock at the Austrian Grand Prix, in mid-August, when Piccinini suddenly buttonholed me.' The paddock, as ever, was alive with journalists and John could see photographers taking pictures as they talked. The story seemed to be threatening to come out and soon the rumour emerged that after the race Barnard had driven down to Maranello. Ron refused to believe it and he wasn't alone, the rumours of defection being met with general disbelief at Boundary Road. 'If JB leaves, pigs will fly,' was one comment John recalls hearing from the factory floor.

The finalised contract, dated 11 August 1986, gave Barnard the title of technical director of Ferrari's racing department, with 'overall charge and exclusive responsibility for all aspects concerning the conception, engineering, design, construction and development of the Constructor's motor race cars (including their chassis, aerodynamics, engines and transmission).'

John was answerable only to Mr Ferrari, and, much to his joy, it appeared that he had complete control over the engine department. What he didn't fully realise at this stage was that Ferrari was riven with political factions. Mr Ferrari had an unspoken but much-practised policy of 'divide and rule' and seemed to some to take special delight in setting one person against another in his efforts to increase competitive spirit. If Barnard thought he was in total charge of the engine department, indeed of anything based in Maranello, he had another think coming.

Now the time had come to break the news to Ron. As John recalls it, he popped into Ron's office in late August.

'Ron, you need to know that I'm leaving at the end of this season.'

'Is it Ferrari?'

'I'd rather not say,' was Barnard's slightly embarrassed but emphatic response.

And that was that — he left the office.

But that was not quite that. According to Steve Nichols, the rows that followed were the worst he had known. Once more, staff in the drawing office winced under the impact of verbal blows raining down from Ron's office.

THE PERFECT CAR

'You would hear the thunder coming through the floor,' says Nichols. 'Ron got in some good licks too. On the day John left, I recall that, for the first time, we could actually make out some of the words. The only sentence I remember was John shouting, "NO, RON, I AM TELLING YOU!" I don't know what he was telling him but we learned subsequently that he had been negotiating with Ferrari and Ron obviously wanted him to stay.'

Ron's full response came less than a week after John broke his devastating news. It came in the form of a letter, little more than a few terse sentences, following a board meeting held in John's absence, which to this day Barnard thinks was 'technically out of order'. Barnard was told that he must not talk to anyone at McLaren, that he could not return to Boundary Road, that his personal effects would be delivered to him, and that he would be paid until the end of the season as per his contract.

Barnard was out two months before the end of the season, on 'gardening leave', which is usually a good deal less relaxing than it sounds. Looking back, he says he understands.

'Ron was distraught. He just couldn't believe it. He thought I'd be there for life — we'd built McLaren together.'

'Why did I do it? Why did I leave?' Barnard still asks the question. 'And now people were asking, "Why leave now, when you're on top?"'

But the simple truth is that he needed a new set of bricks and these bright red ones looked particularly appealing. 'Now I had the whole package. Sure, I had had some control over Porsche before, but this was Ferrari, an engine-based team, where engine was king. It just looked like the right thing to do. I wasn't feeling well-disposed towards Ron and I was being offered a fantastic deal.'

Thirty years on, Barnard still agonises. 'Was it the right decision? Should I have stayed? Could I have stayed? You've only got one life and sometimes you've just got to have a go. Ron has hated me ever since.'

Ron Dennis disagrees about hating John 'ever since' but he certainly hated him at the time because he was terrified of the potential impact of his sudden departure. He feared that McLaren would collapse, and with it the lucrative, successful world that he and John had created together. The split had become a full divorce with all the poison so often associated with such rifts. Suddenly Ron was on his own, fully aware that replacing Barnard was probably going to be impossible. He was faced with the horror of watching his cars slide down the grid.

According to Steve Nichols, Ron turned to him in some despair: 'John had always convinced Ron that he did everything, so Ron asked, "Who's going to do the aerodynamics?" And I said, "Bob Bell will do the aerodynamics, like he has done for the past several years." "But who's going to do the stress analysis?" "I'll do that like I have done for the past several years." "Who's going to do the suspension?" "Tim Wright will do that, like he has done for the past several years. We've got a team here, Ron." "Can you do it?" "Sure we can do it."'

Ron appeared to be unconvinced. His long-term goal of creating the British equivalent of Ferrari was suddenly in the balance, with the man who had made the dream possible walking out, most appallingly, to Ferrari itself. If Dennis had been developing a fixation about Ferrari before, now it became a full-blown obsession.

John's gardening leave involved no pottering around the dahlias or dead-heading the roses. He needed to build a Formula 1 factory immediately. To get things moving, he called Peter Reinhardt, his old Rebaque ally who was now back in England. His brief to Reinhardt was simple: 'Find me factory space near my home in Godalming with sufficient room to build a state-of-the-art carbon car.'

Peter duly found Broadford Park, a smart new industrial estate in Shalford, halfway between Godalming and Guildford, just three miles from John's house. The chosen building, River House, was ideal, with 17,000 square feet and a very modern appearance, with the added bonus of brickwork and window frames in 'a sort of Ferrari red'. Even better, it wasn't quite finished, enabling John and Peter to change some of the layout to suit their peculiar needs.

After opening negotiations with the owner, Reinhardt invited Marco Piccinini over from Maranello to take a look. Piccinini had insisted that Ferrari's new English premises should be classy, not some 'oily rag sort of place with dirty floors'. Ever the humourist, Peter decided to drive Piccinini first to somewhere else: 'I took him to a shabby shithole of an abandoned factory, at which I announced brightly, "This is it, we'll remodel it!" You should have seen Marco's face.' Needless to say, Piccinini was mightily relieved to see the Shalford reality, describing it as 'perfect'.

Piccinini immediately started haggling with the owner, Richard Pickett, a man who spent his weekends huntin', shootin' and fishin' with members of *Genesis*, the progressive rock band that, as it happened, had been formed in Godalming, its five musicians having attended Charterhouse, the nearby public school. Pickett pointed out to Piccinini that they weren't 'in a Moroccan bazaar' and the price was settled. Piccinini returned to Maranello to give Mr Ferrari the good news while Barnard and Reinhardt moved into temporary offices provided by Pickett until the build was complete.

Then John launched a raid on the McLaren pantry. He offered Joan Villadelprat the post of chief mechanic and the Spaniard became the first to defect, quickly followed by chief fabricator Brian Pepper. Villadelprat takes up the story: 'For many years, Ron Dennis had promised me the chief mechanic job at McLaren. Dave Ryan was in that position and our personalities clashed. I felt strongly I should have the job and Ron promised me, but it never happened; always it was "next year".' So when Barnard offered Joan the same job at Ferrari, he jumped at the chance: 'I knew I could learn Italian quickly, it being not so different from Spanish.' He duly popped into Ron's office to tell him he was leaving for Ferrari: 'Ron when absolutely bananas. I stormed out, slamming the door behind me.' No surprise there, then.

But what Ron Dennis did three days later was a surprise. According to Villadelprat, he called him into his office and sat him down with his lawyers, Baker McKenzie, not, as might be feared, to terrify him into submission, but instead to draw up his Ferrari contract: 'He wanted to make sure they didn't stiff me. That's Ron Dennis. He's so loyal to the people he believes belong to him, and I had been with him from the beginning.'

Ron was dealing with the situation rationally and, where he could, generously. But it was getting out of hand. When Gordon Kimball, who had been with Barnard at Chaparral as well as McLaren, prepared to walk out of the door too, Barnard-bound, Ron plunged his finger into the dyke.

He called a meeting with Enzo Ferrari and flew to Maranello. According to Barnard, Dennis threatened to 'bid whatever necessary' for key Ferrari staff if Mr Ferrari didn't make Barnard desist. In the end the two team bosses reached an agreement and Barnard's McLaren recruitment drive was halted.

One consequence was that Kimball was forced to wait some six months before he could make the switch. However, Dennis had no control over Arthur Webb, who had worked unpaid at McLaren in his spare time while at BAe and then migrated to GEC-Marconi, where he had become involved in a project for the Space Shuttle *Challenger* until its ill-fated mission of January 1986 brought an end to the entire programme. As this had somewhat dented Webb's career prospects, it was a relief to get a call from John offering an important job at

Ferrari, as head of materials and composites.

Webb then made a raid on GEC-Marconi's pantry that was little short of grand larceny. Barnard reckoned he needed 30 people, so Arthur started by recruiting composites experts Peter Brown and Ian Weild, plus machinist Graham Saunders. He also found materials expert Andy Smith, whose job, like Webb's, had just come to a sudden end, in his case when the British government cancelled its contract with GEC-Marconi for the development of an Airborne Early Warning version of the Nimrod maritime patrol aircraft.

Another to join Barnard's team a little later was 22-year-old design engineer Diane Holl. Taking her on was a bold move as it was rare indeed in those days for racing teams, let alone macho Ferrari, to employ females as engineers. As Reinhardt colourfully puts it, 'The Italians had never heard anything like it. "A woman! A design engineer! Ridiculous!"' John, perhaps recalling his mother's engineering ability, warmed to Diane's enthusiasm and commitment, such that he offered her a job while she was still in her final year at university, studying mechanical engineering at the University of Plymouth. He recalls applying some pressure: 'I wanted a first, or, at worst, a 2.1.'

Diane had chosen Plymouth because it offered one of only two courses in composites available in Britain. Brought up in Banbury, Oxfordshire, just 15 miles from Silverstone, she already had a modest record in motorsport and was well aware of Barnard's achievements. Her father, a materials scientist, had regularly taken her to watch motor racing and later lent his expertise when she decided to create a carbon-fibre drive shaft for a university project. While a student, she worked part-time for two significant motorsport businesses close to home: first she had a spell with Reynard, then taking its first steps in Formula Ford and Formula 3 but later to become a big manufacturer in those categories as well as in Formula 3000 and Indycar; then she spent six months at March working in the wind tunnel under a young designer called Adrian Newey, who was the team's aerodynamicist and a senior race engineer. Come her finals, she got her 2.1 and was delighted to secure her first full-time job in motorsport at Ferrari — the brightest possible start!

So it was that John began building Team Barnard, his core of experts, many of whom would stay with him for the next 20 years.

It was now November 1986. While Barnard's people were sourcing equipment and putting together their own teams under the oversight of general manager Peter Reinhardt, John flew out to Maranello to take a look at the F1/87, the V6 turbo car being built for the forthcoming season.

Designed by Austrian Gustav Brunner, the car, says Barnard, 'was more or less done. There wasn't an awful lot I could do to it without a total rebuild, so all I did was make some changes to the suspension, specifying new wishbones, and designing some new uprights, hubs and axles.'

He also decided to change the CV joints: 'They were still running standard Löbro CVs, which didn't last long under the strain of turbo power — they were chucking them away like they were shelling peas.' As at McLaren a year earlier, he designed tougher, simpler, longer-lasting versions and went to the same supplier, Kenny Hill at Metalore in California, to manufacture them.

When Piero Lardi Ferrari heard of this, he tried to persuade the English engineer to use an Italian firm. John's response was typically brusque: 'I refused on the grounds that I knew Metalore's quality and trusted it, and so could see no reason why I should take a chance with someone I didn't know.' This put Piero's nose out of joint, and not for the last time. Already seeds of discord were being sown.

Reinhardt reports that Barnard at first wanted nothing to do with Brunner's car, until Peter insisted that he really should make an effort with it. John swept the rear into a coke-bottle shape complete with diffuser, or 'aerodynamic ramp' as he called it, which tidied up the air flowing from under the car towards the rear wing. He even sent the engine for torsion testing, and, after getting the results, ordered the block to be stiffened. This must have come as an unwelcome surprise to the Ferrari engine department, which, until Barnard, had ruled the Maranello roost.

At around this time, Barnard started keeping a form of diary, an *aide-mémoire* that reflected his enormous work load and, sometimes, his personal reactions to the stresses arising from the job. His notebook from this time reveals early difficulties with Maranello people, Piero Lardi Ferrari being a particular source of angst.

On 20 November, John wrote: 'I heard from Gustav that Piero had OK'd building the first type of gearbox oil tank, i.e. the old Ferrari system. Had said nothing to me. Causes undermining of my powers and unnecessary work.'

Despite John being in overall control, Piero was having trouble letting go, as this next paragraph from the notebook reveals: 'Also Techno Magnesio in Italy have been given wheel drawings to make trial wheels. The drawings have not yet been released by me. I had already told Piero I would use Dymag [a British company] first and try Italian people afterwards.' One can understand the younger Ferrari's concern; parts of his existing authority were being usurped and his deals with Italian suppliers were being torn up.

John was also getting grief closer to home, from the Shalford landlord, as in this note: 'No money available for paying rent on temporary office, even after Piero said money had been sent. It had not. 3 weeks ago money was promised.'

By Christmas, John was irritated by the fact that Ferrari staff 'all went on hols for about 2 weeks'. Then there were 'strikes at Maranello in January, with the workshop working only standard hours, no overtime'. By February he was calling Piero 'a bloody nuisance' for interfering with work on the gearbox. He was also becoming irritated with Brunner: 'Beginning not to think much of GB. He does not think the design through from the beginning. He's no engineer either — never seems to think about loads, etc. Only just got them to work extra hours. Much pushing of PLF [Piero Lardi Ferrari] to get this.'

But John wasn't desperately bothered about the 1987 season; his target was 1988, just as 1981 had been when he joined Project Four in 1979. That, of course, wasn't how the Italian press saw it; they were already beside themselves in a fever of expectation.

Through this period, Barnard, still working in the temporary offices, concentrated on the rapid assembly of the new Guildford Technical Office, or GTO. The idea for the name came from Piccinini, who enjoyed its implied reference to the iconic Ferrari 250 GTO, the *Gran Turismo Omologato* first produced in 1962 and widely considered to be the finest Ferrari of all time — and today it is certainly the most valuable.

Under the direction of Barnard, Webb and Reinhardt, River House was being partitioned, painted and equipped with machine and fabrication shops, carbon lay-up facilities, clean rooms, offices and a dedicated, air-conditioned computer room to drive the emerging CAD software, which, reports Reinhardt, was a 'pig' to get working and brought 'terrible problems with IBM'. Webb describes the building of GTO as 'a major undertaking' and praises Peter's organisational skills: 'I've never seen anybody like it; he really was good at it.'

Barnard briefed Webb to design a full-size autoclave big enough to take not just a Formula 1 racer but also a sports car, having in mind Ferrari's planned future use of carbon-fibre on their production cars. One of the biggest challenges was to work out the best method for rapid access 'in order to get maximum utilisation', so the autoclave was equipped with a hydraulic lift and rails to allow tools to be put on trolleys and trundled quickly in and out.

Construction of the autoclave required a large pit to be dug beneath it.

That meant breaking through the concrete floor of the building, a prospect that caused some tense negotiation with Pickett and his insurance company, partly because it required excavators and dumper trucks to work inside. The next problem was getting this machinery into the building: the only way was to remove the entire roof-high glass façade. Peter Brown, one of the GEC-Marconi emigrés, came up with a block-and-tackle system to do this: the massive windows were removed every morning as a single unit, set aside, and put back every evening.

Once through the floor, the contractors discovered that the soil beneath was badly polluted with chemicals deposited by a previous occupant, initiating a time-consuming and expensive decontamination programme. At the same time work began on building an in-house electricity sub-station to provide the enormous quantity of power required by the autoclave and other machinery.

Finally GTO was ready, almost exactly a year after John had accepted the Ferrari job. River House now contained the most advanced facility in motorsport, equivalent to, in Reinhardt's words, 'any aerospace facility', and it would have made Ron Dennis very envious had he been able to view it. Visitors were greeted with, says Peter, an 'attractive and roomy' reception dominated by 'a beautiful stairway' and a 'lovely' Ferrari sign. Further within, the environment was, says Webb, 'of hospital cleanliness'. Barnard and Reinhardt, the two GTO principals, had offices on the top floor commanding views over the River Wey meandering through the surrounding countryside, and new secretary Joanne Woodward occupied an office between them. Barnard had two rooms, one for design ('just a drawing board — no CAD') and one for running the business.

Andy Smith, aged only 25 and in charge of the test laboratory, was very impressed: 'We were doing mechanical testing, checking performances, finding break points and establishing specifications. We had thermal analysis equipment, infra-red spectroscopy, a range of aerospace testing techniques — the first that Formula 1 had ever had and a blueprint for everything that followed. The idea was to push the limits of the materials all the time.'

But Andy, like others, would soon learn that working with Barnard was no picnic. He recalls the boss's uncanny knack for sensing a mistake: 'If everything went right, you wouldn't see him, but as soon as something went even slightly wrong, he'd be there.' He remembers working in the clean room on a car's fuel tank area when a component fell and marked the carbon-fibre at the bottom: 'I thought, "Shit", looked up, and there was John, watching through the window.'

Despite John's sometimes trying nature and demands, his core team remained with him for many years because, says Andy, 'we all had real respect for him'. As with McLaren's Two Rules, 'there was John's Way and the Wrong Way'. John's Way 'always worked because it was efficient and reliable'. As for the famous temper, Smith witnessed a number of blow-ups: 'If you took a short cut, that's when John got upset. If he could, he would have done everything himself, because then he would know for sure that it had been done properly.'

To ease the pressure of this constant vigilance, John bought a waterfront holiday home for occasional breaks. This was in Hythe, Hampshire, across the water from Southampton, and at its attendant mooring he installed a large, brand-new powerboat, a Fairline 50. Patrick Head, who had been a sailor since childhood, went out with him one day for a jolly around Southampton Water and down to the Needles on the western tip of the Isle of Wight.

'He was always adventurous,' says Patrick, 'and for him piloting the Fairline was just like driving a car. He didn't have any sort of chart of where the sandbanks were; it was just, "I'm here and I want to go there!"'

Presumably the sandbanks and shoals of Southampton Water and the Solent spotted who they were dealing with and got out of the way, because neither Barnard nor Head talk of any embarrassing beachings.

John was now having to spend a lot of time flying between GTO and Maranello. Needing someone to take this load off his shoulders, he tasked Joan Villadelprat to oversee his end of the operation in Italy.

'He dropped me in Maranello on my own, the bastard!' is Villadelprat's assessment from the distance of 30 years. 'I was the first chief mechanic at Ferrari who wasn't an Italian — a bit of a shock for everybody. I was 30 years old and my youngest mechanic there was 52. They had all won many championships. And here was this young Catalan telling them what was what.'

So it was that Barnard and Villadelprat began making changes at the Scuderia. As John says, 'I needed to bring to Ferrari a different kind of attitude and I wanted Maranello to operate along the lines we were used to. I do think the old man had seen what had happened at McLaren and thought I was the bloke he needed. He probably got feedback from Marco about what I was like and I think he knew that I was a tough enough character to swing my weight around Ferrari. I know my arrival ruffled feathers immediately. I am sure it ruffled Piero Lardi Ferrari's feathers more than anyone's. He wanted to prove to Fiat that he could take over from his father, who was getting frail.'

Villadelprat: 'To be honest we changed the whole of Ferrari. I remember there was just one long bay, with no separation between the cars. The best mechanics would be on the car expected to do the best, working for the best driver. The other cars got the lesser mechanics. We changed all that, ensuring all the cars were built to the same standards. It was the first time that Ferrari had had such an education. Massive changes, not just to the technology, but to the mentality.'

This change was made a little easier for the young Spaniard by the looming figure of Barnard, be he so often ever so far away. 'They were scared of him,' says Villadelprat. But even more scary was the regular presence of *Il Grande Vecchio*: 'Enzo would come into my office every morning. All the people there were so deferential to him, almost dropping to the floor in his presence. I would say "hello" and carry on working.' This sang-froid helped Villadelprat establish his credentials.

One task undertaken at this time by Villadelprat's mechanics was the construction of a Ferrari Indycar, the Brunner-designed 637. Joan recalls that Barnard walked in one day just as the car was being completed and said, 'Right, that's going straight into the museum.' The Spaniard found this shocking: 'It never even did a lap at Fiorano. It was finished, painted, ready.'

There was an intriguing reason for this, as Barnard reports: 'I had no hand in the decision to mothball the Indycar and anyway it was never intended to race. It was only built to reinforce a threat to pull out of Formula 1. That's what Ferrari did. If they didn't get their way about something, they would start talking about pulling out — which was unthinkable. Formula 1 without Ferrari is like *The Beatles* without John Lennon. You can forget it.'

Fiat, as Ferrari's owner, also insisted on changes, installing their own accountant at GTO. This was Vijay Kothary, who, some 15 years before, had fled the dictatorship of Idi Amin in Uganda. Kothary's arrival bothered John: 'I thought, hang on a minute, I've had no input in this guy at all, I don't know him from Adam. This shouldn't be happening. I should have an input on all the people who work for me here.' Happily it turned out that Vijay was a good guy and he and John worked well together for the next 15 years.

One of the many noses in Maranello that Barnard immediately shoved out of joint belonged to Dr Harvey Postlethwaite, who had been running chassis design until Barnard's appointment. But if Harvey felt snubbed, he didn't show it, agreeing to work as instructed. He had the advantage of several years in the job, fluency in Italian, particularly the Modenese dialect spoken by the mechanics, plus an intimate understanding of Maranello politics. He also knew how to bide his time.

Another significant casualty of Barnard's arrival was long-time designer Mauro Forghieri. As Enzo Ferrari biographer Brock Yates put it, referring to the setting up of GTO, 'The move was but one of a number of outrages that finally ended the long relationship between Mauro Forghieri and Enzo Ferrari. The man who had created more brilliant designs — and more winners — than any other head of the engineering section finally left the place he had called his home for over a quarter century.'[66] He went to Lamborghini.

Perhaps it was to Mr Ferrari's divisive delight that Barnard was busy making himself unpopular with a wide range of people. The Prince of Darkness was back, wielding his scythe like the Grim Reaper through the time-honoured traditions of the Scuderia, or so the Italian press might have put it.

In his private notes, Barnard complained in one, dated 6 March 1987, that he had 'just heard from Peter Reinhardt that Ferrari's asked Dymag for more wheel bolts [for securing a seal to the rim to stop the tyre bead coming off]. Max [Boxstrom, from Dymag] did not understand instruction coming from Italy. HP [Harvey Postlethwaite] or PLF [Piero Lardi Ferrari] involved. Comment went back to Max — "Ferrari is still run from here" (Italy). His attitude is typical of what I expect could happen. Makes for big confusion on all sides.'

At Piccinini's prompting, Barnard began to look at how the team operated at circuits and wasn't overly impressed. For a man who liked to go home for lunch, Barnard wasn't so forgiving of others who enjoyed time-honoured lunchtime traditions — and Ferrari did lunch in style at the races. Between Saturday morning practice and afternoon qualifying, the tables would come out in the paddock, tablecloths would be spread, cutlery laid, and pasta and Lambrusco served.

As Barnard says, 'I found this comical, at best, when I was at McLaren. Vital adjustments would wait for at least an hour, sometimes much longer, at this crucial time. But this had always been the Ferrari way.' Sensing an opportunity, Piccinini asked Barnard what the lunchtime practice was at McLaren.

'Sandwiches, coffee and a ten-minute break.' 'Do you think we should do

---

[66] Yates, Brock, Enzo Ferrari, The Man and the Machine, *Doubleday/Transworld Publishers Ltd, London, 1991, p394.*

that?' asked Piccinini. 'Yes, I do.' 'What about wine?' 'Not at lunchtime. It will slow them down!' 'No wine.'

The Italian press were told and the Italian press were outraged. John caught the media flack but it made little difference to him — he couldn't read it. But he has some stiff words for Piccinini's manipulation: 'What a bastard! Marco obviously wanted to change it, or he wouldn't have asked me. I was the convenient scapegoat.' It also gave him a pretty harsh start with the mechanics, who were now grumbling about the destruction of Ferrari traditions by this English interloper. 'So what?' says Barnard. 'It had to be changed.'

This was one of a thousand examples of how Ferrari used the press to bring pressure to bear on their own people. The Italian press was known as *Stampa* and when they stamped, people jumped. Barnard was beginning to get an inkling of the Ferrari Way.

Other habits were harder to break. Villadelprat recalls walking in one Monday morning and finding that none of his mechanics were there — just a few reception and maintenance staff. When he asked what was happening, he was told, '*Sciopero.*' He had to look up what that meant — strike.

'A Formula 1 team on strike?' says Villadelprat, still spluttering with outrage after all these years. 'I could not believe it. Ferrari belonged to Fiat and there was a strike there so no Italians were allowed into the Maranello factory. Only the foreigners, like me, could stay. So that day I found myself working until three or four o'clock in the morning.'

The following day a man named Benassi, one of the lead engineers, saw the work that Villadelprat had done to build the car that he normally would have been overseeing. 'Benassi asked me who had been building his car. I said, "Me. It's not your car. It's a Ferrari car. And that car will be running round the Fiorano test track on Friday, with or without you."'

That evening, at nine o'clock, Benassi, although still on strike, came in to help. The following evening everybody was working, outside the strike and in their own time. By Friday all three cars were testing at Fiorano.

Otherwise Italy's *Stampa* were full of positives at the beginning of 1987, a year that marked the 40th anniversary of the Scuderia. Barnard was their new hero, despite his incomprehensible attitude to a civilised lunch, and expectations were deliriously high. They dubbed him *Il Mago*, the magician, the wise man, and duly expected miracles.

Barnard had always tried to avoid the press. As he told *Sunday Times* journalist Neil Lydon at the time, 'To be honest, I find the entire PR side of this business a complete pain in the arse, though I recognise the need for it.'[67] At McLaren he had largely side-stepped the media, letting Ron Dennis and even Alan Jenkins handle it, but at Ferrari this was impossible. He was the story and, as far as the journalists were concerned, he was promising a return to Ferrari's glory days, which meant the daily press would sell thousands more copies — and *Autosprint*, the weekly motorsport magazine, might even double its circulation.

Much more was resting on Barnard's shoulders than he could ever have accounted for, including the livelihood and future prosperity of the journalists covering his every move. As he also told Lydon, 'There are times, these days, when I feel as if I've taken a 20-ton weight on my back.'

Wherever Barnard went, *paparazzi* would snap and flash. So Barnard was furious with himself when, in March 1987 after testing Brunner's F1/87 at Imola, a moment's incaution, prompted by fatigue, coupled with wine at dinner, led him to lower his guard with Neil Lydon.

He subsequently took the *Sunday Times* journalist back to his childhood, to the classroom where he had built the speedboat. He revealed the old chips on his shoulders, that the teachers told him he shouldn't have been at a secondary modern but at a grammar school, that he had therefore failed his 11-Plus. He even told Lydon how he lost his rag with his father. Three months later Lydon quoted him in his article: 'There are plenty of people I have to deal with for whom it would be a perfect excuse not to take me seriously if they can see me as an uneducated blacksmith with oily hands. This is a highly sophisticated business where people's qualifications really count.'

That particular phrase — 'an uneducated blacksmith with oily hands' — was telling, all the more so because it reflected not only Mr Ferrari's dismissive label, *garagista*, but also the discomfort Barnard felt in being appointed to a position above the highly educated Dr Harvey Postlethwaite.

But how did Enzo Ferrari himself start? Blessed with far less formal schooling than Barnard, he began work in the bleak aftermath of the First World War driving lorries. Perhaps more pertinent than this, the word 'Ferrari' means 'blacksmith'. It is sometimes said, perhaps not often enough, that 'we hate in others what we hate in ourselves'.

---

[67] Lydon, Neil, *'Ferrari's English Formula'*, Sunday Times Magazine — Quality Cars, 14 June 1987, p37.

Barnard's concern, of course, was only so much paranoia. Formula 1 may have been a 'highly sophisticated business' but the truth was that qualifications didn't count as much as John feared. Despite the good doctor's degrees, Barnard was more successful than Postlethwaite by a country mile, as Ron Dennis was more than Teddy Mayer, and Enzo Ferrari more than all of them. Yet still Barnard continued to fret about his lack of academic status, as does Dennis to this day. And it wasn't necessarily a bad thing — the sickly feeling of inadequacy is probably the best motivator of them all.

Lydon provided an amusing insight into the stresses of Ferrari testing after that session at Imola with Brunner's F1/87: 'It had been a tiring and frustrating day, during which modified parts had arrived late from the factory in Maranello; [John] had spent a significant proportion of his day waving his arms and telling Ferrari's proud artisan mechanics that they weren't following his instructions; Michele Alboreto's car had caught fire while going at high speed down the pit straight; and the gathered legions of spectators and *paparazzi* had hooted their derision.'[68]

What perhaps should have concerned Barnard more, and didn't, was Enzo Ferrari's own angry reaction to other observations in the *Sunday Times* piece. Lydon referred to an 'institutionalised complacency' at Ferrari, a comment prompted by Barnard's evident opinion that, given a free hand, he would sack most of the Ferrari staff.

'Most of the people in this racing team,' Lydon's piece quoted, 'have been with Ferrari since they left school. They don't know anything else and they don't have anywhere else to go, unless they leave the country. The worst that can happen to them is that, if they screw up, they get to move out of the racing division and into production.

'If I could have my way entirely, there's a hell of a lot of them who would go; but to do that, I'd have to get too close myself to the company with the consequence that I might become a victim of the same process.'

The quote could hardly have been better calculated to upset Mr Ferrari. Perhaps even worse was John's criticism in the same article of the Ferrari Mondial road car that he had been given with the job. 'It's incredible that you can get ABS [anti-lock braking] on a [Fiat] Croma and not on a new Ferrari,' he said, while simultaneously declaring that his preferred transport was a

---

[68] Lydon, Neil, 'Ferrari's English Formula', Sunday Times Magazine — Quality Cars, 14 June 1987, p32.

Mercedes 560SEC, which he described as 'the best car in the world'.

John still has little time for Ferrari road cars, as he recently commented: 'If you want attention, drive a Ferrari. Everyone looks at you, from children to grandmas, and it makes a pretty noise. But the Mondial was a nightmare, with its heavy gearbox and crap steering — and it had tiny rear seats.'

Just a few days after the *Sunday Times* article was published, on 14 June 1987, John was in Detroit preparing for the Grand Prix. He was handed a typewritten letter embossed in black with the sign of the Prancing Horse, addressed to '*Gentile Signor Barnard*' and written in both Italian and English:

The commercial department of our Company has drawn my attention to the article 'Ferrari's English Formula' published in the 'Quality Cars' supplement to the Sunday Times Magazine on June 14th, 1987.

Whilst I too have been disappointed by the tenor of this interview, certain specific quotations attributed to you have been indicated to me as being contrary to Ferrari's public image.

I trust that your views have been improperly represented by the journalist, as I believe you will certainly confirm to me, and that this episode will encourage more cautiousness in the future.

The letter was from Enzo Ferrari and its quiet and crystal-clear message was that Ferrari might use the press against Barnard but not the other way round. The Italian version of the letter was signed 'E. Ferrari' in his trade-mark purple ink with a sweeping flourish, the 'E' incorporated into the 'F' in one deft stroke. God had moved his hand. And while Barnard was certainly impressed, he also thought God was wrong. Ferrari's Formula 1 team was a mess and it was going to take years for the English engineer to sort it out. When he finally achieved this aim he would leave the famous Scuderia ready and able to dominate for many years. But that wouldn't be for a decade.

For now Barnard had to cope with the political chicanery of the *Lavoratori Ferrari* (Ferrari workers), also known as the *Patrimonio* ('Ferrari's valued possessions'), as well as those further up the food chain at Maranello. He did it in the way he knew best — by ignoring it for as long as he could. He had bigger fish to fry, namely, creating another series of important innovations. Befouled by their own ludicrous, self-defeating politics, the only people to be slow to appreciate these contributions would be Ferrari themselves.

CHAPTER 21
REINVENTING THE WHEEL
1987–88

Once racing got under way in 1987, Gustav Brunner's F1/87 made a pretty poor showing for Ferrari. After eight of 16 World Championship rounds, its highest finishes were only a pair of third places for Michele Alboreto, at Imola and Monaco, while Gerhard Berger could do no better than fourth, which he achieved on three occasions, in Rio, Monaco and Detroit. Meanwhile, the teams doing the winning were McLaren, where Alain Prost took two victories, and those with the superb new Honda engine, Lotus and Williams, with two and four wins respectively.

Inevitably, John Barnard found himself sucked more deeply into the in-season development process for Brunner's car. It would take most of the year for the difference to become apparent.

The disappointing early results encouraged the *Stampa*, never a patient lot, to blame Barnard, criticising the madness that had made Ferrari spend millions on a facility in England when surely they had a world-class operation in Italy. Come mid-season, even a Ferrari driver was having a go. In an interview with the French sporting paper *L'Équipe* before the German Grand Prix, Alboreto compared Barnard's efforts to direct the Scuderia from a Surrey village to 'a brain surgeon attempting a complicated operation over the telephone'. He had a point, but his outspoken criticism of John was going to have major repercussions for him further down the line.

Alboreto's observation caused some panic in Maranello, prompting Piccinini to summon Barnard to a press conference at Hockenheim. As journalist Alan Henry put it, 'Those present can recall the look of thunder on the Englishman's face throughout the weekend.' Henry added, in a caption to a pertinent photo,

'Trial by press: the ill-judged 1987 Hockenheim press conference where John Barnard… was obliged to waste time which could have been better spent working on the new naturally-aspirated car.'[69]

The reason for Barnard's 'look of thunder', of course, was Alboreto's 'Italian back-stabbing'. The disrespect was mutual, with Alboreto commenting, 'The tensions built up and I thought to myself that I must have a very quiet winter indeed if I'm going to be able to stand another season driving for them in 1988.'

Both cars retired from the German Grand Prix, adding further fuel to the fire. This was the third race in a row where both Ferraris had dropped out. The cars were not only off the pace, but unreliable too.

Changes were made to aerodynamics and suspension, and very gradually progress was made, particularly in qualifying. At the Hungaroring, which followed Hockenheim, Berger put a Ferrari on the front row of the grid for the first time in two years, next to Nigel Mansell's pole-sitting Williams-Honda, but in the race the Austrian was soon stranded with a broken differential.

Three races later, in Portugal, Gerhard took pole position, the first of his career, and led for 64 of the 70 laps, but unfortunately the last lap wasn't among them. With Goodyear tyres shot and under intense pressure from Prost's McLaren, Berger spun it away three laps from the end. It was only a half-spin, but the error allowed Prost to pounce, leaving the Ferrari driver to have to settle for second place.

After two more unsatisfactory races for Ferrari, the Formula 1 circus arrived in Japan, Honda's home ground. Williams-Honda had already secured the Constructors' Championship, such was the team's dominance of the season with nine wins, and by this race, the penultimate one, the Drivers' title was also destined to go to one of the Williams men — the question was which one. That was settled early in practice at the Suzuka circuit when Mansell had a big accident and hurt himself enough to have to miss the race, leaving Nelson Piquet as World Champion with an unassailable points lead.

But the real glory at Suzuka belonged to Ferrari, which trounced all the Honda-powered cars. Berger put his F1/87 comfortably on pole, over half a second quicker than Prost, and Alboreto was up there too, fourth on the grid. In the race Berger did everything right, winning without threat after leading for all but one lap, with second-placed Ayrton Senna's Lotus fully 17 seconds

---

[69] Henry, Alan, *Ferrari: The Grand Prix Cars*, *Hazleton Publishing, Richmond, Surrey*, 1984, pp331–332.

behind. So ended Ferrari's 38-race victory drought. The *Stampa* were jubilant.

It got even better. Two weeks later in Adelaide, the final race of the season, Berger did it again, taking pole and victory, with Alboreto second after Senna's disqualification. A Ferrari one-two to close the season!

As far as the *Stampa* and the *Tifosi* (the Ferrari fans) were concerned, this luminous double victory meant that the stage was set for Ferrari dominance in 1988. Barnard, as ever, took little delight in the end-of-season success, which was to him nothing but a distraction. He was utterly focused on his uncompromising mission to create the perfect Ferrari. To do that meant turning the whole place upside-down.

By now Barnard had made considerable progress on his new Ferrari 639 for 1988. He says, 'I remember Enzo telling me, "When you design Ferraris, I want you to do something special."' Such direction was music to his ears, a conductor's signal for a new step change.

But doing something special wasn't so easy to achieve at Ferrari, whose mechanics were set in some particularly old-fashioned ways. Ferrari didn't even seem to understand the modern way of mounting the engine, which was still being supported in a subframe rather than bolted directly to the back of the chassis as an integral part of the overall structure. The result was that the rear suspension could behave oddly, with the effect of, in Reinhardt's words, 'a dog wagging its tail'. John would soon solve Ferrari's engine-mounting problem but would receive little thanks for it, as will become apparent.

Dr Harvey Postlethwaite comes in for some criticism from Reinhardt: 'Harvey was a very bright engineer, but he was also a politician, inclined to agree where he should disagree. Sometimes he got engineering and politics mixed up. He was a political animal.'

Barnard, of course, was most definitely not a political animal, and insisted upon his meticulous methodology. Like the Team McLaren mechanics before them, those at Ferrari were simply not used to receiving drawings from the drawing office and making parts that were exactly right. They were more used to getting a drawing, making a part and, as Reinhardt puts it, 'hammering, grinding and chiselling it until it fitted'.

Barnard, having already installed Joan Villadelprat in Maranello as chief mechanic, needed more like-minded help there and Gordon Kimball duly became based in Italy, doing his best to learn the language and help teach the staff the Way of Barnard. He was aided in this by Villadelprat and, in particular, Giorgio Ascanelli, an engineer fresh from tyre manufacturer Pirelli who warmed to Barnard's approach. Initially 'very green' according to Villadelprat, 'Giorgio learned quickly and was a brilliant engineer.'

The 639's engine was to be a naturally aspirated 3.5-litre as Formula 1's first turbo era was coming to a close. At the end of 1986 the FIA had announced a two-year transition period, 1987–88, in which the existing turbocharged 1.5-litre engines could be joined by the 3.5-litre normally aspirated engines that would become mandatory in 1989. For the first of these transition seasons, both types of engine had to run to a fuel limit of 195 litres, although the 3.5-litre cars could be lighter, with a limit of 500kg rather than 540kg. For 1988, the rules shifted to favour early adopters of 3.5-litre engines, as the turbos now faced a much lower fuel allowance, just 150 litres, and inevitably it looked as if they would be less competitive.

In view of all this, Barnard saw no point in preparing a turbo car for 1988 and instead ordered the engine department to start building a lightweight naturally aspirated V12 engine according to his design parameters. This was a novel experience for them. No mere chassis designer had ever instructed them in such a thing before. Who on Earth did this Englishman think he was? They had always called the shots on the engine.

None of this was said to Barnard, or at least not in English. Not that the engine department was inclined to quarrel with a V12. Mr Ferrari had famously said, 'I married the 12-cylinder engine and I never divorced it.' And that passion was deeply instilled throughout Maranello, in both its road cars and its racers. Barnard agreed in principle: 12 cylinders could rev higher than six, eight or ten, and should produce more power to compensate for its weight.

But to Barnard's alarm, the 3.5-litre V12 turned out to be underpowered. Reinhardt claims that initially it put out just 300bhp on the Ferrari dynamometer instead of the predicted 700bhp.

To address this thorny problem, Reinhardt consulted Berger, who, as an Austrian driver, had good contacts at Anstalt für Verbrennungskraftmaschinen List, thankfully better known as AVL, an automotive think tank based in Graz in Austria. This company, widely used in Formula 1, was at the cutting edge of electronic engine management and helped restore the much-needed power. One may imagine how the Ferrari engineers were upset by this intervention.

The pressures all around Ferrari were bringing a pot of trouble to the boil. To simmer it down a little and against Barnard's inclinations, Reinhardt invited the entire Maranello racing crew to Surrey, which happily boasted a first-class Italian restaurant, La Baita (now converted into a house), in nearby Bramley.

Just before pudding, Reinhardt suggested 'a real dessert' and took them for a short walk along the high street to Bramley Motor Cars (still there), which proudly flaunted upon its forecourt a range of classic cars, including Ferraris. As Peter recalls, 'They were all moving among the cars, boasting about which bits they had designed or built. It certainly broke the ice.'

Returning to GTO in Shalford, Reinhardt found their mood improved. They were less critical of River House's design, which they considered 'clinical', and slowly began to express enthusiasm about the facility. They even witnessed tourist boats coming along the River Wey announcing, 'And over to your right you can see the new Ferrari factory — yes, ladies and gentleman, Formula 1 has come to Godalming.'

Reinhardt's PR push was beginning to turn the tide, at least among the workforce: 'They could smell that something special was going to happen for the future. Once you have the racing team supporting you, that's half the battle.'

Barnard's 'something special' came one day late in March 1987 when he was sitting at his board in his new office designing the cockpit and rear arrangement of the 639. 'I was draughting away, trying to get a good lean shape, but found myself struggling with the bloody gear linkage, yet again, as I had done on the Chaparral and on the McLarens. The damned thing needed too much room to run back from gear lever to gearbox.' The gear linkage was a perennial design headache, complicating the design of the fuel tank behind the driver.

For Barnard, the absence of ground-effect tunnels under the sidepods didn't prompt him to make the chassis any wider. He knew he could make it stiff enough in its narrower form and he preferred to sacrifice cockpit width for more room in the sidepods for the radiator layouts; from his point of view, the narrower the cockpit, the better for aerodynamics. He considered the possibility of running the gear linkage through the right-hand sidepod *à la* Chaparral but that in itself would compromise the radiator arrangement on that side of the car.

Driven by frustration, a new idea began forming in the depths of his mind: 'Rods running in and out of tubes, with their crappy hook joints rattling around; there was nothing nice about it, nothing aerospace; it was more like bloody Meccano.'[70] He was angry with the awkward complexity of the system: 'This ghastly lever and links game, mucking up my fuel cell.'

When Barnard gets angry, he gets creative: 'Even the gear lever itself was pissing me off; the damned thing made the cockpit several inches wider.' His drivers, of course, had the temerity to require room to grip the gear lever. John recalled Eric Broadley's wise advice and let the problem percolate.

Diane Holl recalls the reaction in the GTO drawing office when Barnard suddenly announced his solution to the gear-linkage problem: 'John, always on the look-out for the next step, announced, "Well, we won't have a gear shift!" Everyone was stunned — it seemed bonkers. No gear shift? The objections were so overwhelming it was hard to know what to say.'

If every inventor craves a Eureka moment, then this surely was Barnard's. With growing excitement, that tremulous joy that comes when a problem solver spots the ghost of a solution, the idea bubbled up in his brain and took solid form. 'Get rid of it! Get rid of the gear lever and get rid of the linkage!' Still the drawing office looked bewildered. 'Get rid of the lot! This is 1987 — surely we can just press a button to change gear!'

The advantages began to flood into Barnard's mind: 'No linkage, no gear lever, no clutch pedal, just a wire and a button on the wheel. A narrower cockpit, a neater fuel cell. And better for the driver! If he could change gear without his hands leaving the steering wheel, what a difference it would make!'

Out of pure frustration with the 'Meccano' linkage, and out of pacing around his office, out of letting the problem take its course around his head, John had turned a vexing problem into a brilliant solution — a device to shift the gears hydraulically. 'It didn't really matter that people said — "No way! You're crazy! It'll never work!" — because it was clear to me that they just didn't get it. To me it was blindingly obvious. I wanted to do it, and if I had to fight for it, then I would. I was used to it. I had to fight for everything.'

Now came the enormous task of making it happen. John drew how he wanted the necessary hydraulics and other equipment on the gearbox, and then gave the scheme to Ferrari's gearbox people, expecting them to move forward with it. To that end, he flew to Maranello to see Fosco De Silvestri, chief of Ferrari's gearbox team, to explain face to face what he wanted. Fosco was an ambitious engineer looking to make a mark at Ferrari, so his eyes lit up at the suggestion and soon they were both locked in conversation. Fosco proposed

---

[70] *Meccano is a construction toy consisting mainly of perforated metal plates and strips, plus rods, clamps, cogs, screws, nuts and bolts. It was conceived by Frank Hornby of Liverpool in 1898. It was sold in America as Erector.*

that Fiat's electronics arm, Magneti Marelli, a division full of talent, should become involved. Hitherto, Barnard's *modus operandi* had been to endeavour to be hands-on and oversee every detail, but this exercise he really did have to farm out, despite his own gearbox expertise learned alongside Pete Weismann.

Why had no one done such a gearbox before? The concept seemed simple enough: just press a button to send an electrical signal down a wire to an electronic actuator on the gearbox that would make the gear change. What could be more obvious? The actuator would operate hydraulics, using the power of oil in a piston to change the gears.

In Formula 1 there can be thousands of gear changes in a race. Monaco requires well over 4,000 and each one, in the old days, required the driver to push in the clutch with his foot, take one hand off the steering wheel and shove the lever into the chosen gear, all the while driving as fast as possible through sharp corners tightly bordered by steel barriers. A 'semi-automatic' gearbox would give the driver the control he needed, but more safely, more quickly and with much less effort.

A further benefit was reliability, which McLaren's Tyler Alexander explained with admirable clarity: 'The big side effect was that it really helped reliability because you couldn't do what everyone did with a manual gearbox. They would go howling down to the hairpin at 200mph and suddenly stuff the car into first gear, revving the shit out of the engine. With John's idea, you had to go down the gears on the sequential gearbox.' The electronics simply wouldn't allow the driver to make a downward gear change if the revs were too high.

As John says, 'Almost all engine over-revving stopped. That's the sort of bonus you never think about at the outset. There are always advantages that you never predicted.' And, as Joan Villadelprat adds, 'You could programme the gearbox according to the track — even skip an entire gear.'

Solving such problems was meat and drink to Barnard. As he adds, 'I find gearboxes absolutely fascinating. I think they're great. I love them, because there are so many options, so many ways of doing things.'

The essence of Barnard's concept was to operate the gearbox's selector forks hydraulically rather than by means of a traditional mechanical linkage to the gear shift. Pistons housed in hydraulic cylinders were linked to the selector forks on the gearbox and actuated by an electronically controlled device called a Rexroth valve, which could open and close hydraulic valves within milli-seconds, giving the whole system the speed necessary to be practicable.

In addition, the electronic control had the capacity to check the speed of the wheels against the speed of the engine and the gear required.

So, instead of having a rod running from the cockpit gear lever through the fuel cell to the selector forks, there was simply an electrical connection between two buttons on the steering wheel and the electronic control box for the Rexroth valve/hydraulic piston assembly. The button on the left of the steering wheel would shift down through the gears, the button on the right would shift up.

Thanks to a thought that popped into the mind of Piero Lardi Ferrari, the buttons became paddles, shaped levers behind the steering wheel that the driver could rapidly click, giving rise to the now-popular name of 'paddle shift'. As Barnard recalls, 'I was talking to Piero about the system and my plans to put buttons on the steering wheel when he said, "Go-karts have levers on the steering wheel. You could use those for changing the gears."' According to John, this bright idea was Piero's most important contribution to the Ferrari operation during the engineer's time there.

Initially John thought that the driver should keep the clutch pedal, just losing the gear lever and its 'horrible' linkage, but soon it became apparent that the semi-automatic gearbox would work better without a clutch pedal. He thought it was important to allow the driver to be able to shift gears out of sequence by moving, for example, from sixth gear straight into second on the approach to a tight corner. To do this required keeping the gearbox's basic arrangements of rods and forks, which enabled the driver to select any gear at will.

But later versions of his gearbox adopted a sequential system, eventually employing an aerospace Moog electro-hydraulic valve to control a hydraulic rotary actuator made at Ferrari by Fosco De Silvestri, of which more later. This system meant that moving from sixth to second would be achieved by rapid clicks on the paddle (5–4–3–2). This proved to be just as fast, if not faster, than manually moving a gear lever from sixth to second, and protected the engine and gearbox from the damage caused by crashing into lower gears.

Although the idea of a semi-automatic gearbox had been around in road cars for decades, Barnard's was the first successful attempt in motorsport, where the stresses and strains are far greater, so great, in fact, that previous attempts at it had either never worked or never shown any advantage. When Barnard's system was being developed, one of the Ferrari engineers told him that some years earlier they had tested a sequential semi-automatic gearbox with a manual gear shift rather than paddles. Gilles Villeneuve tested it at Fiorano, Ferrari's private circuit, but the team, led by technical director Mauro Forghieri, couldn't divine any advantage and dumped the whole affair.

Patrick Head is another who attempted to create a sequential gearbox. In 1982 he studied a Honda racing motorcycle and created a 'barrel actuator' on the gearbox from which a push-pull cable ran forward to the cockpit. Williams never raced it. Head gives full credit where it's due: 'John was the initiator of the semi-automatic transmission — I thought it was a bloody good idea.' Williams were the first to follow Ferrari's lead when they introduced their own semi-automatic in 1990.

The revolutionary gearbox had the full backing of Enzo Ferrari, despite considerable resistance, reports Barnard, from just about everyone else in Maranello, including Postlethwaite. But, barring a total cock-up, with Mr Ferrari's blessing it would be seen through to completion. The highly motivated Fosco De Silvestri knew that if he could make it work, his small department — he had only three on his team — would gain significant kudos throughout the company. Such was the way the Ferrari fiefdoms operated: success was likely to mean higher status, more staff and a bigger budget.

With the semi-automatic gearbox in good hands and well underway, John turned his attention to the bodywork and aerodynamics. When he arrived at Ferrari, the company was midway through building its own new wind tunnel, which for the first time included a rolling road. The project was led by Postlethwaite with French aeronautical engineer Jean-Claude Migeot working under him. Barnard's input was minimal: 'All I did was tell them how to make the model wheels and give them some pointers on the rolling road.'

Pretty soon Barnard hit a brick wall. Much of the time the Maranello wind tunnel didn't seem to be available for testing his model of the Ferrari 639 and, when it was, little worthwhile seemed to come out of it. 'I just couldn't trust the data,' he explains. Something was going on, and he wasn't sure what.

He pressed on. The V12 engine took some considerable cooling, which required bigger radiators — just how much bigger had to be judged by rule of thumb because information from Ferrari's engine department was also a little sparse. As it happened, the increased cooling needs provided more opportunity to improve his coke-bottle shape, which by now had been copied by most of the paddock: 'Because I had narrowed the cockpit by taking out the gear lever, I had more room to play with the shape of the sidepods. I found that if I put the inlet close to the chassis, and then bulged the bodywork around the radiator and brought it in again at the back, I could create an even more extreme coke-bottle shape.' He added a further improvement, bringing the airflow out of each radiator through the length of the sidepod and out of the back of it, under the rear wing.

The result was a car of striking beauty, although, as we shall see, the Italian press found itself in two minds. Italian engineer and aerodynamicist Nicolò Petrucci, who would later work with John, reports being most impressed by this 'double curvature' shape, which he described as not only beautiful but 'very efficient aerodynamically, a completely different shape'.

Looking on from McLaren at his old boss's work, design engineer Matthew Jeffreys was also bowled over when he finally saw the car: 'John's first Ferrari was such a departure from his thinking when he was at McLaren. I was full of admiration that he could not only build GTO in the time frame he did but also design that car at the same time. The 639 moved away from a lot of the McLaren thinking — perhaps he had been keeping the new concepts to himself!

'The 639's plan view seemed to me to be critical. He moved the curvature of the outside quite a long way forward so it swept in quite markedly behind the front wheels. If you compare the plan-view shape to the McLaren of the time, it was very different. Also in side view, the 639 featured a very high-to-low profile to get over quite a forward-mounted water radiator. And then it went downwards again towards the rear wheels. He must have found something in the Ferrari wind tunnel to prove what he settled on. There was much chatter in the paddock: "Oh, that's an interesting idea, I wonder why he's done that?" I was intrigued that he had come up with something different that certainly wasn't in his thought process when he was with us.'

With no meaningful access to a wind tunnel, Barnard was designing by instinct once more, but, of course, Jeffreys and the others chattering in the paddock couldn't know that. Frustrated at the lack of cooperation on wind tunnel and engine, but unwilling at this early juncture to upset tottering apple carts, Barnard decided to keep away from Maranello, assigning his agents — Kimball, Ascanelli and Villadelprat — to keep him informed.

Settled in Shalford, Barnard was doing the part of his job that he 'absolutely loved', working undisturbed on new designs. He promptly came up with another breakthrough, solving Ferrari's 'wagging tail' problem by changing the way in which the engine was mounted in the car. Perfecting a method of engine mounting had been rather an obsession ever since he brainstormed the problem of installing the VW engine in the Super Vee at Lola. Later he became frustrated with the way Cosworth DFV engines were mounted at the bottom of the engine via fixing bolts just nine inches apart. He could never understand those nine inches because he thought the distance far too close: 'It did nothing to help lateral stiffness of the engine.' The top of the Cosworth was secured to the rear of the cockpit via triangular plates that were bolted to the cam covers, the plates being designed to allow for expansion when the engine was hot.

Barnard's simple solution to this irritating problem was to ask the Ferrari engine department to put four mounting points on the front of the new engine. There were two strong points on the top, on each cam cover, with each strong point drilled through, while at the bottom, fixed to the front of the oil sump, he specified a lateral beam with two more holes, one at either end. On the back of the monocoque he arranged four threaded studs in corresponding positions, projecting out to mate with the four holes on the engine. 'It was simple. You slid the engine onto the studs, put a nut on each of the protruding bolts at the top, and on the two on the beam at the bottom. I made an educated guess that engine expansion wouldn't be an issue.' Barnard was right — it wasn't.

But the proposal caused some consternation at Ferrari where, as mentioned, they had always used a subframe to mount their engines. They just couldn't see how four bolts would be strong enough to support an entire V12: 'There was a sort of sucking in of breath, Italian code for, "There isn't a snowball's chance in hell of this working." So I just said, "Yup, that's what we're going to do. Goodbye." Barnard wasn't about to let native breathing habits interfere. The result was entirely successful and, like so many of his ideas, soon spread throughout the paddock as the simplest and best way to mount an engine.

By now Barnard had in place yet another 'nuts and bolts revolution' that would spread throughout Formula 1. During his time at Parnelli he had learned about NAS (National Aeronautical Standard) bolts, high-specification aerospace fastenings designed for extreme conditions and available in just about every conceivable size, and he had used them ever since. NAS bolts were Imperial, measured in inches, but Ferrari worked in metric and Barnard was forced to think again. Try as he might, however, he just couldn't find metric bolts of sufficient quality.

Never a man to stint, he commissioned a French company called Blanc Aero (now Lisi Aerospace) to make bolts according to his design, including specifications for quality, strength, torque and temperature resistance: 'It was an expensive business, but worth it.'

All such key specifications went into Barnard's so-called Blue Book. Created and compiled largely by Diane Holl and Andy Smith, the Blue Book contained ever-growing lists of specifications for bolts and fixings, bonding mixes and other fabrication processes. A copy was presented to each new designer so that he or she knew the best material or subset of material for a given job and exactly which specification should be stipulated on their drawings, not just for nuts and bolts but for components in carbon, titanium, aluminium or steel. This was so useful that it wasn't long before copies began to escape the Scuderia.

'The process of building up these databases went on for years,' says John. 'Over time, as people left my team, they'd pop their copy of the Blue Book into their briefcase and take the bloody list with them! It wasn't long before it dawned on me, "Blimey! We've just created the method for other teams to bloody well design and build these cars!" Before I knew it, there were another ten people ordering parts from our suppliers and Blanc Aero bolts and other materials specs were spreading throughout Formula 1.'

The impact of this should not be under-estimated. While it wasn't a landmark on the scale of carbon-fibre or the paddle shift, Barnard's Blue Book and the metric fixing system contained within it changed the way everyone worked within Formula 1 design, helping them to raise standards throughout and contributing to the creation of better cars and improved driver safety.

Ross Brawn, one of motorsport's very best technical brains who has enjoyed enormous success, particularly at Ferrari and Mercedes, recently paid due homage to Barnard's initiative: 'I think John raised the standard, and all of us recognise that when somebody raises the bar you have to try and get up there yourself. We all recognised that it could be achieved, and therefore that was what we had to aim for. JB was meticulous in his application of the engineering; it was a very strong combination of innovation with very strong engineering standards and principles behind it. His cars never suffered failure due to engineering faults.'

Brawn's comments point to the enormous difference Barnard made to the professionalism of Formula 1. Similarly, Andy Smith makes a useful observation about the contrast between Ferrari before Barnard and afterwards, referring to the cars that followed the 639: 'When we started at Ferrari, we saw that each whole car was full of bespoke parts. You couldn't swap them between the team's three cars because nothing was made accurately enough — there was no concept of interchangeability. When we did the 640 and 641, a wishbone, for instance, could go on any of the three cars. That just wasn't the case in

Formula 1 until Barnard came along. With John it was designed right, and it was machined right, and it fitted. People complained about the cost of a Barnard build, but the truth was his approach actually saved money.'

Ron Dennis backs up this assessment: 'John's approach tended to incur a cost penalty. However, his designs were usually so impeccably wrought that they required little fettling once manufactured, which reduced the need for further spend. So I would describe them as expensive but cost-effective, which was particularly gratifying once we had begun to win Grands Prix and World Championships with them.'

This may sound like Barnard approached his work with little regard for a budget, but that wasn't the case. Reinhardt reports that in early meetings Ferrari were fearful that GTO's cost would far exceed the predicted amount, a Fiat representative saying, 'You say this much, and we know it will be double. Everything that Ferrari touches is double the budget.' So when, at the end of 1987, GTO's operational expenditure came in some 8% under the expected cost, Fiat were unsure how to react. In the end their people closed their gaping jaws and told Reinhardt that it was the first time a Ferrari Formula 1 project had come in under budget.

'John was very particular about this,' says Reinhardt. 'He was always on top of the money, making sure that we got the best quality for the best price and insisting that people keep within the projected limits.' It was another example of Barnard's capacity for good planning creating less angst further down the line, a desire born out of experience gained from his first spell at McLaren.

Be it Maranello or Shalford, everyone at Ferrari was under pressure as the 1987 season came to a close. Newly recruited Diane Holl had tried to raise her game but found she couldn't: 'I was nervous to start with but, having worked for him for a while, it actually got worse. I lost all my confidence. John expected the best of everybody — he was a hard taskmaster. If I didn't grasp something I often felt I wasn't good enough, not of the standard he needed.'

She recalls one incident when she was tasked with drawing a bracket for manufacture, a particularly complex form in three dimensions: 'I must have sat there for hours looking at this piece of paper. I even remember cutting up a bit of cardboard and trying to make it out of that, just in an effort to get my head around it. I got nowhere with it for the rest of the day. When I came back the following day, it had been drawn. I reckon it would have taken John about five minutes. I felt terrible about it.'

Locked in a spiral of self-doubt, she decided to quit. Her parents, horrified by the idea of her leaving Ferrari, warned her that she might never get such an opportunity again. She ignored them, wrote a resignation letter, took it to work and put it on John's desk, intending to say, 'There you are. I'm resigning!' At the last moment she said instead, 'I'm thinking of giving this to you.'

'Well,' said John, 'if you're thinking of giving it to me, then we have something to discuss.' And so they talked. 'I can't take this pressure,' she said. 'It's too much.' 'You're doing far better than you think,' he replied. 'If you weren't, you wouldn't be here.'

Looking back now, John recalls: 'Diane was getting a bit of a ribbing in the office. There were no other females and I thought it was pretty brave of her coming into that world.' He had made it clear that just because she had a bit of paper from a university declaring her to be clever didn't mean she knew much, but he had taken her on — and wanted to keep her — because he considered her sufficiently intelligent and talented to do well. She had a good eye, a good instinct and was a hard worker, and, despite her self-doubt, a feeling he knew only too well, she was, he thought, tough enough to survive in a harsh, male-dominated world.

So he explained to her, as she stood in his office on the edge of tears, that she wasn't to take his criticisms personally, that it was his job to dwell on the problems rather than any good work she did. It wasn't really criticism, he explained, simply a shortage of time: 'I've got to find the problem and we've got to fix the problem, because there's no second chance — we've got a deadline.'

To ease the pressure he offered to 'get off her case' and stop looking over her shoulder. To make this more likely, he put her to work directly for Gordon Kimball, who, based in Maranello, was often ordering parts to be drawn up at GTO. It didn't last. Within weeks she was back working for John. 'I wouldn't say he was any easier on me despite what he said,' she admits, 'but from that moment on it worked a lot better.'

But other things weren't working better. As the new season approached, the 639 wasn't ready, a fact that played into the hands of a frustrated group at the top of Ferrari, people who were planning Barnard's demise under deep cover within the workshops of Maranello. These frustrated players were creating an alternative plan, designed to rescue Ferrari from the clutches of this abrasive Englishman, who showed them no respect and who simply wouldn't listen to a word they said.

CHAPTER 22
THE SECRET CAR
1987–88

Why wasn't the 639 ready for the 1988 season? John Barnard blamed the engine department; the engine department blamed him. But without a working V12 engine, all of his efforts on the new car were pretty pointless.

The result was a big meeting in late 1987 at which it was decided to use an adapted version of the existing F1/87 turbo car for the 1988 season, the last in which 1.5-litre turbos were to be permitted. It was a poor compromise that could and should have been avoided. As Barnard puts it, 'The whole year was a complete cock-up.'

The outdated Ferrari was going to have serious trouble in 1988 against McLaren's new Honda-powered offering, the MP4/4, driven by Alain Prost and spectacular new signing Ayrton Senna. As the MP4/4 owes a debt to Barnard and became one of the most dominant cars in Formula 1 history, famously winning 15 of the season's 16 races, it is important, at this juncture, to reflect a little upon how that car was created — because it knocked Barnard's Ferrari efforts into a cocked hat.

So, what had been happening at McLaren after Barnard's unexpected and sudden departure? The answer is a mixture of panic and brilliance.

Ron Dennis needed to appoint a 'name' as his new technical director and he went for Brabham's Gordon Murray. As Murray confirmed in an interview for this book, he arrived at McLaren at the end of 1986 to find that the new car, the MP4/3, 'had already been designed', largely by Steve Nichols and Matthew Jeffreys. Given the crisis caused by Barnard's departure, the car did pretty well during 1987, McLaren taking second place to Williams-Honda in the Constructors' Championship, with Prost scoring three wins and newcomer Stefan Johansson adding useful results in support. During 1987, Murray then had to organise design of two cars, a brand-new turbo, the MP4/4, for 1988 and a normally aspirated V10, the MP4/5, for 1989, choosing Nichols and Neil Oatley as their respective chief designers.

Nichols recounts the evolution of his MP4/3 to the famous MP4/4, explaining that the earlier car wasn't much different from Barnard's MP4/2: 'There was a lot that we didn't do to the MP4/3 because we didn't feel that we had the time. And in fact the MP4/3's advantage over the the MP4/2 was only slight.

'My ethos for the MP4/4 was to make it small and compact — don't bite off more than you can chew — so it wasn't terribly radical. But the whole aerodynamic package of the sidepods was transformed, compared to John's MP4/2. Aerodynamically, the MP4/4 wasn't much better than the MP4/3, which was a little bit bigger because it had the larger Porsche engine. But making all this more compact really was only a very small aerodynamic advantage.'

Two new FIA rulings had a major bearing on the design of the MP4/4. First, fuel capacity was reduced from 195 litres to 150, meaning that the tank behind the driver could be smaller. With the car's more compact Honda engine, Nichols was also able to reduce the height of the airbox and associated bodywork: 'The real advantage to making it little and low was that it had a low centre of gravity. If you ask your Aunt Nelly which is best — to make a race car higher or lower — she'll tell you that it should be lower. So making the car low was a no-brainer, and it was a given you were going to make it as compact as possible.'

The second ruling concerned safety: the relatively stubby noses of previous Formula 1 cars were lengthened to provide more protection for the drivers' legs. Before this, their feet could extend beyond the front wheels; now they had to be behind the front axles. To achieve this the front wheels were moved forward, with attendant changes to the front suspension.

Nichols's colleague, Matthew Jeffreys, explains more: 'In a way the MP4/4 designed itself. We had these new restrictions and we now had the much smaller Honda engine, so the bodywork behind the driver could be reduced. It was a natural follow-on to have the driver in a low-lying position.'

Another major change for the MP4/4 was a redesign of Barnard's narrow cockpit, creating, claims Nichols, 'a much stiffer monocoque'. The sidepods were duly altered to be 'much lower with side outlets rather than top'. Jeffreys adds that they 'retained JB's male-moulded chassis-manufacturing technique as it offered greater aerodynamic flexibility of the bodywork shape and allowed for a largely flat slab-sided monocoque shape whereby more structurally efficient unidirectional carbon fibres could be utilised rather than heavier cloths.'

Concluding his comments on the MP4/4, Nichols says: 'Gordon Murray had virtually no influence... Barnard's influence, although indirect, was greater.'

Clearly Barnard's legacy was significant in the MP4/4. Murray, Nichols and Jeffreys all concede that its creation would have been harder had it not been for the changes Barnard had wrought at McLaren. Had he not created the carbon car, had he not instituted a *modus operandi* led by the drawing office and kept on track by aerospace accuracy, had there not already been a host of other Barnard innovations on the cars, including the coke-bottle shape, had the systems and the perfectionistic ethos not already been in place, it would have been almost impossible for McLaren to produce such an extraordinarily successful car.

As Barnard says, 'It wasn't my car, it was definitely theirs, but it's fair to say that it was built on the principles that I had established, although they made a breakthrough by making the whole car lower, giving it excellent grip.'

Such was the success of the MP4/4 that even Patrick Head likes to claim a little input: 'At Williams we worked hard with Honda to bring their new engine up to Formula 1 specification. They had taken on a really nice guy called Katsumi Ichida as the main Formula 1 engine designer and he was very good. One problem was the Honda's oil sump arrangement — it was basically a bucket underneath the engine with some pumps in it and a filter at the bottom. I tried to persuade Ichida to use a low-line sump by employing a similar system to the Cosworth engine, which recirculated the oil coming down from the cylinders via a specially designed crank that would sweep the oil into a separate channel where it was gathered by scavenger pumps.

'By the time the Honda was offered to McLaren, Ichida had adopted the idea. So I can at least claim that small contribution to the MP4/4, because its low-line sump was the result of many conversations between Honda and me and it was demonstrated to us at the end of 1986.'

One has to admire Steve Nichols; one can only imagine the pressure applied to him by Ron Dennis in the latter half of 1986 and the following year. He was no Barnard, but, in some ways, as he explains, that was a good thing.

Regarding himself as lacking self-confidence and 'riddled with self-doubt', Nichols describes his approach as highly consultative and he exudes pride in the achievements of his team. He surrounded himself, he says, 'with capable people, with me inviting criticism from all of them. If I had an idea I would be horribly scared that it wouldn't work, so I would ask everybody to pick holes in it. If they couldn't, then I'd think, "Maybe we are on to a winner!" But it was always that lack of confidence, that double-checking of everything and making sure that everybody else had an input that actually pushed things ahead. But to do that you needed a team of people for whom you had immense respect.'

Barnard believes there were two other reasons for the MP4/4's success. The first was the brand-new Honda turbo engine, which turned out to be the most powerful on the grid, with 'probably about 150bhp more than anyone else'. The second was the car's drivers: Ayrton Senna was now in his prime as one of the best drivers on the planet and Alain Prost was at the top of his game. The furious and sometimes dangerous competition between them was a major contributor to McLaren's extraordinary dominance of the 1988 season.

As it turned out, Ferrari's adapted 1987 car, the F1/87/88C, managed to give the Scuderia a respectable first half to the 1988 season. While McLaren won all of the first eight races, and scored one-two results in five of them, Ferrari achieved second and fifth in Brazil, second and third in Monaco, third and fourth in Mexico, and third and fourth in France. McLaren apart, Ferrari were doing better than any other team. Barnard attended most of the races and had a major part in ensuring that the results for the car — still essentially the Gustav Brunner design that he had inherited — were as good as possible.

Meanwhile, John continued to work on his 639, still refusing to spend time in Maranello — despite Joan Villadelprat begging him to — and still working hard to create the perfect paddle-shift Ferrari. Besides his travails with the engine department, another barrier was that he hadn't been able to get enough access to Ferrari's new wind tunnel for testing the 639 in model form. He wondered why.

'You could tell there wasn't the enthusiasm,' he laments. 'You could feel they weren't there to help you. I just had to press on, trying to get them to do more tunnel tests.'

As Arthur Webb reports, 'Ferrari made life difficult with silly things. We'd send them parts for the car and they'd say they hadn't arrived when we knew they had. Or we'd tell them we'd deliver a particular part by a particular date, the earliest we could manage, and they'd insist it had to be a week earlier. It drove John spare.'

Another 'trick' from Barnard's opponents in Maranello was to complain that a part had arrived with damage that must have occurred before transit.

'It was a ridiculous idea,' adds Webb. 'The very notion that John or anyone at GTO would ship a damaged part was daft. We ended up taking photos of everything as it went into the packing cases. It was all a load of cobblers.'

On top of this, despite the fact that GTO was running within budget, Barnard was constantly being told that things were unnecessary or too expensive.

Then, out of the blue, a reason for Ferrari's petulant behaviour suddenly hove into view. One bright, spring day Barnard was sitting in his River House office when he took a call from Joan Villadelprat. His Maranello-based ally had been on a walk around the factory and arrived at the wind tunnel. What he saw there shocked him. Villadelprat takes up the tale:

'The problem we had had with the 639 was that we couldn't get it into the wind tunnel. At the time I was in charge of the race team, the test team, the sub-assembly team and part of the machine shop; I had around 140 people answering to me. Maranello is big; the engine side was in a separate place and the wind tunnel in a separate building as well. One tended to operate in one's own area but I did like to put my nose in everywhere, just to see what was going on.

'So, on that day, I walked over to the tunnel, went inside and to my complete shock I saw another car in there that wasn't John's. I learned that it was a project being run by Harvey Postlethwaite and Jean-Claude Migeot. I called JB straight away and told him that Harvey was no friend of his, that he was trying to cut his legs from under him.'

Barnard, of course, was deeply disturbed by the news.

Very soon after, Peter Reinhardt, the manager at GTO, received a similar call from George Ryton, a Maranello-based British engineer whom he had recently taken on. Reinhardt went to see Barnard and told him: 'You're going to have to go out there. Harvey, Jean-Claude and Piero are building a secret Formula 1 car. It's a different car — a competitor to yours. Ryton says it has a raised nose. It's the reason we can't get in there, why we can't get any cooperation. The Old Man knows nothing about it!'

To Barnard it explained everything, the delays, the lack of cooperation, the continual, wearing sniping, and, critically, why they had been prevented from testing the 639 in the wind tunnel. This was revenge Italian-style and John blamed Piero Lardi Ferrari.

Piero Lardi, born in 1945 to Enzo Ferrari's mistress, Lina Lardi, was widely regarded as a man with a chip on his shoulder and a lot to prove. As Enzo's illegitimate second son, he had had a tough life for a little rich kid, always in the shadow of his older half-brother Dino, upon whom Enzo doted. When Dino, a talented engineer, grew up, he joined his father's company and was both liked and respected, but soon he became crippled with muscular dystrophy and died, in 1956, aged only 24. Enzo never got over it, and Piero, bearing the brunt of being treated like the 'runt of the litter', was determined to find a way to emerge from Dino's eternal shadow and impress his father. It was indeed a long shadow. Barnard recalls hearing tales of how Enzo's wife, Laura Dominica Ferrari, hated Piero's presence when she was at Maranello: 'She'd chase him from the building, screaming abuse at him.'

The last thing Piero needed was an Englishman who might tell his father that he was no good at his job, although this isn't something Barnard ever did. All the same, Lardi evidently decided that the risk existed and that he had to take measures to protect himself.

Lardi got on very well with Postlethwaite, who, a top-flight engineer, was the sort of character who got on with everyone. Both of them had their doubts about Barnard and they both rubbed along with Jean-Claude Migeot. So, some time in mid-1987, the triumvirate formed a mini *cosa nostra* ('our thing'), apparently winning over the necessary Maranello staff, including, says Reinhardt, driver Michele Alboreto. Given his public clashes with Barnard, Alboreto must have been easy to recruit to this parallel plan.

One can only speculate as to what was going through Lardi's mind when he embarked upon this risky course. He was approached during 2017 for an interview for this book but declined on the grounds that he was only granting interviews organised or promoted by 'the company' in celebration of Ferrari's 70th year.

Did he really believe his father would thank him for coming up with such a scheme? Did he really think Postlethwaite was better than Barnard? Was he really hoping that he was doing his father's will, that *Il Commendatore*'s penchant for dividing and ruling, which some believed helped engender creative initiative within the Scuderia, actually meant this effort would be rewarded?

Villadelprat offers some explanation: 'In Ferrari there were two groups: the Old Man and Barnard on one side, and Piero Lardi and his 'secretaries', Harvey Postlethwaite and Jean-Claude Migeot, on the other. Postlethwaite and Migeot were working with a turbo engine while John was trying to make the new V12. The priority, it turned out, was always the secret turbo car.

'Harvey could be a very nice person but also such a politician. He was able to control Maranello very well and was very secure with the Italians. In my view, Piero was always trying to plan things behind John's back... and I think Harvey did everything in his power to screw up John.'

Post-Ferrari, Postlethwaite and Migeot went to Tyrrell and Barnard suspects that the secret car was the precursor to their memorable, innovative but ultimately unsuccessful Tyrrell 019 of 1990. This was the first Formula 1 car with a raised nose, of the style that George Ryton had observed in the Ferrari wind tunnel, and it established a new aerodynamic template that has been followed ever since. This concept served to force high-speed, and therefore low-pressure, air under the car, improving downforce. It was an aerodynamic breakthrough.

'I believe the car in the Maranello tunnel was a pretty good effort,' says John. 'But it meant they were trying to prove they didn't need me.'

It seems bizarre in the extreme that leading people at Ferrari could put together a rival project counter to the express wishes of Enzo, so creating a clear breach of the Ferrari contract with Barnard. But the Scuderia already had a somewhat twisted track record for destructive internal politics, especially when it came to dealing with their 'foreigners'.

Most famous perhaps is the case of British driver John Surtees, the seven-time motorcycle world champion who turned to cars in 1960 and joined Ferrari three years later. Despite being courted by Enzo directly, he seemed unable to get along with Ferrari's aptly surnamed sporting director, Eugenio Dragoni, who made a big point of favouring Italian drivers.

Surtees's first outing for Ferrari was the 12-hour sports car endurance race at Sebring, Florida, his co-driver being Lodovico Scarfiotti. They turned up to discover that the Ferrari 250P that he and Scarfiotti had been testing in preparation for the race had instead been given by Dragoni to three other Ferrari drivers — all Italian. Surtees and Scarfiotti were given the 'scarcely tested' second car. Insult turned to injury shortly after the start of the race when the car they'd been given started to feed exhaust fumes into the cockpit, rendering both drivers extremely nauseous. In spite of their extreme discomfort, Surtees and Scarfiotti crossed the line first, with their preferred sister car second. The winning drivers had to leave the victory rostrum to throw up. But what turned Surtees's stomach even more was the subsequent discovery that their victory for Ferrari was being protested — by Ferrari! Dragoni postulated that Surtees and Scarfiotti were a lap behind and that the other Ferrari had therefore won. Happily, Surtees's wife, Pat, had kept a meticulous record of the laps completed and it agreed with the official timekeepers' record, so the victory stood.[71]

Had he read it, Barnard would have nodded in grim agreement at Surtees's description of this experience as 'a foretaste of what was to come at Maranello'. And, having discovered the existence of the secret car, one might have expected him to leap on the next plane to Italy and storm into the Scuderia. But instead he ignored it, choosing to bide his time, supremely confident that whatever they had come up with, even with the full cooperation of the Scuderia, wouldn't compete with his paddle-shifted masterpiece.

'I said to Peter and Joan,' Barnard reflects, '"Don't worry, I'll sort it out later. Just wait, ignore it. When I have done this car, when it's on its wheels and ready, I'll deal with it."' But of course it bothered him deeply: 'I understood I was competing with McLaren, but Ferrari — I bloody worked for them!'

Although handling politics was always Barnard's big weakness, his decision to make no fuss about the secret car reveals interesting elements of his character. It showed first of all that he refused to allow a plot of such monumental proportions to be a distraction to his number one goal, and it also showed his harder side. He would take his revenge in his own sweet time, revealing nothing of his hand along the way, revenge being a dish, as the epithet has it, that is best served cold.

Arthur Webb recalls further new ideas within the 639's carbon-fibre chassis: 'In John's eternal quest to save space he designed ducting channels that ran through the honeycomb sandwich to carry cables and electrics.' He was probably the first to use a carbon roll bar, made as an integral part of the airbox behind the driver's head. Says Webb, 'It was a real pain to make, a tight horseshoe hoop itself made up of an even tighter horseshoe of carbon, when viewed in section. Getting that to consolidate properly so that the fibres worked was extremely difficult.'

Webb also reports that they had problems making the front bulkhead tough enough for the crash test, the strength of it having been compromised by 'the amount of holes put in it for pedals and other equipment'. Confident they had solved the problem, he flew out to the Fiat test facility in Turin to oversee its performance. It was 14 February 1988, Valentine's Day, and so, inspired by the prospect of a romantic weekend 'swanning around the snowy beauty of the Dolomites', he brought along his wife, Janette. While she 'mooched about' in

---

[71] *John Surtees with Mike Nicks,* John Surtees: My Incredible Life on Two and Four Wheels, *Evro Publishing, Sherborne, Dorset, 2014, p144.*

Turin, he went to watch the test — and the bulkhead failed. Janette returned to their hotel only to find her husband beckoning her straight out again to their hired car and driving not to the wintry splendour of Alpine Italy but instead the 190 miles to Maranello, where he had to burn the midnight oil with Gordon Kimball to work out a solution to the test failure. 'She wasn't particularly delighted,' he says in his laconic style.

Webb recalls that they also spent a lot of time on the 639's carbon undertray, especially at the rear, where exhaust temperatures could exceed 700°C: 'Most composite materials die at 300°C!' By this stage they were using heat-resistant Nomex for the core in the carbon sandwich of the undertray, having overcome bonding issues experienced with the material, although the core of the carbon-fibre chassis itself continued to be the much stronger aluminium alloy honeycomb. To combat the extreme heat, they looked at a range of insulation blankets and even contemplated a ceramic composite, but this technology was judged to be too new. In the end they opted for a metallic-surfaced insulation blanket and made this part of the undertray from a solid heat-resistant laminate, with an air gap between it and the exhaust. As Arthur says, 'John endeavoured to shape the rear of the car, the rear of the tray and the exhaust itself to encourage air through this gap. This was all part of his continual effort to increase downforce and improve cooling where needed.'

In mid-May 1988, well after the start of the season, the first 639 was finally completed at GTO and shipped to Italy. Villadelprat takes up the tale:

'One Saturday I was in the factory. Enzo's bodyguard and driver, Dino, an ex-boxer, called me and asked how many people were in the factory. I told him around 100 people. He asked me to send everyone home. I checked that it was an order from the Old Man and did so.

'Two hours later Enzo's car, a black Lancia saloon, arrived at the main gate. I opened the big doors to the racing department and Dino drove the Lancia inside and parked close to the Formula 1 639 V12. I helped Enzo get out of the back and brought him over to the 639.' Enzo Ferrari, now 90, was weak from kidney disease, and supported himself with a stick.

'I pulled off the cover and he started to touch the car, to feel its lines. As he did so, he kept repeating, "*Bella, bella.*" He was getting so excited that we thought it was dangerous for him, so Dino and I led him back to the car and he was driven home.'

Ferrari test driver Dario Benuzzi was the first to put the 639 through its paces. He did so not at Fiorano but at Balocco, the Fiat-owned Alfa Romeo test track near Turin; Barnard wished to avoid the prying eyes and lenses that always surrounded Ferrari's own test track in Maranello. The Balocco test was going satisfactorily when John realised that his attempt to outfox the Italian motorsport *paparazzi* had failed, presumably because someone had tipped them off. They were present in numbers, hiding, says John, 'in the trees, in the bushes, all round the bloody circuit.'

Barnard, furious at the breach, despatched security guards in vans to chase the photographers away, by all accounts something of a Keystone Cops routine, but he knew he was wasting his time when a photographer flew over in a helicopter, hanging out of the aircraft with a 'sodding great telephoto lens'. Barnard duly 'blessed his celluloid with a few choice gestures'.

That day the new 639 was equipped with a trial version of the paddle shift that employed automatic upshifting, with the electronics calibrated to change each gear at a specific engine speed. The system was not destined to last, primarily because drivers often want to change up at lower revs than the engine might automatically choose — automatic upshifting just didn't offer enough control.

The car finished, now the time was ripe for revenge on the people who had, in Barnard's mind, caused its delay. He had sent a series of memos on the matter to Mr Ferrari, but none had been answered; John suspects they were intercepted. So in late May, just a week or two after the Balocco test, he flew back out to Italy to deal with the problem directly, meeting 'Fiat man' Gianni Razelli, Ferrari's managing director at Maranello.

As soon as Razelli, who spoke excellent English, realised the sensitivity of the issue, he suggested they talk privately at a restaurant away from the factory. As reported by John, the following exchange occurred:

'I told him, "You've got to make a decision, because it's either me or them. I can't operate like this. You can't have it both ways. If you want to pay me off, I will go, but I can't do it like this." Razelli went 12,000rpm — talk about light the blue touch paper! It was obvious that Fiat were dead against Piero Lardi Ferrari. "We want you — the others are just a nuisance," he said, and left before I had finished eating.'

Apparently Razelli went straight to Mr Ferrari, whose reaction was as swift as it was brutal. In a flood of action not unlike the climax to a Shakespearean tragedy, Piero Lardi, Enzo's only surviving son, was effectively thrown out of the Ferrari Formula 1 team. Harvey Postlethwaite and Jean-Claude Migeot also left, to join Tyrrell, taking their secret car concept with them. And, to add insult to injury, the favourite of the *Tifosi*, Michele Alboreto, was duly replaced by another Englishman — Nigel Mansell — and at the end of the season also joined Tyrrell. Another Fiat man, Piergiorgio Cappelli, was brought in as Lardi's replacement.

'Can you imagine it?' asks John. 'Enzo must have been furious. He banned his only remaining son from coming to the races. For anyone, let alone an Italian, that is monumental. He was so hard on Piero. Still, you don't build a business like that by being soft.' John, too, knew how to play hardball.

This turned out to be *Il Commendatore*'s last major decision. Early the following month, June, Pope John Paul II visited the Scuderia, but the Old Man was too ill to leave his home, speaking instead by phone. The Holy Father did benefit from a close-up view of the 639 — photographs reveal him to have been pretty perplexed by the radical new car — plus a ride around Fiorano in a Mondial and a tour of the factory by Piero, who must have been happy to be back inside the gates.[72]

It didn't take long for the storm to break, and Barnard was in serious trouble. The PR department at Ferrari did what they could to control the news of Lardi's departure, but rumours had already started flying at the Mexican Grand Prix at the end of May. At a Maranello press conference the following week, as reported in *La Stampa*, one of Italy's oldest newspapers, 'Piero Lardi confirmed that he was leaving Ferrari sports management "for an important industrial role", gaining the title of Ferrari Vice-President. He is quoted as saying, "I didn't want an official interview... but it's no use hiding. It's not true that I had an argument with my father. We both have different opinions about employing John Barnard. Enzo Ferrari is responsible for the team. He decides.'

The message was clear, Lardi had been sidelined and he blamed Barnard. As the unnamed journalist of the newspaper account commented, 'Ferrari's son has made it clear that he doesn't trust the designer much.' The feeling could not have been more mutual.

Also quoted was Ferrari President Vittorio Ghidella, who headed Fiat's car division and was considered the main force behind Fiat's commercial resurgence thanks to strong sales of the Uno road car. Ghidella was speaking with due caution: 'I won't say anything,' he declared, before adding, 'On 8th

---

[72] *Yates, Brock*, Enzo Ferrari, The Man and the Machine, *Doubleday/Transworld Publishers Ltd, London, 1991, p400.*

June, Ferrari's board will meet. We'll see. I don't think anything will change. Barnard is the technical director.'

In England, this might be called 'damning with faint praise' or, in this case, no praise at all. The same article featured a large heading, 'With the aspirated engine, we are all at sea', a quote attributed to a member of the engine department. This might be read today as verification of Barnard's complaints about the V12 but at the time it was interpreted as being entirely Barnard's fault, since he was, allegedly, in overall technical control.

The battle for power at Ferrari was in full flow as the Scuderia awaited the death of the Almighty. They had to hang on until the evening of Sunday 14 August before Enzo Ferrari finally succumbed.

John Barnard was not invited to the funeral, but, to be fair, no one was, as Enzo's English right-hand woman, Brenda Vernor, testifies: 'He was buried at 7am on the morning of August 15th', explaining that he had asked to be buried quickly by his immediate family and that his death should only be announced after the funeral.[73] He was therefore interred within a few hours of his death.

Thus passed, quietly, the greatest legend that motorsport has ever known, in a manner that was a reflection of his true character. It is thought that only Piero and his wife Floriana were at his bedside.[74]

Like Barnard, Enzo Ferrari may have had a tyrannical image, and, as Brenda Vernor says, 'one had to be careful of his moods', but in fact he was shy, even timid. The trade-mark sunglasses allowed him to be reserved in company, and if, as the head of Ferrari, he found it impossible to avoid the full glare of publicity during his life, he made certain there would be none at his funeral. The Scuderia received over 3,000 letters, cards and telegrams of sympathy — Brenda Vernor says Piero Lardi replied to every one.

The death of a great king often spawns savage internecine battles as potential successors vie for the throne — the Scuderia would be no exception. Piero Lardi, the only man with the Ferrari name, would find his position, so recently hopeless, considerably stronger as Fiat struggled to find the best way to bolster the Ferrari brand.

Barnard realised he now had to protect his interests, so he decided to break

---

[73] *Enzo Ferrari's Right-Hand Woman'*, Motor Sport, *August 1994, p837.*
[74] *Yates, Brock,* Enzo Ferrari, The Man and the Machine, *Doubleday/Transworld Publishers Ltd, London, 1991, p401.*

his habit of a lifetime, daily lunch with his family, by flying out to Maranello to take control. He wasn't impressed by what he found.

August was doubly a dead time for Ferrari. Almost the entire factory was in the continental habit of going on holiday for the month, something that always made Barnard seethe. 'It didn't seem to matter that they were a racing team — almost everyone went on bloody holiday, which was mad, because we had the Belgian Grand Prix towards the end of the month and the Italian Grand Prix coming up in early September.'

Barnard installed himself in his office there and soon found himself looking at a memo from engineer A. Dominici about test results performed at Ferrari on American-made Garrett TP13 turbochargers. Dominici described the performance improvements offered by the new Garretts over the existing turbos as 'very small — not worth bothering with'.

Somewhat disappointed, Barnard looked through the performance charts and saw, to his surprise, that the improvements in turbo-lag time, around 10%, were useful. He tried to get hold of Dominici but discovered that he too was on holiday. That provided no insurmountable obstacle to Barnard, who summoned Dominici to the factory anyway. When he arrived, John let him have it.

'These results are good, so why did you stop the testing?'

'The improvement wasn't big enough,' came the limp reply.

'What are you talking about?' thundered Barnard. 'Ten per cent will make a vital difference! Why are these turbochargers not on the car?'

The proffered explanation was that they came from America and it was vacation time. Barnard made his view clear.

'I want these on the race car! Now!'

Dominici shrugged his shoulders. As John says, 'I just couldn't understand the attitude that the Garretts offered a gain but somehow it wasn't big enough to bother with.' He dismissed the man and got on the phone to Garrett. The turbos were at the Scuderia within the week.

On 8 August Barnard fired off a memo to Cappelli, the new boss, copying Kimball among others, and describing Dominici's analysis as 'ridiculous and bad in the extreme', adding that the 10% improvement amounted to 'a very significant step forward' and berating Dominici for making the decision to stop 'without discussion'. John was gearing up for a major battle with the attitudes at Maranello that were constraining his aims.

He now started thinking about how to combat the McLaren MP4/4, which by now had won all 11 races so far that season. He quizzed the few engineers present at Ferrari on their thoughts about McLaren's Honda turbo engine. One said he believed that Honda had found a way around a new FIA ruling about turbo boost.

In order to limit the power of the turbo cars in their last two years of eligibility, the FIA had, in 1987, capped the allowable boost at 4.0 bar (i.e., four times normal atmospheric pressure). It was generally reckoned that 0.1 bar equalled about 20bhp, so when, in 1988, the FIA reduced the limit further, to 2.5 bar, with the additional loss to the turbo cars of some 300bhp, there was a level of panic, even at Honda. These restrictions on boost pressure were imposed by requiring the use of a pop-off valve that would open to release pressurised air when the limit was exceeded.

The Ferrari engineer reckoned that Honda had found a way around this limit by designing the internal shape of the manifold upon which the valve was mounted in such a way that it created a false reaction. Says John, 'In short, it was thought they had made the air flow faster just beneath the valve, and, as you know, faster air has lower pressure.' The upshot was that, with such a cunning manifold design, a valve set to 2.5 bar would in reality require boost of 3.0 bar or more to open it, allegedly giving McLaren around 100bhp over the rest of the field. It was clever, arguable and extremely hard to detect — what Barnard called 'a creative interpretation of the rules'. Whether or not there was any truth in this speculation, the FIA most certainly was guilty of, in John's words, 'pretty poor policing'.

Certainly there was nothing in the rules that specifically said an engine manufacturer wasn't allowed to alter the manifold geometry. So, could Honda have decided to go with a creative interpretation of the rules? 'Absolutely. I would have done too,' says Barnard. It might not have been within the spirit of the regulations, but that's all the latitude Formula 1 engineers need in their constant and ever more taxing battle to counter a growing and ever more demanding rulebook.

'I believe the Honda engine had at least 100bhp more than anyone else and this, I think, was the reason for their advantage,' says Barnard, despite both Murray and Nichols claiming that no such adjustment was made. 'They had Senna and Prost and this creative interpretation of the rules. It was a good car, but not such a great car, and the adulation it has received really pisses me off. It certainly wasn't as good as the record books make it look.'

His point is that 1988 was a strange season, a halfway house made into 'a fiasco' by the efforts of the FIA to phase out turbo cars. 'It was all about horsepower — and the McLaren had a massive advantage. I'm sorry, but it is hard to judge how good the MP4/4 was. It was very good, but against what? A somewhat under-developed 1987 Ferrari? Because we were the only ones who gave them a real run for their money.'

By the time of the Italian Grand Prix at Monza, Italy was still in grief from the death of Enzo Ferrari four weeks earlier, and the press were upping the ante.

The 639 was ready to go to the races, but Barnard knew that a naturally aspirated car couldn't compete with the all-conquering turbo McLarens. Despite the efforts of the FIA to level the playing field, having turbos racing non-turbo cars was not, to his mind, any such thing.

Reluctantly he shunted the 639 into the wings — and so it became the one Barnard car that never raced. It had served the purpose of preparing for its successor in 1989, the first non-turbo season, but no one was impressed by that. John now had firmly established the most negative part of his reputation, that he would get so obsessed with perfecting an important innovation, in this case the paddle shift, that he would miss racing deadlines. It was an unfair reputation, but life itself is rarely fair.

On the basis of 'if you can't beat them, join them', Barnard agreed to allow the Ferrari engine department to alter the updated 1987 car's V6 turbo manifold along the lines described to him, creating an estimated and 'possibly protestable' boost of 2.9 bar, while simultaneously incorporating the new Garrett turbochargers.

'Our car wasn't as good as the McLarens, that's for sure, but now we had a chance of competing.'

At Monza on the morning of Friday 9 September, the first day of practice for the Italian Grand Prix, the two Ferraris were invited to take to the track first in tribute to Enzo Ferrari. Saturday went as well as could be expected, with Berger and Alboreto qualifying third and fourth behind the two McLarens, Senna on pole. But Sunday morning was marked by a welter of negative reporting in the Italian press, who were expecting disappointment. Who could beat the unbeatable McLarens? And whose fault was it? Barnard was in the crosshairs.

The press's mood was partly inspired by the recent announcement of Alboreto's departure at the end of the season. They had always felt that the Italian driver hadn't fulfilled his potential and considered the highly paid Barnard entirely to blame for not giving him a winning car.

In a big headline on the morning of the race, *La Stampa* announced 'Barnard's reputation is on the line'[75]. Journalist Cristiano Chiavegato quoted Ferrari President Vittorio Ghidella as describing his relationship with John as 'excellent' only to be followed by the somewhat less enthusiastic, 'He is doing the job for which is paid.' Ghidella then noted that the 639 was 'promising, even though we still have some issues to solve. Barnard knows his reputation is on the line, and ours is on the line too.' Then he had a go at Barnard's work rate: 'Up until now he has worked a bit slowly… I am hoping that we'll manage to develop the semi-automatic gearbox, which is a difficult task. This is why we also have a mechanical gearbox, though the car will obviously have to be modified to take it…'

As Ghidella was soon to discover, there was no way Barnard was going to put a mechanical gearbox on the 639 or, indeed, on its successor, the 640.

Ghidella also had a pop at GTO: 'There is Guildford, which we are keeping. It's a technological investment. I'm not saying it's better than Maranello, but hopefully it is useful.' Italian bosses are masters at making statements designed to encourage reading between the lines, and none of it was complimentary to Barnard.

Corriere della Sera, a major paper in Turin, also laid into Barnard, with Nestore Morosino writing under the heading 'Barnard is Ferrari's question mark': 'There are still doubts about the British designer. Up until now, from what he has promised we have seen but little, and the 1989 programme is delayed by six months. Shortly we think Barnard will have to report. If he's not convincing enough there will be black clouds on the horizon and for "Sir John" the threat of drowning will be more real.'

All of this blithely ignored the fact that, actually, under Barnard's direction, Ferrari had had a better season than any of the other teams in McLaren's wake, with their two drivers regularly qualifying third and fourth behind the MP4/4s, and several times finishing in those positions. Understandably, only winning was good enough for Ferrari.

The national newspaper *Il Tempo* headlined its Sunday piece 'Piccinini is leaving, Barnard is risking' with a subsidiary heading stating that Ghidella was being 'Tough with the Guildford Magician', before going on to fan rumours of Barnard's imminent departure and his alleged complaint that 'Ferrari hasn't even respected half the points in their contract'.

---

[75] La Stampa, *Sunday 11 September 1988.*

And so, after the Italian press had been digested by just about everybody within Ferrari apart from Barnard, a classic race got underway at Monza.

Prost passed Senna at the start but almost immediately discovered, to the cheering joy of the *Tifosi*, that his engine was misfiring. Senna took the lead straight back, with Berger and Alboreto close behind Prost in third and fourth places. It is alleged that Prost realised early on that his misfire was terminal and so applied maximum pressure on Senna, consuming more fuel but hoping to force the Brazilian to use up so much of his own that he couldn't finish or would be overtaken by the Ferraris, thereby gaining Alain an advantage in the championship — he wasn't called 'The Professor' for nothing. Perhaps if he were really lucky, Senna might make a mistake under the pressure of the chase.

Halfway through the race, Prost's misfire began to sound worse and both Ferraris passed him on lap 35, at around two-thirds distance. There was fulsome jubilation in the stands as Prost pulled into the pits, the first and only McLaren retirement that season due to trouble with the remarkable Honda engine. Alboreto now found his gearbox was malfunctioning and had to drop back from Berger. A few laps later it recovered and he began to catch Berger again, securing, to the hysterical delight of the *Tifosi*, the fastest lap.

Senna's advantage at the front was 25 seconds when Prost retired. Soon after, he was forced to slow down and save fuel, perhaps because of Prost's alleged tactics. Berger and Alboreto, in line astern, closed in and with three laps to go they were only six seconds behind. By now, the *Tifosi* were starting to believe, offering up prayers *en masse* to their Knight Commander in the sky.

And then, by apparent divine intervention, Senna was struck down. Flying along the pit straight about to start his penultimate lap, he was closing on a backmarker, Frenchman Jean-Louis Schlesser, driving a Williams in his first Grand Prix as substitute for the ill Nigel Mansell. Rapidly approaching the first left-hander in the notorious *Rettifilo* chicane at the end of the pit straight, Senna came up on the inside of Schlesser, who moved wide to let him through while simultaneously making a hash of his braking, locking up and skidding off the track into the gravel on the right-hand side, all in full view of the main stands. As Senna shaped himself for the next bend, a right-hander, Schlesser, still off-track, ran across the corner's apex and smashed into the right rear of Senna's car, nearly flipping it over, before sending it into a lateral spin.

Murray Walker and James Hunt were commentating for the BBC. In disbelief Walker's voice leaped a full octave as he stuttered: 'Spin! Senna! Ayrton Senna spins!' Recovering his manliness, Murray continued: 'What a fantastic situation! I am surrounded by a bunch of cheering, gesticulating, shouting, overjoyed Italians and the atmosphere is unbelievable! We are not only going to see a Ferrari win in Italy, but we're going to see one finish second!'

James Hunt was most amused as he watched the replay and saw Senna spin across the track. 'He's stuck on the kerb,' he giggled. In his classic style Walker talked the BBC audience to the triumphant conclusion: 'Well, what an amazing Italian Grand Prix! The unblemished McLaren record has been well and truly smudged by these two cars, and Alboreto is right up now with Berger and he's going for a win, he can sense the chance of winning! It's going to be a fantastic end to the Italian Grand Prix and history is being made in 1988 — listen to the crowd!'

But the heavenly *Il Commendatore* had other ideas, because Alboreto couldn't close the gap. 'Ferrari wins!' shouted Walker as Berger screamed across the finish line, and 'Ferrari second!' as Alboreto followed just behind.

Walker summed it up: 'And the first Italian Grand Prix since the death of the great Enzo Ferrari has seen his beloved scarlet cars from Maranello honour his memory with first and second places. It's a truly happy crowd.'

The Italian press were equally delighted, declaring it the '*Miracolo a Monza*'. They gave no credit to John Barnard, of course, and little enough to the drivers, making the point that it was Prost's engine failure and Senna's mistake that gifted the Scuderia its first and only win of the season.

It was small consolation that Ferrari came second in the Constructors' Championship and that Berger was the highest-scoring non-McLaren man in the Drivers' Championship. The whole plan had been to take Barnard, *Il Mago*, away from McLaren and thereby make it impossible for the English team to win. Now, according to the national paper, *Il Messaggero*, in its Tuesday edition following the race, 'John Barnard has been put on a leash, a tight rein, from whose undeniable genius the real Ferrari of the future will have to emerge.'

The message was clear. Barnard had to win next season — or leave.

CHAPTER 23
THE MIRACLE OF THE DUCK
1988–89

John Barnard assumed his accustomed posture, returning to his family in Godalming to begin creating a new, improved version of the 639, the 640. Working with aerodynamicist Henri Durand, he refined the bodywork while ensuring that the new car would not and could not have a manual gearshift — plans that soon put him in conflict with Ferrari's President.

Vittorio Ghidella was determined to make Barnard modify the new car to take a mechanical gearbox, repeatedly insisting in messages to the Englishman that he wanted the 640 to have a mechanical option, instructions that John repeatedly ignored. The confrontation came to a head when they bumped into each other in the Ferrari racing department's car park in mid-September 1988, just a week or so after the Monza Miracle.

'Ghidella told me he was worried about the electronic gearbox,' reports John. 'He said, "I cannot afford to have a failure. I've got to take over from Enzo and it would just look too bad for me in Italy if the first thing that came out of my reign was a failure. So we must have a manual gearshift option in the car."'

Barnard's reaction to Ghidella's order was to the point. 'No chance, Vittorio. The car is designed without one and that's the way it's got to be. The car is built around the concept of no gearshift.'

Ghidella insisted: 'I want you to build manual option to test at Fiorano.' Still Barnard refused, explaining that the chassis would have to be widened to accommodate a gear linkage, a mountain of pointless work and a real 'backward step'.

By now the discussion in the car park was becoming a heated row, with

Barnard yelling at the President of the Scuderia. 'We don't have the capacity to do that! And even if we do, I don't WANT to do it, I see NO POINT in doing it and I'm NOT doing it.'

Ghidella, a power player within Fiat and unused to such vehement contradiction of his wishes, continued to insist. John played his ace, reminding Ghidella that his contract gave him technical authority over Ferrari, whatever the President might think and say. 'This is MY decision and I will not compromise this car!'

They parted, the issue unresolved, with Barnard's overriding feeling being a sense of disgust at Ghidella for his 'lack of balls — he was dead scared of what the outcome would look like if it didn't work. He was no Enzo, not by a million miles.' Not for the first time in his career, or the last, Barnard was absolutely furious.

Unsurprisingly, so was Ghidella. Chief mechanic Joan Villadelprat recalls that one evening Ghidella came into the racing department to examine a 639 chassis: 'He had a broomstick pole and started poking around the chassis to see where a manual gearshift could fit into the cockpit. John had designed it to ensure that it was impossible to do that. They were even suggesting putting the gearshift on the outside of the chassis, with the driver reaching out over the side to change gear! Everyone was sure that the semi-automatic gearbox was going to be a disaster. And, to be fair, it was a disaster at the beginning of the year.'

Why it was a 'disaster' will become clear, but, by way of a tease, Villadelprat describes the conflict as 'a typical Ferrari row, with Barnard blaming the alternator and the alternator people blaming the gearbox.'

For John the row in the Maranello car park was the final straw. Under legal guidance, he began to write a series of letters to Gestions Sportives Automobiles S.A. (GSA), the Ferrari entity to which he was contracted, accusing the company of breach of contract.

In a three-page letter dated 30 September 1988, he related the history of his troubled times there, declaring that the 'major problems became more apparent once Maranello became more closely involved with research and development work on the new car. The problems became more difficult due to the failing health of the Chief Executive [Enzo], to whom the Engineer [Barnard] was solely responsible.'

He then fired an accusation at Piero Lardi Ferrari and made indirect reference to the secret car:

It became clear, in particular, that the executives in day to day control, including Piero Lardi Ferrari, had made no real attempt or effort to establish or implement the Engineer's authority there, and not only did they fail materially to cooperate with and support the Engineer, but they utilised essential resources and facilities there for projects of their choosing.

The various difficulties were raised by the Engineer on numerous occasions both in discussion with the Chief Executive and by notes and memos to him.

Nothing was materially rectified despite assurances, and the situation gradually deteriorated to the extent that the Engineer had no real direct authority or influence at Maranello.

Barnard moved on to his conversation with managing director Gianni Razelli, and the sweeping changes that followed:

The problem eventually became so acute that BDC [Barnard Design Consultancy Ltd] decided it was necessary to serve notice of GSA to terminate the Agreement. Before doing so, however, the Engineer was authorised to raise the matter with Fiat, in view of the failing health of the Chief Executive.

This ultimately resulted in Fiat exercising its option, with the consent of the Chief Executive, to acquire control of the constructor and replacing key executives with Fiat-nominated executives and introducing a new structure, agreed with the Engineer, which appeared to be intended to implement the Agreement and establish the Engineer's direct authority, with a proper organisation and chain of responsibility, answerable to him on all technical aspects.

Barnard chose not to name the President, Vittorio Ghidella, as the source of obstruction in his efforts to have technical control of Ferrari, instead citing Piergiorgio Cappelli, whom Enzo had appointed sporting director after the secret car had been exposed. Such was Barnard's low opinion of Cappelli that he even spelled his name incorrectly:

In particular Mr. G. Kimball and Mr. J. J. His [the engine department chief], both of whom had the confidence of the Engineer, were placed in charge at Maranello of the two technical divisions within the Racing Department, and with direct responsibility to the Engineer and a non-technical Chief Executive, Mr. Capelli [sic] was appointed, seemingly to operate in accordance with the Agreement, under which any new chief Executive's powers were to be exercised so as not to infringe on or inhibit those of the Engineer...

Then came the kicker:

However, far from taking the necessary positive action, as outlined above, the opposite has resulted and the reorganisation has had the effect of imposing the authority not of the Engineer but of Fiat and its management.

These events, and in particular direct and indirect instructions from the Fiat management, both contradicting and bypassing the instructions of the Engineer and cutting across the programme of development laid down by him, and a major change in the organisational structure at Maranello contrary to the wishes of the Engineer have seriously damaged the position and status of the Engineer and have undermined the whole basis of the Agreement.

That 'major change of organisational structure' might have been the 'disappearance' of sporting director Marco Piccinini and the appointment of Pierguido Castelli as technical director in Maranello, reportedly charged with overseeing Barnard's activities. 'There was immediate friction between the British and Italian ends of the operation and Ferrari began to look for someone to replace Barnard.'[76]

Indeed, another letter in Barnard's files, from Gordon Kimball to Barnard on 14 September 1988, includes the complaint that Castelli's appointment 'places an intermediate position between you as Technical Director and the three sector managers...' adding, 'When I accepted the position of Car Sector Manager it was with the stated understanding that I would be considered for the post of Technical Director should it become vacant at some time in the future. Under this new structure I believe this is now virtually impossible.' This was an irritant much like a speck of sand in an oyster, and it would soon grow.

John certainly wasn't happy with Castelli's arrival, commenting that he

---

[76] *Constructors: Ferrari (Scuderia Ferrari)*, grandprix.com.

'came in with no racing experience whatsoever'. So he rounded off his letter with a shot across the Ferrari bows, concluding that the 'consequent and continued failure to implement the terms of the Agreement, as outlined in this notice, accordingly constitutes a fundamental breach of the Agreement and of GSA's obligations thereunder.'

As so often happens at such moments, the lawyers were called in. Michael Jepson represented a fuming John Barnard and Dr Henry Peter, a young, super-bright American, represented Ferrari in tension-filled discussions in the Maranello boardroom.

'There was a bit of a stand-off,' says John, euphemistically. 'I could see I was going to have to compromise — you always do when fighting the giants.' The lawyers carried on their discussions throughout the night, Jepson being paid for his highly expensive time out of Barnard's own pocket.

It became clear that Barnard was batting his head against a brick wall, that Ferrari were too big to fight. Against every bristling fibre in his being, Barnard accepted that compromise was the only possible way ahead.

So he agreed to modify the contract, striking a deal whereby, he explains, 'if the paddle shift didn't work, or was deemed to be unsuccessful, they could tell me to get on my bike with no financial compensation for an early departure'. Specifically, the revised contract with Ferrari stated:

> *In addition GSA undertakes to procure that by 10th January 1989 at the latest, the Constructor [Ferrari] shall make a decision (the 'Decision') as to whether it will commence the 1989 FIA Formula 1 World Championship using a 640 car or whether to postpone such use, using a 639 car until the 640 car is considered by the Constructor to be ready for use in such Championship.*
>
> *If the Decision is to postpone such use of the 640 car notwithstanding the fact that both:*
>
> *i) the 640 car is superior to the 639 car on the basis of the wind tunnel tests and*
>
> *ii) the automatic gear box of the 640 car or, if such gear box of the 639 car is shown by means of a circuit test to be capable of both 50 laps on the Fiorano circuit and one Grand Prix distance on each of the Jerez and Monza circuits without any problems in its electro-hydraulic system,*
>
> *SC [for Ferrari] shall have the right to terminate the GSA Agreement by notice with immediate effect given not later than 20th January 1989.*

In other words, if the paddle shift failed, John was out on his ear. He had nailed his colours, and very possibly his future, to his own mast.

'It's the nature of the game,' he says. 'Any time you do something new, you have to be determined and convinced that your idea is right. And then you have to stick your neck out.' There were plenty at Ferrari standing ready with the axe.

Another man standing ready with an axe was an unlikely lumberjack in the form of Arthur Webb.

On the night of Thursday 15 October 1987, the October Hurricane swept through southern England, killing 18 people and taking down an estimated 15 million trees, including many of those in Barnard's nine-and-a-half-acre garden, rendering the Surrey lanes impassable with fallen trunks. The storm also brought down power lines across the region, leaving the Barnard residence without power for ten days; even the phone didn't work.

Once reconnected to the modern world, John, true to his do-it-yourself nature, bought a second-hand JCB. With his big new toy, he began grinding up the Combe Rise lawns as he pushed the fallen trees aside while Arthur busily hacked at the branches like a lean, soft-spoken Paul Bunyan.[77] While this was going on, John's daughter, Jennifer, was running around in high excitement, ignoring Arthur's attempts to shoo her away. An effervescent child, she persisted in running up close and making faces at him, managing at a critical and hideous point to put her head too close to the axe as Arthur was bringing it down on a branch. He was just able to swerve the blade as it flashed down, missing her by inches and striking the wood a glancing blow, the tool flying out of his hands. 'I've never told John that,' he says, shuddering at the thought of what might have followed the decapitation of one of his daughters.

The Combe Rise garden now became a wonderful playground and remained that way for the next five years. Every weekend when John could get away, he would spend the time in the garden with his children, whatever the weather, cutting up trees, making bonfires, and building camps in the bushes and the woods. As Jennifer says, 'If he could get out of going to a race he would — he far preferred doing that with us than having to talk to people who he didn't really want to talk to.'

---

[77] *Paul Bunyan was one of America's early superheroes, a mythical giant lumberjack who battled 'fearsome critters' and displayed extraordinary strength and endurance.*

For John's son, Michael, the youngest of his three children, early memories are dominated by these times: 'Every weekend for the next few years after the storm we were out in the garden chopping up trees, digging out roots.' Even Grandad Ted was out there, now in his 80s, 'wielding a chainsaw', says Michael. 'We loved it — we'd all help out — although probably we slowed it down more than we helped. Such great memories of jumping in the big holes where the trees had been, and Dad driving us round in the bucket of the digger — he'd lift it up and suddenly drop it with us in it. We were all given mini-axes to chop up the wood' — with one of which, according to Jennifer but forgotten by Michael, he nearly removed her fingers.

And so back to work on the 640, flat out at GTO and Maranello. Taking his lead from the 639, Barnard refined what was to become the trade-mark 'extreme' coke-bottle shape, bringing the sidepods out to their maximum regulation width and bulging them around the radiators, which he refashioned to be as large as possible to cope with the V12 engine's cooling requirements, before bringing the bodywork in tightly at the rear.

But the heat generated by the radiators was still causing major problems. As we all know by now, big issues are Barnard's meat and potatoes, and the struggle produced a new idea, as he explains:

'I was trying really to make a step. At McLaren we had the airflow from the radiator rise up and exit over the top of the sidepod. But this flow of hot air heading towards the rear of the car was bad for the wing, causing turbulence and reducing its downforce. We had tried pushing it out of the side of the car but it didn't seem to help.

'The solution was not to let the hot air out near the radiator, but instead to duct it through the sidepods so that it came out lower down at the rear of the car where it wouldn't affect the wing so much. In fact, if it did anything, this low-pressure, hot air would help speed up the airflow under the inverted wing, and so increase the downforce.'

In short he created what he believes were the first enclosed sidepods in Formula 1. Each sidepod had tall air intakes just behind the front suspension and two extra cooling windows low down on the sides to allow more heat to escape from the radiators in climatically hot conditions.

The 640's overall appearance, a design breakthrough at the time, bears some striking similarities to the Ferrari of recent years, designed nearly 30 years later, and marked the beginning of a revolution in aerodynamics. The car's hallmark has been termed the 'double coke-bottle', with the bulging sidepods swept in both at the front and the rear, lending the 640 a fluid beauty more dramatic even than that of the 639. It was, without doubt, the most beautiful car on the grid, a fillip to the *Tifosi* who loved a little Ferrari eye candy.

Journalist Franco Lini, writing in *Il Giorno* on 5 December 1988, described it as 'wide across the hips but very seductive' in the headline to an article that went on to state, 'Certainly she is a beautiful car... her shape is very slender, even though her hips [sidepods] are quite broad, perhaps too voluminous, but they probably have a precise functional reason to be so [quite right, Signor Lini, they did]. Slender, with her narrow nose, her soft rounded lines... the new Ferrari pleases the eye. Will it also please the stopwatch?'

Gerhard Berger waxes lyrical on the subject. 'It was a new-generation car,' he said in an interview for this book. 'I just loved it. It was absolutely beautiful and it was great to drive. Such a fantastic car.'

Some of the car's elegance owes a debt to an intriguing area of inspiration, as Diane Holl explains: 'John explained to me the subject of airship curves and gave me the necessary information from a book. Airship curves came from the first airships of the early 1900s and mathematically described a teardrop, aerodynamic shape. So, in using them, you just scaled them up or down depending on the shape you wanted. John explained how I needed to calculate it all and basically stood next to me as I drew what he wanted. The 640's bodywork was made up from them.'

Diane confirms that neither the 639 nor the 640 had much time in the wind tunnel, being designed more by a combination of John's eye and the airship formulae: 'For John things had to look aesthetically pleasing, and that is something that I have taken on. John always said, "If it looks good, it will probably work well too, because it has the right feel."'

The 640's long nose cone, flattened to a chisel-like tip at the end, prompted a witty mechanic at Maranello to come up with a nickname. He dubbed the car *Il Papera*, The Duck, since the nose bore some resemblance to a duck's bill. Once the Italian press got hold of this little titbit, they called the 640 almost nothing else, partly because the word carried a double meaning, always a delight for any journalist — *papera* could also mean a blunder.

The Ferrari 640 contained one other significant innovation, one that was, after the paddle shift, the most impressive on the car, and one that would, once more, become *de rigueur* throughout the paddock.

Until the 640, the road springs in a Formula 1 car's front suspension had been usually of coil type and mounted either vertically within the chassis or at an angle from a push-rod or pull-rod. The problem for John was that this type of spring wasn't up to his technological standards. Too heavy and too 'old school', coil springs were like the 'crappy Meccano gear linkage' and simply 'not aerospace'. Nor were they efficient: under heavy load, they could expand and contract slightly out of line, transferring forces awkwardly to and from the rocker arms and damper units, causing friction within the rocker/damper system. 'They were old-fashioned, bulky things. I hated them,' says Barnard.

There was another problem too: they threatened to compromise the beauty of the car's design. Diane Holl takes up the story:

'The front torsion bar on the 640 came about because we couldn't fit the springs in — it was a little like the reasoning that led to the paddle shift. John was upset because putting in a road spring would mean we needed a bump in the bodywork to cover it. I can remember drawing these annoying bumps on the car and he was like, "Uh, no." Simple as that — quite short!

'I'm like, "John, they've got to be there!" and he'd just say, quietly, "Uh, no."' So I'm thinking, "Sod you!" I just couldn't see a solution.

'In the end he said, "We'll just have to do something different with the springs." "Like?" "Well, I wonder if we could fit a torsion bar?" My response was, "How the hell can we fit in a torsion bar?" To me they were long unwieldy affairs that could only make the situation worse.

Torsion bars weren't new. The E-type Jaguar, dating back to 1961, used long torsion bars for its suspension, and you may recall that Maurice Philippe put them on his Parnelli, but those were over two feet long and very complex affairs, comprising a compound bar that incorporated an inner tube of steel, with the loads passing through both. There was no way that kind of set-up was going to fit on the 640.

As so often before, John followed the sage advice of Eric Broadley and mulled over the problem for some days: 'When you analyse the movement on a front wheel of a Formula 1 car, there's not a lot. Today it's a maximum of about 50mm. Once you've translated that back through a rocking arm and spring, it's quite a small movement. I suddenly thought, "Hold on a minute, if we haven't got that much movement, why would we need these great long torsion bars?" I did a rough calculation and came up with something much shorter. I asked Arthur Webb to do some sums. He came back saying that the length I wanted required a compound bar — which sounded a bit complicated to me. So I went away and started doing some proper numbers.'

He came up with a torsion bar that was only 20cm long and made of a single piece of tubular steel. It was mounted upright, with the bottom anchored to the inside of the chassis wall and the top located into the rocker arm, which had castellations around its 'trumpet end' for this purpose. The car would corner, load would transfer to the torsion bar, and the bar would twist.

'The new torsion bar was a perfect solution, lightweight, compact, and with much less friction than a coil spring,' enthuses John. 'I looked at it and thought, "Yes, that's really nice, I really like that!" I never used a road spring again.'

Besides being light and compact, the system had another little bonus. It provided a quick method for adjusting the car's ride height, as John explains: 'At the bottom end of the torsion bar I attached carbon rods that reacted against the force through the torsion bar — they were about the size of a person's finger. You could adjust the length of the reaction rod and that would alter the ride height of the car. It was another nice, simple, extra feature.'

The material of choice for the torsion bars was 300M Aeromet steel, a superstrong material developed for the undercarriages of fighter jets thumping down onto aircraft carriers. Says John, 'They could process this in California better than anywhere, so I had Kenny Hill of Metalore make up the torsion bars.'

Still Diane Holl was anxious. She recalls asking John what they would do if the torsion bars didn't work as expected and they couldn't get the right spring rate: 'His response was typical. "Oh, it's only physics. We'll be able to do it. No problem." He seemed so calm about it. Whether he used to go round the corner and scream silently into his knuckles, I don't know, but he did seem supremely unbothered by the risk of failure.' It's an amusing idea, the notion of John Barnard screaming silently into his knuckles, like Basil Fawlty. No chance of that: this particular technological excursion was such small beer compared with the paddle shift that it probably barely registered on his personal Richter Scale of stress.

'Tubular front suspension springs' is not a phrase to set the average human heart racing, but these subsequent iterations of the short torsion bars were things of beauty and efficiency, those happy partners. Arthur Webb says he thought this Barnard innovation a brilliant wheeze, being smaller and lighter than their sprung steel counterparts and so saving significant space and weight while proving considerably stiffer. Arthur is generous in his praise: 'Before, if you chose to go for a stronger or weaker spring on a race car to suit a particular track, you usually had to change the mounting and attachments as well. Barnard's could all fit onto the same mounting, enabling the mechanics to rapidly alter suspension stiffness to suit varying conditions.'

The new torsion bars may have been a Barnard design but it took all the brilliance of his team to make them work. Andy Smith, who headed the GTO laboratory, put in a lot of work to calibrate the springs and ensure they didn't fatigue. They also made the spring housings and retainer units out of carbon, itself a major undertaking. Once more John Barnard was taking Formula 1 excellence to a new level of detail.

John went to some lengths to conceal the new torsion bars for as long as possible. At races, and especially the first race of a season, journalists and other interested onlookers would always drift around the cars between practice sessions, seeing what was what. One person in particular, Giorgio Piola, a celebrated technical illustrator as well as a writer, paid special attention to the front of the 640 when he first saw it, so John decided to mislead people with a practical joke.

'We had a pair of large-diameter aluminium screw caps to hold down the two rocker assemblies. In the normal course of events these were covered by the upper bodywork, but when the bodywork was lifted off you could see these caps — but not a lot else. I watched Giorgio puzzling over the caps, trying to work out what they were for, and clearly trying to locate the road springs.'

So John had a chat with the Ferrari boys, and at the next race the two aluminium caps were marked *Olio* (oil) and *Acqua* (water). 'Giorgio kept making drawings, but he still couldn't work out what it was all about! He must have been thinking it was some form of hydraulic system.' The ploy led observers to deduce erroneously that John had come up with a hydraulic suspension system.

A few races later Piola spotted a torsion bar lying on a workbench and realised what was going on. He approached Barnard to thank him. 'That was a good trick you played on me, but I had the last laugh. I have made a small fortune selling all the sketches I did — I got so many of them published that I've bought myself a boat.'

Peter Reinhardt was particularly fond of Barnard's little technological wonders: 'The torsion bars were like surgical tools. Instead of greasy coiled springs, there were just these little bars that you could pop in and pop out, just by lifting a cover. Berger told me they made the car a dream to drive, and the mechanics loved them too.'

In fact the torsion bars were one of the things that brought the Ferrari mechanics round to Barnard's way of thinking, as Reinhardt explains: 'A driver might say, "Look, I need to change the springs", which would mean a two- or three-hour job. With Barnard's torsion bars, it was the work of a few minutes. It began to dawn on them that he was making their lives easier.'

The idea caused quite a stir in the paddock once everybody knew about the system. John recalls Ron Dennis coming up to him and asking, 'What is it with these torsion bars, what's the big deal? Why are they so much better? Is it the friction caused by the spring?' John replied, 'Yes, they are much better on friction' — which of course wasn't the whole story.

A rocker assembly complete with torsion bar is one of the few specimens of his work that John keeps at home. To him, it was one of his most pleasing pieces.

Nigel Mansell's first acquaintance with the 640 came when he squeezed into one of the monocoques in Shalford. Mansell, who had joined Ferrari as Alboreto's replacement, was a big man by Formula 1 standards. 'Bloody hell, John, it's a bit tight' is John's recollection of his complaint. Barnard replied, referring to the paddle shift, 'Don't worry Nigel, you won't have to take your hands off the wheel.' John didn't think that made Mansell any happier.

In the meantime, Vittorio Ghidella came up with a cunning ruse plucked straight from Enzo Ferrari's book of Divide and Rule. He plotted to stamp his authority upon Barnard, a hopeless task if ever there was one, by trying to get Mansell on his side in their gearbox dispute. Ghidella ordered the Maranello mechanics to modify the 639, cutting the cockpit about to make way for a gear shift, a clutch pedal and all ancillary gubbins. John protested as soon as he got to hear about the changes to his car, but he was overruled and let it go; after all, the 639 was now a museum piece. Ghidella, interpreting this as surrender from Barnard, and triumphant now that his British bulldog was firmly at heel, ordered Mansell to try the converted 639 at Fiorano. According to John, Nigel did four laps, drove back into the garage, climbed out and said, 'No, I don't want that. I want the paddle shift.'

That was the end of that. Ghidella might have been able to make Barnard rewrite his contract, but if his driver thought the President's plan was rubbish, then that pretty much wrapped it up. Ghidella, as John had divined, was no Enzo Ferrari.

By now Gerhard Berger had had a number of runs at Fiorano in the paddle-shift Ferrari 640. In an interview for this book he said, 'I remember doing my first laps in Maranello with the paddle shift. I came back saying, "If this keeps working, nobody will ever drive a car in the future with a different gearshift."'

This was prescient for two reasons. First, paddle shifting is now becoming common in road cars. Second, there was indeed a question mark over its reliability: would it keep working?

Early in December 1988, the 640 was unveiled during testing at Jerez in Spain. The Italian press, eager to get a good look at it, took the opportunity to slide a knife into Nigel Mansell early on — apparently he was not at the test because 'he was having fun playing golf'. However, it was widely agreed that the 640 was a thing of beauty; the burning question was whether it would be a joy forever?

Marco De Martino followed up with an acerbic piece in *Il Messaggero* under the headline, '*Vola la Papera*' ('The Duck Flies'), saying, 'Here it is then, the big duck, the comic conundrum with its flattened nose that cost two years of so-called work by Barnard the magician [the 'm' now in lower case] costing billions of *lire* to Ferrari only to give stomach ache to the *Tifosi*.' Now the title *Il Mago* indicated a card sharp, trickster, con man, mountebank rather than a wise, magical genius.

It didn't help that the 640 only managed 15 laps on the Sunday of the tests, compared with the new non-turbo McLaren-Honda, which completed all of its tests and set a record lap time to boot, prompting journalist Umberto Zappeloni to describe the Sunday as a 'Day of Rest for the Ferrari — under Father Barnard's eyes' beneath the scathing headline 'Few tests for the Reds in Jerez. Record time for McLaren test driver'. Berger also came in for criticism, with the accusation that he had tried to evade Austrian military service by becoming a resident of Monaco, this by way of introducing his 'usual refrain' of criticising the engine, complaining that it lacked the requisite power: 'I don't have any problems any more with the automatic gearbox but the engine tests are really unsatisfactory.' Zappeloni conceded that the paddle shift was a *soluzione rivoluzionaria* but one that, until now, had generated a lot of 'confusion and difficulty'. Perhaps at last it seemed to have 'come to a good point'.

To the surprise of *La Gazzetta dello Sport*, which was also reporting on the test, Barnard 'looks like he's discovered the pleasure of a smile', headlining its piece 'Barnard surprises' with the smaller heading, 'I feel good at Ferrari and the new car will surprise everybody'. This generally positive piece was penned by Giorgio Piola, whom John had so perplexed with his torsion-bar suspension.

Another article, written by Renato D'Ulise, opened with a sarcastic question:

'Mr Barnard, what a nice day! You seem to be available. How is the new Ferrari?'[78] D'Ulise then gave the reader observations about 'the bad relationships and misunderstanding that exist between Barnard and the previous managers, from Lardi Ferrari to Postlethwaite', before quoting Barnard as saying 'some people weren't interested in communicating'. In D'Ulise's piece, Barnard was forced to deny rumours that he was leaving Ferrari and planning to buy the GTO facility to create his own motorsport technology business in Britain — a prescient rumour since just nine years later he would do pretty much exactly that. Asked if he was satisfied with the two years he had spent at Ferrari, he was typically candid:

'To be honest, I would have preferred to have been more successful, to have obtained better results, but you have to consider that I arrived in this team not only to design a car but also to change many things, reorganise work, select new team members and revise problem-solving methods.

'If you consider how things were before and how they are now, how we work on the circuit and at the factory, if you consider there are many changes that people can't really see from the outside, then you will understand that many things had to change and have changed. It was necessary! Now there are a lot of new people who need to be trained, educated. This is the only way to prepare for the future, to have a good technical base. You will see this as time goes by.'

It doesn't take much to imagine the indignation this would have engendered among the *Tifosi*, few of whom would have believed that the constructors of their beloved Ferraris needed educating by an Englishman.

And there was yet more. 'BARNARD: CHRONICLE OF A FAILURE FORETOLD' shouted the headline in *La Stampa*, ominously echoing Gabríel Garcia Márquez's famous novella *Chronicle of a Death Foretold*. For this piece Cristiano Chiavegato caught up with Michele Alboreto, still smarting from his Ferrari departure and struggling to get the money together to join Tyrrell, where co-conspirators Harvey Postlethwaite and Jean-Claude Migeot awaited him. Chiavegato introduced Alboreto's inevitable attack with one of his own:

'Ferrari's mystery man hasn't changed at all in two years. The ex-magician of Maranello maintains the same arrogance towards everyone, and in particular the Italians, who have covered him in money. The English designer arrived at

---

[78] *All of the Italian press extracts in this section are taken from cuttings prepared at the time by Ferrari PR for the team; in the case of Renato D'Ulise's piece, the cutting does not feature the name of the newspaper.*

Maranello on 1 November 1986, when Enzo Ferrari gave him *carte blanche* in order to try to sort the Scuderia's fate. The Scuderia was in crisis. He hasn't succeeded yet.'

Then Alboreto opened fire: 'John Barnard… is not capable of designing a car on his own. At McLaren he had a whole structure behind that made up for his weaknesses. You need only to see the recent results. The English monocoques not only have kept winning without him, but also have dominated the season better than ever.

'In the past two years Barnard has been working on the new Ferrari without obtaining any good results, while other designers have developed new and competitive cars within three months' work.

'I have never before seen certain solutions like the suspension resting on one uniball, which removed all the rigidity that a chassis needs. If it stays as it is, his *'papera'* will never be good.'

John's reaction to Alboreto's outburst is sharp. Referring to the 'uniball' comment, he says: 'I don't know what he was on about. I don't suppose he knew either.'

The British press were not immune from the 'have-a-go' impulse either. A little earlier than all this, on 24 November 1988, *Autosport* ran a piece under the witty headline 'Guildford Bypassed?' claiming that Barnard had been ordered to base himself in Maranello. The magazine following this up the week after, on 1 December, with a piece entitled 'Barnard's Ultimatum' that sent the British engineer potty:

'John Barnard has a deadline of Jan 10 to deliver his new version of the 1989 normally-aspirated Ferrari to Maranello, according to a leading Italian newspaper. Our Italian correspondent, Pino Allievi, well-informed on affairs at Maranello, reports that the new Fiat-appointed head of Ferrari, Piergiorgio Cappelli, visited the Guildford Technical Office last week to talk to Barnard and see how the new car, described as the 'F1-89 Evoluzione' [640], is progressing. The car is said to be profoundly modified from the first version which has been tested with little success at Fiorano.

'The Jan 10 deadline is, apparently, extendable to Jan 15, but Cappelli has reportedly laid down another condition to Barnard continuing with Ferrari — he must work almost full time at Maranello once the car is completed.

'Ferrari has reportedly approached Patrick Head's senior assistant at Williams, Argentine Enrique Scalabroni, with a specific offer to work on chassis development, but he has apparently declined the invitation.'

Mr Allievi was not as well informed as he claimed. John penned a response to the magazine on 2 December, complaining of 'highly damaging implications' that were 'completely untrue and written in a such a way as to be extremely damaging to my career and reputation', before claiming that the ultimatum, if any, was more from him than from Cappelli, and admitting that 'I had told Dr. Cappelli that I did not intend to renew my contract after its expiry in 1989.'

One outcome of those Jerez tests was John's discovery that the Ferrari engine department had given him incorrect data about fuel consumption, forcing him to redesign the 640's fuel tank to increase its capacity.

He chose to pour out his fury to Marco De Martino of *Il Messaggero*, one of the journalists who had so recently insulted him in print. Under the headline, 'They boycotted me, giving me the Wrong Data', a much-animated Barnard is quoted as saying:

> *I have been accused of having messed up the car. I've been accused of having wasted time, and of being a mercenary, looking for money. In other words, I've been Ferrari's ruin.*
>
> *In all honesty I can say instead that I haven't made any mistakes because when Maranello gave me the data for the new aspirated engine, the weight, the length, the width, I took everything as being correct, and I started to work on the new car.*
>
> *In reality the many engineers who have now left the company gave me bad data, so when my first car was finally ready, for example, the airflow taking away the engine heat wasn't enough. Also, there were errors, gaps, in the aerodynamic data.*
>
> *It was a real boycott aimed against me personally. These men have tried to ruin my reputation and to destroy my relationship with Ferrari. Fortunately now it's all over.*

He was also reported as admitting to having 'thought of leaving, quitting, of giving up', a rare public confession of weakness. He added, 'I am aware that my reputation is at risk, but I am not afraid.' He went on, 'I know I am a difficult person and many have tried to put obstacles in my way.'

And then, never a man to pull punches, Barnard laid into his former chief, Ferrari President Vittorio Ghidella, who had just been removed from Maranello, in November 1988. Ghidella's departure from Ferrari — and Fiat — came after he lost a power struggle to Fiat executive Cesare Romiti, who, seven years later, would take over from the long-term boss and chairman of Fiat, Gianni Agnelli:

> *Ghidella was my strongest enemy. He didn't choose me so he couldn't stand me. Ghidella tried in every possible way to make me design the car with a traditional gearbox and for this reason he turned everyone against me.*
>
> *But I resisted and in fact now people are saying that I was right and are giving me credit. Ferrari will run next year with the automatic gearbox and when the system is perfected and the driver is comfortable with the paddles, the advantages will be extraordinary.*
>
> *They tried to impose dozens of controllers on my back, but after Ferrari's death, I was the one who dictated my conditions. I have asked that Maranello be reorganised and I have put Gordon Kimball, my deputy, to oversee and coordinate.*

This is as savage a public attack by an employee on a recent boss as you're ever likely to see, but then Barnard has never been one for taking prisoners. When he loses his rag, consequences are of no consequence to him, as the Moran boy so nearly found to his cost back in John's childhood.

Not content with having a go at his former boss, Barnard tipped into his new one, Piergiorgio Cappelli, describing him as 'the guy who talks and who dictates judgements', before undermining the sporting director's authority still further by denying he had given him 'an ultimatum, that he told me to go and live in Maranello,' adding, 'I wouldn't have accepted even if he had.' In short, whatever Cappelli might claim in the press, he certainly couldn't control Barnard.

In fighting mood, Barnard had another go at the Ferrari engine department:

> *It is our main problem. We can't deny it. Honda is ahead of us, and we are in a bad place. The problem is that we have insufficient horsepower and we also have problems with the electronic engine management — this year fuel consumption has killed us.*
>
> *Our hopes are in Hahn, the man we took from Porsche and who will be able to really help us. Berger is right to complain, but crying won't resolve anything. We need to be patient, even with McLaren I had to wait. My contract? It terminates next Christmas. We'll see. When I start winning, they'll ask me to stay.*

Ralf Hahn, John explains, was a 'hands-on development man out of Weissach. Anything we could do to break up the mafia that was the engine department was worth doing. I brought him in to get involved so at least I knew what was going on.' Barnard had learned the importance of installing his own people in key positions.

It seems remarkable that, following such outspoken public comment, Barnard's contract wasn't terminated on the spot, since he had pretty clearly breached it in this attack. Section Five insisted that that he wasn't allowed to disclose 'anything whatsoever concerning the activities carried out by GSA… or any other information regarding [their] affairs'. But Cappelli was rather over a barrel. He needed Barnard to finish the 640 and so decided against confrontation — and in any case he was far too busy trying to ensure his own survival at Ferrari. As the post-Enzo political storm raged on in the background, Barnard cracked on.

Nigel Mansell first drove the 640 at Fiorano shortly before Christmas, excited to be in a Ferrari for the first time. In the New Year he tried it again at the Paul Ricard circuit near Marseilles. He loved the sound of the V12, calling it 'the most gorgeous-sounding racing engine I had ever heard', but the gearbox caused him a few problems and some confusion:

'The [paddle] on the right controlled the seven speeds up, just like a motorbike, and the one on the left controlled the speeds down. The first time I drove it I pushed the left button instead of the right, went down instead of up and locked the rear wheels. Unfortunately I was going down the straight at the time and the car slid backwards across the grass, getting covered in mud and frost; it was terribly embarrassing.'

He had another 'moment' a little later while cornering, dropping through the gears and expecting to be in first as he pulled away, but instead finding himself in seventh. Said Nigel, 'The gearbox was quite tricky to get used to at first, especially the way that you had to rethink when you had full lock on the steering wheel. It was a tremendous advantage to be able to change gears in mid-corner, but you had to remember which paddle was which when your hands were upside-down.'

He also felt it took him longer to change down, say, from sixth to second when approaching a corner because 'you had to go through every gear when you were downshifting' but conceded that changing up was 'quite a bit faster than a conventional transmission'.

The downshift was indeed a problem early on, as Barnard acknowledges: 'We were still working on the electronics and it took quite a bit of practice to get the coordination between wheel speed, engine speed and what gear you were in exactly right so that you could go bang, bang, bang down through the gearbox.'

Mansell wanted to keep a foot-operated clutch, but Barnard didn't. Instead there were two further paddles on the steering wheel, allowing the driver to operate the clutch with either hand. This system alarmed the English driver, especially in anticipation of race starts, during which he would have to keep the clutch paddle pulled in to keep the clutch disengaged while awaiting the green light.

'Maybe in time it would be the way to go,' said Mansell, 'but I was worried that if you screw up, you go nowhere and that would not only be disastrous for competitiveness, but also extremely dangerous if you were stuck on the grid.'[79]

The road to Rio was rough. The approach of the Brazilian Grand Prix, the first race of the first season in which turbos were banned, was a source of worry for many teams, Ferrari among them. During this period of pre-season testing, the 640's engine, electronics and new gearbox caused a host of failures. The Italian press described Ferrari's testing performance as 'terrible' and anger against Barnard mounted ever higher.

Barnard's frustration was intense and the biggest cause of it was the semi-automatic gearbox's dreadful unreliability at this time. It just didn't seem to work consistently. The drivers would come in from testing, saying 'the gearbox has failed again', and John couldn't understand why. During a test at Estoril, Mansell only managed about ten laps because of repeated gearbox breakdowns.

Chief mechanic Joan Villadelprat is critical of John during this period: 'The semi-automatic gearbox, with its eight electro-valves, was great. Whatever the driver wanted to do with that gearbox, he could do it. But we had a problem with the alternator; it would stop working and not enough power would reach the electro-valve, and sometimes we'd land up with two gears engaged and the box would explode.

'John was convinced that Magneti Marelli had to change the alternator. They kept changing it, making modifications, but the only thing it really needed was

---

[79] Mansell, Nigel, with James Allen, Nigel Mansell, My Biography, CollinsWillow, London, 1995, pp203–204. All quotes from Mansell in this chapter are from this book.

a bit of fresh air because it was overheating, which killed the alternator and in turn killed the gearbox. To convince him to make a hole in the chassis and duct air onto the alternator was impossible. We lost a lot of races because he insisted that Magneti Marelli had to make a better alternator. That was the other side of John — his stubborn head.'

Those are tough words from a man loyal to Barnard, and John dismisses them out of hand: 'With respect to Joan, he wasn't party to all the facts. I know where he's coming from, but it was pretty clear to me that Magneti Marelli simply had to make an alternator that would live in the position they put it on the side of the engine. It had to be made to deal with the temperatures. I couldn't see why I was required to risk ruining my aerodynamics to accommodate an alternator that wasn't good enough. Eventually, they got it right.'

But as it turned out, Barnard wasn't party to all the facts either.

Now it was the end of March 1989, Easter weekend, and the Brazilian Grand Prix was at hand, the *Tifosi*, ever faithful, at prayer, seeking a miracle. This was to be the last time that Formula 1 would use the much-feared Jacarepaguá circuit, a punishing track with an abrasive surface that was as famous for damaging tyres and suspension as it was for its searing temperatures.

The race marked Nigel Mansell's much-anticipated début for Ferrari and he was sure that the team was on a hiding to nothing. For him, practice and qualifying laps were ruined by breakdowns out on track and he hadn't completed more than five laps in a row, thanks to, he reckoned, hydraulic pump failures on the semi-automatic gearbox. On one occasion he fetched up in front of a group of local fans who had no love for him, since, quite rightly, their countrymen Ayrton Senna and Nelson Piquet had their hearts instead. So they pelted the Englishman with bottles and coins. Mansell must have cursed the Barnard innovation that had put him within range. All the same, the 640 was decently quick and in the end Mansell qualified sixth.

The situation wasn't so bad for Gerhard Berger, who had fewer breakdowns and managed to qualify third, half a second quicker than his team-mate. Imperious on pole was Senna in a McLaren, nearly a second faster than his front-row companion, Riccardo Patrese in a Williams.

Maranello politics appeared as faulty as the 640, with Piergiorgio Cappelli replaced as sporting director by the debonair Cesare Fiorio, formerly competitions director at Lancia and Alfa Romeo, both owned by Fiat. Before the race, Fiorio, concerned about the unreliability of the new Ferraris, took

Barnard aside and said something along these lines: 'This doesn't look good, does it? How long do you think the car will last? Do you think we can finish?' Barnard of course, had no definite answer, so Fiorio suggested, 'Why don't we just put in half a tank of petrol and make a real show of it? Just so we can lead for at least some of the race.' Barnard replied, 'Oh come on Cesare, let's fill the cars up — who knows, we might get lucky.'

On Easter Sunday, Mansell found himself standing by his car on the starting grid, sweltering in the thumping 41°C heat and wondering what the hell he was doing there, his car having broken down again during the morning practice, after just one lap. As it happened, the captain of British Airways flight BA244 was also on the grid, due to leave for London Heathrow at 4.30pm, just three and a half hours after the 1pm race start. Ever the chancer, Mansell asked the captain if he would book him and his wife, Rosanne, onto the flight and the captain agreed. The British driver wasn't expecting to make it past lap 15 at best and figured that a 'quick helicopter hop' would get him to the nearby airport with some time to spare. So, internally delighted that he would at least gain some sort of victory by being the first of the Ferrari team back home, Mansell prepared for the race start.

It was a beginning in which the *Tifosi*, some at the circuit, most at home watching on television, felt their hearts soar. As the green lights came on, Berger weaved across the track behind Senna and Patrese, sparks flying from the Ferrari's underbody, before he cut suddenly to the inside for the first bend, the Molykote Curve, at some 180mph and began to pass Senna on the inside, looking to take the lead. Senna, in a daft panic, moved across to block him, forcing the Ferrari to ride with its right wheels on the grass. Now with reduced grip, Berger could only try to hold his line as Senna continued to press until wheels collided. The McLaren's front wing broke away and sliced up into the air while Berger's Ferrari was sent into a terminal spin.

BBC commentator James Hunt was most unimpressed as he watched the replay: 'Now you see Berger comes alongside and Senna starts to move over on him and that is out of order…' Both drivers were out, although Senna was able to limp on for a while before pulling into the pits in tears, his dream of a glorious victory on home soil shattered by his own mistake.

And so *Tifosi* hearts collectively sank to their stomachs, their best hope out of the race. All that praying, and for what? What was left but a *bastardo* car that could barely get round the circuit driven by a *bastardo* Englishman who played golf when he should be practising? Had they known that Mansell had booked an early flight home, they might well have lynched him. True, he was in third place now almost by default, behind Riccardo Patrese and Thierry Boutsen in the two Williams cars, but what possible good would that do?

On the third lap Mansell passed Boutsen, the man who had replaced him at Williams. Some of the *Tifosi* in the crowd cheered, most were quieter, trying to suppress the rising hope. Mansell continued to close on Patrese, and, by lap 15 — his cut-off point for getting the hell out of Rio — he was lining up the race leader on the long Junção straight. Says Mansell: 'Riccardo came across to keep the inside line into the left-hander. I went right and simply drove around the outside of him. I was now leading and couldn't quite believe that the car was still in one piece. The gearbox seemed fine, the engine was pulling well. How extraordinary.'

What were the *Tifosi* to think? Could they dare let themselves believe? As John Cleese said in his film *Clockwise*, released just three years earlier, "It's not the despair... I can take the despair. It's the hope I can't stand...' Hands were clasped together once more, in prayer more than applause.

Then came the pit stops to change heavily worn tyres and Prost took over the lead, one second ahead. Within four laps Mansell passed him with ease, and then, he stated, 'Lap after lap I was just waiting for the car to break.' So certain was he that Barnard's car was going to fail that he was even getting angry about missing the plane.

But the laps kept passing, the car kept feeling good, and he kept stretching his lead. On lap 31, halfway through the 61-lap race, Murray Walker, aware of the dreaded Commentator's Curse, tentatively offered: 'I'd better be careful what I'm saying... if Mansell can just keep this car going, it looks to me as though he's got the Brazilian Grand Prix well and truly tied up.' By the 40th lap even Mansell was beginning to think he might win. Which, of course, is when things went appallingly wrong.

To Nigel's disbelief, the paddle-shift steering wheel was coming off in his hands — a most alarming state of affairs at any speed let alone at 200mph. All three bolts holding it onto the quick-release tube that fitted over the steering column had been shaken loose by the rough track and two had fallen out completely. The fact that this happened at all is still a cause of anger for John: 'That was just neglect by a mechanic — the bolts shouldn't have come undone, however rough the circuit.'

Mansell radioed in the problem: 'The steering wheel is falling off!' This was met with some disbelief, so he repeated himself: 'I said the steering wheel is coming off!' 'Can you keep it going?' asked Barnard. Clearly not, was the answer. It was taking all of Mansell's concentration to steer at all and he was only able to get the car round corners by jamming the steering wheel hub against its quick-release flange to get enough bite on the column.

As Mansell prepared to head for the pits, John ran off to find the team's single spare paddle-shift steering wheel, an untested one stored somewhere in the depths of the garage. Even when he found it, he held out little hope that it would make any difference: 'I didn't for a minute think it would work because of the complex electronics that had to go down through the central plug. I thought there was no way this was going to match up first time.'

When Mansell arrived in the Ferrari pit, the mechanics jacked up the car and began changing the wheels so that if their man got back into the race he would at least have fresh rubber. Struggling with the 'quick-release' mechanism, Mansell removed the broken steering wheel as John leaned into the right-hand side of the car to fit the spare. But he couldn't get it to lock in place — vital seconds were passing.

Joan Villadelprat arrived on the opposite side of the car, leaned over, took the old wheel from Nigel, slung it over his left shoulder, grabbed the new one out of John's hands and slammed it onto the steering column so hard that he cut his hand, dripping blood all over the new steering wheel just as Mansell roared away. John and Joan stared after the car, somewhat incredulous that it was steering at all, let alone changing gear. The pit stop had taken a seemingly eternal 13 seconds, long enough for Prost to have retaken the lead.

All this provided considerable excitement for Murray Walker: 'And there is Nigel Mansell in the pits! He's had the steering wheel off for some reason there. What on earth is happening? He's having a new steering wheel fitted! That is the first time I have seen *five* wheels changed in a pit stop. Four wheels, two at the front, two at the back and the steering wheel!'

'It was a nightmare,' says John. 'We'd never done a fast steering wheel change before. I expected it to give up at any moment.'

What had given up was the radio, the button for which had been broken by the force of Villadelprat's intervention. It was only after the race that the chief mechanic looked at his hand and noticed that the switch was embedded in his flesh. It took a pair of pliers and eyes tight shut to remove it.

Now Mansell couldn't hear the engineers, but the added bonus was that they couldn't hear him either. The English driver had the endearing habit of singing his way around the course, delivering scintillating numbers like 'Daisy, Daisy, give me your answer do' and 'Oh, I do like to be beside the seaside' as he belted down the back straight. For the grouchier among the racing team, radio silence came as blessed relief.

So, uninterrupted and no doubt blithely singing his head off, Mansell went on one of his famous charges, hauling in Prost, who was now experiencing clutch problems. Murray Walker was beside himself. 'Oh what a race! Alain Prost at the wheel has lost none of his motivation, being harried every inch of the way by, in his first drive for Ferrari, Nigel Mansell, 13 times a Grand Prix winner. And he's right on the gearbox of Prost's car now!'

As he had done earlier, Mansell took the leader on the Junção straight just before the Curva Sul, only two laps after he'd blasted out of the pits. Once more the English driver was allowing himself to hope, praying with the *Tifosi* that the car would 'please, please, please keep going'. It had to do so for 14 laps.

Nothing in life is easy. As Mansell came round the final corner, the chequered flag ready and waiting ahead, a spectator ran out in front of his car. 'What a fool running across the course!' rasped Walker. 'A raving lunatic!' But Mansell missed the sun-struck *signor* and crossed the finishing line for an epic victory.

Barnard recalls it all with a big grin: 'After the pit stop I had envisaged him tearing off in first gear and never getting out of it. But, off he went, roaring up through the gears. When he took the chequered flag I could have danced the samba!' It's weird to hear that coming from John Barnard.

'That win was as close to a fairy tale as anything I have ever known,' stated Mansell later. 'Somehow fate had decreed that I would win on my début for Ferrari and it couldn't have been a better start.'

Murray Walker couldn't help but agree. 'Nigel Mansell wins the Brazilian Grand Prix… the most exciting one we have seen for years… a magnificent victory for the new 640 John Barnard V12 Ferrari.'

So it was that Nigel Mansell became the first man to win his first race for Ferrari since Mario Andretti 18 years earlier (in South Africa in 1971), a feat that wouldn't be matched for another 18 years, by Kimi Räikkönen (in Australia in 2007). The Englishman was also the first driver to win with a paddle-shift semi-automatic gearbox, and the paddock duly took note. As soon as they could, all the other teams started working on their own versions.

There was a curious twist in the tail to this story. On the podium Mansell raised the winner's trophy above his head in triumph but, unfathomably, it had razor-sharp edges that cut into his hands, sending streams of blood down his wrists and Mansell himself staggering off stage left. As was said at the time, it was quite literally a case of 'first blood' to Ferrari, and the blood was both Mansell's and Villadelprat's. The début paddle-shift victory had been well and truly christened.

Back in Maranello the Easter bells rang late into the night, the local priest receiving a message of congratulations from the Bishop of Modena for both the Resurrection of Christ and Scuderia Ferrari, and one suspects the latter brought more joy. In Rio as in Italy, the *Tifosi* were in rapture, giving Mansell a new name, *Il Leone*, The Lion, a soubriquet to reflect his courageous, charging, driving style. Peter Reinhardt commented that Italians now had three things they loved: 'Mansell first, football second, the Pope third.'

Utterly against his nature, even John Barnard was celebrating: 'Jesus, was that a win and a half,' he says from the distance of nearly three decades. For Barnard, of course, this didn't last long: 'My celebrations lasted about ten minutes. I congratulated Nigel and went to the airport, leaving the mechanics to get pissed.'

But he does concede the moment's importance, the first big relief from the ever-mounting pressure that had been his experience at Ferrari to date: 'This was probably the most amazing and memorable win of my career. But big highs are dangerous — they can so often be followed by massive lows, so I kept a lid on it.'

Barnard was right to be circumspect, because the very next race brought the biggest low he ever encountered in his professional career.

CHAPTER 24
MAN ON FIRE
1989

A month after the Brazilian Grand Prix, the Formula 1 circus arrived in Italy for the next race, the San Marino Grand Prix at Imola, sold out and brimming with expectant, excited *Tifosi*.

Gerhard Berger was the more fired up of the two Ferrari drivers, clearly determined not to let his team-mate beat him again. Nigel Mansell wasn't optimistic, knowing how lucky he had been in Rio, benefiting from Ayrton Senna's accident and Alain Prost's clutch problems. Nevertheless, the Englishman turned it on in qualifying, ending up third on the grid behind an all-McLaren front row, Senna on pole again. Berger drove conspicuously hard to qualify fifth, riding the unforgiving kerbs that bordered Imola's numerous and notorious chicanes.

On Sunday morning there was a setback when Gerhard's warm-up was compromised by a split gearbox casing. Perhaps the omens were not auspicious.

Senna drove clear at the start with Prost just behind. For a couple of laps Mansell hung on to Prost's tail before deciding to preserve tyres and fuel, easing off a little while keeping a mirror eye on Riccardo Patrese's Williams-Renault just behind him. Berger was taking to the kerbs again, desperate to get past the Italian and keep in touch with Mansell.

Having crossed the line to start the fourth lap, Berger was approaching the long *Tamburello* left-hander when something on his car fell off. As he said later, 'I tried steering — nothing. I tried braking — nothing. I just said, "Shit." Now I brace for impact and just pray.'[80]

---

[80] Smith, Sam and Filippo Zanier, 'Imola 1989 — Saving Gerhard', www.sniffermedia.com.

THE PERFECT CAR

The Ferrari hit *Tamburello*'s concrete wall at 180mph. Wheels, bodywork and carbon-fibre exploded into the air on impact as the 640 bounced and gyrated along the advertising hoardings before coming to a stop. There was a brief moment of silence before the car burst into flames, the cockpit instantly engulfed in an inferno. Unlike Watson's Italian crash eight years before, this fire didn't go out — the fuel tank had been ruptured and it was full.

In the pit lane, John Barnard watched the TV monitor in utter horror. 'I went cold. I was horrified at the thought that I might have killed a driver. He was on fire.'

Berger's life was saved in the first instance by volunteer fireman Gabriel Vivoli, who sprinted some 90 metres from Gate 3C in full fire-protection kit carrying an 8kg extinguisher that he unloaded over the burning Austrian just 14 seconds after flames first engulfed the car. This is Vivoli's account:

'Flames were so high that *Tifosi* who had climbed on top of the advertising board to see the race felt the urge to jump into the Santerno river, metres below. The car was completely engulfed in flames, to the point that I couldn't see which way it was facing. I stepped into the fire spraying my extinguisher, and as flames started to fade I could see Berger's position. I clearly remember seeing heat bubbles forming on his helmet'.[81]

Other marshals arrived and the entire blaze was put out in under ten seconds. In his haste, Vivoli had forgotten to lower the visor on his own helmet and his face was blackened.

Soon after, Berger was lifted from the boiling car. Then came the agonising wait as the unconscious driver, attended now by the brilliant Formula 1 doctor, Professor Sid Watkins, was treated with air and an emergency drip. Berger then woke only to enter a state of 'psychomotor agitation' that forced Watkins to sit on his shuddering chest to keep his spasms under control while a colleague struggled to ease off the melting helmet. He was gingerly lifted onto a stretcher and carried into a waiting ambulance to be taken to the circuit's state-of-the-art hospital. The race was stopped.

To everyone's bewilderment and relief, Berger's injuries were remarkably slight given the severity of the crash — second-degree burns on his hands, a broken shoulder blade or bruised collar bone, and one or two broken ribs (accounts vary). If, as everyone suspected, the accident was caused by some form of technical failure — and this had yet to be established one way or the

---

[81] Smith, Sam and Filippo Zanier, 'Imola 1989 — Saving Gerhard', www.sniffermedia.com.

other — it was clear to all that the extraordinary strength of Barnard's 640 chassis had saved Berger's life every bit as much as the fire marshals. Almost square on into a concrete wall at 180mph — he should have been dead.

Berger himself is unequivocal on the matter. 'The car saved my life at Imola,' he said in an interview for this book. 'Barnard had made it so strong and so safe. It absolutely saved my life.'

Back at the race, and with Berger safely in hospital and out of danger, officials gave warning to the teams that there would be a restart in 30 minutes. Mansell and Fiorio, the new sporting director, had decisions to make and questions to try to answer. Should Mansell get back in the car? What caused the crash? Could it happen again? They both went to the hospital where they found Berger conscious but unable to explain what had happened.

Meanwhile Barnard had heard from Bernie Ecclestone that Berger was all right. 'I was still shaken, and I had already made up my mind. If he had died, I was out of the business. I would have quit on the spot.' Now the pressure came fully to bear: people were losing no time in blaming Barnard. Mansell found himself deeply upset by the way Ferrari were treating the English engineer in these most dreadful of circumstances:

'I was mortified by the accident and by what I witnessed among the team... I went inside the motorhome and it was like a madhouse. All kinds of wild things were being said and in the middle of it all Barnard was being put under this impossible pressure. I couldn't listen to any more of that, so I came away and made the decision I would restart.'[82]

It was a very brave decision, especially as he had only just encountered James Hunt, commentating as ever with Murray Walker for the BBC, who told him it was too dangerous to get back in the car. This opinion carried considerable weight because Hunt was a former World Champion and had witnessed the crash on his TV monitor, whereas Mansell hadn't seen the accident because it had happened behind him. Part of his decision to drive again was because he wanted to support Barnard:

'I knew it was very risky,' said Mansell, 'given that we didn't know why Gerhard had crashed, but from what I had heard, I felt that if I didn't give Barnard the vote of confidence, then the team would suffer in the long term.

'I didn't feel particularly brave, although I might well have thought someone

---

[82] Mansell, Nigel, with James Allen, *Nigel Mansell, My Biography*, CollinsWillow, London, 1995, p210. *All quotes from Mansell in this chapter are from this book.*

else stupid for doing the same thing. You just have to judge the situation as it appears to you... I might still have an accident, but at least I would give myself more margin for error than Gerhard.'

Fiorio was also under immense pressure. He asked Barnard if another crash could happen. Of course Barnard couldn't answer that except to say that no answers would be forthcoming until the full investigation he and Arthur Webb would conduct the next day. Then Mansell found Barnard and said: 'Tell me it's okay, JB, and I'm back in the car and away.' Barnard replied, 'Nigel, as far as I know there isn't a problem with the car. It's okay.'

So, when the race started, *Il Leone* was there, understandably taking considerable care at *Tamburello*, the corner that would claim Senna's life in similar circumstances just five years later. Mansell eventually retired, forced out on lap 23 with the ever-recurrent 'gearbox failure'.

The following day Webb got to work on the crash post-mortem. They quickly found that the front wing, supported by a carbon-fibre tube through the nose of the car, had been fractured. Barnard states: 'It had been broken in a mode that we didn't expect — it had been snapped upward. We hadn't calculated the mounting to withstand upward shock, instead basing our calculations on resisting downforce on the wing.' The only consolation was that the troublesome semi-automatic gearbox had played no role.

They concluded that Berger's penchant for driving over the kerbs and catching the stiff front-wing endplates on the ground had weakened the right side of the wing. When it failed on the approach to *Tamburello*, the front wing had folded under the car, with inevitable consequences for steering and braking. Webb reckoned that the force of the impact was 100G — a testament to the extraordinary strength of the chassis. Had Berger's legs been severely damaged by the accident, no one would have been surprised.

Barnard lays some blame on a rule change that banned flexible endplates on the front wing: 'We had been able to run a flexible part to the bottom of the endplates. If you ran the car with a slight rake, the endplates would touch the ground, which aerodynamically made the front wing work better. But the powers-that-be considered the flexible endplate to be a moveable aerodynamic device and banned it, so we had to make them stiff. At the time it struck me as crazy because I knew the endplates were going to ground all the time, and that meant the load transferred directly into the front wing's tube mounting.

'We just didn't calculate for the endplate lifting half the weight of the car. That was a mistake. If Gerhard had died, it would have been my fault. He was lucky he was in a carbon car, because there were parts of the chassis that were cracked like an eggshell; it had obviously absorbed a lot of energy without deforming, which saved him.'

Berger's main injury was burned hands. How could that have happened when drivers wore fireproof gloves? Peter Reinhardt found out a few days later when he spoke to Gerhard after his transfer to a hospital in his home country, in Innsbruck: 'He told me he had cut the Nomex out of his gloves to give him better feel on the wheel and as a result his hands were burned.' Clearly Berger's determination to beat Mansell had encouraged him to take risks that were at best unwise.

Two weeks later the Austrian was joking: 'I remember everything. I remember I get some technical problems — the car went straight and the big bang. Until the moment I hit the wall I remember everything. And after I sleep a little bit because I was tired!'[83] He went to sleep, of course, as the fire engulfed him.

Revealingly, and testament to Barnard's chassis, Berger told Mansell that he had 'not really been on the racing line before he went off and once the car went, he didn't try to brake or steer out of it, he just "made himself small in the cockpit" as he put it.'

Barnard and his team duly increased the carbon layering in the front wing but this temporary fix proved to be insufficient and at the next race, Monaco, the problem recurred during practice. Mansell takes up the story:

'I was approaching Casino Square, going uphill flat in seventh when I heard something metallic go "clink". My instant reaction was that perhaps it was a drain, you pass over them from time to time on the Monaco streets. I changed down to fifth and turned in to the corner and nothing happened…

'I realised that the same thing had just happened to me as had happened to Gerhard at Imola, except that, luckily for me, I hadn't been going so quickly. The wings had been beefed up since Gerhard's shunt and yet mine had broken just like that. I suddenly felt physically sick.'

Barnard and Joan Villadelprat immediately removed the nose sections from the two cars and took them to Maranello, where they found some steel tubing that could be inserted within the front wing to add strength. As John says, 'It was a bulletproof solution, but it did worry me that I might transfer the problem somewhere else.' They returned to Monaco in time for qualifying.

---

[83] *'Gerhard Berger 1989 Imola crash — with his interview'*, youtube.com.

Why didn't the first fix work? Barnard offers an explanation: 'Mansell drove Monaco by touching the barriers with the front wing. I tried to point out that the idea was not to touch the barriers but Nigel insisted, "No, that's how you have to drive at Monaco — you have to lean on the barriers a bit, you've got to use them." He wanted the ability to touch the barrier without damaging the car. Well, of course, we couldn't calculate for that.'

Barnard was uneasy about reinforcing the wing: 'I remember animated discussions about how to beef it up. If we made the wing support stronger, we'd transfer the problem elsewhere; instead of destroying just the front wing, you could destroy the nose box too.' In the end he decided to put in a thicker tube of carbon-fibre.

He had found the whole experience extremely hard, as Diane Holl points out: 'A Ferrari going off at Imola and bursting into flames — dreadful. John found that pretty tough. People think he was harder than he really was. As a woman working with him for so long, I saw him in a different light, and I saw the family side of him too.'

Barnard describes the 1989 season as 'very up and down'. He had an extra incentive for success in that his contract allowed him to keep a car if the team won five races, but that wasn't to be. Between them, Berger and Mansell failed to finish 21 times out of 30 starts. When they did finish, they were first, second or third, and often they ran at or near the front before trouble struck. Clearly, when it was working, the 640 was highly competitive. But why was it failing so often? The press, of course, blamed Barnard and the gearbox.

John suspected that the fault with the gearbox lay in the electronics. Diane Holl recalls that he had enormous rows with Magneti Marelli's people, all to no avail — the fault couldn't be found. John was certain there was no physical problem with the gearbox and became deeply suspicious of everything the electronics boys did — all fuel to his growing paranoia that Ferrari people were still trying to wreck his career.

Diane reports that he got it into his head that Magneti Marelli had given the Williams team the latest version of their engine control system while leaving Ferrari with the older version, a suspicion that made his blood boil. One race weekend he asked Diane if she could try to check it out, so she wandered down the pit lane and popped her head into the Williams garage. No one was around whom she recognised so she moved closer to the car. A Williams mechanic came up to her.

'It such a nice car,' she said, in the sexiest Betty Boop voice she could muster.

'Yes, isn't it,' replied the lascivious muppet. 'Do you want a closer look?'

She was examining the electronics box when she felt a tap on her shoulder. Her former boss, Adrian Newey, was standing behind her.

'Diane, get out,' he said, in his firm but quiet voice.

She returned to tell Barnard that she was pretty sure Williams had the same version of engine control system. Barnard, apparently, refused to believe it.

And then, at last, the primary reason for the gearbox failures became clear. The problem that had plagued pre-season testing and inhibited the gearbox's development and racing success, that had brought down so much approbation upon Barnard's head and had caused his chief mechanic to become intensely frustrated with his boss, was, as he had long suspected, nothing to do with the gearbox itself. It wasn't even a problem with the alternator getting too hot.

It was over halfway through the season when one of the engineers at Maranello decided to do some high-speed filming of the engine while it was on the dynamometer. Says Barnard, 'To my horror, it showed that the belt to the alternator was jumping on its pulley and slipping' — something that couldn't be seen by the human eye. If the alternator wasn't working properly, then the car's lightweight battery wasn't being topped up, and that meant the electronic gearbox would quickly cease to function. But what was causing the belt to jump and slip? It was all down to a design feature within the V12.

'To reduce friction,' John says, 'the Ferrari engine team had decided to run the crankshaft on only four main bearings. This allowed the crank to bend if the engine was running at high speed — the so-called whip effect. This in turn could make the pulley on the end of the crank wobble, causing the belt to slip or even jump off the pulley, which, of course, caused the electrics to fail. The first effect the driver noticed was that he couldn't change gear.'

If Barnard had made a mistake, it was perhaps in not spending more time overseeing the engine himself. But even if he had, it would have made little difference — he didn't have high-speed cameras for eyes: 'You kind of rely on your engine people to pick up on your engine problems. It was easier for them to blame the gearbox and me, this foreigner, who had come along and done all sorts of things that he shouldn't be doing.'

Reliability began to improve as soon as this problem was addressed. Monaco had been followed by three races that neither Ferrari finished, but then came a string of strong results for Mansell. He finished second at Paul Ricard and Silverstone, beaten in both races by Prost's McLaren-Honda. Third place followed at Hockenheim, this time with both McLarens ahead of him. And then to Hungary.

At the Hungaroring, Mansell found himself only 12th on the grid, by far the worst qualifying performance by a Ferrari thus far that season, while Berger started sixth. The English driver made a great start, elevating himself to eighth place by the first corner, and then set about chipping away at those in front of him. Alessandro Nannini's early pit stop for new tyres on his Benetton promoted Nigel to seventh, and soon he was fifth after overtaking Thierry Boutsen's Williams and Alex Caffi's Dallara in quick succession. Now he was behind Berger until his team-mate pitted for tyres. Next in his sights was Prost and he duly passed the Frenchman to take third. When Patrese's Williams slowed with a punctured radiator, Mansell only had Senna in front of him.

His Ferrari handling beautifully, Nigel put considerable pressure on Ayrton, clearly quicker through the corners but not quite as fast on the straights owing to the extra power of the McLaren's Honda. He had been all over Senna's exhaust for several laps when, halfway round lap 58, they came upon a backmarker, Stefan Johansson in an Onyx. The Swede, nursing a broken gear linkage, slowed unexpectedly and Senna suddenly found himself right on top of the ailing car. He hesitated momentarily before diving right to pass. Mansell, with an extra fraction of a second to react, pounced, pulling out of Senna's slipstream and passing him in a flash. Mansell surged away to win, building up a massive lead of 26 seconds in the remaining 19 laps.

The Englishman described this race as 'one of the most incredibly satisfying wins of my whole career'. And it came at the Hungaroring, known for its lack of overtaking opportunities.

Barnard was very impressed: 'For all of Nigel's melodramas, he was a "big balls" driver. When he needed to, he'd pick the car up by the scruff of its neck and wring a time out of it. His overtaking move in Hungary against Senna to take the lead was quite amazing.'

Having achieved a drive of a lifetime, Mansell also claimed credit for some technical input. He and race engineer Maurizio Nardon were both concerned that the 640 lacked sufficient downforce for such a sinuous track. Knowing that the McLarens, with their Honda V10 engines, could outdo them on the straights, they concentrated on improving performance in the corners.

'I knew that I needed more downforce at the front for it to be really effective on turn in,' stated Mansell. 'Designer John Barnard said that I had the maximum wing available. I sat down with Maurizio and... we came up with the idea of making a Gurney flap to add onto the front wing... It was made overnight and fitted before the warm-up on Sunday. Immediately, the car felt better and I was a second a lap faster than before and easily the fastest car of all in the warm-up.' You may recall that this wasn't the first instance of a race engineer unilaterally popping a Gurney flap on a Barnard car — shades of the 1986 German Grand Prix.

There was one more Ferrari victory that year, an important one at Estoril in Portugal. It fell to Berger, who by this stage of the season, in late September, already knew that he was about to move to McLaren to replace Prost as team-mate to Senna. As it turned out, Prost was heading the opposite way, Ferrari-bound in a rare case of Formula 1 swapsies, propelled by increasingly bitter feuding with Senna.

Berger was on a roll going into the Estoril race. Following his return to action after the Imola accident, having missed one race, he had had to endure a torrid sequence of eight consecutive race retirements, as well as being out-qualified by his team-mate on six of those occasions. But then at Monza, that cauldron of *Tifosi* passion, he finished second.

Estoril brought the very same qualifying outcome as at Monza: Senna on pole, Berger second and Mansell third, the disgruntled Prost fourth. Berger made a great start and led for 23 laps until Mansell passed him. Still leading at the halfway stage, Nigel made his stop for new tyres at the end of lap 39. He came in far too quickly and overshot his pit. Instead of waiting for his mechanics to pull him back to the pit, he engaged reverse, forgetting that reversing is banned in the pit lane — disqualification was inevitable.

Mansell, in furious mood, roared back out, now third behind Berger, the new leader, and Senna. Completely ignoring the black flags telling him he had been disqualified, he closed on Senna. Eight laps after his pit stop, at the start of lap 48, he tried to overtake Senna and the two cars collided, taking them both out of the race. The Englishman, of course, shouldn't have been on the circuit at all, but the crash was clearly the Brazilian's fault because he turned his McLaren into the Ferrari. Berger duly won easily, 32 seconds ahead of Prost. Mansell's foolish behaviour earned him a ban from the following race.

Despite Cesare Fiorio's description of 1989 as 'a fantastic season for Ferrari', it wasn't really. The Scuderia ended up third in the Constructors' Championship behind McLaren and Williams. As for the Drivers' title, which Prost secured in acrimonious circumstances at the Japanese Grand Prix after Senna infamously collided with him, Mansell was fourth and Berger seventh. Although the Barnard-designed 640 had proved to be highly competitive, it simply hadn't been reliable enough, with just nine finishes in 16 races — three wins, four seconds and two thirds. It wasn't enough for Barnard to get to keep a 640.

Following his departure from Ferrari, Berger decided to let rip in the press. He wrote an article for *On Track*, a respected US-based magazine, under the title 'Glad It's Over'. It contained a stinging attack on Ferrari and on Cesare Fiorio in particular.

Berger began by stating how happy he was to have had his last race for Ferrari, or, 'to be more precise, my last race with Cesare Fiorio, somebody I sincerely hope I will never have to work with again.' He went on to complain how, after telling Ferrari mid-season he would be leaving, Fiorio had favoured Mansell over him, allegedly using 'lies and deceit'. Among a host of other objections, he accused Fiorio of providing special fuel for Mansell and refusing to allow Berger to have it, and of refusing him access on one occasion to the spare car, and, at a critical moment, Mansell's car. 'To screw me around was one thing, but what I cannot understand is that at the same time he is doing that, he is spoiling the chances of the Ferrari team.' He added with spitting fury, 'You would have thought that the guy would try and do the best he could for both of us in order to keep Ferrari ahead. The guy is a joke.' If he was, neither Barnard nor Berger were laughing.

Gerhard had supportive words for the designer: 'John Barnard might well have stayed with the team but for the way Fiorio carried on. When we got into trouble [on the track] it was always Barnard who sat down and got things right again.'

And finally: 'If Alain thought there was too much politics at McLaren, wait until he joins Ferrari... It will make my job [at McLaren] a lot easier next year if the team remains under Fiorio... I could write a book on the sort of bullshit that went on.'

Unlike Barnard, Berger was known up and down the paddock as a very easy-going character. The fact that someone like him could publicly vent such rage about Ferrari underlines the enormous difficulties faced by Barnard.

CHAPTER 25
WORK OF ART
1989

In the eyes of the Italian press, John Barnard hadn't fulfilled the promise that had prompted Enzo Ferrari to employ him on such generous financial terms, hadn't justified the massive Italian investment in his home town of Godalming, and hadn't put Ferrari back at the top.

That he had created the most beautiful car in the paddock, that his 640 had been second only to a Barnard-derived McLaren in its 1989 tally of race wins, that he had originated the ingenious paddle shift, and that he had managed, against enormous political and personal opposition, to bring Ferrari bang up-to-date in technologies in which it had been so woefully far behind, were achievements both unappreciated and insufficient to compensate for the fact that he was a foreign interloper who could only be tolerated if he brought victory. Barnard had done everything but win them the championship, and that, of course, and understandably, was the only thing they wanted.

Barnard himself concedes that there were problems with the GTO concept: 'I knew it would be difficult trying to run Ferrari from England. It was pressure on me, the travelling backwards and forwards and trying to handle the politics. Whenever a major part of any operation is based in another country, politics is almost bound to become an issue.

'There's stuff that's kept secret and there are people in one place who will blame the people in the other facility, saying they didn't do this, or they didn't do that, or they did that wrong, or they just didn't listen, or they didn't do what we agreed. And I don't just mean on the Ferrari side, it happened from our side too. It is just too easy a way out, and you end up with mud-slinging backwards and forwards.'

Peter Reinhardt believes fatigue was now affecting Barnard: 'John had delivered what he promised to deliver, but now he was tired. Marco Piccinini was a great help early on, trying to keep everything in balance, but Enzo died, Piccinini left and Piero Lardi didn't do anything.' Reinhardt also explained that the Shalford operation was fundamentally down to 'John being a family man', adding, 'he hated to be outside the UK'.

Just as at McLaren before, John's need for a break was clouding the atmosphere in Shalford. Andy Smith echoes comments made earlier in this book by Matthew Jeffreys of McLaren: 'When John used to fly out to Ferrari, the mood would lift at GTO; there would be a sense of relief and people would feel more chilled out. He used to get paranoid that if he went away we wouldn't work. But of course it just wasn't like that. The pressure was always on, it was just more intense when he was there — that was the nature of his presence.'

Reinhardt believes that Mr Ferrari had it in mind to secure for Barnard a doctorate from a major Italian university, an idea that no doubt would have been appreciated, since deep within John the status of his education always lurked as a problem. Reinhardt adds, 'I thought it would have been good for him to go to Italy — but not after Enzo died. He would have been okay with Enzo alive. Without him, he had no support — the backstabbing did for him.'

Barnard continued to work on the 1990 car, the 641, introducing more fuel capacity, making small changes to the chassis, remounting the electronic boxes, pushing hard to reduce their size and improve their packaging, and smoothing off the 'rough edges' of the aerodynamics. More or less finished by the end of the 1989 season, the 641 was, he says, 'a refinement of the 640, which itself was a fundamental step in Formula 1'.

With his contract due to expire on 31 October 1989, John noticed as the season unfolded that Ferrari wasn't exactly falling over itself to keep him, which is why he was open to an approach from another Italian-backed Formula 1 team, Benetton, operating as a British entity out of the old Toleman works at Witney, Oxfordshire. The approach came in September, in the Monza paddock, just after qualifying.

But it turned out that Ferrari hadn't quite resolved itself to get rid of *Il Mago*. Following Gerhard Berger's victory in the Portuguese Grand Prix, the next race, Ferrari sent a private jet to Estoril to pick up Barnard and Cesare Fiorio, the sporting director, together with an invitation to stay overnight at Fiorio's house. At dinner they briefly discussed Barnard's future, with Fiorio asking if he was going to stay on. John equivocated and soon was feeling that Cesare's heart wasn't in it. So he told him about the approach from Benetton: 'This prompted a big show of asking me to stay — Cesare had obviously been asked by the higher-ups to keep me on board.'

But he recalls no concrete offers, nothing to tempt him to decline Benetton. John now thinks it was Fiorio who didn't want him to stay, 'probably because I was too powerful. Fiorio's a politician; he wanted to be kingpin. All the Italians want to be kingpin at Ferrari.'

Looking back, Barnard sees devices and plots that he feels, with hindsight, were designed to gain control over him at Ferrari. Reflecting on the 1989 Brazilian Grand Prix, he now suspects that had he agreed with Fiorio to put on a show by running the cars with half-filled fuel tanks, it might have become a weapon to be used against him down the line; that, perhaps, somewhere in some Scuderian corridor of power, it might have been whispered that 'Barnard chickened out at Rio'. Barnard's honest, no-nonsense, have-a-go approach that day might well have saved him from a grief even more profound.

He also reports that, astonishingly, no one told him Alain Prost was coming to Ferrari: 'Had I known, I might have stayed. I heard rumours but no one told me for sure.' Fiorio must have known for sure, and negotiations certainly began while Barnard was still in Ferrari's employment.

In his biography of Alain Prost, Maurice Hamilton quotes John Hogan as saying: 'Although Marlboro obviously had strong connections with Ferrari as well as McLaren, Alain's move to Maranello was largely of his own volition. They were after him and we certainly wouldn't have had strong objection to that. The point to remember is that when the negotiations started, John [Barnard] was there and he thought Alain was the best ever.'

This prompted Hamilton to comment: 'Barnard's undoubted respect for Prost was not enough to prevent him leaving Ferrari and accepting a new challenge with Benetton just as the 1989 season was ending. Prost had joined on condition of Barnard being present. He could have torn up the contract but didn't. Such is the romantic lure of Ferrari, even for a reasonably dispassionate driver such as Prost.'[84]

If Barnard's remaining with Ferrari was a condition of Prost's contract, it is strange indeed that the engineer was never told, making it hard to avoid the conclusion that Fiorio was doing all he could to appear on the one hand to

---

[84] Hamilton, Maurice, *Alain Prost*, Blink Publishing, London, 2015, p240.

be tempting Barnard to stay while on the other helping him to leave. On 28 September 1989 the Ferrari press office issued a press release in Italian, English and French:

> *Regarding the possibility of continuing the working relationship with John Barnard, Ferrari confirms the decision taken last June.*
>
> *At the time, no solution to extending the working relationship was reached at the end of a meeting between Ferrari Chairman Piero Fusaro, Cesare Fiorio and John Barnard.*
>
> *This situation has not changed in the past three months and therefore the working relationship with John Barnard will cease on October 31 1989 as specified contractually.*

Barnard had spent too much time looking over his shoulder in anticipation of attack. He was in a world where the competitive approach was devious at best and destructive at worst; he just couldn't bear sneaky behaviour.

The clashes reveal the most challenging side of John. He had a visceral hatred of certain behaviours, people and even peoples, hatreds probably acquired during his relatively sequestered childhood in post-war Britain and all wrapped up in and vented through his lifelong fury with imperfection, which was his creative driving force.

His experiences at Maranello only served to amplify his prejudices. He had done all he could at Ferrari. It had been utterly exhausting and he needed to be re-energised by a new challenge. There had been so much pain during the Barnard transfusion, in fact, that both sides were in need of recuperation.

What else could have happened? In what parallel universe might things have panned out differently? Had Ferrari been able to change its internal politics, had Ferrari been able to fully embrace the English engineer in spite of his tendency to be disrespectful, sneering even, demanding his way as the only way, had Ferrari chosen not to undermine him at so many different turns, had Ferrari honoured the contract by pulling together under Barnard's leadership, be that leadership ever so physically remote, then 1989 could well have been a more triumphant year — indeed all three years of his Ferrari tenure might have been much more successful and more would have followed in short order.

But that was too much to ask. The Scuderia was Latin-proud and Barnard was a bull-headed Briton. Both approaches have brought great achievements in motorsport history, but if ever in Formula 1 there was a case of irresistible force meeting immoveable object, this was it. In equal measure, Ferrari and Barnard wanted each other but repelled each other.

When John learned that Prost was joining Ferrari, he found himself wondering whether he was making a mistake to leave. He knew that with Prost fighting his corner in Maranello, many of his problems would have simply disappeared. Further, the 640 was a good car compromised by the engine's wobbly, four-bearing crank cocking up the electrics, a design error that the engine department acknowledged by rebuilding the V12 with a seven-bearing crank. With that, and the normal end-of-season upgrades, mostly instituted by Barnard, the 641 became an extremely competitive car, winning six races in 1990: 'It's a classic case — I never follow it through to the end.'

As ever, John's old friend, and Best Man, was observing the situation from his lofty seat at Williams, where cars of his design delivered four Constructors' titles and three World Champion drivers during the 1980s.

'In my opinion,' says Patrick Head, 'John really should have based himself in Maranello. He went to America, so he wasn't necessarily averse to going abroad. Perhaps the Italian language put him off, though God knows Ferrari would have paid to have had an interpreter on his shoulder the whole time. He probably thought of the Americans as at least halfway Anglo Saxon.

'John was highly wary of politics, especially corporate politics where the person pulling the strings might not even be visible to him. Not going to Italy and educating them from inside was probably a mistake; I'm sure they would have given him the world. They would have done anything for him once they saw the level he was at.'

Responding to the point that the Italians weren't happy with the Godalming operation, Head says: 'Well, you wouldn't be, would you? I mean they are Italians, and proud people. Inevitably it created factions. John could deal with politics as long as he was at the top of the pyramid telling everybody else what to do. But I don't think complex politics were his bag — you can't deal with that by shouting at people, getting upset and putting pressure on them. Perhaps that's a bit unfair on John. Don't get me wrong, I've got huge respect for him, huge respect for his engineering integrity and the toughness with which he pushes himself.'

Diane Holl hits several nails on their heads when she says: 'John was an Englishman at Ferrari, and no one on the ground floor really wanted him there. It was really the first time that any real English influence had permeated into

Ferrari; Postlethwaite was almost Italian, he embraced the lifestyle, and they loved him. John didn't and, consequently, wasn't loved by the Italians. His thing was, "I'm going to make you a car that's going to win. I will be a Ferrari designer, but it's John Barnard who has done this. And by the way, I live in Godalming, so Ferrari needs to move here." This wasn't really in the spirit of Ferrari where the brand name took precedence over all — it was contrary to their philosophy.'

When observations such as Head's and Holl's are put to John, he accepts the opinions but does point to the extraordinary circumstances: 'The whole story has never been told in this kind of step-by-step detail. It brings home that the hill I was pushing the shit up was even steeper than I realised and shows just how difficult it was, day-to-day, to make progress at Ferrari, where you were faced not just with technical problems but massive political chicanery. That would never have happened at McLaren where, if I was going to do it, I was going to do it, end of story. Ferrari was a whole different deal.'

He speaks with passion when he says how much he loves to sit at his desk 'drawing bits and pieces' but that he never really got the chance to fully lose himself in his vocation: 'Honestly, I was dreading the phone ringing with news of more crap from Maranello. It wasn't as if I could shut the world out and suddenly feel gloriously at ease and be happy.'

By the time Barnard's departure became common knowledge within Ferrari, many people there had slowly come round to the realisation that they were losing a major asset. Even the mechanics had warmed to the Barnard approach, as indicated by Joan Villadelprat: 'We changed the workers' pay structure and improved their pensions. They worked less, they got more money and they were happier. We pushed hard, but we looked after them and we fought on their behalf. I remember putting a radio in the factory, to play music while they worked. An official came and took it away. I went to him, had one hell of a row, and brought the radio back. They appreciated that sort of thing.'

Peter Reinhardt agrees: 'John did a lot to make sure their life was easier. He hated them having to work overnight, and that was common before he arrived. His cars were mechanic-friendly, a dream to work on.'

They were a dream to drive too. Gerhard Berger loved the 640, his only reservation being the V12's inability to put out the requisite power. He was particularly enthusiastic about the paddle shift: 'I'm more than happy with the automatic gearbox… it's really comfortable because it allows us to drive with hands constantly on the steering wheel.'

Ferrari was going to miss Barnard. Word of this later came back to Patrick Head: 'Ferrari was highly impressed by the elegance of John's engineering design — it took them to another level of mechanical design. And even when they were not with John afterwards, the same hubs and spindles and beautiful engineering were carried on.'

Most put out was the incoming Alain Prost, who told John some months later: 'I turned up and you weren't there! I couldn't believe it — one of the main reasons for coming to Ferrari was that you were going to be there!'

The 641 came close to bringing Ferrari its first World Champion driver for 11 seasons but that prospect fell foul of the bitter rivalry between Alain Prost and Ayrton Senna. The Brazilian went into 1990 still smarting from the collision with Prost in the previous year's Japanese Grand Prix that had robbed him, as he saw it, of the World Championship. Twelve months later they were back in Japan, again with the title in the balance.

After qualifying, Senna beat Prost to pole position, just as he had the previous year. Unlike in 1989, however, Senna asked to start from the left side of the track, not the right, because it was on the racing line and therefore 'cleaner'. When the request was blocked, Senna became incensed. He saw French collusion between Prost and FISA President Jean-Marie Balestre.

Come the race, Senna appeared to make a cold decision full of revenge. Prost, starting from the 'clean' position Senna favoured, led by half a length into the first corner but Senna dived inside him and didn't lift off. The McLaren cannoned into the side of the Ferrari, putting both cars out of the race and ensuring that Senna, rather than Prost, became World Champion.

There is a glorious footnote to this Ferrari story. In 1993, Ferrari's new boss, Luca Cordero di Montezemolo, opened a conversation with one of the most prestigious art institutions in the world, the Museum of Modern Art (MoMA) in New York. The subject was a possible Ferrari-focused exhibition, called 'Designed for Speed', that duly opened to the public on 4 November 1993 and ran until 5 April 1994. On display were three Ferrari cars: a 1950 166MM *Barchetta* ('little boat'), a 1987 F40 and... the Barnard-designed 641. John supplied his concept drawings after Diane Holl had inked over the pencil lines to make them more prominent.

Paola Antonelli, Director of MoMA Research and Development as well as Senior Curator at the department of Architecture and Design, explained some of the background in an interview for this book: 'There has long been a continuous connection between MoMA and Ferrari. The 641 represented a marvellous moment in time for them. I imagine there was this moment when there was a person high up at Ferrari who had a passion for the car and what it meant for the Scuderia, who happened to be talking to someone like-minded at MoMA — a perfect conjunction... An exhibition was built around it.'

Antonelli says that, as an Italian, she grew up watching Ferrari and supporting the reds: 'For me, the 641 is the classic configuration for a modern Formula 1 car, perhaps because it coincides with the centre of gravity of my life. But also because it was the time of Alain Prost, the time of Nigel Mansell, the time of John Barnard — all this coincides with my idea of the golden age for Maranello. The 641 condenses the perfect motorsport moment because Formula 1 is the pinnacle of motorsport.'

Which explains in part, perhaps, why the car is still there (at the time of writing). If you happen to find yourself in New York, treat yourself and go to MoMA, and walk through to the outdoor café/sculpture garden on Floor One. There, visible through the massive window of the Education and Research building, you should see the 641 up on the wall like some giant, beautiful, red beetle, the swept 'double coke-bottle' shape of its carapace a perfect expression of aerodynamic elegance. Then go inside the building and down the stairs to take a closer look. You can look up at it as if you're lying on the grid at Monza, with the car about to run you over.

Antonelli puts it like this: 'The 641 deserves to be in the museum because it is absolutely elegant. Aesthetics is important without a doubt, but the thing here is that the aesthetics help it fulfil its purpose, to be a winning car. Its gorgeous form reflects the efficiency of the engineering. Everything works together. There is no fat. Everything is there for a reason and the aesthetics express this absolute determination, that the car must win Formula 1 races. As such, it is the perfect 'racing horse' — fitting for the Scuderia of the Prancing Horse.'

No other Formula 1 car has been so honoured. The only other British-designed car to have received the MoMA treatment is a 1963 Jaguar E-type roadster, but it isn't a permanent exhibit. How long will the 641 stay there? Antonelli explains: 'When you work in a museum, you realise there are a few staples of your collection that people want to see. If the Louvre took down the *Mona Lisa* it would be a disaster. If we didn't have Picasso's *Les Demoiselles d'Avignon* always on view, it would be a major disappointment for so many people who come from so many different parts of the world to see just that painting. And people expect to see the Ferrari.'

How does its designer feel about his car being displayed amid some of the greatest art in the world, rubbing shoulders with the work of Picasso, Matisse, Cézanne, Rousseau, Magritte, Lichtenstein, Warhol, Dali and Mondrian, to name just a few?

'Honoured, of course,' he says, in a tone that suggests he doesn't have a lot of time for modern art.

At the end of 1989, free from the machinations of the Maranello Machiavels, Barnard was, on the whole, feeling delighted to be heading back to life with a British-based team, where, he sincerely believed, people were going to 'play off a straight bat'. He felt that Benetton would be a happy contrast to the ferocious back-stabbing that was par for the course at Ferrari. He would be in England, talking to English people. What could possibly go wrong?

Perhaps he had stumbled under a ladder somewhere, or, unseen, a black cat had wandered across his path, because Benetton turned out to be a good deal worse.

PART 6
BENETTON
AND TOM'S TOYOTA

CHAPTER 26
THE GODALMING SCUD
1989–90

The approach from Benetton at Monza in September 1989 came from none other than the controversial figure of Flavio Briatore, the team's new managing director. Having watched the Ferraris qualify second and third, Briatore invited John Barnard to join him for breakfast on the Sunday, away from the circuit, adding that Alessandro Benetton, son of Luciano, founder of the family's global clothing brand, would be there too. Intrigued, John assented and, over coffees and pastries, the discussion turned to the need for the Benetton team to raise its game.

Four years earlier the Benetton family had bought Toleman, a British Formula 1 team that had never won a race but had wowed the world by providing the début seat for Ayrton Senna. After Benetton took over, results gradually improved and Gerhard Berger secured the team's first win at Mexico in 1986. By 1988, the year of total McLaren supremacy, Benetton had hauled themselves up the Constructors' Championship standings and finished third.

Briatore explained that he wanted to take Benetton to the top. Barnard replied that to beat Ferrari, Williams and McLaren, Benetton would have to dramatically improve its car-making facilities, demonstrating the point with a quick pen-and-napkin calculation. He told Flavio that it would need £14 million to create state-of-the-art facilities and a team that could win championships. Briatore, batting no eyelids, asked if John might be interested in taking on the job. Barnard replied that he would want 20% ownership of any new facility he built plus 50% of the race team. Still no objections. He added that he would want to set up the factory in Godalming, near his home. General assent. He was in, his lunchtime habits once more secure.

Barnard soon received a series of calls at GTO from Briatore asking if he might help Benetton's chief designer, South African Rory Byrne. John pointed out that he simply couldn't, not while under contract to Ferrari. 'But we're worried Rory is going down the wrong road,' replied Briatore. Fearing an initial year marked by racing disaster, Barnard agreed to do what he could. So he sent Byrne a profile of the front wing he had designed for the Chaparral 2K.

The background to this offering lay in Barnard having observed a shortcoming of Benetton's 1989 car, the B189, specifically when driven by Alessandro Nannini in pre-season testing at Jerez: 'It literally leaped five feet sideways coming round corners. I had never seen anything like it. They had this huge tea-tray front wing and it seemed pretty evident to me that they really didn't understand aerodynamics.'

This led him to doubt that Benetton's wind-tunnel facilities were up to scratch: 'I was sure they weren't able to easily adjust the height or pitch of the model car in the wind tunnel. If you set up the model at one height and angle, you can produce things that will make brilliant numbers in that position, and that's what they must have done. As soon as you put a car on the track and it starts bouncing up and down, the pitch angle changes every time the driver brakes and accelerates — 'tea-tray' front wings are just hopeless.'

Barnard elaborates on the effect upon Nannini: 'He would come round a corner on one line and, next time round, he'd be on a completely different one. The poor bloke looked absolutely terrified — he had no idea what the car was going to do. If he hit a slightly different bump or rise in the track then, one lap to the next, the car would end up in a different place on the road.'

Later, someone at Benetton decided to make mischief about the Chaparral wing profile that Barnard had supplied to Byrne, by sending a picture of it to Peter Windsor, a former motorsport journalist who had been appointed by Ferrari to run GTO after Barnard's departure. John didn't feel he had done anything wrong: 'I've passed no Ferrari secrets to Benetton. It's my own creation and I first made it for the Chaparral 2K. Do your worst.' Ferrari declined to do their worst.

Officially John Barnard joined Benetton as technical director and general manager on Monday 6 November 1989, the day after the season's last Grand Prix, although the British national press had apprised the public of the move some weeks earlier.

The *Daily Telegraph*'s story on 30 September opened with the declaration,

ABOVE Gerhard Berger with Piero Lardi Ferrari, son of Enzo. Barnard became infuriated by Piero's 'secret car', a rival to his 639 built under wraps at Maranello. *Getty Images/Marka/UIG* **BELOW** *Miracolo a Monza:* Before Barnard's first Ferrari was ready, Gerhard Berger and Michele Alboreto drove the existing turbo cars to an unexpected victory in the 1988 Italian Grand Prix a few weeks after Enzo's death. *LAT Images*

ABOVE The first Barnard Ferrari to race, the shapely 640, seen with upper bodywork removed before its début in Brazil in 1989. *LAT Images* **BELOW** Pit-lane ecstasy as Nigel Mansell takes an entirely unexpected victory in Brazil with the 640. Cesare Fiorio, Ferrari's sporting director, is already over the barrier, while the car's designer (under umbrella at right) holds his head in disbelief. *Courtesy of John Barnard*

ABOVE The gorgeous 640 in the wet during 1989, Gerhard Berger driving. The shape of the tip of its nose gave rise to the nickname *Il Papera* — The Duck. *Courtesy of John Barnard* BELOW The 640 looked fabulous from every angle — here Nigel Mansell locks a front wheel during the French Grand Prix at Paul Ricard. *Courtesy of John Barnard*

ABOVE The 'nearly' year of 1990: Alain Prost, seen waving to the Monza *Tifosi*, won five Grands Prix with Barnard's 641 that season, by which time the designer had moved to Benetton. *Courtesy of John Barnard* **BELOW** Disaster for Prost, and some disappointment for Barnard, came in Japan when Ayrton Senna took the Frenchman out at the first corner, preventing the 641 from winning the title it so deserved. *LAT Images*

ABOVE John looking happy with his new opportunity at Benetton, alongside Nelson Piquet and Flavio Briatore. *Sutton Images* **BELOW** Rory Byrne's B190, complete with Barnard's front wing and other adjustments, was Benetton's car for the 1990 season; John has always thought its nose looked like Prost's — 'big and broken'. *Courtesy of John Barnard*

ABOVE Barnard's new design for Benetton was the B191 for the 1991 season, seen on the crash test rig at MIRA in Warwickshire. *Courtesy of John Barnard* **BELOW** One of Barnard' team, Arthur Webb, explained carbon's success in absorbing a frontal impact as a 'continual shattering as the crush zone moves along the structure... snap, snap, snap, all in a microsecond, with large amounts of energy dissipating with each snap'. *Courtesy of John Barnard*

ABOVE Press launch for the B191: evident is Barnard's advance on Tyrrell's 1990 innovation of the raised nose, by simply using one long, flat wing rather than the Tyrrell's moustache-like dihedral arrangement. *Courtesy of John Barnard*

RIGHT Roberto Moreno was delighted that Barnard had, once more, come up with 'something new'. *Sutton Images*

ABOVE As the B191 wasn't ready for the first race of 1991, the United States Grand Prix at Phoenix, the old B190 ran with new wing and new colours, Nelson Piquet driving here. *Sutton Images* **BELOW** At Monaco in 1991, Gerhard Berger's McLaren rammed the back of Piquet's B191 in the scrum at the first corner, putting the Benetton out of the race. *LAT Images*

'John Barnard, whose efforts put McLaren firmly on the map and has now brought Ferrari back in the forefront of Formula One, is joining Benetton at the end of the season.' The report underlined Barnard's growing reputation for taking his time, stating, 'And knowing how Barnard works it will probably be some time — 1991 — before the real fruits of his labours bring the first all-Barnard Benetton', quoting the engineer as saying, cautiously, 'I hope it will be a substantially different direction.'

The *Sunday Times* reported that the Benetton/Barnard deal was 'an impressive one, both in terms of finance and of commercial vision' with Barnard overseeing 'a research centre which will concentrate on composite materials — space-age stuff.'

An early task was to find a location for that new research centre, which would be called Benetton Advanced Research Group (BARG). With an architect friend, Tom Miller, John scouted out Henley Park, a 'big old country house with plenty of land' near the village of Wanborough, five miles north-west of Godalming. Miller's plan was to keep the original façade of this semi-derelict house and build a factory behind it, complete with a wind tunnel. Meanwhile, temporary premises were found at Langham Park in Godalming.

John spent so many hours on facility specifications and layout that he decided to have the results printed up in book form, providing Benetton, and himself, with a blueprint for possible future use: 'I was drawing office and factory layouts, listing all the machines I wanted, designing the wind tunnel, specifying computers and software while running the team in Witney and Godalming and working on the race cars. I had so many balls in the air.'

Although the plan was for the Witney facility also to be upgraded, Barnard fully intended to move the vast majority of Benetton's design and build operation to Godalming. This was a concept that didn't go down well with Benetton employees. In his book *The Mechanic's Tale*, Steve Matchett accuses Barnard of ignoring the needs of the majority to satisfy his own:

'Meanwhile the entire staff of the old Witney factory was invited to Godalming so they could observe the temporary facility, witness for themselves the picturesque beauty of the Surrey landscape, and see what an irresistible, golden opportunity they were about to be offered by having their place of employment shifted two hours' drive away.

'If the staff didn't relish such a long trip, ten or fourteen times a week — we knew one chap who didn't — then they could always look to relocate. That generations of their families have lived in Oxfordshire; that their children were happily settled at school; that their lifelong friends and cricket clubs and gardening societies were all within a short stroll away; surely all of these things were just minor irritations? "Earth calling Planet Formula One, we're losing contact with you, can you still read me?"[85]

Barnard's answer to this was straightforward: 'Okay, the Godalming facility was near my home, but I had a good crew of guys at GTO who lived around there, and I didn't want to lose them.' Clearly, as Matchett indicated, the proposed migration wasn't a move calculated to win hearts and minds, but John had never been a hearts and minds kinda guy: 'Either they liked me and what I did, or they didn't. I couldn't really care less.' This uncompromising approach may have taken McLaren to the front row but it hadn't won him many friends there, or at Ferrari, and the early indications were that it might cause troublesome tensions at Benetton, serving to fan the flames of opposition, signals of doom that entirely passed him by.

John was less than impressed with Witney work practices, a fact that further motivated the move: 'I thought their mechanical design prehistoric. They were intimidated by carbon-fibre, didn't really know how to use it, how to transfer loads into it. They used machined blocks of aluminium within the carbon-fibre sandwich to carry the loads, rather than carbon stock-block inserts. To me they were mixing up metal design structures with carbon design.'

Barnard was planning to change the way his carbon cars were made, replacing his initial method of using a male mould and instead adopting a female mould, a move that had already been made by other teams. This would mean breaking his 'no-joins' rubric. Two moulds would be made for the chassis, one for the top and one for the bottom, and the carbon pre-preg would be laid up on the inside of each mould before the two were joined together. The big advantage of this was that when the mould was released, the outer surface would be smooth, which meant that he could dispense with much of the car's covering bodywork.

He looked around Witney for another Andy Smith who could oversee the carbon operation and lay down the aerospace standards — but he found no one. This increased his determination to make Godalming the Benetton centre of excellence.

During a visit to Witney he witnessed one of the design team drawing a

---

[85] Matchett, Steve, *A Mechanic's Tale: Life in the Pit-Lanes of Formula One*, London, Orion Books Ltd, 2001, pp84–85. *All quotes from Matchett in this chapter are taken from his book.*

pick-up for a front suspension wishbone in the form of a massive aluminium insert into the carbon-fibre monocoque. Instead he proposed a much simpler, lighter method, using a lightweight steel bracket fixed with glue and anti-peel bolts, and drew a quick sketch: 'They just couldn't understand that. I heard later that they created a rig to test what loads my lightweight bracket could take, expecting that it would pull apart, but they couldn't fail it. That told me that their level of understanding of how to connect to a carbon structure simply wasn't there.'

In Benetton's defence, the paddock was still catching up with John's level of aerospace excellence — which was precisely why he had been hired.

John had been brought into Benetton over the head of chief designer Rory Byrne, a talented South African who, since 1977, had been designing cars for Toleman and then Benetton. Barnard's input into Byrne's B190 for the 1990 season was necessarily limited: 'I made a few adjustments to suspension geometry and pick-up, but the car was more or less finished.' Byrne would spend the next few months smarting from the experience of having Barnard's beady eye glancing over his shoulder, before going to Reynard to work on an abortive Formula 1 project.

While Barnard has very positive opinions about Byrne's later genius displayed at Ferrari, he was, at this time, unimpressed by aspects of his design philosophy: 'I don't think he had much time for aesthetics back then. If you look at the B190 in profile, it had a nose like Prost's [i.e., big and broken]. He'd brought the lines of the car along until he had to lift them up to accommodate the front suspension springs. He then dropped the lines down like a hooked Roman nose; I thought it was exceedingly ugly.'

To be fair to Byrne, who would become a pillar of Formula 1 design before the decade was out, Barnard also had good things to say about his work, commenting in a Ford press release of the time: 'With the Benetton B190 Rory Byrne has created one of the best-balanced chassis currently contesting the World Championship.'

Checking out Benetton's wind tunnel at Shrivenham, a facility belonging to Cranfield University located in Wiltshire about 20 miles south-west of Witney, John was, once more, appalled by what he saw: 'I couldn't believe it. They were in the dark ages, years and years behind, and they didn't seem to know it. So crude, so basic — only a quarter scale. The wind tunnel was a plywood affair, like a university student might make as a final-year project. At least it had a rolling road, but really, it was more *Blue Peter*[86] than Formula 1.'

There was no means of altering the model car's ride height or attitude while the tunnel was running. To do so, they had to turn everything off, let the fans run down, unscrew the existing struts and adjust them: 'The whole point was to be able to map the differences as ride height changes, while the tunnel was running. This is why they didn't predict how the tea-tray front wing would be so sensitive.' When he suggested installing a moveable strut for the model, the response was that they couldn't afford one: 'Utter rubbish — it would only have cost a few hundred quid!'

By this stage Barnard had started assembling a proper aerodynamic team in Godalming. He duly tasked new recruits Mark Handford and James Allison to design and make a moveable strut system and install it at Shrivenham: 'It made all the difference. Now the team could see what happened to the car when pitch and attitude changed at high speed, which meant they could start developing an aerodynamic map. It's essential to simulate how a car bounces and yaws on a track — they just didn't seem to get how sensitive these cars could be. But it was still a crappy little wind tunnel.'

Barnard now began forging an arrangement with British Aerospace at Farnborough to create a testing facility in one of their spare wind tunnels: 'It was a much bigger tunnel and therefore much more accurate. The plan now was to fully attach the wheels to a 60% model of the car and dispense with the strut. I was going to install measuring equipment on the suspension inside the car, together with battery-powered, radio-controlled motors that would adjust the suspension and therefore the attitude and ride height. This way the model would be able to sit on the moving belt like a real car, broadcasting its data via a radio link.'

Barnard found himself in public conflict with the team before the year was out. The 12 December 1989 edition of *Autosprint*, the Italian weekly, featured this headline: 'Benetton is Late with Financing and Barnard Raises his Voice'. The unnamed journalist was reporting John's absence from a Benetton test session: 'They were waiting for him at Estoril and there was a rented car booked for him — the new technical chief of Benetton, John Barnard — but nobody could see him in the pits. Rapidly, some rumours spread in the Portuguese autodrome

---

[86] Blue Peter *was a popular BBC TV programme that taught children how to make toys out of household objects.*

about violent discussions between the little diplomatic English engineer and the Benetton family. The reason for the discussions… was Barnard's insisting on having an immediate approval of some funds, which must have been quite substantial considering the projects… at the moment of the official agreement.'

The phrase 'violent discussions' was how much of the Formula 1 world now presumed that Barnard conducted his negotiations; the 'little diplomatic English engineer' was designed to sarcastically convey a diminutive man draped in a Union Jack and with all the diplomatic skill of a snarling bulldog. It was all wide of the mark: apart from anything else, at 5ft 11in Barnard is above average height.

The piece then described Barnard flying to Detroit to meet the new Ford chief, Bob Polling, before quoting a reassuring Flavio Briatore saying that 'everything is going according to plan'. Briatore was also quick to deny 'rumours of disputes' between Barnard and Byrne: 'The work between Rory Byrne and John Barnard is going very well. The former will be responsible for the 1990 car. Barnard, however, has already reviewed something of this project, but he will be working first of all on the 1991 single-seater with the new 12-cylinder motor.'

The purpose of the Detroit trip was for Barnard to put his view that, for Benetton to be more competitive, Ford needed to supply its *de facto* works team with a V12 rather than the existing V8, the HB, itself a new design that had only been introduced midway through the 1989 season. Quite quickly it became apparent that the whole matter of engine development was a briar patch of similar prickly consistency to the one cultivated by his opponents in Maranello.

His problem was Cosworth Engineering, which had developed the HB V8 engine on Ford's behalf. Although he had support from Ford, he got none from Cosworth.

Early conflict arose over John's wish to introduce a fly-by-wire throttle. Known as Electronic Throttle Control (ECT), this system would replace the traditional mechanical linkage to the engine by electronics, rather like the way semi-automatic transmission had replaced the old gear linkage. The ECT would combine the driver's instructions, as given by his foot on the accelerator pedal, with the engine's electronic brain to adjust fuel flow according to the engine's needs as dictated by variables such as temperature, track altitude, cornering loads and gear changes; in a perfect world the driver wouldn't notice any difference and the powertrain would be all the more efficient for it.

John recalls a meeting with Cosworth in the temporary offices in Godalming attended also by Ford representatives from Detroit: 'The Ford technical people were pretty receptive to the idea of a fly-by-wire throttle, although they did tend to talk in years instead of months. But Cosworth were impossible, saying, "We're not having anything to do with electric throttles; if you want an electronic throttle, then when it gets to the engine you will have to have a mechanical cable!" They were unbelievable!'

Beyond this issue, he was deeply dismayed about their general approach to electronics: 'They insisted on running a mixed bag — one bit was theirs, another somebody else's. You can't have that for a race car: it must all be integrated! Their electronics were prehistoric.' The conflict resulted in some spectacular rows: 'I used to kick off about their attitude all the time. It was as if they expected me to roll over and wave my legs in the air. Instead I'd be: "If you want a face-to-face, boys, I'm your man."'

Barnard also found himself bridling at the control Cosworth demanded at races: 'We'd be in a qualifying session and pushing the car to the limits; I can't remember the figures, but let's say the specified rev limit on the engine was 11,000rpm. The driver might be doing 11,100 for a while and these Cosworth boys would step in and say, "That's it; you've got to stop the car!" I'd say, "Hang on a minute, we've got time for some more runs — we need to get up the grid!" And then they'd threaten to pull the ignition box off the engine if I tried to run the car again — that was their attitude!'

Barnard suspects with good reason, as we shall see, that Cosworth went to Mike Kranefuss, Ford's man in charge as boss of Special Vehicle Operations, to complain about the recalcitrant technical director. Barnard's uncompromising approach was failing to win friends and influence people.

John thus had less control over the engine than he had had at Ferrari and McLaren. Cosworth didn't see him as their overlord in any way, and, no doubt, given his combative style, took some pleasure in telling him so. So a fly-by-wire throttle for the Benetton never saw light of day while Barnard was there.

Barnard could draw some consolation from his growing team of proven allies. Ferrari chief mechanic Joan Villadelprat joined him, taking over as manager of the Witney factory while running both the race and test teams. Giorgio Ascanelli also defected from Maranello. Peter Reinhardt was project coordinator, in charge of all new development, alongside Vijay Kothary, the financial controller whom Fiat had installed at GTO. In Godalming, the machine shop was run by Graham Saunders, composites by Peter Brown, fabrication by Brian Pepper, electronics by Rob Wheeler, aerodynamics by Mark Handford, research and development by Pat Fry, materials testing by Andy Smith.

One arrival was Mike Coughlan. Two years earlier he had joined Barnard very briefly at Ferrari from Lotus before announcing that he had been made a better offer by Lotus and wanted to return. John was put off at the time by this fickleness, but let it pass. He considered Coughlan a 'good engineer who worked hard', so hard, in fact, that his dedication to racing 'probably destroyed his family life', and thought him an attractive character: 'He enjoys life, he's got a good sense of humour and he's a practical joker.'

Soon John put Coughlan in charge of the drawing office to which he brought 'quite a vibe'. There are, in certain circles, those who like to give Coughlan co-authorship of the new Benetton car, the B191, but Mike himself said in an interview for this book: 'That was a JB car. I had more experience by then and I had taken on a greater role, but John did all the concept work. He laid the car out and handed it over to me for the detail work. But by that time John and I had a good rapport and I understood the kind of detail he wanted.'

There were no quarrels between these two and Coughlan had nothing but respect for his boss: 'At that time he was THE engineer. There was him, Gordon Murray and Patrick Head. John was the person to work for; he had a tremendous reputation especially for detailed design. He also had a reputation for being hard, but if you wanted to push yourself, if you were young and wanted to improve, then you had to work with the best.'

So BARG, in general, was a happy team of people all versed in the Barnard Way and most of them used to working with each other. Of course there were still tensions, but that was par for the course. Diane Holl, another who came with John from Ferrari, recalls an entertaining example:

'JB had come out of his office to have an argument with one of the designers. There was a lot of shouting going on and loud table-banging, mainly from John. I kept my head down but then thought I'd take the opportunity to pop into his office and collect something I needed.

'What I hadn't realised was that John had left the argument and had gone back into his office himself. When I walked in, I saw him hopping up and down, his right hand under his left armpit. He had hit his hand so hard on the table that he'd really hurt himself. He was going "Ahhh, ahhh, ahhh", obviously in agony. I looked at him and he looked at me and he mouthed, "Don't you DARE tell anyone!" I turned around and walked out laughing, and, no, I didn't tell anyone. Not right away, anyway.'

On 5 April 1990, Barnard signed a Joint Venture Agreement that basically stated he would work in partnership with Benetton for the next five years, with a review after three years, within the new entity, Benetton Formula Limited (BFL), the aim being to 'develop and expand the existing Formula One racing team operated by BFL into a championship-winning team and to engage in certain related joint activities calculated to assist such development expansion and the separate commercial exploitation thereof.'

The main 'vehicles' of the joint venture would be Benetton Formula (BF) Holdings, which would be owned equally by Benetton and Barnard, and Benetton Properties, ownership of which would be 80% by Benetton and 20% by Barnard. The role of Benetton Properties would be 'to invest in freehold land and buildings in the United Kingdom' so that new Formula 1 facilities could be built.

The agreement outlined the flow of money from Benetton into BFL, and had various clauses to ease the pain of separation. If the two parties decided to part company early, or Barnard dropped dead, then under certain circumstances Barnard, or his family, could expect a handsome pay-off, up to $2.7 million for his shares in the operation, plus 20% of certain net profit. All looked good.

But there was one fly in the ointment. Under the title 'Organisation of the Joint Venture Companies and Conditions Precedent', Clause 2.1(c) declared that: 'Immediately after this agreement has been signed by all the parties... Benetton and Mr. Barnard shall determine the Budget of the Companies for the Financial Year ending 31st December 1990.'

It sounded most sensible if only because it was difficult to be exactly sure what that budget might be, since a site had yet to be bought, and clearly it would be better to sign it off once things were a little clearer.

However Clause 2.4 stated: 'None of the remaining provisions of this Agreement shall come into effect until the satisfaction of the conditions set out in sub-clauses 1 and 2... In the event that they do not come into effect, the Parties' rights and obligations prior to the signature thereof shall remain unaffected.'

In other words, if Benetton decided not to sign off the 1990 budget, the entire 65-page contract would be rendered null and void.

Sensing a potential issue, John added a letter at the end of the contract clarifying that the budget referred to in clause 2.1(c) was the one relating to 'the expenses and income of Witney and Godalming *excluding* any projects which it is not possible to quantify with reasonable precision at this juncture [emphasis added].'

Within two weeks John had sent 'details of the proposed budget to Benetton', as his lawyer Michael Jepson told David Mills of Carnelluti, the Italian legal firm representing Benetton, in a letter dated 23 April 1990. Jepson optimistically concluded that the details were being discussed 'and presumably being agreed with John this week'. Among a list of worries about promises not yet fulfilled, Jepson also expressed concern that Barnard 'had not yet been appointed a Director, although you have indicated that this was to be put into effect straight away'.

Barnard was becoming concerned: 'Luciano Benetton hadn't actually signed anything to say that he had agreed for me to spend this money.' John reports that over the following months he contacted Flavio Briatore repeatedly about signing off the 1990 budget: 'I'd say, "Flavio, what's going on?" and he'd reply, "Don't worry, John, they'll do it!" And I'd call again and get, "Oh sorry, yes of course. We'll speak to Luciano, we'll get round to it. Relax."'

While the seeds were being sown for another harsh harvest, the British media was providing Barnard with a welcome contrast to his previous Italian experience by actually being positive about him. The situation at Benetton was summed up brilliantly in a piece by Joe Saward, published on 1 May 1990.[87]

Under the headline 'The tale of Two Theories...: Uncivil war at Benetton', Saward described the rise of the Benetton Formula 1 team, the recruitment of Briatore, how team manager Peter Collins, a brusque, no-nonsense Australian, was ousted, followed by the appointment of another bruiser, John Barnard, whose 'uncompromising style has left him with some detractors, but there is little doubt that he has produced the goods.'

Saward revealed that Briatore's arrival 'threatened to transform the team from British-based control to a system of more direct input from Italy' and talked of support from Mike Kranefuss, who, impressed by Barnard's GTO operation, had declared that he wanted to see at Benetton 'an outside development design area that supplies a very small racing team with fully developed products'.

---

[87] Saward, Joe 'The tale of two theories...: Uncivil war at Benetton', grandprix.com

It detailed how Kranefuss had offered to set up 'a Ford-funded technical group for Barnard' prompting 'pitlane jokers' to refer to Benetton as 'BBK Racing — Briatore, Barnard and Kranefuss'. This triumvirate was, apparently, 'keen to rebuild the Benetton team in their image — an image of cold, calculating professionalism — an image to rival that of McLaren.'

Saward also talked about the 'steady stream' of new people arriving at Benetton, most being assigned to Godalming where 'the project was shrouded in extreme secrecy', how, 'over the winter as more and more people began to appear at Benetton, it became something of a joke around the racing scene to try to work out what they were all going to be doing'. Saward was right about the numbers: by now the newly formed Benetton Formula Limited had 185 staff, unusually high for that time, with 79 in Godalming and 106 in Witney.

The piece concluded that Benetton's transformation was 'perhaps an indication of the general change which F1 has been undergoing since the 1988 season, with the move towards a more corporate structure being necessary to compete at the sharp end of F1. Detractors will tell you that it has little to do with the sport, but few can deny that it is necessary.'

More praise came from other quarters. In the *Daily Telegraph* of 12 July 1990, Alan Lis described Barnard as 'universally regarded by his peers as the best designer in the business'. Under the headline 'Barnard's eye-catching designs attract the very best', Lis quoted Barnard as saying, 'With the projects I undertake I think there is a three-year cycle; to make changes, to get the changes integrated into the existing set-up and then to see the benefits.'

Wherever John moved, this was the mantra: 'Don't expect anything for three years.' People would sign on the dotted line and in pretty short order would become upset that the results weren't immediate; John's perfectionist ways didn't fit in with the 'win now' demands of Formula 1.

As if to underline the point, the *Daily Telegraph* piece concluded, 'Under the Barnard influence the Benetton cars have already shown more consistently competitive form than in the past, and great things are expected in the near future, not least by Ford who provide a large part of the team budget.' So much for three years.

But it was true the team was becoming more competitive. By this time, the mid-point of the 1990 season, Benetton's new star driver, three-times World Champion Nelson Piquet, had achieved a promising run of results in the B190, finishing in the points in seven of the first eight races, with a best placing of second, in Canada.

At around this time, Lis also wrote a magazine feature headlined 'The Expert's Expert — Grand Prix Car Designers'[88] in which he interviewed most of the leading Formula 1 designers about each other. Almost everyone agreed that John Barnard was the design hero of the paddock, with Patrick Head a close second. Steve Nichols, Rory Byrne, Harvey Postlethwaite and Jean-Claude Migeot got a number of mentions, while Gordon Murray, by then retired from Formula 1, was praised just the once. Nichols was the most complimentary, describing Barnard as 'at the pinnacle'.

It may come as a surprise that Barnard, not a touchy-feely kind of chap, was ahead of the motorsport curve on environmental thinking, but in a piece in *The Independent* on 11 July 1990 he was described as an 'advocate of ecology'. Under the headline 'Barnard condemns pursuit of power', he was quoted as saying, 'I think fuel should be carefully regulated... if anything, we should be using fuel that's more "green" than the fuel you can buy at the pumps.' He also explained that the modern fuel developed for Formula 1 to increase horsepower in the post-turbo era was possibly damaging the health of the mechanics, describing it as 'fairly anti-social stuff', and adding, 'I don't think people are fully aware of the harm this fuel can cause.' His argument was that Formula 1 should be about 'efficiency rather than brute force', concluding, 'Grand Prix racing can't simply stand on an island and say all we want is brute power and sod the rest of you.'

Soon after, in *Autocar & Motor* dated 25 July 1990, Mike Doodson asked the question 'Should F1 go green?' and concluded that it 'would be well-advised to listen to Barnard' and 'stay at the forefront of research if it is to survive the criticism that its demands on the resources of the earth are out of proportion to its usefulness as a human activity.'

Meanwhile Barnard was hard at work on the new Benetton B191 for the following season. Like everyone else in Formula 1's design offices at that time, he had observed the Tyrrell 019 with its innovative raised nose, derived from the style that had been described to him on Piero Lardi Ferrari's secret car. John knew that the concept of a raised nose forcing more air under the car at high speed was an aerodynamic breakthrough and he sought to improve it.

Looking rather like a handlebar moustache, the Tyrrell design had flat wing

---

[88] *The publication was probably the* Sunday Telegraph Magazine, *but this cannot be confirmed as the available cutting, in John Barnard's files, carries no identification.*

sections on either side that bent upwards in the middle at 45 degrees to attach to the underside of the raised nose. Says John, 'I couldn't see any reason why it had to have this handlebar design — it looked so vulnerable.' So instead he schemed a single front wing that ran uninterrupted across the full width of the car, suspended on two curved, aerodynamic struts that dropped down from either side of the nose. He evaluated this in the wind tunnel and also, for comparison, made a version with a Tyrrell-like nose.

His solution was more elegant by far: 'As far as I could see from our wind-tunnel tests it was better to have this complete wing section than to have a dihedral section with a bit missing in the middle. From what the numbers told us, having the bit we added in the middle improved the performance.' Barnard therefore claims that, while the raised nose wasn't his idea, the twin-strut method of supporting the front wing certainly was — an important, if incremental, development that has been the norm in Formula 1 ever since.

This was typical of the way Barnard came up with ideas. To him, the Tyrrell 'just didn't look right'. Its ugliness annoyed him, so, while tipping his hat to the aerodynamic breakthrough, he immediately improved it, solving the aesthetic, aerodynamic and mechanical aspects of the problem at a stroke.

One thing he couldn't do, however, was install his most remarkable recent invention, the paddle-shift semi-automatic gearbox. 'We just didn't have the electronics technology at Benetton to build such a thing,' he explains. So it was back to a wider cockpit to accommodate a manual gearshift for the B191.

The frustrations generated tensions and out of it came a new nickname for Barnard. At McLaren it had been the Prince of Darkness, which offered at least a certain majesty; the moniker created at Benetton didn't. It emerged at the time of the Gulf War, when the Iraqi dictator, Saddam Hussein, was firing his unreliable Soviet-made rockets at coalition bases in Israel and Saudi Arabia. As Andy Smith reveals, 'They gave him the nickname Scud, which he didn't like.' One time, upon overhearing someone using the nickname, he butted in saying, 'The difference between me and a Scud is that when I land, I explode!' But in truth, he rarely heard the word; it was usually used to announce his imminent arrival, prompted by the dread sound of his car driving into the BARG car park. 'Scud Alert!' would be declared, or even 'Godalming Scud incoming'.

In late 1990, John came up with an innovation so simple that it beggared belief and was soon adopted throughout Formula 1. It arose from a simple dilemma: during a race weekend, the teams had to repeatedly remove and attach the bodywork and sidepods. For obvious reasons these had to be securely fastened, which made removal and refitting quite time-consuming. John's solution was a flush-fitting screw that was turned into place not with a spanner or a socket, but with a two-pronged key — now bodywork and sidepods could be off the car in seconds.[89]

Curiously, the one team that refused to persist with this time-saving quick-release catch were Benetton themselves, as mechanic Steve Matchett complained in his book: 'John Barnard is a perfectionist, his attention to detail is legendary, and there were some fine details to the design of the B191... Barnard's team had developed a flush-fitting quick-release catch... I have never understood the real reasons why, but those catches were never carried over to any other Benetton designs since the '91. I don't know if it was just a matter of pride ('I can't use that idea because I didn't think of it first') or what it was, but it was a superb idea that has since been wasted.'[90]

But one idea that even Benetton couldn't ignore was his solution for the B191 nose cone and front wing assembly. This was far more vulnerable than bodywork or sidepods — barely a race goes by that doesn't see one or more damaged front wings being changed after a dust-up at the start or on a tight corner. Before Barnard came up with his new method for the B191, changing this assembly could take several minutes even under race pressure, as Matchett explains: 'The nose of the B190 was secured by four small pins, retained in the chassis by internal spring clips. The idea was to grip the head of the pin with a pair of pliers, pulling them out of the nose in order to detach it. They were terrible. The pins would either stick in the nose, resulting in the pliers constantly slipping on the tiny removal flange, or, occasionally, the pins would work loose and disappear out on the circuit somewhere.'

To address this, John came up with an idea that was, as it happened, increasingly popular in the DIY industry and familiar to anyone who has ever assembled flat-pack furniture. He screwed four metal lugs into the nose cone at the connecting points to the chassis, the protruding tip of each lug flared out like a little mushroom. When the nose cone was being mounted, these lugs were lined up with four snail cams — small metal cylinders set into the chassis to receive the four mushroom heads. As soon as the nose cone was in place, a mechanic would use an Allen key to twist the snail cams through 180°, thus

---

[89] *'Nose Cone — Technical F1 Dictionary'*, www.formula1-dictionary.net.
[90] Matchett, Steve, A Mechanic's Tale: Life in the Pit-Lanes of Formula One, *London, Orion Books Ltd, 2001, p82.*

drawing the lugs in tight and locking them in place. Bingo: the nose was secure and yet quick to release.

This is the only Barnard innovation to bear his name, the Barnard catch, or as he termed it a little more prosaically, the Eccentric Quick Release Fastener. Diane Holl delighted in calling it the 'MFI catch', after the cheap and cheerful DIY superstore chain that supplied self-assembly furniture.

Of course, having been designed by Barnard, these catches were anything but cheap and cheerful, being made especially by Kenny Hill at Metalore in California out of 300M high-carbon steel. Matchett the mechanic comments: 'This was another brilliant piece of ingenuity, and one which should have won his team a trophy for Formula 1 design excellence.'

As far as Benetton were concerned, 1990 ended well, despite a tragedy for driver Alessandro Nannini in early October when his right forearm was severed in a helicopter accident; it was subsequently reattached with microsurgery and he was able to return to racing, but not Formula 1.

Nannini was quickly replaced by Brazilian Roberto Moreno, but, as Barnard reveals, it could have been Ayrton Senna. Four months earlier, at the Monaco Grand Prix, Senna had called Barnard and they had lunched at the driver's apartment overlooking the harbour. Says John, 'He began to sound me out about Benetton, saying, "Now that you've arrived, it seems they've got great potential. Do you think I should join the team?"'

John was tantalised by the prospect of having 'the best talent to have emerged in the sport in recent years' at the wheel of one of his cars. But he did the right thing, saying, 'No, Ayrton, not now. Now is not the time. We're just not ready for you yet.' Both were disappointed but, adds John, 'I'm glad I said it — it was the professional thing to do. I could foresee his frustrations and it just didn't seem right.'

Just a week after Nannini's accident, Benetton arrived at Suzuka for the Japanese Grand Prix, the penultimate race of the season, and scored an unexpected victory. This race was the one made famous by Senna's vengeful decision to use his McLaren to shunt Alain Prost's Ferrari off the track at the first corner, putting both cars out of the race but securing for himself the World Championship. In fact for Benetton it was a one-two, Piquet from Moreno, the best result achieved by the team up to that point.

Piquet went on to win the final race of the season as well. Senna looked certain to win the Australian Grand Prix in Adelaide but in the latter stages missed a gear and crashed out. Piquet inherited the lead but for the final laps he had a charging Nigel Mansell in Barnard's Ferrari 641 right up his exhaust, the Englishman nearly taking them both out on the final lap with a desperate lunge down the inside.

These two end-of-season victories elevated Piquet and Benetton to third place in both the Drivers' and Constructors' standings. It was an auspicious start for Barnard, with his team having picked off Williams in his first full year there, and with McLaren and Ferrari firmly in his sights. Ford was most impressed, with letters of congratulation coming from Lindsey Halstead, Ford of Europe's chairman of the board and, a few days later, from Ford Motor Company President Philip E. Benton Jr., who had just been appointed to the position and who duly and gleefully wrote:

Let me offer you and your team my congratulations on the outstanding victory on Sunday in Adelaide.

The two consecutive victories have certainly been a boost to the Benetton Ford program, and we're hopeful it's just a sign of even better things to come in 1991. Certainly, 1990 has been a watershed year for you. Thank you for bringing Ford to third place in the manufacturer's championship.

Once again, congratulations on an outstanding season. We're proud to have you and your colleagues as part of the Ford program.

Which just goes to show how important good performance in Formula 1 was to the major car manufacturers — 'win on Sunday, sell on Monday'.

To which end, Kranefuss wrote to John on 13 December, copied to Briatore, declaring that Cosworth was now briefed to create a V12 engine for the 1992 season as a result of 'recent changes in Cosworth's operating philosophy and attitude', following apparent pressure from both Ford and Benetton for Cosworth to 'demonstrate a commitment to a winning F1 program'. Barnard's messages were getting through.

However, the letter revealed that money was going to be an issue, appealing to Barnard to ensure that 'Benetton share a portion of the funding burden while enjoying the rewards', given that the 'resulting vehicle should potentially be a very competitive and unique one which could command even greater sponsorship contributions'.

Briatore's written response was to say that Kranefuss's letter was 'certainly good news' but that finances were a problem for Benetton too, revealing that

Japanese electronics giant Sanyo was reducing promised sponsorship by 50% and that 'in the last six months Benetton has spent approximately £7 million trying to bring the team to Ferrari and McLaren level'. The letter concludes by asking for an exact cost breakdown of the new V12 and wishing Kranefuss a Happy Christmas on his holiday in the Bahamas.

Now Benetton was looking good for Barnard, who recalls Briatore's endeavours to bring him in on a number of deals from which he could personally benefit, including a tyre contract with Pirelli. 'We were best of buddies at the time,' says John. 'I said to Flavio, "Do we take a chance with Pirelli?" It would be a calculated gamble. Tyres are the only things you can bolt on a car which could gain or lose you seconds.'

While John has always had a good head for money, he was never comfortable with business risks. Towards the end of the year, Flavio set up a meeting between himself, his financier, Barnard and team owner Guy Ligier. 'The idea was to do a deal with them that had the potential of making us all a lot of money,' says John. It involved Barnard taking 'a piece of the Ligier team' in return for technical help, although fundamentally it was a business deal — 'but something about it didn't smell right'.

The plan seemed to Barnard to be a proposal to pass Benetton technology on to Ligier: 'I was playing it pretty straight, explaining that we couldn't really run exactly the same stuff in both teams because it wasn't FIA-legal, that we'd have to set up a separate design office to service Ligier.' He was getting well outside his comfort zone and talking the wrong language in a world of risk, and in the end he stepped away: 'I guess I just didn't fit the mould for that kind of business.'

Perhaps Briatore wasn't impressed, perhaps this was a test. Was Barnard a 'player'? Could he stretch a few rules to make everyone money, doing business in the more 'flexible' Italian style? The call for such flexibility would feature significantly in the reams of correspondence that would flow between Barnard and Benetton.

In a letter to Luciano Benetton dated 13 December 1990, the English engineer declared himself 'very disturbed' by a 'direction from Benetton' to his accountant to 'apply some of next year's budget income to cover current year expenses. Especially when Benetton have not yet covered the properly budgeted expenditure for the Godalming operation.'

His contract, the Joint Venture Agreement, had stated that Benetton would provide the necessary funding, but instead Benetton Formula Ltd had been forced to borrow money to pay for much of the equipment and property, debts with which John, director and major shareholder, felt increasing discomfort.

Worse, the crucial 1990 budget still hadn't been signed off by Benetton, which meant that Barnard's contract hadn't been ratified despite the fact that he had been operating in accordance with the budget for eight months. John's letter continued: 'The Witney budget was produced at the normal time and the Godalming budget was included later, in accordance with the Joint Venture Agreement. This was submitted and Benetton Formula Ltd has operated on the basis of these since then. We have in fact operated largely within those projected figures, although, when Benetton responded, a number of items, for example, legal charges, were switched into another category.'

Barnard's growing concern focused on the fact that there was going to be, he stated in the letter, 'a substantial deficit for the year to 31 December 1989. Joint Venture responsibility for this deficit was no part of our arrangements, since it built up principally before I joined Benetton.' He further complained that 'Benetton appears to be changing the deal and the financial arrangements without any consultation or agreement with me.'

Aware of his partners' mindset, Barnard conceded that Benetton might have needed some 'flexibility' in the way it presented its figures but pointed out that 'Benetton Formula and the Property Company is part of a joint venture, arrived at after much discussion resulting in carefully negotiated and agreed terms.' He called for a meeting to resolve the issues.

On 20 December, Luciano Benetton replied, saying the issues were 'fairly simple and easily solvable', adding that 'it seems quite reasonable to us that any company would have to cover its losses, incurred during unfortunate times, with contribution from profitable years.'

Reasonable it may have been, but Barnard's point was that it wasn't part of the deal and that as a partner in a new joint venture, he shouldn't have to be responsible for old debts, or indeed, borrowings that he had been assured wouldn't be necessary.

Luciano continued, 'I believe this is particularly true in our case, considering that Benetton has accepted to give up almost completely its presence in the car', meaning that space for Benetton logos had been given over to other companies to generate income. 'This,' declared Luciano, 'is an enormous cost to Benetton and we consider it a substantial contribution in making this operation profitable.'

To Barnard it was all so much smoke and mirrors. As far as he was concerned the deal was being breached, and Benetton was seeking to fund the operation entirely by sponsorship and loans, which was fine in theory, but in practice it left him feeling partially responsible for mounting debts — the money that he supposed was to come direct from Benetton simply wasn't arriving.

Luciano had more bad news: 'With regard to the budget, we haven't approved it formally yet. I do not believe it is possible to approve anything as long as your estimates are subject to such wide fluctuations. In fact, your first estimate for 1991 was $25 million US last July. Today it is $35 million US.'

This, again, seemed evasive to John. The issue wasn't discussions about the 1991 budget, it was the critical 1990 budget that needed approval. Luciano concluded: 'Although we believe that you have done a superb job in the development of the team, and the improvement of the quality of its members, there is a limit to what we can do. Logic must have predominance here. We are looking forward to share with you even more successful years, but more flexibility must be considered on your side.'

'More flexibility' to John meant more risk, it meant agreeing with changes that he had not agreed to, going back on a deal that he had painstakingly thrashed out, a deal that was not yet ratified. It meant trusting Benetton. He was doing his part; every day he was developing the team, improving 'the quality of its members'.

But what was to stop Benetton deciding that, once he'd done a little more of that, once he'd got the team into championship-winning shape, that it would be a good idea to dump their difficult partner, the one who had 50% of the action and who wouldn't play the game according to their apparently moving goalposts? Surely they wouldn't do that? Surely that was just so much paranoia? Barnard tried to put these ominous prognostications to the back of his mind.

On the personal front, 1990 turned into a dreadful year for John. In the summer his father, aged 86, had a stroke and was rushed to hospital. Rosie reports that John spent as much time as he could with him but that Ted gradually deteriorated. 'We looked into getting him back to the house but it would have ended up being too complicated,' she says. 'He ended up being unable to speak. It was so bad; it was a two-man job to get him from one place to another; he was a big man. So we moved him into a nursing home and I think he just gave up.' He died on 12 September.

John was greatly affected: 'It really set me back; it was such a blow. I felt alone — that was the way I felt.'

Rosie concurs: 'John was absolutely devastated. Ted was the only person he had known all his life — the only child in such a close unit; I think Ted's death was more intense for John than for most, partly because he had no brothers or sisters to share it with. I was there but of course my relationship with Ted obviously hadn't been the same. It was the final anchor of his youth being ripped away.'

Gillian, eight at the time, is eloquent about the emotional impact upon her father: 'When Mum told me at our kitchen table, I remember Dad standing up on the other side of the kitchen with his back to us looking out of the window with his hands on the counter and just being quiet. I remember knowing and feeling all the sadness and emotion that he was going through without him having to say anything. That is generally how it is with us and Dad — generally we don't have to say anything to understand.'

The original tight family unit, the three-legged table, now only had one leg left, and it was tottering.

Looking back over his time with his father, whom he loved deeply, John recently reflected upon arguments that he occasionally has with his gifted and perfectionist older daughter, Jennifer, also a designer. 'Sometimes we have these rows in which she calls me all the names under the sun, telling me I'm an idiot, that I know nothing. I find myself reeling, thinking, "God, is that how I spoke to my father? Is that what it was like?"'

No doubt memories of those awful rows amplified Barnard's grief. Jennifer says: 'Most of the arguments with his Dad were about him not doing something to an acceptable standard. As a child I just thought, "Oh, Dad's being a bit mean to Grandad", because Grandad was so nice, so patient.' On her loving if stormy relationship with her father, she says, 'We have always rowed. When I asked for homework help and then didn't grasp it quickly enough, I was an idiot. During my Further Maths A-Level or Engineering studies, there were occasionally times when he could no longer help and I found that quite satisfying!'

Certainly he drew comfort from his family, but on the day Ted died John also received a thoughtful message from an unexpected source. Bernie Ecclestone wrote: 'John, I have just heard about your father and, as regretful as these things are, unfortunately this is the way life is. Although I am quite sure it is difficult for you at the moment, time heals all wounds.'

John soon found himself thinking, 'I've got to get up and get on with it.' So he cracked on, working so hard that he had little or no time for his children, who, being at school, wouldn't see him at lunchtimes, and then would be in bed by the time he got home in the evenings. Even at weekends he wouldn't see much of them, being so often away at races.

In mid-October his Gillian took matters into her own hands, taking to an electric typewriter to compose a formal letter from herself and five-year-old Michael to their father:

To Mr. John Barnard.
If you would not mind my manager (Michael Barnard) and I (Gillian Barnard) are wishing you could send us both a letter saying what you would like for CHRISTMAS. We would like it to be back by the end of November. You can send it to M.B's room and G.B's room. When you are wrighting this letter we would like it to be in printing or on the computer. That is if you have one. Thank you so much.

The letter was signed by G.A. Barnard ('secutery') and, in a cute, higgledy-piggledy scribble, Michael (manager), who happened to be a fan of the Teenage Mutant Ninja Turtles. Dad duly replied on Benetton-headed paper:

Dear Ms. Barnard and Mr. Barnard
Thank you very much for your recent enquiry concerning my thoughts for a Christmas Gift.
I have much pleasure in advising you that I would be very happy to receive a tie or possibly some Turtle underpants.
Thank you again for your kind enquiry.
Yours sincerely
J E Barnard
Technical Director

CHAPTER 27
THE TRUE COLOURS OF BENETTON
1991

It was proving to be a cold winter in the northern hemisphere and cold too was the tone of a letter from Ford's Mike Kranefuss to Flavio Briatore and John Barnard, dated 6 February 1991.

Kranefuss stated: 'Current events, such as a slumping world economy and a war in the Middle East, are having a severely negative effect on our business. At a time when we are closing plants, cancelling product programs and laying people off, it is difficult enough to keep any program going, let alone something as seemingly discretionary as a racing program.' The context set, he went on to make three telling points.

The first was an accusation directed at Benetton and therefore Barnard of failing to deliver 'absolute cooperation and completely open communication' to Cosworth and that 'Cosworth has spent the past three months working on the general package without any concrete support from Benetton'.

The second point was a complaint about delay in Barnard's B191. While its lateness wasn't a surprise, 'the way you chose to communicate this development certainly was... Apart from purely technical implication and the effect this will have on Cosworth, I reassured Ford management as recently as last month that the new car would appear at Phoenix [the first race of the 1991 season] and would serve as the focal point of planned media activities there. Obviously I was the only one who thought so.'

The third point was delivered with surprising fury. Kranefuss stated that he had spent the past year enjoying the 'questionable pleasure' of reading in the press about the 'enormous power disadvantage' of the Ford V8, and was 'completely baffled' by Benetton's apparent failure to 'motivate' its partner,

Mobil, in their production of specially blended fuel — Barnard's 'fairly antisocial stuff'.

Kranefuss concluded that there was 'clearly something fundamentally wrong in this relationship,' that 'in reflecting on the past 12 months, I remember to be filled with Benetton's criticism of Ford and Cosworth, at times justified and with good reason' but that 'it is now your responsibility to change and to adopt a more constructive and cooperative attitude'.

The message from the top was clear: you may not like Cosworth, but you had better find a way to work with them or Ford would pull out. Taken aback by the letter's tone and content, John suspected that all sorts of 'fabricated' complaints had been delivered to Kranefuss via his enemies at Cosworth.

There was much else on Barnard's mind. Against his expectations and wishes, going into 1991 he found himself immersed in legal advice from Michael Jepson over the status of the Joint Venture Agreement. Jepson wrote to him on 5 February advising that he himself had sought further advice, a 'conference with Counsel', whose opinion was that, despite the 1990 budget not being signed off, the contract was 'binding'.

Jepson stated in that letter: 'He considered that this was not something which would now prevent the Agreement being operative particularly bearing in mind that 1990 has now passed and we are therefore moving onto the 1991 budget. The Agreement provides that this should be agreed by 1st February and of course this has not been agreed partly because of disputes as to what should be included in that budget and what should be included in the previous budget...'

A key point was that, added Jepson, 'It should not be possible for Benetton to rely on technicalities to argue that the Agreement is not yet effective. First of all you and they have effectively acted on the basis of the Agreement as if it had become effective and in particular you have billed and been paid in accordance with the Services Agreement.'

Jepson also pointed out that 'at this stage you do not have 50% interest in Benetton Holdings'. Counsel's opinion was that the situation had reached 'breach or deadlock and arguably both' — meaning that Barnard would be within his rights to terminate.

So, on 12 February John renewed his correspondence with Luciano Benetton, complaining that the company's Alessandro Signorini had demanded that 'some income from 1991 must be used in 1990, and on top of that a huge "roll over" figure from 1990 to 1991 must be budgeted for'. John reminded Luciano that 'it was very much part of the agreement that Benetton would finance any deficit', that the current situation 'undermines the whole basis of the joint venture agreement', that the date had passed for agreeing the 1991 budget and that although considerable progress had been made 'I do need to feel that I have your full financial backing and support…'

It cut no ice. Luciano's reply was polite but evasive, concentrating on the fact that the 1990 budget still hadn't been signed off — the great weakness in John's position. Luciano proposed a meeting at Benetton's headquarters in Italy. He suggested a date when John would be in Phoenix for the United States Grand Prix, the first race of the 1991 season, as he must have known. Attempts to find another date resulted in yet more delay.

John replied on 15 February in a firm if conciliatory tone, warning that as a result of the cash-flow delays and other impasses, the deal to buy the Henley Park site in Wanborough was probably dead, a fact that didn't seem to bother Luciano one jot. It bothered Barnard; he'd put heart and soul into the design of this planned new facility.

As the snow fell in this freezing winter of discontent, Barnard trudged on. Diane Holl remembers a bitter night in February when she, Mike Coughlan and John were working late at Langham Park to prepare the new B191 for its first shakedown run at the Pembrey circuit in South Wales in the hands of Roberto Moreno, who had by now been confirmed as Nelson Piquet's permanent team-mate.

At 1.00am and with Diane yawning at her post, John told her to go home and leave him and Mike to finish up before the car was taken to the circuit just a few hours later, adding that she would have to drive them to Pembrey in his Ford Sierra Cosworth and needed to get some sleep. Arriving at the freezing circuit at around 9.00am, all exhausted, they soon discovered that the B191 wouldn't start.

This wasn't going to stop Barnard and Coughlan. They put Moreno in the B191, attached a long tow rope to the back of the Sierra Cosworth and started hauling the racer around the circuit, trying to bump-start it. Diane explains what happened next: 'When Roberto let his foot off the clutch the race car leaped forward. He slammed on the brakes and stopped short of the back of the Sierra by about two inches. I often remember this moment and think, "God, were we that stupid?" It was all pretty bizarre, and typical of the gung-ho, hands-on side of John's character that seemed such a contrast to his fastidious perfectionism.'

It turned out that a new starter mechanism had been made incorrectly — an error that had escaped John's eagle eye. The test at Pembrey also revealed another mistake: 'We weren't running power steering then, so in an effort to take some load off the steering I had overcooked the front suspension — and got to the point where the steering didn't self-align in corners. It actually ended up steering itself towards the wall. We hastily changed the geometry and made new uprights.'

It was some comfort to Diane that even the Great Barnard could make a suspension cock-up, because she was about to make a major one herself. Aged a mere 26, she had been given the responsibility of designing the rear suspension and felt the weight on her shoulders. Two nights before the car was to be unveiled to the media at a hotel near Heathrow, she says, 'Everything was coming together like clockwork'. The suspension was in place and one of the last tasks was to install the exhaust pipes: 'When they offered it up, an exhaust pipe hit the rear leg of the lower wishbone and wouldn't clear it. I thought, "That's it. I'm fired!"

This big error had Diane quaking in her pop socks, in dread of a Barnard explosion, but it never came: 'John's reaction was amazing. He didn't shout. He didn't say anything bad to me at all. He just said, "Okay, Diane, what do we need to do to fix it?" So, we went back to my drawing board. Both he and Mike Coughlan sat down and helped me redesign the suspension that bit lower, so it would miss the exhaust. We moved around some suspension blocks — the points at which they joined the chassis — and got the design to the fab [fabrication] shop. Then John said to me, very gently, "You go home, everything's okay, we'll see it through the fab shop, come back in the morning and you can see the rest through when you come back." By the morning it had all been done. John never mentioned another word about it. So he used to erupt on the small stuff, but, with the big ones, he went completely calm and dismissed them.'

John recalls the incident and explains his calm: 'The more major design work you do, the more experienced you become. You get a feeling when things are going well that something is bound to go wrong, so, approaching the final build of any car, I was always waiting for the clanger — you do tend to wait for the big one.'

He adds that this is why he has always been so proud of the Chaparral

2K, 'because there was no clanger — not even a small one'. He treasures the memory of Bob Sparshott saying, 'I can't believe it. We've made everything to drawing and it all fits!'

John agrees that it was always the little things that sent him up the pole: 'The small stuff tends to be because someone just hasn't thought it through, just dashed it off. That's what winds me up.'

Barnard was never particularly satisfied with the B191: 'There were so many compromises on it. Sure, it was soundly engineered but I considered it to be pretty much bog standard, just an interim car to get us going.'

Benetton, however, were delighted with it, and so was Moreno when he first saw it at the press launch on 28 March, as John explains: 'Everybody said a few words, the car was unveiled, there was a gasp, and Roberto's comment was, "Well, John has done it again, he's come up with something new" — all because the front wing was different!

'But in the back of my mind I was thinking, "Roberto, if only you knew how bog standard that thing really is!" It was prudent not to be pushing out too many things as we simply didn't have the capability at Benetton at that time to deal with rapid innovation. It would have been stupid of me to have buried ourselves in that sort of complexity.'

Mechanic Steve Matchett was impressed with the beauty of the car: 'It looked nothing like anything else that Benetton had ever produced but this wasn't surprising. Barnard had started the design work of the B191 with a completely clean sheet; it was intended that nothing should be carried over from previous Benetton creations. The only way to move forward is to innovate, I suppose. It must be said that what he came up with was a beautiful-looking car, endowed with some very sleek body lines. In essence it looked much more like a Ferrari than a Benetton; the shape could have been a perfect successor to Ferrari's 1990 car, the 641.'[91]

Meanwhile, for the first two races of the new season, the existing B190s were wheeled out. Kranefuss regained some face in Phoenix when he watched Piquet take third place behind Ayrton Senna's McLaren and Alain Prost's Ferrari, but in Brazil Piquet only managed fifth with Moreno seventh.

There was then a five-week break before the San Marino Grand Prix at

---

[91] *Matchett, Steve*, A Mechanic's Tale: Life in the Pit-Lanes of Formula One, *London, Orion Books Ltd, 2001, pp81–82. All quotes from Matchett in this chapter are taken from his book.*

Imola but even so the mechanics faced a series of all-nighters to get the B191s ready, as Matchett explained:

'We were slipping behind schedule and needed more time, but try telling that to the FIA. The races will happen when they're planned, and no one is going to put the San Marino Grand Prix back a couple of weeks because Benetton isn't quite ready. We had problems with the gearbox, problems with the engine's cooling system and constant problems with fuel pressure. The knock-on effect of all this was that the Imola race was much worse than 1990. There was not so much as an hour's sleep for anybody throughout the duration of Thursday, Friday and Saturday.'

All that effort was to little avail. Moreno and Piquet qualified only 13th and 14th. Neither finished the race, Piquet spinning out on the second lap and Moreno retiring on lap 52 of 61 with a broken gearbox.

The Monaco Grand Prix two weeks later was another trial of endurance for the Benetton mechanics. A gearbox problem revealed itself on this circuit of many gear changes, requiring a rush to construct a gearbox jig followed by remedial work with mills and lathes borrowed from Riva Boat Services. Working late, fighting against Time's fell march, people became so exhausted that, as Matchett reports, one gearbox mechanic fell asleep on his feet in the pit lane during the race.

Barnard explains: 'We had to take the shift rods out of the gearbox and file tiny radiuses on the gate corners, because when you go from second to third, you have to cross the box in a rapid S movement. The guy drawing the box — I can't blame him — had drawn square edges on the shift rods. So we just had to take the corners off. It was one of those things that a few tests would have sorted out. But we never had time for testing — everything was last minute.'

So hearts fell into stomachs as Piquet, who qualified fourth, failed to make it round the first corner after Gerhard Berger's McLaren smashed into the back of his B191, breaking Diane Holl's carefully designed suspension as well as whacking the carefully rebuilt gearbox. Moreno, however, managed to go some way to make up for it, coming home fourth.

Why was everything so last minute? Joan Villadelprat, loyal to his very boots, was becoming frustrated with what he saw as a boss distracted by business: 'I had a very high regard for John, but we did have arguments. One was about his being more worried about making the factory in Godalming than he was about designing the car... To me, he seemed more into his relationship with Benetton and the possible business opportunities.'

The truth, however, was that Barnard was becoming demoralised.

It had all begun so well. Briatore had chosen to base himself in Godalming, travelling there in chauffeur-driven splendour from his expensive apartment in London's Cadogan Square. He was, in a sense, the Ron Dennis of the relationship, the deal maker, the money man.

John recalls Briatore's early warmth saying, 'You know, John, I think of you as my brother', which perhaps didn't bode well for any real-life siblings because Barnard's overwhelming sensation by this time was that Briatore was getting ready to knife him in the back.

The tone of John's letters to Luciano Benetton became more robust, the replies ever more measured, but always oozing power. In a letter dated 25 February, Barnard complained again about the proposal to roll over from 1990 to 1991 an 'impossibly large "work in progress" figure of £2.75 million. I cannot in any way justify a figure of this size and do not agree with this accounting practice.'

He added that if he were asked to 'sign off the audited accounts as a Director and principal person responsible for the budget, I would not be able to do so', adding that he did 'not believe that any Director can or should sign accounts if these items are included as required by Benetton. In my view, work in progress at the level you propose cannot be justified and it is totally misleading to carry back into 1990 income that clearly relates to 1991', and warning that 'there could be serious implications under the Companies Act and the directors' obligations and liabilities'. He received a reply by fax on the same day in which Luciano declared himself 'disappointed' by Barnard's approach.

Luciano then suggested that since Barnard was refusing to sign the accounts, another director should do so. As for the budget for the year 1990, he pointed out that the continuing impasse about this remained the reason why the Joint Venture Agreement still could not be put into effect. John felt the slow twisting of the knife.

With the end of the tax year approaching, the accounts had to be submitted to the Inland Revenue. In mid-March, Vijay Kothary received a letter from the Guildford office of the big accounting firm Arthur Andersen, copied to Benetton in Italy. There was something not quite right about the BFL accounts. The particular concerns raised by the accountants were threefold: a) the nature of the connections between the various companies around Benetton Formula, i.e. who was due to benefit; b) the sponsorship deals — they wanted to look at the contracts with all ten primary sponsors; and c) the rollover amount — how it was calculated and whether there would be 'sufficient revenue to cover costs in 1991' as projected in the budget forecast for that year. The companies around Benetton Formula Limited that interested them were Research and Development of Sponsorship Ltd, Sponsorship Corporation (International) Ltd, Rubino Caribe Ltd, Ben Marketing and Sponsorship Ltd, and one called Stockton — quite a web.

This sort of stuff made John nervous: 'Arthur Andersen wouldn't sign off the accounts because they weren't happy with the way they were presented.' He sought Jepson's advice, telling him 'we've operated to the budget as we promised. Benetton have suggested that I sign off the accounts because I'm a director. Should I? Can I?'

Barnard was told not to, for two good reasons — Arthur Andersen weren't happy and Benetton themselves wouldn't sign off the 1990 budget. Which presented a problem. Barnard was the key director, the man who oversaw the budget process and who spent the money. Eventually he would have to sign the accounts.

On 25 March, Barnard wrote to Luciano once more, expressing his disappointment about the delayed meeting and complaining that BFL's balance sheet 'shows that it is excessively over-borrowed and it is this that concerns me as a director. Whilst this might suit Benetton from its own group accounting point of view some of the assets, especially work in progress, do not have real value until the profits are carried to cover them. Furthermore ever since we set up the joint venture, all funds which Benetton have required have been borrowed, not just to cover its deficit, but to cover all the plant equipment and other expenses' — this at a time when Bank of England interest rates were running at over 10%.

He added, 'I am particularly concerned about the way in which you seem to be forcing us to have to operate… entirely on borrowed money. This is creating a resultant balance sheet and profit and loss situation which, in terms of the Joint Venture Agreement, means you have put no more real money into BFL since we signed up.'

Borrowed money, as we've established, was anathema to Barnard. He accuses Benetton of offering 'no evidence at all… that you are really serious about fulfilling our Joint Venture Agreement… The evidence so far points very strongly to the impression that you are interested in my input and expertise only as part of the Benetton group and therefore at the end of three years, you intend to buy me out.' And what would BFL shares be worth then, saddled, as it already was, with enormous debts?

The meeting in Italy that Luciano Benetton had suggested finally took place on 6 April. Accompanied by Vijay Kothary, Barnard flew out to Benetton's headquarters in Treviso, 20 miles north of Venice, within a vast and beautiful Italian villa, built in white stone and marble, flanked by arcades around a magnificent reflecting lake, buried beneath which was an entire complex of Benetton stores designed to show employees and visitors how the Benetton franchise worked. That day, however, the beauties of the place entirely passed Barnard by as he sat down with Luciano.

The meeting was brief and ended, says John, 'on bad terms'. The debilitating row had become deadlocked.

But still Barnard struggled to find ways to go on. The B191 was a car full of potential. Beyond the B191, there was still the prospect of a V12, and there would be new, younger, better drivers, a semi-automatic gearbox and aerodynamic advances. Benetton was nearly up to scratch. It seemed madness to end it all now.

John began thinking about signing off the 1990 accounts, trying to find a way to make that possible, but he was haunted by the possibility that even if he did, Benetton in return might not sign off the 1990 budget. He felt trapped.

He was now convinced that Benetton's refusal to sign the budget was the plan all along; that they'd always intended to take a look at him, milk his expertise to lift Benetton to new heights and — should he prove to be the sort of fellow they couldn't do business with — simply remove him. There was only one way this was heading, and that was out of the front door. Still he tried not to believe it.

And so, after weeks more of correspondence, much of it between lawyers, it came to the crunch. At the end of May, Barnard had a meeting, a cold affair, with Flavio Briatore, who told him there had been a board meeting at which it had been decided that John would have to leave on the grounds that he refused to sign off the 1990 accounts.

John went straight to see to Jepson. 'I was supposed to get a multi-million pound pay-off if I went early. Should I fight this?'

He could, replied Jepson, but he should also keep in mind that if he fought the Benetton group, it would be all he had time to do, because it would take over his life, that right and wrong wasn't the issue, that it would be relatively effortless for them to keep him tied up for years.

John considered his options — but there weren't any. As far as he was concerned, he had been tricked.

'Flavio knew Benetton was now on an upward curve, and the idea of giving 50% of that success to me was clearly becoming unacceptable,' says John. Now it was a question of negotiating from a weak position, a David against a Goliath. He was out, and the struggle now was to salvage something.

The news of John's departure reached Diane Holl on the evening of her birthday, 5 June, just after she had returned from a London theatre, celebrating with her mother by watching a performance of *Annie Get Your Gun*. 'When I got home, there was a message on my answer machine from Mike Coughlan, at around 10pm. It said, "When you come in tomorrow, John won't be here. I'm helping him pack up."'

She found the news deeply upsetting. She knew things hadn't been going well, but hadn't realised that it was completely over. 'I can remember being so angry that they had done this to John. I didn't really know what had gone down, but I remember being so upset. And, sure enough, next day, I went in and John was gone, his stuff cleared out. He called me the day after and said, "Hey, hang tight, I don't know what I will be doing next, but there will be something." As soon as I could I joined him at his home, working for Barnard Design Consultancy.'

Andy Smith had a similar response: 'I remember John coming to the test lab and saying, "I feel like Caesar having just been stabbed by Mark Antony." After that we at the manufacturing site decided that Benetton would never be our future and we remained in touch with John to see what he was planning to do next. It was such a pity: Benetton was probably the most fun I've had in Formula 1 — it was a brilliant team of people at Godalming.'

On 2 June, three days before Barnard left, the fates handed him a gift at the Canadian Grand Prix, a race that also saw Piero Lardi Ferrari take over the running of the Ferrari Formula 1 team from Cesare Fiorio. The Williams-Renaults were the class of qualifying, Riccardo Patrese taking pole with Nigel Mansell alongside him, while Moreno and Piquet started fifth and eighth in their B191s. Mansell led away and stayed there. In his wake others dropped out, including Moreno — after a spin on lap 10 — and both McLarens and Ferraris. Eventually Piquet found himself second to Mansell, albeit nearly a minute behind. Steve Matchett takes up the tale:

'In the closing stages of the race Nelson was in second position trailing behind Mansell, who had rejoined Williams for his push to become World Champion, and they stayed in this order until the final corner of the last lap. Suddenly, as Mansell prematurely waved to the crowd, his Williams ground to an undignified stop, with Piquet nipping past to take the chequered flag. Very bizarre!

'Afterwards, Mansell absolutely, categorically and unconditionally denied that he had flicked the ignition switch by accident as he lifted his hand from the cockpit. Well, we're all only human and make mistakes from time to time. After carefully inspecting the car, I understand the Williams mechanics never found fault with it. Conclude from that what you will.'

Mansell, of course, takes an entirely different point of view of how he handed the race to Piquet, blaming Patrick Head's revolutionary FW14 with its active suspension and brand-new paddle shift. Describing it as 'one of the worst mechanical failures I ever suffered,' he says that as he came through the final hairpin 'I couldn't find a gear to save my life'. He adds, with some fury:

'My engineer David Brown and I were trying to get over it as quickly as possible, when we read some truly idiotic suggestions in the press that I had switched the ignition off while waving to the crowd. It was a pathetic notion and it really hurt.

'Let's face it, you don't push as hard as you can for 68 laps and then switch your own engine off. It was bad enough losing the race through mechanical failure, but to have insult added to injury in that way was too painful to describe.'[92]

Whatever the reason for Mansell's demise, it was a sweet first victory for Barnard's B191: 'At least I can say that my car won a race. Up to that time I don't think I'd done a car that hadn't won. So at least I kept the record going.'

Steve Matchett wrote of his sadness about the departure of 'our illustrious technical director, John Barnard'.

'The B191 was supposed to take the world by storm,' stated Matchett, 'the car to catapult Benetton amongst the dogfights of McLaren, Ferrari and Williams for race victories. Maybe it was not the car to clinch the Constructors'

---

[92] *Mansell, Nigel, with James Allen,* Nigel Mansell, My Biography, *CollinsWillow, London, 1995, p79 and p236.*

Championship in its first year, but the next evolution of it, the B192, should have been in a position to have the bounties of glory heaped upon it. A contract had been signed with Pirelli, and they had agreed to help Benetton develop a tyre for the B191 which should challenge the dominance of Goodyear, and in 1991 a shot at second place in the Championship should have been a distinct possibility… It was a great pity to have parted with John Barnard when we did. Given sufficient development time I'm convinced that the B191 would have proved its full potential and perhaps we could have squeezed more than just a single victory out of it.'

Another gutted by the news was chief mechanic Nigel Stepney, who, according to Matchett, had joined Benetton precisely because he would have the chance of working with Barnard: 'Nigel jumped at the chance of promotion and the possibility to work alongside the great man himself… with the finance in place, Barnard as designer, and Piquet in the car, it was now quite obvious that Benetton was looking to Formula One big time.' Stepney left Benetton immediately after Barnard, later to join him at Ferrari.

The motorsport media, too, were sympathetic to Barnard. Nigel Roebuck of *Autosport* was mystified, his observations appearing under the headline 'Was it just too good to last?' in one of his respected 'Fifth Column' comment pieces.

'My understanding from other sources is that [Barnard] did not flounce out of his office in a resignation rage; rather his departure was orchestrated by individuals he considered colleagues, even friends.

'If this be true, they will surely one day rue their actions. "Working with him was no trip to Paris," Mario Andretti once said of Colin Chapman, "but you're always going to have problems with a genius, right?"

'Right. There are times when the entire paddock seems populated only by folk in Benetton-Ford schmutter, yet when they trim the staff, the man shown the door is the most successful race car designer of the modern era. There is curious logic at work here.

'Whatever forces conspired to engineer Barnard's removal, the fact remains that the move was sanctioned by someone at the highest level in the company — presumably Luciano Benetton himself…

'It took little time for Barnard to emerge as the man calling the shots, for such is his way, and perhaps this went ill in a team where the chiefs previously seemed to outnumber the Indians.

'For the moment everybody involved is buttoned up on the subject, leaving us on the outside merely to speculate. But to me, the whole matter is unfathomable at a time when Benetton appeared poised to join McLaren, Williams and Ferrari at the top level.'[93]

In that same issue of *Autosport* there was a news item headlined 'Barnard quits Benetton'. Written by Tony Dodgins, it quoted Benetton's explanation that there had been 'a basic contrast of ideas in the running of the company on a day-to-day basis' but that they fully recognised 'the many skills and talents of John Barnard', an admirably accurate if euphemistic summary of the intractable situation. Dodgins stated that 'Barnard's departure is the consequence of a "palace revolution".'

Benetton were, according to the article, conciliatory, expecting to 'negotiate an agreement satisfactory to him and it [Benetton]'. John was quoted too: 'I hope Benetton and I can reach an amicable agreement,' he said, before revealing that he wanted 'to take two or three months off, give myself a little time to see if I want to be involved in Formula One any more. I'm a bit disillusioned at the moment, to be honest. Maybe I'll stay in F1, maybe not.'

John's broken heart was on his sleeve, the piercing arrow revealed in the article's opening paragraph: 'Replacing him will be Gordon Kimball, the man Barnard regarded as his protégé.'

Kimball had stayed on at Ferrari after Barnard left, but then, realising 'it wasn't going to work' with incoming Fiat technical people whom he considered 'buffoons', he returned to McLaren, initially working to get the team back into Indycar and then, when that got sidelined, upon the F1 road car. At the end of 1990, as he puts it, he 'fell victim to Flavio Briatore's sales pitch and got sucked into Benetton for a year.'[94]

He took over as Benetton's technical director in time for the Mexican Grand Prix on 16 June. The news came as a shock to Barnard, who considered it 'treachery'. What he found particularly grievous is that, despite a long friendship, Kimball never indicated what was coming: 'I didn't mind him making the move, advancing his career if you like, but he could at least have phoned me and asked if I was leaving, what was going on, would you mind if I took over? Then I could at least have warned him about the problems he'd face.' He felt Kimball had been 'sneaky'.

---

[93] Roebuck, Nigel, 'Fifth Column: Was it just too good to last?' Autosport, *13 June 1991.*
[94] Kirby, Gordon, 'Bernie did all he could to help Ferrari. I guess he wanted somebody to beat McLaren...', Motor Sport, *September 2015, p94 (and also www.motorsportmagazine.com).*

Kimball had been one of Barnard's detail-design men since the Parnelli days and had followed him everywhere. As a consequence, John thought he had a very good relationship with him; their children had played together and their wives were friends. 'He just turned up and took my job. I was dumbstruck. I felt it was a total betrayal, such an unbelievable bit of back-stabbing.'

For Kimball, the move proved to be a giant leap, in fact, a bridge too far. Matchett says in his book that Kimball seemed 'a pleasant enough chap. I had never heard of him before… but it was as if the team's management had decided that they just needed someone (anyone) to carry the mantle of Technical Director until they had more time to reorganise. Poor Gordon Kimball was replaced by the end of the year.'

Kimball blames his rapid departure upon politics and a lack of funding: 'Tom Walkinshaw didn't have a nickel to put into the team, so he took authority by putting his own people in place. I had some other offers, but we had moved to England, then to Italy and back to England. Between the politics and uprooting the family again, I'd had enough of Formula 1. I was an engineer, not a politician, and thought it was no longer fun.'[95] He returned to America where he set up his own design consultancy business and so stepped out of Barnard's world.

Also stepping out of Barnard's world was Arthur Webb, who couldn't conceive of working under Kimball because he was 'a character I couldn't take to at all'. Webb returned to developing his consultancy. He had enjoyed a great ride with Barnard and made a major contribution to motorsport. Without Webb's expertise, Barnard would have found it far harder to complete the carbon-fibre project — Arthur was absolutely the right man in the right place with the perfect temperament for working with John.

Kimball was replaced as Benetton technical director by Ross Brawn, who had designed the Ford V8-powered A11 for the Arrows Formula 1 team. Talented, intelligent and one of the best people managers in the business, the affable Brawn had a calm disposition and a good strategic mind. He was destined to take the refurbished, upgraded Benetton team to new heights.

Brawn could speak the language of business to Briatore and the language of car design to returning chief designer Rory Byrne. Neither Brawn nor Byrne

---

[95] Kirby, Gordon, 'Bernie did all he could to help Ferrari. I guess he wanted somebody to beat McLaren…', Motor Sport, September 2015, p94 (and also www.motorsportmagazine.com).

were designers of Barnard's stature, but Brawn had qualities that John lacked and was able to protect Byrne from the political machinations that caused so much distraction and destruction for Barnard. They inherited an upgraded Benetton and their heydays were upon them.

Breaking contracts whatever the stipulations is never easy. As their statements in the press revealed, Benetton didn't want John flying off the handle and bad-mouthing them in the media; their legal position might have been strong, but the same was not so for their image within the small world of Formula 1, or indeed the wider world of a sport followed by hundreds of millions of fans. So John's reputation for apoplectic fury and damn the consequences here worked in his favour and strengthened his hand. Benetton struck a deal in which Barnard received a pay-off, not what was promised, but enough to salve the wounds.

Those wounds were deep. He had been forced out. This was an utterly new experience for John who, thus far, had always moved onwards on his own terms. 'It was so disappointing for me to have to leave on the cusp of success,' he says, ruefully, 'but I wasn't sorry to leave behind the sharks there.'

As anyone does in such a situation, he began to worry about his future, for his life seemed to be coming apart around his ears. So much promise, all dashed from his hands as he was raising the cup of victory to his lips.

Could it have gone better? Could Barnard have handled Benetton with more skill? These were the same questions that had arisen after McLaren and Ferrari.

Would it have been better had he upped sticks and moved to Oxfordshire? Would that have been such a burden for his family to bear? It would still have been in the heart of England, after all. It's possible that the Witney team would have been far more welcoming, and there may have been less opposition to his contribution, which might have then percolated upwards.

Perhaps Luciano Benetton and Flavio Briatore would have valued him more if he had been considered less of a threat to the personal futures of so many team members, if he had secured more support throughout the team. As it was, Barnard made it pretty easy for them to dump him.

On the other hand, the canny move of creating what Barnard saw as a tripwire clause in his contract gave them all the power they needed. If Benetton didn't like him, they could drop him like a hot rock and with minimal cost. If they loved him, if he was a player, if he was their kind of guy, if they could do business with him after their own style, they would keep him — although the 50% ownership was always going to be an issue.

It was, indeed, a clash of styles: Barnard's straight-dealing, frank-talking, sometimes brutal Anglo-Saxon honesty against the evasive grace of Briatore and Benetton; Austin Reed verses Versace; Honest John fighting the moneyed, smiling might of 'flexible' Benetton.

And if it didn't work out, well, Benetton knew what he'd done for McLaren and Ferrari in pretty short order. It was a calculated risk to give him a year or two. Benetton was certain to benefit, as indeed they did, if only because the staff had learned vital new skills and Rory Byrne, when he returned, benefited from Barnard's pioneering understanding of aerodynamics, wind tunnels and car design.

'Rory said to me once,' states Mike Coughlan, 'that he learned an awful lot from John, but John never thought he learned anything back. Rory saw the benefit of most of what John had put in place and was a willing learner. Personally I think John did learn from Rory; certainly he took some good ideas from him.'

'I didn't go there just to design them a car,' reflects Barnard. 'I went there to lift their whole team up, to improve their entire technical expertise. To do that I told them what sort of budget we'd need to spend, and I wasn't wrong.

'It was the same old story,' he continues, with some bitterness. 'What I left McLaren, Ferrari and Benetton was this whole new design ethos and team of designers and mechanics with much more understanding and experience of designing and working in composites.

'This uplift,' he adds, 'made them much more attractive to big-name drivers. Schumacher came into Benetton at the end of the year, attracted in part by the fact that their car facilities were now state of the art. If you look at that period of Benetton cars through to 1995, they were all developments of the B191.'

'Maybe with what they had with Byrne before I arrived,' he angrily concludes, 'they knew they weren't going to move forward. Maybe it's why they hired me — to set them up and then get rid of me. Did I put Benetton on the right road? Absolutely I did. I left them a palette with the right colours in the right places for a world-class painting.' The colours of Benetton as painted by Barnard.

John now feels that his time with the Anglo-Italian outfit was pointless. Looking back, he believes that he would have been much better off staying at Ferrari developing the 640 with Alain Prost.

Barnard's people had called him the Godalming Scud but in truth the epithet is better applied to his entire experience at Benetton. It had launched full of promise but when it landed, as far as Barnard was concerned, it was a dud.

CHAPTER 28
TOMFOOLERY
1991–92

Now John Barnard was on his own and out of work. The pressure of creating the menu for a masterpiece and being sacked for his efforts proved too much. He decided to take that well-overdue break.

'I went home and I thought, "I'm going to stop for a while. I'm going to go home; I've got an office at home, I've got drawing boards at home, I'm just going to play around at home. Before I do that, I'll go on holiday, to France for a month with the family, do some dinghy sailing." When you're living with constant pressure, and at Formula 1's pace, I think you're working on adrenalin much of the time. You don't know it, you don't realise it, but that's going on.'

Barnard's choice of language is moving. The repetition of going 'home', where he would just 'play around', harks back to that seminal moment on his first day at school when he couldn't face the pressure and went home for lunch. Except now both his parents were dead and home wasn't Peel Road held down by his life-long anchors, Ted and Rose Ellen, but Rosie and the children instead.

The family's French destination was a beautiful house commanding a view over the picturesque L'Arguenon estuary by Saint-Jacut-de-la-Mer on the north coast of Brittany. Ten days into the break and for the first time in his life, John was hit by a serious illness: 'I thought that the stress had lifted, but suddenly I was feeling worse than I had ever done. I couldn't get up; I was really hit for six. It was as if my body had gone on holiday as well.'

Rosie explains: 'He always seemed to get ill if we went on holiday. I think it was the stress draining away as soon as he was able to relax. This time he was very, very ill; at the time I didn't realise how bad it was. The kids were unwell too and at first I imagined he'd caught the same thing, so I thought, "This is just man flu!" But it was worse than that. It was pneumonia and pleurisy. He went through a really bad patch when he could hardly breathe.'

Back at home and in recovery, John busied himself with converting part of Combe Rise into a base for Barnard Design Consultancy Ltd, creating an office between his six-car garage and the main house, complete with drawing boards, desks, filing cabinets and lay-up tables — 'a nice comfortable office with an indoor swimming pool'.

In the garage by now were two handsome classic cars, further fruits of his handsome earnings. His 1933 Lagonda M45 Tourer, with its prominent vertical-barred grille, large stand-alone conical headlights and graceful running boards, sat alongside a newly acquired Aston Martin DB6 Volante Mark 2 that harked back to his youthful days with the DB4 except that this was the ultimate specimen of the breed, the last of the DB4-to-DB6 line and the convertible version too.

So in the bosom of his family, John decided to 'play around a bit and do some thinking'. His cogitation brought him back to gearboxes. What troubled him was the size of the gear package: if he could make it narrower and lighter there would be more scope at the rear of the car to improve aerodynamics and reduce weight.

He recalled that Getrag, the German transmission manufacturer, had created a ball-bearing system that allowed the gears to spin alongside each other without dog rings in between. The Getrag method was, he judges, 'a lovely idea' but, as Lotus had discovered, with a powerful Formula 1 engine it was hard work for the driver to change gear, requiring too much strength and effort, and gears had a habit of popping out as well. So, as it was impracticable to eliminate dog rings, he began to think how to reduce their size. Thus was born something that most people have never heard of but nevertheless brought significant change in the way gearboxes are made — and a good example of the sort of innovation that seemed obvious only after it had been done. Barnard called his idea the 'inside-out dog ring'.

A standard dog ring is a steel ring about 14mm thick carrying six 4mm teeth, known as dogs, positioned on the face of the ring rather than the outer circumference. As the selector fork pushes the dog ring into place, the tapered dogs slide and lock into the corresponding teeth on the face of the adjacent gear. Together, the gears and dog rings in a six-speed racing gearbox had a width of about 168mm — just over 6½ inches.

John reduced this width by 18–20mm and in doing so was able to make the gearbox casing smaller: 'It doesn't sound a lot, but everything is useful.' He achieved this by increasing the circumference of the dog ring and putting the dogs on the inside circumference rather than on the face — 'inside' rather than 'outside'. When pushed by the selector fork, the dog ring would slip over the teeth on the face of the gear cog, the dogs on the inside of the dog ring meshing with the teeth and effectively wrapping them in a band of steel, eliminating the width of the dog teeth; he was also able to reduce the number of dogs from six to three. This all served to make the dog ring's grip stronger, much in the way that grasping a tube around the outside is more secure than trying to grip it on the inside, while also increasing the inherent strength of the dog ring and making for quicker gear changes.

More to the point, it was neater, cleverer, more perfect. Diane Holl, who joined John in his new offices at home, drew up the idea up and admits: 'It would never have occurred to me.' She became part of domestic life at Combe Rise, working long hours there with occasional interruptions: 'Michael, John's young son, used to creep in when I was working at the drawing board, throw a rope over me and start tying me to the chair, reassuring me that "Daddy won't mind."'

From time to time John would entertain an approach from people who were well aware that he was a major talent at a loose end. In mid-1991 he met up with James Hunt and Anthony 'Bubbles' Horsley, former team manager of Hesketh Racing, for a pub lunch. They were looking to raise funding for a new team, talking about 'big money from Boeing'. After several more pub meetings and much laughter — 'that's what happened when you went out for a drink with James and Bubbles' — the scheme died.

Towards the end of the family's French holiday, John having recovered from his pneumonia, he took a call from someone he absolutely had not been expecting to hear from. It was Ron Dennis.

'I'm looking to develop carbon-fibre commercially,' said Ron, 'and I'm talking to Courtaulds. I thought you might be interested in getting involved. I'll send you some bumf.'

Ron's way of 'sending bumf' was to fly into Dinard airport in the company jet to drop off a box of papers before taking off immediately to some other exotic business destination. Says John, 'It was a serious proposal and I looked at it all very carefully. But the more I read, the more I realised that he didn't want a technical director, he wanted a business manager. So I called him and said, "Sorry, Ron, but this isn't me."'

Not long afterwards and back at home, John received another call, this time from Glenn Waters, a former Team Lotus mechanic who, in the early 1980s, founded Intersport, a team that raced in Formula 2 and Formula 3. In 1987 Waters had struck a canny deal to create a European arm for Tokyo-based Tachi Oiwa Motor Sport, more usually known as TOM'S, a race car tuning business with close contacts within the upper echelons of Toyota.

When he called Barnard, Waters had just finished setting up TOM'S GB Ltd in Hingham, Norfolk, not far from Lotus, and Toyota's Le Mans cars were being prepared there. Waters told John that Toyota was seriously considering a move into Formula 1 with its own car — would John like to design and build it?

It all sounded rather marvellous so Barnard visited the new factory and deemed it 'a decent set-up, with no F1 capability, but plans for a clean room and a composites facility'. The level of Toyota investment was evident and further encouragement was provided by the fact that the operation was now called TOM'S Toyota.

All the signs were propitious: an out-of-the-blue approach that would be thoroughly funded by a massive corporation. He could start from scratch, something he loved to do. And, the biggest relief, he could create 'a non-political team of people who weren't bringing a load of baggage with them'.

Barnard gave Waters the cost estimates, they agreed a preliminary deal and the project got underway, with Waters apparently assuring him that there was enough slack in the existing budget to start improving the facility straight away. Soon Barnard was on the phone to some of his trusted people, mainly still at Benetton and Ferrari. He called materials expert Andy Smith, aerodynamicist Mark Handford, designer Kevin Taylor, long-time McLaren man Leo Wybrott, composites expert Peter Brown and machine-shop manager Graham Saunders. Soon his team were assembling in temporary digs near the Norfolk factory.

Barnard and Waters flew to Tokyo to discuss budgets with Toyota executives. As John recalls, 'It was a typical Japanese meeting, in which we were always outnumbered five to one. There must have been ten TOM'S and Toyota people sitting around this long board-room table, with just us two representing the British operation.' Barnard told Toyota that the budget to build a successful team was likely to be around £20 million, on the basis that Benetton had cost £14 million and that was to upgrade an existing team rather than establish an entirely new one. There was general nodding around the table.

Back in Norfolk, Barnard's crew got busy equipping a clean room, arranging the installation of an autoclave and putting in five-axis milling machines. John went house-hunting with the intention of buying a weekday place nearby, a dormitory house — 'I had no plans to move the family to Norfolk just yet.'

Now John and Diane Holl were making the four-hour trip to Hingham every week, Diane driving them up in Barnard's 'hundred grand' Mercedes on the Monday and him driving them back on the Friday 'like the gentleman he was' when both were exhausted. She relates that driving the expensive Merc made her nervous: 'I had a big struggle getting it into first gear and I used to land up crunching it in. In the end he'd wait for me to press the clutch pedal and then reach across and put in into first gear himself! It used to make me laugh.'

One task for Diane was to plan and equip the drawing office, designing for each person a partitioned bay containing a drawing board, a CAD computer and a ten-foot table with storage drawers below and a sloping lay-out top for drawings, all built by Bob Sparshott. It wasn't good enough for Barnard: the lay-out tables ran the length of each bay but left a gap of an inch to the partition wall at either end — and he complained.

'You saw the drawings!' was Diane's confident response, a victory made a little sweeter when she discovered that he had ordered one of the lay-out tops for his office at Combe Rise and it had turned out to be two feet too long. 'At least it wasn't two inches too short,' she told him, brightly. Diane was finding ways of coping with the perfectionist.

Back at Combe Rise he asked her in passing if she might help brighten the office by hanging some framed photos of his time at Lola, Parnelli, Chaparral, McLaren and Ferrari. When he had gone, the full horror of the task dawned on her: 'There was no way on earth I was going to get that right!' Taking the bull by the horns, she hammered in nails at random — different heights, varying distances apart — and had all the pictures on the walls within ten minutes. Shortly after John walked in and 'did a double-take'.

'Oh,' he said, 'you've put the pictures up.'

Diane, busying herself with a drawing, didn't look up, but answered enthusiastically, 'Yeah! Artistic, eh?'

'Um, yeah', was his doubtful reply as he scanned the higgledy-piggledy arrangement, his mind busy with how he would have measured each picture in relation to its neighbours, the floor and the ceiling — all of which, he concedes, 'might have been too regimental'. He never changed Diane's arrangement.

In the spring of 1992 it all went wrong with the Toyota project. John was on a second visit to Japan, rocketing towards Mount Fuji on the Bullet Train for an appointment at a Toyota executive's luxurious holiday home halfway up the mountain. During the meeting it began to dawn on John that the figures he had quoted were causing alarm at Toyota and no one was going to commit the £20 million needed to enter Formula 1 in winning style. 'I just wasn't getting answers from these guys and started to believe they weren't really on board; no one round the table seemed prepared to stick their necks out for the project. We needed the men at the very top to get behind the decision, and they weren't there.'

He was faced with pushing ahead 'on a shoestring' on an off-chance, hoping against hope that Tokyo might change its mind. But Barnard had never been a man for shoestrings in Formula 1 and he wasn't going to start now.

He flew home with a heavy heart and gathered his team to tell them the bad news. He said, 'I'm sorry, I don't think this is going to happen. We're going to have to wind this all up and I'm afraid you guys will all need to find work elsewhere.'

Fortunately none of them had made a permanent move to Norfolk and all would have little trouble finding new employers, but the situation was nevertheless disheartening for John: 'I felt responsible. I had told people this could work. I think everyone was aware it was risky, but that didn't make much difference to how it made me feel, and I didn't feel good about it.'

Toyota did eventually enter Formula 1 with its own team ten years later, in 2002, basing itself in Cologne, Germany. John's view of that effort chimes with other criticisms at the time: 'They jumped in at the wrong place and with the wrong people, whose expertise seemed mainly in spending big budgets. What we had asked for a few years before was peanuts compared to what they ended up spending.' And all for a meagre outcome: after nine dismal seasons without a single race victory Toyota withdrew from Formula 1.

Diane, who continued to work with Barnard at Combe Rise, has this conclusion: 'Toyota cocked it up: if they had gone with John, they would have been Formula 1 World Champions without a shadow of a doubt.'

And so it came to pass, in the summer of 1992, that Barnard spoke on the phone to Niki Lauda, who was now working as a consultant to Ferrari. Diane recalls that John had been reluctant to take calls from him: 'Niki used to phone quite a lot and I'd whisper, "John, it's Niki Lauda!" and he'd say, "Oh, tell him I'm out!"' When they did finally speak, Lauda made it clear that Ferrari was very keen to have John back on board, but that they would need him to base himself in Maranello. John replied that it was worth continuing the conversation.

As Diane recalls, 'He toyed with the idea of commuting to Maranello each week in a private jet, flying out on the Monday to be back on the Friday. I remember him asking me, "What do you think, Diane? Could I persuade my designers to do that?"' She was doubtful, especially after the TOM'S Toyota débâcle. 'John, you'll get the ones who are single, but that's it. And you yourself will do it for a month, get fed up and it'll all be over. You just won't want to do it.' John thought about it and conceded she was right.

But the lure of Ferrari is powerful bait indeed. Could it happen again? Could John face again the switch-blade, switch-back chicanery of Maranello? Could Ferrari have swallowed sufficient pride to take on *Il Mago* once more? It turned out that they both could — if only because no one else was currently knocking on John's door, and, as Diane rightly divined, they needed him.

PART 7
FERRARI (2)

CHAPTER 29
PURE GENIUS
1992–94

Mid-July in 2015 and Maranello is wincing beneath the ringing hammer of an Italian summer sun, the road its melting anvil, the temperature 38°C in the shade. The Ferrari T-shirts and Ferrari caps stroll slowly along its leafy pavements, stopping only to admire the roar of another Ferrari engine, turning to drink in its sleek red curves and envy the driver, proud as Berlusconi at the wheel.

Then the still air is shaken by an even greater roar: for the entertainment of well-heeled clients, the Scuderia is running Michael Schumacher's 2000 championship-winning Ferrari around the Fiorano test track a short walk away. Ears cocked, people sweat their way up Viale Alfredo Dino Ferrari, a road without shade, to Via Marsala. There, holes torn in the netted high fencing at its dead end afford brief glimpses of the iconic machine ripping through the gears as it screams and stutters around the southern hairpin.

Maranello is a living shrine to Enzo Ferrari. Almost every street and roundabout is adorned with icons at which the *Tifosi* may worship: statues of Enzo, images of the Prancing Horse, roads named after the Scuderia's international heroes, flags, road signs, shops, buildings, sculptures, pictures in the gravel. Even the baby store, Brum Brum Bimbo, features an infant, complete with dummy pacifier in his mouth, sitting in a Ferrari Formula 1 car beside a script that boasts *Tutto per il neonato e per la mamma* — everything for the newborn and for mum. The pushchairs and the pillows are, of course, in Ferrari red, for they start the *Tifosi* young in Maranello.

When they are old enough to walk, *piccolo Tifosi* are taken for their first visit to the Museo Ferrari. Those going there in 2015 and 2016 walked into a foyer dominated by a wall-mounted row of wind-tunnel models, most of which were designed by John Barnard between 1986 and 1997.

The theme of this exhibition is 'Genius and Secrets' but the only man of the eight celebrated design heroes of the Scuderia who is described unequivocally as a genius is Barnard himself, to whom a room on the first floor is entirely dedicated. Here is *Semplicemente Geniale*, helpfully translated for visiting foreigners into 'Pure Genius'. Barnard talks to the crowds from a video screen that is set, somewhat incongruously given his complete disinterest in youth culture, within a giant Nintendo Game Boy, which also, as the supporting legend suggests, 'ushered in a whole new era' in the same year, 1989. The subject of his discourse is the tricky tale of the semi-automatic gearbox, its conception, development and eventual ubiquitous success. Beneath him and to his left is Nigel Mansell's Ferrari 640, the one in which he so memorably won the Brazilian Grand Prix. Its revolutionary gear-shifting paddles — flat plates with a kink for the fingertips on each side of the steering column — are almost invisible behind the wheel.

On the other side of the room is a display explaining the modern Formula 1 steering wheel, upon which is mounted all the controls that were previously on the race car's dashboard. It is, of course, an obvious idea, the natural progression from the paddle shift, which, strangely enough, somehow failed to occur to the paddock's brilliant engineering minds until, in 1995, it popped into Barnard's. Such is the case with so many of his inventions: they're blindingly obvious after he has come up with them, so obvious that most people have forgotten where they came from.

The display demonstrates the complexity of the modern race car steering wheel. Without taking your hands off it, you can change gear, alter the fuel mix, deploy DRS (Drag Reduction System), check the pressure and temperature of the tyres, set up the brake and accelerator pedals for wet, dry or intermediate conditions, engage the 'pit limiter' that stops you speeding in the pit lane, make changes to the differential for different parts of a corner, speak to the pit crew via radio, change the clutch bite point and, among an array of other settings, even take a drink through a tube in your helmet.

As the awed audience study this massive graphic, they can hear the conclusion to Barnard's five-minute video: 'So now you ask what's been passed from Formula 1 to the road car? Well, not too many things spring to mind, but one of them is the paddle-shift gearbox, which is becoming standard on road cars. When I'm driving my road car and I'm using the paddles on the steering wheel, I think, "Yeah, I think I started this revolution."'

Museum director Antonio Ghini, who was Ferrari's head of communications in 1992, explains the reversal of fortunes at that time that prompted Ferrari to swallow its pride and ask Barnard back:

'At the end of 1991, Luca Cordero di Montezemolo arrived. The company was in trouble with its road-car production. The Testarossa was an old model, too old for the new requirements of the market. The Ferrari 348 was a difficult car but it proved to be the basis of the 355, which was a big jump forward.

'When Montezemolo arrived here he took a brilliant decision. The 1991 season had been disastrous for Ferrari in Formula 1, but, instead of concentrating his activity there, Montezemolo decided to focus instead on the road cars, saying, "If I make good road cars, then I will make enough money to relaunch Formula 1." So he concentrated on the 355, the 550 Maranello, and other cars that all delivered a world-wide message that Ferrari was producing cars that clients wanted.'

The son of an Italian aristocrat, Montezemolo started his professional life as a racing driver before joining Fiat and moving to Ferrari in 1973, where he worked as Enzo Ferrari's assistant before taking over the management of the Formula 1 team. He duly brought glory to Maranello by overseeing the two World Championships won by Niki Lauda in 1975 and 1977. Returning to Fiat, he rose through the ranks until, in November 1991, he was appointed to the Ferrari Presidency by Fiat supremo Gianni Agnelli.

In June 1992 John was still mulling over the idea of rejoining Ferrari. By the end of the month, Niki Lauda persuaded him to speak to the new Formula 1 team manager, engineer Claudio Lombardi, a conversation that largely consisted of John telling Lombardi what he wanted. Lombardi was acquiescent but insistent that John come out and meet his boss, and so, within days, Barnard was on a plane to Milan to see Montezemolo.

The meeting at Fiat's HQ was short and sweet, unfolding along these lines, with Montezemolo making the opening gambit, telling Barnard that the arrangement couldn't work if it were to be along the lines of the previous engagement. 'I'm not coming back if I can't be based in England,' was Barnard's line in the sand.

Montezemolo told him he understood, that both Lombardi and Lauda had told him that Barnard wouldn't move to Maranello, but that, equally, they didn't consider it possible for him to run Ferrari Formula 1's technical operation from Godalming. Montezemolo then made a proposal, that Dr

Harvey Postlethwaite, who was back at Ferrari, could run the Maranello operation including the car he was building for 1993, while Barnard could concentrate on a car for the 1994 season in Godalming. Postlethwaite would be technical director in Maranello, Barnard in England. Postlethwaite would not have authority over Barnard, and vice versa.

To Barnard this sounded manageable. He had already learned that it was impossible to control Maranello from Godalming. If Harvey was running the Italian end, then that was fine by him, as long as there was more cooperation and no more 'secret cars'.

Talk then turned to a new facility in Godalming. GTO still existed and was still run by Ferrari, but it was coming up to a five-year break in the lease and Ferrari intended to sell it to McLaren. Ron Dennis wanted to use it to build his famous 'F1', a three-seat supercar conceived by Gordon Murray and the first road car to have a carbon-fibre monocoque. Selling GTO to McLaren made no sense at all to John, who said: 'Do not do a deal with McLaren. They're your competitors, both on the track and now in road cars.' John predicted, with remarkable accuracy, that road cars would distract Ron and make winning in Formula 1 far harder. 'Why make Ron Dennis's life easier? And anyway, you need it for yourselves! I need it!'

Barnard argued that building a new facility could delay the production of a competitive race car: 'Why sell an existing state-of-the-art facility; how does it make sense to build a new factory from scratch?' Montezemolo nodded, but the gesture was non-committal; no doubt other considerations were holding sway. The meeting ended on good terms, with Montezemolo giving John a batch of Teenage Mutant Ninja Turtle videos, much to the surprise and delight of Barnard's son, Michael — apparently Luca had made an investment in the franchise.

The next meeting was in London, at the Berkeley Hotel in Knightsbridge on 13 July. In Barnard's files, there is a fax addressed to Niki Lauda confirming details of the meeting and asking him to inform a fictional 'Mr. Jones' about the rendezvous with 'Mr. Lombardi, Mr. Postlethwaite and Mr. Montezemolo'. Barnard, knowing Ferrari to be as leaky as a sieve, had insisted his name was not to be used.

Barnard's first problem was meeting the man who had previously tried to build a rival car at Ferrari and he confesses to having had 'some bad feelings' when he first saw Harvey Postlethwaite. Watching the tension rise, Montezemolo said: 'You two need to get on together if this is going to work. I think it would be a good idea if you went into another room and talked about it.' They did so, closing the door behind them. John said, 'Well, Harvey, what do you think? Can we work together?' Harvey replied that he was prepared to give it a go if John was. They both agreed that the money was good, that they'd keep themselves to themselves, not interfere in each other's work, and cooperate as and when needed.

John didn't trust Harvey, but, a little older and wiser now, he thought the deal could actually work if both showed some willing. Barnard wanted it to work: he still had unfinished business at Ferrari and plans for his next iteration of the perfect car were already bubbling up in his head. They came out of the room together, smiling. Montezemolo allowed himself a sigh of relief and the deal was passed into the hands of lawyers.

As is the way with all things Ferrari, and despite the 'Mr. Jones' red herring, the news leaked out, much to Barnard's irritation: 'It felt like I was stepping back into the Ferrari-style political mire.'

Just two days after the meeting *The Times* ran a story by journalist Norman Howell entitled 'Ferrari court Barnard', declaring that 'Ferrari is on the verge of agreeing terms with John Barnard, the designer who fathered the all-winning McLaren in the late 1980s. Sources at Fiat, Ferrari's parent company, have confirmed that Barnard met secretly with Luca di Montezemolo, Ferrari's president, who was in England for the British Grand Prix.'

Barnard duly penned an irritable fax to Lauda written entirely in capitals with the article attached: 'NIKI, I THOUGHT YOU WOULD BE INTERESTED IN THIS ARTICLE — IT SHOWS THE PROBLEMS WE FACE TRYING TO KEEP A SECRET AT FERRARI.' Not the best of starts, then.

The key to the Postlethwaite/Barnard plan was Montezemolo himself. Unlike the ailing Enzo back in 1988, Montezemolo was able to keep an active eye on the two Ferrari operations, ensuring that he got the best from both. Montezemolo duly told Barnard that the deal with McLaren had advanced as predicted, that GTO was sold and that there was no getting it back, so it was up to John to find a new facility in which to build a factory for making the new car.

This new facility was to be called Ferrari Design and Development (FDD) and Barnard found the ideal location for it — next door to the old GTO. And so it was that Team Barnard began to assemble once more in Godalming, in Northfield House, girding its loins for a second stint at Ferrari. This time it was going to be different. This time they had learned the lessons of the past. And this time they had a British ally in Maranello in the form of Dr Harvey

Postlethwaite. Surely the days of Ferrari chicanery were over? Surely those lessons had been learned on both sides of the border?

So what had been occurring at Ferrari in Barnard's absence? At first things had gone well on the track, with Alain Prost winning five races in 1990 with Barnard's 641 and narrowly losing the World Championship to Ayrton Senna, but the following year brought a severe slump and Prost, winless with the 642 and 643 designs, was fired before the end of the season for his public criticism of the team.

On the design front, Steve Nichols had followed Prost from McLaren, arriving in late 1989, and two years later Jean-Claude Migeot, like Postlethwaite, had returned from Tyrrell. Together, Nichols and Migeot created for the 1992 season a most unusual and potentially revolutionary car, the double-floored F92A, which was designed to channel air between the sidepod and the floor. Aerodynamicist Nicolò Petrucci reports that the F92A was one of the most aerodynamically efficient cars ever measured in the Ferrari wind tunnel and showed 'even higher values' on the test track.

However, the performance of the F92A in 1992 fell woefully short of Patrick Head's Williams-Renault FW14B with its pioneering active suspension. Nigel Mansell won eight of the first ten races and secured the World Championship at the 11th, in mid-August, with five races still to go. Ferrari's best results, meanwhile, were two third places for Jean Alesi. This disaster led to a big clear-out of personnel in the drawing office and chassis department, including Nichols and Migeot.

Barnard wasn't impressed by the double-floor concept. He observed that the car was 'super sensitive to ride height', a factor that could in theory be corrected by active suspension but not at Ferrari because they still hadn't mastered the technology in Maranello.

At the insistence of Montezemolo and much to Barnard's suspicious irritation, four young Italian design engineers were exported to Godalming. Tiziano Battistini, Angelo Camerini, Cristiano Altan and the aforementioned Nicolò Petrucci were awed by Barnard's reputation but delighted to have the opportunity, as Petrucci confirms: 'We were to work closely with John and learn as much as possible from him. I will always be grateful to Mr Montezemolo and Ferrari to have had the chance of such a marvellous life experience both personally and professionally.' Doubtless part of Montezemolo's motive was to ensure that if the relationship with John went wrong, there would be something substantial to show for it at the end.

For his part, Barnard at first had no time for them whatsoever: 'I just considered them spies and really rather ignored them.'

Camerini recalls Barnard's attitude on his first day in Godalming: 'I turned up at the Shalford office and sat there for a whole day before JB ever came along and said hello. It wasn't surprising; I'd heard about his character.' There was also a moment of nervous embarrassment: 'I didn't make a great first impression. He called me into his office and asked me to sit down, but my knee struck the leg of his table and sloshed his tea all over his drawing. He said, "Well, if you don't do worse than that, it's not too bad a start." He's probably forgotten it, but I never will.'

Battistini had a similar experience and learned pretty much immediately that John considered him a Montezemolo plant. He remembers John calling him into his office and telling him, 'If you're here because you want to work with us, fine, but if you're here just to see what we're doing so you can report to someone in Maranello, then this is the wrong place for you. Either you're with me or you're not.'

The Italian quartet learned quickly that talking among themselves in their native tongue was a no-no. Petrucci: 'It became clear that John thought we were speaking in Italian to keep secrets from him. So we decided to only speak Italian outside work.'

There were other difficulties. By now computer design systems were well-established in Formula 1 but the British CAD system used in Godalming was different from the Italian version they were used to. Camerini remembers telling Barnard he didn't understand the British CAD. 'He had no sympathy! "What's the problem?" If you can't use it, there's a drawing board right here!" So I went out of the office, picked up some paper and got on with it.' Times had changed: drawing boards were being consigned to the dustbin of history, but to Barnard they were babies being thrown out with the bathwater and he liked to insist that his designers used them to get a sense of real scale. As Battistini says, 'It was the first time I had used a pencil for professional design work. I think it was a bit of a test — would we call Maranello and complain?'

Each of the Italians had to prove his spurs. Camerini recalls his breakthrough moment: 'I remember after a couple of months I found myself alone in the drawing office when a supplier called saying there was a problem with a suspension part designed in Shalford that they were trying to make — it was too long. The person who designed the part wasn't there. I had a flight that evening so I was short of time, but quickly decided to draw the modification myself. When John heard about that, I think he really appreciated it. It was probably the first time I had really impressed him, shown him that I was committed to the team. After that his attitude started to change: he realised we were there to work, to help, to build a Formula 1 car and not to spy!'

Cristiano Altan recalls two key moments when he stood up to the Great Barnard. The first was a tentative and polite confrontation that ended in an openness to criticism that few associate with John: 'In the beginning I didn't know him, and didn't know what he wanted. I remember him telling me once to do a detail on the steering rack one way, but I had another idea. So I said to him, 'Look, John, I think it would be better this way!" He became angry, his face was red! I quickly understood that I hadn't made the right approach.

'So, quietly and in parallel, I also developed my own solution. Every morning when he came in, he went through the drawing office, table by table, to see the improvements each designer had made on the drawings from the day before. So he came to me, asking, "How are we doing on the steering rack?" I said, "Okay, John, you asked me for this", and I showed him the design he wanted. I watched him carefully before I said, "Okay, there is also this", and showed him my solution. He took the paper and went off with it. I thought, "I've made a mistake doing that and now he is angry." But he came back, smiling and said, "Carry on with your idea."'

The second confrontation almost turned into a resignation on the spot: 'In early 1993 JB told me to make a cardanic junction for the steering wheel [the joint where the steering column changes angle]. I decided to use smaller bearings because there wasn't much load. At the time the engineer George Ryton was visiting FDD and he and John came to my table late in the afternoon. John asked me what I had done and I showed him. John said, "Bullshit, Cristiano, you should use a bigger bearing!"

'I said, "No, look John, the forces are very small. The joint will become too big — and it's unnecessary weight. The small bearing is fine." He then said something that I didn't understand because my English wasn't up to it. George Ryton started laughing. I said, "May I laugh too? Can you explain?" Well, what he said was offensive. "Okay John," I said, "if this is your approach to me, then it's not going to work. I will return to Italy because I'm not here to be offended." He turned red. And then he said, "Cristiano, I'm sorry, it's just a joke." I replied, "You may think it's a joke, but please don't call me that again."'

And then came a moment that Cristiano will never forget, one that stands as powerful testament to Barnard's better side: 'He went out with George Ryton, and I guess he discussed it with him. Then he came back and said to me in front of the whole drawing office, "Look, I need to say sorry again to you, because, in the end, you were right." It's not easy to find such a guy. He realised he'd made a mistake and admitted it, not just to me, but to everyone, which he didn't have to do.'

The Italians also well remember his seething hatred of interference from Maranello. Battistini: 'Top people from Maranello visited in a sort of procession to see how the project was going. They were asking questions, because they knew nothing about what was really happening there. JB was always on edge then and hated them coming, worried they would try to interfere.'

As time passed, Barnard began to recognise the talent and worth of the four Italians. They began to blossom, and to see the advantage of a contrasting way of working. Barnard: 'You can't keep a good engineer down and soon they were getting involved in the design and build. And it brought a change in them. Before, they were utterly Ferrari-ised. They were highly political, careful of what they said, endeavouring to gauge the political lie of the land. But when they discovered that the politics in Godalming were small beer and that if you worked hard, you didn't have to watch your back, that sniping and point-scoring weren't appreciated at all, they began to appreciate their new-found freedom to design without political comeback.'

It was gradually dawning on the young Italians how the relatively politics-free world of British Formula 1 operations helped to bring rewards. Says Barnard, 'They began to see why British design teams were so successful. There was no manoeuvring — everything was played off a straight bat. Italians don't play cricket — perhaps they should.'

Now the Italians felt 'like family'. Barnard now had no real concern that they would learn his methods; now it was exactly what he wanted. Once he came to trust them, he did everything he could to fulfil Montezemolo's desire for them to learn as much as possible, as Petrucci explains: 'I learned two things from John. One was attention to detail and the other was innovation. Working with him was one big push for innovation. He wanted something new from you all the time you were there. He was always pushing everyone to come up with new solutions, better solutions. Having worked with this Master, I still find myself pushing for innovation, practical solutions that you can make on the car.'

While beavering away on the car for the 1994 season, John was doing what he could at Montezemolo's request to help improve the 1993 car, the 644 Bis, which was Postlethwaite's creation, fitted with active suspension.

'Trying to integrate active suspension was extremely hard,' says John. 'It was hopeless trying to catch up with Williams and the others. The trouble with active suspension was that you were always at the mercy of the software writers.' He never found himself in a position to master it, describing his efforts at Ferrari to get a grip on it as like 'being in a haystack throwing hay over my shoulder looking for a needle'.

A few years later, in *Motor Sport* magazine, Barnard became eloquent about the frustrations of the 1993 season, describing it as 'one of the most difficult I have ever had, complicated by the need to develop an active suspension system just before such systems were banned. But in the back of my mind, I'm just passing through that season, like a train on the way to the terminus. I'm looking out of the window, if you like, and it's all going past in a blur. I can't do anything. I can't stop the train and get off at that particular station, because I don't want to be at that station, I want to be at the end of the line'[96]. The end of the line, of course, was the new car he had been commissioned to build.

It shouldn't have been so difficult to develop active suspension because Ferrari had had the opportunity to be ahead of the curve with it, as Nicolò Petrucci explains: 'They were working on this at Ferrari in 1989. But at some stage the project was stopped because someone up high decided there wasn't enough advantage.'

Petrucci grew to despair of the way senior Ferrari bosses with limited technical knowledge still insisted on calling the shots: 'If the technical director takes a decision after full and fair discussion and approval from all his assistants, there is no reason not to do it, if it is possible to do it. It shouldn't be the case that someone who isn't part of the technical group, but who is in upper management, can take a decision not to make an innovation because they fear it won't work. John's experience with the paddle-shift gearbox proves the point.'

There are always two reasons for not doing something innovative. They are the reasons that have so often prevented both glorious achievement and terrible mistakes. They are money and fear of failure. The trouble at Ferrari was that the culture of covering backsides suppressed innovation, so the wrong people landed up making the wrong decisions for the wrong reasons.

---

[96] Henry, Alan, 'No More Excuses', Motor Sport, February 1997, p110.

By now, John found himself harried once more by the full force of Ferrari politics. Montezemolo had appointed Frenchman Jean Todt, a former rally co-driver, to the post of sporting director. Barnard never warmed to him.

'I suppose he was okay, good at his job, but he could be so self-important. He surrounded himself with a little entourage — a driver, a "gofer", among others. He definitely played the part of "I am Mr Big".' Pompous Frenchmen had always made Barnard seethe, ever since FISA's Jean-Marie Balestre pronounced against ground-effect to mollify Ferrari, causing him no end of grief and pain at McLaren.

On 19 August 1993, Barnard received a stiff fax from Todt, copied to Montezemolo, declaring, amid various complaints, 'If I have been properly informed, one of the fundamental reasons and objectives of your being hired by Ferrari last summer was to produce a very short-term and radical improvement of the poor results that were being achieved at the time.' This observation followed: 'It cannot be ignored that none of these objectives have been met: to the contrary, notwithstanding huge financial and other efforts, no new competitive car is available yet and the current results are worse than those of one year ago.'

John replied that, indeed, Todt hadn't been properly informed, that his involvement was not a 'a quick fix but a long-term plan to achieve good design with proper schedules which allowed for serious development before being raced.' Barnard pointed out that Ferrari hadn't helped by selling GTO, a move that in itself had caused unnecessary delay. He added that Maranello had then tried to get him to commit to producing his first car much sooner than agreed, by the San Marino Grand Prix at Imola in April 1993.

Then he explained how events conspired to slow him down because he had been forced to take over the 1993 car, the 644 Bis, a remodelled version of the F92A of 1992, from Postlethwaite and Ryton, leading to 'the inevitable delay of an all-new car'. He explained to Todt that the 644 Bis was meant to feature fully active suspension, something that required massive effort but seemed pretty pointless given that a ban on the technology was expected for the 1994 season. He stated that he had proposed alternatives that were rejected as being too expensive, that the resulting compromises made for poor results, that he didn't have a magic wand.

Todt was limited in his power here. He knew he couldn't sack the best designer in Formula 1 without making everything even worse. Barnard, Montezemolo and Todt met in Maranello on Monday 23 August and some level of peace was re-established. Perhaps the sacrificial lamb — there always had to be one — was Postlethwaite because he was out within weeks of the meeting.

Postlethwaite died of a heart attack in 1999 aged only 55. As quoted in an obituary by his friend Roger Horton, he said of his second stint at Ferrari: "I was beginning to find the whole thing a little too cumbersome for my taste. I'd had some good times with Ferrari, especially when the old man was alive, but by the end I had too many memories of sitting in planning meetings with some 40 other people, all talking, all getting nowhere."[97]

Postlethwaite's departure created for John an immense headache. He recalls a somewhat panicked call from Montezemolo just ahead of the Italian Grand Prix: 'What are we going to do for the next race, John? You've got to help more with the current car!' Barnard agreed, but it was problematic: the terms of his contract didn't give him the level of power he had enjoyed in his previous spell with Ferrari and this, as he euphemistically puts it, 'created problems'.

'From that moment on I was floored,' he says, 'I was thinking, "Christ, here we go, we're back where we were, except I don't have the power I had."'

Ferrari's results in 1993 were pretty much as dismal as they had been the previous year. The technologically sophisticated Williams-Renaults sailed on almost as serenely as before, now with Alain Prost and Damon Hill aboard instead of Nigel Mansell and Riccardo Patrese. Prost became World Champion and they took ten victories, seven for Prost and three for Hill, while the only man in the same league was Ayrton Senna, whose McLaren, now Ford-powered, won five times. The season's other winner was Michael Schumacher for Benetton. As for Ferrari, their best result was Jean Alesi's second place at Monza — the race following Montezemolo's request to Barnard for more help — and a pair of third places earlier in the season, one each for Alesi and Gerhard Berger. There were 16 retirements in 32 starts.

Ask anyone, and they will tell you that among the most beautiful machines ever made is Britain's iconic fighter aircraft, the Spitfire. No surprise then to learn that it inspired what Barnard considers his own most beautiful creation, the Ferrari 645 (or, as Maranello would have it, the 412T).

At home one evening John was reading an old book on aerodynamics and happened upon a description of the work done by Supermarine on the development of the Spitfire's trade-mark cooler — which Airfix model-makers

---

[97] Horton, Roger, 'Farewell to a Friend, April 1999, atlasf1.autosport.com/99/apr21/horton.html.

may remember as a fiddly pod that had to be glued to the underside of the starboard (right-hand) wing. The principle was ingenious. Cool air would rush into the relatively small 'letterbox' opening of the radiator pod. Once inside, the air would be instantly energised by radiator heat, expanding rapidly as the duct widened and reducing in density as it went through the radiator core. Ever more energised, it would stream out of the back of the pod pretty much at the same speed it had entered the front. In effect this meant that there was no system drag — zero drag is the Holy Grail for aerodynamicists.

Barnard began to think how it might be applied to a car, how he might create interior architecture for the sidepod that allowed the air to exit at the same speed it came in. He would need bigger radiators to get more air through reasonably quickly, and that would mean bigger sidepods. Calculations told him that the increase in drag around the outside of the pod created by bigger radiators would be compensated by internal drag of almost zero.

In the end he decided to make the radiator system asymmetrical, with the water radiator in one sidepod twice the size of the one in the opposite sidepod, leaving room there for a smaller radiator to cool the engine oil. This asymmetric design would cause severe problems later on, but not because of any mistake on Barnard's part.

He briefed a new recruit, aerodynamicist Dominic Smith, to work on the concept using test rigs at the MIRA (Motor Industry Research Association) facility in Nuneaton, Warwickshire: 'By cycling hot water through the radiator system and blowing air through a representative sidepod, we could measure the effectiveness of the radiator and the effective drag of the system. Once the car went on track it appeared to have good top speed. Of course all the engine people said this was because the engine had more power than others, but I knew it was also due to the fact that it was a very slippery car.'

Barnard designed the entire car around this concept and the result was undoubtedly gorgeous from just about every angle. With a high nose like a bright red missile warhead, its fluid lines gave the illusion that, in profile, the car was ovoid, tapered at both ends, an illusion prompted by the arched curvature of the top of the sidepod.

Just forward of the driver and in the upper part of the front of each sidepod, the 645's distinctive radiator air intakes looked like the openings of torpedo tubes, reminiscent of the nostril-shaped ducts in the bow of *Stingray*, the vessel in the 1960s children's TV series of that name. Behind the driver's helmet a high, gently concave airbox resolved itself into a long, falling rearward arc with all lines flowing aft in sculpted sweeps to form a tight aerodynamic package around the engine. One Italian writer described it as 'a pebble washed by the sea'.

The 10 February 1994 edition of *Autosport* devoted the front cover and eight pages to the car under the headline 'One from the Heart'[98], referring, of course, to Barnard's passion for beauty. 'The stunning new Ferrari 412T1 has to be the one that puts the most famous marque of all back among the Grand Prix elite,' crooned James Allen and the writing team. 'This John Barnard-designed car, unveiled at Maranello last week, must restore the tattered pride of Italian motor racing and bring the *Tifosi* flooding back to Monza and Imola.' Contrasting the 'bucking broncos' of the Ferraris produced in the Barnard interregnum to the engineer's 'prancing horses', the piece looked forward with hope: 'Should the old adage "if it looks right, it is right" hold true, the beautiful 412T1 will quickly transform Ferrari back into winners… Indeed, the 412T1 is the automobile as art.'

Barnard's cutting of this *Autosport* article holds another surprise — it has been annotated by his children in black ballpoint. A picture of Montezemolo is adorned with fangs, Christopher Lee sideburns, Frankenstein stitches across his forehead, and spiky eye make-up reminiscent of Christiane Kubrick's work for *A Clockwork Orange*. There's even a caption: 'Wanted — Dead or Alive — reward £10,000,000.' In the text Montezemolo's and Todt's names are scribbled out, while those of Barnard, Alesi and Berger are underlined.

One can imagine the scene. At home Dad was venting to Mum about 'bloody Montezemolo' and that 'toad Todt' while young Michael sat in silence over his breakfast, absently doodling on a magazine that happened to be lying open. There was trouble brewing at Ferrari and the Barnards are nothing if not ferociously loyal.

How do you hold the front wheels on a race car? By suspension arms running out from the chassis to support the upright, which has a central bearing on which the wheel hub runs. How do you fix the suspension arms to the upright? This had always been done with ball joints, spherical bearings sitting in cup-like fixings, allowing movement in any direction. How do you fix the suspension arms to the chassis? Same system… until Barnard decided there was considerable room for improvement.

---

[98] Allen, James, 'The Ferrari Renaissance' Autosport, 10 February 1994.

The idea arose during 1993 after conversation with Berger, who told Barnard that towards the end of a race he could feel the front ball joints beginning to 'clap out'. John was sceptical at first, but when Berger reiterated his observation, insisting that in the second half of a race he could feel extra play through the steering wheel, the engineer examined one of the ball joints. He found that it was undamaged, its hard plastic liner in perfect condition. So when Gerhard complained yet again after the next race, John 'did an Eric' and went home to think about it. Sitting in his armchair one evening, it dawned upon him that the plastic liner might gradually heat up with the prolonged loads sustained during a race. Could it distort and then reshape itself?

The plastic of choice for the liners was Teflon, as used for non-stick frying pans. A vital property of Teflon is its ability, with heat, to expand at the same rate as adjoining metal and then similarly contract when cooled. So, thought Barnard, it was quite possible that the heat generated by the spherical bearing twisting and turning inside the liner might soften the Teflon and even cause it to squish and spread under load, which would certainly make the joint looser.

Barnard concluded that Berger was right — so what to do? His solution was brilliant, game-changing and very simple. He applied it, in the first instance, to the lower wishbone arms, which come in from the bottom of the front uprights and all but meet in the middle beneath the chassis, where they were normally connected with the spherical joints. John was playing with one of the joints in the drawing office when he turned to Diane Holl, who takes up the story: 'This was classic John. Looking at a spherical bearing with all these motions, he said, "Why don't we just do a flexure?" "What do you mean?" "Well, it only has to move up and down at bit. It doesn't need all this freedom."'

Diane could see he had a point. The wishbone only really needed to move up and down where it attached to the chassis; any forward and back movement could be handled by the ball joints out on the uprights. And as the wheels only moved up and down by 50mm, when that movement was translated down the length of the wishbone the angle change was just a few degrees — 'not very much at all'.

'So I just dumped the ball joint,' explains Barnard. 'I could make the end of the steel wishbone into a thin, flat plate, about 3–4mm thick, and bolt that flattened section straight to the chassis.' The wheels would move up and down, flexing the flattened end for ever more, provided, of course, that the elastic limit of the material wasn't exceeded. Thus was born one of Barnard's many unsung inventions — the suspension flexure.

Everything about the idea was better. Now he could dispense with the large carbon inserts in the chassis used to support the spherical bearings. Instead, all he needed were two smaller inserts containing screw threads to receive the bolt holding the two overlapping flexures in place under the chassis. It was the sort of simplicity that John loved.

Others didn't see it as simple at all. Diane Holl admits, 'Even now I would hesitate to do it, because it is so complex. But John wasn't fazed by complexity, especially if it created a solution.' Its complexity arose from the choice and methods of manipulating the materials and from working out how to make the steel plate resist the continual flexing under high load. To John this was straightforward, a question of picking a material that he intuitively knew would be strong enough and then doing the stress calculations.

He explained to Diane: 'If the wishbone is x long with y load in z axis, then the material must be capable of... Just draw one up and we'll try it, and test it.' She looked doubtful: 'Oh, you can do it; just draw it like this' — and he did a quick sketch on her pad. Still Diane was confused, so Barnard added: 'Well, it's only got to go up and down a bit, Diane.' 'What about fatigue?' 'Oh, we'll be under the fatigue curve, don't worry about that. It's only physics.'

Diane was, once more, amazed: 'He always had this confidence when stepping off in a new direction, a confidence that so few designers have.' Even now she keeps the first Formula 1 flexure ever made at home, in Charlotte, North Carolina.

Mike Coughlan, who rejoined Barnard after a short spell as Tyrrell's chief designer, also remembers the invention of flexures, crediting it in part to a 'What If' day: 'Every Saturday morning John would come in and devote his time to way-out stuff. We wouldn't concentrate on specific problems with a car; instead it was a time for fundamentals, for vision, for considering the next step rather than the detailed grind of getting work out. Flexures came out of discussions with clever people whom he had employed. He generated the mindset that produced the ideas. And John was always more relaxed on Saturday mornings.'

Coughlan thinks that the flexure concept had its roots in the making of the wind-tunnel model for the 645, specifically the need to reduce friction between the wheels, supported from the outside on stalks, and the chassis: 'We ended up grinding rod ends to reduce the friction, and one day they broke, so John said, "This is ridiculous — what do we want here?" So we drew something with tiny little blades. That transformed the wind-tunnel model.'

ABOVE Back at Ferrari for a second term, John Barnard shows the way ahead to Fiat supremo Gianni Agnelli (left) and aristocratic new Ferrari boss Luca Cordero di Montezemolo. *Walter Iscra* **BELOW** Dr Harvey Postlethwaite, team manager Claudio Lombardi and John Barnard at the Fiorano test track in Maranello for the launch of the 1993 644 Bis. *Walter Iscra*

ABOVE At the races during 1993 Barnard had the devil's own trouble trying to integrate active suspension into Postlethwaite's 644 Bis; Gerhard Berger patiently waits for the action to start. *Courtesy of John Barnard*
BELOW Enjoying a joke with Alain Prost, with Jean Todt, newly arrived at Ferrari as sporting director, in affectionate mood. *Sutton Images*

ABOVE The Fiorano launch of Barnard's 645 — the car that he considers his most beautiful — with Gerhard Berger (left), Jean Alesi (in cockpit) and test driver Nicola Larini (right). *Courtesy of John Barnard*

BELOW The 645's machined titanium gearbox case, precursor to the successful carbon/titanium set-up used the following year. *Courtesy of John Barnard*

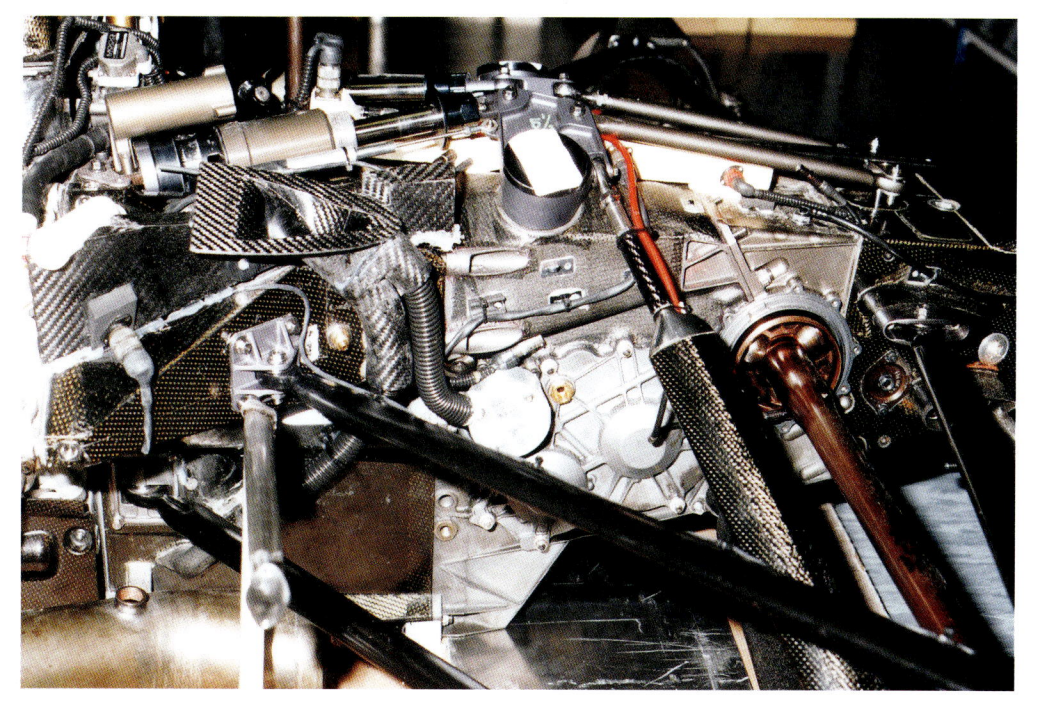

ABOVE John caught in a beaming smile outside the Ferrari motorhome early in 1994. Come May, things got a lot worse: just three weeks after the tragedies of Imola, where Roland Ratzenberger and Ayrton Senna were killed, the Barnard family suffered a traumatic, violent burglary while at home one evening. The experience had a particularly deep impact on John and daughter Jennifer. *Courtesy of John Barnard*

ABOVE An early wind-tunnel model run at Filton, Bristol, a facility set up by Barnard, shows one of the 1994 645's distinctive intakes for its Spitfire-inspired 'zero-drag' cooling; extra outlet slots are also being tested. *Courtesy of John Barnard*
BELOW Those intakes are visible on the finished 645, seen at Imola in 1994 in the hands of second-placed Nicola Larini. *LAT Images*

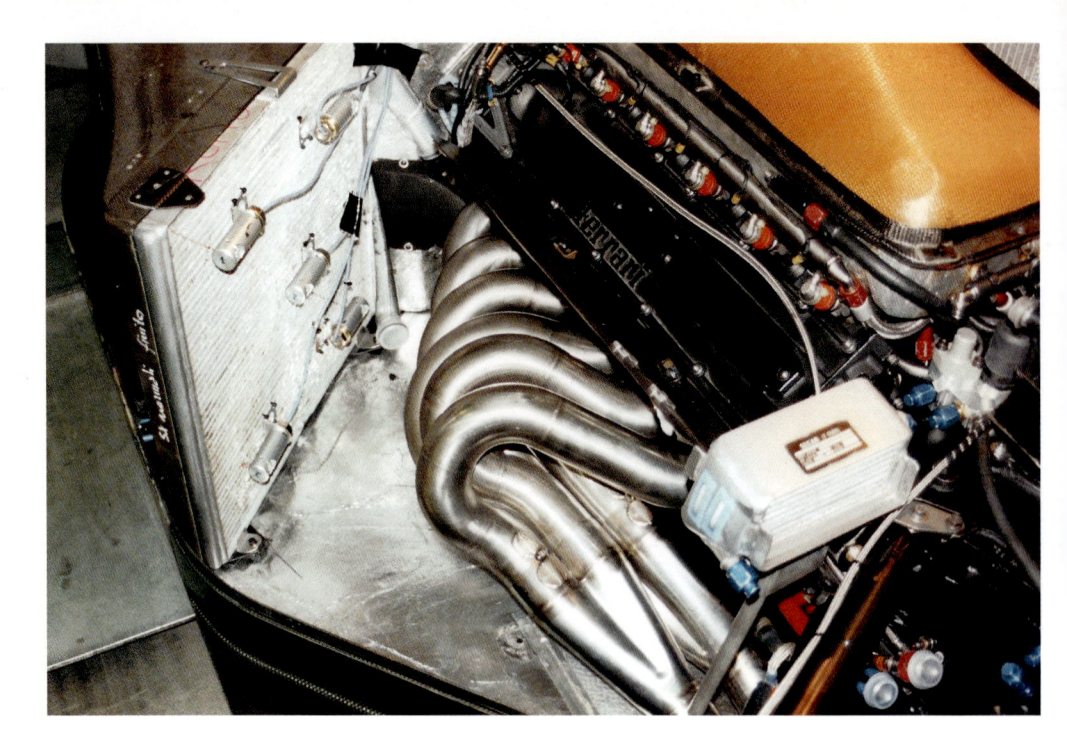

ABOVE Full-size cooling tests of the 645 in Ferrari's road car wind tunnel in Maranello; in due course Barnard's innovative and beautiful asymmetric radiator and ducting system was discarded but wrongly so because the engine department had failed to measure coolant flow correctly. *Courtesy of John Barnard* **BELOW** Berger winning the 1994 German Grand Prix, complete with Gustav Brunner's bargeboards. *LAT Images*

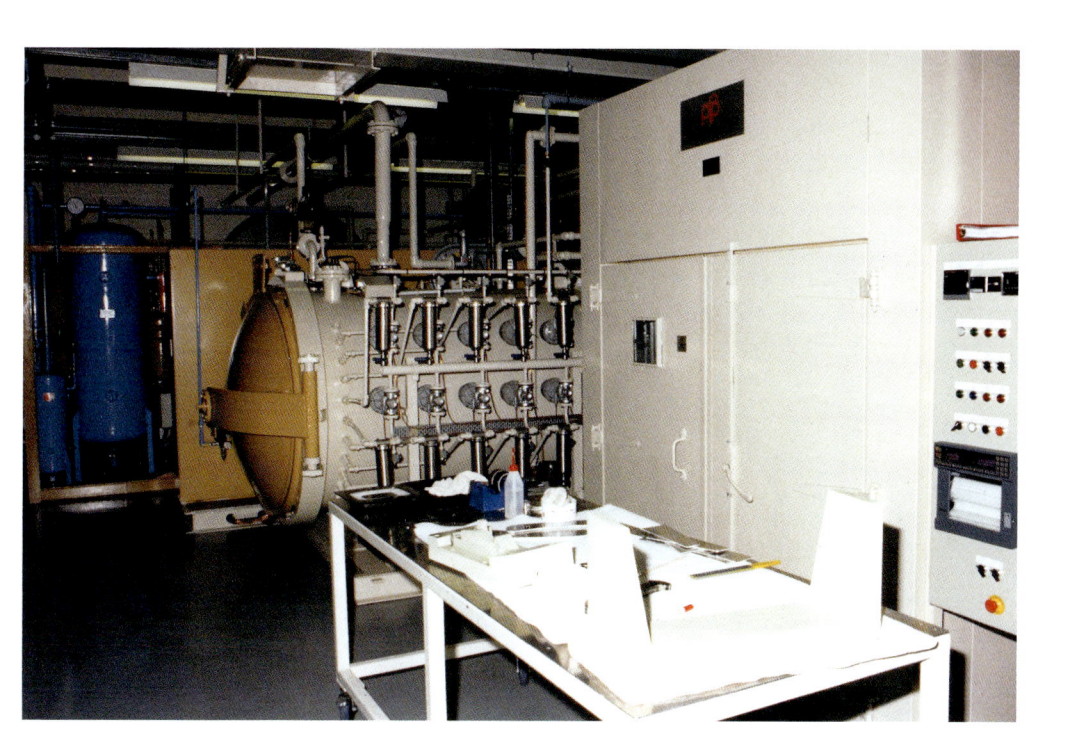

ABOVE Just as with GTO, Barnard based himself and his team in Godalming for his second Ferrari stint, the operation being named Ferrari Design and Development (FDD); this view of the facility shows the autoclave. *Courtesy of John Barnard*

BELOW Typical of the sophisticated carbon-fibre components turned out by FDD in the mid-1990s is this oil tank and gearbox spacer. *Courtesy of John Barnard*

ABOVE A wind-tunnel model of the 646 at Filton in early 1995, showing the car's completely altered sidepod design. *Courtesy of John Barnard*
BELOW Jean Alesi riding to victory in the 646 at the 1995 Canadian Grand Prix in Montréal. It was the last Formula 1 win for a V12 engine, and, as such, the end of a much-loved era. *LAT Images*

Barnard was delighted with the clean simplicity of the new suspension connection to the chassis: 'So now my chassis is dead clean underneath. I've got no ball joints, no bits and pieces, I've got no play here at all, none. Can't have any play. It's dead simple. It hadn't been done on any other vehicle to my knowledge.'

Flexures soon spread throughout Formula 1, but not before they had encountered massive political resistance at Ferrari. Barnard soon changed the material from steel to titanium, riveting the titanium flexure to the steel wishbone. Then it occurred to him, in 1995, to have carbon-fibre wishbones and have the flexures in carbon too. He believes he was the first to opt for carbon-fibre wishbones.

Another innovation on the 645 spread through Formula 1 more slowly, largely because of its complexity. To accommodate the tight aerodynamic packaging around the V12 engine, Barnard decided to bring the gearbox forward to improve weight distribution.

'With a race car,' he explains, 'it's critical to get the weight distribution right so that the tyres work with their correct loadings. And it's always better to put the heavy bits within the wheelbase of the car.'

Seeking to reduce gearbox length, he created a transverse gearbox like the one he had developed at Parnelli, but this time it included his paddle-shift semi-automatic technology and the space-saving inside-out dog rings that he had developed in 1991. But the big step forward was the material he used for the gearbox casing.

The primary function of any gearbox casing is to provide solid support for the gear shafts, so that the gears will mesh and run accurately at every gear change, without fail. This means the casings have to be strong, and strong usually means heavy. Together with the engine oil tank and the bellhousing that contains the clutch, these units typically weighed around 50kg. By making components from magnesium, as was the wont of racing gearbox engineers, the weight could be reduced to around 27kg, but magnesium is weaker than steel and liable to fatigue at high temperatures and under racing loads, resulting in cracks.

Barnard thought hard about building the gearbox casing in carbon-fibre but quickly realised that the technology wasn't yet up to making it strong enough. So, for the start of the season, he plumped for a cannily milled steel casing that weighed a similar amount to a magnesium version but was stronger. All the while in his mind were the next steps: to make the gearbox casing out of titanium, and then, eventually, carbon.

The transverse titanium gearbox, made at FDD, went into the cars halfway through 1994, and for the 1995 car was bolted into a CFRP (carbon fibre/reinforced polymer) bellhousing/oil tank unit to which fixings were attached to support the rear suspension, creating 'an immediate 40% weight reduction'.[99]

Titanium is hard to work, requiring welding in an atmosphere of argon gas and, preferably, the use of expensive milling machines blessed with Computer Numerical Control (CNC). It needed all the collective skill of Team Barnard at FDD to make it possible. With each welded section having to cool between each step, the titanium gearbox was slow to build compared with a magnesium casting. Says John, 'They had to make their own argon-welding chambers to do this job and it was extremely tricky. They were very proud when they got the system to work.'

The advantages brought by all this monumental effort were significant. Titanium is lighter and stronger and much less liable to distort under high temperatures and loads. This meant that gears could be made more finely, resulting in more accurate meshing and more reliable gear changes — the gearbox would therefore be more durable even in extreme racing conditions.

John, now far ahead of his competitors in gearbox design, had it in mind to create a fully carbon-fibre gearbox, but that breakthrough would have to wait a while.

He also leaped a year ahead of the rules by creating a CFRP rear impact crash structure. In his words: 'The same basic arrangement has been in use at Ferrari ever since 1998 — CFRP bellhousing, titanium fabricated gearbox case, CFRP rear case and impact structure — but in a longitudinal layout.'

The 645 also featured another hallmark of Barnard's genius — beautifully crafted titanium uprights with a suspension system largely made of titanium too. 'I wasn't the first to run titanium suspension,' he says, 'but I was the first to run it successfully.'

Fresh thinking didn't always go according to plan. Gerhard Berger was put into a sticky situation when Barnard tried to improve the procedure for moulding a seat to the driver's body. The established method was to pour liquid foam into a large plastic bag placed in the cockpit. The driver climbed in, made himself

---

[99] Wright, Peter, 'John Barnard on Gearbox Case Design', grandprix.com, 2 September 2001.

comfortable and stayed there until the foam hardened. But the process too often resulted in a wrinkled finish that needed to be smoothed out.

In a moment of inspiration, John decided to reverse the process and ensure a smoother fit by putting a plastic liner into the seatless cockpit and then spraying the liner with a releasing agent. The crew then dressed the victim, Gerhard Berger, in a bin bag, poured the liquid foam and put him in the car.

Coughlan takes up the tale: 'The guy preparing the liquid foam mixed up too much. As it expanded it went everywhere, even into Gerhard's freshly trimmed hair. Of course, he wanted to climb out but John told him to say where he was until it set. The problem was that the chemicals were getting hotter.' This all took place late one evening and poor Berger was stuck there, sitting in the middle of an increasingly hot bubble bath that had gone completely out of control. It took two hours for the foam to set sufficiently to cut him out. As Berger stated, 'John was always bringing new ideas into the game. Most of them worked, but not all of them. Some were crazy.'

'It was brilliant fun,' says Coughlan, who still laughs at the memory. 'If the correct amount had been prepared it might have worked a treat. As it was, Gerhard had a burned arse and a ruined haircut. He was not a happy bunny.' The experiment was never repeated. As Coughlan concludes, 'It was a classic example where JB's lateral thinking backfired because someone made a simple mistake.'

Happy bunnies would be in short supply as 1994 progressed, a year that would turn out to be terrible for Formula 1 and for the Barnard family as well.

CHAPTER 30
DEATH AND DAYLIGHT ROBBERY
1994

And so to the races. Jean Alesi scored a creditable third place for Ferrari at the opening race of 1994, the Brazilian Grand Prix at Interlagos, while Gerhard Berger dropped out with engine trouble. A week later Alesi smashed his back in a testing accident at Mugello and was sidelined for some months. He was replaced by test driver Nicola Larini, who managed seventh to Berger's fifth at the Pacific Grand Prix in Japan on 17 April. That was followed at Imola on 1 May by a most impressive second in the San Marino Grand Prix, a home race for Ferrari, but Berger retired again with engine problems.

Not that it mattered. Nothing in Formula 1 mattered any more, because the race at Imola was shattered by the most appalling double tragedy.

The omens had been bad. Rubens Barrichello had been very lucky to escape with just superficial injuries when he lost control just before the pit entrance during Friday practice, his Jordan taking off, landing on its nose and rolling.

The following day, Saturday qualifying, was worse by several orders of magnitude. Austrian novice driver Roland Ratzenberger came off the track in the new Simtek car at 180mph after taking the notorious *Tamburello* left-hander, the one that had so nearly killed Gerhard Berger in Barnard's Ferrari five years before. Still alive, Ratzenberger was taken to Imola's medical centre and then helicoptered to hospital in Bologna, where he succumbed to massive head injuries.

On Sunday, Ayrton Senna, visibly affected by Ratzenberger's death and full of foreboding, went off at the same spot. He was killed instantly by the impact, probably by a piece of his Williams-Renault FW16's front suspension that struck his helmet and penetrated it. With photos seemingly showing his steering wheel subsequently lying by the side of the car still attached to a length of shaft, rumours began to circulate that the steering column had failed, that responsibility lay not with Senna but instead with Frank Williams, Patrick Head, Adrian Newey and the design and manufacturing team at Williams.

The Italian authorities impounded both Ratzenberger's and Senna's cars, and within days notices were served on Imola track boss Frederico Bendinelli, plus representatives of Williams, Simtek and Bell helmets — they were told that they might be investigated 'on suspicion of culpable homicide'.[100]

The impact of Senna's death on John Barnard was profound: 'I remember going quite cold. It brought back the horror of the Berger accident a few years before.' When he realised that Senna was dead he recalls feeling, 'Oh boy — this is the end of the line we are on. Something big is going to change now. It was a bit like watching 9/11, the aircraft flying into the towers. You thought, "This is going to change the world."'

The nightmare had come true and his long-time friend, Patrick Head, was going through it. Perhaps the greatest driver who had ever sat behind a wheel had been killed and more and more people were saying it was a cataclysmic mechanical failure, the fault of the people who designed and built the car.

John and Patrick have never really talked about the incident. All John will say on the tragedy is this: 'It must have affected Patrick. Whether he took responsibility, took the blame for it personally, I don't know. He has never said so to me. There have been lots of theories about what happened and I still don't know. Hand on heart, I still can't say it was this or it was that.'

Nor can Patrick, who said in an interview for this book: 'After the weekend, we investigated all the data, but never fully understood what had caused the accident. There was a civil court case in which I represented Williams; it started with many being accused, but ultimately I was the senior technical person at Williams. It was a very difficult time for everyone, and not one that I care to think about much. It is a great regret that any driver should be killed in one of our cars, and I am sure that this responsibility also weighed on John's shoulders. John always designed solid cars.'

As widely expected, the immediate impact was a flurry of rule changes. As Barnard says, 'These big flat-floor cars had to be run low. Perhaps the most likely theory was that during a yellow flag, they all slowed down, the tyre temperatures dropped, the tyre pressures dropped and the cars were even

---

[100] Henry, Alan, 'The mystery behind Senna's accident', Autocourse 1994–95, p127.

closer to the ground. So, it was thought, when Senna took *Tamburello*, the car bottomed out and he lost his steering.'

An emergency meeting of the Formula 1 Technical Working Group was called, Barnard being one of a number of technical directors and chief designers in attendance. Around the table with FIA representative Charlie Whiting, they made a rapid analysis and proposed changes.

The first consequence was two immediate changes to come into force for the next race: the diffuser at the rear was chopped off to reduce downforce, thereby making the car ride a little higher, and holes were required in the airbox to bring down top-end speed. Many more changes followed in short order: to increase ride height, front-wing endplates were raised and the size of the front wing was reduced, both measures lowering overall downforce by about 15%; in addition the minimum weight of the car went up by 25kg, higher cockpit sides were required to provide more protection for the driver's head, and crash barriers were improved.

And, *Tamburello*, the corner that previously couldn't be tamed because a river ran by it, was changed. In a flash of the blindingly obvious, it suddenly occurred to someone that the installation of a chicane before the turn would stop cars approaching it at such high speed. Where there's a will, there's a way.

So, of course, people who a few days before Senna's accident had been perfectly happy with the deadly excitement provided by *Tamburello* were now running around like headless chickens claiming that they had seen the solution all along, and, as always happens, a scapegoat was sought. The Italian authorities decided it couldn't be the most obvious culprit, the Italian track owners who had refused to redesign a dangerous corner. Therefore the Englishman must be investigated.

It was so much rabbit-in-the-headlight nonsense and hypocrisy. Since Barnard had arrived and driven all the construction standards into the stratosphere, designers were less and less tempted to cut corners with sub-prime materials, so fatal accidents were proportionally rarer. Four people died in Formula 1 in the first decade of the carbon car, the last, Elio De Angelis, in 1986. The pre-carbon 1970s brought 12 deaths, the 1960s 14. Every effort to improve safety had to be made; it seemed daft to hound one top designer for what may or may not have been an error committed by one of his team.

But hounded Head was, by press and Italian legal process, with the whole affair coming to trial in 1997. The result was acquittals all round but a retrial was ordered in which the Italian Supreme Court of Cassation delivered Verdict

Number 15050, which declared that 'the cause of the accident was due to the failure of the steering column, that this had been caused by the changes badly designed and badly performed, such that erroneous changes were traced to wrongful conduct, commissive and omission [by] Head, and that the event was predictable and avoidable.'[101]

It was a matter of some relief for Patrick Head that this verdict came 13 years after the accident, which meant the declaration that he was, in effect, guilty of manslaughter/culpable homicide fell outside the Italian Statute of Limitations which was in this case seven years and six months.

It's worth noting that designer Adrian Newey, who had been working for Head at the time, is convinced that the steering column, which had been rebuilt after Senna had complained about the steering wheel's position, had nothing to do with the crash. In 2011 he told *The Guardian*: 'The honest truth is that no one will ever know exactly what happened. There's no doubt the steering column failed and the big question was whether it failed in the accident or did it cause the accident? It had fatigue cracks and would have failed at some point. There is no question that its design was very poor. However, all the evidence suggests the car did not go off the track as a result of steering column failure.'[102]

The evidence he refers to is camera footage from Michael Schumacher's car that shows the rear of Senna's Williams stepping out, possibly because of low tyre pressure or a puncture.

May 1994, then, began horrendously. Who would have thought it could have ended up even worse for John Barnard?

Tuesday evening at Combe Rise on 24 May 1994 found Rosie Barnard in the kitchen with Gillian, aged 13, helping her with Latin revision. It was around 8pm and Rosie was just beginning the nightly debate about bedtime. John was in the adjoining sitting room off the kitchen dozing in an armchair. Jennifer, 15, was upstairs in her bedroom studying for her French GCSE. Michael, eight years old, was asleep in his bedroom.

Suddenly a group of men wearing stocking masks and dark blue shell suits burst into the kitchen, carrying fence posts and metal swing-ball poles they had found in the garden. One grabbed Rosie around the face and pulled her off her

---

[101] *'Senna, Head Responsabile'*, La Gazzetta Dello Sport, *13 April 2007.*
[102] *'Ayrton Senna's death "changed me physically", says Adrian Newey'* The Guardian, *16 May 2011.*

stool, causing her nose to bleed. Another took hold of Gillian and a third went into the sitting room to confront the dozing John.

John sleepily noticed a masked head appear round the door and thought it was one of the children messing about. Before he could put two and two together, the attacker, a short man, was at the back of his armchair with a metal pole across his throat, pulling it backwards. John got his fingers underneath the pole, pulling it away from his neck as he stood up. He bent forwards in an effort to throw the assailant over his head, but then a taller man, who seemed to be the gang's leader, hit him over the head with a fence post. John raised his hands to protect himself only to have them repeatedly hit. He feared that his knuckles might be damaged permanently.

Out in the kitchen Rosie and Gillian could hear the struggle and his daughter shouted out, 'Don't fight them, Dad! Do what they say.' Soon the blows ceased.

In the meantime another burglar had gone upstairs to Jennifer's room. As he entered, her reaction was similar to her father's, thinking it was someone messing around. He grabbed her from behind, pulled her from her chair with his hand over her mouth and dragged her backwards down the stairs to the kitchen. The first thing she saw was her mother bent over a pool of blood, which scared her, but it was no more than one of the nosebleeds to which her mother was prone. Jennifer then saw her father, a bruise evident on his chin.

The family border collies, Jess and Bracken, started barking loudly from their refuge under the kitchen table. Gillian was told to shut them away.

Now the burglars started shouting at John to take them to his safe. This was problematic: the Barnards had a safe but never used it and John didn't know where the key was. He took them to the study at the other end of the house and hunted in vain for the key. One of the men returned to the kitchen to make Rosie go through a bag of keys but this was fruitless too.

John told the burglars there was cash and jewellery in the bedroom, so they took him back to the kitchen. There the leader forced Rosie to kneel and take off her engagement ring, a blue sapphire surrounded by diamonds. Then she was taken upstairs to find the rest of her jewellery, one of the two escorts poking her with a metal pole as they went. While they loaded up their pockets, she said, 'Please keep your voices down, my son's asleep in the other room.' Complying with this instruction, they asked her for cash and she gave them all she had — £60.

Concerned that this didn't seem enough, she then remembered John's collection of expensive watches that he had been given over the years, a solid gold Ebel chronometer among them, and showed the intruders where they were. 'I don't think John has forgiven me for that, but at the time I just thought, "Take what you can and leave us alone. I don't care about this stuff!" I just didn't want them to do anything horrible to the girls.'

Apparently satisfied, the burglars took her back downstairs to the kitchen where John, Rosie, Jennifer and Gillian were made to kneel with their hands behind them so they could be tied up, with garden twine and cord found in a shed. The phone was ripped out and the family were bundled into the cupboard under the stairs. Soon everything was quiet. John wanted to get out straight away and contact the police, but the girls insisted they all stayed longer to be sure the men had gone.

Happily, no one had been badly hurt — John refused medical attention — and the value of the stolen jewellery and watches amounted to about £30,000.

'The worst part of the burglary,' recalls Jennifer, 'was when they took Dad or Mum off somewhere and we didn't know where they had gone or what was happening to them.' For John and Rosie, the fear, of course, was the other way round.

The main item on the front page of the *Surrey Advertiser* the following Friday was headlined 'Burglars tie up family in night robbery', playing fast and loose with what was, in fact, daylight robbery.

To this day John fumes about the ghastly experience that he and his family were put through: 'It was very, very nasty. If I had had a gun, I would have shot them. I wouldn't have thought twice about it. If I knew who they were I would probably go and shoot them now.'

Much of his lasting fury is down to the effect the burglary had on Jennifer. Her pressing problem that evening was her French GCSE the following day. Kept up all night by anxiety, police and forensics, she was in no state to do the exam and her father told her she didn't need to. That elicited the expected response: 'No, I must do it.'

She scored an A*, as she did in all her GCSEs, such was her perfectionist, obsessive character. She is so much her father's daughter. But it's a character trait that can have a downside, as she readily admits, and the incident caught her at a very sensitive age.

'For some reason,' she says, 'I associated the fear and trauma of the burglary with food, so I would have panic attacks and flashbacks when I was trying to eat.' Perhaps this was related to the fact that most of the horror took place in the kitchen. Whatever the reason, she stopped eating and quickly went downhill towards full-blown anorexia. 'I was in such a strange place, very isolated and very afraid. I went through a phase of being extremely close to Mum where I was almost her shadow and wouldn't want any communication with Dad. But then there was a time when I was close to Dad.

'I wasn't thinking of other people really. In that state you're so cut off and isolated from everything going on around you, too cut off to consider how they were dealing with it. I was taken over by the thing and I didn't have a rational point of view. I would flip from one extreme to the other.

'I shut a lot of people out and I think I shut family out. We'd never been an overly emotional family in terms of talking about stuff. There was never any doubt that we all loved each other but it wasn't done through a verbal process, it was done through actions and being there.

'I probably needed to find a way to talk about things that arose from the burglary but I didn't know how to and also didn't want to. The shock had been too great to deal with. I had been terrorised in my own home and I lost trust in everyone. I lived in survival mode for quite some time. I shut everyone out of my life.'

To date, John Barnard's life had been all about two things that amounted, really, to one thing: building the perfect race car in order to create the perfect home for the family he so loved to be with.

Now the goal of all his missions was sullied because the impact of Jennifer's illness was enormous.

'She was already a difficult teenager,' says Rosie, 'but this was the straw that broke the camel's back. We were very worried. She wouldn't even see her brother or sister. It was awful — angry exchanges, pleading exchanges, tearful exchanges. We tried every emotion in the book to talk to her about it. It's a very strange thing — it's more talked about now than it was then.'

Gillian, two years younger, found it difficult too: 'It was pretty all-encompassing and really very difficult to live with. As a girl at that age, a lot of comparison stuff goes on, and part of the illness meant that Jenny was always trying to feed everyone around her. She'd get very distressed if I didn't eat. It was terribly stressful all the time. Food and meals are such a big part of family life. Every time we had a meal there was a fight or an argument.

'She would come home, go out for an hour's run and only eat a few beans for supper. She got very ill and very thin. It was horrendous, like living with a skeleton. She just wasn't on the same wavelength as us. When we went out, people would be horrified by how she looked. It impacted everything.'

Within a few years the dogs died, Jess first. Gillian recalls the dam bursting when Bracken also went: 'Dad and Michael dug Bracken's grave next to Jess's in the woods at the back of our land and Dad carried Bracken's body over to bury her. He was in tears to see her go as she was such a big character and part of the family. It was one of the very few times any of us has seen tears from Dad. He's definitely a big softie really. He's like a porcupine — prickly on the outside but soft on the inside.'

The show must go on. After Senna's death Formula 1 duly rolled into Monaco like a funeral cortège, mourning the undisputed king of Monte Carlo. Journalist Alan Henry wrote: 'Mechanics worked in near-silence as they prepared the cars, their familiar chatter reduced to a subdued whisper. The sense of trauma and loss was still very much to the forefront of their minds.'[103]

Gerhard Berger drove his Ferrari 645 into third place behind Michael Schumacher's winning Benetton and Martin Brundle's McLaren, but the overwhelming feeling attending the chequered flag was, as Henry put it, 'one of unbridled relief that F1 had got through the race free from another serious accident' — although Karl Wendlinger had been badly injured during practice.

Barnard's 645 was also lacklustre, experiencing major cooling problems. Maranello's engine department immediately blamed the radical inlet design on the sidepods, believing what might work for Spitfires in a dogfight doesn't necessarily work for Formula 1 cars on a race track. Barnard asked Dominic Smith to check and recheck the calculations, getting him to retest using the hot-test rigs at MIRA, but he couldn't find any fault, and nor could the radiator manufacturer when asked to verify the calculations. It was a mystery — but something was wrong somewhere.

Luca di Montezemolo and Jean Todt began to panic. Now the full force of the Maranello blame culture came into play as the Ferrari top brass demanded a head on a platter. Barnard's radical new sidepod didn't work and that, of course, was ultimately his fault, but it would cost too much and be too disruptive to sack him. Someone else would have to take the fall.

'Who's responsible?' asked Montezemolo, in one of a series of stressful phone calls. John, to his eternal shame and lasting regret, found himself pointing to the young engineer on his team who knew most about the calculations behind the design of the cooling system and the airflow through the sidepods: 'In

---

[103] Henry, Alan, 'Monaco Grand Prix', Autocourse 1994–95, pp131–32.

the end I decided to fire Dominic, assuming his calculations were at fault.' It was the first and only time in Barnard's career that he sacked an employee at someone else's bidding.

Montezemolo and Todt were calling for major changes to the car. Every instinct in Barnard's body told him they were wrong, but he couldn't convince them — and he had no evidence to back up his instincts. They, on the other hand, had plenty of evidence, all drawn from the results sheets.

Sensing Barnard's reluctance, Todt briefed someone else to come up with solutions. This was Gustav Brunner, whom Todt, much to Barnard's dismay, had brought back into the Scuderia just a few months earlier. In due course Brunner changed the front wing, reduced the length of the sidepods, replaced the radiators and made the inlets bigger.

Following a growing Formula 1 fashion at the time, Brunner also introduced aerodynamic barge boards behind the front wheels, not unlike the turning vanes Alan Jenkins had come up with at McLaren to improve airflow around the front wheels. Barge boards were still such a new concept that they were described in *Autosport* as 'two-piece aerodynamic deflectors'.[104]

John found himself having to support the changes: 'Todt was talking to Brunner, who was saying we should do this and we should do that. Todt effectively made the decision that it was going to happen. I said, "Fine, okay, I understand we have to do something. Let's do that." So, if you like, I endorsed it, but I wouldn't say I was behind what was happening.'

Brunner's work on the 645 yielded a shocking result, as Barnard discovered later, and far too late: 'When they started modifying the sidepods to run the turning vanes, they had to revise the radiator set-up. In doing this the engine people took the trouble to put it on the engine dynamometer and measure the water flows. It turned out that they had never originally balanced the flow of the hot water going from the engine to the radiators. The car had been overheating because two thirds of the water was going through the small radiator with the oil cooler next to it and just one third through the big radiator. We had been trying to cool it with one third of the required radiator area.'

For want of a nail the shoe was lost. In Barnard's opinion all the pain could have been avoided had the Ferrari engine department done their job and checked the flows in the first place: 'Then they would have discovered all they needed was a little restrictor in the pipe going to the small radiator, which

---

[104] Henry, Alan, 'French Grand Prix', *Autocourse 1994–95*, p149.

would have automatically forced most of the water to the larger radiator. But they just hadn't looked at it. Can't have looked at it.'

Like so much of what happened in John's career, he still boils at the memory: 'I started wondering if it was done on purpose to screw me over. The 645 didn't get the respect it deserved, and, to my lasting regret, Dominic paid the price. Those bloody engine people again — they screwed us royally.'

Had John's zero-drag theory been sound? The unjustly sacked Dominic Smith, who went on to a fine career in motorsport, has no doubt that the theory was sound. As he stated in an interview for this book, 'Several years later I was fortunate to be able to use the experience with an Indy 500 winning car that featured a similar inlet, this time without problems.' How did he feel at the time of his sacking? 'I felt very let down.' But there was a silver lining that he expresses politely and nobly: 'The experience I gained in the two years I worked for JB helped develop not only my engineering skills but also how I deal with young inexperienced engineers as we pass on our experience to the next generation. I am very grateful for the opportunity he gave me.'

Barnard winces when he recalls his decision to make a scapegoat of Smith: 'I greatly regret it. It was a terrible thing to do considering, as it turned out, that it wasn't Dominic's fault.'

Should he have spotted the problem behind the overheating? In an ideal world the answer is clearly 'yes', but working at Ferrari was no utopia. John admits that he should have personally overseen the engine department running the same water pipes on the dynamometer that they ran on the car: 'We might have been able to spot the water-flow problem. But it's like everything else; I wasn't in charge of the engine department. They didn't care, all they had to do was keep throwing the ball back to the chassis people saying there's not enough cooling, it's running too hot.'

The situation wasn't helped by the fact that soon after Brunner's first round of changes were made, Gerhard Berger and Jean Alesi qualified first and second for the German Grand Prix at Hockenheim, and Berger won by nearly a minute — a huge margin — after leading from start to finish. Of course, this seemed to underline the idea that Montezemolo, Todt and Brunner were right and Barnard was wrong.

Still Barnard is angry at the stupidity of the saga: 'It was all such a waste of valuable time — we'd spent half a season trying to resolve the problem. We could have concentrated on the car's performance, but instead we got lost in incompetence and politics. The thing that really guts me is that the cooling problem could have been solved with the installation of a control valve on the engine water outlet — a ten-minute job costing tuppence ha'penny. It was immensely frustrating.'

Had John had more clout in Maranello, had his father not died, had the burglary not happened, had he retained the will to fight for what he knew was a brilliant idea, had he not been plagued by his own self-doubt, had Todt and Montezemolo trusted him more, had the engine department been more willing to really try and help, then the 645 might have achieved what its beauty told John it should achieve.

It was a great car murdered by internal politics and bad decision-making.

The upper echelons failed to sufficiently respect the genius of the technical director they had appointed. Managing geniuses is never easy, but Jean Todt and Luca di Montezemolo made a complete mess of it with John Barnard.

Another management mistake, in the same season, occurred with the front suspension flexures. Montezemolo was sceptical, Brunner disliked them, and the drivers were divided — Berger liked them but Alesi didn't. In fact Alesi refused to drive a car fitted with them.

Barnard puts this down to driver psyche: 'If Alesi's going out there thinking everything that's wrong with his car is because of the flexures, a thought reinforced by the fact that the rest of the paddock weren't using them, then they're going to get the blame. But everyone uses them now.'

Alesi decided it was a good idea to complain publicly about how useless flexures were. A fax from Todt in Barnard's files dated 27 July 1994 reveals that Todt agreed that 'Jean Alesi should abstain from… divulging any technical information regarding the car' and that the 'necessary steps' had been taken to ensure it didn't happen again. The fax concludes by stating that 'it is also fundamental for Ferrari's image to present ourselves to the outside as a team which has no internal conflict and which has a unitary vision on all issues.'

For Barnard, the growing stresses within the Scuderia were making his position increasingly unworkable. The top brass at Maranello seemed to think that he had lost his touch. He had never felt so undermined. But a change was coming that had the potential to turn everything around.

CHAPTER 31
THE LAST V12
1994–95

Wind tunnels are dangerous places, a fact illustrated currently by the one at the University of Brighton. The far wall of theirs is scarred with gashes made by 10p coins dropped by students into the airstream when it's blowing at full speed, 190mph, when the wind flings them so powerfully that you wouldn't want to be in the way — which is why this party trick is usually monitored from behind a thick glass window.

John Barnard didn't encourage such play at the British Aerospace wind tunnel in Filton, Bristol, where, as 1994 unfolded, he became hands-on in developing a new type of rolling road. It was a project fraught with danger.

Until then, he had been using the Southampton wind tunnel for his Ferrari work. This could only offer 500 hours a year with a third-scale model, but Filton could provide more than twice that, 1,200 hours, and it could also take a half-scale model. But even this was only half the time enjoyed by McLaren, Benetton and Williams in their own exclusive facilities, the Benetton set-up being the one Barnard had created for them at Farnborough.

In Maranello, meanwhile, there were two tunnels, one of which could take a full-size road car but was somewhat behind the times and lacked a rolling road. Barnard duly advised Luca di Montezemolo, therefore, that Maranello should build a bespoke, state-of-the-art facility specifically designed for a full-size Formula 1 car. The result, with some Barnard input, was the striking Galleria del Vento, opened in 1997. Designed by celebrated Italian architect Renzo Piano, the building remains the centrepiece of the Scuderia.

Back in Filton, Barnard persuaded 'Bob the Builder', the man who did all the work on his houses, to help him install a three-tonne cast-iron bed for the rolling road. Barnard says of the installation process, 'This bed was suspended on a web of rigging that, had one of the pins in the pulleys gone, would have squashed us flat.'

Behind this escapade was John's solution to a fundamental problem with rolling roads in wind tunnels. When a rolling road — a giant loop like a conveyor belt — was running at high speed, low pressure under the car tended to suck the belt off its bed and play havoc with the readings. The standard solution was to perforate the bed with holes, attach tubes to the holes and run them to a vacuum pump, but there was a drawback: the high-speed struggle between suction and friction caused the model's wheels to wear a groove in the bed under the belt, leading to more friction and inaccurate readings.

Barnard's answer was to set aluminium wheels into his cast-iron bed flush with the surface and under the belt, directly beneath the model's wheels. This automatically stopped the wear in the bed, with the wheels on the bed and those on the car effectively acting like printing rollers to keep the belt taut. This also provided a means of measuring forces between the model's wheels and the belt. Says Barnard, 'We could fit load cells or strain gauges — instruments that could measure the downward pressure on the model's wheels — to the wheels set in the bed. Now we could measure any wheel lift.' It was a difficult thing to do and Barnard doubts anyone in Formula 1 had taken this route before he did.

Diane Holl recalls the effort and the dangers: 'We spent days at Filton putting in the belt and trying to get it to track properly — and we nearly set it on fire. John was there with us all the time. He did everything from negotiating the use of the tunnel to crawling underneath the rolling road and putting in bolts to hold the thing together. Nothing was beneath him. Designing, negotiating or putting nuts on bolts — JB did it all.'

The Filton tunnel should have helped Barnard's next car, the Ferrari 646, to secure a series of victories in 1995. Like everyone else, he had to design it around further measures to slow down the cars in the aftermath of the Imola tragedies. Downforce was now reduced to 60% of pre-Imola levels by reducing wing area, lowering the rear wing, and requiring cars to have a stepped underside, with a 50mm step running down the centreline for most of the car's length. Engine size was now reduced from 3.5 litres to 3.0 litres.

The 646 featured a number of advances, one of which was the redesign of the carbon-fibre composite oil tank and bellhousing in a combined unit that could take the main rear suspension loads — Barnard regards this as 'a really nice set-up'. A difficulty, however, was that oil was finding its way through the carbon into the aluminium honeycomb centre. The answer was to introduce tank sealant, a rubbery solution swilled around the inside of the tank and left to set. The threat of leaks prompted the engineer to think again about the use of honeycomb for building tanks.

As Barnard hadn't yet been told the true story behind the apparent fault with his 'Spitfire' sidepods, he decided to go for a more conventional sidepod and radiator design, but still featuring a version of the tear-duct sweep of its predecessor. At the rear there was a wider 'coke-bottle' exit and at the front the inlet was larger. The inlet was set back deep inside the aperture's top and bottom ridges, which themselves were formed by C-section carbon-fibre beams to provide much better protection in a side-impact accident. The revised treatment was carefully tuned in the Filton wind tunnel to ensure it provided sufficient cooling at all circuits.

Barnard also eschewed the high-nose format, in order to return more downforce to the front wheels, and reintroduced an earlier success, the transverse gearbox, now made from a carbon composite — 'a very neat package'.

Some writers have credited Gustav Brunner with a major hand in the design of the 646 but Barnard says that is completely wrong: 'Gustav had nothing to do with this car.'

The 646 was the last 12-cylinder Ferrari Formula 1 car. Its 3-litre V12, a wonderful example of Ferrari's genius with the configuration that Enzo always preferred, is also widely touted as the Formula 1 engine with the finest sound. It is worth hunting down and easy to find. Just Google 'The Best Sounding F1 Engine'. Or, better still, pop into the Ferrari Museum in Maranello where it is featured as a sound exhibit.

Why did the V12 have to go? The answer is that advancing technology had led to ever lighter engines made of exotic alloys, ceramics and titanium, such that a contemporary ten-cylinder engine could now could generate as much power as a V12 for less internal friction and less weight. With the banning of turbos for the 1989 season, Honda and Renault brought the first V10s into Formula 1, and by 1995 Ferrari was the only front-line team without one — although rectification of this was under way by then and accelerated by the trouble experienced that year with the V12.

Engine problems rather ruined the 1995 season for Ferrari and its drivers. Reliability was unsatisfactory and both Gerhard Berger and Jean Alesi found the V12's dramatic engine braking unnerving. As Barnard explains: 'They didn't like it in fast corners. The engine had so much internal friction that as soon as the foot came off the gas, the revs would drop like a stone. It felt like someone had yanked on the handbrake, making the back of the car suddenly feel loose to them, like they were going to skid. It made the car feel unstable.'

For all that, however, Gerhard states: 'I loved the V12. It always gave good top-end performance, but it was heavier at race starts because of the weight in the back.'

The season brought just one victory, for Berger in Canada. There were also ten other podium placings, split neatly — and a little oddly — as four second places for Alesi and six third places for Berger. In the Drivers' Championship Alesi and Berger were only fifth and sixth respectively, but their combined efforts put Ferrari third in the Constructors' Championship. Benetton's Michael Schumacher became World Champion for the second time and his team won the Constructors' title for the first time. Things were moving in the right direction, but not fast enough for Todt or Montezemolo.

There was, however, one bright ray of sunshine in 1995 when the Royal Society for the Encouragement of Arts, Manufactures and Commerce (RSA) bestowed upon Barnard the design industry's highest honour by electing him to the faculty of Royal Designers for Industry (RDI), in recognition for helping lay down 'the design guidelines for a whole generation of Grand Prix machines'.

The press release cited the 'first Indy racing ground-effect car', the Chaparral 2K, the first all-carbon-fibre chassis, radical aerodynamics and the paddle shift, or the 'electro-hydraulic shifting gearbox' as the RSA termed it. Barnard joined Williams's Patrick Head and Jaguar's Jim Randle in the faculty, and others so honoured included Sir Alec Issigonis, designer of the Mini, and Colin Chapman, both by this time deceased.

In July 1995 John answered the phone to Ron Dennis, concerned that his cars were slipping down the grid. Would John consider returning to McLaren as technical director? The approach came utterly out of the blue.

This could have been a dream come true, for McLaren was built in the Barnard image, English through and through, and he knew its ways intimately. But something in John's self-destructive armoury began to interfere in the process.

He soon learned that he would be answerable not to managing director Ron Dennis but to head of operations Martin Whitmarsh, an engineering graduate who had risen through British Aerospace to a senior managerial position and then joined McLaren in 1989. This was unacceptable, Barnard told Ron: 'Whitmarsh is a manager, not a racer. I will not work under him.' John had already had more than enough of working under people he regarded as managers rather than racers at Ferrari and Benetton.

Ron Dennis, as is his way, assured the engineer that all was going to be fine, that he would speak to Whitmarsh and make the position clear, that John would be answering to Ron directly.

Indeed, the draft service agreement sent to Barnard's lawyer, Michael Jepson, made this crystal clear: Clause 2.8 stated: 'The Technical Director shall be responsible only to the Managing Director… No appointment will be made… which would or could have the effect of changing or prejudicing the direct line of authority'. Clause 2.7 even stated: 'The Technical Director shall be consulted and due consideration shall be given to his views in relation to the overall conduct of the company, including strategic non-technical business activities.' It looked like the dream deal.

Ron and John duly met to sign it off, but, as Barnard's hand hovered over the signature page, a bolt of doubt shot through him. He looked up at Ron and asked, 'You've told Martin Whitmarsh that I won't be working under him, haven't you?' Ron, says John, looked evasive and wouldn't answer the question. John's temper flashed: 'You haven't! You haven't told him!' That was it. The deal was over. Barnard stormed out, taking a nonplussed Jepson with him.

What if Barnard hadn't asked the question, deciding instead to hold Ron to his word and the contract once back within McLaren's walls? He might have had a good working relationship with Whitmarsh, whom he didn't really know. He might have found a way around any chicanes; certainly he was experienced enough by now.

Had he done so, he might have helped restore McLaren to the level of dominance that his groundwork laid in the 1980s, something McLaren has never repeated. Probably he would have found himself working in a much less politically charged atmosphere than he had found at Ferrari and Benetton. He might have been given the freedom to get on with developing the perfect car. It all might have been so very good.

Instead, all the ghosts of clashes past came welling up into his head as his hand hovered over the contract.

Flouncing out was, quite possibly, Barnard's greatest professional mistake. 'I should probably have signed,' he now admits, 'and I might still be earning big money.'

CHAPTER 32
THE COMING OF THE KING
1995–97

Had Ron Dennis's approach been made public, it would have been one of the biggest Formula 1 stories that year. Instead, the big story of 1995 was about Michael Schumacher. The young German had joined Benetton towards the end of 1991, soon after Barnard's departure, and immediately made his mark. He narrowly beat Damon Hill in 1994 to become World Champion, and did it again in 1995, this time in dominant style with nine race victories.

During the 1995 season rumours began to spread around the paddock that Ferrari was trying to poach Schumacher from Benetton, which, despite its success, was showing signs of coming apart at the seams amid a flurry of accusations of cheating at races and political turmoil within. Luca di Montezemolo watched with interest.

At the end of July, shortly before the German Grand Prix, Montezemolo told *La Stampa*, the Italian newspaper widely regarded as the official mouthpiece of Fiat, that there were three prerequisites for victory: 'To win in Formula 1, you need... a good organisation, a great car and a great driver. In my role as President I have a duty to bring home the best. Schumacher is undoubtedly the best...'

The piece also stated that Montezemolo expected to have a decision by mid-August, which was, more or less, when Schumacher signed for the Scuderia for a rumoured and staggering salary of $30 million, replacing Jean Alesi, whose nose was now right out of joint. Before leaving for Benetton, Alesi made some public comments about Ferrari chicanery that prompted Montezemolo to say: 'I have told him this and I say it again: it is important not to make accusations about treachery and not to behave like a little baby.'[105] Barnard wasn't the only one with Ferrari knives in his back.

So it was that Schumacher came to Ferrari trailing clouds of World Championship glory. His chin-up, sniffy arrogance seemed to warm him to Ferrari's Italians as much as it horrified the Brits, Barnard chief among them.

But the air was full of promise. Schumacher declared himself to be really looking forward to working with Barnard, who recalls a telephone call from his old friend Gerd Kramer, a man who played a significant role in the development of the German driver's career. Says Barnard, 'Kramer told me, "Schumacher really wants to work with you, and if you two hit it off together, the sky's the limit."'

Barnard's first meaningful encounter with Schumacher came during a winter test at Estoril, where two Ferrari 646s were presented to the German maestro for his evaluation. One had a V12 in the back as raced by Gerhard Berger and Jean Alesi all season. The other was powered by a hastily installed example of Ferrari's new V10 engine. Schumacher climbed into the V12 and set off.

Within five laps, he was almost a second quicker than Berger and Alesi had been. He came into the pits, stepped out and announced: 'Wow, I could have won the championship far easier in this V12 than in the Benetton' — which, of course, was music to Barnard's ears.

Ross Brawn, who followed Schumacher to Ferrari from Benetton at the end of 1996, adds a fascinating further dimension: 'Michael said to me at the time that the V12 was a super car and he couldn't understand why Ferrari hadn't won the World Championship with it — but that wasn't down to John.'

So why did Berger and Alesi consistently fail to beat the German ace during 1995? The answer, thinks Barnard, lay in their contrasting driving styles. You may recall that Berger and Alesi disliked the V12's tendency to unsettle the rear of the car as soon as they lifted off the throttle in a corner. Schumacher, on the other hand, loved the way the car shoved its back end out and oversteered. He loved it because he could use it.

In fast corners Schumacher was uniquely able to finesse the rear-end drift with rapid micro-touches on the accelerator, using the engine braking to create

---

[105] Henry, Alan, 'Montezemolo wants Schumacher — and signals Alesi's departure', Autocourse 1995–96, p161.

the perfect grip for the bend, allowing him to come round the corner faster and exit more quickly than his competitors. It was a unique style, requiring acute sensitivity. As Barnard puts it, 'You need lightning reactions and big balls to drive that way. He could lift off the throttle to force the car into oversteer and then press it again to compensate with understeer. It really was amazing.'

Amazing it may have been, but Barnard was bothered by it: 'It just didn't seem right to me. I called it "driving off the front of the car". John Watson's approach was better. He wanted a nailed back-end so he'd get round the corner in one piece and feel more relaxed about opening the throttle earlier. That I understood, because at the end of the day traction is what makes it go quicker.' The fact was that Schumacher could achieve better traction with this unique driving method, but still it made Barnard's flesh creep.

Barnard had plenty of other problems with Schumacher and he feels they began at that Estoril test. 'I respected his talent but I found him incredibly hard to work with. He laid down the law despite having so little experience. I found that very hard to handle.'

'I had years of experience over him but it didn't stop him from questioning everything I did: "Why that, why this? I don't like that, I don't like this." At the time I was up to my eyeballs in Ferrari problems and found myself thinking, "Jesus, why can't this young guy just listen to me for a bit and try to understand what I'm saying and the way I would prefer to set up the car?"'

'There was no point in standing there and arguing with him. That was my first encounter and really it kind of defined my relationship with him thereafter.'

Schumacher was less positive about the new V10, expressing disappointment that it couldn't offer the same level of engine braking. So Barnard proposed a compromise, offering to change the gearbox from six-speed to seven-speed for the V10. The idea was straightforward: more gears meant more options for high revs in the corners, which, for Schumacher at least, meant more control.

As Mike Coughlan recalls, 'It immediately became crystal clear that anything Schumacher asked for he was always going to get.'

One example of just how overboard it could go occurred even before Schumacher drove a Ferrari, when, trying out the cockpit, he asked for the steering wheel to be moved towards him by 6mm. Coughlan recalls that they had spacers, 'relatively complex pieces', of 5mm and 7mm for the steering column, and to create a new one of 6mm would have been unnecessary work. He reports that Barnard, keen to avoid having a driver dictate everything, said to the team, 'Listen, one or the other is good enough for his first drive here.'

But Maranello was horrified and an Italian engineer was duly appointed to give Schumacher exactly what he wanted, working through the night to create a 6mm spacer.

Another aspect of Schumacher's arrival upset Barnard: 'Each year we would present the following year's budget and Maranello would ask for 20% savings. Now we had Schumacher and suddenly Todt was telling us to buy whatever we wanted: "What do you need? A new machine? Go and buy one. £300,000? That's fine!" It was night and day. And that was annoying because we should have been building up to this.'

And so it began to become evident to all around that the star engineer and the star driver didn't seem to get on.

Now a little more world-weary and not so full of fight, Barnard decided to do what most of his rival designers did and delegate more of the detail to others.

A new man, Tony Tyler, came in to run the new V10-powered car's aerodynamics programme in Godalming, and was soon given a wider role in the car's creation. His first suggestion was to have radiator pods just aft of the driver, with their front halves separated from the floor of the car in a manner somewhat reminiscent of Migeot's double floor. Barnard duly briefed Tyler to do the job.

A new rule for 1996 aimed to improve driver protection by requiring a U-shaped collar behind and alongside the driver's head. It looked like an integral part of the car but was in fact a special foam-filled section around 100mm thick. Working in the Filton wind tunnel, Tyler discovered that if he made the collar taller all round, it produced 'better numbers'. Barnard accepted the good news at face value but was soon to rue the decision.

It turned out that Tyler had failed to take into account the way in which the air flowed over the collar into the airbox. As Barnard says, 'The combination of the high collar, the driver's helmet and the position of the airbox meant that the airflow into the engine was disrupted.' That meant that engine performance was affected, and the only way to deal with that was to have Schumacher drive along with his head cocked to one side to let the air flow more easily. This was an embarrassing requirement and Barnard, as boss, obviously had to take the blame.

The situation created a management conundrum for him: 'If you start going over the top of people you've put in these positions, you're kind of wasting your time.' Barnard had decided to delegate but he disliked doing it.

There was no mistake in the next landmark in Formula 1 technical history, when Barnard came up with an innovation so brilliant and yet so obvious that it's hard to comprehend why it hadn't been done before. Like so many of his innovations, this one was born of frustration.

The trouble was the dashboard. Formula 1 cockpits were getting smaller and more crowded. By the time the steering wheel was locked into place, it was quite difficult to read any of the dials and pretty tricky to flip the switches. As John explains, 'I was getting fed up with trying to make the dashboard more accessible.'

The solution bounded out of the problem like a gazelle at a leonine lunchtime: 'The logical thing was to make our own carbon steering wheel with the dashboard instruments on the steering wheel itself.' He briefed junior designer Kevin Taylor to come up with a design, standing at his shoulder. Taylor suggested using the Ferrari shield shape for the hub, a wheeze that Barnard rather liked.

The steering wheel dashboard wasn't an essential step. His drivers weren't complaining that they couldn't see the dashboard or use the switches. And, to his knowledge, no one else was trying to solve the dashboard problem. All of which prompts him to ask: 'When other people were still building dashboards in the car, why did I bother to take all the stuff off the dashboard and put it on the steering wheel? What did it do for me? If I'd continued to put dashboards where drivers could see virtually nothing and hardly reach anything, they wouldn't have complained because everyone else had the same. I could have made my life easier and not done it. But for me there was a problem there — it wasn't right.'

Barnard's quest for perfection was continual, despite the cost to him politically and personally. Shortly before the steering wheel dashboard, he had worked with Maranello colleagues to make a series of improvements to the paddle-shift system. He improved the actuator that operated the gears, coming up with the first rotary hydraulic version — 'a very difficult thing to build'. This was in contrast to other people's efforts: 'They used a more linear system, like a steering rack with teeth and a piston on each end shuttling back and forth to operate a barrel system, not unlike a motorbike gear change.'

There's no need to get lost in the detail here. Suffice it to say that the new 'Moog' system, devised mostly by Fosco De Silvestri with Barnard in oversight, had the high-speed rotary actuator fixed directly to the end of a 'shift barrel', which amounted to a much neater package than having separate pistons upon the selector rods: 'It did away with a lot of bits and pieces in the gearbox. Now gears could be shifted in the realm of milli-seconds.'

His drive for perfection, the pursuit of what was right, put himself and many others under a lot of pressure — but that was and remains the cost of progress. He concedes that he could have been more successful in terms of Grand Prix victories if he hadn't taken this approach.

As he says, 'I was taking up time and resources and pushing people hard to do more work in the same length of time that other teams were tweaking this and that. I was trying to create something new all the time. In a sense I'd made a rod for my own back because that's what everyone expected. Montezemolo would phone me up and ask, "What have you got that's new? What's coming?"'

It was Barnard's way, the only way he knew, the only way that interested him. 'I found tweaking really boring,' he says, with some passion.

The new car was launched with due fanfare at Maranello. To everyone involved in its creation, it was called the Ferrari 647, but Ferrari PR insisted on it being known as the F310, referring to the engine's 3-litre capacity and 10 cylinders. It was hailed as another beauty, 'more like a jet fighter than a race car' as one commentator put it. Speaking at the press conference, Schumacher declared, 'It would be too optimistic and unrealistic to say we will fight for the championship. I would like to fight for a couple of victories. If I could achieve that I would be perfectly happy. If you go back, Ferrari has won two races in three years and if it could win two or three races in one year then it would be a major success.'[106]

Schumacher duly achieved his target. The first of his three wins came in a rainy Spain, where he drove brilliantly in appalling conditions at Barcelona's Catalunya circuit, earning himself the nickname *Regenmeister* (Rain Master). The second was at Spa in Belgium, after a long tussle with the Williams of Jacques Villeneuve, son of Gilles, in which Schumacher never expected to prevail. The third, and perhaps the most memorable, was at the next race, the Italian Grand Prix at Monza.

Out in front and with just 13 laps to go, Schumacher suffered a rare loss of concentration at the first chicane and clipped the tyre wall. The same mistake

---

[106] Warren, Peter (director), Michael Schumacher, The Red Baron, *4Digital Media Ltd, 2008, at 16m 30s.*

had already put Damon Hill out of the race, but such were Schumacher's superfast reactions that he and the car survived the impact intact. Three laps from the end he laid down the race's fastest lap and took the chequered flag over 18 seconds ahead of Jean Alesi in a Benetton.

It was a victory to be cherished — the first Ferrari win at the Italian Grand Prix since the 1988 *Miracolo a Monza* when Gerhard Berger and Michele Alboreto, driving Barnard's 640, crossed the line first and second as if in tribute to the recently deceased Enzo Ferrari. The *Tifosi* went berserk.

Schumacher was third in the 1996 Drivers' Championship and, even better for Barnard, Ferrari were second in the Constructors' title, behind Williams and ahead of Benetton and McLaren. Everything was coming up roses.

Barnard, however, wasn't satisfied with the 647: 'It never drove with quite the same ease and balance as the 1995 car. Although it did win, it never realised its potential. It was never the step forward from the 1995 car that it should have been, never the improvement I wanted.' He blames himself: 'I should have dumped everything else, gone down to the tunnel and got involved. I was questioning them, but I was trusting their figures.'

Someone he could trust, and perhaps his closest colleague, decided to move on at the end of the season. Diane Holl, frustrated that Ferrari wouldn't accede to her burgeoning desire to become a race engineer, left for the United States and Indycar racing: 'They were Italians, I was female, I was English and I hadn't done race engineering before.' John felt the move was good for her: 'I told her she would learn more by going race engineering with Indycar teams.' So she did just that at Tasman Motorsports and continues to carve an impressive career as a designer/engineer within NASCAR.

The new Ferrari for 1997, the 648, was replete with all the advances and refinements that Barnard had brought to Ferrari over the previous four years, which meant it was special enough to vie for the 1997 World Championship — but Barnard regarded it as 'nothing special'.

Schumacher won five races during the season and led the title battle by one point from Villeneuve going into the final race, held at Jerez in Spain on 26 October. Williams already had the Constructors' Championship in the bag but Villeneuve had to beat Schumacher to achieve the World Championship crown as well. Schumacher, of course, had other ideas.

It's an infamous story that has been told many times, so we can be brief. Villeneuve qualified on pole in his Williams-Renault with a lap time of 1 minute 21.072 seconds. Schumacher posted an identical time but did so after Villeneuve and therefore lined up second. Somewhat infuriated by this, Schumacher beat Villeneuve to the first corner of the race and stayed in the lead, more or less, until lap 48, the moment of one of the most controversial incidents in Formula 1 history.

Villeneuve, his tyres failing, was less than a second behind — he knew that if he didn't get in front soon, he might as well kiss goodbye to the championship. Six corners into the lap they were both approaching the Dry Sack right-hand hairpin. Schumacher, still ahead, left space on the inside of the corner and Villeneuve dived in for the gap. Schumacher turned in to close the door, realised it was too late, but turned in again with the evident intent of shunting his championship rival off the track.

It was a moment of madness and he utterly botched it. His right-hand front wheel hit Villeneuve's left-hand sidepod, which, instead of pushing Villeneuve out of the way, shoved Schumacher himself off the track and out of the race. Villeneuve, damaged but not disabled, carried on to finish third and became the World Champion.

This type of behaviour made Schumacher one of the most hated men in sport, that is when he wasn't being the most loved. It wasn't the first time he had become so entangled out of apparent fear of losing. He had done exactly the same to Damon Hill in 1994, winning the World Championship for Benetton in an equally deliberate attack aimed at ending his rival's race. As Barnard says of that offence, 'It was such a calculated move. I've never seen one like it. There's no doubt in my mind at all that he hit Damon's car on purpose.'

Unlike in 1994, Schumacher's misdemeanour of 1997 was punished, and severely. The FIA disqualified him not only from the race but also the entire 1997 World Championship. This, you might have thought, would have compelled Barnard to give the 'arrogant German' a piece of English mind.

But no. Things had changed dramatically at Ferrari by the end of the season — Ross Brawn was in and John Barnard was out.

A year earlier, in September 1996, Jean Todt had a tricky message for John Barnard. He decided to deliver it personally. One day John walked into his Godalming office to find Todt sitting in his chair: 'John,' he said, 'I want to take Ferrari back to Maranello. I need to know if you are going to come. You'll still be technical director, of course.' Barnard wasn't surprised to hear the plan; the writing had been filling up the wall for several years.

'No, Jean, is the short answer,' he replied. 'My contract makes it clear that I am to work from here. You know the reasons. My family is still Number One.'

'Okay, John, I understand. It's what I expected. Who do we replace you with — we're thinking about Ross Brawn from Benetton?'

Barnard agreed Brawn would be the ideal choice, suggesting that Todt should take Rory Byrne too: 'The two together would be a powerful combination.' So that's exactly what happened: 'Todt went to Brawn and Byrne with his cheque book and before the year was out the deal was pretty much done.'

John had no counter-argument to Todt's proposal and didn't try to make one. The Godalming experiment had run twice now, and while it could be said to have worked up to a point — by improving results, technical standards and know-how in Maranello — it did make good sense to have all of Ferrari based at Ferrari. As Barnard says, 'It was logical and I couldn't say anything against it.'

The decisive factor from John's point of view was Michael Schumacher. He just couldn't bow either to him or his apparent power over Todt and Montezemolo: 'If there was something Schumacher didn't like, if it wasn't working the way he wanted, he would go to Todt, tell him he didn't like it and it would get changed. In effect we were all working for Schumacher. I didn't particularly go for that.'

Was this a case of the pot calling the kettle black? Was there in Barnard a hatred for the very thing that people disliked in Barnard himself — his distance, his arrogance, his superiority? Could Barnard be every bit as difficult as Schumacher? It wouldn't be hard to find people in the paddock who would say that he was.

Both Barnard and Schumacher proved to be geniuses in their way but there was a vital difference between the two. Barnard was a backroom boffin who preferred to keep out of the limelight, while Schumacher was a superstar who revelled in it.

News of the severance became public early in 1997. 'Barnard and Ferrari to part company' announced *Motoring News* on 12 February, declaring that 'Barnard is currently thought to be negotiating with his employer to buy out FDD's Shalford premises, which we understand will be used as a design base for Alain Prost's Peugeot-powered French "super team".'

Autosport ran a three-page colour special in its 20 February edition, entitled 'Barnard and Ferrari', in which John outlined his reasons for leaving. Talking about FDD, he explained the Godalming philosophy: 'This place would be forward thinking, and would be looking at the design of the next car, and more futuristic development work. Since Harvey Postlethwaite left... there hasn't really been a proper technical leader in Maranello. And therefore the thing hasn't really been operating in the original way it was conceived, because we had to be more involved in day-to-day stuff. That's something I clearly told Ferrari at the beginning of the deal. I said based on previous experience, it cannot operate as a day-to-day thing.'

In the *Autosport* piece Barnard also revealed just how much he was being undermined at Ferrari: 'There were a number of things that made it impossible for me to operate in the way I wanted to. One of them was that in the middle of last year the decision was made to take all the aerodynamics back to Maranello, which left us virtually zero-handed on the wind tunnel side. We couldn't really continue properly the development of this car, which is why it has come out with things like standard steel front suspension, when it really needed aerodynamic stuff on it. So there's an instance where I know there's more performance, and we haven't been able to do it. And I get the blame for the whole lot.'[107]

So, for Barnard, the 1997 season amounted to a prolonged departure from Ferrari. While Ross Brawn and Rory Byrne were settling in at Maranello, John and his FDD team were busy finishing off the 648, the car that would take Michael Schumacher tantalisingly close to the 1998 World Championship title, as in 1997. There was little contact with the new men. Says Barnard, 'I never really worked with Ross — there was just a bit of correspondence between us. I also heard from a number of people that they had no plans to do any development on the 648 because it was my car.'

Ross Brawn confirms this, up to a point, saying: 'I inherited what was a very nicely engineered car. I think Rory and I had a few different ideas on what might help its performance — you have your own paths you tread in terms of engineering. I remember John had a very simple fuel system, for instance, and we introduced a fuel tank with a more complex baffling system because we didn't want the fuel moving around so much; John didn't think that was such an important factor. So we introduced things that were more aligned with our philosophy of race cars.'

He adds that he thought the 648 a good car to which they were able to add

---

[107] Cooper, Adam, 'Barnard and Ferrari', Autosport, 20 February 1997.

a few enhancements: 'It was a good basis to work from in terms of what then became the Rory Byrne car the year after and thereafter.'

Brawn praises Barnard's professionalism during the changeover, commenting that what could have been a difficult transition turned out to be fairly smooth: 'John was very mature and objective about what was happening and recognised the change that was coming.'

It wasn't, however, entirely stress-free. Brawn has etched forever in his mind a bewildering moment during a meeting between himself, Barnard and Roberto Dalla, head of the Ferrari electronics department:

'John had the reputation for being pretty fiery, not afraid to call a spade a shovel if occasion demanded. But I hadn't seen that; he'd been very quiet and placid in all the meetings I'd been in. John and I and Roberto sat down and the meeting kicked off and everything was normal. Suddenly John brought up a topic that had obviously been irritating him for some time, to do with the weight of an electronic component, and then blew his top.

'And then Roberto blew his top, because he was that sort of guy as well. And I sat there watching Roberto and John screaming at each other, trading insults. It reached this pitch, from calm and pleasant to total fury, in about ten seconds, with both of them hurling insults at one another at high volume.

'And suddenly, it just stopped! It was almost like a switch got turned off again, and the meeting carried on as if nothing had happened. I found it most amusing. It was the only occasion that I saw John explode; I'd never seen it before and have never seen it since.

Barnard doesn't recall the incident, but he does remember a pre-season test at Jerez: 'Brawn, Todt and Schumacher were there, all telling me what we were going to do, discussing the design like it was a committee. I found that ridiculous, too much, all these people telling me what they wanted. I just went back to England, sorted out the problems revealed by the test and handed it over to Brawn to take it racing.'

And so began the era of Ferrari dominance. The new team took another year or more to reach its full potential despite the boost Barnard had given them, but when they hit their stride in 1999 they became truly awesome. That year Ferrari won the Constructors' Championship for the first time in 16 years, and they went on to win it six years in a row, the best run in the history of the sport. These were the Schumacher years, of course, in which his driving genius reached its glorious apotheosis, so all-conquering that everyone who wasn't a Ferrari fan became bored with his procession of victories.

Barnard concedes the brilliance of the team: 'It was ideal really. They had Ross Brawn, a superb manager with a strong design background, able to massage Schumacher's enormous ego and attend to his every racing need, while standing between the back-stabbing busybodies in the Maranello boardroom and Rory Byrne's increasingly brilliant aerodynamic and mechanical talent.'

Their job was to keep ahead of the game, and with Schumacher in the driver's seat and Brawn displaying prowess in his racing strategy, that was, perhaps, not such an onerous task. No major risks were taken, no step changes were made. Byrne never came up with the equivalent of a semi-automatic paddle-shift gearbox, a carbon-fibre chassis, a new form of upright, a dashboard on the steering wheel — because he didn't need to. Barnard had done all that. Byrne's job was to take a good car built by a good system and tweak it and refine it and make it better and better. Revolutions were not his brief; winning was. Montezemolo probably didn't ask him, 'What have you got that's new?' The whole focus was different and, with the groundwork laid, the new approach paid off handsomely.

But what of Barnard? What on earth was there left for him to do?

PART 8
B3 AND BEYOND

CHAPTER 33
THE LAST BARNARD CAR
1996–98

John Barnard's next step had been incubating in his mind for some years, indeed, had been outlined as a possibility in the contract he signed in 1992. Now he sat down with his lawyer, Michael Jepson, and drew up his exit strategy in detail.

Barnard would negotiate to take over Ferrari Design and Development (FDD), take it off Ferrari's hands for a peppercorn payment and set up his Plan B, a technology company to service motorsport and aerospace, keeping his key staff in their positions, ensuring the top-class team that he had built up with such care over 20 years would stay together

But what should he call this Plan B? That resolved itself, he says, when Vijay Kothary brought in a marketing company to produce a brochure: 'They came up with B3,' reports Barnard. 'I liked it because I took it to refer to my having three children.' Andy Smith, soon to be promoted to managing director of the new enterprise, adds that there had been a competition to choose a name: 'Everyone suggested ideas but we heard nothing until the announcement of a name that hadn't come up in the competition.'

The B3 concept had various advantages. No longer would he have to jump to the demands of a prima donna driver, no politics above him would compromise his work, he would be able to choose his projects, he could continue working for Ferrari on a freelance basis — and, most important of all, he could still go home for lunch.

And, for Ferrari, Barnard saw advantages too: 'Ferrari gave me a very generous deal, but my plan saved them a lot of aggravation because closing down a company and getting rid of people is never a nice thing to have to do.'

On 19 March 1997, Tom Walkinshaw, former engineering director at Benetton and owner of Tom Walkinshaw Racing (TWR), wrote to Barnard. Walkinshaw had just bought the Footwork Arrows Formula 1 team, having pulled out of a deal to buy Benetton. The letter reveals that Barnard was buying FDD from Ferrari for 'one pound sterling' with the added sweetener of an £800,000 loan. Walkinshaw was offering to buy the operation from John for the same, including a monthly fee of £250,000 for Barnard and his team to design a Formula 1 car for Arrows, the idea being to integrate B3 into Arrows to create another revenue stream while providing access to state-of-the-art Formula 1 technology.

In return Barnard would become the technical director of Arrows Grand Prix International with an annual salary of £360,000, plus an extra £250,000 'finder's fee' payable to Barnard Design Consultancy for teeing up the FDD purchase by TWR. The letter concludes, 'If you are in agreement with the points laid out above, please sign the attached copy of the letter.' The copy in Barnard's files bears his signature.

But then things went wrong. Nine months later, in a draft fax to Walkinshaw dated 29 December 1977, Barnard stated that a press leak, presumably from Walkinshaw, had caused panic at Ferrari, who had asked Barnard to assure them that he wouldn't sell B3 to TWR. This, and the fact that various monies hadn't yet been received by B3 from TWR to pay off the Ferrari loan, prompted Barnard to change his mind.

He would now keep ownership of B3, thank you very much. And, by the way, he no longer wanted to be technical director for Arrows — Mike Coughlan could have that pleasure — because he 'found it very difficult being away from my family'. He now intended to work as technical consultant to Arrows two days a week at the team's base in Leafield, Oxfordshire.

John was fully ensconced in B3 by late April 1997 and, apart from a few of the usual aggravations, was enjoying the new-found freedom. He immersed himself in the effort needed to get Arrows up the pecking order.

He worked directly with Damon Hill, who, despite being the reigning World Champion, had fetched up at uncompetitive Arrows after four years with super-successful Williams. The son of racing legend Graham Hill, Damon had been thrown into the limelight as team leader after Ayrton Senna's death but rose to the occasion by winning six races in his battle for the 1994 title with Michael Schumacher, only to lose out by one point when the German driver pushed him off the road at the last race. Damon's time did come in 1996, when he took eight victories, but his 1995 season had been so troubled that Frank Williams had already decided to get rid of him upon contract expiry.

In an interview for this book, Damon recalled: 'John's opening line was, "Damon, the first thing we need to do is make it safe!" Things like that stick in drivers' minds! I'm sure it was safe but John set the standard really.' John is surprised by Hill's recollection: 'I'd have thought I'd have said, "Let's make it quick." Perhaps I put it something like, "The damned thing is slow, so let's make sure it doesn't kill you."'

John remembers talking to Hill over the radio during Friday practice at the 1997 British Grand Prix at Silverstone in July: 'It became clear that Damon wasn't going anywhere, so I brought him into the pits and told everyone we were going to make some fundamental changes — spring rates, ride heights, front wing settings.' After all that, Barnard recalls a happy Damon commenting that 'the front end is really working now'. Given the power disadvantage of his Arrows A18's Judd/Yamaha engine, he drove a fine race to sixth place for his and the team's first point of the season.

As Barnard says, 'Once you make a step like that, everyone perks up because the car goes up the grid. You can start to generate the interest and get the team and driver behind you.' He went on to rework the suspension and improve front-end downforce by putting lead weights in the wing to get the Bridgestone tyres working better. He also increased the size of the airbox to bring more air into the engine, giving a bit more top speed.

The highlight of Arrows's 1997 season came in Hungary. Damon drove a brilliant race and towards the end was leading Jacques Villeneuve's Williams by 31 seconds when he struck trouble, a throttle problem closely followed by difficulty in changing gear. What should have been a spectacular victory became second place. Barnard was upset: 'It was a tuppenny ha'penny failure. Someone had installed a faulty O-ring; it failed and that cocked up the hydraulics, which meant the paddle-shift system wouldn't work properly.' It would have been a maiden win for long-time under-performers Arrows: in 296 races between 1978 and 2002 the team never won a race.

As Bob Constanduros put it in his end-of-season review of the teams in *Autocourse*, 'Barnard had blown into Leafield not so much like a breath of fresh air as like a gale.'

While helping to get Arrows up the grid, Barnard worked on the new A19 for the 1998 season. His first problem was that he lacked a wind tunnel:

'Unfortunately we lost our wind tunnel facility in Bristol, because Ron Dennis had previously done a deal with BAe insisting that we were kicked out.' So early work on the A19 was done with a ⅓-scale model in a tunnel at Milton Keynes while a new rolling-road set-up for a 60% model was built on the Royal Aircraft Establishment site in Bedford.

It was at Arrows that Barnard finally perfected the carbon gearbox, solving the problem of leakage through the bonded joints by eschewing honeycomb. Now the gearbox was significantly lighter, weighing just 9kg. Together with the rear crash assembly, the total weight was 14kg as opposed to the 25kg offered by the previous magnesium structures. 'This was the time when everyone was trying to save weight at the back and move ballast forward to make the new front tyres work,' explains John, referring to new regulations that made the cars narrower and required their slick tyres to have deep grooves, the aim being, as ever, to address escalating speeds.

The carbon gearbox, like so many of Barnard's innovations, would have been impossible had he not surrounded himself with such a talented team. He delighted in the fact that at B3 he felt he could stretch his wings with a team around him that was prepared to push the boundaries as far as he was: 'That's part of the reason why lots of the guys at B3 who worked there for a long time liked working there — I would always be throwing them a new challenge.' B3's facilities also played their part as there were so many components he couldn't have designed — might not even have thought of making — without them: 'I had a composite shop good enough to lay up difficult components and do it well, and a machine shop who jumped at the chance of doing complex machining of carbon — not something that most machine shops relish.'

But there was a problem with the carbon gearbox. Barnard had turned to an old and trusted ally, Kenny Hill at Metalore in California, for the manufacture of some of the gearbox internals. Unfortunately the gear hubs came out fractionally too small, by 40 microns, about 0.0016 of an inch. This meant that under racing conditions the gears tilted on the shaft and began to damage the meshing dog ring teeth, leading to gearbox failure. But the problem had first to be discovered.

'It was the start of the bad feeling at Arrows,' says Barnard, citing a row he had over the issue with Mike Coughlan, who was still with him at B3. 'We were standing in the gearbox shop looking at the package set up on the bench. The problem was that the dog rings were knocking the corners off the dog teeth and this meant it wouldn't stay in gear. We just couldn't figure out what was going on. I said, "Okay, let's redesign the ratchet mechanism on the gearshift barrel." He asked why, and I said, "Because I can't think of anything else to do!" He reckoned it was a waste of time but when I asked what he would do, he didn't answer. So I said, "Well, I'm your boss and I'm telling you what you're going to do." He told me that I wasn't his boss, that Walkinshaw was his boss.' That didn't go down well.

The carbon case was, indeed, being questioned by Walkinshaw. Behind John's back, Walkinshaw had it tested for strength. The tests showed that it was, in fact, stronger than a standard magnesium case.

Barnard's feelings on this are still raw: 'It's no good saying it's the bloody carbon-fibre gearbox. You have to go with your technical director, help realise his vision, have faith in his ability. I'm not saying you can't question him or make suggestions, but the aim is to work together, not against each other, behind each other's backs. If you don't go with the guy who's making the decisions, then it's not going to work.'

Eventually, the carbon gearbox did work; so well in fact that, as Barnard reports, 'Arrows ran not just the same design, but the same actual cases into the second season. That was unheard of.'

The A19's performance was made more problematic by its unproven new engine, a V10 made by Brian Hart, who had a small engine company in Essex. Barnard went to see the operation but wasn't impressed: 'Hart had a good reputation, but his new 10-cylinder engine was really an upgraded Cosworth V8 and it was in its early stages. I didn't think he had a strong enough electronics department.' Engine power, once more, was going to be an issue. At least Barnard had some influence over the engine design, and his team at B3 designed a new set of pumps on the side of the engine to scavenge oil from the gearbox.

But shortage of money plagued the Arrows project and really began to surface when it came to Barnard's plan for titanium brackets to support the rear suspension. It was some weeks before he noticed that the parts he had designed hadn't shown up. When Barnard checked with general manager Gordon Message, he was told the parts had 'got stopped'.

'It was too much for me,' says Barnard. 'The bottom line was that Tom Walkinshaw didn't have the money to make the changes I wanted and couldn't face telling me. Had he said that we had to stop doing development and making bits, I'd have said, "Fine, we'll stop. In fact I can find a way to save you money, never mind spending more." But nobody came to me.'

Walkinshaw, an ex-racing driver, was a man with a thumb in many pies, ever on the hunt for the perfect plum. For many years his TWR operation had run teams on behalf of manufacturers and enjoyed many successes, most notably Jaguar's triumphant return to endurance sports car racing with two wins in the Le Mans 24 Hours. By the time Walkinshaw added Arrows to his portfolio, in 1997, his TWR Group employed 1,500 people world-wide. He was hugely successful — but he had a reputation for exaggeration at best and being economical with the truth at worst.

Chicanery, of course, was never exclusively an Italian province, as Barnard was finding out. He believes Walkinshaw was in the habit of pretending the money was there when it wasn't, a fact not helped by Damon Hill's departure at the end of 1997, a loss that was never going to be helpful in raising sponsorship. As Barnard says, 'Losing Damon meant we lost our driving edge. As we also didn't have an engine edge, it became clear that we wouldn't be going anywhere in 1998.'

Which, says Damon, was a real pity: 'Had we got the budget together, we would have become a competitive team. I left before I got to drive the car John Barnard designed and it was an absolute peach, one of the most beautiful-looking cars. I'm sure if it had had a bit more power it would have been very, very competitive.'

Beautiful indeed. Jet black and blessed with flowing lines that dipped and rose over the sidepods to flood in and down from the curvaceous airbox into the coke-bottle waisted rear, with its high-rise nose giving it a panther-like, leaping stance, the A19 looked gorgeous — sexy even.

The A19 was also Barnard's last race car — not the last he consulted on or contributed to but the last he devised in full. Deeply frustrated by the underfunding, he pulled out of Arrows.

Where could Barnard turn next? He already had a plan, choosing an old friend, the man in Formula 1 for whom he had the most respect, Alain Prost.

CHAPTER 34
PROST GOES POP
1998–2002

The Professor now had his own Formula 1 team. Alain Prost had created Prost Grand Prix by buying the Ligier team from Flavio Briatore in early 1997. He approached John Barnard in the middle of 1998. The plan was to have Barnard as technical consultant and use B3's technical facilities to augment Prost's team, which was based near Paris.

Perhaps Prost had other ideas, but, as with Tom Walkinshaw before him, cash proved to be the biggest stumbling block.

The first obstacle was Prost's chief designer, Loïc Bigois, who had built his reputation in aerodynamics. Barnard's job was to 'steer him in the right direction' but he soon found that Bigois was struggling, a fact that became evident when he asked Bigois for a copy of the car's overall scheme so that B3 could design the suspension.

When it finally arrived Barnard wasn't impressed: 'He sent me an outline, just the car in side view, with information about height, length and width at various points along the car. It was bloody enormous, way outside the minimum dimensions required by the rules. The first rule of building a race car is to make it as small as possible, unless you have a particular reason to make it big.'

When Barnard asked the French designer if he really wanted the car to be so large, Bigois agreed to make it smaller — which didn't exactly fill Barnard with confidence.

Then began the blame game. During testing at Catalunya John observed Bigois altering the front-wing endplates, to give more grip, and also reducing ride height. The result was severe understeer. To Barnard's irritation, Bigois announced that the suspension design was at fault, that B3 had got the geometry wrong. Barnard pointed out that the changes Bigois had made were obviously the problem, but the Frenchman denied that he even made the changes.

'But I could see he'd made them,' says Barnard. 'It was a classic situation and I should have known better. When you make stuff in England and ship it to France, they're always going to blame your design rather than their input. You just can't go forward like that. I thought, "Oh dear, here we go again with the blame game."'

It was a warning of what was to follow: 'I didn't design the car, I was just the consultant. Yet Bigois's instinct was to blame me without even thinking about it. I found myself thinking, "Hello, I'd better be a bit careful with this character."'

But despite this the omens were good, so good that John and Alain began discussing the possibility of Prost later buying B3 to create an entity called Prost Grand Prix UK.

Barnard was still recruiting, and one summer intern he took on was his daughter Gillian. Bright, breezy and easy to talk to, she looked after reception and generally got along well with everyone. Sometimes the B3 staff would try to get the lowdown on her father, asking what he was like at home, how she handled his legendary temper, whether she was scared of him. 'Scared of him?' she'd reply. 'Not likely. He's scared of me!'

Another recruit with a personal connection was Dan Fleetcroft, the son of John's doctor, who joined in the summer of 1999. Dan, who now runs his own highly successful technology business, had done a week's work experience at FDD several years earlier and recalls his youthful joy: 'You can imagine how good that was for a schoolboy to tell his careers master that he'd arranged work experience with a Formula 1 team.' Dan later got a Saturday job and did holiday work at FDD, with the upshot that Ferrari duly sponsored his degree course in aerospace engineering at the University of Bristol. After his graduation, Barnard immediately dropped him into B3's deep end.

Fleetcroft's first brief was to solve the perennial problem of the in-car fire extinguisher. At the time Formula 1 cars were equipped with extinguishers similar to those used in aerospace, comprising a weighty pressurised aluminium bottle filled with foam. New regulations required an increase in the amount of extinguishant, which inevitably meant a bulkier, heavier bottle that would be difficult to fit in the cockpit. Barnard hated the prescribed increase in size and weight and decided he wasn't going to put up with it — yet another example of an irritant sparking innovation in his brain.

'The extinguisher bottle was a nasty, old-fashioned piece of technology and was begging to be updated,' John says. So he teased at it, possibly during one of those Saturday 'What If' sessions. The creative analysis went something like this: 'What are the facts? This bottle has to be big and strong because it's under pressure. Why is it under pressure? Because it is compressing large amounts of extinguishant into a small space. Is the pressure only about keeping a large amount of extinguishant into a small space? No, it's more about delivering it at high pressure over distance onto a fire. So it only needs to be under full pressure at the time of delivery? Yes.'

Eureka! If the bottle's full-time job was only to store uncompressed extinguishant, Barnard could make it weaker and lighter and shape it more or less how he liked. He could, in fact, make it out of carbon. How? Lay pre-preg carbon cloth over a soluble plaster mould, cure it and wash out the plaster with hot water. Hey presto, a container capable of coping with temporary high pressure. They would later discover that the fastest way of washing out the plaster was by putting it in B3's dishwasher — to the machine's cost.

But what about delivering the extinguishant it contained? Surely this required more pressure? Surely the only way was to return to the time-honoured metal bottle design? The solution to this quandary was as simple as it was brilliant, and it involved borrowing from technology that was becoming increasingly common in road cars — the dashboard airbag.

The bottom of the carbon container was attached via plastic tubing to an electrically activated common-or-garden car airbag inflator, which itself was contained in a specially designed titanium housing measuring roughly 150mm x 70mm and tucked away below the driver's legs. Should the fire extinguisher be needed, the airbag inflator would be activated by either driver or rescuing fire marshal, and, having been 'detonated', would shoot high-pressure gases down the tubes leading to the carbon container, increasing the pressure inside until a 'burst disc' in the neck ruptured, allowing extinguishant to flood along two tubes — one to fill the cockpit and the other to flood the engine bay. Because a carbon container could be fashioned in a shape that fitted in the car more conveniently, the eventual installation in fact comprised two flattened carbon bottles placed either side of the driver's hips.

The system proved to be a nightmare to make, as Fleetcroft explains: 'It was an absolute monster of a project because the extinguishant kept leaking. We couldn't find the cause.' He and engineer Brian 'Wols' Wallis spent a month trying to get it to work, putting in 80 hours or more each week, including all-nighters, because they themselves were under pressure, with an imminent FIA deadline to test and approve the system. In somewhat cavalier style, Barnard suggested a solution, as Fleetcroft recalls: 'He told us to try it without the bladder in the carbon bottle. We were slightly nervous of this, but we went ahead as requested.'

It was 1.00am by the time the test was ready. The two engineers took the sensible precaution of hanging their system — 'all very Heath Robinson' — out of a window because they didn't want it going off inside the lab, so the loaded carbon bottle was suspended outside on tubes for the airbag inflator and on wires that ran into the lab for data-logging. What could possibly go wrong?

'I was in the lab and Wols was outside in the car park with a stopwatch to time how quickly the extinguishant was expelled,' explains Fleetcroft. 'The FIA required three litres of extinguishant to be expelled in under 30 seconds. Wols then began a shouted countdown: "3–2–1–Go!"'

Fleetcroft hit the button and the gases rushed down the tubes in a flash, pressurising the carbon bottle. But without the internal bladder to act as an extra seal, the extinguishant exploded out of the bottom of the bottle instead of breaking the burst disc at the top.

'The whole thing shot off towards Wols like a rocket,' says Fleetcroft, 'dragging all the data-logging cables with it and chasing him across the car park. It actually forced him to dive for cover as two McLaren engineers, standing outside the old GTO building on a late-night cigarette break, were looking on. I could hear them laughing from the lab.'

They eventually found that the leakage problem was caused by osmosis through the bladder. Fleetcroft: 'It took us ages to find out; we'd be sealing things and bonding things, we'd even have the bladder out of the bottle on the desk and pumped full of air — it wouldn't leak. We'd fill it with water and it wouldn't leak. But put it back in the bottle and fill it with extinguishant and after a while it would start bubbling.'

The breakthrough came after a bladder full of extinguishant was left on a desk and in time a dark patch became visible on the bladder's neck — evidence of osmosis. The solution was simple enough — to use thicker material for the bladder and coat it in a black shiny PVC.

Eventually this remarkable system was adopted throughout Formula 1.

In the late summer of 1999, Alain Prost decided to appoint a technical director for his Gauloises Prost Peugeot team to oversee development of the AP03, the new car for the 2000 season. He chose Barnard's old McLaren staffer, Alan Jenkins, who had been in a similar post at Stewart Grand Prix.

'It was difficult at Prost because John worked for me!' recalls Jenkins. 'Can you imagine? I said to him once, "In theory, you're working for me now. But we won't pursue that!"'

Jenkins based himself in Paris and from time to time John would fly over. He felt that Alan was trying to start from the ground up, spending too much time thinking about the layout of the factory. His advice was that Alan should instead 'establish his technical director credentials' by concentrating on 'making the new car go faster'.

But the AP03's performance in 2000 was lacklustre to say the least. Its aerodynamics were poor — Jenkins states that 'the aero side of Prost didn't work' — and its Peugeot engine lacked power. By season's end it was as far off the pace as it had been at the beginning. It's no coincidence that its only decent display came at Monaco, where shortcomings in power and aerodynamics come least into play. Here Jean Alesi qualified seventh, way better than anywhere else, and Nick Heidfeld brought his car home eighth, the best result of the year.

Barnard's instinct was that the wind tunnel, in central France, was a primary factor: 'I felt there was something not quite right with the numbers it was generating and thought that Alan should have spent more time there. They kept making new aerodynamic parts and putting them on the car but they didn't seem to work. The numbers indicated that the changes should have been better but they didn't make a difference on the track. The team went nowhere aerodynamically.'

Prost fired Jenkins mid-season and replaced him with Henri Durand, whom Barnard had known as a young aerodynamicist during his first stint at Ferrari. Durand took on the title of technical director and so, as a consequence in Barnard's view, he also didn't spend enough time in the wind tunnel, which is where the English technical consultant continued to feel the technical director was most needed.

Eventually Jean-Paul Gousset, who ran the design office for Prost, went to investigate the wind tunnel and discovered that, according to Barnard, 'most of the vacuum holes that sucked the rolling road down to keep it flat were blocked up.' This, of course, would have caused false readings.

Barnard is vociferous about the dangers of excessive reliance upon computers: 'Too many people at Prost were in the habit of taking numbers produced in the wind tunnel and running them through a computer to come up with the answers that they wanted, rather than questioning the numbers the wind tunnel was producing.

'But you've got to check the mechanics that generate those numbers and get to the bottom of discrepancies between track performance and wind-tunnel data. No amount of number crunching is going to help you do that if you don't have a feel for the mechanical aspects. In my opinion it's a common shortcoming in people whose main racing experience has been learned in a university.'

Besides all this, Barnard felt that the Prost team's uncompetitiveness was in danger of harming his reputation: 'There was this expectation that if I was at a Formula 1 team, I'd run everything, but that wasn't the deal and wasn't my job.' Fairly early on Barnard started to learn from third parties that Alain Prost was blaming both he and Alan Jenkins for the team's woes, and he considered that most unfair: 'I wasn't in a position to say to people, "Don't do that, do this, change that!" I could only advise — if they ignored my advice that was their concern. I did what I could and what I was asked to do. You can take a horse to water but you cannot make it drink.'

And then things took a turn for the worse financially. B3's accountant, Vijay Kothary, reported that things were getting tight for the company because the money wasn't coming through from Prost. Emails began to go unanswered and John's telephone conversations with Alain were increasingly brief.

Finally, just before the start of the 2002 season, Prost went pop, owing Barnard personally £65,000 and B3 a great deal more than that. After much evasion and a long legal struggle, it was discovered that the money to pay people on individual contracts did in fact exist and Barnard eventually received what was due to him. B3, however, was £700,000 in the hole.

To find a way out, Barnard decided to seek advice from Ron Dennis; if anyone knew how to deal with a problem like this, he would; perhaps Ron might even be interested in buying B3. But Barnard's intent was misunderstood. When they met, Ron told him, 'I can't lend you that sort of money.' 'I'm not asking you to, it's not why I'm here!' responded John. The encounter never recovered from that moment.

The fact that Ron Dennis's door was open at all shows that at least he was receptive to healing the wound that had opened up nearly two decades earlier. Barnard, however, watching the press from time to time, became convinced that Ron was still making every endeavour to write him out of the history of McLaren. The two remained at loggerheads.

CHAPTER 35
BYE BYE B3
2002–08

B3 restructured and there were casualties, but John Barnard tried to look after his people as best he could. As Dan Fleetcroft recalls, 'When times were tough he really dug deep to keep people's jobs safe.' But by now Barnard was developing an exit strategy.

'At the time, my goal was to run B3 at arm's length,' he says. 'Then I could have the best of both worlds. I could still do nice, intricate Formula 1 bits and pieces, but I could be my own boss as well. I just liked being able to come and go when I felt like it and not feel that I was under pressure. I had never felt I could just go home when I wanted.'

In the meantime his company continued in its innovative vein.

B3 invented a smart new method for making the tricky foam cockpit collar introduced to protect drivers' heads after the Senna accident. Such collars were usually made of layers of foam glued together and hand-carved into the requisite shape, but B3 came up with a far more accurate, 'aerospace' method. They froze a foam block with liquid nitrogen and then machined it to the required complex shape — which sounds easy and obvious but was, in fact, elaborate and ingenious. The foam was then covered in two layers of carbon-fibre and Kevlar to take any impact from the helmet. Ferrari were B3's principal clients for these 'nitrogen head rests'.

Another B3 'first' was the carbon brake pedal, developed for Prost. By this time brake pedals were normally made of titanium, but John saw that it was possible with carbon to create a wider range of shapes with the same strength but up to 40% lighter. He recalls B3 making a particularly huge one, 'about five or six inches wide', for David Coulthard at McLaren, with the intention being that 'presumably he could choose to brake with either foot'.

Barnard came up with a rather brilliant solution to the thorny matter of carbon loading eyes. Not a problem that would ever burden most of us, this was a difficulty that arose when drilling a hole through a carbon plate, such as a flexure, to provide a fixing to the chassis or an upright. As John explains, 'By drilling through, you inevitably break some of the carbon fibres. The problem was to carry the loads through to the bolt without compromising the strength of the plate.' He considered various methods, including wrapping unidirectional carbon-fibre around the hole, but this was a messy solution that didn't meet his instinctive requirement for simplicity and elegance.

It suddenly occurred to him that the solution lay in placing thin plates of titanium, around 0.4mm thick, between the layers of carbon cloth in a composite sandwich, all glued and cooked together: 'We used six or seven layers, which allowed us to make the loading eye of a decent size. We were pretty chuffed with the solution.' His daughter Jennifer, then in the final year of an engineering degree at the University of Bristol, made the study of the problem and the solution the core of her final project.

B3 further developed the Barnard catch — the bodywork fastener he conceived at Benetton — and supplied these widely within motorsport.

'These were nice little bits and pieces,' says John of his swansong in motorsport. 'Even though we were now only partially involved in Formula 1, the team still enjoyed designing and building them. We probably should have pursued this more and become a centre of excellence for this sort of thing.'

B3 also turned outwards and upwards, specialising in aerospace. Fully equipped with clean rooms and high-end machining kit, the company was ideally placed to capitalise on know-how from the extreme environment of Formula 1. One client was Surrey Satellites, a ground-breaking company spin-off from the University of Surrey for which B3 made components, including super-accurate carbon tubes for space cameras.

One noteworthy and ingenious space project was a gyro-guidance system, which used four spinning discs mounted back-to-back to turn a satellite in the weightless vacuum of orbit by means of gyroscopic forces, thereby saving on propellant. Designed by Surrey Satellites and made by B3, the system also operated as a generator: when the satellite was in sunlight its solar panels would provide the energy to spin up the discs and, as it moved into shadow, the spinning discs would recharge the batteries.

B3 made the saucer-shaped main casing for the ill-fated *Beagle 2*, the archetypically British Mars lander, built on a shoestring but packed full of ingenuity. Sadly and memorably *Beagle 2* crashed into the planet on Christmas Day in 2003 after suspected parachute malfunction.

There was more. B3 took on some development work for a prosthetic limbs company, coming up with an idea that involved flexure technology. At the 2006 Winter Olympics the skeleton bobsleighs of Britain's Kristan Bromley and Shelley Rudman used B3-made carbon undertrays. And so on.

As Fleetcroft states, 'These sort of projects often came from clients who had only sketched the concept on a napkin. Happily we were good enough and experienced enough to solve the problems and turn them into practical reality.'

Even Barnard himself occasionally took advantage of his facility. Says Fleetcroft, 'We made some titanium reservoir caps for his Aston Martin DB6. We made him furniture, window frames and a state-of-the-art barbecue. I think he even fixed his shower tray with a carbon patch — well, you would, wouldn't you, if you had a facility like B3 at your beck and call?'

'B3 did okay,' says Barnard. 'It wasn't making me millions but it was keeping me chugging along. We did interesting high-end things and we had such a nice crew of talented people.'

Barnard did poke one more toe into the world of motorsport. This was MotoGP, the pinnacle of motorcycle racing. His client was the Proton team run by American Kenny Roberts, the three-time world champion who had been Barry Sheene's great track rival in the 1970s. John dedicated a lot of time to this in the 2002–04 period, for a while spending most of his working week at the team's base in Banbury, Oxfordshire, with Dan Fleetcroft usually at his side.

He made it clear from the outset that he had no professional experience of motorcycle racing, telling Roberts that he saw his job as introducing high-level engineering principles and getting the drawing office properly organised. It proved to be a tall order.

'In the first place,' says John, 'they'd be whispering behind their hands, "What does he know about bikes?" It felt a bit like… if I didn't have a leather jacket, boots and tattoos, I was no use. But as far as I was concerned it was all about engineering. Yes, of course, tuning a bike is a different animal and manifestly different from a four-wheeled car, but initially it was all about basic engineering.'

The increasingly jaded Proton team seemed unimpressed by his introduction of high-spec carbon-fibre, his moving of the engine air intake to the front of the nose fairing, his redesign of the headstock so that air could flow uninterrupted around the spindle holding the front forks ('a beautiful piece of aerodynamics'), and his beautifully designed aluminium swing arm.

The main problem was the V5 engine. The Proton team made their own, but, despite pouring time and money into it, they couldn't make it competitive.

John found it all a chaotic and alien world, but Fleetcroft loved it, partly because his employer gave him much more responsibility: 'John let me get on with defining and designing the bike, the bodywork, the composites, the tanks. It was also a lot more visual — I was styling the bikes too, with ample input from JB of course. You can't really show people your work on a fire extinguisher but you can show them the fairing you designed for a motorcycle. It gave me massive personal satisfaction.'

As the years passed at B3, John seemed to be slowly slipping into neutral and coasting towards an early retirement.

'It was late 2007, I was 61 years old and the trouble was that B3 wasn't making much money,' he reveals. 'It was housed in state-of-the-art Ferrari facilities that we could no longer afford. The answer was to move to a facility with a lower rent.'

Andy Smith found alternative premises in Bordon, Hampshire, half an hour from Godalming. 'It was 25,000 square feet,' says John, 'which was far more than we needed and yet we could save quarter of a million a year in rent if we took it.' But he also calculated it would cost £400,000 to move and decided to pull out, at quite a late stage.

Not long after, two offers to buy B3 emerged, both originating within Barnard's team. The first was put together by his sales and marketing man, John Minett, with business partner John Allen. The other was a proposed management buy-out led by Andy Smith with involvement from Roy O'Mara, who ran the machine-shop, and composites expert Ian Weild. The Minett/Allen bid won the day and they duly took over on 5 March 2008, bringing in, to Barnard's considerable surprise, Steve Nichols as technical director supported by Matthew Jeffreys — both men Barnard knew well from McLaren days a quarter of a century earlier.

As their employment of Nichols and Jeffreys indicated, Minett and Allen had renewed Formula 1 business in their sights. They were getting up to speed just in time for it all to go terminally wrong. That September the giant American investment bank Lehman Brothers filed for the largest bankruptcy in history and so opened the seething Pandora's Box of sub-prime mortgages and banking malfeasance, bringing the entire, tottering, global financial system crashing to the floor.

As Jeffreys says, 'It was the perfect storm of unfortunate events. The business relied a lot on Formula 1 and at the end of the year Honda, which was 50% of our customer base, withdrew completely. At the same time the world-wide crash hit us and the banks stopped lending.' The company was bust before the end of the year.

Like a scene out of *Pulp Fiction*, John Barnard, always a man to avoid being in the wrong place at the wrong time, had dodged not just one bullet but a veritable strafing.

'Making a go of B3 was always a cause of anxiety,' reflects John. 'By the time I got to the end of it, I was in a mood to divest myself of so much material stuff, which, I thought, was making life complicated. I just wanted to simplify things. The kids were growing up; I was done with the pressure of business. It was time to downsize my worries.'

His first worry was his massive house, Combe Rise, in which he and Rosie were beginning to rattle around as their children took wing. They decided to sell it and look at moving to Switzerland, where they visited an old friend, Graham Bogle, who used to work for John Hogan at Marlboro, and went house-hunting. They found a modest but comfortable three-bedroom house on a ¾-acre plot in the village of Féchy, 40 minutes north-east of Geneva, commanding a stunning view southwards across the famous lake towards a snow-capped Alpine backdrop, with Mont Blanc visible on clear days.

Such is John's nature, he soon decided that the house wasn't good enough as it was: 'We thought we'd modify it a little, and ended up knocking it down and building a house bigger than we really should have done.' Of course, they had to have at least four large bedrooms with en-suite bathrooms, so that the children could stay with their partners, plus a large modern kitchen, a drawing room, a private study and a dining room. And, naturally, a basement home cinema and games room in which he could display his Formula 1 memorabilia — front wings, wheels, favourite pieces of technology, models of his cars built for him and lovingly displayed in glass cabinets. Oh yes, and garaging for four cars.

Less than ten years later, in 2017, Barnard was getting itchy feet, a lifetime complaint. He duly put his magnificent Swiss retreat on the market, but not before buying a house in Wimbledon (which he completely gutted and rebuilt) as a comfortable London *pied à terre*. At the time of writing he is searching for a country house in the middle of land as far away from 'pesky neighbours' as is possible. He would have it in deepest Cornwall if he could, but Rosie, far more gregarious, wants to live within striking distance of London.

John Barnard has done extremely well financially from motorsport design. It has given him the freedom to do exactly what he wants.

What he wants, increasingly, is to be a loving grandfather; he has three grandchildren so far. And he loves to do DIY at the homes of his children, Jennifer, Gillian and Michael, painting and decorating to such high standards that it creates some domestic pressure as the days tick by, the living room still shrouded in dustsheets as John reaches the decision to take off all the skirting and sand it down to the bare wood.

Rosie continues to love him and stand by him, enjoying his sense of humour and passion for life, tolerating his anger, frustration, and occasional moods — the modern Barnard is a good deal more mellow than the Prince of Darkness or the Godalming Scud.

What else does he do? As mentioned at the outset, he has achieved award-winning innovation in furniture design: 'Terence Woodgate talked to me about his plans for a minimalist dining table and soon we were working together on the idea, using B3's facilities.'

Their first attempt featured a thin steel skin covering a foam sandwich for the table top, but it didn't work: 'The legs were so thin that if you knocked against it, the weight of the table top was such that it would resonate and just wouldn't stop.' The B3 boffins considered a variety of solutions, including mass dampers inside the table. In the end they plumped for a carbon skin over a foam core set on four elegant steel legs. The supremely elegant Surface Table was born.

What use a dining table without dining chairs? Terence and John duly created the thoroughly minimalist Surface Chair to go with the Surface Table. The table is offered by Established & Sons in three lengths — 2.4, 3.0 and 6.0 metres. At £42,000, £46,000 and £190,000 respectively, prices are eye-watering but there is evidently a significant market for people wanting large, strong tables that look gorgeous, are easy to move, can seat up to 24 comfortably, can bear the weight of a truly enormous banquet, and will probably last forever.

Their designs won awards from the magazines *Wallpaper* (2008), *Design Week* (2009) and *Homes & Gardens* in association with the Victoria & Albert Museum (2009). To boost sales, Woodgate, Barnard and Established & Sons put a six-metre table on show at the Biennale Interieur in Belgium during October 2010, drawing attention to it by planting a contemporary McLaren Formula 1 car on its surface, courtesy of Ron Dennis and Martin Whitmarsh. One six-metre prototype spent time in Modena at the Museo Casa Enzo Ferrari and sold for over £230,000 when auctioned by Sotheby's in New York in late 2016.[108]

And what else? Barnard continues to dabble in design for carbon road cars at the behest of partners in far-off countries and to develop new thinking in areas of transport that he would prefer, for now, not to reveal. He is ever secretive, as ever. His mind is ever active, as ever. You just can't keep a genius designer down.

---

[108] *'Terence Woodgate and John Barnard — Prototype 'Surface Table', www.sothebys.com.*

CHAPTER 36
WAS HE ALL THAT?
1969–2008

Within the Formula 1 paddock it is commonly thought that John Barnard's cars could have won many more races and many more World Championships had he been less fixated upon creating the perfect car and more focused on winning races. Certainly the bald statistical summary looks a little meagre compared with the records of his most celebrated peers, confined as it is to three Drivers' titles (1984–86) and two Constructors' titles (1984–85), all during the McLaren years. Two of those peers, Ross Brawn and Patrick Head, gave interviews for this book and offered their thoughts on the reasons.

Ross Brawn's distinguished career has embraced a good few teams, including Williams in the early days, but three phases stand out like beacons. First, his time at Benetton brought two World Championships with Michael Schumacher, in 1994 and 1995. Second, an extraordinary period of Ferrari supremacy delivered six consecutive Constructors' Championships, from 1999 to 2004, and saw Schumacher become World Champion five times. Third, his own Brawn team achieved a surprising, stunning and popular World Championship success in 2009 with Jenson Button, evolving from there into the awesome Mercedes-Benz Formula 1 operation of today. This is Ross's summation:

He was game-changing in terms of his influence and involvement in Formula 1. His period at McLaren was incredibly impressive and his periods at Ferrari too. It was the innovation — he definitely introduced some things that changed Formula 1 forever… He raised the standard of engineering in Formula 1… He was a hugely influential character both on me and Formula 1 generally.

> *John has a very strong vision and that can be a strength and sometimes a weakness, in the same way that I am perhaps more accommodating — that can be a weakness as well… So if there was a trait that brought John into conflict with drivers more often, it was that he had a very clear view of how he felt a car should be and what balance it should have and how it should be driven. That, I know, didn't suit all drivers.*
>
> *There's no getting away from it: his tendency to call 'a spade a shovel' was too much for too many people but this uncompromising honesty was an essential part of what made him such a brilliant engineer.*

Patrick Head, John's old friend from Lola days and Best Man at his wedding, spent his entire front-line career at Williams. Seven times his cars produced World Champions, from Alan Jones in 1980 to Jacques Villeneuve in 1997, and in that same period Williams won the Constructors' Championship nine times. This is Patrick's summation:

> *I think John's pure approach to engineering meant he suffered from great frustration when engineers failed to achieve his standard. There are plenty of examples where talented engineers work in partnership with more people-oriented managers and for him, I'm sure, that would have resulted in a more positive working environment.*
>
> *He would have had a much bigger career had he bitten the bullet and gone to Italy. I'm sure Rosie would have supported him. The trouble was that he couldn't abide schemers; particularly schemers who didn't talk English. Had he found a way to cope with that, the sky would have been his limit.*

Drivers, too, have their opinions about John Barnard. Let's take just two who speak well of working with him.

Gerhard Berger had a closer association than any other driver as he totalled six years in Barnard-designed Ferraris, during the periods 1987–89 and 1993–95, and in between he experienced at McLaren what had been built upon Barnard's foundations. This is Gerhard's verdict:

> *It's very simple for me. During the 1980s John Barnard was the best race car designer in the world. He was the master. He not only built quick cars but also beautiful cars.*

His Ferrari 639 and 640 were so special. If I came across one I would buy it. This is one of the most beautiful Formula 1 cars ever made, and the first with a paddle shift. So special.

Damon Hill, World Champion in a Patrick Head-designed Williams FW18 in 1996, drove Barnard's last Formula 1 car, the Arrows A19:

John was one of the heroes. When you're a young racing driver, you look up to these guys. I'm very fortunate, I've worked with him… it was just nice working with the man. People who are demanding are difficult to work with, because they require people to do things that perhaps are at the limits of their ability, which is tough. But that's why things don't get better, because people don't want to step outside the comfort zone. Barnard was one of most truly innovative and meticulous designers in Formula 1.

The views of colleagues, of course, are also relevant in assessing Barnard's legacy in Formula 1 design. Diane Holl, who was at his side for so long, from early in his first spell with Ferrari to late in his second, says this:

I do believe that John has had nothing like the level of praise he deserves. He fell prey to setting up three teams — McLaren, Benetton and Ferrari — and then the politically smarter people stepped in and reaped the success.

He knew how to design a fast car, and how to set up the systems to make it so — the parts, the machining, the aerodynamics. But once that is all in place and moving, all you really needed was a manager to smooth it along and a half-decent designer to keep topping it up.

John was also one of those engineers — and I don't think they come along very often — who knows load paths. They know, almost by instinct, where the loads are coming and going. In between the two you need to put structure. The aim is to make it as light as possible for what you're trying to achieve — that will lead to the most efficient design. This was second nature to him. So his designs were light, strong and very functional.

Andy Smith joined Barnard in 1986 as head of materials and composites when GTO was being set up and stayed with him for over 20 years, all the way through to B3, where he was managing director until the sale of the company in 2007. This is his view:

John was one of the last dictators in Formula 1. He knew everything that was being done, down to the last nut and bolt.

He loved to keep pushing things. It was always his desire to do things better, to make them lighter, more efficient, better, faster. He just wasn't interested in treading water. I was amazed at how we dumped everything each year. We'd throw away the design and start again. How John came up with the ideas to do it differently, to do it better, God alone knows.

Joan Villadelprat also worked with Barnard for many years. He was a mechanic with Project Four and McLaren, then John took him to Ferrari as chief mechanic, and later he joined Benetton as factory manager in Witney. The Spaniard says this:

What was really good about John Barnard was that he was never happy with anything he did. He was always trying to make it better, to do something new. I believe motor racing owes a lot to him.

No other designer took John's step-change approach to Formula 1 so wholeheartedly and single-mindedly, and no living engineers can claim to have had quite the revolutionary impact that Barnard had, not Patrick Head, not Gordon Murray, not Ross Brawn, not Adrian Newey.

And who among the dead? Probably only Colin Chapman of Lotus, and he achieved his creative advances too often at considerable risk to his drivers.

So why haven't more Formula 1 engineers produced more technological innovation? Some would say that it was just too expensive to do so. Barnard says it's all about design management, his approach compared with that of others. How did his approach differ? This is Patrick Head's overview of his own methods at Williams:

I would write a brief to our project engineers rather than directly to the designer, and I'd keep an eye on the progress, seeing how they were solving the problems. Sometimes I wouldn't be able to find a better solution, but sometimes I could.

I would always write a very specific brief, and the first page of it would have all of the targets in order of importance. I'd get them to stick it up on the top right-hand corner of their drawing board, telling them to look at it at least twice a day and ask themselves whether what they were designing

ing to meet the targets. This was because people so readily go off into ₹ something that may be beautiful, filigree design but doesn't actually achieve what you wanted.

Here, in potted form, is Barnard's guide to making a Formula 1 car:

You make a list: here's the wheelbase I want, here's the track, here's the centre of gravity position, this is the aero percentage of improvement I want over last year's car, we want this gearbox with this internal gear train, but in a smaller box, etc... But there's a point at which you can't put it down on a list, you can't write design down on paper in a list.

So I would decide on the basics at my drawing board— wheelbase, engine, gearbox, rear wheel centre-line positions, estimated centre of gravity positions — so much being defined by regulations. I would generally define everything and my 'pencils', later CAD operators, would draw it in detail.

With CAD, you have to define the axes, setting as zero the centre line down the middle of the car, and positioning the elements off that. Other zero reference points would be the bottom of the chassis and the front chassis bulkhead.

I would then draw a plan view of the car at, say, ¼-scale and then create a side view to give the profile. I would give this to a CAD person and sit at their elbow and they would transfer my drawing board scheme into a CAD model under my guidance.

Certain things form themselves. The driver's space is naturally formed around a CAD model of your driver. You can adjust his position as you see fit. Then the fuel tank — how much fuel you are going to carry — which is usually defined by rules. There are rules about where the fuel can't be put, e.g., not alongside the driver or the engine. What shape? Wide, short, tall, long? Driver's space. Fuel. The rest of the car you would make as small as possible.

This procedure left him freer to concentrate on major change. He realises this differs from how others went about their work: 'If I had spent less time coming up with steps and more time in meetings going through lists of problems, delegating people to fix the problems, that might have meant I would have had a more successful Formula 1 career. But I wanted to make big steps all the time, and it cost me in results.'

The major steps couldn't be delegated: 'If you said to someone, "I want you to find a whole new solution to changing gear", that's like saying to a young artist, "paint me a masterpiece."'

The innovations invariably required determination, drive and commitment to push them through, especially the really big ones: 'Take the paddle shift. Had I not stood my ground at Ferrari, had I not put my contract on the table, my job on the line, the paddle shift wouldn't have happened, possibly still wouldn't have happened — who else would have done it? Who else would have risked their job to further a big innovation? I don't think that's the way other top designers play the game.'

Looking back, Barnard thinks that leaving McLaren was his biggest mistake: 'What I should have done was kept my McLaren shares and retained the same shareholding clout as Ron to keep us on a level footing. I shouldn't have worried where he was and what he was doing, whether he was enjoying himself, because at the end of the day Ron comes up with the money and he's not a bad manager.'

He also feels angry with himself for turning down the second chance of returning to McLaren when Ron approached him in 1995: 'I could be living in the lap of luxury.' When it is pointed out that he is, in fact, ensconced in just such a lap, he adds, 'Well, more luxury.' At McLaren in the modern era he might have been able to forge a place for himself where he was mentally free to concentrate on fundamental design thinking, contemplating the next steps.

Barnard did his best to achieve this nirvana anyway. When he arrived at each team he always told them it would be at least two years, possibly three, before he had improved the systems there to build a car that had any chance of winning consistently. The teams never liked this news and would always put him under pressure for quicker results. The result was that he would soak up too much pressure and, when he was full, he would detonate.

The other factor in his short-term residencies was boredom. If he wasn't finding new steps he didn't want to play. That and the fact that, day by day and month by month, the people around him, especially those in power above him, would drive him completely potty.

So he walked out of McLaren when the team had hit its stride and with much more to come; he walked out of Ferrari just before Alain Prost should have secured the 1990 World Championship; he was pretty much sacked from Benetton just before Michael Schumacher came in to win; and he walked out of Ferrari when Schumacher should have won the 1997 World Championship and just prior to their six years of extraordinary dominance.

The truth is that Barnard, like most creative geniuses, is simply not made for routine. Going racing every weekend bored him out of his mind: 'Living in hotels, staying at the circuit late, sitting there looking at computer graphs and print-outs, trying to figure out whether I should increase the ride height by 3mm or change the front wing angle by half a degree…' All that was mind-numbing for him, however fascinating others may have found it.

He was much happier when testing at a circuit: 'I could make a fundamental change to a set-up, run it, and then make another fundamental change and run it again. That was interesting. But going racing and all the crap that goes with it, all the bullshit, simply didn't hold my attention.'

If things go on the way they are in Formula 1, there will never be another Barnard. As he says, 'In those days it was easier to make step changes because a) the rules were a lot looser and b) the sport was more in its infancy. It's much more difficult now. Now if anyone proposes a step change, there are enormous discussions as to whether it should be allowed. If anyone had the balls, and the money, they should make the change and then argue it at the races. Changes now are driven by group decisions, such as the drive to make Formula 1 greener, more relevant.'

My choice for the person to deliver the last comments in this book is Murray Walker, who commentated on so many of John's races:

> *What has always surprised me about John is that he was able to walk away from something in which he had been so involved and which was so dependent upon him, and go away and design bloody furniture! I mean, what a difference! I'm sure he designs brilliant furniture, but to a Formula 1 enthusiast like me it really doesn't matter very much compared with what he used to do… John Barnard is one of just a handful of the true greats.*

So, was he all that? Yes he was. And he still is.

EPILOGUE
AND THEN? WHAT HAPPENED NEXT?

Something quite remarkable happened next. There came a moment in writing this biography when I had to broach with John Barnard a difficult subject — the need for me to interview Ron Dennis.

John had long harboured deep disappointment in Ron, a feeling that he felt sure was reciprocated. One of the main reasons why John agreed to cooperate with me on the book was his total conviction that Ron was trying to write him out of McLaren history, and, indeed, there is evidence for this. There were plenty of opportunities when Ron might have sung Barnard's praises, but didn't, especially for his contribution to the birth of the new McLaren organisation and his work on the carbon-fibre car.

When I first visited a Formula 1 paddock, at Silverstone during the 2012 British Grand Prix, I was agreeably surprised that I was welcomed so openly by the best journalists there, especially David Tremayne, who did everything in his power to help a rookie, and the late Alan Henry, whom I already knew because he lived near me. So many journalists asked of me, with a glint in their eye, 'Ah, how is the Prince of Darkness?', revealing a playful fondness for one of the great characters of the sport, one who had given them so much fascinating copy over the years.

Mike Doodson gave me a stern warning. I told him that one of my most difficult challenges was to get Ron Dennis to agree to an interview. Mike said: 'Well, you've got to get him. It won't be much of a book about Barnard if you don't get Ron's view. I don't think I'd bother reviewing it.'

But John didn't want me to interview Ron, arguing that he would have nothing to say but 'negative, inaccurate rubbish'. John considered Ron to be such a control freak that even if he agreed to the interview, he would never allow me to go to print without approving every word. In short, John said I was a fool for even trying.

I pushed on because Doodson was right: the book had to have Ron Dennis. I had hoped that John might approach Ron for me, but he made it clear that if I wanted Ron, I had to get him myself.

Over the next two years I made various approaches through McLaren's PR people but my phone calls and emails elicited nothing. I found myself dreaming, as writers do, of a perfect scenario: that Ron would say 'yes', that he would be open to my questions, that he would want to put the 30-year row with Barnard behind him, that Barnard eventually would too. The fantasy developed. I dreamed that I could be the hero, that I could do the impossible, that I could bring them back together, be the catalyst to their working together again. What a fairy-tale ending to the book that would have made.

It was, of course, a stupid dream, and subsequent conversations I had with long-established journalists in Formula 1 made me feel silly for even thinking of such a thing. I began to mentally prepare myself for a book about John without Ron Dennis, composing phrases about how his refusal just went to prove how right Barnard was about him. At one point I even convinced myself that the book would be better without him.

At the 2014 British Grand Prix I tried in vain to have a word with Ron but I did chat to McLaren's head of PR, Matt Bishop, who invited me, as is par for the course these days, to send an email. Ten days later I eventually got a reply:

'I'm sorry but it isn't something that Ron is going to be able to devote time to, I regret to say.

'We receive many such requests but, as CEO of McLaren Group, which comprises much more than only a Formula 1 team nowadays, Ron has to divide his time very judiciously; as a result, although reminiscing about the past is interesting and sometimes enjoyable, it isn't something he has time to do any more really.'

The tone was a trifle irritating, but, having burned my fingers before in similar circumstances, I resisted the instant curt reply, that heady danger of email, and resolved to leave it for a week. I didn't have to — five days later, and entirely out of the blue, came this:

'Good news: it so happens that Ron may be able to squeeze you in after all!'

So it was both with trepidation and excitement on a cold morning in late

ABOVE The V10-engined 647 at its Fiorano launch early in 1996. The press described the car as 'more like a jet fighter than a racing car'. Ferrari's new star driver, Michael Schumacher, predicted a couple of victories, and got three. *Courtesy of John Barnard* **BELOW** The wind-tunnel model of the 647 undergoing testing at Filton. *Courtesy of John Barnard*

ABOVE The steering wheel dashboard first appeared on the 647 of 1996. Barnard: 'I was getting fed up with trying to make the dashboard more accessible.' *Sutton Images* **BELOW** Michael Schumacher in the 1996 Belgian Grand Prix at Spa-Francorchamps, chalking up one of his three wins that season. *LAT Images*

ABOVE The Filton wind-tunnel model of the 648, Barnard's last Ferrari, looking pretty much identical to the finished car as it ran during 1997. *Courtesy of John Barnard*
BELOW Schumacher driving the 648 to victory in Monaco, one of five wins for Barnard's car in 1997, after his departure from Ferrari. Schumacher might have won the World Championship had he not tried to take out rival Jacques Villeneuve in Spain. *LAT Images*

ABOVE Post-Ferrari, John Barnard took over Ferrari's Godalming facility as the base for his new company, B3 Technologies, keeping many of his trusted and long-serving team. *Courtesy of John Barnard* **BELOW** Barnard with his smart-looking Arrows A19 at its 1998 launch, with drivers Pedro Diniz (left) and Mika Salo, plus team owner Tom Walkinshaw. *Courtesy of John Barnard*

ABOVE Carbon/titanium suspension parts made at B3 for Prost Grand Prix. The company made parts for several Formula 1 teams, including Ferrari, and also built and designed components for satellites. *Courtesy of John Barnard* **BELOW** Barnard's innovative carbon-fibre fire extinguisher system dispensed with the traditional extinguisher bottle. *Courtesy of Dan Fleetcroft*

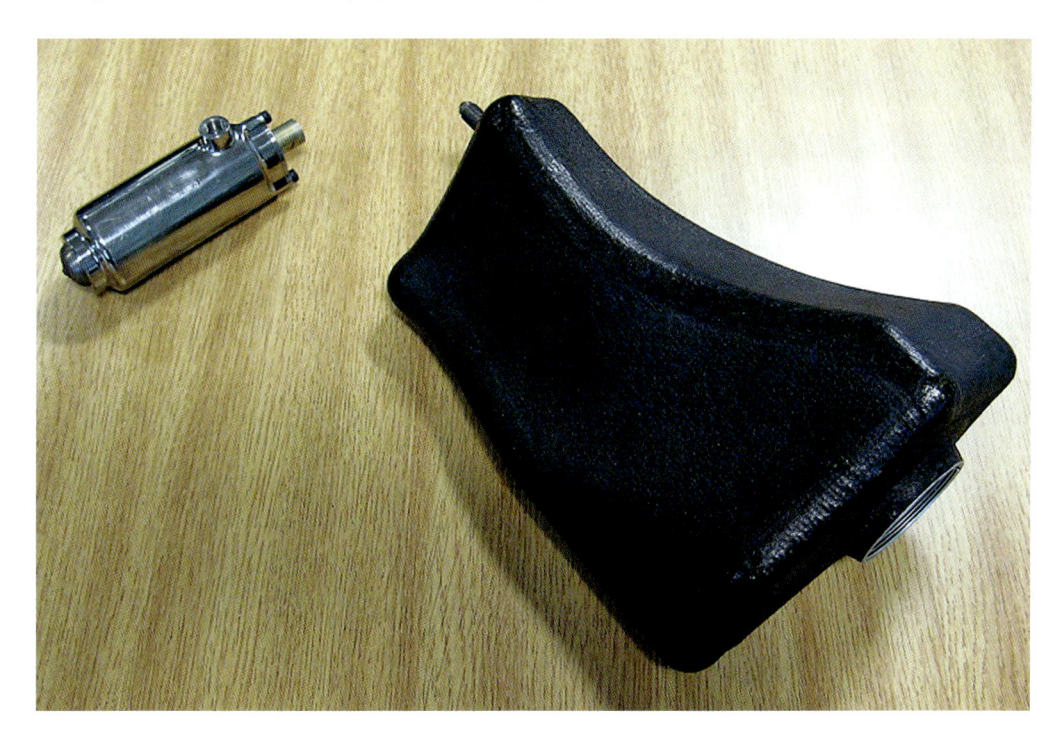

ABOVE A display of nine wind-tunnel models at Maranello's Ferrari Museum includes six of Barnard's cars. *Author* **BELOW LEFT** Barnard talking about his paddle-shift gearbox in the Ferrari Museum on a giant representation of a Nintendo Game Boy — an invention of the same period. The exhibition described his work as 'pure genius'. *Author* **BELOW RIGHT** Barnard's Ferrari 641 on display at New York's Museum of Modern Art. *Author*

ABOVE Barnard seated on a carbon Surface Chair at the carbon Surface Table he helped design. *Greg Pajo*
BELOW Barnard at a more traditional table, checking his memory against the motorsport press at his Geneva home. *Author*

ABOVE After 30 years of anger and minimal contact, John Barnard and Ron Dennis met at the McLaren Technology Centre. *Author* **BELOW** Looking like an alien spacecraft, Barnard's MP4 carbon-fibre monocoque revolutionised motorsport. *McLaren Technology Centre*

EPILOGUE

September 2014 that I arrived outside the white wrought-iron gates of Kingsbourne, Ron Dennis's multi-million pound home in the heart of fashionable Surrey. I was to join him in his car on a journey into London, an estimated 90-minute ride, more than enough for the likes of me.

I rang the intercom bell at the precise appointed time, 7.30am, and the large gates swung open. I walked up the long gravel drive amid immaculate lawns, trees and privet hedges trimmed in perfect topiary. Some way ahead of me was the main entrance, flanked by two 12-feet evergreens shaped into Christmas tree cones growing out of giant square marble tubs. The front door was behind four massive unfluted pillars topped off, some 16 feet up, by ornate Corinthian capitals supporting a vast and heavy-looking triangular portico. The wings on either side featured neat, perfect, oblong, 12-pane, sash windows. In fact, Kingsbourne bears more than a passing similarity to the White House as seen from the Rose Garden.

The door was already open when I got there, attended by David the butler, a fresh-faced, lean young man, who politely asked me to remove my shoes. I tiptoed over the immaculate carpet in the large entrance hall to the kitchen off to the right, itself dominated by a massive white granite counter, upon which David started to make me a strong coffee.

I looked around the room. To my right was a living room space. It seemed homely, a place where Ron could relax. There was a large TV on which BBC Breakfast News was playing, a top-of-the-range music system, a host of remote controls, expensive-looking furniture, bookshelves and artwork. Everything was tidy but not OCD-tidy. The room had a comfortable, lived-in look.

I gazed across the room to the window overlooking the drive and became transfixed by the odd behaviour of Tim, the chauffeur, who was, for no apparent reason, running up and down outside as 8am approached, clearly in some distress and not unlike a character from *The Benny Hill Show*.

At 8.07am, Ron arrived in the kitchen, looking smart and trim in an expensive, tailored dark blue suit. We chatted about the news — dominated by the cruelty of so-called Islamic State — and then went off to the car, a luxurious, black, immaculate Mercedes S-class.

The interview began stiffly, with Ron self-effacingly asserting that any transcription of the recordings would 'probably be gobbledegook', before answering questions about how he had first come to hear about John, all in a language that has been dubbed by the paddock as RonSpeak. This is the somewhat bombastic way he often answers questions, using long, rambling statements, and employing long words, sometimes inappropriately, where shorter and fewer words would be far more clear.

As the minutes ticked by, with Ron describing John's achievements at Chaparral in meticulous detail, it occurred to me that RonSpeak was a defence mechanism, a function of his insecurity about his academic credentials, but I could see that it also serves another purpose. It stops interviewers, or anyone else, from interrupting: it is indeed a challenge to cut across a Ron Dennis monologue, however long it might already have been.

I had to get him to relax, and I decided to try that by the simple device of pointing out what a wally John Barnard could be at times. Soon we were both laughing at John's excesses, and Ron began to talk more freely about the plusses and minuses of working with a perfectionist genius with an explosive temper.

And then we had a car accident — a deeply weird experience. During the middle of a conversation about the Hercules facility in Utah, Tim the chauffeur pulled into a McDonald's. Were we to have an Egg McMuffin for breakfast in the car? It seemed most unlikely.

Tim piped up: 'I've got to use the loo, Ron, I'm very sorry.' A few seconds after Tim had rushed off, with Ron in mid-sentence, the car was shaken by an impact. The driver of a Thames Water van had reversed into the left rear wheel arch of the Mercedes, buckling it, and providing a spectacularly novel way of interrupting RonSpeak.

'Oh shit!' was Ron's perfectly natural response. He threw open the door and yelled at the driver as he climbed out: 'It's my brand new Mercedes!' Fearing a fracas, I too climbed out of the car, thinking how good it could be for me if I had to step in to defend Ron in a punch-up. But it was not to be. The van driver was all apology: 'Sorry mate, it was an accident. I'll get my details. Sorry.'

Ron, showing admirable self-control, said: 'Yeah well, you know. If you had just paid more attention — literally two weeks old!' The driver apologised again. Ron gestured me back into the car.

When Tim emerged from the building, he performed a classic double-take. Why was his boss out of the car? Who was that bloke? He paced over, his face white with anxiety. Ron directed him to get the van driver's details.

When Tim got back in the car, his day went from bad to worse. The two-week-old Mercedes had decided not to work properly: 'I can see a bloody alarm', he said forlornly, pointing to a warning light on the dashboard. 'Bad morning.' By way of explanation, Ron leaned over to me and said: 'My driver will feel bad because he basically just said "I have to go to the bathroom." If he had had a pee before we left, then we wouldn't have been parked here.'

Eventually we resumed our journey. As far as the interview was concerned, I found myself back at square one. But in time, and following some more laughter at Barnard's expense, the mood softened again.

When it came to the crucial question of what Ron considered to be the cause of his break-up with Barnard, things became frosty. I found myself severely quizzed about John's view of what had happened, rapid terse questions: 'Let's hear his version... And so, then what? And then? What happened next?'

Satisfied by the truth of my answers, that John was frustrated, unreasonably jealous of Ron's lifestyle, in need of a change of scene, upset by Ron's lack of response to his request for a dramatic pay rise, and having secured, with some initial disbelief, my promise that the less complimentary aspects of John's behaviour would be in the book, Ron revealed his accusation of industrial espionage when John departed for Ferrari.

'I received a phone call from a person... a night watchman... paid by us, who was living across from the factory. He said, "There is someone at McLaren very late at night." John was copying drawings to take with him... You could say that was the ultimate betrayal for me.'

And so we came to the crunch.

NICK: Do you think it's a repairable relationship?

RON: Of course. Completely, completely. I don't harbour... life is too short and you mature. You don't just mature in terms of age. Your thinking changes, you're more tolerant, and you are more attuned to the weaknesses of man.

NICK: What do you like about John?

RON: Oh, you know the, er... it wasn't a huge sense of humour, but it was a good one, is a good one. I loved his family loyalty. His attention to detail. I mean we both had that as character traits, and I think everything we did complemented each other and I didn't have to worry about whether we were going to have an elegant, competitive race car. When you are part of a Grand Prix team, that is a huge part of the challenge. We were pioneering together. When it came to concepts and everything, I was just one of the tools in John's tool box. But I still remember being quite hands on...

NICK: What did you not like about him? What were the things you found difficult to work with?

RON: Well, he was hot-headed. He could lose his temper before he got his brain into gear. And very often the reason he lost his temper didn't substantiate his reaction. But things were relatively quickly forgotten — not instantly. So it is strange when you ask me effectively, do I regret that we don't meet? We have actually met I think one or two times.

NICK: You have, he has mentioned it.

RON: But yes, I do… Maybe out of this comes… it would be great if he came to McLaren. I would, I think, quite like him to come to McLaren. The only thing I hope is, in showing him McLaren, that he would be looking at it with the right mindset.

NICK: Yes that is true, of course, he is hyper-critical.

RON: Yes, I don't mind as long as he doesn't harbour any negative emotions, I am more than happy to welcome him to McLaren.

NICK: Because his mind is still razor sharp. I think he is still the creative genius he was, he just hasn't got that outlet.

RON: What does his son do now?

NICK: He has Jennifer, Gillian and his son Michael. I am not sure, I think it is in legal. But I will let you know.

RON: But he lives in Switzerland still?

NICK: John has a lovely place in Switzerland on Lake Geneva. Living opposite Alain Prost's son, next to Phil Collins, bizarrely. He is probably as content as he ever will be. He has done well financially — not in your league but nevertheless he has done well and has been able to set his kids up and give them everything that his early ambition wanted. He has achieved those ambitions… And of course he was all about producing the perfect car.

RON: Well you know, if he wants to design things, I am absolutely happy to create the opportunity for him to design things.

NICK: Wow! Okay, well, I will let him know.

RON: And 'things' means 'anything'.

NICK: Yes.

Soon the Merc drew up outside offices on the south side of Fleet Street, Ron slipped back into his professional shell, shook my hand and stepped out of the car. Tim drove me back to Surrey, telling me tales of his boss and how good he was to work for, giving me insights into the world of Formula 1 that will have to remain, as he and I agreed, between the two of us, for fear of getting him into trouble.

But he did explain the story behind the McDonald's stop, an explanation that shed light on his Benny Hill routine before we left. He had been running around because he had been trying to help another of Ron's employees to fix the staff lavatory, but they hadn't been able to get it finished in time — so he hadn't been able to have a pee before departure and was hoping for the best.

A good man, it struck me, working for another good man.

I sent John an email summary of the interview and followed up with a transcript. His only response was angry denial of the accusation of theft. He had never heard this before and was most unhappy about it.

'In my spare time,' he explains, 'I had been making drawings at the factory of oak built-in furniture for my home office. Those were some of the drawings I was copying.' He added that he had also copied drawings of the 1985 MP4/2B, because he had been given one of the cars, as his contract stipulated, for winning that year's World Championship and knew he might need them in the future: 'If you want to build some spares, you're going to need some drawings.'

As for Ron's offer of renewed collaboration, John didn't mention that.

I also sent the transcript to Ron for approval. The only changes he made were to the first section about Chaparral. Oh, and he suggested cutting out the story of the car accident, a story that caused John much mirth when I finally told it to him: 'If you put it in, there will be hilarity up and down the pit lane I can tell you.' I decided that it revealed no secrets and was accurate — and I felt that Ron wouldn't mind really.

Almost a month after the interview, John called to go through Ron's transcript in detail. Towards the end of the conversation, which in part consisted of an analysis of McLaren's Formula 1 woes at that time, I asked him what he thought of Ron's offer. He said he found it 'confusing' and asked for my view. I told him that I thought Ron was serious. John replied, 'The first thing that came into my head when I read it was, "Oh good, maybe I could go there and finish some projects I've got going. They've got all the resources."'

I replied, 'That's exactly what he'd want! It would be a marvellous story if you two got back together. But just don't do it until the book's out.' John came back with a typically terse quip: 'Well, you'd better finish the bloody book!'

So I emailed Ron, via his personal assistant, Justine Bowen, telling him that John, whom I copied, was interested in talking to him about possible future collaborations. An appointment was duly confirmed by Justine: 'Ron wondered if 12.30 on Friday 13 February [2015] would work for a get together.' To which John observed, for my eyes only: 'A cunning trick — he knows I am superstitious and is trying to get me on the back foot before we start.'

So the arrangements were made, I met John in Guildford and we drove to Woking together in a hired car. The Great Barnard was nervous — something I hadn't seen before.

At the main entrance to the McLaren Technology Centre (MTC) we were directed left, a route for VIP visitors around the formal lake that forms the ying of the 'ying and yang' layout of this breathtaking place, cunningly devised to ensure that important guests drive round in full view of the facility's huge windows. Once parked, we were shown up to an impressive, private, spacious, circular reception room walled in curved glass and flooded with natural light. The uncluttered space featured stylish white sofas and armchairs set off by charcoal grey carpet and decorated with abstract sculpture. Five minutes later, Justine Bowen came through from the inner sanctum of offices. She told us that she had joined shortly after John's departure and had immediately been dubbed JB herself — it had taken her a while to get what everybody kept laughing about.

Ten minutes later Ron Dennis strode in, looking super-smart in a tailored dark blue suit that made him look even taller than he actually is. He came up behind John's seat and announced, with a clown of a smile, 'Well, one thing, you've got more hair than me!' I started to take some pictures as Ron helpfully quipped, 'I'm the one with a tie on.' John Barnard was having none of that:

JOHN: Well, you wouldn't expect me to wear a tie!
RON: Nooo! Don't be silly, I'd never see you! So, let's go and look around.
JOHN: Yeah, if you like. As long as I don't meet anyone I know.
RON: Doesn't matter, does it?
JOHN: I suppose not really. Just gets them talking. You know what it's like.
RON: Let them talk. What have you been doing?
JOHN: A lot of DIY.

Ron laughed, clearly assuming that John was joking. Oblivious, and never an apologist for his life in retirement, Barnard continued, 'I started off at Gillian's house in Dulwich, did about three days there, and then I've been to Michael's in Wandsworth — I've just come from there.'

Ron listened to this vivid contrast to his own 24/7 workaholic lifestyle and commented, 'I don't think anyone is going to feel threatened by that.'

And so the banter began, two highly competitive old friends who had once conquered the world together, actually happy to see one other; the first time they had enjoyed each other's company for 30 years. We entered a tubular glass lift, for all the world like a giant piston inside a crystal cylinder, and descended to McLaren's famous Boulevard with its giant windows looking onto the lake, the inside wall lined with McLaren's illustrious race cars, each worth millions of pounds.

Ron spent the next three hours walking us around his massive, space-age technology facility, opening the countless locked doors with what is probably the company's only universal electronic pass, explaining first how his three children, Charlotte (a doctor and head of an A&E unit), Christian (who graduated in 2015 in engineering product design) and Frankie (studying architecture) were doing well, how their nickname for him was ATM. We were soon to learn how Ron, perhaps unconsciously, was taking McLaren into fields that were of interest to his children, although he made a big point of the fact that none of them were in motor racing, which, he said, was 'by design'.

And then we entered the world of cutting-edge automotive technology — McLaren being vertically integrated (providing its own supply chain) — the inner secrets of the astounding, if problematic, energy recovery system on the Formula 1 car — the various supercars, their supreme quality, how everything is measured and measured again to make sure of perfect fit and function first time — unwrapping the latest, secret road car for us — sleek and predatory beauty — a sniffy dismissal of LaFerrari F150, the Scuderia's million-pound-a-shot, hybrid supercar competitor — the waiting lists for McLaren supercars — the financial corner having been turned, making money — 'killing everybody on weight and stiffness' — 'the P1 [McLaren's road car flagship] is a megacar' — the business, the stock control, the immaculate design of the facility — 'no-one can compete'. Clearly the dream that John and Ron had conceived back at the launch of the first carbon race car had found solid form; carbon-fibre was revolutionising the motor industry and, as predicted, McLaren was leading the way. It was also, I noted, using paddle-shift technology.

In effect, Ron was boasting to John, showing his old partner how far he had come. John couldn't fail to be impressed, although, with his arms folded at every stopping point, he was in no hurry to show it.

We walked up and down the production line, with Ron revealing how McLaren had mastered the complexities of carbon-fibre — dry lay-up, inflation and injection, getting the optimum flow paths and viscosity — how he'd reduced the cost of high-quality composites production by enormous factors — now like 'shelling peas' — everything new is patented — control and perfection is all — getting it right first time is five times cheaper than correcting something in the field — economies of scale — award-winning hybrid engines — no carbon car production line like it in the world. Even John was impressed by the way the rubber door seals are inserted. 'Wonderful,' he said.

We continued our ever-more fascinating tour, admiring the pristine precision, the tidy complexity, the brilliant organisation. We passed the cleanest imaginable paint shop, with glass walls and white floor. There was no paint anywhere but on the cars — not on the glass, not on the painters' overalls. 'We don't use robots to paint, they're not good enough,' said Ron. 'Only highly skilled humans can get the finish I require.' I found myself thinking that Ron is a man who might feel most at peace in an aerospace clean room.

It suddenly dawned on me that all the staff were in uniform, but not just any uniform. The blue and grey trainers were fashionably chic, the black trousers and black fleeces designer-labelled, the light grey overalls smart and neat.

So when we emerged into yet another endless, curving corridor to pace past a forlorn, lost-looking man with long, unkempt hair, a straggly beard, grubby clothes and a backpack, Ron understandably performed a classic double-take, spinning on his heel to quiz the unhappy hippy.

It turned out he was a Spanish contractor doing some insulation work. 'Lagging,' he said, which sounded more like a description of his status than his job. Abruptly Ron turned away: 'There are 3,000 people here. He's just cruising around. He's not where he's meant to be.' Truer words were never said. I also wondered whether I was where I was meant to be.

We approached a corner at which point Ron looked up and down the corridor before pushing the wall, which opened as if by magic, revealing itself as a Narnian doorway into a dark and secret world. A long suspended walkway on the left rose beside a wide, curving, dark passageway above a line of McLaren Formula 1 cars down on the right, the space below dominated by a temporary wooden module, part of a proposed 'immersive educational experience' that led through to a state-of-the-art multi-media theatre in-the-round, one of Ron's many prides and joys.

This was the grandly titled McLaren Thought Leadership Centre, with 150 terraced seats behind curving desks equipped with multiple screens looking over a central, hydraulically operated, rotating, rising podium, the room illuminated all around by natural light falling from high windows. 'You could have three neuro-surgeons explaining an operation sitting in the middle,' said

EPILOGUE

Ron, 'or a car raised up a metre and slowly turning.' He then admitted, 'I've toileted so much money trying to get this right!'

John suddenly turned to Ron, his face set:

'What about Formula 1?'

'That's a good question!' replied Ron. 'Formula 1. I've changed the model. These are my last years. No one in the Formula 1 team has any responsibility at all other than winning in Formula 1. Completely ring-fenced. Dedicated, complete resource, for them. No responsibilities other...' A dog with a bone, John interrupted:

JOHN: Who's running it?
RON: Who's running it?
JOHN: Yeah. You?
RON: Ultimately I take responsibility. But I've got individuals...
JOHN: Are you in there, running it?
RON: Of course, of course. I'm just showing you some of the toys.
JOHN: I know, but if you are not in there running it...
RON: But you see, the problem is, the answer is I am running it, but I'm running it using really good people. Technical people — there's a structure. I go to all the races. I stand back, I'm plugged into the guy who's running the team. He's the Sporting Director. I don't have Team Principal any more. The roundabout never stops, John. The system has to accommodate 24/7, 365, total, even in August, in close down, when a whole army goes in and resets the entire building. Cleans everything, deep cleans, all the rest of it.

Ron, it seems, was taking refuge in cleanliness, a source of comfort and control when under pressure.

RON: Formula 1 is a cost centre.
JOHN: Sure...
RON: So what happens is, they negotiate with me their racing budget. I have the ability to dive down into bills of materials, uprate costs, all these sorts of things. Sectioned into months. I look every month at the maths, my CFO looks at it every month... Any Formula 1 team will spend exactly what you give it.
JOHN: Yeah, sure...

RON: It has an infinity. So then you've got to see productivity, you've gotta look at that, you've gotta look at this. You've gotta say, 'Is it quality?' I don't think we've made a better race car in history, both conceptually and everything. And it's always the key technical people. How you operate it? The way I look at it, you make a fighter plane…

JOHN: But does anybody join those key technical people together?

RON: Yeah. Yeah. Structure.

JOHN: You?

RON: No, not me, because basically that would be worse. Everything other than aero is under one person. These two people have to be able to function completely together, respect each other…

JOHN: So two people look after it?

RON: Two people look after it, but, because, if you let the engineer take over aero, or the other…

JOHN: Yes of course…

RON: It's a complete disaster.

JOHN: Sure…

RON: But the challenge is packaging. And the packaging is everything. Honestly, you've got to hit all the stiffness, things…

JOHN: Of course…

RON: We have all the performance numbers. It's going to weigh this…

JOHN: Yeah, yeah…

Ron appeared to be struggling under the onslaught. Nothing he was saying was having any impact on John whatsoever. Another pause, another sense of awkwardness, a feeling that our generous host has been under attack and was on the defensive. John uttered yet another cynical-sounding 'Hmm'.

Ron wandered off. A big screen showed waves crashing on a big rock, threatening to wash a man into the sea. It did so. The man was driven repeatedly up against the iron shore.

In a conciliatory tone and in an effort to soften the attack, to help Ron take on board the point, I interjected:

NICK: I think John's point was about that focal person who's the driving force, which obviously is you, but you don't have time to be that person in Formula 1.

RON: No, no, I am hands-on on many, many things. But the reality is, if I can't demonstrate to a third party that this can ultimately work without me, then basically, how do I get out?

JOHN: Wow. Yes.

RON: How do I get out?

How does he get out? He wants to get out? I'm a little lost. But these men are ten years older than me, have had brilliant careers and understandably sometimes just want the speeding train to stop. There was a pause, but John didn't let up:

JOHN: That question still remains, though, Ron.

RON: Yeah I know, I know.

JOHN: Because, if you get out, who's going to do what you do here? No one.

RON: That's true. It's a night... it's a sort of compliment, I think.

NICK: It is a compliment.

RON: I don't know... I wouldn't be here if it wasn't for one thing. Divorce!

We all laughed, nervously in my case. We all knew that we had reached the human crux of the issue. In 2008 Ron separated from his Californian wife, Lisa, in what was by all accounts a deeply painful experience, and then went through a hideous battle over his money. Talking to me, he laughed again and said of John, 'He told me she'd be off in five minutes — well actually it was 25 years!'

We emerged from this extraordinary facility and John returned to his favourite theme: 'I can see you've got to have different arms in different spheres. My only fear, as it always was, is that I do think Formula 1 is a different animal to the normal concept of a company or an industry. I just think that there's something about the person who is pulling it together having that fundamental...'

Ron, unused to having such a special VIP tour interrupted with such penetrating questions, smiles, and in a laughing voice that betrayed some irritation, says:

RON: John, I'm 24-frigging-seven!

JOHN: I know.

RON: I hovered over a golf ball and I thought, 'I don't like this as much as I like working.' So I threw myself back into it. For me, it's just such a pleasure to spend some time with you, because, actually, it's cool to have like-minded people. Most people don't get it.

We emerged into the corridor through the 'secret' door. Ron turned and said to John, smiling, 'I'll give you a proposition over lunch.' But John continued his devastating analysis. Ron repeated the phrase three times before John dropped the subject.

Ron took us into a small glass-partitioned room and, with some excitement, pointed out a brake calliper to John, who was impressed by the pocketing, the aeration holes used for cooling and making it weigh less.

> RON: How about that!
> JOHN: Nicely pocketed.
> RON: That's how it comes! You'd never believe where that gets made. Well you will believe it now. This is an exclusive contract we have — we develop all this. This is with a Japanese company called Akebono. They're just pieces of jewellery.
> JOHN: Mmm...
> RON: The structural effort. Do you remember all that thing we went into about not spreading...
> JOHN: Oh yeah...
> RON: And getting wedging on the pads...

As ever, John, who could see that the basic design was unchanged, spoke his mind and made his mark:

> JOHN: Well, that's why I designed that calliper in 1984. To get rid of all that.
> RON: But, but...
> JOHN: And this is all there...
> RON: And...
> JOHN: All the vents round the cylinders. And all the rest of it.
> RON: Look at this!
> JOHN: Yup.
> RON: Different loads.
> JOHN: We didn't have machines that could make that.

EPILOGUE

For John, this wonderful brake calliper was just as he would have designed it 30 years ago had today's equipment been available to him. After our departure, he added: 'It hadn't really changed. Sure, it was pretty, shiny and lots of little bits of metal had been whittled out with expensive numerical-control machining, but it isn't actually different. Move on, do something new, was my thought. I didn't say it, because that would have been rude.'

And so to lunch, an hour late and a very private affair, in a dedicated room above the staff restaurant, with a large oval table dressed in a white tablecloth, a flower display and silver cutlery. Windows provided views over both the lake and the Boulevard within the building.

As whispering waiters served white wine and a first course of perfect scallops, Ron and John chatted through the early days of McLaren International, analysing what Teddy Mayer did wrong, what they both did right, how they coped with the resistance put up by the old-school mechanics.

Ron recalled their finest hour: 'We made a few mistakes along the way. Do you remember when we were trying to get our heads around how to make a carbon-fibre chassis? And there was nothing out there. We invented it. Male/female tooling.'

When John mentioned the disappointment of the first carbon chassis, Ron continued, 'It was ugly, but boy it was strong. You just think, body fit. Let's look at body fit now John. It was mind-blowing. All the effort we went to, because all the bucks were hand-made.'

Which prompted a sharp retort: 'Sure, but look at all the machinery you've got now! If you can't get it perfect with all that gear, then it's never going to happen.'

A main course of roast duck followed, perfectly prepared and cooked, of course, served with a glass of full-bodied red wine poured from a bottle with an expensive label.

And then we came to the point of it all — Ron's proposal. I cannot give detail, except to report that Ron Dennis leaned back in his chair and said, 'I think "John Barnard for McLaren" could be a pretty powerful brand. So I tell you what, John, you bring me your ideas and anything else that shows sales potential, and we'll have a deal.'

The dream, ladies and gentlemen, the ludicrous fantasy, had come true. I smiled into my wine and did a little internal punch in the air.

John resolved to send over some drawings and lunch concluded, at around 4pm, with a delicious dessert of lemon ice cream and a chocolate pudding to die for.

THE PERFECT CAR

Walking back to the reception area along the Boulevard's upper gantry, we paused to look down on three Barnard cars, which hadn't been there on my previous visit a few months earlier, when I had interviewed Andy Smith. I suspect that Ron had ordered them to be wheeled out specially. The cars prompted further discussion about the old days. Leaning over the balustrade, Ron began talking about the multi-million-pound value of the cars along the Boulevard before suddenly remarking to John, 'You sold a car, didn't you?'

'Yes, I sold my MP4/2B,' replied John. 'I sold it to Gerhard [Berger].' And then he added, referring to Ron's so far unmentioned accusation of industrial espionage, 'And he's got the drawings.'

There was a moment's silence before Ron laughed, saying, 'No comment!' John, ever the devil, laughed a little as well and spoke further:

JOHN: I thought I'd send him drawings because I knew he was going to get the car. So I thought what am I going to do if I haven't got the drawings?
RON (laughing): So anyway!
JOHN: But nothing I ever do is a copy...
RON (laughing a little less): Move on!
JOHN: No, I won't move on! It's all in my head, Ron. It's all in my head!
RON: Do you remember when we took that car to Long Beach for the first time?
JOHN: Yeah. The bodywork caught fire...

And so Ron, ever the diplomat, steered the conversation back to the old days, when they worked together and conquered the world, while I backed away, taking pictures, feeling an immense sense of privilege of having been party to and witnessing a most remarkable reunion.

But will they work together ever again? Now Ron has been forced out of McLaren and it's unlikely he has access to such facilities. But if they do, if that fighting unit comes together once again, both more mellow with age, now a pair of wise old owls, then surely British engineering and perhaps Formula 1 itself will be the better for it.

We drove away contented, me blissful, John, as ever, thinking of the problems, which is about as blissful as he ever gets.

TECHNICAL MILESTONES

This listing records the technological milestones in John Barnard's career. All of these he invented broadly single-handedly, alongside his team. Many were certainly firsts, although some may have been developed independently and concurrently at other teams. There currently exists no definitive, reliable record of technological innovation in Formula 1.

Lola
1970
- First-semi-stressed mounting for a Super Vee engine revolutionises Lola's engine mountings.

McLaren
1973
- Aerodynamic single post for the rear wing.
- Foam-injected lightweight sidepod.

Vel's Parnelli Jones
1976
- Helped with the first turbocharging of a Cosworth DFV and designed the first car to win with one.

1977
- Pathfinding transverse gearbox.

Chaparral
1979
- First ground-effect car for Indycar racing.
- Possibly the first out-of-the-box 'perfect car' in motorsport.

Project Four
1980
- Carbon-fibre executed to aerospace standards for the first time in motorsport.
- Creating the first carbon-fibre chassis, ensuring lighter, stronger, safer construction, and that cars of the same model were identical.
- Narrower chassis for aerodynamic advantage.

McLaren
1980
- Aerospace standards introduced to motorsport (the mechanics sidelined).
- First time all car parts are drawn for a Formula 1 car.
- Double-barreled, spooled uprights, allowing cooling air onto the brakes.
- Wind-tunnel wheels on outriggers.
- First use of foam tyres for wind-tunnel models.

1981
- Wind-tunnel advances: control of pitch, yaw, roll and ride height while the tunnel was running.
- Directing Porsche to design a Formula 1 engine tailored to a specific car.

TECHNICAL MILESTONES

1982
- The 'coke-bottle' shape, which still defines the shape of Formula 1 cars.

1983
- The first successful carbon brake discs, radially drilled for cooling.
- Sliding mounting system to fix aluminium bell to carbon brake disc.
- Barge boards and turning vanes — not pursued.
- Stronger, lightweight callipers designed to run with carbon brakes.
- Integral CV joint/wheel hub package.

1985
- Titanium slips between calliper and carbon brake pads.

1986
- Carbon clutch plate.

Ferrari
1987
- Paddle-shift semi-automatic gearbox.
- Double 'coke-bottle' shape: bulging sidepods, swept in both fore and aft, a design feature still used in Formula 1.
- New engine-mounting system, using four bolts and fixing the cam covers directly to the chassis.
- Metric fixings system, and his Blue Book standardising high-specification aerospace parts throughout Formula 1.

1988
- Possibly the first 'enclosed' sidepods in Formula 1.
- Carbon roll bar incorporated into the airbox.

1989
- Short torsion bars replacing road springs.

Benetton
1990
- Pioneering promoter of clean fuel in Formula 1, helping the sport to become more environmentally aware.
- Front wing supported on two struts for a high nose.
- The Barnard catch — for nosecone and bodywork. Plus quick release catches for sidepods.

Barnard Design Consultancy
1991
- Inside-out dog ring.

Ferrari
1993
- Flexures replacing suspension ball joints.
- No-drag sidepod radiator system.

1994
- Carbon composite gearbox/oil tank/bell housing.
- Titanium uprights — first successful design.
- Wind tunnel under-belt wheel system.

1995
- Carbon flexures.
- Carbon wishbone.
- Steering wheel dashboard.

1996
- Moog rotary hydraulic actuator for semi-automatic gearbox.

B3
1996
- 'Nitrogen' head rest for Ferrari.

1997
- Carbon gearbox for Arrows.

2000
- Carbon brake pedals for Prost.

2002
- Carbon/titanium loading eye.

2003
- Carbon fire extinguisher system.
- Proton MotoGP: nose cone intake for airflow through new headstock.
- Proton MotoGP: Machined aluminium swing arm.

GLOSSARY

This listing explains all the terms you are likely to need while reading this book. It also explains, if you jump around the italicised cross-references, how engines work.

Active suspension This uses computers to control the up and down movements of the chassis. Also known as adaptive suspension. See *suspension* and *passive suspension*.

Actuator This turns electronic signals into physical action. So, an actuator on a *semi-automatic gearbox* turns the signals coming from the *paddle shift* into physical force that causes the *gearbox* to select the correct *gear*.

Aerodynamics The study of how air flows over a vehicle. The aim of race car aerodynamics is to make best use of that airflow to improve the car's performance, and often involves the use of inverted wing shapes to force the car downwards. See *downforce* and *ground-effect*.

Aerofoils Most *open-wheel* race cars have aerofoils ahead of the front wheels and above and behind the rear wheels that help create *downforce*. Also known as *wings*.

Air jack A system for lifting the car up in a *pit stop* so that the wheels can be changed. It involves inserting an air hose into the rear of the car, which activates pneumatic jacks to raise the car off the ground.

Airbox A cowling, similar in shape to a ship's ventilation funnel, which sits above and behind the driver's head and sucks cooling air back towards the engine.

Alternating Current (AC) An electrical current that periodically changes direction, as opposed to *Direct Current (DC)*, which flows only in one direction; AC is used to power your home.

Alternator This generates electricity from the engine by spinning a magnet around a coil of wire (a standard way of generating electricity). It generates an Alternating Current (AC), hence its name.

Anti-roll bar A device in the *suspension* that compensates for the car's tendency to *roll* when it goes round a corner, helping to keep the car flat and level. It also compensates for the upward movement of each wheel as it goes over a bump.

Apex The apex of the corner is the very tip of the inside curve. Racing drivers like to 'hit the apex' of each corner because it's the shortest way round the bend.

Aquaplaning When a car aquaplanes, it literally floats on the film of water on the track surface, often causing a crash.

GLOSSARY

Autoclave A large oven that uses heat and pressure to 'cure' (set) *carbon-fibre* structures.

Axle Typically a rod of steel supporting the wheel at its centre. F1 axles tend to be short, entirely independent and attached to the *upright*, which itself is connected to the *suspension*.

Balance A well-balanced car will be fast on the straights while also having good grip through the corners. Motorsport engineers are in a continual battle to achieve perfect balance by making fine adjustments to the suspension to meet the demands of each circuit and the individual driving style of each driver.

Barge board A vertical panel that tidies up the airflow coming through the front suspension of an F1 car before it moves through the *sidepods* and towards the car's rear. Sometimes they are horizontal. Also known as a *turning vane*.

Bearings At their most simple, bearings are devices to help objects rotate or slide. Ball bearings are devices to help shafts rotate and typically consist of a circular channel filled with metal balls: the shaft, say, an axle, is pushed through the centre and rotates easily against the balls.

Bellhousing A substantial, curvaceous metal container attached to the engine that usually contains the *flywheel* and *clutch*.

Belt drive The system of pulleys that runs the *drive belt*.

Bodywork The panels of aluminium, glass fibre or, more recently, carbon fibre, which cover the *chassis*, improve the *aerodynamics*, protect the driver and which are usually covered in sponsors' logos.

Boundary layer When air flows in a wind tunnel and encounters the floor or walls, it behaves differently to its performance in the middle of the tunnel. This border between air and floor/wall is known as the boundary layer. It can also refer to the point at which moving air contacts any surface, e.g., the rear wing of a race car.

Brake horsepower BHP. See *Horsepower*

Brakes See *Outboard brakes* and *Inboard brakes*.

Brickyard The nickname for the Indianapolis Motor Speedway, which hosts the annual *Indy 500*. In 1909 the oval circuit had been paved with over three million bricks. When these were asphalted over in 1961 a strip of the original bricks was left uncovered, one yard wide, to mark the start/finish line.

Buck A wooden *mould* often created to help make a second mould.

Bulkheads These are frames inside a chassis or an aircraft fuselage that help provide rigidity, and onto which the bodywork is attached. In a boat the bulkheads are usually solid divisions separating the various compartments, often incorporating watertight doors.

Bush A metal lining for a round hole, especially one in which an axle rotates. It can also be a bearing for a rotating shaft or a sleeve to protect a cable from chafing.

CAD-CAM Computer-Aided Design and Computer-Aided Manufacture. Often the two are directly linked, so that a designer may draw a component and send it immediately to a machine which will create a prototype, or even the finished component.

Calliper The calliper is usually a U-shaped control device mounted over a *disc brake*, containing two disc pads that can grip each side of the disc itself. When the driver applies the brakes, a Piston inside the calliper, powered by hydraulic fluid, forces both disc pads onto the spinning disc and grips it. It is not unlike a bicycle braking system, which often uses similar pads.

Cam belt The cam belt, or timing belt (or chain), connects the crankshaft to the camshaft, and so controls the opening and closing of the engine's *valves*. The cam belt can also be used to drive the water pump and oil pump.

Camshaft The camshaft carries a number of cams (elliptical or eccentric, i.e. imperfectly circular, metal plates) which open and close the engine's *valves* as it rotates. The eccentric cam shape allows the spring-loaded engine valves to spring open at one part of the rotation and be pressed closed on another. An overhead camshaft is positioned on top of the engine and operates the valves without having to use a complex system of rods and 'rockers' which are used if the camshaft is placed alongside or below the engine. It is covered by the cam cover, or rocker cover.

Can-Am The Can-Am series took place in Canada and America. The cars were allowed, more-or-less, unlimited engine sizes, full *turbocharging* and *supercharging*, unrestricted *aerodynamics*, and, in short, were as close as any major international racing series has ever come to 'anything goes'.

Carbon Fibre Composite (CFC) Carbon Fibre Composite cloth is made up of strands of purified carbon woven into a material that can then be mixed with an epoxy resin, laid up on a mould and heated under pressure in an *autoclave* to produce one of the strongest materials known to man. Light and flexible it is ideal for making high-performance vehicles.

Carburettor A device for delivering the right mix of fuel and air into the cylinder, where it explodes (via a spark from the *spark plug*), forcing the *piston* down and making the *crankshaft* rotate.

Cardan A type of joint — see *Universal joint*.

CART Championship Auto Racing Teams. Founded in 1979, this regulatory and sanctioning body for single-seat *open-wheel* race cars, often called Indycars, was created by American racing team owners after a row with *USAC* over the use of a Cosworth engine, among other complaints. CART is also known as Champcar.

Central element Often a way of referring to the *chassis*.

Centre of gravity If a car has a high centre of gravity, it means the car may roll more in the corners. The aim is to keep the centre of gravity low by keeping the heaviest parts of the car as close to the ground as possible.

Centre of pressure The point through which the all aerodynamic forces can be said to act.

CFRP Carbon-fibre-reinforced polymer.

Chassis The basic skeleton of a car, onto which is mounted the *engine*, *suspension*, *cockpit* and *bodywork*. See also *monocoque* and *stressed engine*.

GLOSSARY

Chicane A double corner in the track that requires skilful braking and handling to negotiate. Chicanes usually take the form of a left hand bend followed immediately by a right hand bend, or vice versa. The pejorative term 'chicanery' comes from the quick movements from side to side; suggesting evasion or deceit. Often used to slow cars down before a dangerous bend.

Circuit Another name for a race track.

Clutch The clutch on a car allows you to change *gear*, i.e. move from one size of cog in the *gearbox* to another. This is difficult to do without using a clutch because the cogs are mounted on the *drive shaft* and are spinning. So the clutch's mission is to separate the drive shaft from the engine while you are changing gear. The gearbox has attached to it a *pressure plate*, a disc of metal which itself is fixed to the drive shaft that runs through the gearbox. This presses against and engages with the clutch plate, which is fitted snugly inside the *flywheel*, so that the flywheel, clutch plate, pressure plate and drive shafts all spin together. When you push the clutch pedal down, you disengage the pressure plate, which moves away from the clutch plate on powerful springs, allowing the engine to keep on turning and the gearbox drive shaft to slow down so you can more smoothly change to a larger, or smaller cog. You let the pedal out to re-engage the pressure plate and reapply the rotational power, or *torque*, from the engine to the car's road wheels.

Cockpit The tub-like container in which sits the driver of a vehicle.

Coil A coil, also known as an ignition coil or spark coil, transforms the battery's low voltage to the thousands of volts needed to create an electric spark in the *spark plugs*, which ignite the fuel.

Coil Spring A conventional suspension system in which the weight of the chassis and engine is supported by coiled springs, rather than, say, *torsion bars*.

Composite A form of construction making the structures from a variety of materials. Glass Fibre Composite consists of glass fibres woven into a cloth and epoxy resin. *Carbon Fibre Composite* consists of carbon-fibre cloth and epoxy. Aluminium honeycomb and Kevlar may also be included.

Computational Fluid Dynamics, (CFD) The study of the movement and behaviour of fluids, such as air. Used for *aerodynamic* calculations. Computer technology has become so advanced that CFD is beginning to make *wind tunnels* redundant.

Con rod A connecting rod, linking the *piston* to the *crankshaft*.

Constant Velocity (CV) joint These allow the rear wheels to continue to turn unimpeded even if their *drive shafts* are rising up and down with the suspension as the car rides over bumps or the wheel drops into potholes.

Crankcase The housing for the *crankshaft*.

Crankshaft This is the steel shaft system that is connected directly to the *pistons* via the *con rods*. As the piston goes up and down, it pushes round the *crankshaft*, which, eventually, via the *drive shafts*, turns the car's wheels.

Cure To cure something is to make it set. *Carbon-fibre*, for example, is cured in an *autoclave*.

Cylinder The super-tough metal barrel that contains the *Piston*. It's where the fuel explodes thousands of times a minute, forcing the piston up and down the cylinder and spinning the *crankshaft*.

Cylinder head This is typically the upper part of the engine block that houses the *valves* and *spark plug*. It is bolted on top of the engine over the cylinders and is sealed with a head *gasket*.

Cylinder liner These metal tubes slide inside the cylinder and serve to reduce engine wear caused by the rapid movement of the *piston*.

Damper A device for controlling or reducing movement, usually in the car's *suspension*. See also *springs*.

Differential Often a large egg-shaped container typically on the rear *axle*, of a standard car or lorry, the differential, or diff, houses gearing that drives the rear wheels while allowing the outside wheel to turn at a different rate to the inside wheel. When a vehicle turns a corner, the outside wheel travels more distance than the inside wheel, since the inside wheel is describing a tighter arc, i.e., travelling a shorter distance. The differential cleverly compensates for this. It is connected to the gearbox via a *propshaft* and to the two driving wheels via separate *drive shafts*.

Diffuser A device to accelerate the flow of air under the car and out of the back. This helps create an area of low pressure at the rear and increase *downforce*.

Disc bell Also known as a 'top hat', this is an aluminium bowl, fixed to wheel hub, which provides a mounting point for the *disc brakes*.

Disc brakes These are a highly efficient means of slowing a car down. They consist of three main components: the *calliper*, the brake pads and the disc itself (also called a rotor). Put simply, the rotor is a large disc normally attached to the wheel hub via the *disc bell*. The calliper controls two disc pads that grip the disc when the driver applies the brakes. See also *outboard* and *inboard brakes*.

Distributor A device that passes electric current to each spark plug in turn, from the *coil*, which itself amplifies the car's battery power.

Double valve springs Double *valve springs* are more powerful than single valve springs, helping the engine valves seat more firmly, increasing power by creating a tighter seal.

Downforce This is an *aerodynamic* effect that forces the car's wheels onto the track surface to increase grip when cornering at speed. See *aerodynamics* and *ground-effect*.

Drive belt A drive belt is a loop of rubber, or similar material, used to drive engine parts such as the *alternator*, water pump and power steering pump.

Drive shaft The thick rod of steel that runs out of the engine. It is spinning, and that spin is transferred to the wheels through a system of cogs called the *gears* and the *differential*. It also refers to the shafts that emerge out of either side of the differential to each rear wheel. It also refers to any shaft that drives the wheels.

Drive train The components of the *transmission* system between the engine and the wheels. A drivetrain typically includes the *clutch, gearbox, propshaft,* *differential*, *drive shafts* and *axle*. See also *Powertrain*.

Drag Reduction System (DRS) This is a system whereby the rear *wing* can be allowed to spill air through a slot, reducing the *downforce* and so decreasing the car's grip to the track, thus increasing its speed on the straights. It is closed for cornering.

Dynamometer A machine, usually installed in an engine shop, used for measuring engine power.

Endplate Vertical plates or *winglets* fixed to each end of a horizontal *wing* are called endplates. They help guide the airflow over the wing, keeping the flow even and preventing vortices that can create drag.

Engine block The basic carcass of an engine, minus *pistons*, *conrods*, etc.

Epoxy resin Usually a synthetic polymer adhesive, that is typically liquid at room temperature until it is set by mixing with a catalyst and/or *curing*.

FIA The Paris-based Fédération Internationale de l'Automobile is the governing body of Formula 1 and many other categories of motorsport.

Finite Element Analysis A method for calculating approximate displacements, stress and strains on each point of a material. In simple terms, it is a method for dividing up a very complicated problem into small elements that can be solved mathematically in relation to each other. It requires advanced computing.

FISA Between 1978 and 1993 the Fédération Internationale du Sport Automobile, run by Jean-Marie Balestre, was the body to which the *FIA* delegated all Formula 1 governance.

Five-axis milling machine A cutting or milling machine that can shape a component from a variety of angles into a wide variety of shapes.

Flange A protruding rim or collar on a tube or pipe, often used to add strength to the tube and provide a fixing point to secure the tube in place.

Flat engine format An alternative to the V format is the flat format — such as Ferrari's Flat 12, in which the angle of the V has become so obtuse (180°) that the cylinders are lying on their sides. This has the advantage of lowering the racing car's *centre of gravity*. See also *V8*.

Fly-by-wire This describes systems that use wires and electronics rather than mechanical linkages to operate. A semi-automatic gearbox is fly-by-wire, since the gears are moved not with a traditional manual gear lever, but via electronic signals sent to *actuators* on the gearbox from the *paddleshift* steering wheel.

Flywheel This is usually a heavy, large diameter wheel that is attached to the *drive shaft*. Its rotation helps dampen engine vibration. It is usually contained in the engine *bellhousing*. A flywheel can also be used to store energy.

FOCA Run by Bernie Ecclestone, the Formula One Constructors' Association was a group of mainly British teams that represented their interests during the 1970s and 1980s.

Four-stroke A four-stroke engine has, as the name implies, four movements of each *piston* in each *cylinder* to complete a cycle of fuel/air intake, ignition, compression and exhaust. See also *two-stroke*.

Gasket A compressible piece of material, such as rubber or a heat-resistant material, which provides a seal between the faces of two joints. E.g., a head gasket — see *cylinder head*.

Gearbox Control Unit (GCU) The electronics system that controls the movement of *gears* in a *semi-automatic gearbox*.

Gear Usually, a toothed wheel, also known as a cog. Typically meshes with other gears to change the speed of the wheels in relation to the speed of the engine. Typically cars start in first gear, with the gearbox allowing the wheels to turn once for multiple rotations of the drive shaft. At speed, say in sixth gear, the relation between the drive shaft rotations and the wheel rotations is much closer. The car needs to be at speed before this can happen. The more gears you have, the more control you have over performance at each speed.

Gear train See *Gearbox*.

Gearbox A metal box that contains a row of cogs that are mounted on the *drive shaft*. The row of cogs, or *gears*, are known as the gear train. See also *semi-automatic gearbox*

G-Force A measure related to the force of gravity. Modern F1 cars subject drivers to as much as 6G during cornering, i.e., they feel like they are six times heavier as they go round a corner. This is why F1 drivers need such strong neck muscles.

Grid The grid, or starting grid, is the place where cars begin the race. A car's position on the grid, be it 1st or 24th, is determined by *qualifying*, typically, in F1, on the Saturday before the Sunday race.

Ground-effect A means of designing the underside of the car by using *Venturi tunnels*, so the airflow causes the body to be sucked down onto the ground, improving grip on corners. Typically involved the use of *skirts* to preserve low pressure under the car. See also *downforce*.

Gurney flap Developed by American drivers Dan Gurney and Bobby Unser in 1971 for the Indycar series, this simple aerodynamic device usually consists of a small flap along the trailing edge of a car's wing, situated on the high pressure (concave) side. It sticks up at right angles to both the wing and the airflow, helping create more *downforce*.

Horsepower (hp) The work that a steam engine could do was originally compared (by James Watt and others), to the work a horse could do; an 8 horsepower engine could do the work of eight horses. Watt came up with a measure for power; 1 horsepower (hp) = 756 Watts. Ever since then, engine power has been measured in hp, which is now calculated by the following equation: hp = *Torque* x *RPM* ÷ 5252. Brake Horsepower, also known as True Horsepower, is a measure of the engine's output before it is diminished by other elements such as the *differential*.

Hydraulics Hydraulics is a collective name for systems that use oil under pressure as a means of control. A *cylinder* is filled with oil, the pressure of which is controlled by a moving *piston*. Often used in *suspension*, or in *actuators* which can move cogs and levers by remote control.

Inboard brakes These are usually fixed

GLOSSARY

to the *chassis* rather than the wheel, where brake pads grip a spinning *disc* attached to a brakeshaft that is connected to the wheel. See *outboard brakes* and *disc brakes*.

Indy Racing League The IRL governs Indycar racing in America, a body which grew out of the various legal suits and takeovers between American car racing regulatory bodies.

Indy 500 The Indianapolis 500-mile race is the biggest motor race in the USA. It is held annually on the last weekend in May (Memorial Day weekend) at the Indianapolis Motor Speedway in Speedway, Indiana. The race forms the centrepiece for the Indy Racing League series. Also see *Brickyard*.

Indycar The term used in America for single-seat, *open wheel* racing cars. They are similar to F1 cars but with some important differences; they generally race on oval tracks, engine specifications differ, they use methanol for fuel, their bodywork is more all-enveloping and, unlike in Formula 1 and since John Barnard's introduction of ground-effect tunnels with the Chaparral 2k, they continue to use sculpted underbodies to increase *ground-effect*.

Intermediate tyres Half way between *slick* and *wet tyres*, these are often used when light rain is falling or when the track is slightly wet.

Kinetic Energy Recovery System (KERS) This system enables cars to take the heat energy generated during braking, store it in a flywheel, and reapply it later to increase the engine power, facilitating faster overtaking on a *straight*. See also *flywheel*.

Kevlar High-strength synthetic material used in *composite* construction.

Lifing systems Racing car parts only survive the rigours of racing for a limited time. A lifing system ensures there is a record of what must be replaced before it is likely to fail. Parts that are 'lifed' should not be used again in racing.

Lift A measure of a car's tendency to rise up from the track.

Mandrel See *Mould*

Monocoque A chassis that is created as one self-contained unit, rather than being made up of a network of girders, tubes and struts. The monocoque is the main body of the car, containing the cockpit, onto which everything else is fixed.

Mould A 'tool' for making components, into which you can pour liquid metal, glass, plastic, etc., or over which you can lay carbon-fibre or fibreglass cloth. Moulds tend to come in two forms: a male mould, or mandrel, has the material, such as carbon cloth, laid over the outside, whereas a female mould has the material laid on the inside. Mandrels are easier to work with for composite applications, but usually have rough exteriors; the smooth surface being the one upon which the cloth is laid, which remains smooth when the mould is removed.

Naturally (normally) aspirated A car that uses natural airflow to provide air for combustion in the engine, rather than the enhanced airflow that comes with a *turbocharger*.

Open-wheel An open-wheeled car is one that has its wheels outside the body of the car, as in F1 racing and Indycar.

Outboard brakes These are the most common form of brakes, usually consisting of a disc attached to the wheel which is gripped by brake pads controlled by *callipers*. See *Inboard brakes* and *Disc brakes*.

Oversteer If a car tends to turn too quickly into a corner, it is oversteering. This is usually caused by the front wheels having more grip than the rear wheels, causing the rear to slide, skid, or 'step-out'. See also *balance* and *understeer*.

Package Packaging generally describes the way in which various elements are fitted within the bodywork.

Paddle shift The gear-selection system invented by John Barnard in which the driver flips levers, or paddles, on the steering wheel to select which gear is needed, rather than using a clutch pedal and gear lever. It is connected to a *semi-automatic gearbox*. This was eventually adopted throughout motorsport and is now widely used on road cars too.

Passive suspension Passive suspension is suspension that is not computer-aided, and in which the *heave, roll, pitch* and *yaw* of a car are determined by the road surface.

Pencil A draughtsman or woman tasked with making detailed drawings of the chief designer's concept drawings, so the parts can be manufactured.

Pick-up Mounting points. A designer might say, 'the new specification made it really difficult to pick up the engine' — in this example the designer means 'mount' or 'secure'.

Piston This is a cup-like piece of metal that pumps up and down inside a *cylinder*. Emerging from the bottom of the piston is a *conrod* which is attached to the *crankshaft*.

Pit This is the team's trackside garage — each team has its own pit at each race track. Here the team monitor the cars' *telemetry*. See also *Pit Stop*.

Pit lane The lane that leads into and away from the *Pits*.

Pit stop Racing cars leave the main track and drive into the pits at a limited speed, so they can change tyres, repair damage or retire the car. Tyre pit stops (usually to change all four tyres) now typically take under 3 seconds, excluding the time it takes to drive in and out of the *pit lane*.

Pitch, pitching When the rear of a car moves up and the front moves down, or vice versa, it is said to be pitching. See also *porpoising*.

Planform The shape of a racing car or aircraft as seen from above.

Plank Literally a plank of wood, or, more accurately, of Jabroc, which is fitted beneath an F1 car to protect it should it hit a kerb or a bump. Jabroc is compressed, laminated, glued wood that is 80% lighter than steel and is cheaper, and wears much better, than *carbon-fibre*.

Pole position The car that *qualifies* with the fastest lap time is put at the front of the *grid* for the start of the race and is said to be 'on pole' or 'in pole position'.

Porpoise This is dramatic *pitching*, and takes its name from a porpoise's tendency to swim in a series of waves, rising up out of the water and then down under it.

Powertrain The components of a car that deliver power to the road, including the engine, *drive shafts*, *gearbox*, *differential* and *axles*. Similar to *Drivetrain*, except that it also includes the engine.

Pre-preg This is *carbon-fibre* cloth that has been pre-impregnated with epoxy resin.

Pressure plate See *Clutch*.

Propshaft Part of the drivetrain, this is a rotating rod that transfers rotating engine power from the *gearbox* to the *differential*.

Pull-rod/push-rod Pull-rods and push-rods are the diagonal bars between the chassis and the *upright* (where the *suspension arms* are attached to the wheels). When the car goes over a bump, the push-rod, which runs from the lower part of the upright to a *rocker arm* positioned high up in the chassis, pushes the rocker arm and so twists the *torsion bar*, which untwists after the bump. Pull-rods tend to be attached to the upper part of the upright and run down to a rocker arm situated low in the chassis, and they pull on the rocker arm to twist the torsion bar. The decision to use either pull or push-rods depends on how you want to *package* the suspension and other elements in the car, and, of course, what rules permit.

Qualifying The cars have to qualify for *grid* position by racing against the clock, usually on the Saturday before the Sunday Grand Prix. The car that gets the best lap time goes on *pole position*. There are normally three stages. The first two stages eliminate drivers until the final 'Top Ten Shoot-Out' for *pole*.

R&D Research and Development.

Rake The angle of the car in relation to the ground when viewed from the side. In most F1 cars the front is set slightly lower than the rear.

Ride height This defines how far the bottom of the chassis is from the ground, and can be adjusted for each track — a bumpy track might need a higher ride height than a smoother one. The adjustments are typically made by lengthening or shortening the *push-rod* or *pull-rod*. Also see *suspension* and *rake*.

Rising rate suspension This describes a system in which the suspension effectively become stiffer as the car goes faster and the ride gets rougher. Achieved by adjusting the suspension geometry and using springs, or their equivalents, that can change tension under compression. It helps maintain consistent *balance* and ride.

Rocker arm A lever that converts the in or out movement of *push-rod* or *pull-rod* into a rotary movement that then twists the *torsion bar*. The rocker arm can also amplify wheel movement to the *dampers*, so if the wheel moves 1cm upwards, the damper will move, say, 3cm. This helps the car feel stiff and stable. Rocker arms are also known as bell cranks or linkages. See *suspension*.

Roll This describes the tendency of a car to roll from left to right, or right to left, as it goes around a corner. See *Suspension*.

Roll bar See *Anti-roll bar*

Rolling road A road-like surface, often a wide, flat, rubber-impregnated canvas belt, which runs under a model car's wheels in the wind tunnel to simulate driving on a track at high speed. This is usually set in the wind tunnel floor and runs over a series of rollers mounted in a frame.

Roll-over bar This is usually an 'n'-shaped hoop of steel typically situated behind the driver's head and fixed to the *chassis*, designed to protect the driver if the car flips upside down. Often incorporated into the *air box*.

RPM (Revolutions Per Minute) This is a measure of each rotation of the crankshaft, i.e., each time a piston goes up and down. A family car will cruise at around 2,000rpm, often less. An F1 car can do 18,000rpm, about 300 revolutions per second. In *four-stroke* engines, each of the cylinders fires once for every two revolutions of the crankshaft.

SCCA Sports Car Club of America, a racing regulatory body.

Semi-automatic gearbox The gearbox invented by John Barnard in which the driver uses a *paddle shift* to send electronic signals to tell the gearbox what gear is required. See also *paddle shift*.

Set-up Set up on racing cars is primarily about suspension adjustment, ensuring the car is well-*balanced* and as perfectly suited as possible for the individual vagaries of each race circuit and the different driving styles of the drivers. See also *oversteer* and *understeer*.

Shock absorber A form of *damper*, this is usually a hydraulic device designed to absorb the shock of running over a bump or other sudden jolts to the car. See also *suspension*.

Sidepod These are box-like units attached to the sides of the *monocoque* alongside the cockpit. They typically house the engine's radiators, usually including ducting that funnels air over the radiators, helping them dump excess engine heat.

Skirts These plastic panels, much like stiff curtains, were positioned along the sides of the car between the bottom of the chassis and the track. They helped trap air under the car, helping to create lower pressure, so increasing *ground-effect* and grip. See also *Venturi effect*.

Spark plug An electrical device, which, under the control of the *distributor*, delivers thousands of rapid sparks into the *cylinder* each minute. The sparks ignite the fuel and air mixture, forcing the pistons down the cylinders, again, thousands of times per minute.

Spring rate Spring rate is a measure of how much pressure, in pounds, it takes to compress a *spring* one inch. For example, if it takes 500lb of pressure to compress a suspension spring one inch, it is said to have a spring rate of 500.

Springs Usually a length of coiled metal that compresses under pressure and then resumes its original shape. Used in *suspension*. Often called road springs.

Sprung mass (or spring weight) The main weight of the car — i.e., everything — chassis, bodywork and engine — except the *tyres, wheels, axles, brakes*

GLOSSARY

(*outboard*), *uprights*, and parts of the suspension between the *uprights* and the *chassis*. *Unsprung Mass* is the weight of everything on the car that isn't 'sprung' i.e., isn't supported by the suspension, e.g. the *wheels* and *axles*.

Stampa Collective name for the Italian press.

Straight The long, straight stretch of racetrack, without corners, upon which you can achieve the car's top speed.

Stressed engine A stressed engine is installed in such a way that rather than being a burden to the *chassis*, it adds strength and stiffness to it. The same is true, to a lesser degree, for a semi-stressed engine.

Structural fuse This is a structure that has been designed to fail at a given point, once a critical load has been reached. For example, engine mountings can be designed to fail and thereby effectively jettison the engine away from a racing car during a high-speed accident.

Sump A low-lying hollow into which liquid drains. In a car, the oil sump is a reservoir of oil at the bottom of the engine.

Supercharger A device to force compressed air into the engine to make the petrol explode with more energy. Similar in some respects to a *turbocharger*.

Suspension The system which effectively 'suspends' the *chassis* between the wheels. It is designed to cushion the car as it goes over bumps and to keep it level as it takes corners. Suspension is traditionally made with powerful *shock absorbers, springs* and/or *torsion bars*, among other devices. See also *anti-roll bar, coil springs, damper, pull-rod, push-rod, rocker arm, suspension arms, upright, wishbone.*

Suspension arms Struts that attach the wheels to the *chassis* and so effectively 'suspend' it between the wheels.

Team orders When a team orders one of their drivers to hold station or let a team-mate pass, often because that team-mate may have a better chance of winning the championship by doing so, he is said to have received team orders. Generally, F1 crowds consider them unsporting, and they are periodically banned.

Telemetry A radio system which broadcasts dashboard data back to the *Pit* (e.g. fuel remaining, engine *revs, hydraulic* pressures, tyre pressure, temperature, etc.)

Tifosi Collective name for Italian fans.

Top hat See *Disc bell*

Torque Torque is turning, or twisting power. If you (unwisely) try to grip a spinning *drive shaft* while the engine is running, you will get a vivid and painful impression of the power of *torque*. Engineering bolts are often tightened to a specific torque (i.e. a measure of how much twisting power has been applied).

Torsion Torsion is all about twisting. Torsional loads on a racing car are usually experienced during cornering at speed, when the forces try to twist the *chassis*.

Torsion bar These are used in motorsport *suspension* systems instead of *coil springs*. A bar of metal or carbon-fibre is attached to the chassis and the wheels. When load is applied (e.g. by the car going round a corner or over a bump) the bar twists to known and adjustable limits, acting, in effect, like a coil spring. Torsion bars usually take up less space than a coil spring. First used in F1 by Colin Chapman in 1970 on the Lotus 72.

Track The distance across the width of the car between the wheels, and also another word for a race circuit.

Traction Road grip, adhesive friction between the *tyre* and the *track*

Transaxle The unit containing the *differential* and the rear, driving, axle.

Transmission This system transmits power from the engine to the wheels and typically encompasses the whole *drive train*.

Tread The part of a *tyre* that is in contact with the road surface. A *slick* tyre is tread only, with no grooves.

Turbo lag *Turbochargers* cannot work efficiently until the engine is producing enough pressure in the exhaust to spin both the exhaust turbine and the air intake turbine, say, above 2,000rpm. The time it takes for the turbine to spin up (or spool up) to optimum speed is referred to as the turbo lag.

Turbocharger A device for pumping air into the engine under pressure. It's the same principle as blowing air onto a fire — increasing the combustion rate. A turbocharger usually consists of two turbines, or fans; the first is spun round by exhaust gases, causing the second to rotate and force more air into the engine.

Turning vane Curved vertical plates mounted between the front wheels and the sidepod air intakes to tidy up the turbulence coming off the front wheels and to protect the airflow through the sidepods to the radiators. See *bargeboard*.

Two-stroke A two-stroke engine has, as the name implies, two movements by each *piston* in each *cylinder* to complete a cycle of fuel/air intake, ignition, compression and exhaust. Generally a simpler option all round, if less powerful. See *four-stroke*.

Tyre Note the British spelling. Americans spell this word *tire*, which sounds exhausted… But given that the word comes from the French word 'tirer' (to pull, a reference to how tyres were made), then we must accept that the Americans have it right. In F1 there are various types of slick tyre, currently ranging from 'Hypersoft' to 'Superhard', and also 'wet' tyres with grooves to remove water in wet conditions.

Tyre deflection The amount a *tyre* is crushed down by the weight of the car where it touches the road.

Undercut If a driver makes a quick, well-timed pit stop, e.g., stopping earlier than an opponent for fresh tyres, a decision which ultimately puts him ahead, he has 'overtaken on the undercut'. Or, if the car overtakes on the inside of the curve, it can be said to have 'undercut' the opponent.

Understeer If a car is difficult to turn into a corner and tends to run wide, it is said to have understeer. Often caused by the rear wheels having more grip than at the front wheels, forcing the driver to work the steering wheel hard to get the car round the bend. See also *oversteer* and *balance*.

GLOSSARY

Universal joint Also known as a *Cardan joint*, or Cardanic joint, this is a means of connecting two rotating rods in such a way that one or other of the rods can move in pretty much any direction.

Unsprung mass See *Sprung mass*.

Upright This is usually a vertical metal fabrication to which the wheel is connected and which provides mountings for the upper and lower *suspension arms*, *axle* and *disc brake*.

USAC The United States Auto Club is a sanctioning body for single-seat, *open-wheel* racing in America such as Indycar.

V8 A V8 describes an engine with two sets of four *cylinders* arranged in two lines opposite each other, joining at the bottom (around the *crankcase*) to create a V shape when viewed from either end. V6, V10 and V12 are also common cylinder arrangements. See also *Flat*.

Valve Engine valves are typically on the top of the engine, in the *cylinder head*. Inlet valves let in fuel and air, exhaust valves release combusted gases. They are sring-loaded to allow them to open and close. See also *cambelt* and *camshaft*.

Venturi effect When a fluid, such as air, rushes through a wide pipe into a narrower pipe, it speeds up in the narrower section, which means its pressure drops. A *ground-effect* car features inverted wing-shaped 'tunnels' beneath its side pods which narrow towards the rear of the car. The resulting lower pressure allows the rear *wing* to press down more effectively, giving more grip in the corners.

Weight distribution This is a measure of how the weight of the chassis is distributed across all four wheels.

Wheelbase The distance from the centre of the front wheel to the centre of the rear wheel is called the wheelbase.

Wind tunnel A facility often like a large tube, at one end of which is a massive fan to generate winds of over 200mph, and in which vehicles can undergo *aerodynamic* testing. See also *CFD*.

Wing F1 cars have inverted wings in front of the front tyres and above and behind the rear tyres that help create *downforce*. Also known as *Aerofoils*.

Winglet These tend to be small wings that are, in F1, usually mounted on the bodywork in front of the rear wheels.

Wishbone Both front and rear *suspension* systems are made up of upper suspension arms and lower suspension arms, which are fixed to the wheels via *uprights*. These are often called *wishbones*, because their forked shape, joined at the upright and spreading to upper and lower anchor points on the *chassis*, is reminiscent of a bird's wishbone. See *suspension arms*.

Yaw When cars (or aeroplanes) move sideways, they can be said to be yawing.

ACKNOWLEDGEMENTS

First of all I must thank John Barnard, who has given unstintingly of his valuable time. His knowledge is, of course, second to none on the subject of his own life and innovations. To make this book possible, I should record here that JB paid me for the time I spent writing it (money he will gain back from royalties) while insisting on my editorial independence and agreeing that I was free to include criticisms of his work and character and any contradictions of his recollections and points of view.

My thanks also go to the following people, in alphabetical order (with deep apologies to anyone I have inadvertently omitted):

Tyler Alexander, now sadly deceased, who gave me some of the inside story of Team McLaren; **Cristiano Altan** for his time and information in Maranello; **Gillian Barnard**, JB's second-born daughter; **Jennifer Barnard**, JB's first-born daughter; **Michael Barnard**, JB's son — all three gave me an avenue into the domestic Barnard; **Rosemary Barnard**, JB's wife — who did the same and who was vital in persuading her husband he wasn't wasting his money on me; **Tiziano Battistini**, for organising the interviews in Maranello; **Gerhard Berger**, who granted a second interview even after traffic and error meant I missed the first one; **Justine Bowen**, Ron Dennis's very approachable and helpful PA; **Ross Brawn**, who took time out of a manic schedule to give his honest and open impressions of JB; **Angelo Camerini**, for his entertaining tales from Ferrari days; **Jim Chapman**, who provided valuable insight into JB's time at Lola and Vel's Parnelli Jones; **Gordon Coppuck**, who so kindly granted an honest and insightful interview about his time with JB at McLaren; **Mike Coughlan**, for the rich insight he provided; **David Coulthard**, for granting an interview on the fly at a Silverstone event; **Ron Dennis**, who provided two lengthy, open and crucial interviews; **Dan Fleetcroft**, for the vital information and colour he provided about B3; **Antonio Ghini**, for kindly granting an interview, with little warning, at the Ferrari museum; **Ronnie Grant**, the cabbie-cum-racing driver who gave so much information about John's and Patrick Head's time at Lola; **Shyam Gupta**, for helping me get my head round Smith numbers; **Sir Patrick Head**, who granted a lengthy interview; **Alan Henry**, journalist and author, sadly deceased, who was immensely helpful and encouraging; **Damon Hill**, who kindly granted me an interview at Silverstone;

ACKNOWLEDGEMENTS

John Hogan, who provided unparalleled insight into the workings of Formula 1; **Diane Holl,** who had such entertaining stories about JB; **David Hughes,** author, writer and musician, for his creative inspiration; **Mark Hughes,** for being such a brilliant editor; **Matthew Jeffreys,** for his valuable contribution on the challenges of working for JB; **Alan Jenkins,** for the three hours he gave me during the 2013 British Grand Prix, despite my being late for the interview; **Gordon Kirby,** who provided so much useful information on JB's time in America; **Gerd Kramer,** for the information he provided about Porsche and McLaren; **Paul McKenzie,** school friend and chemicals executive who provided important contacts at Hercules; **Robin Miller,** for information about the Chaparral era; **Gordon Murray,** who was good enough to give an interview and concede carbon-fibre chassis priority to JB; **Tim Murray,** F1 enthusiast who helped provide background information; **Steve Nichols,** for his entertaining, informative discourse upon Chaparral and McLaren; **Jane Nottage,** journalist and author who helped secure my interview with the late Tyler Alexander; **Barbara Pani,** who provided such excellent translations of Italian and French press reports; **Nicolò Petrucci,** for providing expert information on JB's Ferrari cars; **Luciano Prandini,** for his time and willingness to help; **Bob Randolph,** former head of R&D at Hercules who related the American side of the carbon chassis story; **Peter Reinhardt,** for his wealth of anecdotes about working with JB; **Neil Robinson,** former sports editor-in-chief at *The Independent* group who helped secure journalistic access to the Silverstone paddock at three British Grand Prix and who put me in touch with Alan Henry; **Sue Skeens,** my sister, who laboriously transcribed so many interviews; **Andy Smith,** who gave such excellent detail on working with the Godalming Scud, **Dominic Smith,** for contributing despite JB having sacked him, in error; **Sir John Sorrell,** for bringing me into the world of design writing; **Luke Steele,** who provided some entertaining information about wind tunnels; **Sir Jackie Stewart,** for allowing me to mine his memory for information from JB's Lola era; **David Tremayne,** journalist and author, who very kindly introduced me to the players in the F1 paddock at the 2012 British Grand Prix and who also provided important contacts; **Joan Villadelprat,** for his honest appraisal of JB's strengths and weaknesses; **Murray Walker,** for his incisive summary of JB's contribution to motorsport; **John Watson,** for his hilarious, no-nonsense openness about his time at McLaren; **Arthur Webb,** for his patience, information and checking of the carbon-fibre explanations in this book; **Terence Woodgate,** a leading furniture designer who first put me in contact with JB; and **Peter Wright,** for setting me straight on some of the history of F1 wind tunnel development.

INDEX

A Clockwork Orange
(film) 478
Absalom, Hughie 98, 101,
117, 119, 125, 126, 127,
133, 138, 139, 147, 157
Adams, Douglas 154
Agnelli, Gianni 384, 467
Airfix (models) 476
Alboreto, Michele 263, 302,
334, 336, 337, 338, 355,
360, 364, 366, 367, 379,
381, 382, 506
Alesi, Jean 470, 476, 478,
484, 493, 494, 497, 498,
500, 501, 506, 525
Alexander, Tyler 54, 96,
100, 101, 202, 207, 210,
211, 214–215, 218, 220,
221, 222, 245, 259, 260,
265, 266, 267, 268, 269,
270, 342
Alfa Romeo (cars) 237,
240, 387
Alfa Romeo (team) 231,
256, 359
Allen, James 478
Allen, John 530
Allievi, Pino 382, 383
Allison, James 420
Altan, Cristiano 470,
472–473
American Express 315
Anderson, Gary 204–205,
272
Andretti, Mario 108, 109,
110–111, 116, 126, 237,
240, 263, 391, 448
Arnoux, René 240, 241
Antonelli, Paola 409–410
Arthur Andersen
(accountancy firm)
443–444
Arrows (cars)
A11 450

A18 517
A19 517–518, 519,
520, 536
Arrows (team) 315, 450,
516–520
Ascanelli, Giorgio 339,
345, 422
Ascari, Alberto 26
ATS (Auto Technisches
Spezialzubehör) 166
Autocar & Motor (British
magazine) 427
Autocourse (British annual)
233, 240, 244, 281, 288,
301, 517
Autosport (British magazine)
41, 56, 135, 136, 158,
382, 448, 449, 478, 492,
508–509
Autosprint (Italian magazine)
333, 420
Avak (engineering company)
190
AVL (Anstalt für Verbrennungskraftmaschinen) 339

B3 Technologies 515–520,
521–533, 536
Bacon, Roger 173
Baja 1000 (Mexican
road race) 111
Baker McKenzie (law firm)
269, 324
Baldwin, John 102, 216, 236
Balestre, Jean-Marie 231,
232, 233, 270, 271, 290,
409, 475
Balocco (Alfa Romeo
test track) 359
Barnard, Edward 'Ted'
William (father) 23–39,
41–48, 75–76, 88–89, 102,
103, 143, 165, 304, 374,
434–435, 454

Barnard, Gillian Ann
(daughter) 77, 236, 304,
435, 436, 487–488, 489,
490–491, 522, 532, 550
Barnard, Jennifer Ellen
(daughter) 151, 165,
304, 373, 435, 487, 488,
489–491, 528, 532
Barnard, John Edward
Dogs
Bracken 488, 489, 491
Buster 37–38
Jess 488, 489, 491
Education
Park Lane Infants 25, 26
Wembley Manor Junior
26, 31
East Lane Secondary
Modern 32, 33–35, 36
Acton Technical College
38, 42, 45, 53
Brunel College of
Advanced
Technology 38
Watford College of
Technology 53
Furniture 529,
Surface Chair 532
Surface Table 10, 11,
532–533
Homes
(chronological order)
99 Llanover Road, North
Wembley, London
23–26
3 Peel Road, North
Wembley, London
27–39, 40–47, 61, 75,
79, 140, 143, 210,
297, 454
15 Weir Road,
Hemingford Grey,
Huntingdonshire 64,
79, 102

578

INDEX

151 Ambleside Road, Lightwater, Surrey 102, 103, 140, 165, 170, 210
Redondo Beach, California (rented apartment) 109
Torrance, California 132
Rawdon, Heath House Road, Worplesdon, Surrey 263
Combe Rise, Munstead Heath Road, Godalming, Surrey 304, 373–374, 455, 456, 458, 459, 487–489, 531
Hythe, Hampshire (holiday home) 329
Féchy, Switzerland 531
Innovations (most significant)
Carbon-fibre gearbox 518–519
Carbon-fibre monocoque 12, 15–19, 172–202, 234, 245–247, 498
'Coke-bottle' body shape 12, 272–274, 278, 374, 375
Ground-effect in Indycar 141–145, 146–147, 159, 498
Paddle-shift gearbox 12, 341–345, 359, 365, 368, 372, 373, 379–380, 384, 385–386, 387, 391, 392, 398, 403, 408, 428, 466, 474, 498, 504–505, 539
Steering wheel dashboard 12, 466, 504
Wind-tunnel technology 223–225
Jobs before racing
Geest banana-packing factory 46

General Electric Company (GEC), Osram Lamps, Wembley 53–54
Hoover Company, Perivale, Middlesex 55–56, 57
Nicknames
Il Mago (The Magician) 332, 367, 380, 404, 460
Prince of Darkness 11, 156, 214, 218, 221, 331, 428, 532, 543
Scud (or Godalming Scud) 428, 453, 532
Road cars
Personal cars
Aston Martin DB2/4 45–48, 54
Aston Martin engine 46
Chevrolet V8 engine, 46–47, 54
Ford Zodiac straight-six engine 54
DB4 54–55, 73, 76, 455
DB6 Volante 455, 529
Austin A35 van 42–43
Ford Escort 103
Lagonda M45 Tourer 455
Morris 10 (father's) 41
Rover 14 sports saloon 44
Standard Vanguard estate (father's) 55
Triumph TR3A 45
Company cars
Ford Sierra Cosworth 439
Mercedes 560SEC 335
Porsche 928 279, 304, 314
Renault 30TS 140, 143

Volkswagen Golf GTi 198
Workplaces
Lola (1970–72)
Yeovil Road, Slough, Berkshire 57, 58, 64
Huntingdon 64, 65, 68
Team McLaren (1972–75)
David Road, Colnbrook, Berkshire 79, 90, 92, 93, 94, 99
Vel's Parnelli Jones (1975–78)
Indianapolis, Torrance, California 103, 107, 108
Chaparral (1978–79)
3 Peel Road, North Wembley, London 140, 143
Project Four (1979–80)
Poole Road, Woking, Surrey 169, 172, 191, 199, 208, 209
Rabbit Hutch 172, 185, 186, 198, 199, 210
McLaren International (1980–86)
Boundary Road, Woking, Surrey 209, 212, 221, 243, 251, 279, 283, 287, 291, 292, 297, 321, 322
Ferrari — Guildford Technical Office (GTO) (1986–89)
River House, Broadford Park, Shalford, Godalming, Surrey 323, 327–328, 340, 341, 345, 348, 349, 354, 358, 365, 374, 378, 381, 382, 403, 404, 416, 418, 422, 425, 468, 469, 475, 524, 536

579

Benetton — Benetton
    Advanced Research
    Group (BARG)
    (1989–91)
    Langham Park,
        Godalming, Surrey
        417, 422, 423, 426,
        428, 432, 439, 442,
        443, 446
    Ferrari — Ferrari Design
        and Development
        (FDD) (1992–96)
        468, 469
        Northfield House,
            Broadford Park,
            Shalford,
            Godalming, Surrey
            469, 470–474, 482,
            503, 507, 508, 509,
            515, 516, 522
    B3 Technologies
        (1997–2007)
        Northfield House,
            Broadford Park,
            Shalford,
            Godalming, Surrey
            515, 516, 522, 530
Barnard, John 'Jack'
    (uncle) 24
Barnard, Rose Ellen (mother)
    (née Martin) 23–39, 40,
    42–48, 88–89, 143, 454
Barnard, Rosemary 'Rosie'
    Elizabeth (wife) (née Irwin)
    89–91, 99, 102–103, 109,
    127, 137–138, 140, 143,
    151, 152, 165, 210, 236,
    269, 282, 303–304,
    320–321, 434, 435,
    454–455, 487–489,
    490, 531, 532, 535
Barnard Design Consultancy
    (BDC) 165, 370, 446,
    455, 516
Barrichello, Rubens 484
Battistini, Tiziano 470,
    471, 473
Baxter, Raymond 86
Beagle 2 (Mars lander) 529
Bell, Bob 299, 307, 323

Bell (helmets) 485
Bellamy, Ralph 142
Bellof, Stefan 290
Bendinelli, Frederico 485
Benetton, Alessandro 415
Benetton, Luciano 415, 425,
    432, 433, 434, 438–439,
    443, 444, 445, 448,
    451, 452
Benetton (cars) 400, 491,
    501, 507
    B189 416
    B190 419, 426, 429, 441
    B191 423, 427–429,
        439–442, 445, 446–447,
        448, 452
    B192 448
Benetton (team) 283,
    404, 405, 411, 415–436,
    437–453, 457, 458, 476,
    498, 499, 500, 506, 507,
    508, 516, 528, 536,
    537, 539
    Benetton Formula Ltd
        (BFL) 424, 426, 433,
        443–445
    Benetton Formula (BF)
        Holdings 424
    Benetton Properties 424
Benton, Philip E. Jr 431
Benuzzi, Dario 358–359
Beresford, Don 'Mother' 81,
    91, 219, 225
Berger, Gerhard 303, 336,
    337, 338, 339, 364, 366,
    367, 375, 379–380, 387,
    388, 393, 394–395,
    396–397, 398, 400, 401,
    402, 404, 408, 415, 442,
    476, 478, 479, 482–483,
    484, 485, 491, 493, 494,
    497–498, 501, 506,
    535–536, 558
BFGoodrich (tyres and brakes)
    264
Biennale Interieur, Belgium,
    2010 533
Bignotti, George 114
Bigois, Loïc 521
Bishop, Matt 544

Blanc Aero (French aerospace
    company) 346, 347
Blue Book 347
Blue Peter (British TV
    programme) 420
Bluebird (record car and boat)
    141, 320
BMW (company) 315
BMW (cars) 252
    M1 Procar 168, 169, 172,
        179, 186, 191, 198, 248
BMW (engines)
    Turbo 252, 278, 283, 288,
        291, 293
Bogle, Graham 531
Bonnier, Joakim 'Jo' 71–72
Bosch (electronics) 253, 254,
    282
Boulton, Matthew 171
Boutsen, Thierry 389, 400
Bowen, Justine 549, 550
Boxstrom, Max 331
Brabham, Jack 168
Brabham (cars) 86, 167,
    170, 240, 247, 262,
    274, 282, 283, 289,
    290, 291, 293
    BT49 183
    BT49C 232
Brabham (team) 168, 177,
    203, 230, 232, 257, 263,
    278, 315, 350
Bramley Motor Cars (dealer)
    340
Brands Hatch (British circuit)
    145, 281, 302, 307
Brawn, Ross 347, 450, 501,
    507, 508, 509–511,
    534–535, 537
Brembo (brakes) 285
Briatore, Flavio 415, 416, 421,
    425, 426, 431, 432, 437,
    443, 445, 446, 449, 451,
    452, 521
Bristol Rotorway
    (manufacturer of
    helicopter rotor blades) 191
British Aerospace (BAe) 15,
    179, 180, 199, 287, 324,
    420, 495, 498

INDEX

British Aircraft Corporation (BAC) 180
British Hovercraft Corporation (BHC) 91
Brittan, Nick 283, 284
BRM (cars) 87, 141
BRM (engines)
H16 60, 61
Broadley, Eric 56–57, 58, 59, 60, 61, 62, 64, 66, 68, 71, 72, 73, 75, 78, 92, 341, 377
Bromley, Kristan 529
Brown, Creighton 168, 210, 266, 267, 268, 269, 298, 299, 315
Brown, Dan 171
Brown, David 447
Brown, Peter 325, 328, 423, 457
Brundle, Martin 491
Brunner, Gustav 326, 327, 333, 334, 336, 353, 492, 493, 494, 497
BS Fabrications 143, 158, 167
Bunyan, Paul 373
Burns, Peter 143
Buzzi, Aleardo 235, 277, 278
Byrne, Rory 416, 419, 421, 427, 451, 452, 508, 509, 510, 511

Caffi, Alex 400
Caine, Michael 55
Caldwell, Alastair 80, 268
Camerini, Angelo 470, 471–472
Campbell, Donald 141, 320
Cappelli, Piergiorgio 360, 362, 370, 371, 382, 384, 385, 387
Carbon Industrie (carbon composites) 283
Castelli, Pierguido 371
Catalunya (Spanish circuit) 505, 521
Cavallino restaurant (Maranello) 319
Cézanne, Paul 411
Challenger (space shuttle) 324

Chaparral (cars) 133, 138
2E (Can-Am) 138
2F (sports car) 138
2J (Can-Am) 138, 142
2K (Indycar) 140, 141, 142, 143–154, 155, 157, 158, 159, 160, 166, 172, 179, 185, 192, 203, 209, 255, 288, 340, 416, 441, 498
Chaparral (team) 133, 139, 285, 297, 324, 458, 546, 549
Chaparral Cars UK Ltd 140, 160
Chapman, Colin 13, 60, 64, 80, 108, 111, 113, 141, 228–229, 230, 231, 232, 233, 252–253, 297, 448, 498, 537
Chapman, Jim 57, 58, 66, 101, 102, 109, 110, 115, 117, 119, 120, 121–122, 123, 126, 127–128, 130, 131, 132, 135–136
Chapward Racing Services 57, 58
Cheever, Eddie 261, 263
Chevrolet (engines)
V8 46–47, 54, 98–99
Chiavegato, Cristiano 365, 381
Ciba-Geigy (Swiss chemical company) 192, 196
Citroën SM 131
Civil Aviation Authority (CAA) 246
Clark, Jim 53, 228, 303
Cleese, John 389
Clermont-Ferrand (French circuit) 276
Clockwise (film) 389
Cockerell, Sir Christopher 91
Coles, Bob 190
Collins, Peter 229, 230, 425
Collins, Phil 548
Concorde 175, 180
Constanduros, Bob 517
Cooper, John 13
Cooper (cars) 41, 168, 234

Coppuck, Gordon 79, 80, 81, 82, 83, 84, 85, 87, 88, 89, 92, 93, 94, 95, 99, 100, 101, 102, 139, 202, 203, 204, 205, 210, 211, 212, 214, 216, 299
Corriere della Sera (Italian newspaper) 365
Costin, Mike 114
Cosworth (engines) 114–115, 119, 231, 275, 277, 278, 280, 281, 282, 421–422, 431, 437, 438
DFV V8 16, 17, 60, 61, 98, 172, 235, 236, 239, 246, 251, 252, 346
Parnelli's turbo version 114–115, 117, 119–124, 126, 129, 130, 133–134, 135
DFX V8 (turbo) 133, 145, 147, 150
DFY V8 275–276
Cottingham, Mick 41–42
Coughlan, Mike 423, 439, 440, 446, 452, 480, 483, 502, 516, 518
Coulthard, David 527
Courtaulds (manufacturing company) 174, 192, 456

Daily Telegraph (British newspaper) 209, 416, 426
Dali, Salvador 411
Dalla, Roberto 510
Dallara (cars) 400
Dallenbach, Wally 126, 150
Dassault Falcon 900 317, 320
Davey, Tom 63
De Adamich, Andrea 86
De Angelis, Elio 292, 293, 486
De Cesaris, Andrea 16, 200, 235, 236–240, 243, 245, 246, 247, 248, 256, 258
De Martino, Marco 380, 383
De Silvestri, Fosco 341, 343, 344, 504
DeLorean (cars) 228
Dennis, Lisa 555

581

Dennis, Ron 100, 160,
  168–171, 179, 186, 187,
  190–191, 192, 193, 194,
  197, 198, 199, 201, 202,
  204, 205, 206, 207, 208,
  209, 210, 211, 213, 215,
  216, 220, 221, 223, 225,
  228, 229, 235, 236, 237,
  238, 241, 242, 243, 244,
  248, 249, 250, 252, 254,
  256, 262, 263, 265, 266,
  267, 268, 269, 270, 274,
  275–276, 277, 278, 279,
  284, 287, 288, 289, 291,
  292, 295–297, 298, 299,
  304–305, 309, 313–314,
  315, 316, 317, 320,
  321–323, 324, 328, 333,
  334, 348, 350, 352, 379,
  443, 456, 468, 498–499,
  500, 518, 526, 533, 539,
  543–558
Dernie, Frank 272
Design Week (magazine) 533
Desoutter (drills) 253
Detroit (American street
  circuit) 261, 277
Detroit Engineer (American
  magazine) 181
Dijon-Prenois (French circuit)
  238, 244, 289
Dodgins, Tony 449
Dominici, A. 362
Donington (British circuit)
  167, 245, 249, 250, 264
  Donington Collection of
    Single-Seater Racing
    Cars 303
Donohue, Mark 98
Doodson, Mike 427,
  543, 544
Douglas, Pauline 64
Dragoni, Eugenio 356
Drake, Sir Francis 318
Duckworth, Keith 114–115,
  119, 133, 253
D'Ulise, Renato 380
Dunham, Robert 'Bob' 34
Dungl, Willy 250
Dunlop (tyres) 175

Durand, Henri 368, 525
Dymag (wheels) 326, 331

Eagle (cars) 115, 119, 123,
  124, 125
Ecclestone, Bernie 11, 101,
  167, 177, 231, 232, 395,
  435
Economaki, Chris 153
Edison, Thomas 173
Edwards, Guy 71
Edwards, John 109, 117, 128
Elford, Vic 72
Equipe Renault Elf
  — see 'Renault (team)'
Established & Sons (furniture)
  532–533
Estoril 293, 386, 401, 404,
  420–421, 501, 502
Evening Standard (London
  newspaper) 201

Fabi, Corrado 290
Fairline 50 (powerboat) 329
Fallert, Jane (cousin) 103
Fallert, Joan (mother's sister)
  (*née* Martin) 88, 103
Fallert, John (cousin) 103
Fangio, Juan Manuel 25, 26
Fawlty, Basil 377
Ferrari, Alfredo 'Dino'
  (Enzo's first son) 355
Ferrari, Enzo 233, 270,
  316, 317, 318–320,
  321, 324, 330, 331,
  333, 334, 335, 338,
  339, 344, 354–355,
  356, 358, 359, 360,
  361, 364, 367, 368, 369,
  379, 382, 385, 403, 404,
  465, 467, 469, 497, 506
Ferrari, Floriana (Piero's wife)
  361
Ferrari, Laura Dominica
  (Enzo's wife) 355
Ferrari, Piero Lardi (Enzo's
  second son) 319, 326, 327,
  329, 331, 343, 354, 355,
  359, 360, 361, 369–370,
  381, 404, 446

Ferrari (cars) 16, 86, 103, 237,
  239, 240, 244, 274, 302,
  441, 446–447
  166 MM *Barchetta* 409
  250 GTO 327
  250P 356
  312T 129
  348 (road car) 467
  355 (road car) 467
  550 Maranello (road car)
    467
  F1/87 325, 333, 334, 336,
    337, 350
  F1/87/88C 353
  F40 (road car) 409
  F92A 470, 475
  LaFerrari F150 (road car)
    551
  Mondial (road car) 334,
    335, 360
  Testarossa (road car) 467
  Tipo 637 (Indycar) 330
  Tipo 639 338, 339, 340,
    344, 345, 349, 350, 353,
    354, 357, 358–359, 360,
    364, 365, 368, 369, 372,
    374, 375, 379, 536
  Tipo 640 347, 365, 368,
    372, 374–380, 382, 383,
    385, 386, 387, 391, 394,
    395, 398, 400, 402, 403,
    404, 407, 408, 453, 466,
    506, 536
    Il Papera ('The Duck')
      375, 380, 382
  Tipo 641 347, 404, 407,
    409–410, 430, 431, 441,
    470
  Tipo 642 470
  Tipo 643 470
  Tipo 644 Bis 474, 475
  Tipo 645 (*aka* 412T) 476,
    477–478, 480, 481, 482,
    491, 492–493, 494
  Tipo 646 496–498, 501
  Tipo 647 (*aka* F310) 505,
    506
  Tipo 648 506, 509–510
Ferrari (engines) 253
  V6 turbo 350, 355, 364

INDEX

V10 501, 502, 503
V12 339, 344, 346, 350, 355, 358, 361, 374, 385, 391, 399, 407, 408, 481, 497, 498, 501
Ferrari (team) 10, 96, 97, 108, 143, 185, 209, 231, 232, 233, 244, 251, 252, 255, 256, 260, 262, 263, 271, 302, 316–321, 322–335, 336–349, 350–367, 368–392, 393–402, 403–411, 415, 416, 417, 422, 423, 431, 432, 448, 449, 451, 452, 458, 460, 465–483, 484–494, 495–499, 500–511, 515, 516, 530, 534, 535, 536, 537, 539, 540
Ferrari Museum 465, 497
Fiat 330, 332, 342, 348, 357, 359, 360, 361, 369, 370, 382, 383–384, 387, 422, 449, 467, 500
   Croma (road car) 334
   Uno (road car) 360
Fiorano (Ferrari test track) 332, 344, 359, 360, 368, 385
Fiorio, Cesare 387–388, 395, 396, 401, 402, 404–405, 406, 446
Fittipaldi, Emerson 85, 87, 88, 95, 96–97, 103, 176
Fleetcroft, Dan 522, 523–524, 527, 529, 530
Fletcher Racing (team) 124, 150
Flohr, Hans-Peter 315
Flying Scotsman (locomotive) 24
Footwork Arrows
   — see 'Arrows (team)'
Ford 421, 422, 431, 437, 438
   Special Vehicle Operations 422
Ford (engines)
   Cosworth V8 — see 'Cosworth > DFV V8'
   HB V8 421, 437
   V8 Indycar engine 119

V12 421, 431, 432, 445
Forghieri, Mauro 252, 331, 344
Foyt, A.J. 114, 131, 135, 137, 150, 154
Franco, General Francisco 176
Frankenstein 478
Friday Island (TV game show) 35–36
Fry, Pat 423
Fusaro, Piero 406

Gabriel (shock absorbers) 117–118, 144
Gardner, Frank 62, 66–67, 76
Garrett (turbochargers) 362, 364
   TP13 362
GEC-Marconi (aerospace) 287, 324, 328
General Motors 148–149, 152
Genesis (rock band) 323
Gethin, Peter 63
Getrag (gearboxes) 455
Ghidella, Vittorio 360, 365, 368–369, 370, 379, 383
Ghini, Antonio 467
Gleason (differential) 291
Goodwood (British circuit) 79, 187
Goodyear (tyres) 302, 337, 448
Gousset, Jean-Paul 525
Grand Prix+ (electronic magazine) 229
Grands Prix
   Argentine
     1958 234
     1980 205
     1981 233, 237
   Australian
     1986 308–309
     1987 338
     1990 430–431
     2007 391
   Austrian
     1974 96
     1975 110
     1984 292–293
     1985 302, 303

Belgian
   1973 85
   1982 257, 265
   1983 276
   1984 289
   1985 302
   1988 362
   1996 505
Brazilian
   1981 237
   1982 256, 257
   1983 274
   1984 287, 288
   1985 302
   1986 306
   1987 336
   1988 353
   1989 386, 387–392, 393, 405, 466
   1991 441
   1994 484
British
   1973 86
   1975 110
   1979 147
   1981 238–243, 244
   1982 261–262
   1983 277
   1984 292
   1985 302
   1989 399
   1992 469
   1997 517
   2012 9, 543
   2014 544
Caesars Palace (Las Vegas)
   1981 247
   1982 262–263
Canadian
   1973 88
   1974 96, 108
   1980 212–213, 247
   1983 277
   1984 291
   1985 302, 303
   1986 315
   1990 426
   1991 446–447
   1995 498

583

Dallas
  1984 291
Detroit
  1982 261, 275
  1983 277
  1984 291
  1985 302
  1987 335, 336
Dutch
  1980 205, 209
  1981 245
  1983 278, 281, 282
  1984 293
  1985 302
European
  1983 281–282
  1984 293
  1985 302
  1997 506–507
French
  1975 109
  1981 238, 244, 258
  1983 275–276
  1984 289
  1985 302
  1988 353
  1989 399
German
  1973 87
  1974 96
  1975 110
  1982 262
  1984 292
  1985 301
  1985 302
  1986 307, 401
  1987 336–337
  1989 400
  1994 493
Hungarian
  1987 337
  1989 400
  1994 283
  1997 517
Italian
  1970 70
  1974 96
  1975 110
  1978 203
  1980 201

1981 15–19, 245, 249
1983 281
1984 293
1985 302
1988 362, 364–367, 506
1989 401
1993 476
1996 505–506
Japanese
  1976 111
  1987 337
  1989 401, 409
  1990 409, 430
Mexican
  1986 415
  1988 353, 360
  1991 449
Monaco
  1979 183, 205
  1981 237
  1982 261
  1983 276
  1984 290–291
  1985 302
  1987 336
  1988 353
  1989 397–398, 399
  1990 430
  1991 442
  1994 491
  2000 525
Pacific (Japan)
  1994 484
Portuguese
  1984 293
  1985 302
  1987 337
  1989 401, 404
San Marino
  1981 237
  1982 257
  1983 276
  1984 289
  1985 302
  1987 336
  1989 393, 393–397
  1991 441
  1993 475
  1994 484
South African

1971 391
1973 85
1976 111
1983 282, 284
1984 289
Spanish
  1975 176–177
  1981 237–238
  1996 505
Swedish
  1973 85
  1975 108
United States
  1974 97
  1975 110–111
  1980 213, 232
  1991 437, 439, 441
United States West
  1976 111
  1978 135
  1981 236–237
  1982 256–257
  1983 274–275
Grant, Ronnie 74–77, 78, 89, 90, 116
GTO (Guildford Technical Office) 327–328, 330–331, 340
Gurney, Dan 77, 134, 158
Guthrie, Janet 131, 153

Hahn, Ralf 384, 385
Hailwood, Mike 95, 96
Hall, Dick 149
Hall, Jim 133, 138–139, 145, 147, 148, 149, 151–152, 153, 154, 157, 158, 214
Halstead, Lindsey 431
Hamilton, Maurice 405
Handford, Mark 420, 423, 457
Hart, Brian 519
Hart (engines)
  V10 519
Harvey, Dr John 65, 141
Head, Patrick 63, 68–69, 70, 71, 73, 74–76, 77, 78, 84, 102–103, 108, 135, 146–147, 159, 169, 183, 224, 229, 257, 272, 307, 329,

INDEX

344, 352, 382, 407, 408, 409, 423, 427, 447, 470, 485, 486–487, 498, 534, 535, 536, 537–538
Heidfeld, Nick 525
Henry, Alan 250, 306, 314, 336–337, 491, 543
Hercules Inc. (aerospace) 174, 192–195, 196–198, 199, 201, 216, 237, 246, 262, 287, 546
Herd, Robin 166, 205
Hesketh, Lord Alexander 87
Hesketh Racing 456
Hewland (gearboxes) 118, 246, 278
Hilborn (fuel injection) 121
Hill, Benny 545, 549
Hill, Damon 476, 500, 506, 507, 516–517, 520, 536
Hill, Graham 42, 100, 176, 516
Hill, Kenny 326, 377, 430, 518
Hill (cars)
  GH1 176–177
Hirashima, Chickie 117, 119–121, 133
His, J.J. 370
Hitchcock, Alfred 45
HITCO (carbon composites) 264
Hobbs, David 96
Hobden, Nigel 224
Hockenheim (German circuit) 262, 292, 307, 336–337, 400, 493
Hogan, John 168–169, 191, 192, 198, 201, 202, 203, 204, 205, 206, 207, 208, 210, 213, 214, 232, 236, 238, 242, 248, 249, 250, 262, 265, 268, 274, 277, 278, 283, 284, 302, 305, 405, 531
Holl, Diane 215, 299, 325, 341, 347, 348–349, 375, 376, 377, 398–399, 407, 408, 409, 423–424, 430, 439–440, 442, 446, 456,

458–459, 460, 479, 480, 496, 506, 536
Homes & Gardens (magazine) 533
Honda (engines)
  V6 turbo 302, 308, 336, 337, 350, 351, 352, 353, 362, 363
  V10 400, 497
Horsley, Anthony 'Bubbles' 456
Horton, Roger 476
Howell, Norman 469
Hulman, Mary 153
Hulman, Tony 152–153
Hulme, Denis 'Denny' 85, 86, 87, 88, 95, 96
Hungaroring (Hungarian circuit) 337, 400
Hunt, James 19, 87, 103, 111, 203, 249, 366–367, 388, 396, 456
Hussein, Saddam 428
Hustedt, Wolfgang 254

Ichida, Katsumi 352
Ickx, Jacky 87, 88, 290, 291
Il Giorno (Italian newspaper) 375
Il Messaggero (Italian newspaper) 367, 380, 383
Il Tempo (Italian newspaper) 365
Imola (Italian circuit) 237, 257, 260, 276, 289, 333, 334, 336, 393–397, 398, 401, 441, 475, 478, 484, 485, 496
Indianapolis Motor Speedway 115, 151
  Hall of Fame Museum 157, 159
  Indianapolis 500
    1963 107
    1969 108
    1972 97
    1974 98
    1975 98, 115
    1976 98, 124
    1977 131

1979 143, 149–153
1980 157, 209
Indianapolis Star (newspaper) 130, 158
Interlagos (Brazilian circuit) 484
Interscope (film production company) 125, 132, 135
Intersport (team) 457
Irwin, Elizabeth 'Betty' Sherrard (mother-in-law) (*née* Fulton) 89
Irwin, John Walker Sinclair (father-in-law) 89
Irwin, Sir Samuel T. (grandfather-in-law) 89
Issigonis, Sir Alec 498
Ive, Jonathan 171

Jacarepaguá (Brazilian circuit) 387
Jackson, Peter 61
Jaguar 498, 520
  E-type 376, 410
Jarama (Spanish circuit) 237–238
Jardine, Tony 213
JCB 373
Jeffreys, Matthew 184, 216–217, 218, 219, 279, 291, 314, 345, 350, 351–352, 404, 530, 531
Jenkins, Alan 168, 178, 180, 185, 189, 190, 196, 199, 211, 214, 216, 218, 224, 225, 226, 227, 236, 241, 242, 244, 260, 271, 272–273, 286, 292, 294, 295–296, 299, 300, 318, 333, 492, 525, 526
Jepson, Michael 269, 320, 372, 425, 438, 444, 445–446, 499, 515
Jerez (Spanish circuit) 380, 383, 416, 506, 510
Jobs, Steve 171
Johansson, Stefan 351, 400
John Player (cigarettes) 292
Johncock, Gordon 125, 126, 150

585

Johnson, Bill 173
Jones, Alan 239–240, 247, 535
Jones, Rufus Parnell 'Parnelli' 107, 110, 111, 112–113, 114, 115, 132, 133, 134, 158
Jordan (cars) 484
Judd/Yamaha engine 517

Kimball, Gordon 128–129, 143, 152, 159, 167, 324, 338, 345, 349, 358, 362, 370, 371, 384, 449–450
Kirby, Gordon 108, 114, 134, 158, 159, 160
Koinigg, Helmuth 97
Kothary, Vijay 330, 422, 443, 445, 515, 526
Kramer, Gerd 254, 501
Kranefuss, Mike 422, 425, 426, 431, 432, 437, 438, 441
Kubrick, Christiane 478
Kyalami (South African circuit) 85, 282, 289

La Gazzetta della Sport (Italian sports newspaper) 380
La Stampa (Italian newspaper) 360, 365, 381, 500
Laffite, Jacques 240, 274–275
Lamborghini 331
Lancia 358, 387
Lardi, Lina 354
Lardi, Piero — see 'Ferrari, Piero Lardi'
Larini, Nicola 484
Lauda, Niki 87, 96, 97, 103, 111, 129, 168, 191, 248, 249, 250, 254, 256–257, 258–259, 261, 262, 263, 264, 273–277, 280, 281, 282, 283, 284, 288–290, 291, 292–293, 301, 302, 306, 307, 315, 318, 460, 467, 469

Le Mans 24 Hours 252, 520
1972 72
Learjet 147, 183, 280, 317
Lehman Brothers (bank) 531
Lennon, John 330
Leonard, Joe 126
L'Équipe (French sports newspaper) 336
Lee, Christopher 478
Leston, Les 41
Lichtenstein, Roy 411
Ligier, Guy 432
Ligier (cars) 240, 263, 521
Ligier (team) 432
Lini, Franco 375
Lis, Alan 426
Löbro (CV joints) 326
Lock, Mike 236
Lockheed Martin (aerospace) 122
Lola 56–78, 79, 80, 99, 101, 116, 141, 144, 167, 346, 458, 535
 T192 (Formula 5000) 66
 T212 (2-litre sports) 71
 T220 (Can-Am) 58
 T242 (Formula Atlantic) 66
 T250 (Formula Super Vee) 59–62, 73–74, 98, 346
 'Taurus' 75, 76, 77
 T260 (Can-Am) 64, 65, 69, 108
 T280 (3-litre sports) 66, 71, 72
 T290 (2-litre sports) 66, 71
 T300 (Formula 5000) 66, 80
 T310 (Can-Am) 66
 T500 (Indycar) 145
Lombardi, Claudio 467, 468
Long Beach (American street circuit) 111, 236, 256, 257, 259, 274–275, 558
Longford (Australian circuit) 79
Lotus (cars) 85, 87, 167, 228, 290, 292, 293, 337, 455
 Seven 57
 Type 43 60
 Type 49 60, 108

Type 56 107, 113
Type 72 70, 80, 108
Type 78 139, 142, 166
Type 79 111, 166, 205
Type 88 228–231, 232, 233, 239
Lotus (team) 64, 65, 101, 111, 135, 141, 166, 177, 203, 224, 232, 336, 423, 457, 537
Louis Schwitzer Award 157
Lucas (fuel injection) 121
Lydon, Neil 333, 334

Magneti Marelli (electrical components) 342, 386, 387, 398
Magritte, René 411
Mansell, Nigel 239, 290, 293, 302, 308, 337, 360, 366, 379, 380, 385, 386, 387, 388, 389, 390, 391, 392, 393, 395–396, 397, 398, 400, 401, 402, 410, 431, 446–447, 466, 470, 476
Mansell, Rosanne 388
March Engineering (cars) 87, 166, 223, 260, 325
 'The Orbiter' 166
Marlboro (cigarettes) 88, 95, 96, 168, 169, 191, 192, 198, 201, 202, 204, 205, 206, 207, 209, 211, 213, 235, 238, 242, 262, 265, 266, 268, 269, 277, 278, 281, 282, 283, 292, 302, 405, 531
Marquart, Jo 56
Márquez, Gabríel Garcia 381
Marston, Bob 68–69, 70, 78
Mason, James 214
Mass, Jochen 96, 260, 261
Matchett, Steve 417, 428, 441, 442, 447–448, 450
Matisse, Henri 411
Mayer, Teddy 36, 79, 82, 87, 88, 95, 96, 99–100, 101, 202, 204, 205, 206, 207–208, 209, 210, 211, 213, 214, 215, 219, 221,

INDEX

222, 232, 243, 247, 251, 258, 259, 260, 264–269, 270, 334, 557
Mayer, Timmy 79
McLaren, Bruce 56, 79, 207
McLaren (cars) 167, 202, 337, 340, 387, 388, 399, 400, 403, 430, 441, 442, 446, 476, 491, 533
  F1 (road car) 468
  M10A (Formula 5000) 98
  M16 (Indycar) 80, 97–98
    M16C/D 98, 125, 126
    M16E 98, 124, 125
  M19 84
    M19C 85
  M23 79, 80–88, 91–97, 98, 102, 103, 122, 129, 203
  M25 (Formula 5000) 98–99
  M26 203, 204–205
  M28 203, 204, 205
  M29 205, 236, 237, 246
    M29B 205
    M29C 205, 212
  M30 205, 206, 209, 212
  MP4/1 15–18, 202, 207, 220, 222, 230, 231, 233, 236–243, 244–248, 249–251, 254
    MP4/1B 255, 256–260, 273
    MP4/1C 272, 273, 274–277
    MP4/1D 278, 281, 282
    MP4/1E 278, 280, 281–282, 285
  MP4/2 270, 284, 285, 287–291, 292–294, 351
    MP4/2B 300–303, 558
    MP4/2C 306–308
  MP4/3 350, 351
  MP4/4 350, 351–352, 353, 362–364, 365
  MP4/5 351, 380
  P1 (road car) 551
McLaren (team)
  Team McLaren (to 1980) 56, 79–103, 116, 134, 135, 139, 148, 177, 201, 203–210, 211, 212, 213, 219, 238, 266, 267, 269, 299, 338, 348
  McLaren International (from 1980) 11, 17, 160, 177, 207, 209–222, 225, 235–309, 313–315, 317, 318, 320, 321–323, 324, 326, 331, 333, 336, 345, 350–353, 357, 365, 375, 382, 401, 402, 404, 405, 408, 415, 417, 422, 426, 428, 431, 432, 448, 449, 451, 452, 458, 468, 469, 492, 498–499, 506, 526, 527, 530, 534, 536, 537, 539, 540
  McLaren Technology Centre 550–558
    McLaren Thought Leadership Centre 552
McNally, Patrick 'Paddy' 191
Mears, Rick 150, 153, 154, 157
Meccano 340, 341, 376
Mercedes-Benz 347
Message, Gordon 519
Metalore (racing components) 326, 377, 430, 518
Mezger, Hans 252, 253
Michelin (tyres) 235, 244, 264, 266, 274, 276, 302
Michigan International Speedway (oval)
  Norton 200 1977 132
  Norton Twin 125 1979 154
Migeot, Jean-Claude 344, 354, 355, 356, 359, 381, 427, 470, 503
Miletich, Velko 'Vel' 107, 113, 115, 119, 133, 134, 139–140
Miller, Harry 130
Miller, Robin L. 158
Miller, Tom 417
Mills, David 425
Milwaukee Mile (oval)
  Milwaukee 150 (1976) 124
  Tony Bettenhausen 200 (1976) 125
Minett, John 530
Ministry of Defence 174, 178
Mint 400 (Las Vegas off-road race) 112
MIRA (Motor Industry Research Association) 93, 476, 491
Mobil (fuel and oil) 437
Mondrian, Piet 411
Monroe (shock absorbers) 117–118
Montezemolo, Luca Cordero di 409, 467, 468, 469, 470, 471, 473, 474, 475, 476, 478, 491, 492, 493, 494, 495, 498, 500–501, 505, 508, 511
Montjuïc (Spanish circuit) 176–177
Montréal (Canadian circuit) 212, 229, 247, 315
Monza (Italian circuit) 15–19, 96, 245, 246, 247, 249, 281, 293, 401, 404, 415, 476, 478, 505
Moog valve 343, 504
Moore, George 130
Moran, Michael 32–33, 384
Moreno, Roberto 430, 439, 441, 442, 446
Moreton, Roger 173
Morgan Crucible 174
Morosino, Nestore 365
Mosley, Max 231
Mosport Park (Canadian circuit) 96
Moss, Stirling 234
MotoGP 529
Motoring News (British newspaper) 508
Motor Sport (British magazine) 74, 474
Mugello (Italian circuit) 484
Murray, Bill 206

Murray, Gordon 175–176,
   177, 178, 183, 187, 230,
   232, 233, 257, 263, 264,
   278, 350, 351, 352, 363,
   423, 427, 468, 537
Museo Casa Enzo Ferrari,
   Modena, Italy 533
Museum of Modern Art
   (MoMA), New York
   409–411

Nannini, Alessandro 400,
   416, 430
Nardon, Maurizio 400, 401
NAS (National Aeronautical
   Standard) 346
National Research
   Development
   Corporation 174
Newey, Adrian 325, 398, 485,
   487, 537
Newman, Paul 214
Nichols, Steve 117, 144, 192,
   194, 214, 216–217, 218,
   241, 242, 279, 286, 292,
   293–294, 321–322, 323,
   350, 351, 352, 363, 427,
   470, 530
Nimrod (aircraft) 325
Nintendo Game Boy 466
North, David 175
Nürburgring (German circuit)
   87, 96, 249, 293, 301
Nye, Doug 256

Oatley, Neil 351
Offenhauser (engines) 98, 115,
   119, 123, 124, 130, 134
Ogilvie, Martin 230
Ojjeh, Akram 254
Ojjeh, Mansour 254, 294,
   298, 299, 304
O'Mara, Ray 530
On Track (American
   magazine) 402
Ongais, Danny 125–126, 132,
   135, 150, 152, 154
Ongaro, Derek 74
Ontario Motor Speedway
   (oval) 147

California 500
   1976 125
   1977 132
   1979 154
Datsun Twin 200
   1979 150
Onyx (cars) 400
Österreichring
   (Austrian circuit) 96

Parkes, Mike 256
Parnelli (cars) 192, 376
   Chevrolet Baja Blazer
      111–112
   VPJ-4 108–110, 117
   VPJ-6 (Indycar) 110,
      114–115, 117
   VPJ-6B 117–126,
      131, 132
   VPJ-6C 128–132, 135,
      144, 145, 146, 154
Parnelli (team) — see 'Vel's
   Parnelli Jones (team)'
Patrese, Riccardo 274–275,
   282, 387, 388, 389, 393,
   446, 476
Patrick, Pat 134
Paul Ricard (French circuit)
   71, 230, 287, 302, 385
Peggs, Mr R. 33–35
Pembrey (Welsh circuit)
   439–440
Pennzoil (oil) 140, 149,
   152, 160
Penske, Roger 98, 134
Penske (cars) 150, 153, 167
Penske Racing (team) 125,
   126, 135, 150, 154, 166
Pepper, Brian 324, 423
Peter, Dr Henry 372
Peterson, Ronnie 85, 86, 87,
   203, 228
Petroleum Museum
   (Midland, Texas, USA) 157
Petrucci, Nicoló 345, 470,
   471, 473, 474
Peugeot (engines) 508, 525
Philip Morris Inc (owner of
   Marlboro) 168, 206, 213,
   235, 250, 275, 277, 278

Phillips, Leslie 173
Philippe, Maurice 80,
   101, 108–110, 113,
   114, 115, 117, 118,
   122, 123, 136, 376
Phoenix (American street
   circuit) 1991 437, 439, 441
Phoenix International
   Raceway (oval) 126
   Bobby Ball 150
      1976 126
      1978 135
   Jimmy Bryan 150
      1976 124
   Miller High Life 150
      1979 156–157
Piano, Renzo 495
Picasso, Pablo 410–411
Piccinini, Marco 316–317,
   318–319, 321, 323–324,
   330, 331, 332, 336, 365,
   371, 404
Pickett, Richard 323–324, 328
Pininfarina, Sergio 319
Piola, Giorgio 378, 380
Piquet, Nelson 183, 240, 247,
   257, 262, 283, 289, 291,
   293, 308, 337, 387, 426,
   430–431, 439, 441, 442,
   446–447, 448
Pirelli (tyres) 224, 339, 432,
   448
Pironi, Didier 16, 240, 260,
   261, 262, 263
Pocono International
   Raceway (oval)
   Pocono 500 (1976)
      124, 133
Pollard, Dave 144
Polling, Bob 421
Pope John Paul II 360
Porsche 252–253, 254, 278,
   280–281, 306, 322
   956 280
Postlethwaite, Dr Harvey
   255, 256, 260, 261, 317,
   331, 333, 334, 338, 344,
   354, 355–356, 359, 381,
   408, 427, 468–470, 474,
   475, 476, 509

INDEX

Price, Tommy 42
Prince Michael of Kent 292
Procar — see 'BMW > M1 Procar'
Project Four 168, 169–172, 178, 179, 180, 186, 189, 190, 196, 198, 199, 201, 202, 206, 207, 208, 209, 210, 214, 223, 225, 232, 327, 537
Prost, Alain 205, 206, 208, 209, 212, 213, 235, 237, 238, 240, 284, 287–291, 292–293, 295, 299, 300, 301, 302, 307, 308–309, 336, 337, 350, 351, 353, 363, 366, 367, 389, 390, 391, 393, 399, 400, 401, 402, 405, 407, 409, 410, 419, 430, 441, 453, 470, 476, 508, 520, 521, 524, 526, 539, 548
Prost (cars)
  AP03 524–525
Prost (team) 508, 521–526, 527
Proton (motorcycles) 529–530
Pulp Fiction (film) 531

Quill, David 79, 81, 85

Racing Car Show, Olympia 1971 63
Räikkönen, Kimi 391
Randle, Jim 498
Randolph, Bob 192–193, 194, 196, 200–201, 246, 262
Random Design (model makers) 190, 224, 271
Rattlesnake Raceway (Chaparral test track) 148
Ratzenberger, Roland 484, 485
Razelli, Gianni 359, 370
Rebaque, Héctor Jr 166
Rebaque, Héctor Sr 166
Rebaque (car)
  HR100 166–167
Rebaque (team) 166–167, 242, 315, 323

Reddy, Tom 63
Regazzoni, Gianclaudio 'Clay' 96, 97, 147
Reinhardt, Peter 166, 167, 315, 323, 324, 325, 326, 327, 328, 331, 338, 339–340, 348, 354, 355, 357, 378–379, 392, 397, 404, 408, 422
Renault (cars) 237, 238, 239, 240, 243, 251, 289, 290
Renault (engines) 251, 290, 292, 393, 446, 476, 497
Renault (team) 206, 213, 231, 232, 244, 248, 284, 308
Reutemann, Carlos 17, 18, 86, 240, 241, 247
Revell (models) 29
Revson, Peter 58, 85, 86, 87, 88
Rexroth valve 342, 343
Reynard (cars) 325, 419
Ricardo (engines) 252
Richardson, Geoff 78
Rindt, Jochen 70, 228
Riva Boat Services 442
Road Atlanta (American circuit) 58
Roberts, Kenny 529
Rockwell, Norman 23
Roebuck, Nigel 233, 448
Rogers, Troy 152
Rolls-Royce (aero engines) 174
  RB211 179, 182
Romiti, Cesare 384
Rondel Racing 168
Rosberg, Keke 257, 259, 261, 262, 263, 293, 306–308
Rosche, Paul 252
Rousseau, Henri 411
Rousseau, Pasquali 143
Rowe, John Saunders 126
Royal Aircraft Establishment (RAE) 173, 178
Royal Designer for Industry (RDI) 11, 498

Royal Society for the Encouragement of Arts, Manufactures and Commerce (RSA) 11, 38, 498
Rudd, Tony 141
Rudman, Shelley 529
Rushbrook, Robbie 63, 64, 67, 78
Russell, Dick 112, 113
Rutherford, Johnny 98, 124, 125, 126, 150, 157, 158, 159
Ryan, Dave 279, 301, 324
Ryton, George 354, 356, 472–473, 475

Sagan, Carl 156
Sanyo (consumer electronics) 432
Saunders, Graham 325, 422, 457
Saward, Joe 425–426
Scaglietti, Sergio 319
Scarfiotti, Lodovico 356
Scalabroni, Enrique 382
Scheckter, Jody 86, 87, 92, 96, 97, 125
Schlesser, Jean-Louis 366
Schumacher, Michael 283, 465, 476, 487, 491, 498, 500, 501–503, 505–507, 508, 509, 510, 511, 516, 539, 540
Scuderia Ferrari
  — see 'Ferrari (team)'
Sebring (American circuit) 356
SEP (carbon composites) 264, 283, 306
Senna, Ayrton 290, 293, 302, 315, 337, 338, 350, 353, 363, 364, 366–367, 387, 388, 393, 396, 400, 401, 409, 415, 430, 441, 476, 484–485, 486, 487, 491, 527
Serra, Chico 186–187
Shadow (cars) 100
Sharp, Hap 152
Sheene, Barry 529

589

Shell (fuel and oil) 315
Signorini, Alessandro 438
Silverstone (British circuit) 9, 16, 76–77, 87, 145, 236, 238–243, 244, 247, 256, 277, 302, 399, 517
Simtek (team) 484, 485
SKF (Svenska Kullagerfabriken) (bearing manufacturer) 131
Slobodinsky, Roman 130
Slutter, Larry 117, 119–121, 133, 134
Smallman, Andy 68, 176
Smith, Andy 325, 328–329, 347–348, 378, 404, 418, 423, 428, 446, 457, 515, 530, 536–537
Smith, Colin 236
Smith, David 201
Smith, Dominic 476, 491, 492, 493
Smith, Harold 155
Snetterton (British circuit) 41, 62, 76–77
Sneva, Tom 125, 132, 135, 150, 153
Southgate, Tony 78
Spa-Francorchamps (Belgian circuit) 276, 302, 505
Sparshott, Bob 143, 148, 151, 159, 167, 441, 458
Specialised Mouldings 61, 65, 71, 81, 143–144, 145
Spirit Racing 299
Spitfire (aircraft) — see 'Supermarine > Spitfire'
Stepney, Nigel 448
Stewart, Jackie 64, 65–66, 69, 70, 85, 86, 87, 108, 153
Stewart Grand Prix 525
Stingray (children's TV series) 477
Stokoe, Ray 79
Stollery, Prof John 141, 142, 147
Stommelen, Rolf 176
Sunday Times (British newspaper) 332–333, 334, 335, 417

Supermarine (aircraft) 474
  Spitfire 476–477, 491, 497
Surrey Advertiser (newspaper) 489
Surrey Satellites 528
Surtees, John 256, 356–357
Surtees, Pat 356
Surtees (cars) 86, 97
Suzuka (Japanese circuit) 337, 430
Swan, Dennis 139
Swan, Sir Joseph 173

TAG (Techniques d'Avant Garde) 254
  TAG-Porsche turbo engine 263, 270, 277, 281, 282, 284, 289, 294, 299, 308, 351
Tambay, Patrick 240, 274, 289
Tauranac, Ron 170
Taylor, Kevin 457, 504
Team Lotus
  — see 'Lotus (team)'
Techno Magnesio (wheels) 326
Teenage Mutant Ninja Turtles 436, 468
Texaco (fuel and oil) 95
Thatcher, Margaret 291
The Beatles 330
The Benny Hill Show (TV comedy) 545
The Birds (film) 45
The Chequered Flag (team) 46, 56
The Crimson Pirate (film) 37
The Guardian (British newspaper) 209, 487
The Independent (British newspaper) 427
The Italian Job (film) 55, 198
The Mechanic's Tale (book) 417
The News (local newspaper, London) 34
The Sun (British newspaper) 209
The Times (British newspaper) 209, 469

The Verdict (film) 214
Todt, Jean 475, 478, 491, 492, 493, 494, 498, 503, 507–508, 510
Toleman (cars) 290, 293, 404, 415, 419
TOM'S (Tachi Oiwa Motor Sport) (team) 457–458, 460
Tom Walkinshaw Racing (TWR) 516, 520
Toray Industries (Japanese manufacturing company) 192
Toyota 457–458, 459, 460
Tremayne, David 229, 230, 233, 543
Trenton Speedway (oval) Trenton Twin Indy 1979 154
Trojan (van) 42
Trojan Cars 98
Trundle, Neil 168, 179, 225
Turland, Pete 'Buttie' 195
Tyler, Tony 503
Tyrrell (cars) 85, 86, 96, 102, 236, 263, 290, 356, 360, 381, 470, 480
Type 019 356, 427–428

Union Carbide 173, 192
Unser, Al 116, 118, 124–126, 131, 132, 133, 139, 145, 147, 150, 151, 152, 153, 154, 157, 158
Unser, Bobby 124, 125, 150, 153, 157

Vel's Parnelli Jones (team) 98, 101–103, 107–136, 216, 221, 346, 450, 458, 481
Vernor, Brenda 361
Vickers (aircraft)
  VC10 92, 180
Victoria & Albert Museum, London 533
Villadelprat, Joan 294, 324, 329–330, 332, 338–339, 342, 345, 353, 354, 355, 357, 358, 369, 386–387,

INDEX

390, 392, 397, 408, 422, 442, 537
Villeneuve, Gilles 237–238, 239–240, 247, 260, 261, 316, 344, 505
Villeneuve, Jacques (Gilles's son) 260, 505, 506–507, 517, 535
Villeneuve, Joanne (Gilles's wife) 260
Villeneuve, Melanie (Gilles's daughter) 260
Vivoli, Gabriel 394
Völker, Herbert 250
Volkswagen 59
  Camper van 282
  Type 3 engine 59
  Type 4 engine 59–61, 346

Walker, Murray 9, 18, 366–367, 389, 390, 391, 396, 540
Walkinshaw, Tom 450, 516, 519, 520, 521
Wallis, Brian 'Wols' 523–524
Wallpaper (magazine) 533
Warhol, Andy 411
Warwick, Derek 260, 290
Waters, Glenn 456
Watkins, Prof Sid 394
Watkins, Susan 177
Watkins Glen (American circuit) 97, 110, 203, 213, 229, 232
Watson, John 15–19, 23, 203, 204, 205, 206, 212–213, 220, 235, 236–243, 244, 245, 246–248, 249, 250, 256–257, 258–259, 260, 261, 262, 263, 265, 271, 274–277, 280, 281–282, 283–284, 289, 394, 502
Watt, Bill 173
Watt, James 171
Webb, Arthur 180–181, 182, 183–184, 185, 187, 189, 194, 195, 196, 197–198, 199, 200, 246, 287, 314, 324–325, 327,
328, 353–354, 357–358, 373, 377, 396, 450
Webb, Janette 357–358
Weild, Ian 325, 530
Weis, Franz 147, 148
Weismann, Pete 118–119, 129, 130, 146, 147, 342
Weismann (gearboxes) 118–119, 153
Weissach (Porsche test track) 252, 280, 385
Wendlinger, Karl 491
Weslake (engines) 252
Wheeler, Rob 423
Wheelock, Bob 63
Whiting, Charlie 486
Whitmarsh, Martin 498–499, 533
Wilansky, Albert 155
Wildcat (cars) 125, 126
Williams, Frank 135, 485, 517
Williams, Glyn 63
Williams (cars) 17, 67, 239, 240, 247, 257, 259, 261, 274, 293, 302, 306, 337, 366, 387, 389, 393, 400, 446, 447, 476, 505, 517
  FW06 135
  FW07 146
  FW11 308
  FW14 447
  FW14B 470
  FW16 484, 487
  FW18 536
Williams (team) 135, 169, 224, 254, 272, 308–309, 336, 337, 344, 350, 352, 398–399, 401, 407, 415, 431, 447, 448, 449, 474, 485, 498, 506, 516, 535
Wind tunnels
  British Aerospace, Farnborough, Hampshire 420
  British Aerospace, Filton, Bristol 495–496, 497, 503, 518
  British Hovercraft Corporation, Isle of Wight 91–92
Cranfield University, Shrivenham, Wiltshire (Benetton) 419–420
Ferrari (Galleria del Vento) 495
Ferrari (road car facility) 344, 345, 353, 354, 356
Imperial College, London 65, 141, 142, 147
Lockheed Martin, Atlanta, Georgia, USA 122, 123
MIRA (Motor Industry Research Association) 93
National Maritime Institute, Teddington, Middlesex 225–227, 244, 271, 272, 286, 299–300, 318
Prost Grand Prix, France 525–526
R.J. Mitchell Wind Tunnel, Southampton University 223, 225, 226, 495
Specialised Mouldings, Huntingdon 65
University of Brighton 495
Windsor, Peter 416
Woodgate, Terence 10–11, 532–533
Woodward, George 57, 58, 66
Woodward, Joanne 328
Wright, Peter 65, 139, 141, 142, 147, 224–225, 229, 230
Wright, Tim 299, 323
Wybrott, Leo 87, 457

Yardley (cosmetics) 85, 88, 95
Yates, Brock 331
Yeager, Bill 126–127

Zandvoort (Dutch circuit) 303
Zappeloni, Umberto 380
Zelkowitz, Dave 191, 192, 198, 277
Zolder (Belgian circuit) 237, 258–260, 265
Zucker, Udo 253–254

591

THE AUTHOR

Nick Skeens started writing about creativity for the Design Council with publications on subjects ranging from design education to creative thinking. He is the co-author of *Future Present* (2000), *Creative Island* (2002) and *Creative Island II* (2009), books that celebrated British design genius by focusing on creative process. Before this he was a news editor and producer for TV-am and GMTV. A freelance journalist, he lives on a barge in Burnham-on-Crouch, Essex, that he designed and helped build.